Antebellum Jefferson, Texas

Everyday Life in an East Texas Town

by
Jacques D. Bagur

UNIVERSITY OF NORTH TEXAS PRESS
DENTON, TEXAS

©2012 Jacques D. Bagur
and the Historic Jefferson Foundation

All rights reserved.
Printed in the United States of America

10 9 8 7 6 5 4 3 2 1

Permissions:
University of North Texas Press
1155 Union Circle #311336
Denton, TX 76203-5017

The paper used in this book meets the minimum requirements of the American National Standard for Permanence of Paper for Printed Library Materials, z39.48.1984. Binding materials have been chosen for durability.

Library of Congress Cataloging-in-Publication Data
Bagur, Jacques D.
Antebellum Jefferson, Texas : everyday life in an East Texas town /
by Jacques D. Bagur. -- 1st ed.
p. cm.
Includes bibliographical references and index.
ISBN 978-1-57441-265-9 (cloth : alk. paper)
1. Jefferson (Tex.)--History--19th century. 2. Jefferson (Tex.)--Social life and customs--19th century. 3. City and town life--Texas--Jefferson--History--19th century. I. Title.
F394.J3B34 2012
976.4'193--dc23
2011047218

This book was made possible by a generous donation from an illustrious Jeffersonian, Lois Moseley Waters.

For my wife Joy,
my daughters Eugenie and Michelle,
and my son Andre.

The Bayou is rising—the weather charming—gardens flourishing—fishing excellent—wives smiling—husbands happy—children healthy—trade increasing—city growing—and every thing in general wears the appearance of prosperity in, around and about Jefferson, suburbs, Paradise and tributaries. (*Jefferson Gazette*, March 25, 1859, as quoted in the April 1, 1859, Marshall *Harrison Flag*)

CONTENTS

Introduction 1
1. Background 9
2. What Jefferson Was 18
3. Foundations 28
4. Townsite 43
5. Emergence 76
6. Development 93
7. Censuses 116
8. Women 123
9. Slaves 129
10. Roads and Bridges 140
11. County Seat 151
12. Municipal Affairs 163
13. Wharves 184
14. Navigation 194
15. Navigation Controversies 205
16. Market Area 212
17. Primary Business Types 223
18. Commodity Markets 241
19. Warehouse District 257
20. Earliest Merchants 276
21. Early 1850s Merchants 298
22. Middle 1850s Merchants 317
23. Late Merchants 329
24. Miscellaneous Businesses 342
25. Manufacturing 353
26. Packeries 371
27. Structural Features 382
28. The Professions 393
29. Politics 403
30. Fraternal Organizations 424
31. Religion 429
32. Education 439
33. Hotels 446

34. Stables	463
35. Stagecoaches	470
36. Newspapers	475
37. Postal Services	502
38. Telegraph	513
39. Railroads	517
40. Sports	524
41. Culture and Entertainment	530
42. Balls and Dances	541
43. Crime	546
44. Vice	555
45. Health and Welfare	562
46. Mortality	567
Appendix: Sources	575
Index	597

INTRODUCTION

Jefferson is located in Marion County in northeast Texas about 20 miles north of Marshall, 150 miles east of Dallas, and 40 miles west of Shreveport, Louisiana. It is a small town, but well known for the quality of its historic resources, its bed-and-breakfast operations, and its antique stores; and it is achieving increasing prominence as an educational center.

The town is situated on a cypress-fringed bayou called Big Cypress, which enters Caddo Lake, through which the boundary between Texas and Louisiana runs. During the 1800s, Caddo Lake was connected with Soda Lake (now extinct), which was drained by Twelvemile Bayou. The latter bayou (which is still in existence in a modified form) entered the Red River slightly above Shreveport. The Red River emptied into the Mississippi River, which passes by New Orleans shortly before entering the Gulf of Mexico (Fig. 1).

During much of the 1800s, New Orleans was the center of trade for the Mississippi Valley, bringing in merchandise from the East Coast and Europe and carrying out the produce of the valley (primarily cotton) to the East Coast and Europe. It was this water connection with New Orleans that enabled the emergence of a number of ports and landings west of Shreveport that carried out cotton and carried in supplies to their respective market areas.

The waterborne commerce of this system of ports and landings was conducted by steamboats. The application of steam to water trans-

Fig. 1. Study Area

port was second in importance to the invention of the cotton gin in the spread of cotton agriculture in the antebellum South. Cotton production was useless without the ability to transport to market. Overland transport by ox-wagons was slow and costly; waterborne transport by flatboats and keelboats was inefficient; and the antebellum South did not have a well-developed rail system in its lower and western components. Shallow-draft steamboats penetrated every navigable waterbody, carrying out cotton from within 150 miles, beyond which the cost of overland transport made cotton production unremunerative.

Jefferson, which came into existence in 1845, was the most important of the ports and landings on the navigation route west of Shreveport, which was called the Cypress Bayou and the lakes route. It was the most important because it was the port farthest upstream on Cypress Bayou, which enabled it to command a large market area extending from the Indian Territory on the north to Dallas on the west. This was not fortuitous, but rather the primary reason for the selection of the town's location. This market area and its attendant cotton production expanded rapidly through immigration, enabling Jefferson to prosper.

From the 1840s to the 1870s, hundreds of steamboats made thousands of trips to Jefferson, carrying out cotton and animal products (primarily hides and pickled beef in barrels) and carrying in merchandise for the plantations, farms, and towns of its market area. Jefferson was an import and export center, serving as the transfer point between interior ox-wagon transport and exterior steamboat transport. Simple transfer would not have produced a town of importance. Import and export items needed to be stored and serviced, which gave rise to receiving, forwarding, and commission merchants who dominated the landing area. Sales to interior merchants and planters were carried out by large wholesaling houses. These two distinctive business types established Jefferson as an important mercantile center.

Jefferson's importance is illustrated by the following facts:

1. Jefferson ranked fourteenth in population (988) among Texas towns in 1860 and sixth in population (4,190) among Texas towns in 1870, exceeded only by Galveston (13,818), San Antonio (12,256), Houston (9,382), Brownsville (4,905), and Austin (4,428).

2. Jefferson was among the top three ports in Texas in terms of number of boat landings. Galveston was a much larger port. A comparison cannot be made to Houston because of an absence of comparative data.

3. Jefferson may have been the largest steamboat port in Texas, reaching a high point in 1870 when 53 boats made 295 trips to Jefferson. Comparative data are not available. Galveston was serviced by a large fleet of seagoing steamships and sailing vessels, but also by steamboats that ran in the coastal trade and upstream to Houston. The establishment of a rail line between Houston and Galveston prior to the Civil War reduced the number of steamboats that would otherwise have run between them.

4. In 1870, Marion County ranked second after Galveston County in total manufacturing output and value added. All of the Marion County industries appear to have been located in Jefferson.

5. Knowledgeable opinion estimates that one-fourth of Texas trade passed through Jefferson. Regional comparative statistics for Texas trade are not available. However, documented cotton exports for Jefferson around the time of the 1870 agricultural census suggest that this is a good order-of-magnitude estimate.

6. In 1906, one of Jefferson's earliest businessmen wrote that it had been "the largest place, commercially speaking, of its size in the United States." This statement, which refers to volume of trade in comparison to the size of the population, may be true and may have been Jefferson's defining characteristic, given similar statements by external observers through the 1870s.

Jefferson's commercial primacy lasted only 30 years and was ended through the capture of its market area by the railroads, a process that was consummated through a tie-in between the Texas & Pacific and the Cairo & Fulton at Fulton, Arkansas, on the Red River in March 1874. The trade of northeast Texas shifted from New Orleans by steamboat to St. Louis by rail. Although the rail ran through Jefferson, it did little to contribute to the economic life of the town. Businessmen abandoned the town, and the population declined rapidly.

The present study is an outgrowth of *A History of Navigation on Cypress Bayou and the Lakes*, which covered all of the ports and landings west of Shreveport and all navigation activities from 1800 to the present. A large amount of information on Jefferson obtained from regional newspapers could not be incorporated into that text. As a result, the Historic Jefferson Foundation asked me to write a history of Jefferson and provided financial support for the effort.

This history was originally intended to cover the period of Jefferson's commercial primacy, from 1845 to 1874. The intention was abandoned with the discovery of the extraordinary resources available for local histories in the federal censuses; city records; and county tax rolls, deed records, probate records, district court minutes, and commissioners court minutes. The volume of materials and the detailed analysis needed to make them useful required that the present text end with the advent of the Civil War.

This history is essentially a weaving together of various bits of information from the local and regional newspapers and the city, county, and federal records, supplemented by maps, journal accounts, documents in special collections, and histories of particular subjects such as medicine. The information is largely presented topically rather than sequentially because of the nature of the sources and because the only story that can be told about antebellum Jefferson is the growth of the town.

For Jeffersonians, it offers a detailed analysis of people, places, and events within the context of the major features of the town. For persons external to Jefferson who are interested in its history, it offers a perspective on the functional dimensions of the town, with particular emphasis on its mercantile operations in a regional trade context. For persons interested in local history, it offers an insight into the potentials available in public documents, most of which are available on microfilm.

Footnotes have not been included because they would have been burdensome and complex. Critical sources have been identified in the text, and the major sources and how they were used are discussed in an appendix. For persons desiring more information, copies of advertisements and accounts transcribed from regional and Jefferson newspapers are on file with the Historic Jefferson Foundation.

In the absence of a sequential narrative, the basic facts concerning Jefferson's history are presented to position the reader:

April 1835—Removal of raft on Red River up to mouth of Twelvemile Bayou

July 1835—Caddo Indian treaty

March 1836—Formation of Republic of Texas

December 1837—Establishment of Red River County

Early 1838—Early settlements in the Port Caddo and Ray's Bluff (Benton) areas

June 1838—First steamboat on Caddo Lake (to Swanson's Landing)

Late 1838—Establishment of Port Caddo on Big Cypress Bayou

December 1838—First steamboat to Port Caddo

By 1839—Formation of Smithland on Big Cypress Bayou

June 1839—Probable selection of the Jefferson townsite by Allen Urquhart

By November 1840—Creation of Jefferson Town Company

November 1840—Corners established on Cypress Bayou for Urquhart property

December 1840—Formation of Bowie County out of Red River County

Late 1840—Construction of log cabin by Berry Durham at Jefferson townsite

Early 1841—Establishment of ferry operated by Berry Durham

May 1841—Probable first mention of Jefferson in a document

November 1841—Survey of Allen Urquhart's headright

January 1843—Probable creation of Jesse Cherry town plan

Late 1843—First sale of lots at townsite

April 1844—Daingerfield meeting to discuss removing obstructions in Big Cypress Bayou

July–December 1844—Removal of obstructions in Big Cypress Bayou

December 1844—Beginning of construction at townsite

March 1845—Arrival of first steamboat at Jefferson

By April 1845—Completion of the first structure

April 1845—Probable first sale of merchandise

1845—Erection of log hotel

Mid-1845—Probable operation of first sawmill

Between June and September 1845—Erection of first warehouse in landing area

December 1845—Entrance of Texas into the Union

March 1846—Resolution of property dispute between Urquhart and Durham

April 1846—Formation of Cass County out of Bowie County

May 1846—Establishment of post office in Jefferson

July 1846—Jefferson beginning to serve as temporary seat of Cass County

November 1846—Beginning of operation of Soda Lake Hotel

May 1847—Publication of first newspaper

By January 1848—Erection of private toll bridge over Big Cypress Bayou

March 1848—Incorporation

Late 1850—Formation of municipal government

March 1852—Linden designated as seat of Cass County

By late 1852—Establishment of stage line between Jefferson and Marshall

February 1853—Minor smallpox epidemic

Late 1853—Jefferson's opposition to steamboat monopoly

Early 1854—Erection of first public wharf

Early 1854—Unsuccessful attempt to secure telegraph

August 1854–December 1855—Extreme low water on Big Cypress Bayou

Late 1854—Initiation of second bayou clearing effort

February 1855—Establishment of free public bridge

February 1855—Completion of first brick structure

1857—National financial panic

July 1857—Initiation of third bayou clearing effort

Late 1857—Establishment of first meat packery

Late 1857—Establishment of first academic institution within city limits

September 1857–August 1858—Export of 25,000 bales of cotton through Jefferson

Late 1858—Establishment of second meat packery

Late 1858—Jefferson's oppostion to draining of Cross Lake

Early 1859—Jefferson's opposition to removal of raft on Red River

February 1860—Formation of Marion County out of Cass County

By late 1860—Establishment of racetrack in Jefferson

Late 1860—Erection of private wharf in landing area as extension of public wharf

Late 1860—Beginning of construction of first railroad

Late 1860—Jefferson's population reaches 988

It should be noted that the Jefferson area was originally part of Red River County and then became part of Bowie County in December

1840, part of Cass County in April 1846, and part of Marion County in February 1860. Thus, most of Jefferson's antebellum history is contained in Cass County records. Much use has been made of a set of materials called the Transcribed Deed Records. These were hand transcriptions made in the 1870s of deeds (primarily land transactions) from previous county jurisdictions that were relevant to Marion County. These transcriptions are particularly fortunate because all of the original Bowie County records were lost by fire.

Many dollar figures are used in the text. The significance of these amounts is not clear without an understanding that a dollar was worth a lot more before the Civil War than it is today. A good rule of thumb is to multiply all numbers by 20. This means that a bale of cotton valued at $50 would be valued at $1,000 today, that a lot sold in Jefferson for $200 would cost $4,000 today, that a slave sold for $1,000 would cost $20,000 today, and that a person with real estate and personal property valued at $50,000 was a millionaire.

Lastly, anyone who has dealt with these old records has had to struggle with the problem of variant spellings in personal names. Anglicizing explains some of this variance, but it was far outweighed by almost universal indifference to how names were spelled. This is particularly evident in single legal records that contain more than one spelling, in newspaper advertisements that carry obviously incorrect renditions for many months, and in census errors where the census taker knew the person whose name was misspelled. I have made best guesses where necessary, used one spelling throughout (except in quotes), and dropped the middle initials to avoid formality.

1. Background

The area in which Jefferson came to be founded was once part of New Spain and from 1821 part of Mexico until the Republic of Texas was established in 1836. Although there was early Spanish settlement to the south in Nacogdoches, there was never a hint of Spanish influence in the Jefferson area. Although Jefferson came into existence before Texas entered the Union, it cannot be characterized as a Republic of Texas settlement. While the town was emerging in early 1845, Texas was well on its way to entering the Union, with annexation approved by the U.S. Congress in March 1845 and Texas formally admitted as a state in December. Jefferson was an American settlement whose origins were coterminus with the achievement of statehood by Texas. As a matter of coincidence, the first steamboat reached the emerging town during the same month that annexation was approved.

When the Louisiana Purchase took place in 1803, the western boundary between the United States and New Spain was uncertain. The 1819 Adams-Onis treaty established part of the boundary as a line running north to the Red River from the point at which the 33rd degree of longitude struck the Sabine River. Although this line was correctly run by William Darby in 1816, this was not an official survey; and in any case the line was incorrectly delineated (for political reasons) by Darby's map publisher John Melish. The line was not firmly fixed until the U.S.-Republic of Texas boundary survey in 1841, which ran the line through Caddo Lake to the east of the Jefferson area. Until that time, there was a strip of disputed territory in which political jurisdiction was uncertain.

Trammel's Trace, which extended from Fulton, Arkansas, to Nacogdoches, Texas, was blazed by Nicholas Trammel around 1815 and was joined above Hughes Springs by another trail blazed by Trammel that extended south from Jonesboro, Texas. The trace crossed over Big Cypress Bayou five miles west of Jefferson slightly above the confluence with French Creek. The trace was the major early entranceway into northeast Texas.

In 1825, Frost Thorn was provided a land grant by Mexico extending from the Sabine River on the south to the Red River on the north, with a provision to respect rights established by prior settlement. Thorn was the son-in-law of Haden Edwards, who was provided a grant that included most of East Texas south of the Sabine with the right to settle 800 families. A map apparently prepared for Thorn in 1826 shows the immediate Jefferson area inked-in (as a rectangle) by a later hand (Fig. 1-1). The map is important because it shows that in the late 1820s there was nothing between Sulphur Fork and the Sabine other than the Caddo Indian village, which is shown incorrectly south of Caddo Lake. The early surveys for the Jefferson area shown on the map were probably moot after the abortive Fredonian Rebellion in November, which was led by Edwards and resulted in his removal to Louisiana.

The general area in which Jefferson came to be founded was a wilderness until it began to be settled in the late 1830s. The reason for this wilderness status was twofold: the Great Raft and the Caddo Indians. The Great Raft was a logjam on the Red River about 80 miles in length that moved continuously upstream at about a mile a year as its head gained additional timber and its foot decayed. Boats could not penetrate the raft, and settlement along the Red was limited to the area free of the raft. Natchitoches was founded as a French post and as a counterpoint to the Spanish post of Nacogdoches near the foot of the raft in 1714. The Campti settlement on the east side of the river and the Cane River settlement on the west side of the river were established above Natchitoches and expanded upward as the foot of the raft regressed.

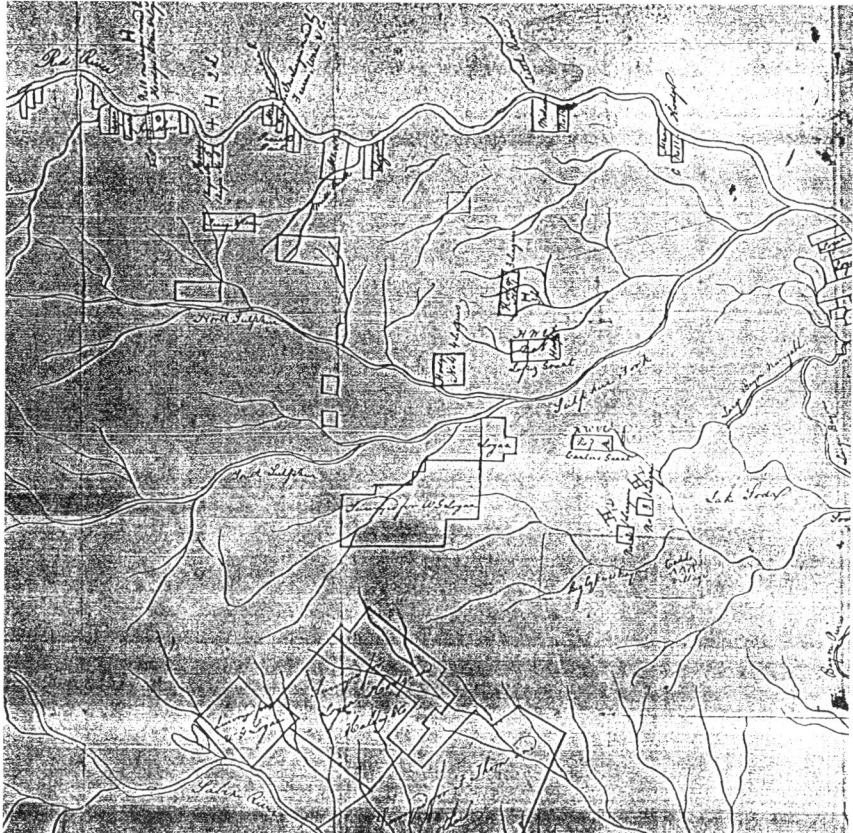

Fig. 1-1. Northeast Texas in 1826

Because the raft acted as a dam on the river, the water had to go somewhere, and distributaries formed continuously on its floodplain, leaving the river above the head of the raft and entering back into the river below the foot of the raft. A navigation route around the raft to the upper Red River was available through a series of streams and lakes on the east side of the river. This route was accessed at the northern end of the Campti settlement and led back into the river above present-day Shreveport. Keelboats began using this route in 1816, but it was closed by the head of the raft in 1828.

The upper Red River area northeast of the river was part of the Louisiana Purchase and began to be settled soon after 1803, with accelerated settlement after Arkansas became a territory in 1819. The area southwest of the river was within the disputed territory, but assumed to belong to the United States by the early settlers, with thrusts across the river beginning in 1811. However, this land was occupied by the Caddo, and their claims were intermittently enforced by federal authorities.

The planters, farmers, and merchants who settled southwest Arkansas and northeast Texas were anxious to have secure water access to New Orleans, and the federal government was anxious to have secure water access to Fort Towson, which was founded in southeastern Oklahoma in 1824 in what was then the Indian Territory. This led to federal efforts beginning in 1825 to establish a navigation route around the raft on the west side of the river above present-day Shreveport, which were successfully completed in 1831.

However, the route was dangerous and costly, and Arkansas citizens wanted the raft removed to provide better navigation by way of the river and to eliminate flooding of farmlands as the raft moved upstream. A project to remove the raft was initiated by the federal government in 1832 and was carried out by Capt. Henry Shreve of the Corps of Engineers from 1833 through 1838. Although Shreve was successful, a new raft formed at the old raft's head above Shreveport in 1839 and built upward until it nearly reached the Arkansas line in 1873 when it was permanently removed. Although Shreve was not interested in the area west of Shreveport, his actions had the fortunate consequence of opening the navigation route west of Shreveport in April 1835 through removal of the raft up to the mouth of Twelvemile Bayou.

The Caddo Indians had lived for centuries on the south bank of the upper Red River. Their hunting range extended from the Red River on the north to (another) Cypress Bayou below Shreveport on the south and to Texas' Blackland Prairie on the west. They were forced by disease and a hostile tribe to leave their traditional village area in 1795, locating first on the east side of the river above Shreveport, then briefly on the west side of the river, until they established a permanent village in 1800 on Jim's Bayou, which enters Caddo Lake from the north. Recognizing that Shreve's raft removal effort would lead to an unstoppable influx of white settlers, they signed a treaty agreeing to their removal with the United States in July 1835, shortly after Shreve removed the raft up to the mouth of Twelvemile Bayou.

Although Shreve's raft removal effort was important to the area west of Shreveport, little would have happened in that area had it not been for the raft. Prior to 1800, Caddo Lake and Soda Lake, which were essential components of the Cypress Bayou and the lakes route, were nonexistent. Cypress Bayou ran at its lower end through a forested valley that was eventually to become Caddo Lake and through a Red River floodplain depression that was eventually to become Soda Lake. These lakes were formed in 1800 when the raft, acting as a dam on the river, caused a break in the banks of a river bend above Shreveport, sending Red River water into the Caddo and Soda lakes areas through a distributary. This was before the 1811 New Madrid earthquake, which is often assumed to be the cause of the formation of the lakes.

These areas did not immediately drain because the raft had trapped sediment, raising the bed of the river at the outlet of Twelvemile Bayou, thereby making it an inefficient discharge point. As the raft moved upstream, new distributaries were formed, sending water constantly into the area of the lakes, at least when there was water in Red River. All of the early federal surveys are in agreement that the Cypress Bayou and the lakes route would not have been navigable, particularly in the Soda Lake area, had it not been for this infusion of Red River water.

With the removal of the raft and the Caddo Indians in 1835, the area west of Shreveport was available for settlement, with water access to the Red River, thence to the Mississippi and New Orleans. Conditions for settlement were enhanced through the formation of the Republic of Texas in March 1836, which acquired the southwest part of the upper Red River area. Farmers, planters, and merchants began arriving in the late 1830s; the fertile agricultural lands north and south of Caddo Lake and Cypress Bayou were settled by planters and farmers; Robert Potter and his mistress Harriet Page (later Ames) became the first white settlers on Caddo Lake (on the north shore at Potter's Point); Peter Swanson settled with his family and established a landing on the south shore of the lake; and merchants became established in the Cypress Bayou ports of Port Caddo, Benton (under the name of

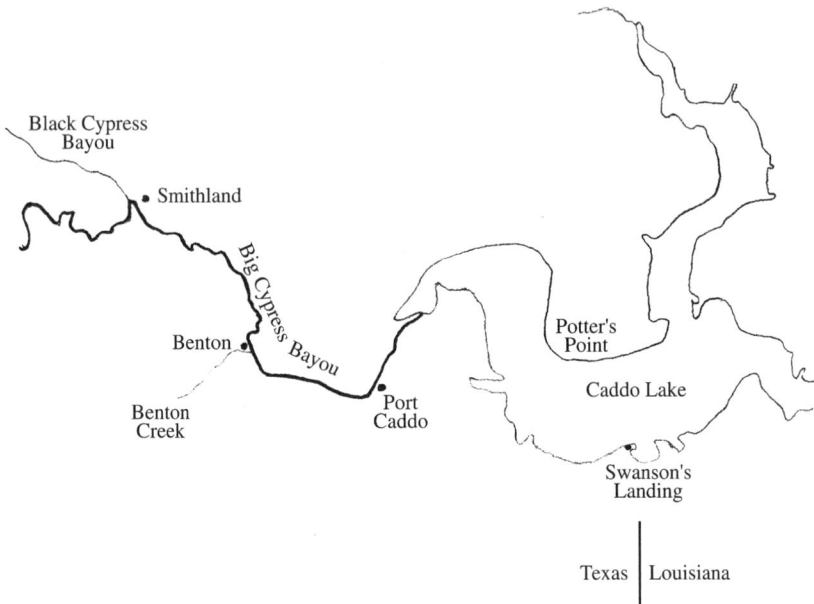

Fig. 1-2. Early Ports and Landings

Ray's Bluff), and Smithland, which was just six miles below the site of what was to become Jefferson (Fig. 1-2).

North of Cypress Bayou was Red River County, established by the Republic of Texas in December 1837. Clarksville, which was homesteaded in 1833 and was functioning as a town in 1835, became the county seat in 1838. Part of Red River County became Bowie County in December 1840, and the southern part of Bowie County became Cass County in April 1846. South of Cypress Bayou was Shelby County, which was established by the Republic of Texas in 1836. The northern part of Shelby County became Harrison County in 1839. Peter Whetstone offered land for a county seat in 1841 that became Marshall in 1842.

Some of the early settlers who moved to the Cypress Bayou area were from the southwestern part of the Republic of Texas. Others were from the northeastern part (the upper Red River area). However, most appear to have been new arrivals, moving overland through Arkansas (which had become a state in June 1836) by way of Washington and Fulton or by water through New Orleans to Shreveport, which was recognized as a steamboat destination by 1837. Steamboats did not run west of Shreveport immediately because there was insufficient development to attract their interest.

By early 1838, flatboats were operating to a small settlement that was to become Port Caddo. Capt. W. W. Withenbury, who brought the first steamboat to Jefferson, indicates in his reminiscences (published as a series of letters in the 1870–71 *Cincinnati Commercial*) that the only steamboats to penetrate Caddo Lake prior to December 1841 were the *Echo*, which made two trips to Port Caddo, and the *Manchester*, which made one trip to Swanson's Landing and Rives' Landing. Harriet Ames in her memoirs indicates that the first steamboat on Caddo Lake brought her brother and James Rives to Potter's Point. This was obviously the *Manchester*, which made a side trip to what was to become Rives' Landing on the east side of the Potter's Point peninsula after visiting Swanson's Landing on the south shore of Caddo Lake.

The trip by the *Manchester* was part of an extended voyage to the upper Red River in June–July 1838. The *Manchester*, a 114-foot by 20-foot sidewheeler, brought freight to the newly formed Swanson's Landing in June and made the side trip to Rives' Landing to enable Harriet's brother to reach Potter's Point at the birth of his niece Lakeann. The first trip by the *Echo* was part of a voyage to the Red River in December 1838. The *Echo*, a 152-foot by 19-foot sidewheeler, brought freight to the newly formed Port Caddo, which was then occupied by Republic of Texas troops. The second trip by the *Echo* was part of an extended voyage to the upper Red River in March–May 1839, with the boat probably reaching Port Caddo in April. The March 25 *New Orleans Commercial Bulletin* advertisement for the *Echo* to Fort Towson, Jonesboro, Fulton, and Port Caddo is the first extant advertisement for a boat west of Shreveport.

Withenbury also indicates that the first bale of cotton was taken out of Port Caddo in December 1841 aboard the *Relief*. Withenbury was a clerk on this boat, which was captained by Joseph Ross. Assistance in navigating the lake, which included a stopoff at Swanson's Landing, was provided by Hiram Bails, known as "Bails the Bee Hunter," a Caddo Lake recluse who earned a living by collecting honey and acting as a pilot for keelboats and steamboats. The cotton at Port Caddo was owned by John Kitchen, whose plantation was north of Port Caddo. Withenbury also mentions the merchant William English, who commissioned the voyage to obtain supplies; the Indian family of Larkin Edwards, who had served as interpreter for the Caddo; and the planter Spire Hagerty, whose Scotch-Indian wife Rebecca was to become one of the wealthiest persons in the south, owning plantations north and south of Cypress Bayou.

Withenbury also says that the bayou was clear for six miles above Port Caddo (that is, to the Benton area), but that the first voyage beyond Port Caddo was 10 miles upstream to Rose's Gin and was made by the *Robert T. Lytle*. This could only have occurred (from the New Orleans newspaper records) in late 1843 or early 1844, with Withenbury suggesting that the latter was the case. Rose's Gin was apparently immediately below the shallow, convoluted area of Cypress Bayou called Dougherty's Defeat. The progressive movement of steamboats upstream was not rapid. In fact, there is nothing to indicate that any steamboat other than the *Robert T. Lytle* ran above Port Caddo until Withenbury took the first steamboat to Jefferson in March 1845, in spite of the fact that the *Farmer* advertised for Benton in June 1841 and the *Star* advertised for Smithland in February 1842.

In the meantime, Port Caddo capitalized on its role as the primary outlet for the cotton of Harrison County, which was the second largest Texas producer in 1849 according to the agricultural census. Boats returning to New Orleans from Port Caddo carried 909 bales in 1842, 1,557 bales in 1843, and 6,391 bales in 1844. At least two boats made at least three trips to Port Caddo in 1842, at least four boats made at least six trips in 1843, and at least five boats made at least 28 trips in 1844, including nine by the *Bois d'Arc*. In addition, the *John H. Bills* made a trip to Swanson's Landing in 1843, carrying out 163 bales of cotton.

In early 1838, the settlement at Ray's Bluff that was to become Benton was actually larger than the settlement that was to become Port Caddo and included a boarding house. Although little is known about Benton during its early years, it was important enough to have a public road, which was established in November 1848 and eventually ran all the way across the county to the west; and it was initially considered as the starting point for a railroad spur line that eventually was constructed out of Swanson's Landing.

Smithland was located at the confluence of Big Cypress and Black Cypress bayous and had a post office in September 1839. It was visited by Josiah Gregg in August 1841 when it had half a dozen houses. Gregg observed that the townsite of Jefferson about six miles upstream was the highest feasible point for navigation on Cypress Bayou and would capture all of the business to the west if the bayou was improved above Smithland. Gregg recognized the potential of the townsite and the conditions for its realization. Because Gregg had not visited the townsite, this recognition appears to have been common opinion among the people of the area in August 1841.

2. What Jefferson Was

The business of America has always been business. Towns during the 1800s were places where people congregated to engage in economic activities, with the notable exception of political centers such as county seats. The character of a town was largely determined by the nature of its business activities. Most towns in Texas were agricultural service centers whose merchants sold retail to nearby farmers and planters, as well as to resident populations. Jefferson had retail stores; but if that was all it had, it would have been similar to thousands of other towns. To classify Jefferson simply as a port town is misleading. The vast majority of ports and landings in Texas never developed into towns; and of those that did, only a few became towns of Jefferson's dimensions. Jefferson would not have become an important town if it had not been a port, but port status does not clarify its distinctive character.

Jefferson was a commercial center—that is, a place where large volumes of commodities that were transported from one point to another were exchanged or bought and sold. These were the export commodities that were produced in Jefferson's market area and the import commodities that were demanded by Jefferson's market area. Export commodities were sent out of the market area by ox-wagon and placed on steamboats at Jefferson for carriage to New Orleans. Import commodities were brought to Jefferson by steamboat from New Orleans and sent to the interior by ox-wagon. Jefferson was as much an ox-wagon destination and point of departure as a steamboat port.

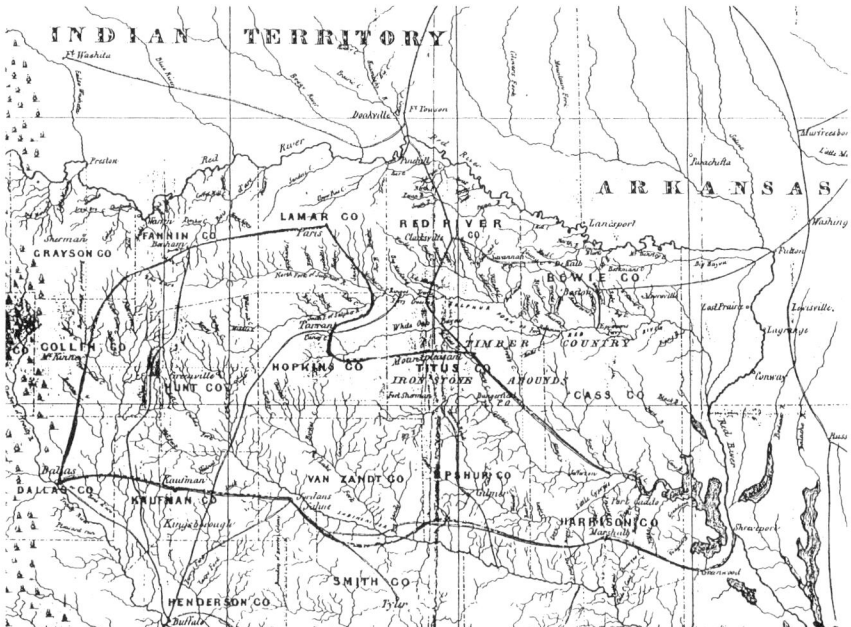

Fig. 2-1. Jefferson's Market Area. Source: Courtesy Archives and Information Services Division, Texas State Library and Archives Commission.

Jefferson was a commercial center because large quantities of merchandise and agricultural products passed through it and this happened because of the high volume of production and demand in its market area. Jefferson's market area encompassed the whole of northeast Texas, extending to the Indian Territory on the north and the Dallas-Bonham axis on the west. The market area is best represented by the map accompanying Edward Smith's *Account of a Journey Through North-Eastern Texas Undertaken in 1849* (Fig. 2-1). Although impressive, the size of the market area was not important in itself. Jefferson was a commercial center because of the dimensions of supply and demand in its market area. Without the large supply produced by agricultural operations and the large demand produced by the agricultural population in its market area, Jefferson would not have developed into anything of importance.

Cotton production was the dominant economic activity in Jefferson's market area. Cotton needed to be exported from the market area because there were no cotton mills. Planters and farmers normally did not bring their cotton to Jefferson before the Civil War. The interior movement of cotton was carried out primarily by slow and expensive commercial ox-wagons and secondarily by producers who wanted to personally sell their cotton in Jefferson. Ox-wagon transport placed severe limitations on the geographic extent of cotton agriculture because the expense of transport made cotton unprofitable if it had to be moved more than 150 miles over land. Waterborne transport was much lower in cost than overland transport. Cotton would not have been grown in northeast Texas without the capacity to export by water. Cotton producers sought the nearest water outlet to minimize transport costs. For most of northeast Texas most of the time, that meant Jefferson.

In addition to exports, cotton was the basis for imports. Cotton was produced on plantations, which were large-scale agricultural operations dependent on the skilled labor provided by slaves. Workers needed such things as clothing; cotton production required tools and such things as rope and bagging; and the wealth generated by cotton gave rise to demands for refined articles. In addition, there were smaller farms that produced cotton and other agricultural products, cattle ranches, and small towns with their own resident populations. All of these elements provided demands for merchandise that was not produced in Jefferson's market area or in Jefferson itself and therefore needed to be imported. Planters, interior merchants, and citizens normally did not go to Jefferson to pick up the merchandise destined for them. The high cost of ox-wagon transport also determined that imports would enter the market area through the nearest point.

Cypress Bayou, on which Jefferson was located, was the only stream penetrating northeast Texas that offered viable waterborne transport, and it had the additional advantage of being navigable for a considerable distance into the interior. As the port farthest upstream on the bayou, Jefferson had a natural command as an export and import center for the market area to the north and west. This command was disturbed only by the intermittent ability of upper Red River planters to transport their cotton directly down the Red River. Jefferson essentially had a lock on its market area and was largely noncompetitive with Shreveport with the exception of the upper Red River trade.

Jefferson's dominance of its market area should not lead to a misplaced emphasis. Jefferson needed its market area. The market area did not need Jefferson in the sense of a particular port at that precise point. What it needed was access to waterborne transport and particularly to the capacity of steamboats to efficiently carry export bulk commodities such as cotton and import bulk commodities such as barrels of whiskey. Jefferson was able to serve this function only because it was a port. However, if Jefferson had not come into existence, the function would have been served by Smithland six miles downstream.

Jefferson was the destination and point of departure for two transport modes that operated in conjunction with each other. Cotton was sent out of Jefferson to New Orleans by steamboat. The commodities destined for Jefferson's market area were picked up by these same steamboats at New Orleans and brought back to Jefferson. Steamboats operated in a circle between Jefferson and New Orleans, taking cotton out and bringing commodities in. Transport costs were reduced because steamboats generally had the opportunity to operate loaded in both directions. The movement of ox-wagons in the interior was also circular. Ox-wagons brought cotton to Jefferson for transport by steamboat and also returned to the interior loaded with merchandise that had been brought into Jefferson by steamboats. Transport costs were reduced because ox-wagons generally had the opportunity to carry full loads in both directions.

Jefferson was the transfer point for the commodities carried by these two circular modes of transport. If transfer had been instantaneous, no value would have been added, and Jefferson would never have been a commercial center. The key elements in value added were the receiving, forwarding, and commission merchants and the wholesale merchants. As their name suggests, these merchants received and forwarded merchandise and sold various items on commission, of which cotton was the most important. The receiving and forwarding activities were in both directions, from and towards Jefferson's market area and from and towards New Orleans. The receiving and forwarding merchants were agents of safe passage between the two transport modes.

Cotton was brought to these merchants by ox-wagons from the interior where it was weighed, marked, and stored in the merchant's warehouse. Storage was necessary because steamboats were not always available, because the receiving and forwarding merchants tried to get the best transport costs for their customers while keeping an eye on the cost of storage, and because ox-wagons could not offload directly to steamboats, which would have created a transportation nightmare with attendant costs. The receiving and forwarding merchants were located in the landing area and transported cotton to the landing by drays, where it was offloaded to the landing and carried onto the steamboats by deck hands.

When cotton was ready for transport, a deal was made with a steamboat clerk for the cost of transport, and a bill of lading was prepared. The bill of lading identified the number and condition of the bales of cotton to be shipped, the Jefferson shipper (and usually the planter who owned the cotton), the New Orleans receiver, the boat that would provide the transport, and the transport cost. The bill of lading was signed by the captain or the clerk of the steamboat, indicating acceptance of responsibility for safe transport. Cotton arriving in New Orleans was listed in a consignments column in the newspaper showing the intended destination.

Movements in the opposite direction followed the same procedures. Commodities destined for Jefferson were loaded on steamboats at New Orleans with bills of lading, transported to the landing where they were offloaded by deck hands, picked up by drays, and transported to various warehouses. The Jefferson newspapers contained a consignments column showing commodity destinations, including Jefferson citizens, wholesalers, and retailers and interior merchants, planters, and citizens. Commodities destined immediately for the interior were stored at the receiving and forwarding warehouses and picked up by ox-wagons.

Of equal importance to the commercial life of the town were the wholesale operations, most of which had retail components. Jefferson wholesalers bought such things as groceries, dry goods, and drugs in

New Orleans, Boston, and New York from wholesalers, with shipments arranged for the time the commodities would be needed. Commodities from the Northeast passed through New Orleans before reaching Jefferson. Unlike the receiving, forwarding, and commision merchants who transferred commodities in both directions, wholesalers bought from one direction and sold in another.

Interior merchants were the primary customers of Jefferson wholesalers; but they also sold to planters, whose large-scale agricultural operations required purchases in high volume. As was common for the period, these transactions were based largely on credit but could be covered by cotton, other agricultural commodities, or cash as payment. Wholesale prices were low because of competition among Jefferson firms and potential competition from Shreveport and New Orleans. Prices were also low because wholesalers pursued a business strategy of profit maximization through high sales volumes, which resulted in fairly rapid turnovers of stock and increased the amount of trade that passed through Jefferson.

Every port in northeast Texas had receiving and forwarding capacities, even if it did not have businesses specifically devoted to those activities. Jefferson's uniqueness was constituted by its large number of wholesale operations, and Jefferson was the only town in northeast Texas to list prevailing prices for wholesale commodities in its newspapers, indicating a formal wholesale market. Because receiving and forwarding merchants carried merchandise for advances to planters, they often entered into the wholesaling business. The receiving, forwarding, and commission house that sold dry goods and groceries at wholesale and retail was the quintessential Jefferson business establishment.

The third feature that characterized Jefferson as a commercial center was not a business type but rather a market for the agricultural commodities produced in Jefferson's market area, particularly cotton, hides, and cattle. Jefferson's commodity markets were not institutionalized through such things as a cotton exchange. However, the markets were formal and unique in the sense that no other town in northeast Texas listed prevailing prices for agricultural commodities in its newspapers.

Prior to the Civil War, most of the cotton that was produced in Jefferson's market area was sent to cotton factors in New Orleans who acted as bankers, suppliers, and sales agents for planters. Factors had better knowledge of the volatile cotton market and sufficient cash reserves to hold cotton until the best price could be achieved for the planter. There were no cotton factors in Jefferson prior to the Civil War. However, Jefferson's receiving and forwarding merchants usually had close working relationships with New Orleans factors and were able to make cash and merchandise advances (e.g., bagging and rope) to the shipping planter on behalf of the factor. This was a partial form of sale.

There were two primary forms of full sale. Planters and farmers who wanted to sell their cotton in Jefferson without actually going to town could send their cotton to commission merchants, who fulfilled the sales agent role of the New Orleans cotton factor. The commission merchants were the primary institutional components of Jefferson's cotton market, displaying samples in their facilities. The primary buyers in this market component were speculators and probably agents of New Orleans cotton brokers who bought for the mills. Planters and farmers who were willing to bring their cotton to Jefferson sold it primarily off of wagons in the streets. The primary buyers in this market component were speculators, broker agents, and merchants. The wholesalers of dry goods and groceries usually offered a mix of goods and cash for cotton. Most of the buying activities were highly speculative because they were based on guesses about resale prices in volatile downstream markets that were obscured in Jefferson by the absence of a telegraph.

Although Jefferson was primarily a commercial center, it also had important industries. The second most important export commodity from Jefferson's market area was cattle and cattle products, primarily hides. The production of cattle in the northeast portion of Jefferson's market area gave rise to meat packing facilities in Jefferson. These were industries rather than commercial operations because they involved the production of commodities rather than their transfer. Meat packeries were located in town and across the bayou before the Civil War. Packery products were not distributed to Jefferson's market area, but rather to external markets, which significantly raised the level of steamboat arrivals at Jefferson. Meat packeries would not have developed at Jefferson had it not been first a commercial center and if steamboats had not been available for transport of pickled beef in barrels to the New Orleans market and beyond.

Economic activity provided the occasion for a fairly large resident population given the standards of the day. The resident population was supplemented by immigrants who arrived by steamboat on their way farther west, merchants and planters from the interior who came to town to inspect wholesale stocks, businessmen passing through, construction workers, steamboat crews, ox-wagon drivers, and the general drift of humanity. Jefferson grew because its market area grew in agricultural production and demand for merchandise. However, it did not grow very large, reaching a population of only 988 in 1860. This was in large part because its defining businesses were not labor intensive. Immense quantities of bulk commodities were moved with the assistance of steamboatmen and ox-wagon drivers who were not Jefferson residents. High commodity volumes with a small resident population gave rise to a trade-to-population ratio that was recognized as Jefferson's distinctive feature.

Jefferson was not commercially active during the summer. Cotton from the previous year had already been shipped out, and boat access to Jefferson was negligible or nonexistent. Planters were busy with their crops, and merchants were away from town securing fall and winter stocks. Cotton was a summer crop, with the first bale generally received at Jefferson during September. However, the bulk of the staple took a long time to get to Jefferson because it needed to be harvested, ginned, baled, and transported over fairly long distances by slow-moving ox-wagons. Receipts picked up in the latter months of the year and reached a crescendo in the first few months of the next calendar year.

The height of economic activity was in the winter. This was when ox-wagons from the north and west glutted the access roads and streets of Jefferson, producing a quagmire when it rained and clouds of dust when it was dry. Steamboats arrived and departed at all hours of the day and night, loading and offloading freight. Drays ran between the landing and the warehouses, and ox-wagons offloaded and loaded at the warehouses. Receiving and forwarding merchants ran round the clock in conjunction with the constant activities of steamboats. The wholesale and retail establishments on Dallas and Marshall streets were alive with activity during the day.

Apart from the dimensions of its commercial activities, the amount of traffic that passed through town, and the fact that it was a port, there was little to distinguish Jefferson from the other towns of the day. Houses were modest. Streets were dirt, with raised wooden sidewalks. Buildings were of one-story or sometimes two-story frame construction, giving way to brick in 1855, which was first used in warehouse construction for fire protection. Water was from wells. Sanitary needs were met by privies. The primary feature that was not shared by many other towns was the landing area, which was dirt until 1854 when sloped wooden wharves were introduced. What was most striking to repeat visitors was the liveliness of Jefferson's economy, the constant growth in the number and size of its commercial establishments, the optimism and enthusiasm of its citizens, and the fact that Jefferson appeared destined for greatness.

Major crimes were few and seldom perpetrated by Jefferson residents. Although there was a modest leaven of vice, it was largely restricted to one part of town. Ox-wagons encamped four miles outside of town, and steamboat crews seldom had an opportunity for mischief because steamboats were constantly on the move. Jefferson was widely recognized for the quality of its civil order, even enviously by towns like Marshall. This was attributed to staunch enforcement of ordinances by city officials; but the impetus for this enforcement came from the mercantile class and its desire for efficiencies in commercial operations.

Jefferson was a magnet for commercial talent from the beginning because of the opportunities it offered and increased as an attractant as it grew in size and importance. Merchants came from other towns such as Marshall, Clarksville, Shreveport, Smithland, Port Caddo, and New Orleans to seize these opportunities. Partnerships were formed and dissolved, new businesses opened, and businesses passed from one hand to another in a dynamic commercial setting. This was what we would call an entrepreneurial economy, but in the language of the day was referred to as the spirit of enterprise, which was manifest in town improvements as well as in business operations.

The mercantile class was comprised of sophisticated men with large business operations, many of whom were very young. They were well read, politically active, litigious, generally leaders in church activities, and involved in the affairs of the community. Their distinctive virtues, in the terminology of the day, were cleverness (shrewd, skillful, mentally quick, practical, energetic, and capable of overcoming obstacles) and liberality (generous, openhanded, and broadminded). Business relations were regional, national, and international in scope, producing a cosmopolitan perspective. Men of talent in an opportunity situation generally engaged in more than one trade and often entered into radically different types of businesses.

Jefferson was a businessman's town. Merchants and clerks constituted by far the largest occupational categories, and all of these were male. Slaves constituted more than one-fourth of Jefferson's population, and male slaves contributed to the economic life of the town as freight and stock movers for the stores and warehouses and as skilled and semi-skilled craftsmen. Like most frontier towns, men outnumbered women in Jefferson; and like most southern towns, female occupations were restricted to extensions of domestic activities such as teaching. The only female business owner-operator was a hotelier. Women were seldom seen on the streets of Jefferson because few were employed and because the port activities and the movement of cattle and ox-wagons was incompatible with their presence. The greatest contribution made by women to the ambiance of the town was sociability and hospitality, which were two of Jefferson's main virtues according to external observers.

3. Foundations

Headrights

Land was given away through headright grants by the Republic of Texas to encourage settlement. Most grants were for 640 acres to unmarried men and 1,280 acres to men with families. In most cases, a conditional headright certificate was issued to qualified applicants, land was selected, a survey was conducted, an unconditional certificate was issued after a residency of three years, and a final patent on the land was provided some years later. These materials were filed with the Texas General Land Office.

The vast majority of headrights were acquired for farming or were sold by their owners to other persons who used the land for farming. Land naturally appreciated gradually in value over time; but in the early circumstances when it was given away for free, the only ways in which an immediate appreciation of value could be secured were through land clearing and other farm improvements or through the founding of a town. Starting a town with lots that could be sold individually provided the best means of making money, but the number of opportunities for town formation was small. Many were envisioned that were never realized.

To understand the inception of Jefferson, it is necessary to review the land acquisitions of Allen Urquhart and Daniel Alley, who are considered the town's co-founders, with the former accounting for the eastern portion in which the port was located and the latter accounting for the western portion that was largely devoted to residential development. It is also necessary to understand the activities of Stephen Smith, from whom Alley acquired his contribution to Jefferson by purchase.

According to General Land Office records, Allen Urquhart arrived in Texas on April 11, 1837, and appeared before the Board of Land Commissioners for Red River County in Clarksville on August 3, 1838, to claim a headright of 1,280 acres, which he was granted conditionally. Urquhart was to eventually choose two 640-acre pieces of land, one that became the nucleus of Jefferson and the other that became the nucleus of Daingerfield 30 miles to the northwest, where he spent his life.

A survey for the land that was to become Daingerfield was conducted by William Hamilton, the deputy surveyor for Red River County, on June 10, 1839, and filed with the county surveyor, J. T. Harmon, in Clarksville on February 26, 1840. Urquhart began to pay taxes on this land in 1840, as indicated by the Red River County tax rolls. He appeared before the Board of Land Commissioners of Paschal County (a short-lived judicial district) in Daingerfield on August 23, 1841, and was granted an unconditional headright certificate on the 1,280 acres, having lived in the Republic of Texas for three years and performed all of the duties of a citizen. A patent on this land was granted to Urquhart by the State of Texas on April 14, 1851.

It appears from this sequence that Daingerfield began to be settled after June 1839, achieving formal existence in January 1841 when the Texas Legislature stipulated that a town to be known as Dangerfield would be selected as the seat of Paschal County. Urquhart appeared before the Board of Land Commissioners in Daingerfield in August, and the town acquired a post office in December.

The survey of the 640 acres that was eventually to become Jefferson was not conducted until November 19, 1841, more than two years after the Daingerfield land survey and shortly after the grant of the unconditional headright. The 1841 survey, which was conducted by Urquhart himself as deputy surveyor of Paschal County, describes the land as situated "on the North Bank of Ferry lake at Jefferson." Ferry Lake was the old name for Caddo Lake, which was considered to

Fig. 3-1. Urquhart's 1841 Survey. Source: Courtesy Texas General Land Office, Austin

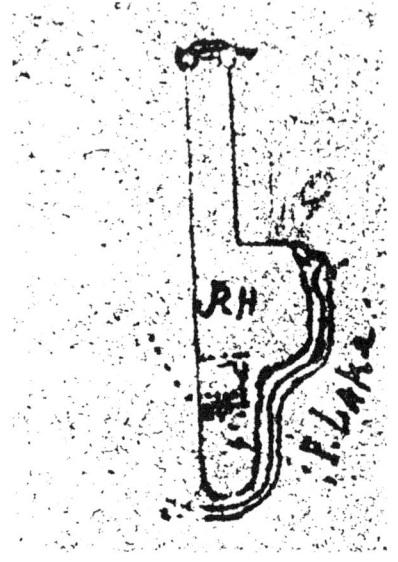

extend far up Big Cypress Bayou in all early records. The use of the name "Jefferson" is important because it shows that Urquhart envisioned this portion of his headright as a town from the earliest time. The inset map that accompanies the survey notes shows a northwest-southeast tending trail crossing Cypress Bayou through the survey (Fig. 3-1). This indicates that a road from Daingerfield to Shreveport with a ferry crossing at Cypress Bayou was in existence by at least November 1841. The ferry was operated by Berry Durham.

The 1841 survey was filed with the county surveyor, Levi Jordan, apparently shortly thereafter (the date of filing is illegible). Although the survey shows a piece of land extending from Big Cypress Bayou on the south to Black Cypress Bayou on the north, the configuration is not the same as that which eventually was adopted. The survey was apparently defective, because the survey lines needed to be closed, which was accomplished through a resurvey on June 27, 1842. Although the text is nearly illegible, the revised survey appears to have been recorded by Levi Jordan, Bowie County surveyor, in September 1842. Urquhart began paying taxes on this land in 1842.

There were some remaining problems with the 1842 survey in relation to contiguous surveys. Another survey was conducted for

Fig. 3-2. Urquhart's 1849 Survey. Source: Courtesy Texas General Land Office, Austin

Urquhart by William Kimbell on November 21, 1849, describing and showing by an inset map the final land configuration. The land is described as that "upon which the Town of Jefferson now stands," and the location of the town is shown in the southern portion of the survey (Fig. 3-2). Urquhart received a patent on this land from the State of Texas on April 14, 1851.

In choosing these two pieces of land, Urquhart was thoroughly acquainted with the development opportunites afforded by various parcels of unclaimed land in northeast Texas. The survey records in the Marion County courthouse, which account for only a small portion of Urquhart's activities, indicate that he was deputy surveyor for Red River County from at least April 1838 to at least June 1840. Moreover, this was a long-term occupation, because he also appears as deputy surveyor for Bowie and Cass counties in 1846 and 1848.

The reason for the selection of the Daingerfield land in 1839 is apparent, because Urquhart was a farmer who was also interested in founding a contiguous town. The Jefferson land was selected in 1841 because of the opportunity it offered for the founding of a port, because it was the highest point upstream where it was feasible to locate a port, and because it was well known throughout the region that the port highest up on Cypress Bayou would capture all of the commercial business to the west. Urquhart probably became aware of the unique opportunities afforded by the Jefferson site for a turning basin and landing when he conducted a survey of the land immediately to the east for the heirs of John Humphries on June 19, 1839 (Fig. 3-3). The

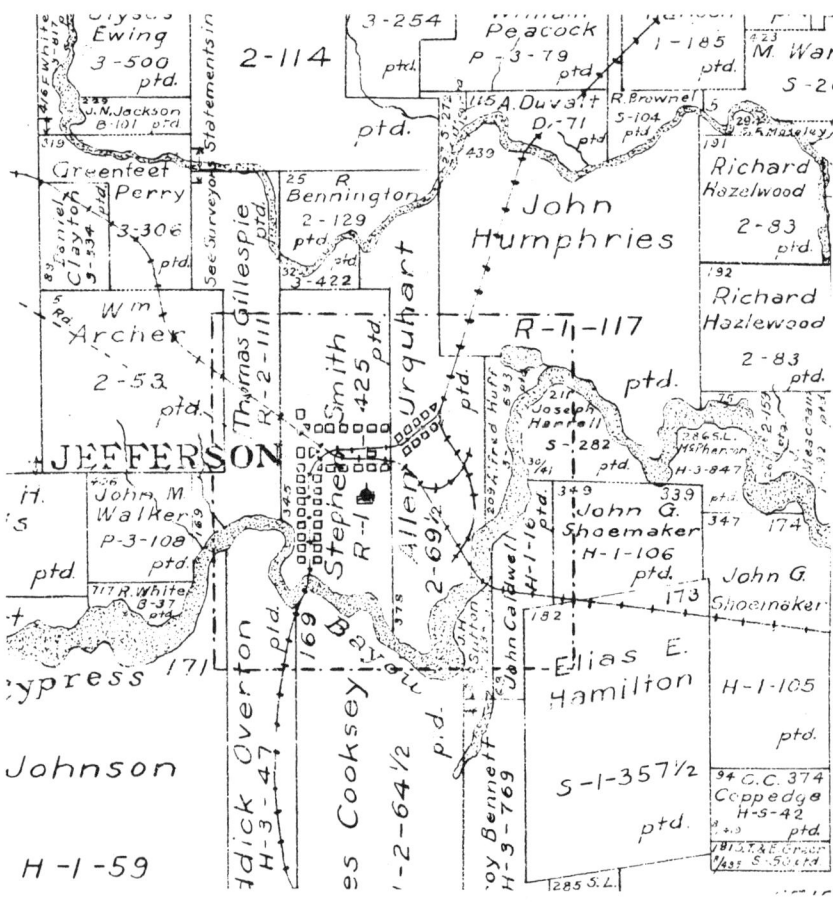

Fig. 3-3. Headrights. Source: Courtesy Texas General Land Office, Austin

streets in this section of town were laid out to run from the northeast to the southwest to maximize access to the landing area.

When Urquhart selected his land on Cypress Bayou in November 1841, the land to the east had already been acquired by the heirs of Humphries, and the land to the west had already been acquired by Stephen Smith. This accounts for the irregular and vertical elongation of the Urquhart headright, which extended north to Black Cypress Bayou. Only the southern portion of the headright was used for the early development of Jefferson.

The other half of early Jefferson was the result of a purchase by Daniel Alley of the Stephen Smith headright in 1845, encompassing the land immediately to the west of Urquhart's. Smith had entered what was to become Texas before the formation of the Republic and acquired one league and one labor of land on December 5, 1839. The land on Cypress Bayou that was eventually acquired by Alley was surveyed by Levi Jordan on July 31, 1841, and contained 586 acres. Smith and his wife lived in Lamar County and apparently had no special interest in the property, because they sold it to Alley for $2,000 on August 29, 1845, with the description using Smithland rather than Jefferson as a point of reference. This was not the full price of the land, because Smith had previously sold half interest in the land to Levi Jordan, and Jordan had sold that interest to James Alley (Daniel's father) in March 1845.

Alley had himself acquired a conditional certificate for 640 acres on Alley's Creek to the west of the area that was to become Jefferson on April 5, 1839. This land was surveyed on November 1, 1839, and Alley acquired an unconditional certificate on October 15, 1841. After Alley acquired the Jefferson property from Smith in August 1845, he commissioned a new survey, which was conducted on January 2, 1851, and revealed that the plot of land contained 660 acres rather than 586 acres. Alley received a patent for this land as assignee of Stephen Smith from the State of Texas on August 6, 1851.

Alley's reason for purchasing the land in August 1845 is obvious, because Jefferson was already under development. The north-south orientation of the streets indicates that he was interested in developing a residential area to complement Urquhart's business area. Paying

$2,000 for a tract of land next to a promising port was a wise investment. It should be noted that Urquhart did not seize the opportunity to purchase the Smith tract, even though he was involved in many major land transactions throughout his life. This indicates that his interest in the Jefferson area was not as strong as has generally been assumed, which was soon to be confirmed by his virtual abandonment of the development of the town to Berry Durham.

Daniel Alley pursued a path of disinvestment (apparently for financial reasons). Thomas Alley's (Daniel's brother) 1860 estate inventory includes numerous lots in Jefferson and 543 acres in the Smith headright not laid off in town lots. There are no deed records concerning the transfer of this property from Daniel to Thomas; but the Cass County tax rolls indicate that this was accomplished by 1858, when Daniel is listed without property and Thomas is listed with 540 acres in the Smith headright valued at $6,400 and 15 town lots in Jefferson valued at $750. In the 1860 Marion County tax rolls, Daniel is listed without property, and the estate of Thomas lists what appears to be 65 lots in Jefferson valued at $20,500. The 1861 tax rolls include 510 acres in the Smith headright in Thomas' estate.

<u>Surveyor Records</u>

The activities of the surveyors William Hamilton and Levi Jordan are critical to an understanding of the sequence of events concerning Jefferson's early history. Hamilton conducted the survey of the Daingerfield property for Urquhart in June 1839. The Stephen Smith survey was conducted by Jordan in July 1841, and Urquhart's November 1841 survey of the Jefferson property was filed with Jordan as the county surveyor.

In the 1850 district court case of William Hughes versus William Perry, Hamilton stated that as deputy surveyor for Red River County he conducted a survey on November 9, 1840, for the Jefferson Town Company that involved setting the property corners on Big Cypress Bayou for Urquhart, Jordan (immediately to the west), and Thomas Gillespie (to the west of Jordan). It is obvious that these corners established the divisions along Cypress Bayou between Urquhart's Jefferson property (which was not fully surveyed until November 1841), the Stephen Smith headright that was eventually acquired by Daniel Alley, and the Thomas Gillespie headright immediately to the west of the Smith headright.

Hamilton's testimony indicates that there was a Jefferson Town Company and that the name "Jefferson" was in use prior to November 1840. If Urquhart selected the Jefferson property on the basis of his June 1839 survey of the contiguous Humphries headright, it is probable that he began using the name "Jefferson" between June 1839 and November 1840, and it is certain that the Jefferson Town Company was formed during that period. Moreover, it is highly unlikely that the road from Daingerfield to Shreveport and the ferry across Cypress Bayou would have been established until the property corners were set. These events and the subsequent operation of the ferry by Berry Durham occurred sometime after November 9, 1840.

Hamilton also states that he went to the same area later with Jordan, Urquhart, and Joseph Lilly and surveyed 640 acres respectively for Urquhart, Jordan, and Robert Hughes, surviving assignee of Thomas Gillespie. What is unclear is why Jordan had corners set for the Smith headright in 1840 and later had the entire headright surveyed. These actions make sense only if Jordan had a proprietary interest in the Smith property.

In a bond for title dated March 11, 1841, Jordan of Houston County sold to James Alley his undivided half of the Stephen Smith survey of 586 acres for $900 and in consideration of a $5,000 loan. This deed also gives the year as 1845. The year 1845 is correct, because the document states that the land when originally surveyed was in Paschal County but was then in Bowie County. On December 4, 1844, Jordan gave power of attorney to Daniel Alley concerning Jordan's interest "in the land located on the Bluffs of the main Cypress known as Jefferson at the head of the Lake about two or three miles below where the Old Trammel Trace crosses said stream which land was located by authority of the Headright Certificate granted one Stephen Smith."

In addition, in a document dated August 25, 1844, Jordan relinquished his title to any part of the land known as the Jefferson land. The relinquishment apparently should have been dated 1845, because Jordan's power of attorney to Daniel Alley in December 1844 spoke of his interest in the property. The relinquishment was filed in connection with Smith's August 1845 conveyance of his headright to Alley. Relinquishments were generally made in conjunction with land transactions to insure that a title would not be contested. Jordan was simply confirming that he had already sold his interest in the Smith property to James Alley.

The deed by which Jordan secured an interest in the Smith property has been lost. Smith probably selected the property shortly after his December 1839 grant, because he was not subject to a waiting period. Jordan probably bought half interest in the property in early 1840, certainly before Hamilton established the corners in November 1840. Smith's headright was surveyed by Jordan in July 1841. Daniel Alley was given power of attorney in December 1844. Jordan sold his half interest in the Smith property to James Alley in March 1845. Jordan relinquished any claims that he might have to the property in August 1845; and during the same month ownership was transferred from Smith to Daniel Alley. There are no deed records concerning James Alley's transfer of half ownership to his son (or to his son's wife and children).

Town Company

Town companies were practical mechanisms to develop towns and were quite common during antebellum times. They were usually legal entities in which the participants held stock, which established a financial interest in what transpired. There are three documents in the Transcribed Deed Records that refer to a Jefferson town company, all of which were prepared during 1842 and 1843 and are among the earliest deed records concerning Jefferson.

The first mention of a Jefferson town company in the deed records is in a February 3, 1842, bond for title from Allen Urquhart, Agent, Town Co. of Jefferson, to Berry Durham. The bond is concerned with the transfer of town lots and part ownership in the ferry to Durham. Urquhart describes himself as lease administrator, part owner, and agent for the Jefferson Company, with lease administration referring to the operation of the ferry. The company is said to be composed of John Russell, William Hulphoides, Redie Robert, Vaden Hughs, and others, and five proprietors are later mentioned.

The names are not clear in the original text and were corrupted in transcription. No one by the name of Redie Robert appears in any early documents. There was a Reddick Overton who owned a headright immediately south of Jefferson, and he is called Redie or Reedie in the early documents. Vaden Hughs may have been William V. Hughes.

The second document is an October 2, 1842, agreement between Urquhart and Durham concerning land transfers and ownership of the ferry. Urquhart describes himself as "part owner and agent of the Jefferson town and Ferry Company." The third document, which was signed on January 28, 1843, is concerned with the lease of the ferry operation to Berry Durham and Tinsly Weaver. Urquhart describes himself as "part owner and Agent of the Jefferson Town Company."

That the company preceded the deed records is known from the affidavit submitted by William Hamilton in connection with the 1850 district court case of William Hughes versus William Perry in which Hamilton indicates that he conducted surveys of the corners for the Urquhart, Smith, and Gillespie headrights for the Jefferson Town Company on November 9, 1840. Present were John Robbins, William Humphries, Leonard Ward, and others. The five principals were probably Urquhart, the three mentioned by Jordan, and William Hughes. Humphries' participation in these activities is confirmed by the September 1, 1876, *Jefferson Jimplecute*. All of these men are listed in the 1840 Red River County tax rolls.

There are no documents concerning a Jefferson Town Company in the official records in Austin, there is no consistency in the naming of the company in the deed records, and there is no certainty with respect to the named principals. Most importantly, it is not mentioned in the commissioners' distribution of properties between Urquhart and Durham in 1846. It is possible that this was never a legal entity, but merely an idea that was never brought to full realization by Urquhart. Durham, who was in a position to know because he was a participant in all of the relevant transactions, apparently was uncertain about the composition and perhaps even the existence of the company. When he sold his interest in the ferry operation to John Withee in December 1843, the transaction is couched in terms of properties that had been obtained from "Allen Urquhart &c.—and others if there were any."

Whatever the status of the Jefferson Town Company, it ceased to play any part in the development of Jefferson after January 1843.

First Mention

When Urquhart surveyed the land that was to become Jefferson on November 19, 1841, his notes describe the property as situated "on the North Bank of Ferry Lake at Jefferson." This was not the first recorded usage of "Jefferson," and it can be presumed that the term was used verbally before it appeared in a document.

The Transcribed Deed Records contain a bond for title from Berry Durham to Richard Peters concerning four lots and two half lots "in the town of Jefferson" that is dated January 16, 1841, and recorded as such in the index. The lots are numbered according to Jesse Cherry's town plan, which was not in existence in 1841, and Urquhart's survey was not conducted until November 19 of that year. There is a second date in the document, January 16, 1845, which is obviously the correct one. The first was probably a transcription error, which cannot be checked because the early Bowie County records were destroyed by fire.

There is also a bond for title from Levi Jordan to James Alley dated March 11, 1841, in which Jordan of Houston County sells to Alley for $900 his undivided half of the Stephen Smith survey of 586 acres "on Big Cypress at or near the head of the Lake about five miles west of Smithland" together with his "entire remaining unsold interest in the Ferry granted license and located at the town site of Jefferson on Big Cypress near the head of Ferry Lake and known as the Jefferson Ferry." This document also contains a second date: March 11, 1845. The second date is the correct one, because the document mentions that the land when surveyed was in Paschal County but was then in Bowie County. If the transaction had taken place in 1841, the land would have been in Paschal County.

Josiah Gregg visited Smithland in August 1841 and mentions the proposed site of Jefferson and its economic potential relative to Smithland. Because Gregg was writing a popular account for national publication, it is obvious that use of the designation "Jefferson" for the townsite was common practice by August 1841.

Jefferson had been named by at least November 1840 when William Hamilton set the corners for the Urquhart property for the Jefferson Town Company. It was apparently not named by June 1839 when Urquhart conducted the survey for the heirs of William Humphries, because Urquhart used Smithland rather than Jefferson as a locator for the Humphries property. The name was probably introduced verbally between June 1839 and November 1840.

If there were any articles of incorporation for the Jefferson Town Company, they have not survived. Urquhart used Jefferson as a locator for many of the surveys that he conducted in the area. The earliest in time that I have found is for Burrell Parker's headright, which was surveyed on May 26, 1841. Other early mentions of Jefferson include Thomas Wilson's June 25, 1841, survey of the William Archer headright for assignee R. C. Graves. The earliest recorded usage was probably in one of Urquhart's surveys and may have been the one conducted in May 1841.

The Name "Jefferson"

The name "Jefferson" was a common name for counties and towns throughout the United States, all in honor of Thomas Jefferson, the author of the Declaration of Independence and the third president of the United States. Although it can be presumed that Urquhart named his proposed town in honor of Thomas Jefferson, there is no documentation to that effect. If the name had been chosen for some other reason, it would undoubtedly have been mentioned by someone at sometime. On the other hand, the fact that no direct reference to the reason has surfaced simply indicates that people are not in the habit of stating the obvious. Given these circumstances, it is reasonable to assume that any reference to Jefferson that might be discovered would be oblique rather than direct and that it would be discovered accidently.

One reference has been found through a review of the Clarksville, Marshall, and Shreveport newspapers. The July 25, 1867, Marshall *Harrison Flag* contains a letter dated the 23rd from Marshall under the pseudonym "Town Boy" addressed to the editor, William Barrett, bemoaning the fact that all the young ladies had left Marshall and gone to Jefferson. The brief references to the name of the town suggest only that it was a reminder of Jefferson Davis:

DEAR BARRETT.—Gone to Jefferson. Yes, all the world has gone to Jefferson. There must be about the little burgh some fascination not to be resisted—some magnetic attraction for the fair inhabitants of our own little town, for they are all gone—from the dark-eyed, earnest beauties, to the fairest flowers of our surrounding hills—all gone to Jefferson, and our only avenue of escape from the darkness which succeeds this migration of the stars, is the road to Jefferson. I have been repeating over and over the name of this little neighboring town, to see if I could find the charm that wields such prodigious power. Can it be that it reminds them of the loved leader of our people in the late struggle for independence, and that this is a quiet pilgrimage to a shrine which bears the name of the sole martyr of the Rebellion, or is it the haunt of some syren whose sweet deceptions have fanned the delusion that pleasure and would-be husbands with fast horses which they manage so skillfully are abundant there? Or have the beaux found some new talisman, with power to lure them from us, and keep them there? If any or all of these causes have effected this departure of the glory from Israel, I call upon you as a public journalist to dispel the illusion, and tell them Jefferson wont do; that the song of that syren is all a fable; that there ain't any concert or pic-nic there; that the very atmosphere of the place is the concentrated essence of malaria; and that if they stay there a week their beauty will never recover from the shock it must sustain; that 'twill be with their soft cheeks and bright eyes a death, without the prospect of resurrection. Call on some poetic friend to pour into their ears, in Milton's lofty strain, the horrors that inevitably attend a long sojourn there, and tell them to come back home. If I just knew they had gone to see the Jefferson Times, I would bear much more patiently the loss, but I can't believe it. Tell them 'tis dark as

Erebus in their absence here; that the roses wither and the emerald grasses bleach beneath the all pervading gloom. So come back.

Who named Jefferson is uncertain. Fred Tarpley in his book on Jefferson indicates that some members of the Alley family maintain that the town was named by James Alley because the Alleys had previously lived near the Jeffersons in Virginia. This is highly plausible if the Alleys had an early interest in the land that became the Alley Addition. However, a proprietary interest was not established until March 1845.

Trammel's Trace

Trammel's Trace, which extended from Fulton, Arkansas, to Nacogdoches, Texas, was blazed by Nicholas Trammel around 1815 and was joined above Hughes Springs by another trail blazed by Trammel that extended south from Jonesboro, Texas. The trace crossed over Big Cypress Bayou five miles west of the Polk Street Bridge slightly above the confluence with French Creek (Fig. 3-4). After crossing Big Cypress

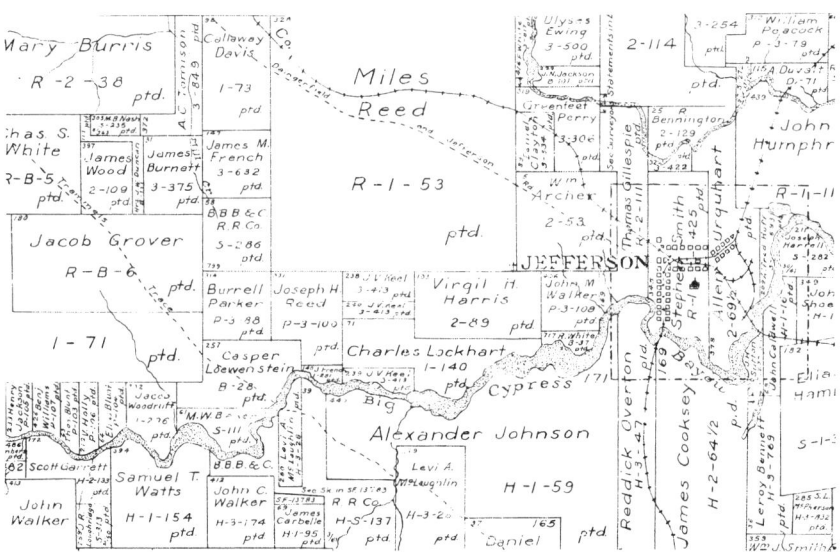

Fig. 3-4. Trammel's Trace. Source: Courtesy Texas General Land Office, Austin

Bayou, it proceeded to the southeast toward Caddo Lake, crossing Little Cypress Bayou at Highway 59, then to the southwest, looping around Marshall.

The antiquity of the trace and its proximity to Jefferson have led to the assumption that the trace influenced Jefferson's location and, in the extreme case, that Jefferson was founded on the trace. With respect to the latter assumption, early and late maps are definite with respect to the delineation of the crossing. With respect to the former assumption, there is no evidence that the trace played any part in Jefferson's formation or development.

The trace was in its earliest configuration a horse trail that did not accommodate the ox-wagons that were basic to Jefferson's commercial activities. Like all early trails, it meandered to minimize the expenditure of horse and human energy, usually passing through the headwaters of streams. Bridges and ferries were not essential because horses could ford streams. Ox-wagon roads were straighter, with minimization of the time spent in travel and its attendant costs as the primary consideration. Jefferson's earliest roads were ox-wagon roads that did not utilize any portion of Trammel's Trace and were created to serve entirely different purposes.

The trace intersected the Big Cypress Valley Road running west out of Jefferson about one mile west of French Creek and crossed Big Cypress Bayou at the southeast corner of the Casper Lowenstein headright, entering the northwest corner of the Levi McLaughlin headright. As the area developed, the trace began to be used as an ox-wagon road. During the January 1844 term of the Harrison County Commissioners Court, Stephen Smith's license to operate a ferry across Big Cypress at the trace was renewed for another year; and during the January 1845 term, the privilege was transferred to Levi McLaughlin. Traffic was sufficient for the trace to be designated a public road during the January 1848 term of the court. Langford's Bridge was established at this point by 1850, with the road to the south leading to Shreveport.

4. Townsite

Ferry

A ferry was in operation across Cypress Bayou at the foot of Houston Street for years before Jefferson came into existence and for years afterward, even after it was replaced by a bridge as the major mode of conveyance. A ferry was simply a means of conveying men, animals, produce, and equipment across a waterbody. Its existence indicates that people were traveling from one place to another. Thus, a ferry operation needs to be understood in the context of the overland route of which it was a part.

The earliest history of Jefferson, which appears in the September 1, 1876, *Daily Jimplecute*, says that the first person to live within the boundaries of what was to become Jefferson was Berry Durham in 1840, with the land then being in Paschal County, and that "He built his cabin on the bank of the river near where the Marshall road so long crossed by ferry and bridges, under an arrangement or lease with Allen Urquhart, for the purpose of establishing a ferry at that point." The comment concerning Paschal County in 1840 cannot be correct, because it did not come into existence until January 1841; but the year 1840 is probably correct for the building of the cabin and 1841 and Paschal County for the beginning of the operation of the ferry.

Urquhart conducted a survey of the property that was to become Jefferson in November 1841. The inset map accompanying this survey shows a northwest-southeast tending road crossing Cypress Bayou through the survey at the right place. The existence of the road on the map indicates the existence of a ferry. This road was not in existence on October 24, 1840, when a map of Harrison County now in the General Land Office was prepared for Chief Surveyor Richard Hooper.

The ferry probably was established after Urquhart's survey of the contiguous Humphries tract in June 1839, which apparently gave rise to the selection of the property that was to become Jefferson, and after William Hamilton set the corners for Urquhart's property on November 9, 1840. The road to Jefferson, implying the existence of a ferry, was mentioned by Urquhart in his May 26, 1841, survey of the Burrell Parker headright. Durham does not appear in the Red River County tax rolls completed in July 1840, but does appear in the 1841 rolls completed in July, with a notation that he was in the Paschal County division. It can be assumed that Durham began operating the ferry for Urquhart between November 1840 and May 1841, apparently building his cabin in late 1840 and beginning operation of the ferry in early 1841.

In order to operate a ferry, it was necessary to construct a boat and facilities, to own or lease the landing area on both sides of the bayou, and to secure the privilege of operating the ferry from the county commissioners courts, because the commissioners were responsible for transportation facility licensing and road maintenance. Unfortunately, the commissioners court minutes for Red River and Bowie counties are not available for these early years, and the commissioners court minutes for Harrison County (the other side of the bayou) do not begin until July 1843. Thus, it is necessary to turn to the deed records for evidence, with the recognition that some early deeds were not filed and others have been lost.

The first documentation of a ferry occurs in a February 3, 1842, bond for title from Urquhart to Durham, with Urquhart acting as part owner and agent of the Jefferson Town Company and lease administrator of the Jefferson ferry. Durham is to have half interest in the ferry and a lease for six years to cultivate the 30 acres contiguous to the ferry and to remove timber for building or fencing. It is apparent from this document that Durham had already been operating the ferry for Urquhart and that he was securing a new or renewed proprietary interest in the boat.

A new agreement was signed on October 2, 1842, nullifying the former. Urquhart transferred ownership of the boat to Durham, with the stipulation that it not be sold for five years; and Durham would have the privilege of operating the ferry for two years from the previous June, apparently with Urquhart retaining some interest in the revenues generated by the ferry operation. This agreement does not appear to have been consummated.

The ferry was reconsidered on January 28, 1843, in a Lease of a Ferry Boat from Urquhart to Durham. Urquhart, as part owner and agent of the Jefferson Town Company, leased the ferry operation to Durham and Tinsly Weaver jointly until June 1, 1844, with one-third of the proceeds to go to Urquhart in his official capacity and the other two-thirds to be divided equally between them. Durham and Weaver bound themselves jointly to return the boat to the owners at the end of the term.

Weaver does not appear to have ever participated, and Durham began operating the ferry under this agreement on March 1, 1843. In October, the Harrison County commissioners court granted Durham a license to operate the ferry with the following tolls: $1 for road wagon; $1 for two-horse wagon; 50 cents for two-wheeled carriage; 25 cents for carryall; 12½ cents for man and horse (women and children were never included in ferry rates); 6¼ cents for man on foot; 6¼ cents for horses; and 3 cents for sheep and cattle. A conflict over proceeds from the ferry operation developed and resulted in an undated 1843 agreement between Urquhart and Durham. Durham had paid Urquhart $42 during the intervening period. By August 1, 1844, Logan Henderson and M. W. Matthews were to review Durham's books and decide on an equitable distribution of monies received from March 1, 1843, to June 1, 1844.

Apparently after the undated agreement, Durham secured a three-fourths interest in the ferryboat, land, and privileges. On December 2, 1843, he sold to John Withee of Lamar County for $100 "one fourth of Jefferson Ferry and boat and its landings and all of its many privileges that is contained in and through one fourth of the above mentioned ferry &c." Durham's operation of the ferry was not renewed. On December 29, 1844, Urquhart developed an agreement with William Bishop to operate the ferry for one year in exchange for one-third of the proceeds.

On October 11, 1845, Durham in a bond for title sold to Bishop for $150 "one undivided half of the interest in the Ferry Landing and Ferry Boat which interest is to continue and remove to all points that may be selected for Ferry Landings across the Big Cypress Bayou near the Town of Jefferson on Allen Urquhart's headright survey;" also an interest of one-half of the lands obtained by Durham from the Harrison County commissioners court. Bishop transferred this bond to James and Asa Johnson on November 28, 1846.

On January 17, 1846, Urquhart sold to Bishop for $100 "one undivided fourth of the Ferry privileges and Ferry landings on both sides of the Big Cypress or Ferry Lake," including privileges that may be granted, such as for a toll bridge. On October 28, 1846, Bishop sold to the Johnsons for $100 "one undivided fourth of the Ferry privileges and ferry landings on both sides of the Big Cypress or Ferry Lake, it being the stream or lake opposite and running by the town of Jefferson and the landing on the Jefferson side of said Lake or stream"; also "all privileges that is or may be granted to the joint owners of said property for continuing said Ferry across said stream or for the erection of a Toll Bridge over the same and does hereby transfer all the land heretofore conveyed to me by Allen Urquhart for the purpose of abutments for a bridge or Ferry Landing."

These transactions mark the end of participation by the townsite residents Durham and Bishop in the operation of the ferry and indicate that a bridge was soon to replace the ferry as the primary crossing over Cypress Bayou.

The reason for the establishment of the ferry in the early 1840s was complex. The most important reason was to secure a linkage between Daingerfield and areas to the north on the one hand and Port Caddo and Shreveport on the other. Steamboats did not begin to arrive at Jefferson until March 1845. Before that time, import and export items for the Daingerfield area and above needed to proceed through Port Caddo and Shreveport, traveling overland by wagon and across Cypress Bayou by the ferry. Horses could ford a stream, but ox-wagons needed a ferry or bridge. Thus, the route of which the ferry was a component was a wagon road rather than a horse trail.

The old road from Daingerfield to the townsite and later the town of Jefferson is shown on a December 16, 1943, Marion County map produced by the General Land Office, which contains historic information (Fig. 4-1). It can be seen today as a heavy indentation in the landscape crossing the present road to Daingerfield at various points. It entered the townsite north of present-day Broadway Street and cut south toward the ferry after reaching present-day Owens Street, as shown on Graham's 1869 *Plan of the City of Jefferson, Texas* (Fig. 4-2).

The ferry site at the foot of Houston Street is not easily accessible today because Houston Street ends at Cypress Street on the ridgeline fronting the floodplain of Cypress Bayou. The present route over the Polk Street Bridge was not taken because of the lowness of the area south of the bridge that Business Route 59 passes through. There are no maps delineating the ferry crossing. However, a late map of the area on page 231 of Book D of the deed records shows a new delineation for the ferry after a bridge was constructed at the foot of Houston

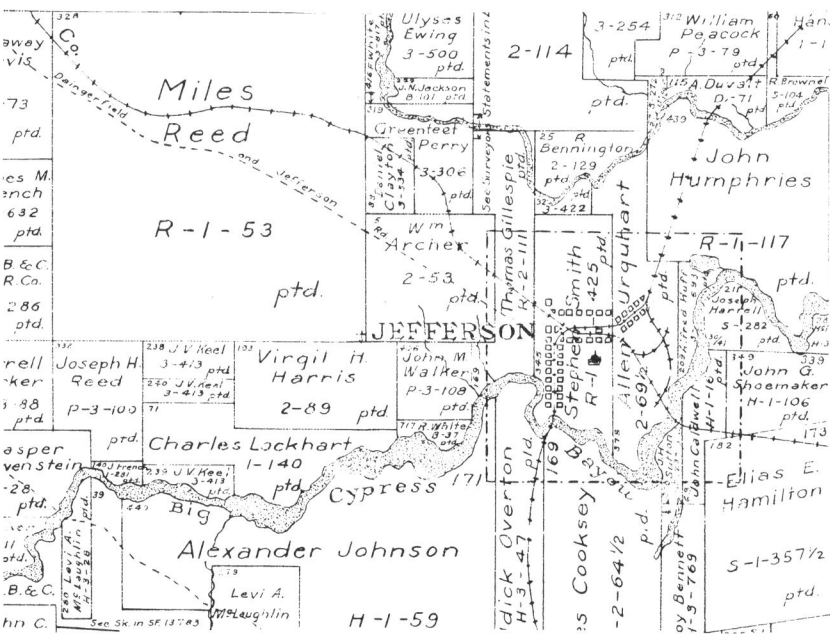

Fig. 4-1. Old Daingerfield Road. Source: Courtesy Texas General Land Office, Austin

Fig. 4-2. Old Daingerfield Road. Courtesy Historic Jefferson Foundation

Street and suggests that one of the reasons for the original delineation was the existence of a small embayment that would have provided protection for the ferryboat (Fig. 4-3).

The ferry crossing linked at the south shore of the bayou with a road that ran through present-day Bayou Maison property. The road hugged the bluffs west of the highway until slightly past the road that cuts to the east toward Caddo Lake State Park and then ran southeast, crossing Little Cypress Bayou about three-fourths of a mile east of Highway 59, crossing over the old road from Marshall to Port Caddo, and proceeding down to Greenwood, Louisiana, and thence to Shreveport, as shown on captured Confederate maps from the Civil War period (Figs. 4-4 and 4-5).

It was not absolutely necessary to establish a ferry at this point, because access to Shreveport from the Daingerfield area could have been secured through a ferry that was already in existence at Smithland, six

Townsite

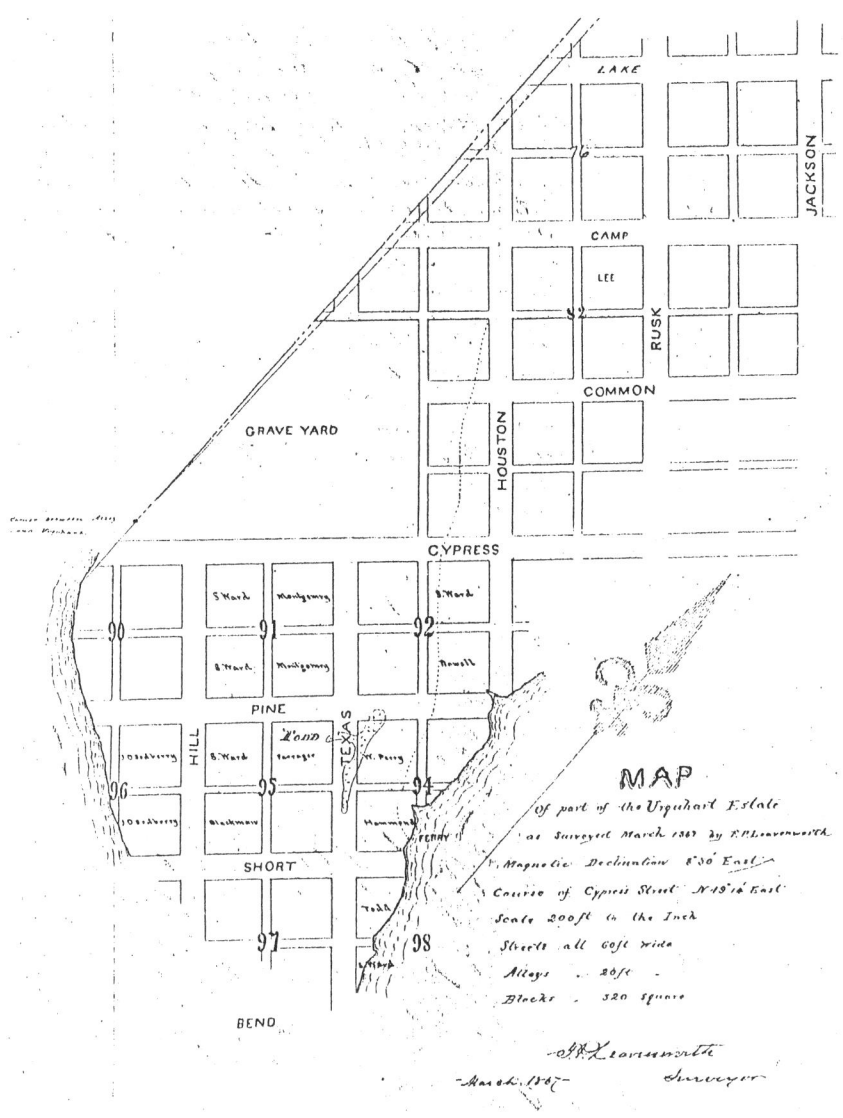

Fig. 4-3. Embayment at Foot of Houston Street.

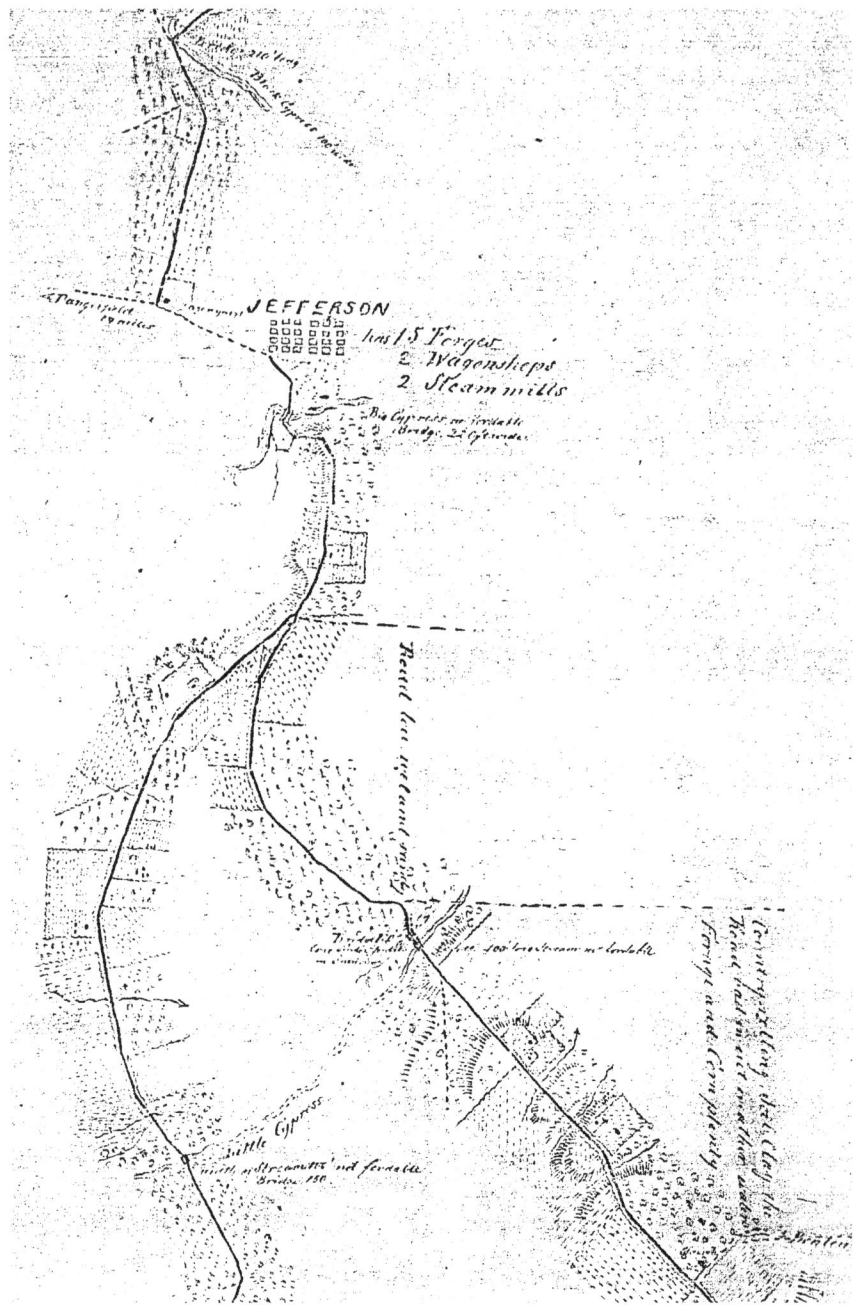

Fig. 4-4. Roads South Out of Jefferson. Source: Courtesy Louisiana Secretary of State, Division of Archives, Records Management and History

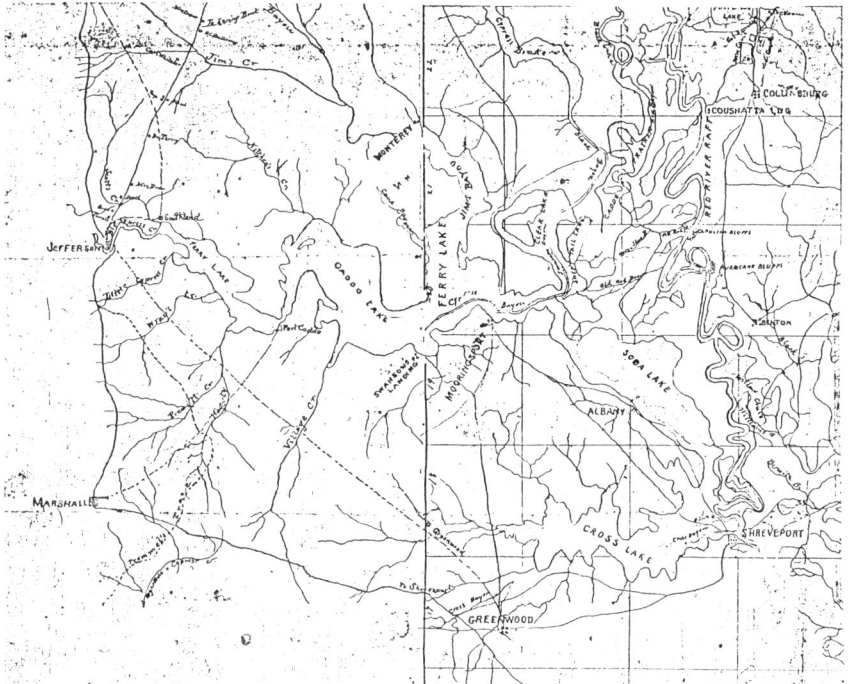

Fig. 4-5. Road to Greenwood and Shreveport. Source: Courtesy Louisiana Secretary of State, Division of Archives, Records Management and History

miles downstream from Jefferson. The ferry was in part established to secure primacy for the townsite in relation to Smithland. In addition, it provided a linkage between Daingerfield and Marshall. The road to Marshall would have been established at the same time as the road to Shreveport.

The old road to Marshall is shown on the captured Confederate maps as the western branch proceeding out of Jefferson. It was continuous with the road to Shreveport until reaching the intersection of Business Route 59 and the present-day road to Caddo Lake and then followed the path of Business 59, crossing Highway 59 at State Route 2208 and then proceeding directly south to Marshall, crossing Little Cypress Bayou about three-fourths of a mile west of Highway 59.

As for the ferryboat itself, it was probably of simple plank and log construction. The bayou is fairly shallow and restricted at that point.

The ferry was probably poled, with a rope stretched from bank to bank providing stability of crossing during periods of rapid flow. The only glimpse of the ferry in operation is given by Charles DeMorse of the Clarksville *Northern Standard*, who visited Jefferson in June 1847 and reported that "The flat at the crossing of the Cypress, places one in Harrison county in two minutes, and it is but fifteen miles to Marshall."

There was a second ferry at the townsite that operated in what became the Alley Addition. In March 1845, Levi Jordan sold to James Alley for $900 his undivided one-half of the Stephen Smith headright of 586 acres along with his "entire remaining unsold interest in the Ferry granted license and located at the town site of Jefferson on Big Cypress near the head of Ferry Lake and known as the Jefferson Ferry." In August 1845, Jordan relinquished his title to any part of the land known as the Jefferson land, including "the first boat built there, ferry, ferry Landing, &c." This document was filed in connection with Stephen Smith's August 1845 conveyance of his headright to Daniel Alley.

The Alley Addition ferry is shown on an 1846 map of Harrison County. Although the town is not positioned correctly, the upper (Alley) and lower (Urquhart) ferries are clearly delineated, and the upper ferry crosses Big Cypress Bayou in the Alley Addition (Fig. 4-6).

On August 12, 1846, the Cass County commissioners court in its first year of operation granted Daniel Alley a license to operate a ferry across Big Cypress Bayou at the termination of a road laid out by Levi Jordan, J. D. Lilly, and others, said road terminating in the town of Jefferson, at the following ferryage rates: man and horse (12 ½ cents); one-horse carriage (25 cents); four-horse or four-ox wagon (25 cents); horses and cattle (six cents); sheep and hogs (three cents); man on foot (six cents).

This ferry probably serviced a road that ran from Alley's Mills (to the northwest on Alley's Creek) along Cypress Bayou south of the Daingerfield Road and was called the Big Cypress Valley Road (Fig. 4-7). Joseph Lilly, who participated in the creation of the road, had property ten miles west of Jefferson on Big Cypress Bayou in the Noah Lilly headright. A portion of this road can be seen at the Freeman Plantation. It apparently entered Jefferson south of the Daingerfield Road

Townsite

and proceeded directly south to the ferry, running west of the Daingerfield Road. After crossing Big Cypress Bayou at the ferry, it probably joined the road to Marshall and Shreveport.

When the ferry in the Smith headright was established is unknown; but it was in existence by at least sometime in 1844, because Jordan's sale in March 1845 was for a ferry already in operation. Jordan refers to it as the first ferry at Jefferson, but he may be speaking about

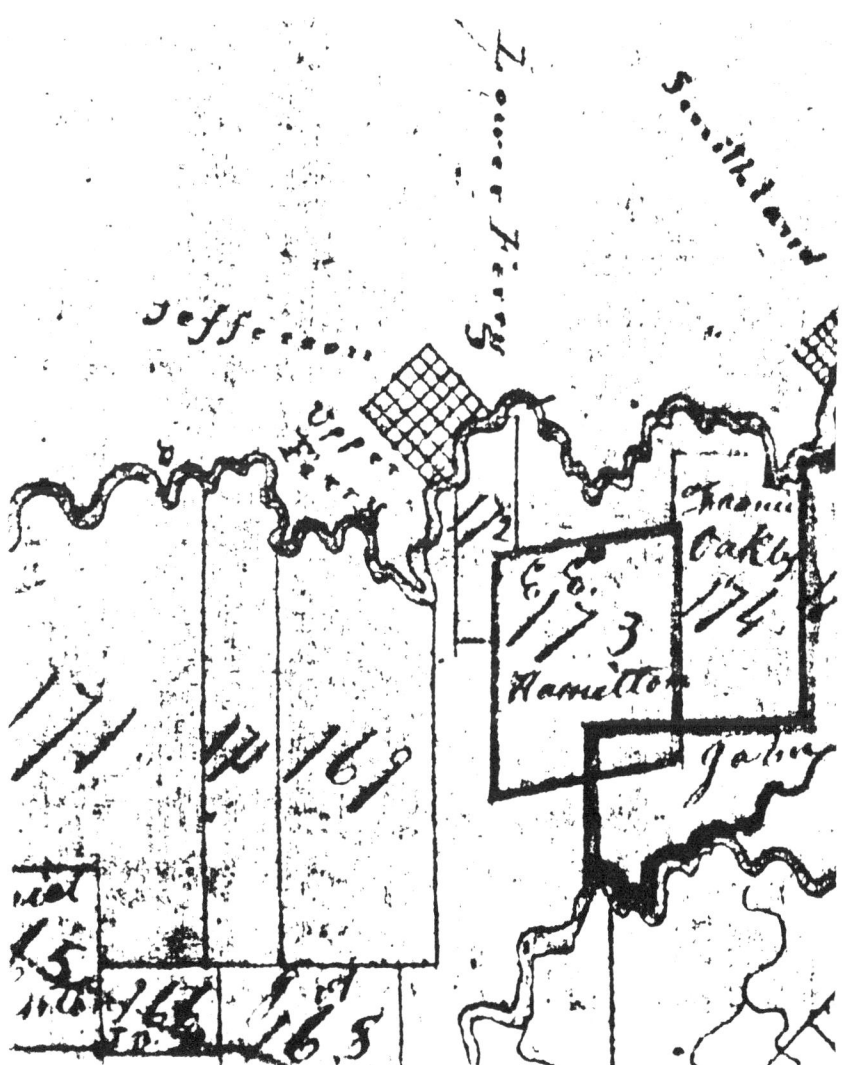

Fig. 4-6. Jefferson's Two Ferries. Source: Courtesy Texas General Land Office, Austin

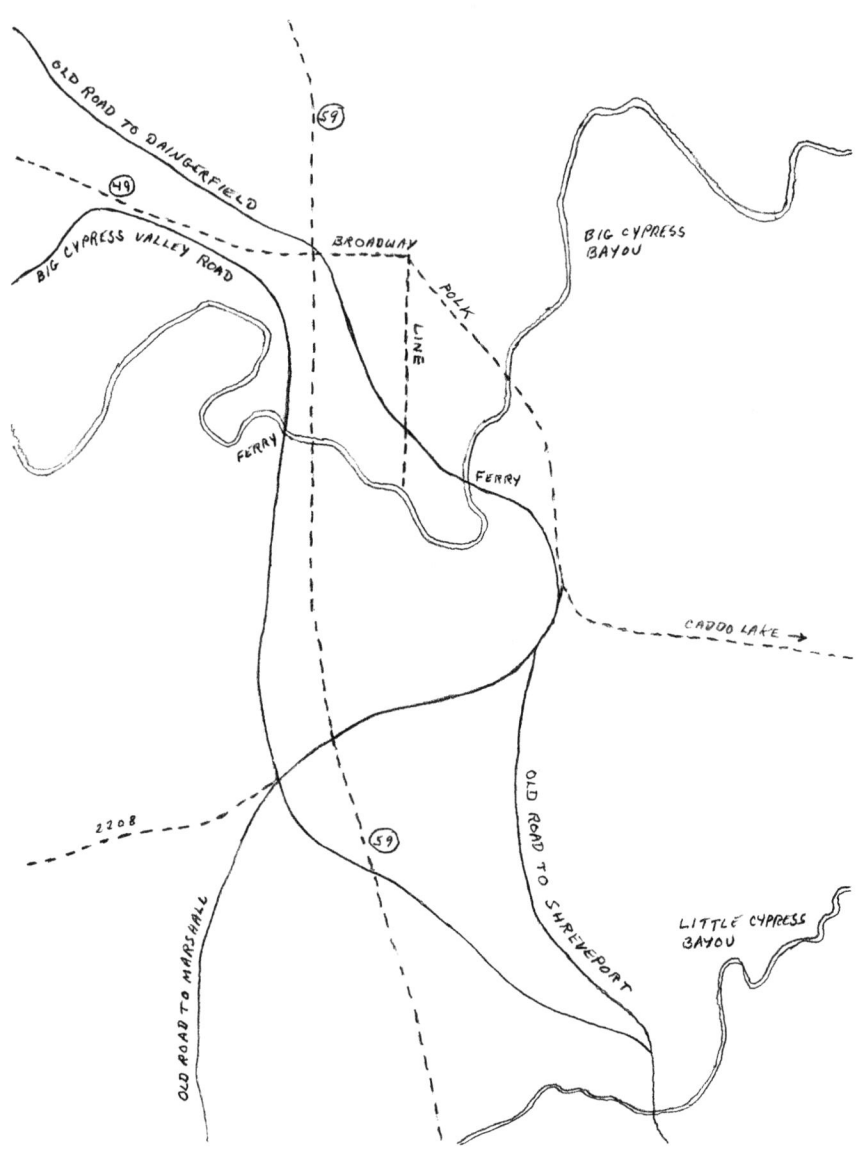

Fig. 4-7. Early Roads and Ferries

the first ferry in the Alley Addition. If it was very early, it probably did not come into existence until after Hamilton set the corners for the Urquhart, Smith, and Gillespie properties in November 1840. If the ferry in the Alley Addition preceded the Urquhart ferry, it did not have a resident operator, because the 1876 *Daily Jimplecute* clearly states that the first person to reside within the boundaries of Jefferson was Berry Durham, the operator of the Urquhart ferry.

The function of the ferry in the Alley Addition is intimately connected with the activities of Levi Jordan, Stephen Smith, and James and Daniel Alley, which remain unclear. Jordan was postmaster of Tuscumbia on Little Cypress Bayou southeast of Jefferson from at least February 1840 and continued in this position until the post office was terminated at the end of the year. He was in attendance when the property corners were set in November 1840 because he was part owner of the Smith property. In April 1843, he was living five miles south of Daingerfield according to the *Northern Standard*. Smith and one or both of the Alleys may have had a proprietary interest in the ferry before Jordan's transfer of his part ownership to James Alley in March 1845. However, it is also known that Smith operated a ferry at Trammel's Trace in 1843 and 1844.

It is probable that the ferry in the Alley Addition was established sometime in 1844 when Smith abandoned the Trammel's Trace ferry, which was operated by Levi McLaughlin by at least January 1845. Although the Big Cypress Valley Road continues to be mentioned in later documents, there is no mention of the ferry in the Alley Addition after 1846. It probably found itself noncompetitive in relation to the Urquhart ferry and was simply abandoned.

During the late 1840s, the ferry established by Urquhart was operated by Bishop and the Johnsons. Urquhart resumed operation in November 1850 and continued in operation during the 1850s, in spite of the existence of a bridge (owned by Urquhart himself during the early 1850s) and a free public ferry. In October 1846, the Harrison County commissioners court granted a license to Isaac Stephens, William Baker, and John O'Hara to establish a ferry across Big Cypress Bayou at the foot of Marshall Street, on which their steam mill was located; and in January 1847, a road from Marshall to Jefferson was proposed beginning at the foot of Marshall Street. Whether the road and ferry were established is not known.

The tolls charged by Urquhart on the bridge and ferry were much resented. In February 1852, the Harrison County commissioners court renewed Urquhart's ferry license, but also made provisions to establish a road to Jefferson from the fork of the Shreveport and Marshall roads about three-fourths of a mile south of town so that a free public ferry could be established. This road was established during the same month beginning 70 yards south of Weaver's slaughter pen and running to Cypress Bayou across from Williamson Freeman's warehouse, which was located on the east side of the landing area. The free public ferry began operation in May 1853.

Town Plan

The first map of Jefferson was a town plan prepared by a professional surveyor, Jesse Cherry (Fig. 4-8). Who commissioned the plan is unknown, but it must have been either Urquhart or Durham. There are no extant copies of this map, and it was never filed in the courthouse. However, the approximate time of its preparation and what it contained can be reconstructed on the basis of the Transcribed Deed Records.

According to evidence in the deed records, the Cherry town plan was not in existence in November 1842, probably in existence by January 1843, and definitely in existence by March 1844, when it began to be used as a reference in land transactions. It was the reference for all land transactions through January 1846, when it was replaced by a new town plan, and continues to be mentioned in some land transactions beyond that point. All of the transactions that used the Cherry plan as a reference are recorded by block number in an appendix to the Urquhart Addition contained in an untitled volume in the Port Jefferson Abstract and Title Company.

The Cherry plan encompassed 21 blocks and at least 219 lots. There were also 13 warehouse lots in present-day Block 9 and the northern half of present-day Block 8, indicating that Urquhart envisioned a warehouse as well as a business district. Unlike later maps, which begin with Block 2, the Cherry plan began with Block 1, which

Townsite

Fig. 4-8. Jesse Cherry Town Plan

was the northern half of present-day Block 75, bounded by Lake, Rusk, Jackson, and an alley. Also unlike later maps, the Cherry plan numbered lots consecutively, rather than beginning with a Lot 1 in each block.

Lot 1 in the Cherry plan is present-day Lot 6 in Block 75 at the southeast corner of Lake and Rusk. The last lot whose location can definitely be determined from the property descriptions is Lot 186 in Block 16 (present-day Lot 4 in Block 2) at the southeast corner of Henderson and Marshall. There are a sufficient number of property descriptions in between to determine the general layout of the lots and the boundaries of the Cherry plan.

Blocks 1–3 and Lots 1–18 ran from Rusk to Market, encompassing the northern half of the present blocks between Lake and Camp. Blocks 4–8 ran between Austin and Lake from the Urquhart survey line to Polk and included the southern tier of Lots 19–51 and the northern tier of Lots 52–81. Blocks 9–14 ran between Lafayette and Austin from the survey line to Walnut and included the southern tier of Lots 82–116 and the northern tier of Lots 117–147. Blocks 15–19 ran between Henderson and Lafayette from the survey line to Walnut and included the southern tier of Lots 148–178 and the northern tier of Lots 179–208. The remaining blocks (through 21) and lots (through 219) were apparently encompassed by the trapezoid formed by the survey line and Vale, Orleans, and Henderson streets. The warehouse lots ran between Dallas and Austin and were numbered from one to 13 beginning on the east at Soda and ending on the west at Polk.

Henderson Street was High Street in the Cherry plan, and Rusk was Clarksville. High Street was not used subsequently as a name for a street in Jefferson, but Clarksville came to be used for a street one block north of the northern boundary of the Cherry plan. Marshall Street was also known as Spring Street by residents of Jefferson during the early years, but it did not appear as such on the Cherry plan and is always referred to as Marshall in the early deed records. There is one mention of a Wharf Street in the deed records, but this was probably another name for Dallas, which appears in all the early deed records and would have been in the Cherry plan.

Urquhart and Durham

The relationship between Allen Urquhart and Berry Durham preceded the formation of Jefferson in 1845 and was at first based on the operation by Durham of Urquhart's ferry at the townsite, which apparently extended from 1841 through 1844. The operation of the ferry was the reason why Durham located at the townsite; but with Durham at the townsite and Urquhart in Daingerfield, it soon became the occasion for Durham to develop an interest in Jefferson as an investment opportunity. The property relationship that was established between these two men in 1842 and 1843 was the decisive factor in Jefferson's earliest development as a town.

The first documentation of a property relationship occurs in a February 3, 1842, bond for title from Urquhart to Durham, with Urquhart acting as part owner and agent of the Jefferson Town Company and lease administrator of the Jefferson ferry. Durham is to have five lots in Jefferson after the town is laid off, with sufficient room for a stable and warehouse. Two of the lots are to be had at Durham's choice, with the other three obtained by chance with the five proprietors of the Town Company.

A new agreement was signed on October 2, 1842, nullifying the former. Urquhart agreed to purchase 130 acres of Durham's headright in Smith County for $300 to be paid in installments ending in June 1845. Durham agreed to purchase 100 acres with an option on 60 from any part of Urquhart's headrights in Jefferson and Daingerfield for $2 an acre. Durham was also to have two lots of his choice after the town was laid off, as per the previous agreement, one for business and one for a warehouse.

This agreement was consummated in a January 18, 1843, bond for land in which Durham purchased 160 acres of the Jefferson land for $2 an acre, with the land to be in two parcels. One parcel for 100 acres was to begin at the two ironwood (bois d'arc) trees below where the ferryboat was built at a spring and to run north and west. The other parcel for 60 acres was to be taken north of the 100 acres laid off for the town and joining one of the lines, apparently referring to the Jesse Cherry town plan. Durham was also to have the five lots designated in the 1842 bond for title.

The significance of this purchase is not apparent until it is realized that the 160 acres constituted one-fourth of Urquhart's headright and that they were located in the lower three-fourths of the headright, of which Durham had acquired a third. More importantly, the 100 acres were approximately one-half of the Jesse Cherry town plan and were at the heart of the town in its earliest development. In essence, Urquhart had sold a major part of his interest in Jefferson to Durham. The location of the two ironwood trees is, of course, unknown; but the ferryboat must have been built in the extreme southern portion of the headright, because it operated at the foot of Houston Street.

Urquhart and Durham began to enter into conflict over the meaning of their January 1843 land agreement, particularly about the precise location of the 100 acres, which is not surprising given the vagueness of the description. Durham had begun selling lots in Jefferson by at least March 1844 in accordance with the Jesse Cherry town plan, which appears to have been commissioned by him. He was not acting as Urquhart's agent but rather on his own account and in terms of his understanding of the 100 acres that had been sold to him. Urquhart did not sell any lots on his own account until January 1846. During the intervening period, all land transactions were by Durham or by persons to whom Durham had sold lots.

By late 1844, the situation had become critical, with William Perry nearing completion of the bayou clearing effort that would make the townsite accessible to steamboats and insure its primacy with respect to trade to the west. Edwin Rogers, Richard Crump, and Ennis Ury were chosen as referees to resolve the dispute. In December, Urquhart and Durham agreed to the referees' basic finding concerning the 100 acres, which stated that "the commencement of said land shall be at the two Iron wood trees marked with the letter H at the spring as agreed upon by the parties and run due north until it strikes the South East boundary of the town of Jefferson survey. Thence with the said line of the town survey in a north eastern direction to such point as will include all the lots surveyed by Jesse Cherry, thence North and West for complement."

The southeast boundary referred to was that of the Jesse Cherry town plan and ran along the alley between Lake and Camp streets. The point of departure in the description was apparently near the intersection of Houston and Common streets. The line ran due north from the two ironwood trees until it struck the southeast boundary of the Cherry plan, then northeast to the southeast corner of the Cherry plan, then north and west, passing through the northernmost point of the Cherry plan at the intersection of Henderson and Walnut. Apart from the specific mention of the Cherry plan as a point of reference, this was simply a clarification of the meaning of the January 1843 agreement and resolved nothing. The problem for the referees was that much of this land had already been sold by Durham, so that it was impossible to simply allocate a parcel of 100 acres. The referees were therefore faced with the task of assigning lots within the context of the specified boundaries.

A new agreement was signed by Urquhart and Durham on December 20, 1845, in which Urquhart conveyed to Durham one undivided fourth (i.e., 160 acres) of his Jefferson property and agreed to make title to all lots that had been sold by Durham or donated by Durham "for opening the Lake or other improvements of said town or given with a view to enhance the value of the same." Durham was to give an account of the lots he had sold and the price, and Urquhart would receive lots of equivalent value as well as lots to cover money owed to him by Durham from their original agreement. Ennis Ury, William Bishop, and Edwin Rogers were appointed commissioners to select these lots and to class and divide all other properties in contention.

The report of the commissioners covers 25 pages in the Transcribed Deed Records, including Hugh Hensey's 1846 town plan, which was used to record the commissioners' property allocations. The report is essentially a series of allocation decisions made between January 5, 1846, and the filing of the report in March. The report begins with a list of 64 lots that had been sold by Durham for $2,360 as of January 5. In addition, Durham owed, with interest, $299.94 to Urquhart from the purchase of 160 acres at $2 an acre. The commissioners assigned 66 lots to Urquhart to cover these two amounts. Durham provided a list of the 46 lots and two half lots donated for the improvement of Jefferson to which Urquhart had agreed to give title, but only two of these had been sold according to Durham's list of sales.

Durham had also sold 25 lots conditionally to Jesse Nave, and there were two unknown ownership lots that were eventually determined to have been sold to Nave. When Nave failed to fulfill the conditions, the lots were divided evenly between Urquhart and Durham. Durham had also sold nine lots to David Hill, for which Urquhart was assigned equivalent value through one block, five lots, and a small parcel of land at the foot of Rusk Street. Of the remaining lots delineated in the Hensey plan, 31 were assigned to Urquhart and 11 to Durham. All remaining properties extending south to the bayou and north to the present-day Howell Addition were assigned as blocks and portions of blocks, most of which went to Urquhart.

At the time of the allocations, the most valuable properties in Urquhart's survey were those that had been delineated as lots at the center of town in its earliest development, most of which were within the boundaries of the Jesse Cherry town plan. Durham had sold 64, donated 46, acquired 13 from Nave, sold nine to Hill, and was assigned 11 by the commissioners, for a total of 143. Urquhart received 66 through equivalent value, acquired 13 from Nave and five from the Hill consideration, and was assigned 31 by the commissioners, for a total of 115. The significance of these determinations is best understood by a comparison of the boundaries of the Jesse Cherry town plan with the boundaries of the lots sold by or allocated to Durham as shown on the Hensey map, keeping in mind that the latter boundaries included lots that had been allocated to Urquhart (Fig. 4-9).

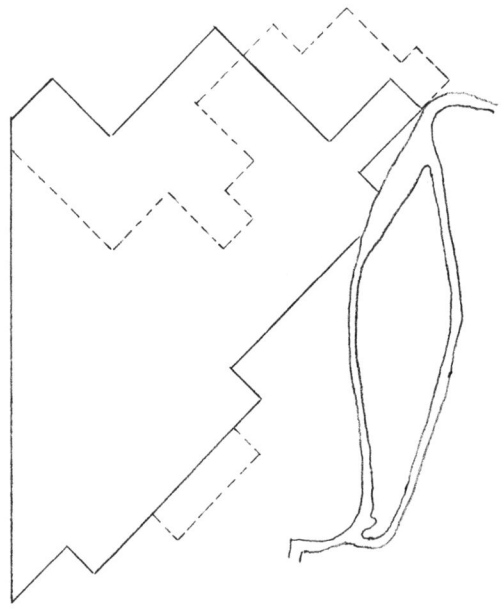

Fig. 4-9. Cherry-Durham Comparison

——— Jesse Cherry Town Plan
- - - - Durham Lot Boundaries

Durham was obviously the dominant factor in the distribution of properties at the heart of Jefferson in its earliest development. What Durham had in mind in his October 1842 and January 1843 transactions with Urquhart was a shrewd land deal. Urquhart's participation in these transactions appears strange only because of the assumption that Urquhart was Jefferson's founder and that founders have certain qualities. Urquhart never lived in Jefferson and appears to have been much more dedicated to the promotion and development of Daingerfield. Moreover, Urquhart was involved in a number of major land transactions, including four on Cypress Bayou above and below Jefferson on both sides of the bayou. He should be classified as a major land speculator, but with the understanding that almost everyone with money back at that time engaged in land speculation.

Although the sale to Durham involved a portion of Urquhart's headright, it was thought of by Urquhart as merely one of his land transactions. Most importantly, it was not a land sale in the normal sense, because Urquhart was not seeking revenue. Rather, it was essentially a land swap in which Urquhart agreed to pay Durham $300 for 130 acres in Durham's Smith County headright, and Durham agreed to pay Urquhart $320 for 160 acres in Urquhart's headright. It must be concluded that Urquhart thought of the Smith County property as at least of equivalent value and that his status as a town founder has been overestimated.

The vagueness of the initial agreement between Urquhart and Durham and Durham's inadequate record keeping for the earliest lot sales were to have long-term consequences for the development of Jefferson. In speaking about the earliest years, the September 1, 1876, *Jefferson Jimplecute* states that "Various troubles and disputes arose about the titles to property, which has, until recently, been the greatest drawback to the city."

Berry Durham

Berryman Hicks Durham was born on January 19, 1807, in Rutherford County, North Carolina, and died in Jefferson on November 7, 1848, at the age of 41. He was one of nine children of Charles Alexander Durham and Patience Davis. Charles Durham was the son of

Achilles Durham and Mary Cates, who had five children. One of these was Elizabeth, who married Berryman Hicks about 1800. Berry Durham was, therefore, named after one of his uncles. Berry Durham's wife Eliza was born in 1819 in Norh Carolina. They had four children (John, Mary, Louisa, Delina), all of whom were born in Texas. The eldest (Mary) is shown as 12 years old in the 1850 census, suggesting that the Durhams were in Texas at least by 1838.

The September 1, 1876, *Daily Jimplecute* article on the history of Jefferson contains a few comments on Berry Durham. The article says that the date of the founding of Jefferson cannot be determined, but that "the first man who ever settled inside of her present limits was Berry H. Durrum, in 1840. He built his cabin on the bank of the river near where the Marshall road so long crossed by ferry and bridges, under an arrangement or lease with Allen Urquhart, for the purpose of establishing a ferry at that point. This territory was then in Paschal county."

The article goes on to say that "Berry Durrum was the first Postmaster, and for many years this was the only post office for a long distance north and west. Mr. D. was a great fisherman, and often when persons came for their mail they would have to go down the river until they found him—but he always had the mail in his hat and had only to take it off and look over the list of letters." William Bishop was actually the first postmaster in Jefferson, having acquired this position in May 1846. Durham became postmaster in January 1847.

The profile suggests a simple man, and there were elements of simplicity about him. However, the mere fact that he assumed the responsibilities of both ferryman and postmaster suggests that there were larger dimensions to his character. These dimensions are revealed through the deed records and through the few available accounts of his activities, particularly in the Clarksville *Northern Standard*.

Durham does not appear in the July 1840 Red River County tax rolls, but does appear in the 1841 tax rolls (under Paschal County), without property in that county but with one slave. Durham probably built his cabin at the foot of Houston Street in late 1840 and began operating the ferry for Urquhart in early 1841. The cabin site was on the east side of Houston Street a short distance from the bayou on the first rise in elevation above the floodplain (Fig. 4-10). Durham acquired

Townsite

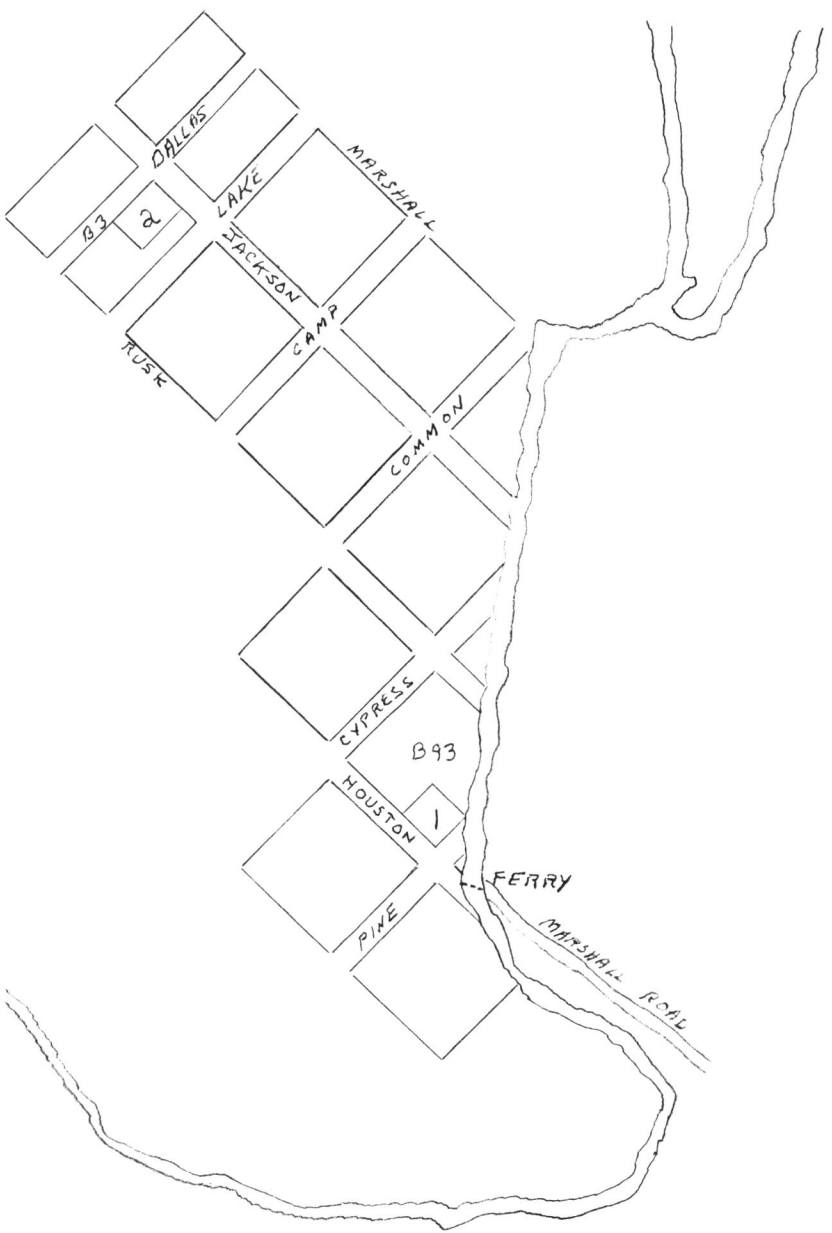

Fig. 4-10. Berry Durham's Locations
KEY:
1. Durham's late-1840 log cabin
2. Durham's 1848 residence

part ownership in the ferry and operated the ferry through 1844, when Urquhart transferred operation to William Bishop.

It is obvious from the article and the deed records that Durham was Jefferson's first resident, because his residency long preceded the formation of the town, and he was in residence when the town came into existence in 1845. However, by early 1845 he was no longer living in the cabin on the bayou, because operation of the ferry had been transferred to Bishop in December 1844. In 1845, Durham was apparently living in a structure slightly to the north in property dedicated to the ferry operation. By March 1848, he had established a permanent residence on Lots 8 and 9 of Block 3 fronting Jackson Street at the corner of Dallas.

In the January 1843 purchase from Urquhart, as determined by the commissioners, Durham acquired one-fourth of the 640 acres of Urquhart's headright on Cypress Bayou. The town was located in the lower portion of the headright. Hensey's 1846 town plan covers about three-fourths of the headright, which means that Durham acquired about one-third of the properties shown on the map. More importantly, Durham acquired more than half of the properties in the area that was the nucleus of Jefferson and largely encompassed by the Jesse Cherry town plan, including all of the warehouse lots at the center of the landing area.

Durham's property ownership in early Jefferson was at least equivalent to that of Urquhart. In addition, Durham was the basis for all lot sales in 1844 and 1845, a process that Urquhart did not begin to participate in until January 1846. With Durham as a major property holder and selling lots in Jefferson and Urquhart in Daingerfield and not involved in the process, it is obvious that Durham was responsible for the early development of Jefferson and that he should be considered a third founder, after Urquhart and Alley.

As with Urquhart, the founding function should not be sentimentalized. Like Urquhart, Durham was a land speculator, although not anywhere near the same magnitude, and his land transactions indicate that he was not totally focused on the development of Jefferson. When Durham conveyed 29 lots in Jefferson to Jesse Nave in June 1845, this was a land swap for 640 acres owned by Nave in Nacogdoches County.

In January 1846, Durham deeded his properties to his children, with Ennis Ury, John Howell, Robert Arberry, and James Durham acting as trustees. Durham retained the right to sell properties with the consent of one trustee. In June 1846, his wife Eliza filed a schedule of separate property that included every fifth lot in Jefferson "which belonged to B. H. Durham by virtue of the right of location or purchase from A. Urquhart &c." These actions were preceded by Durham's initial agreement with Urquhart in December 1845 and followed by the report of the arbitrating commissioners in March 1847.

Durham first appears in the newspaper records in the *Northern Standard* in June 1847, giving a speech in connection with a proposed project to made additional navigation improvements to Cypress Bayou. The newspaper article indicates that he carried the title "Colonel" and that he spoke "in his peculiar and amusing style, occasionally interrupted by ejaculations from some warm admirers of his."

Durham was running for office. In early July, the newspaper announced his candidacy for the Texas Legislature to represent the Second Senatorial District, composed of the counties of Red River, Bowie, Titus, and Cass. Durham was attacked anonymously in late July by one of his opponent's supporters, but the text of the letter is largely indecipherable. Durham's response in August reveals that he had been a member of the North Carolina Legislature (from which office he derived his title), that when he first came to Texas he was poor and lived in a small cabin on Shawnee Creek in Red River County, that he was not wealthy, that he was apparently ugly, and that he had been involved in a trial of some notoriety.

Durham's claim of membership in the North Carolina Legislature is substantiated by the Department of State's 1981 *North Carolina Government 1585–1979: A Narrative and Statistical History*, which lists a Bremen H. Durham as representative of Rutherford County in the 1834–35 General Assembly (now Senate). This was also the same session in which Robert Potter served his third (non-consecutive) term, representing Granville County in the House of Commons (now House of Representatives). The trial mentioned by Durham was not the famous Potter trial, but rather a trial for murder that apparently precipitated Durham's removal to Texas.

That Bremen Durham was Berryman Durham is confirmed by the "Reminiscences of Christenberry Lee 1823–1895" (available online). Lee was a resident of Rutherford County. He relates that Berryman's older brother Achilles had taken a dislike to the incumbent county representative in the upper house and encouraged his younger brother to run for office around 1835. Lee says that "This young man was entirely unknown by the people, having just grown up, and had not been before them for any office. He was looked upon and regarded by the people as an ordinary young man, not rating above mediocrity in point of natural endowments." Nevertheless, Berryman won by a handsome majority because of Achilles' widespread influence.

Durham was soundly defeated in his bid for office in the Texas Legislature in August 1847. However, he immediately purchased the *Jefferson Democrat* from William Bishop, with land used as partial payment for the very expensive printing press. This was Jefferson's first newspaper, with a prospectus published in May 1847 and the first issue received in Clarksville in June. With Durham was Robert Loughery as editor and publisher, who was shortly to establish the Marshall *Texas Republican*. The *Jefferson Democrat* is last mentioned in June 1848 and was definitely out of existence in November, when the *Spirit of the Age* begins to be mentioned as Jefferson's newspaper.

Durham was apparently quite ill and soon to die. He prepared a will in April 1847 leaving all of his properties to his wife Eliza, his son, and his two daughters (corrected in February 1848 to include a newborn daughter). His last lot sale was in August 1848, and Eliza was appointed administratrix at his death in November. Although some town lots are listed in the will, only one-fourth of the property settlement with Urquhart was conveyed to his heirs, apparently because the other three-fourths had already been conveyed to them by 1846. These previous transactions, which involved his wife and children, are why Durham did not die a very wealthy man. I have been unable to determine why the one-fourth was included in the will, and it does not appear in the estate inventory. Eliza conveyed most of the lots to John Speake, Charles Schaff, Sidney Neal, Israel Leavitt, and Samuel Moseley in May 1850. Durham's widow and four children are listed in the 1850 census.

William Bishop

William Bishop was one of Jefferson's earliest and most prominent citizens, although only for a few years. The records concerning his activities in relation to Jefferson extend only from 1844 through 1848.

Bishop succeeded Berry Durham as operator of the Jefferson ferry in December 1844, became part owner of the ferry operation in October 1845, and increased his ownership in January 1846. When Bishop succeeded Durham as the ferry operator in 1844, it is reasonable to assume that he took possession of the cabin at the foot of Houston Street. Thus, Bishop is the second documented resident of Jefferson when it emerged in early 1845. He left the cabin by late 1846 when operation of the ferry was transferred to Asa and James Johnson.

In December 1845, Bishop was appointed one of the commissioners to resolve the land dispute between Urquhart and Durham. He began to purchase lots in Jefferson in January 1846 and became one of the primary lot holders, as is evident from the deed records and the frequent occurrence of his name on the Hensey map.

One of the lots purchased in January was Lot 4 in Block 8 near the landing area and fronting Polk and running along Dallas and Austin (Fig. 4-11). This lot is shaped like an inverted L and is one of the two non-standard lots in town (apart from the fractional lots on the Urquhart-Alley line). The configuration of the Bishop lot was determined by an Urquhart sale in July 1845 of a 60-foot-square lot fronting Polk and Dallas to William Pertle and Albert Manker. The reason for this unique choice of dimensions is unknown and apparently extended back to the period of the Jesse Cherry town plan.

The 60-foot square left a larger inverted L-shaped lot fronting on Polk and running on Dallas and Austin. Bishop established his house fronting Polk Street on this lot and created a fenced garden in the rear. This was in the warehouse district, and one of William Russell's stables adjoined to the east. Usage of the "Manker lot," as it was commonly known, is uncertain.

Bishop was among the commissioners appointed by the Texas Legislature in April 1846 to select a permanent location for the county seat of the newly formed Cass County. He became Jefferson's first postmaster when he was appointed to that position on May 22, 1846,

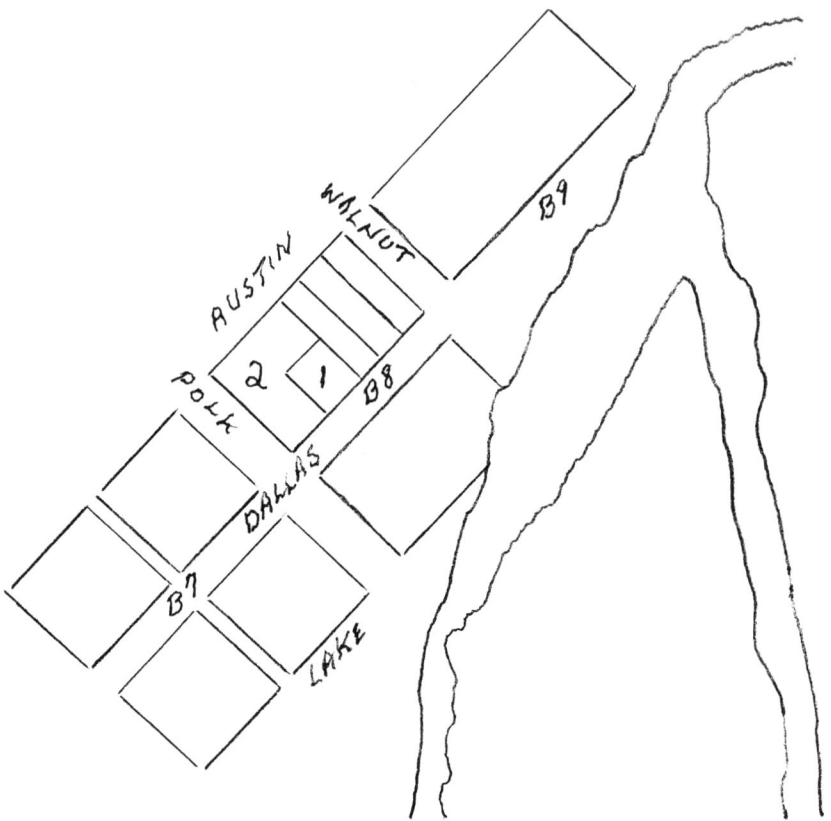

Fig. 4-11. William Bishop's Residence
KEY:
1. Manker lot
2. Bishop's 1846 residence

and apparently established the post office in his house. Although Cass County, in which Jefferson was located, had been formed out of Bowie County statutorily on April 25, the post office was part of the Bowie County system. When the system was changed on January 26, 1847, Durham was appointed postmaster. He was succeeded by Bishop on June 15, and Bishop was succeeded by Perry Graham on February 26, 1849.

Bishop was editor and publisher of Jefferson's first newspaper, the *Jefferson Democrat*, which appeared in June 1847. The newspaper had an elegant and very expensive printing press. Bishop was highly respected by Charles DeMorse, the editor of the Clarksville *Northern Standard*, and they were apparently personal and political friends. Bishop published this weekly newspaper for only a few months, selling out to Durham in August.

Bishop was appointed in early 1847 by the Cass County commissioners court as one of the persons to select a location for a courthouse in the Alley Addition. His work in connection with the Urquhart-Durham dispute was completed in March of that year. The lot and residence in Jefferson was sold to James French and Prentiss Stetson in December 1848 in exchange for carpentry work and 10,000 shingles, apparently in relation to the construction of a home in Paradise. The deed record states that this was the lot on which Bishop recently resided. Bishop does not appear in the county records after 1848, but was not replaced as postmaster until February 1849.

First Sale of Lots

Early land sales in Jefferson were conducted through bonds for title rather than direct sales because Urquhart did not receive a patent on his property until April 1851. The earliest record of a sale of a lot in Jefferson is a March 3, 1844, bond for title from William Brown to John Withee, in which Brown sells to Withee for $90 Lot 33 in Block 5 of the Jesse Cherry town plan. This is present-day Lot 12 in Block 4, a corner lot bounded by Dallas, Lake, and Marshall, on the west side of Marshall. The bond was transferred to Berry Durham on May 17, 1844, and then to Enoch Crow on June 5, 1844.

There are two problems with this transaction. The first is that it does not explain how Brown acquired the lot. There must have been a previous transfer of ownership, either from Berry Durham or Allen Urquhart, who were the original owners of all lots; and, because Urquhart did not participate in any of the early lot transactions, the lot must have been sold to Brown by Durham or by someone to whom Durham had sold the lot.

The second problem is that Durham sold to Brown the same lot only two months later, on May 9. Because this was part of a larger transaction in which Durham sold Brown 12 lots for $600, it might be assumed that the first transaction was simply voided by the second, which was not uncommon when a larger transaction occurred later. However, this assumption is incompatible with the bond transfers to Durham and Crow.

Durham was required to provide a list of his early land sales to the commissioners in his dispute with Urquhart. Persons and amounts of sales are given, but lot numbers and dates are not. Brown is not listed, as is the case with some other persons who appear in the deed records. Conversely, some persons are listed who do not appear in the deed records. In cases of correspondence, the amount given is often below what appears in the deed records. Because the listed transactions are not dated, there is no reason to assume that any occurred before March 1844.

However, there is a July 20, 1844, bond for title from Durham to Brown for 10 lots stating that these lots had been bonded to George Wynne on March 5, 1844. More importantly, there is a January 18, 1844, bond for title from John Withee to Durham in which Withee sells back to Durham 11 unnumbered lots plus one fraction of a lot, stating that these are not all of the lots that he had purchased from Durham. Although no location is given, it is almost certain that these lots were in Jefferson.

It can be concluded that the March 3, 1844, transaction was not the first sale of a lot in Jefferson and that the first sale cannot be documented. The first lots probably began to be sold in Jefferson in late 1843.

First Map Appearance

Jefferson's first map appearance is on Sidney Morse and Samuel Breese's 1844 map of Texas (Fig. 4-12). This map could be used to suggest that Jefferson was in existence before 1845; however, it says just the opposite. The dominant entity in the area is Smithland, with roads leading south by ferry over Big Cypress Bayou to Marshall and north to DeKalb, Clarksville, and Jonesboro. Jefferson is isolated, with no roads passing through it. Other maps produced in 1844 such as Lt. William Emory's *Map of Texas and Countries Adjacent* do not show Jefferson, but include Smithland, Port Caddo, Daingerfield, and Marshall in the immediate area and Clarksville, DeKalb, Jonesboro, and Boston

Townsite

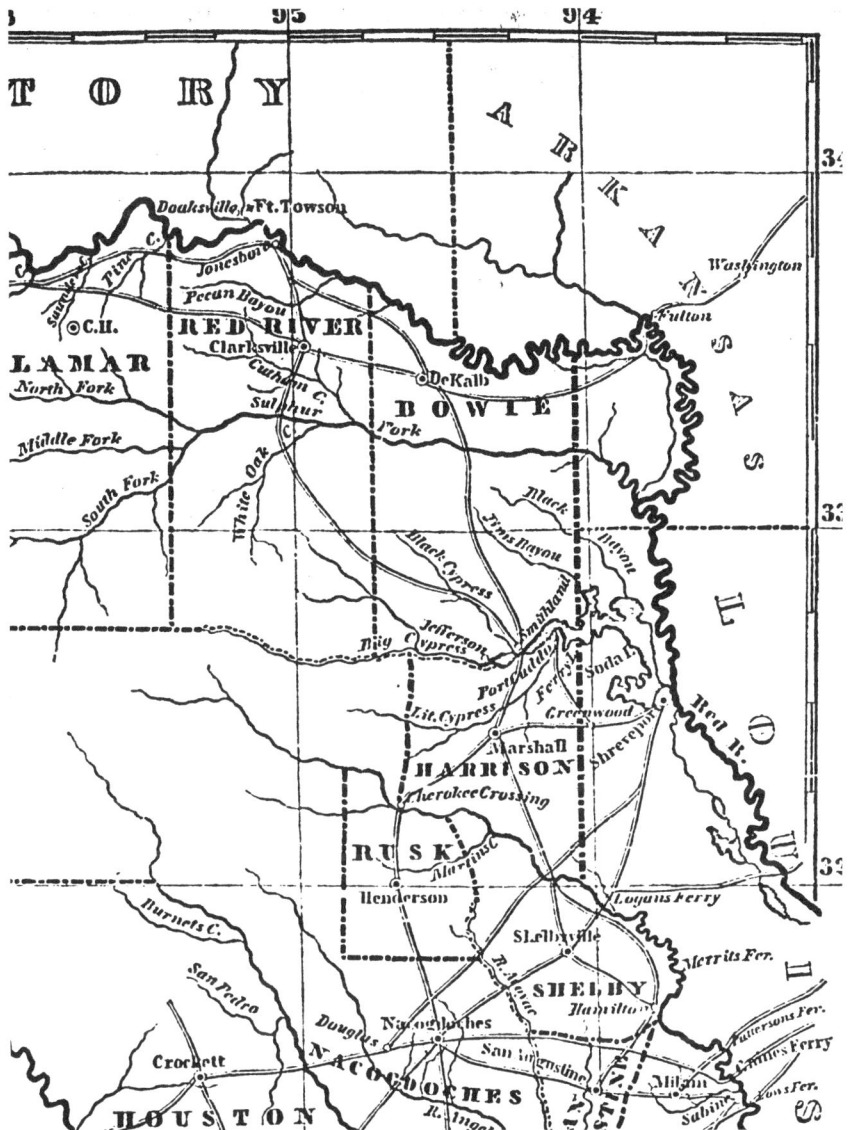

Fig. 4-12. Jefferson's First Map Appearance

to the north. The Morse and Breese representation of Jefferson is obviously a representation of a townsite on its way to becoming a full-fledged town.

Townsite Commerce

The ferry was established across Big Cypress Bayou at the Jefferson townsite in early 1841 to transport cotton from the Daingerfield area to Port Caddo and Shreveport, where it could be taken by steamboat to New Orleans. John Salmon "Rip" Ford indicates that some flatboats were operating by early 1838 between Shreveport and the settlement that was to become Port Caddo; but the first steamboat did not arrive at Port Caddo until December 1838. W. W. Withenbury's reminiscences indicate that the first bale of cotton was not taken out of Port Caddo by steamboat until December 1841, and it was not Jefferson cotton. Steamboats did not begin to make regular trips to Port Caddo until 1842, and during that year there were only two certain arrivals.

The distribution patterns of cotton that passed through the townsite cannot be determined, but included overland transport to Port Caddo and Shreveport and also apparently water transport from the townsite by flatboats to Port Caddo, where the cotton was taken out by steamboat. More importantly, by late 1843 Jefferson had become at least a minor collecting point for cotton that was transported overland or by water, providing an incipient form of the commercial activity that constituted the town's essence.

Writing in April 1844, Charles DeMorse of the *Northern Standard* stated that "There has already been boated off from Jefferson, the present season 350 bales of cotton, and there are 60 more there to ship." DeMorse is referring to the commercial season, which began on September 1 and therefore is indicating that 350 bales had been shipped between September 1843 and April 1844. DeMorse also says that "At present, those who wish to procure goods or realize something immediately for their cotton, are obliged to haul it to Port Caddo or Shreveport." This indicates that the cotton was shipped by flatboats that operated only downstream during high water. Persons desiring import items or who did not want to wait for high water to ship cotton had to operate through Port Caddo or Shreveport by overland transport.

Reece Hughes ran a large plantation northwest of Jefferson. In the 1848 district court case of Jesse Nave versus Reece Hughes, Nave, who was then resident in Missouri, contended that in November 1844, Hughes promised to deliver by December 1844 five bales of cotton weighing 2,550 pounds and valued at $300 to Samuel Ticknor at Jefferson, but then changed his mind and promised to deliver the cotton to Nave instead for a valuable consideration. Nave, who at the time of the transaction was living south of Jefferson in Harrison County, claimed that he never got the cotton. Hughes submitted two receipts showing that the five bales had been delivered on November 29 and December 5, 1844, to Nave through his agent Berry Durham for delivery to Ticknor.

In the 1847 district court case of James McCown versus Reece Hughes, receipts and testimony indicate that McCown of Harrison County received on February 26, 1845, at Jefferson from Hughes 55 bales of cotton weighing 23,418 pounds. McCown was to send the cotton to New Orleans and sell it under his own name. He freighted (apparently by ox-wagon) the cotton to Port Caddo at a cost of $20.62, where it was received by the firm of Todd & Brander and shipped aboard the *Bois d'Arc* at a freight cost of $68.75 to Brander, Williams & Company of New Orleans, where it was sold for $1,270.63 on March 27, minus total expenses of $172.86, for a balance of $1,097.77.

The evidence presented in the second case is particularly interesting because it shows how expensive overland transport was compared to steamboat transport, given the fact that Port Caddo was fewer than 15 miles from Jefferson and hundreds of miles from New Orleans. The need to bring steamboats to Jefferson was pressing. McCown received the cotton at Jefferson on February 26, 1845. That was the same day that Capt. W. W. Withenbury in New Orleans decided to take the *Lama* to Jefferson.

5. Emergence

Daingerfield Meeting

Although Jefferson was firmly established as a townsite through Urquhart's November 1841 survey, it did not become a town until 1845. The Clarksville *Northern Standard* provides a running account of the emergence of the town in late 1844 and early 1845, and all contemporary sources agree that the first structures were completed in 1845.

Jefferson was a relative latecomer to the area. It was preceded by the Louisiana towns of Shreveport and Greenwood, by the northeast Texas towns of Clarksville, Boston, DeKalb, Jonesboro, and Marshall, and by the downstream Cypress Bayou ports of Port Caddo, Benton, and Smithland.

Lots may have begun to be sold at the townsite by late 1843; but the first recorded transaction is from March 1844, after which sales were fairly continuous. There were 22 transactions in 1844, most of which involved multiple lots; but the only things at the townsite by the end of 1844 were William Bishop's cabin for the operation of the ferry and Berry Durham's cabin slightly to the north on the ferry operation property.

The ferry had been established by Urquhart in 1841 as part of a transport system running from Daingerfield to Shreveport, with a lateral to Port Caddo. The purpose of this system was to enable planters in the area northwest of the townsite, which included Daingerfield, to transport cotton by ox-wagon to Port Caddo and Shreveport, where it could be taken out by steamboats, and to bring back plantation supplies by the same route.

Smithland was in existence about six miles downstream by 1839, but there is no evidence that any steamboats had gone up Cypress Bayou that far by 1844. Smithland was a better place than the Jefferson townsite for a port because of higher ground and the fact that Caddo Lake hydrologically extended up to that point, making access by water fairly good during most of the year when the Red River was navigable.

The six miles between Smithland and the townsite were shallow and, more importantly, congested with living and dead cypress trees, logs, and accumulated debris that steamboats could not penetrate. The townsite's major advantage was that it was six miles upstream, and it was well known to everyone in the area that the port farthest upstream on Cypress Bayou would capture all of the business to the west because of the cost and slowness of overland transport by ox-wagon.

The townsite had an excellent turning basin; and, more importantly, the bayou above was more constricted and did not offer an opportunity for an extension of navigation. The townsite was the natural terminus of the Cypress Bayou navigation system and offered excellent navigation facilities; but it could not be reached by steamboats unless the bayou was cleared out. Without steamboat access, people were not interested in investing in town lots or building anything at the townsite.

In April 1844, a meeting was held in Daingerfield to devise a plan for removing the obstructions in Cypress Bayou from Smithland at least up to the townsite of Jefferson and even farther if practical. The meeting was attended by Allen Urquhart, Mansell Matthews, Jeptha Crawford, Benjamin Gooch, Byrd Gray, Bennett Martin, Isaac Hughes, William Peacock, Edwin Rogers, Dr. Isaac Tabor, and John Withee. The meeting was almost certainly called by Urquhart and conducted at his house, but Hughes was the chairman and Gray was the secretary.

A committee of nine was appointed to decide on a plan of action, and a subcommittee of three was appointed to examine the bayou and to estimate the cost of clearance. The subcommittee examined the bayou and determined that some work would be needed between

Port Caddo and Smithland, with the bulk of the work between Smithland and the townsite. The cost was estimated at $2,000, which was reported to the larger committee at a general meeting in May. A motion was made and carried by the attendees that the bayou be cleared out, that work specifications be published in the *Northern Standard,* that the work be let to the lowest bidder at Daingerfield on July 4, and that the work be completed by December 25, with payment in cash or cotton. The choice of dates obviously had symbolic significance.

Two reasons were given by Charles DeMorse of the *Northern Standard* for the initial meeting and the decision to clear out the bayou. The first was the cost and inconvenience of hauling cotton to Port Caddo and Shreveport. The second was a desire to secure the benefits of trade for the general region rather than allowing them to be realized in distant places like Shreveport.

All but two of the men who attended the meeting were large landholders in Bowie County, with most concentrated in the Daingerfield area. The exceptions were Byrd Gray, a Mt. Pleasant attorney in 1848 who played a role in Jefferson's politics, particularly as a judge during the Reconstruction period, and Dr. Isaac Tabor, who was an early lotholder in Jefferson and practiced medicine in Jefferson and Hickory Hill. In addition to Allen Urquhart, Isaac Hughes, Mansell Matthews, and Edwin Rogers had headrights in the Daingerfield area; and William Peacock, who is listed in the 1840 Red River County tax rolls as a slaveholder, was probably the brother of Atlas Peacock, whose headright was in the Daingerfield area.

In addition to Urquhart and Tabor, Jeptha Crawford, John Withee, Bennett Martin, Edwin Rogers, and Mansell Matthews were early lotholders in Jefferson. Crawford was one of Jefferson's earliest and most important merchants. Withee was a Mt. Pleasant merchant in 1854. Martin was a Clarksville attorney in 1844 and became the primary merchant at Benton. Rogers was a Daingerfield attorney in 1844 and moved to Jefferson in 1851. Matthews was a prominent doctor, preacher, and politician, representing Red River County in the first and seventh congresses of the Republic of Texas. Benjamin Gooch held large tracts of land in more than one county; but his primary orientation appears to have been Clarksville, with a farm to the west and town lots.

Because most of these were men of substantial means, $2,000, which was equivalent to about 40 bales of cotton, would not have been a burden, and there is no evidence that additional subscriptions were sought. Most peculiarly, there is no evidence that town lots in Jefferson were used to finance the bayou clearing effort. Durham had donated 46 lots and two half lots "for opening the Lake or other improvements of said town or given with a view to enhance the value of the same." When this donation was made is unknown, but the donation was mentioned in December 1845 and would have been available for payment for the bayou clearing effort. In his report to the commissioners who were dealing with the Urquhart dispute, Durham indicated that only two of these lots had been sold. Actually, two more had been sold by December 1844. There is nothing to indicate that any of this money was used for opening the lake; and, more importantly, the two lots sold in December 1844 were sold to William Perry for cash.

The work effort extended from Port Caddo to the townsite but concentrated on the area above Smithland. Most of the work was conducted during the summer low-water period when obstructions were easily reached for cutting. There is no evidence that any digging was involved, and the project was almost certainly conducted entirely with hand labor. The obstructions in need of removal would have included trees that had fallen into the water from the banks, embedded and floating logs, stumps, mats of branches and small logs, and living cypress trees on the fringes of the channel. The sawn and chopped timber that was floatable was left in-channel to be carried out by the next rise of water on the bayou.

The work was conducted between July and December 1844 and completed on schedule. There is no documentation with respect to who conducted the work, but the likely candidate is William Perry. Perry was the preferred contractor for later bayou clearing efforts and met the first steamboat to Jefferson at Shreveport to guide the boat up the newly cleared channel. Perry began purchasing lots in Jefferson from Durham in December 1844.

The initial Daingerfield meeting was held on April 9. The first record of a lot sale in Jefferson was on March 3 to John Withee. It is obvious that the initial lot sales were stimulated by the intent to clear out the bayou, which probably would have been a topic of conversation by at least the end of 1843. The investigations of the subcommittee were directed toward the cost of removing the obstructions, not whether the project should be conducted. The decision for removal had already been made by the time of the April meeting. As a consequence, concrete plans for the construction of facilities at the townsite began to be made immediately, as reported in the April 17 *Northern Standard*:

> Whenever, as is now projected, warehouses shall be built at the place, and establishments of goods, offering the usual trading and advancing facilities shall be established, Jefferson commanding the trade of a large and fertile section of country, will necessarily become a point of importance. Such houses we are informed will be established within the next six months.

By October, as the work progressed, houses began to be erected at the townsite, as reported in the *Northern Standard* for the 16th:

> Jefferson.—We are told that several houses are now going up at this point, which, our readers will recollect, is the head of navigation on Big Cypress, and several stocks of goods will be opened there within the next two or three months. Jefferson is, we think, destined to be a place of considerable trade. It must necessarily command all the business which has hitherto gone to Shreveport and Port Caddo, from the section of country north and west of the lake.

By January 1845, the town was emerging into reality, as reported in the *Northern Standard* for the 16th:

> The town of Jefferson, in the Southern Division of our own County, was but yesterday a mere name upon paper, and now we are told, quite a number of buildings are going up—several persons will have goods there directly—the navigation of the Cypress has been cleared, so that the first rise of water will take out the

logs and leave the passage free to steamboats of moderate size, and a town will be there immediately; a town *de facto* and one destined to concentrate a large inland commercial business.

Without occupied structures, it is meaningless to speak of the existence of a town; and, for a town intended as a commercial center, that meant operational businesses. It should be noted that in speaking of houses, DeMorse is referring to commercial establishments rather than residences, as in the commonly used terms "warehouse" and "storehouse." DeMorse cites the erection of mercantile and export facilities as the essence of the emergence of Jefferson.

The first structures began to be built at the townsite in October 1844 after the major portion of the bayou clearing effort had been successful. The last report from the *Northern Standard* in January 1845 does not mention any completed structures. On April 11, 1845, Buck Barry arrived on the second steamboat to Jefferson and reports several houses under construction and one completed but unoccupied, a log cabin without a nail in it. It can be inferred that structures were occupied by at least the end of 1845 from the *Houston Telegraph*'s 1847 comment that "Two years ago there were but one or two cabins in Jefferson" and Edward Smith's 1849 comment that "Jefferson four years ago possessed only three log houses."

The first mention of a completed structure in Jefferson in the deed records is an April 30, 1845, bond for title from John Withee to William Perry. In exchange for two lots, Withee secured from Perry "one Lot of ground and house No. 116 and Block 9 of the said Perry Known by the name of the 'Grocery haus' and lot." Block 9 in the old town plan was present-day Block 23. This was probably a log structure and may have been the one completed log structure in Jefferson when Buck Barry arrived on April 11. It apparently was not operational on April 12 when Buck Barry was in search of breakfast. There is nothing to indicate that a grocery house operated in that area at any time, and the structure may simply have been intended as a grocery house. More importantly, the term at the time also referred to a place that sold ardent spirits.

In a July 10, 1845, bond for title from Berry Durham to William Pertle and Allen Manker, mention is made of "Russell's bottom shed." This was a livery stable on Lot 3 in Block 8, one of the lots presently occupied by the new Cypress Valley Alliance building. As the document indicates, this was a shed and not a building. The document also indicates that Russell had another shed farther to the west. This upper shed was also a livery stable and was located on Lot 7 in Block 74 at the northeast corner of Jackson and Camp, probably serving travelers on the road to Marshall.

The third, and final, mention of a structure in 1845 occurs in an October 8 bond for title from Berry Durham to William Perry that uses Amos Ury's warehouse on the west side of the landing area as a point of reference. It preceded the bond for title and was already in operation by October. It is also known from other records that Ury operated a storehouse on Lot 9 in Block 5 by at least the end of April 1845. In addition, a hotel on the south end of Block K in the Alley Addition must have been in existence by mid-1845 because it was a log structure.

Jefferson came into existence in 1845 as the result of a navigation project that was sponsored by planters in the Daingerfield area primarily to secure a closer export point for cotton. This does not mean that these men had no interest in the founding of Jefferson, which was the focus of attention from the beginning. However, it does mean that they would not have been adverse to the extension of navigation beyond the townsite, which was entertained as a possibility at the initial meeting. Because steamboat navigation above the townsite was not feasible, the emergence of Jefferson at the townsite in 1845 was assured.

First Steamboat

The bayou clearing effort from July through December 1844 enabled the first steamboat, the *Lama* under Captain W. W. Withenbury, to reach the emerging town of Jefferson on March 5, 1845. There are two early Jefferson sources that describe this event. The first is from the March 17, 1872, *Jefferson Daily Democrat*:

> The steamer Lama was the first boat that ever arrived at Jefferson. She was commanded by Captain Withen-

bery, with Geo. Alban as pilot, and _____ Wortham as engineer. This was on the 17th day of June 1844. On her return to Shreveport, she was obliged to anchor out in the stream, to avoid being seized upon by the United States Commissioner for having crossed the line.

The second is from the September 1, 1876, *Daily Jimplecute*:
    The first steamboat that ever landed at Jefferson was the Lama, Capt. Withinberry, in the winter of 1844–5, (the exact date we cannot ascertain from the fact that the records of the town, or many of them, was burned during J. S. Elliott's administration as Mayor).
    Capt. Wm. Perry met her at Shreveport and assisted in bringing her through. John Speake, Amos Ury and a few other citizens were also on board of her.

The date of March 5, 1845, is from the October 28, 1870, *Cincinnati Commercial*, which contains one of a series of autobiographical reminiscences published by Withenbury as letters to the newspaper in the city in which he lived. The New Orleans *Daily Picayune* contains a fairly detailed record of the trips made by the *Lama*. These records indicate that the *Lama* could have made the voyage to Jefferson only in March or April 1845. April can be excluded because the *Lama* cleared for Port Caddo on the 12th, and Buck Barry arrived on the second boat to Jefferson on the 11th. March is confirmed by a bill of lading for 154 bales of cotton that were picked up by the *Lama* at Smithland on the 23rd, obviously on the down trip from Jefferson.

The *Lama* was a 68-ton sidewheeler built in Cincinnati in September 1844, which excludes from possibility the June 17, 1844, date given by the *Jefferson Daily Democrat* for the arrival of the *Lama* at Jefferson. Besides running on the Red River, this boat operated on the Yazoo River in Mississippi, on the Vermillion River in Louisiana, and to Pensacola, Florida. She removed to the Rio Grande in 1846, where she exploded at Camargo, Mexico, on May 29, 1847.

Wellington W. Withenbury was a well-known figure in the Red River trade, running many boats besides the *Lama* under the initials W.

W. He was clerk aboard the *Relief* in December 1841 when it brought the first bale of cotton out of Port Caddo. After 1845, he was responsible for opening the passage to Clinton on the upper end of Caddo Lake and for bringing the first steamboat, the *Monterey*, from Caddo Lake up Jim's Bayou to William's Landing, which was immediately renamed Monterey.

George Alban, the pilot, first appears in the early 1840s as a businessman and nominal head of a team of ox-wagon drivers at a portage around the raft on the Red River. He later became one of the most famous Red River pilots, established a toll route around the raft in the 1860s, and participated in the Corps of Engineers' improvements to Cypress Bayou in the 1870s.

The first voyage of a steamboat to Jefferson was not a demonstration project. It was a commercial voyage undertaken to obtain cotton that was ready for shipment at Jefferson and Smithland and secondarily to bring supplies to those points. Withenbury was chosen for the job because his boat was at New Orleans, and he was one of the few captains already acquainted with Caddo Lake. The *Lama* had actually advertised for another port but seized the opportunity when it was offered because of the assured commercial success of the voyage and because Withenbury was an adventuresome person who took pride in opening new routes.

Withenbury suggests in his reminiscences that the highest penetration of Cypress Bayou prior to 1845 was only 10 miles above Port Caddo, so that the *Lama* would be running through virgin territory most of the way. The *Daily Jimplecute* says that William Perry met the *Lama* at Shreveport to assist in bringing her through. As a result of the bayou clearing effort, Perry was the only person with intimate knowledge of what would be encountered in the voyage above Port Caddo. This intimate knowledge would have been important to Withenbury and Alban because the route was confusing at a few points and there would have been many remaining hazards.

The *Daily Jimplecute* also indicates that John Speake, Amos Ury, and a few other citizens made the trip from New Orleans. Speake began purchasing lots in Jefferson from Berry Durham in October 1844, including the fifth warehouse lot at the landing, and was soon to become one of Jefferson's leading merchants. Speake had family business connections in New Orleans, where he was to return after the Civil War. Ury had been operating with his brother as a merchant in the Daingerfield area and was to become Jefferson's first merchant, with a store in early 1845 and a warehouse in the landing area by October. Both of these men were regular vistiors to New Orleans on business. Speake, for example, was one of the signers of a February 1842 card thanking the *Bois d'Arc* for a successful trip from New Orleans to Shreveport, with the boat destined for Port Caddo.

Another person who was probably on board the *Lama* from New Orleans was James Todd, who was a partner in the firm of Todd & Brander at Port Caddo in 1841 when the *Relief*, with Withenbury as clerk, brought the first bale of cotton out in December. The firm was a branch of Brander, Williams & Company of New Orleans. In 1845, Todd was in the process of establishing himself at Smithland, where he became the primary merchant. The March 23, 1845, bill of lading for the 154 bales of cotton picked up by the *Lama* at Smithland was issued by Todd & Brander of Port Caddo, with the words "Port Caddo" scratched out and replaced by "Smithland." The New Orleans destination was the firm of Brander, Williams & Company. The fact that a Port Caddo bill of lading had to be used is another indication that no steamboat had reached Smithland before March 1845.

It is not difficult to envision what happened. Perry completed the bayou clearing effort in December 1844, leaving floatable debris instream, which was carried out by a rise in the stream in February 1845. Speake, Ury, and Todd went to New Orleans in late February to secure supplies for their mercantile establishments and to arrange with New Orleans cotton factors for the transport of cotton out of Jefferson and Smithland on the newly opened route. Withenbury was willing to accept the challenge and cancelled his advertised trip to Vermillionville (now Lafayette), Louisiana, on February 26.

There is no record of a departure or return for the *Lama*. It probably took a few days to load and left New Orleans at the end of the month with Speake, Ury, Todd, and other persons destined for Shreveport, Port Caddo, Smithland, and Jefferson on board. The *Lama* picked up Perry at Shreveport at the beginning of March and took a few days getting to Jefferson, with a stopover at Smithland to discharge freight. The *Lama* reached Jefferson on March 5, discharged freight, and took on cotton, perhaps as many as 400 bales according to Withenbury in a brief account of his life that was published in the July 10, 1878, *New Orleans Daily Democrat*. The *Lama* stayed at Jefferson more than two weeks, probably waiting for cotton to be transported overland to Jefferson.

On the way back, the *Lama* stopped off at Smithland to pick up the 154 bales, which were signed for by Withenbury. The *Jefferson Daily Democrat* indicates that the *Lama* could not dock at Shreveport on the return voyage because she would have been seized by the United States Commissioner. This was because she had not secured the appropriate papers at New Orleans for entrance into the Republic of Texas (which was then a foreign country) and therefore had engaged in an illegal voyage.

Second Steamboat

The second steamboat to Jefferson was the *Gazelle*, in April 1845. This is known to be the case because Withenbury in the brief account of his life says it was and because Buck Barry, Texas Ranger and frontiersman, who made the trip, says that it was. The *Gazelle* cleared the Port of New Orleans on April 2 under the captaincy of S. W. Vandergrift and arrived at Jefferson on the night of the 11th. There were 130 passengers on board, most of whom were immigrants bound for various parts of Texas. This was the first indication of the large role that Jefferson would play in the movement of settlers into Texas.

Because the *Gazelle* was the boat that took the place of the *Lama* when it cancelled its trip to Vermillionville, it can be presumed that there was a close relation between the boats and their captains and that Withenbury provided to Vandergrift sufficient information to leave for Jefferson only a few days after the *Lama* arrived back at New Orleans. There is no record of a return of this boat to New Orleans and no indication that any cotton was taken out, which is reasonable because the fruits of the previous years' crop had been taken out by Withenbury.

Barry notes that "There were several houses under construction but there was only one finished. It was a log cabin built without a nail in it. It was covered with split boards and they were weighted down and held in place by small logs on top of them. It had a puncheon floor and a stick and mud chimney." The finished log cabin was apparently unoccupied, because Barry does not mention anyone in connection with it. It may have been a structure built by William Perry as a grocery house on Jackson Street in Block 23. Perry had purchased the lot from Berry Durham on December 17, 1844, and sold the lot and structure to John Withee on April 30, 1845. Because it was not operational on April 12, the sale on April 30 that mentions the structure probably simply means that Perry had intended it as a grocery house but never ran it as such.

Barry's brief comments are important because they indicate that there was only one completed and apparently unoccupied structure in Jefferson by April 1845 and that there were only several under construction. It also indicates that the first structures were probably all log cabins and that there was no sawmill in Jefferson or nearby. These were probably business structures and not residences, although it is difficult to tell because the word "house" was used for both at the time. Berry Durham and William Bishop were residents at the time in the southwest portion of the town, which could not have been seen by Barry from the landing area.

Because the steamboat rations had all been eaten, it was necessary for Barry to obtain breakfast on shore. He went ashore, inquired about where he could get some food, and was directed to where smoke was coming from brush about 200 yards distant. In company with a young Tennesseean, he made his way through the brush to the smoke "where a man served us with meat, bread and black coffee, using a very large pine log for a table." The man was probably Berry Durham, operating an open-air concession. The meat was bacon, and the fare was standard for almost all meals in Texas at the time.

Barry does not mention anyone in Jefferson other than the man who served breakfast, the man he asked where he could get something to eat, and a farmer by the name of Steward who lived 20 miles away and with whom Barry was forced to seek lodging, traveling by wagon through timber country with few settlers. This does not mean there were no other people in Jefferson. Barry does not comment on who was doing the construction or the activities of the 130 persons who departed the boat. His account does indicate, however, that Jefferson was only an emergent town in April 1845 in the midst of an area that was only beginning to be developed.

First Merchant

Because Jefferson was a commercial town, the opening of the first mercantile establishment was an event of great significance. The September 1, 1876, *Daily Jimplecute* says that Amos Ury was the first merchant to operate in Jefferson, in 1843 or 1844, and that he was one of the persons who participated in the first steamboat voyage to Jefferson. The statements are correct, but the indicated years are probably incorrect.

Ury first appears in the 1838 Red River County tax rolls, as an individual and also in conjunction with the firm of Ury & Brother, the other half being Ennis. Amos had a headright north of Daingerfield and Ennis had a headright southeast of Daingerfield and slightly west of Alley's Creek. Ennis was one of the commissioners in the dispute between Urquhart and Durham and died in early 1847 while the commissioners' report was being prepared.

An October 8, 1845, bond for title from Berry Durham to William Perry refers to "a certain lot lying at the Lake on the South East side of Dallas fronting said Street fifty five feet running back one hundred feet to the waters edge fronting Colonel Urys warehouse on the South west." This transaction refers to Amos' warehouse, which was on Lot 10 in Block 8 south of Dallas Street and west of Walnut Street on an 80-foot lot running to the bayou purchased by Ennis from Berry Durham on May 28, 1845 (Fig. 5-1).

In January 1846, Allen Urquhart and Berry Durham sold to Amos Ury for $350 the west half of Lot 9 in Block 5 fronting 25 feet on Dallas Street and running back to Lake Street, with the houses and buildings thereon. A March 1847 conveyance from Urquhart and Durham to Jeptha Crawford mentions part of the east half of Lot 9 in Block 5 fronting 25 feet on Dallas and running back 75 feet toward Lake as adjacent to Ury's storehouse. Ury's store was thus on Dallas Street on the west half of Lot 9 in Block 5. The property description and purchase price in

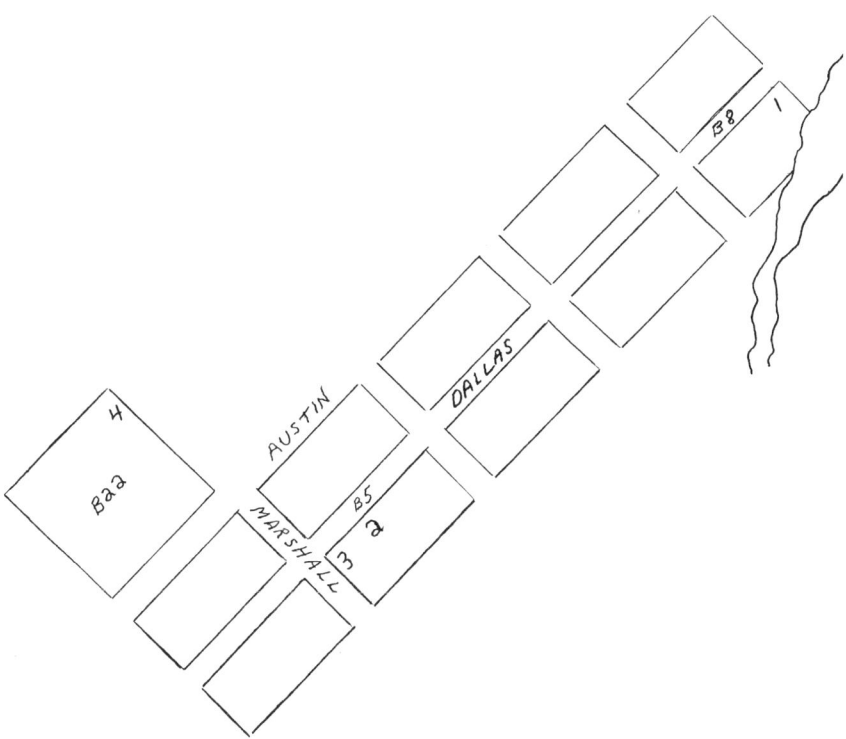

Fig. 5-1. Amos Ury's Locations

KEY:
1. Amos Ury's warehouse (1845)
2. Ury's storehouse (1845); Ury & Ward (1847)
3. Ury & Ward (1851)
4. Ury's residence (1845)

the 1846 transaction indicate that Ury had been operating out of buildings owned by Urquhart and Durham. Ury is shown in the 1846 Cass County tax rolls as owner of 4 ½ lots in Jefferson valued at $2,000.

In the 1846 district court case of Amos Ury versus Reece Hughes, Ennis swore that he had never been in business with Amos in Jefferson and submitted as evidence a letter written on November 28, 1844, in Jefferson, head of Soda Lake, Bowie County, Texas, to the New Orleans merchant Gladden Goren concerning his brother Amos' intent to start a business in Jefferson with William Blythe, a clerk who lived with Amos for three years:

> My brother Amos Ury, who will hand you this, is about to commence business at this point with his friend William Blythe. This is a new place just springing into existence situated on the Big Cypress a few miles above the head of Soda Lake and about thirty miles by water above Port Caddo, a place to which Steam Boats run regularly all last season. We have had the trees, logs and stumps cut clean from the channel and banks of the Lake and bayou up to this point and will be floated out so soon as the water rises, which will render the navigation to this place altogether as safe and easy as it is to Port Caddo. This is a point that I have no hesitation in saying must command the trade of an extensive section of Country. Much of the upper Red River on account of the difficulty of navigation through the Raft, all the Sulphur Fork, all the Cypress must trade to this place. The capital of my brother and his friend is but small and they are resolved not to transcend and to do basically a here one and there the other business, and on that account it has occurred to me that they would do well to keep some heavy articles on Commission, particularly Iron and castings. If you could be the means of throwing such a business in their way, the favor would be duly appreciated. As to myself, you are aware no doubt that I have suffered the fate of the thousands that the great commercial hurri-

cane has just swept over; but I flatter myself that from the acquaintances I have in this section, I will be able to turn much of the business through your house. Any facilities you will be able to afford my brother will be duly appreciated.

This letter indicates that Amos Ury was not in business by late November 1844, with early 1845 being a reasonable time for initiation. Also submitted in evidence are 1845 and 1846 accounts with Reece Hughes, a wealthy planter about 25 miles northwest of Jefferson who came to the area with his father in 1839 and after whom Hughes Springs was named. Hughes is known to have sent cotton to Jefferson as early as November 1844 and sent 55 bales to James McCown and 51 bales to Amos Ury in February 1846. The 1845 account runs from April 1845 to February 1846, listing 41 purchases on 17 occasions, cash advances, and payment of small debts owed by Hughes. The commodities were typical plantation purchases and included bagging, rope, twine, flour, salt, coffee, tobacco, whiskey, bed ticking, cloth of various types, thread, paper, pots, sifters, turpentine, shaving soap, razors, plates, buckets, nails, and allum.

The date of the first purchase is uncertain and may be April 11, 18, or 28, with the latter being the most probable. On that date, Hughes bought a Panama hat and a pair of shoes, which would have been brought to Jefferson by the *Lama* on March 5 or the *Gazelle* on April 11. This may be a record of the first mercantile transaction in Jefferson. When Buck Barry arrived at Jefferson on the *Gazelle*, he reports that several structures were being erected, but that only one had been completed. Ury's store may well have been completed within the next two weeks and opened for business on Monday, April 28. The account also indicates that Ury paid William Perry 75 cents for the storage of six barrels of pork destined for Hughes, suggesting that Ury's warehouse at the landing was not in existence at that time. Perry's warehouse was on the corner of Austin and Jackson, only a short distance from Ury's storehouse. By February 1846, Ury was storing cotton for Hughes in his own warehouse, probably the one at the landing, which had been completed before October 1845.

The March 1847 conveyance from Urquhart and Durham to Crawford that mentions Ury's storehouse was probably shortly before the formation of the firm of Ury & Ward, because the 1847 tax rolls show this firm with $3,000 in merchandise. Ury is also listed as owner of 3 ½ lots in Jefferson with property valued at $2,000. The partner was Matthias Ward, usually referred to simply as Matt, who was soon to become involved in politics. The firm is not mentioned in the deed records until June 1850, with Ury and Ward referred to as traders. However, the firm is shown to have had $3,000 in merchandise in 1849 and $11,000 in merchandise in 1850, by far the wealthiest of the earliest enterprises in Jefferson according to the evidence in the tax rolls.

Ury is listed in the 1850 census as a 40-year-old merchant from Kentucky with a 26-year-old wife and three young sons born in Texas. Listed with them in the census (and therefore residents in their house) are Matt Ward, 37, merchant; Hiram Tomlin, 23, clerk; and A. M. Ward, 20, clerk. Ury's residence was on Lots 1–3 in Block 22, on the corner of Marshall and Lafayette, about one block from his store.

A November 26, 1850, conveyance from McFarland and Peters to William Brooks concerning the west half of Lot 8 in Block 5 indicates that Ury & Ward was erecting a building on the west. The only property owned by Ury & Ward as a company was Lot 7 in Block 5, which was obtained from Speake & Willard in October 1850. The advent of this new store is advertised in the October 4, 1851, Clarksville *Northern Standard*. The advertisement mentions a large stock of fall and winter goods embracing almost every article needed in the hinterland. The articles are to be sold at wholesale or retail and only slightly above New York costs.

The last mention of this firm in Jefferson in the deed records is in March 1852. A July 31, 1852, *Northern Standard* advertisement indicates that the firm had moved to the south side of the public square in Clarksville. This was a retail store selling strictly for cash. Ury sold the west half of Lot 6 in Block 9, which was the location of his original store, to Nelson Trawick in September 1852. By January 1854, Ury was living in Titus County, and the properties owned jointly by Ury and Ward in Jefferson were being divided. Ury died sometime before April 1856, probably at the age of 45.

6. Development

Maps

Jefferson has never encompassed all of Allen Urquhart's headright, which extended from Big Cypress Bayou on the south to Black Cypress Bayou on the north. The midpoint of Urquhart's land was approximately on the line of present-day Broadway Street. Of the five maps of Jefferson that were produced prior to the Civil War, the third and fourth in time (1847 and 1848) were devoted to the Alley Addition. The first, which was the 1844 Jesse Cherry town plan, represented only Urquhart property and was devoted to an area well below this midpoint line. The fourth, prepared by John Eppinger in 1850, extended slightly north of this line. Only the second, prepared by Hugh Hensey in 1846, extended a substantial distance north of this line, encompassing about three-fourths of the Urquhart headright; but this was a special purpose map that only accentuates the fact that all early maps represented the developmental potentials of the town as much more restricted than what would be suggested by the upper boundary of Urquhart's headright.

All of these maps provide numbers for blocks and lots, because their primary purpose was to serve as a reference for land transactions. They are best understood in relation to a contemporary *Lots and Blocks Map*, which can be seen at the city hall or at the courthouse.

Hugh Hensey's January 5, 1846, *Plan of the Town of Jefferson* deals only with the Urquhart property (Fig. 6-1). A copy of this map can be seen on pages 194–198 of the Transcribed Deed Records. This is a photographic copy of a five-page hand-drawn map in the basement vault of the Marion County courthouse, which contains the original Transcribed Deed Records. The hand-drawn map is a transcription of an original five-page hand-drawn map in the vault of the Cass County courthouse in Linden.

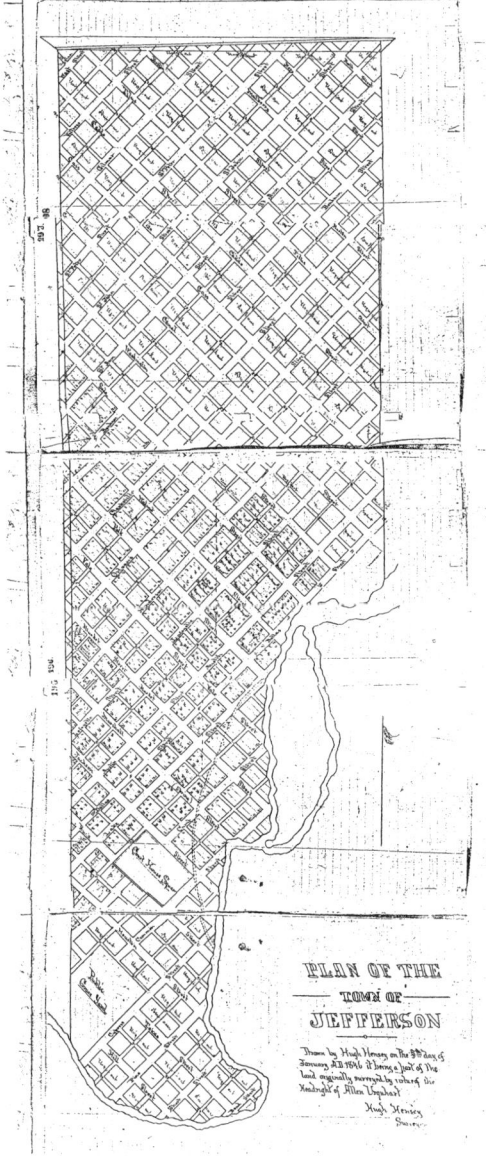

Fig. 6-1. Hensey 1846

Development

There does not appear to have ever been a single hand-drawn map, as is suggested by the fact that street names are repeated on subsequent pages. It was prepared by a professional surveyor to record the determinations of the commission that had been appointed to resolve the land dispute between Urquhart and Durham and apparently was prepared in five sheets so that it could be recorded in the deed records. The determinations were placed on Hensey's base map by the commissioners, which is why the map contains more than one style of writing. The initial part of the commissioners' report and the map bear the same date, and the map and final commissioners' report were filed in March 1847, indicating that the map was intended as a legal document.

The map shows a Court House Square on the south fronting Jackson Street and, farther south and abutting the survey line, a Public Grave Yard. The western channel around St. Catherine's Island is clearly delineated, and the island does not contain any lot or block designations. There is a double-dashed line running from the foot of Polk Street to the foot of Rusk Street. This is not a road, trail, or levee, but rather an indication of the ridge line along the floodplain of Cypress Bayou. No ferry is shown at the foot of Houston Street because the ferry did not enter into the property dispute.

The Hensey map, as is emphasized in the caption, does not encompass the whole of Urquhart's headright, but rather about three-fourths, with the northern boundary at the present-day Howell Addition. This is not a property ownership map, but rather a property allocation map. For example, Durham had sold many lots in Jefferson by January 1846. These lots are not designated by their owners, but rather by the letter "S," which indicates that the lot had been sold by Durham. In addition, the allocations shown on the map were made between January 1846 and March 1847, so the map cannot be used to identify ownership at any particular point in time.

The commissioners' task was to provide an equitable distribution of properties in the light of the January 1843 sale by Urquhart of 160 acres to Durham and subsequent land transactions in which Urquhart did not play any part. The base for these distributions was the set of lots previously sold by Durham and the money still owed by Durham from the original agreement, for which Urquhart was assigned lots of equivalent value. The lots that are marked "U" on the map are those that were assigned to Urquhart to secure the equivalent value or else as part of the general division of properties. Those that are marked "D" were lots donated by Durham for opening the bayou and other improvements to Jefferson or assigned to Durham by the commissioners as part of the general division of properties. The "D Nave" and "U Nave" lots are those that had been sold conditionally by Durham to Jesse Nave and that were divided equally by the commissioners between Durham and Urquhart when Nave failed to fulfill the conditions. The Hill lots were an uncertain set sold by Durham to David Hill for which the commissioners eventually provided equivalent-value lots to Urquhart. Most of the land outside the downtown area was not divided into lots and was assigned by the commissioners to Urquhart and Durham in terms of blocks and portions of blocks, as shown on the map. The area between the double-dashed line and the bayou was considered lowland unsuitable for development and was not assigned.

The delineation of the lots shows that the town proper was considered to extend only from Soda with a dogleg to Washington on the north to Camp on the south, with the Courthouse Square on the southern fringe and the Public Grave Yard even farther to the south. From the perspective of lots that were considered valuable enough to be allocated separately, it can be seen that the town proper was considered to extend only to Henderson on the north with doglegs up Market and down Washington. The numerous "S" and "D" designations for lots within this restricted area, including the eight warehouse lots in Block 9, show that Durham was the dominant factor in the early development of Jefferson (Fig. 6-2).

On July 15, 1847, Robert Graham was paid $15 by the Cass County commissioners for preparing a town plan for the Alley Addition, which was nearly two years after Alley had purchased the land from Smith. Graham surveyed the dividing line between the Urquhart and Alley properties and laid out lots and a courthouse square. This was the first map representation of the Alley Addition. There are two deed records that refer to this early plan, and the lot and block designations indicate that there were no major differences between this plan and

Fig. 6-2. Hensey 1846 Detail

the one that was to follow that was the basis of almost all early land transactions.

Francis Baker's plan of the Alley Addition was the second representation of that portion of Jefferson. Although it was a lithographic map, which means that copies were made, none appear to be extant. It was in existence from at least November 1848, which was the first mention of the sale of an Alley lot in the deed records. From the deed records it is apparent that the block and lot numbers were as they are today. One of the significant features on the Baker map must have been the Public Square on Line Street, because this was used as a reference point for many early land transactions.

John Eppinger's 1850 *Map of Jefferson* (Fig. 6-3) deals only with the Urquhart property and was prepared in conjunction with the establishment of the municipal government during that year. The Eppinger map is much greater in geographic scope than the Cherry map and much more restricted in geographic scope than the Hensey map, because its northern boundary is slightly below where Washington Street strikes North Line. Eppinger was a promising lawyer who was killed in a hunting accident shortly after the map was completed. A copy of this map can be seen in the Jefferson Museum.

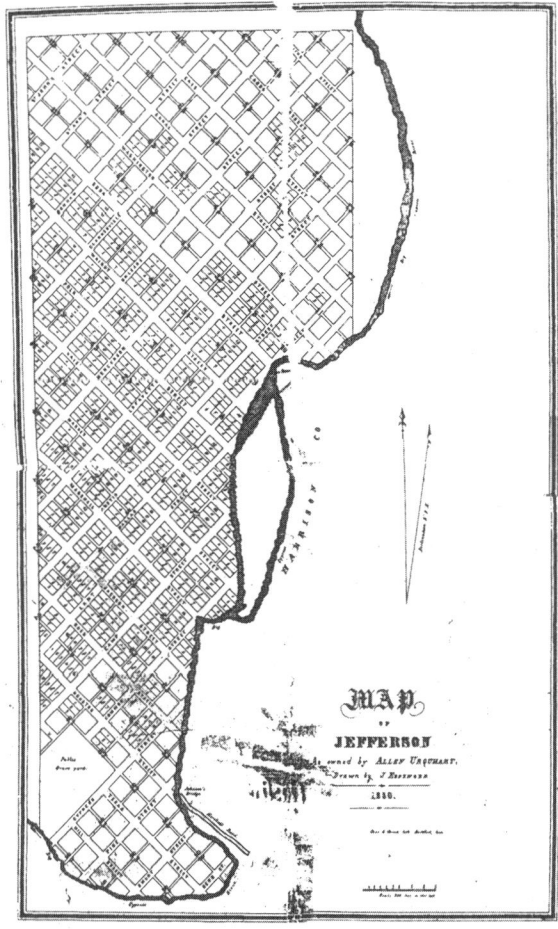

Fig. 6-3. Eppinger 1850. Source: Courtesy Texas General Land Office, Austin

As with the Hensey map, the Eppinger map provides a clear delineation of the western channel around St. Catherine's Island, and there are no lot and block designations within the island. Unlike the Hensey map, the bayou is extended upward the entire length of the map and includes a blank area that was later to become the Perry Addition. A "Landing for Steamers" is indicated at the upper end of the island, and warehouses are indicated contiguous to the landing. Farther downstream, Johnson's Bridge is clearly delineated at the foot of Houston Street leading into the old road to Marshall. The Public Grave Yard continues to be shown in the same place, but the Court House Square has been eliminated.

The Eppinger map has an increased delineation of lots at the southern end, indicating the growing importance of the lower portions of Jackson, Rusk, and Houston streets as commercial traffic to Marshall increased. However, there is also increased development at the northern end. All blocks are numbered, and lots are delineated sporatically to the northeast beyond Soda. Warehouse Lot 8 continues to be shown as extending into Walnut Street, and the Warehouse District continues to expand through the creation of Lots 1–3 in the northern quadrant of Block 11 fronting on Dallas, Austin, and Canal.

Street Names

The streets shown in Hensey's 1846 town plan for the Urquhart property are the same as those of today. In the Jesse Cherry town plan, which was in existence by at least March 1844, Henderson Street was High Street, and Rusk was Clarksville. High Street apparently was so called because it was the upper boundary of the Cherry plan. It was not used subsequently as a name for a street in Jefferson. Clarksville came to be used for a street one block north of the Cherry plan.

Marshall Street was also known as Spring Street by residents of Jefferson during the early years, but it did not appear as such on the Cherry plan and is always referred to as Marshall in the early deed records. The street was so called because of a spring at its head, and this early usage apparently preceded the creation of the Cherry plan. There is also one mention of a Wharf Street in the deed records, but this was probably an early name for Dallas, which appears in all the early deed records and was in the Cherry plan. The usage "Wharf Street" probably also preceded the creation of the Cherry plan. The term "wharf" in the early records did not refer to a wooden structure, but rather was a common name for any dirt landing.

The distinctive feature of the street names in the Hensey plan is that they were eclectic and, insofar as they can be grouped thematically, were randomly distributed, which is somewhat strange for a town that was totally planned. The dominant theme was Texas (Texas, Dallas, Austin, Bonham, Clarksville, Boston, Gilmer, Henderson, Titus, Cass, Marshall, Rusk, Houston). The second most important theme was New Orleans, which was Jefferson's primary trade connection (Canal, Camp, Common, St. Peter, St. John, St. Ann). The New Orleans derivation is obvious in the fact that there was no canal in Jefferson and it was not a Catholic town.

There were three streets related to the large waterbody that was conceptualized as extending from the Shreveport area up to Jefferson and variously know as Soda Lake, Ferry Lake, and Caddo Lake (Lake, Soda, Caddo). Trees were represented (Cypress, Pine, Mulberry, Walnut), as were figures of national importance (Washington, Polk, Lafayette, Jackson), geographic features (Hill, Short, Bend, and probably Vale), and directions (West, North), with Victress and Nero thrown in for no particular reason. Market Street may have been derived from New Orleans, but was more likely an incorrect anticipation of business development.

Population Estimates

Anyone who has attempted to deal with early population estimates is aware of the problem of large discrepancies in personal accounts. The census, for whatever its deficiencies, offers the only fixed point of reference, the only generally systematic recordation, and the only basis for comparing one town to another. Unfortunately, Jefferson was not included as a separate entity in the 1850 census. In 1860, Jefferson's population was 988, of whom 266, or 27 percent, were slaves.

Before 1860, it is necessary to rely on personal accounts, which are often vague with respect to the year and geographic area being described. Personal accounts intend to provide an estimate of the resident population (as the census does), but they appear to be highly influenced by what was seen on the streets, perhaps excluding slaves. The number of people one saw on the streets of Jefferson was seasonally variable. The summer months were dull, with planters on their farms attending to their crops and businessmen away from town securing their fall and winter stocks of goods. The streets became alive in fall and choked in winter as the summer cotton crop was brought to market and steamboats arrived to take it out.

Jefferson always had a large transient population composed of incoming ox-wagon drivers, construction workers, boat crews, immigrants, and businessmen. What a person saw was highly dependent on when he was there, so that discrepancies even for the same year are not necessarily indicative of misinformation. Residential structures were, of course, fixed and not seasonally dependent. Accounts of the number of houses in town almost certainly excluded slave cabins.

The problem for Jefferson begins with the first account of 200 residents provided by Withenbury in the brief sketch of his life, which apparently refers to what he saw when he arrived on March 5, 1845. This estimate is incompatible with some later estimates and particularly with what Barry saw in April. It is not even certain that Withenbury is referring to 1845. He may simply be talking about Jefferson during his early trips. On the other hand, it is highly possible that there were 200 people in Jefferson when the *Lama* arrived, including ox-wagon drivers, construction workers, and people who came to greet the first arrival.

Other suggestions of population levels for 1845 include Barry's April mention of several houses under construction but only one completed and unoccupied, the *Houston Telegraph*'s 1847 mention that "Two years ago there were but one or two cabins in Jefferson," and Edward Smith's comment that "Jefferson four years ago possessed only three log houses."

A. W. Moore visited Jefferson in June 1846 and describes it as a small town just springing into existence with a population of two or three hundred. Charles DeMorse of the Clarksville *Northern Standard* visited Jefferson in July 1846 and had nothing to say about it, although he provides a commentary on Daingerfield and was quite complimentary about the appearance of Jefferson in 1847. The Rev. John McLean visited Jefferson in 1846 (or perhaps 1847) and says that it "sprang up in 1846" and that it contained "three or four stores and shops of different kinds, with a population of probably fifty or sixty people." Later in the same account he says that Jefferson "was just beginning, only a few residences and two or three stores."

Edward Smith arrived in Jefferson in May 1849 and reported "somewhat near sixty good houses and several large well-supplied stores, also one warehouse for the shipment of merchandise, and a small saw and grist mill." Smith also reports 300 families in Clarksville and that Marshall was the most flourishing town in the region, with many shops, industries, and hotels.

All Jefferson residents are contained within Precinct 1 in the 1850 census. As with all censuses, households are covered sequentially. Known Jefferson residents are at the beginning and end of the precinct enumeration, with most at the beginning. There are 52 households containing 282 persons in the beginning section, which ends with John Eppinger, who is known to have been a resident of Paradise. The 5.4 persons per household is high because of the large number of hotel residents and employees in the homes of merchants. Melinda Rankin visited the region in 1850 but had nothing to say about Jefferson.

Albert Leonard lived in Jefferson in January 1852 and describes it as a "small and unattractive village." William Logan, a resident of Jefferson, provides a January 1856 population estimate of 3,000 in a letter to his brother. The 1860 census lists 722 whites in 191 family units and 175 houses, equating to about four persons per house and 3 ¾ persons per household. There were 66 slave owners with 266 slaves. Almost all of the slaves lived in separate cabins, of which there were 73 in Jefferson in 1860.

It appears that Jefferson contained a handful of white residents in 1845, about 50 in 1846, about 200 in 1849, and about 250 in 1850. The years 1854-55 were ones of low water, little navigation, and stymied development, as pointed out by Logan in the letter to his brother, and there were national financial difficulties in 1857. The October 9, 1859, *Daily Picayune* references the *Jefferson Gazette* to the effect that the population had nearly doubled in the last 18 months. The white population was probably around 400 in 1857, increasing to 722 in 1860. With the addition of 266 slaves, the total population was 988.

Spatial Development

When Jefferson was coming into existence, Cypress Bayou was essentially what it is today, a narrow cypress-fringed stream. The cypresses would have been more abundant, and the stream would have been narrower, because it was widened by dredging during the 1870s. Water levels were essentially what they are today, with the exception that the extremes between high and low water were greater, a feature that has been mitigated by the reservoir upstream.

The dominant in-stream feature was St. Catherine's Island, which was formed by two channels of the bayou. St. Catherine's Island is no longer an island, because the western channel has disappeared. It is now simply the low area west of the Polk Street Bridge. The eastern channel was dominant, and the island was covered with water during high-water periods as it is today.

At the downstream end of the island, there was an embayment at the confluence of the two channels that offered sufficient room for a steamboat turning basin. The present scene is deceptive because it suggests that the turning basin was between Polk and Walnut and that it was not very wide. Although this was part of the turning basin, the center lay between Walnut and Soda immediately downstream of where the old railroad track is today and extended to the alley between Soda and Washington. The bayou in the vicinity of the turning basin was much closer to Dallas than it is today and impinged on Dallas near its intersection with Soda. Much of the turning basin has since been filled with sediment.

Fronting the east and west portions of the turning basin were low areas that were subject to flooding but nevertheless suitable for development with raised structures, including the present-day open area east of Polk and south of Dallas. To the north were the bluffs along which Dallas ran, with the land sloping gradually downward towards the bayou. The part of Dallas fronting the turning basin can no longer be seen because it has been obliterated by a levee. Dallas was lower than it is today and was raised by filling after the Civil War. Dallas and the area to the north were subject to flooding during extreme high water.

To the west, between Polk and Market, the land was similar to that north of the turning basin in that it was subject to flooding in extreme high water. To the south of this area was a low area subject to flooding that ran in a broad arc from the foot of Polk to the foot of Rusk, as shown on Hensey's map. This area was not suitable for development. To the west of Market the land was much higher and not subject to flooding even during extreme high water.

The higher areas were covered with virgin pines. The lower areas were covered with bottomland species such as cypress, oak, walnut, and hickory. Land clearing was the first order of business. The first trees to be removed were the bottomland hardwoods in the landing area and the pines on the higher elevations fronting the landing and to the west. When Charles DeMorse visited Jefferson in June 1847, he reports that "the trunks of the first pines felled, still lie in close contiguity to the town."

To understand the development of Jefferson, there are four different areas that must be considered separately: 1) the landing area; 2) the area in which businesses developed; 3) the area known as Paradise; and 4) the Alley Addition. The first three of these areas developed simultaneously during the earliest years.

The landing area was the area contiguous to the turning basin and therefore ran between Polk and the alley between Soda and Washington. This area included the landing proper as well as the facilities that made use of it. Through most of the years prior to the Civil War, the landing was dirt. A public wharf was constructed between Walnut and Soda in 1854. It was extended to the east by a private wharf in 1860, which was soon acquired by the city.

The land north of Dallas and between Walnut and the alley between Soda and Washington was always the heart of the landing area and developed rapidly. The land west of Walnut and south of Dallas was the site of the first warehouse, in spite of the fact that it extended down into the floodplain. There is no evidence for any facility development south of Dallas between Soda and Washington. William Perry constructed cotton sheds in August 1860 south of Dallas and immediately west of the Perry Line and had a cotton shed before that time east of the Perry Line. These were the only structures east of the alley between Soda and Washington.

The only official warehouse lots in the Jesse Cherry town plan were the 13 in Blocks 8 and 9 between Polk and Soda. The eighth actually extended out into Walnut, making the lower end of that street an alley. However, unnumbered warehouse lots were sold to the east and west during the earliest years (1844–1845), eventually transforming the whole of the area south of Austin and between Polk and Washington into a warehouse district.

A port was of little use without warehouses, because import and export commodities needed to be protected from the elements. It is not surprising, therefore, that warehouses began to be constructed immediately. The first warehouse was constructed between June and September 1845 by Amos Ury on the west side of the landing area and south of Dallas in the floodplain. There were at least four warehouses by the end of 1848, as evidenced by an article in the December 16, 1848, *Spirit of the Age*. These were frame structures, with the article mentioning the dimensions of one being built as 40 feet by 70 feet.

These structures should not be thought of simply as warehouses. Probably from the beginning they were the business offices of receiving and forwarding merchants and may even have embraced some retail dimensions. In addition, the warehouse district was not devoted solely to warehouses. Some of the earliest structures in Jefferson were William Bishop's residence on Polk between Austin and Dallas and William Russell's stable on Dallas between Polk and Walnut, which serviced the ox-wagons, drays, and buggies that dominated the warehouse district.

The September 1, 1876, *Daily Jimplecute* says that prior to the Civil War, most of the business was conducted on Dallas and Marshall. This statement is confirmed by the deed records, which contain sufficient information to determine the exact location of many businesses. The deed records indicate that by the advent of the Civil War, there was almost a solid string of businesses along Dallas from the warehouse district to Marshall and extending up Marshall Street and down Marshall a short distance.

The earliest records indicate that the higher land west of Market was favored by the merchants and that the most-favored block was Block 5, bounded by Marshall, Market, Austin, and Lake, with Dallas running in between. Block 5 was the location of the first business in Jefferson, which was owned by Amos Ury, and its successor Ury & Ward. Also operating businesses in Block 5 during the earliest years were George Butt, John Speake, Clinton Willard, Samuel Friou, Horatio Walcott, John Waskom, Thomas Crockett, and Nelson Trawick.

There do not appear to have been many businesses away from the blocks through which Dallas and Marshall ran, and most of these appear to have been non-mercantile operations such as blacksmith shops, stables, and a saw mill. Residences were occasionally interspersed among the businesses, but residential development appears to have taken place largely in the outlying areas, particularly to the north of Austin.

The evidence for early business development along Dallas and Marshall has disappeared, and everything west of Market is presently devoted to residences. In addition, the historic buildings in the present

Fig. 6-4. Brosius' 1872 *Bird's Eye View of Jefferson, Texas*. Source: Library of Congress

downtown area are a reflection of post-Civil War development, which was much larger but concentrated on the port area, as shown in Brosius's 1872 *Bird's Eye View of Jefferson, Texas* (Fig. 6-4).

The reason for the early southwest orientation of businesses, which was anticipated by Urquhart in the Jesse Cherry town plan, appears to be a reflection of more than one factor. The businesses to the west were intimately related to the activities in the landing area. Dallas provided direct connection to the landing area, which was called the Dallas Street Landing in the navigation records. Businessmen appear to have favored the routes west through Marshall and Gilmer, which were accessed through the Houston Street ferry and later the bridge. The Marshall-Dallas axis was the closest high ground to the landing area.

The Alley Addition, with its north-south and east-west street orientation, is generally thought of as Jefferson's early residential area, which is somewhat true if the perspective is on what lay within the town boundaries. However, Jefferson's earliest and most important residential development took place to the west of the town along the road to Daingerfield in the area called Paradise. Paradise was an area of indefinite boundary whose center was the Archer headright, which began at the present-day town boundary. It included at least the Gillespie headright to the east and part of the Reed headright to the west.

Paradise was the home of many of Jefferson's prominent businessmen, including Williamson Freeman, Clinton Willard, Horatio Walcott, William Perry, Robert Nesmith, Frederick Schluter, John Eppinger, Job Baker, and Josiah Hill. This does not mean that these men did not maintain homes in town. It is known, for example, that Frederick Schluter had a home in Jefferson from the earliest years. But, he is listed in the 1850 census as a farmer because he maintained a 320-acre tract in the Greenleaf Perry headright, which was part of Paradise.

Paradise was also the home of the Cass County Male and Female Academy, which was in existence by at least March 1850 and was probably the oldest school in the Jefferson area. It was also the home of at least one sawmill and probably the earliest location of the Figures

Hotel, which appears to have been on the road to Daingerfield slightly outside of the early town boundaries.

Robert Loughery of the *Texas Republican* visited Jefferson in March 1851 and reports that "We were particularly struck with the improved condition of the country on the route leading to Daingerfield. It looks almost like a village, with neat cottages, and buildings of more pretending character. Many of these residences are owned by the business men of Jefferson, and are well improved. This region is called 'Paradise;' a name given it, we suppose, from the fact that it contains a majority of the young ladies." A correspondent to the *Republican* passed through Jefferson in late June on the way to Daingerfield and noted that "For several miles on the road leading north from Jefferson, residences are very numerous. It is said to be the case for some distance off the road, on both sides. This region, having no specified boundaries, is called Paradise."

That Paradise should have developed quite early is understandable because it was bisected by the road to Daingerfield and offered sufficient land for Jefferson businessmen to engage in farming operations, itself a reflection of the multiple occupations that characterized men of talent. The lasting and increased importance of Paradise is obvious in Brosius' 1872 *Bird's Eye View*, which shows only a portion of the heavily developed area extending to the northwest out of Jefferson (see Fig. 6-4 above).

The first land transaction in the Alley Addition was in November 1848. Almost all of the land transactions in the Alley Addition through the early 1850s, of which there were not a great number, centered on the public square bounded by Line, Main, Jefferson, and Taylor streets. The Alley Addition was devoted almost entirely to residences and contained only a few isolated businesses before the Civil War.

Closely related to the town was the ox-wagon encampment west of Paradise on the Daingerfield Road four miles outside of town at the Four Mile Branch of Cypress Bayou. Nothing is known about this encampment other than that it was the waiting place for ox-wagons on the way to town. If the encampment was similar to the one at Houston, it was a commercial operation with log cabins for teamsters, sheds for oxen, a well, and whiskey.

Residential Development

There are a number of mentions in the deed records of residences or places where people lived. These are arranged by date. The dates should not be taken as indicators of when residences were built. For the earliest records, the Jesse Cherry town plan numbers have been changed to their modern equivalents.

On December 14, 1846, John Sharp sold to Solomon Garner Lot 9 in Block 22 fronting 25 feet on Austin Street and running back 150 feet on which Martin Watson was then residing.

On January 1, 1847, Daniel and Lucy Alley sold to Frederick and Ann Schluter Lots 7–9 in Block B of the Alley Addition fronting on Line and Taylor streets. This property had been enclosed and improved (generally indicating construction) by Schluter.

An April 13, 1847, transaction between Daniel Alley and the Cass County commissioners mentions Ennis Ury's estate contiguous to the public square.

A December 1847 transaction concerning Carey Ragan's estate indicates that the merchant Charles Dunn was living in his storehouse on Lot 6 in Block 5 at the corner of Dallas and Marshall streets.

On March 24, 1848, Wesley White sold to Berry Durham half of Lots 8 and 9 in Block 3 fronting Jackson and Dallas streets on which Durham was then residing.

A December 27, 1848, transaction between William Bishop and James French is concerned with Lot 4 in Block 8, including the house in which Bishop recently resided.

On March 26, 1849, Charles Stanley and Mortimer Ward relinquished to Israel Leavitt claims to a portion of the east half of Lot 8 in Block 4 on which the dwelling house and kitchen of Leavitt then stood.

A December 22, 1849, transaction between Richard Peters and John Speake mentions Amos Ury's residence across the alley from Lot 11 in Block 22. Ury resided on Lots 1–3 of Block 22.

A December 3, 1850, transaction between Caleb Ragan and Gilbert Ragan concerns the estate of Carey Ragan, deceased, fronting 25 feet on Marshall Street and running back 50 feet and then occupied by Caleb Ragan.

Eliza Smith's May 9, 1851, schedule of separate property mentions Lot 8 in Block 5 fronting 25 feet on Dallas Street and running back to Lake Street as the lot on which she and her husband George were then residing, including a storehouse.

A November 11, 1851, transaction between George and Cynthia Slaughter and Anthony Owens mentions that the Slaughters were living on Fractional Lots 9 and 10 in Fractional Block 23.

A January 10, 1852, deed of gift from Samuel Friou to Thurzia Jones (his mother-in-law) concerns Lots 3–6 of Block 91 of the Alley Addition fronting on Broadway and separated by an alley from the lots on which Friou then resided, which was Lots 7–9.

A January 31, 1852, transaction between Urquhart and William Brooks concerning Lots 11 and 12 in Block 82 fronting on Houston Street and running back on Camp Street mentions the adjoining residence of Charles Dugan, which apparently was on Lot 10 fronting on Houston and running back along the alley.

A March 1, 1852, transaction between Walter and America Mitchell and Justice Ferris concerns Lots 10 and 11 in Block 7 of the Alley Addition, including the house in which the Mitchells then resided.

On April 23, 1853, Nelson and Sarah Trawick sold to John Murphy Lots 7–9 in Block 7 of the Alley Addition fronting on Friou Street and containing a dwelling house, kitchen, smoke house, corn crib, and stable.

The former residence of George Smith occupying two lots on Friou Street was advertised for sale or rent in the May 14, 1853, *Jefferson Herald*, with the advertisement noting that the residence was located in a high and healthy part of the town.

On August 12, 1853, Lot 12 in Block 21 containing the residence of A. E. Samplin was sold at a sheriff's sale to Daniel McKay.

On November 17, 1853, Urquhart sold to Amos Ury Lots 1–3 in Block 22, which was Ury's former residence but at that time the residence of Robert Nesmith.

On December 8, 1853, the sheriff sold to Sarah King Lot 9 in Block 3 fronting 33 feet on Jackson Street and running back 85 feet on which J. W. C. Northcott (alias Jo Williams) formerly resided.

On August 31, 1854, Charles and Louisa Peel mortgaged to Thomas Smith the west half of Lots 1–6 in Block O of the Alley Addition fronting 75 feet on Delta Street and 312 feet on Alley Street, including their residence.

On December 2, 1854, Charles and Susan Schaff sold to William Towers Lots 11 and 12 in Block N of the Alley Addition, including the dwelling house thereon.

On December 9, 1854, Nelson Taylor sold to Thomas Turner Lot 7 in Block 31 fronting 55 feet on Lafayette Street and running back 150 feet on Walnut Street on which Taylor's home then stood.

On March 1, 1855, Alley sold to John Murphy Lots 4–6 in Block 7 of the Alley Addition on which Murphy then lived.

On March 1, 1855, Alley sold to James Murphy Lots 1–3 in Block 7 of the Alley Addition on which Murphy then lived. The Murphy brothers lived next door to each other.

On March 1, 1855, John Morgan and Hiram Tomlin mortgaged to Jackson Morgan various properties, including Lot 12 in Block 47 on which Tomlin then resided.

On August 13, 1855, Abraham and Emily Kohn sold to William and Sardinia Perry Lots 11 and 12 in Block I of the Alley Addition fronting on Bridge and Line containing the Kohns' home.

On September 17, 1855, William and Martha Baker sold to Francis Clark Lot 10 and the south half of Lot 11 in Block M of the Alley Addition occupied by Edward Jones; also, Lot 7 and the south half of Lot 8 in Block M and the southwest corner lot of Block L, together constituting the residence of the Bakers.

On September 24, 1855, John and May Murphy sold to Jeremiah Wardell Lot 9 in Block 7 of the Alley Addition fronting 55 feet on Friou Street and containing their present dwelling house.

On November 10, 1855, August and Fanny May sold to Henry Schluter Lots 9 and 10 in Block I of the Alley Addition fronting 55 feet on Bridge Street and running back 150 feet to Line Street containing the Mays' home.

On December 18, 1856, William and Matilda Brooks sold to David Taylor the parallelogram bounded by Lake, Dallas, Rusk, and Line streets, it being the homestead in which they then resided.

On February 23, 1857, George Ury sold to Charles Graham Lots 1–3 in Block P of the Alley Addition, it being the late residence and homestead of Perry Graham.

On March 30, 1857, William and Job Baker sold John Dollahite Lot 4 in Block 76 adjoining Dollahite's residence.

On June 15, 1857, John and Christiana Kolster mortgaged to Moses Steinlein Lot 9 in Block 75 fronting 40 feet on Rusk Street and running back 140 feet on Camp Street containing the Kolsters' homestead. The property description does not relate to Lot 9, but rather to the south 40 feet of Lots 7–9.

On January 18, 1858, Consider Sabine agreed to sell his residence in Jefferson to William Todd.

On November 23, 1858, John and Victoria Sabine sold to John Ligon the west half of Block R in the Alley Addition, it being the homestead and premises upon which the Sabines then resided.

On December 21, 1858, John Speake sold to John Ligon Lots 4–6 in Block N of the Alley Addition, "it being the place generally known as the Ochiltree place." Ligon sold the lot with the same reference to Ochiltree to Gus Hodge for $1,800 on December 13, 1859.

An April 15, 1859, transaction between Urquhart and Robert Hughes mentions the residence of John Murphy in the northwest corner of the Humphries survey.

On February 4, 1860, John Winslow sold to his wife Amanda Lots 1–5 in Block 68 on Bonham Street containing their home.

A September 4, 1860, statement signed by Samuel Moseley indicates that he was established as trustee for William and Francis Baker on January 22, 1855, in relation to various properties, including a house and lot in the Alley Addition formerly occupied by Harmon fronting Friou Street opposite the then residence of Prentiss Stetson.

On October 8, 1860, Robert and Olive Nesmith mortgaged to Thomas Ferrell their homestead on Lots 7–9 in Block 46.

A January 6, 1861, transaction between Sarah Moore and Shadrach Eggers mentions Lot 10 in Block R of the Alley Addition adjoining the residence of William Todd on the west, which was on Lot 11.

On March 6, 1861, J. T. Warner and Prentiss Stetson sold to John Porter Block 70 with the exception of Stetson's homestead and Lots

6 and 7 in Block 44 running 100 feet on Henderson Street to Warner's homestead, which apparently was on Lot 8.

On March 11, 1861, Shadrach and Sarah Eggers mortgaged to George Walker Lot 10 in Block R of the Alley Addition containing their residence.

On October 14, 1861, George Terry quit to Urquhart his claim to Block 52, with the exception of the quarter block on which Terry's house was situated and in which he was then living.

On October 30, 1861, Anderson and Eliza Jane Booth sold to Benjamin Terry and David Culberson Lots 11 and 12 in Block 10 of the Alley Addition, it being the land upon which the Booths were residing.

A November 8, 1861, transaction between J. H. Sutton and George and Martha Robinson suggests that the Robinsons lived on Lots 1–3 in Block 51.

On November 15, 1861, Frederick Richards sold to his wife Martha Lot 12 in Block 46 fronting 50 feet on Vale Street and running back 150 feet on Henderson Street containing a house.

On December 20, 1861, John and Martha Aikin sold to Chester Bulkley Lot 1 in Block 15 of the Alley Addition that was then occupied by the Aikins as a homestead.

On December 4, 1862, James and Martha Murphy sold to Sarah Smith Lots 1, 2, 10, 11, and 12 in Block Q of the Alley Addition in which the Murphys then resided.

On March 3, 1863, Hugo and Frederica Fox sold for $2,500 to John Robinson parts of Lots 1 and 2 and the whole of Lot 3 in Block Q of the Alley Addition. The price and location indicate that this was the Foxes' residence.

On March 6, 1863, John Speake sold to Joseph McDermott Lots 10 and 11 of Block 7 of the Alley Addition with a dwelling house thereon.

On April 8, 1863, Richard and Margaret Figures sold to A. L. Kottwitz Block 120, it being their homestead.

On April 7, 1864, William and Mary Todd sold to Bass Nichols Lots 8 and 9 in Block R of the Alley Addition fronting on Jefferson Avenue, it being the Todds' homestead.

On September 21, 1864, Alley sold to John Fisher Lots 5 and 6 in

Block 10 of the Alley Addition west of and adjoining Fisher's residence, which obviously was on Lot 7.

On July 13, 1865, William Perry sold to Ellen Allen Lots 11 and 12 in Block I of the Alley Addition known as Abraham Kohn's house.

These documents suggest that there was an initial sprinkling of residences in the business section of town, particularly homes of businessmen, and that this gave way by the end of the war to a concentration of residences in the Alley Addition and, to a lesser extent, in the Urquhart Addition outside of the business section, particularly to the north.

On the other hand, the documents also suggest that the status of the Alley Addition as the residential section of town has been overemphasized and that the business section of town, which centered on the Dallas-Marshall axis, was a favored location for residences. This is confirmed by the delineation of the town's five wards and the voting patterns for those wards. Wards were typically delineated to achieve equitable representation of residents on town governing bodies. Ward 2 was the second smallest of the wards in size, extending from Vale Street to Jackson Street in the Urquhart Addition. Ward 2 also had the largest number of residents, as indicated by the number of votes cast in the October 1861 city elections.

There are no descriptions of Jefferson's residences, individually or collectively. Construction contracts offer the only insight into what some of the residences looked like. There is some evidence in the public records as to what these residences contained, but they are almost all content listings. I have found only one record that lists furniture on a room-by-room basis.

Abraham Kohn was one of Jefferson's most important merchants. He and his wife Emily originally lived on Lots 11 and 12 in Block I of the Alley Addition. This property was sold to William Perry in 1855 as part of a divesture of properties brought about by the failure of May & Kohn resulting from the low-water conditions of 1854–1855. He established a residence during the same year in the Archer headright on the old road to Daingerfield and went back into business. By 1860 he was in financial difficulties again, mortgaging many of his properties, including his residence and its contents, to a Cincinnati firm for $10,000 and selling his entire stock of groceries, pelts, cotton, and a slave to D. C. Phillips. A court judgment for debts to a New Orleans firm led to a January 1861 sheriff's sale of Lots 7–9 in Block 8 containing Kohn's warehouse and cotton sheds. Foreclosure by the Cincinnati firm led to the sale of the mortgaged property to William Prewitt in November 1860, including the contents of the Kohn house:

> Furniture in hall—longue and mattress, sofa, two maps; furniture in parlor—fine carpet, sofa, ricking chaise and eight green velvet chairs, marble top center table, glass marble top table, small candle stand, broken looking glass, eight pictures, four curtains and blinds, fire screen; furniture in Mrs. Kohn's room—high post bedstead, bureau looking glass, center table, candle stand, fire screen, clock, four curtains and blinds; second bedroom—bedstead, two mattresses, wash stand, bowl, pitcher, wardrobe, two curtains, two pitchers; furniture in dining room—three dining tables, fire screen, looking glass, safe, two curtains, knives, forks, crockery, tableware; third bedroom—bedstead, two mattresses, bureau, wash stand, small table, two looking glasses, fire screen, basin, pitcher, two curtains; fourth bedroom—two bedsteads, three mattresses, lounge, sewing table, fixtures of bed and candle sticks, lounge and cover; balance of household and kitchen furniture, except the feather bed pillows, bolsters, bed clothes, and piano.

7. Censuses

1850 Census

The 1850 Cass County census was conducted by Charles Graham from September through November. Jefferson and the other towns of the county were not enumerated as separate entities. The county was divided into seven precincts. All Jefferson residents are included in Precinct 1, which extended from the mouth of Black Cypress Bayou on the east to Trammel's Trace on the west and apparently to near the present-day Marion County line on the north. Jefferson was the only large population center in this area. The Precinct 1 census was conducted from September 17 through October 18. Graham obviously began in Jefferson and ended in Jefferson, apparently moving in a clockwise direction. Precinct 1 contains 151 households, which may be divided into thirds, with the first and third sections containing almost all Jefferson residents (i.e., persons who lived within the town limits), but also many others.

The census begins with the wagon maker James Smith, who is known to have operated a business in Jefferson from at least 1847 but lived in Paradise. Sardinia Perry, who also lived in Paradise, is shown without her husband William, who had gone west for the gold rush. The first section ends with the lawyer John Eppinger, who practiced in Jefferson but lived in Paradise. However, the first section includes persons such as James Todd and John Pitkin, who operated a store in Smithland. The second section is comprised largely of farmers. However, it includes persons closely associated with Jefferson who lived in Paradise such as the gunsmith John Porter, the teacher John Steel, the farmer Williamson Freeman, the minister Josiah Hill, and the lawyer Martin Rogers. It also includes the dentist George Slaughter, who is known to have been a Jefferson resident in 1851. The third section begins with Amos Ury, who is known from other sources to have been a Jefferson resident, and runs to the end of the census.

Although the Precinct 1 enumeration (and particularly its first and third parts) includes all Jefferson residents, it cannot be used as a Jefferson census and therefore is not useful for statistical analysis.

1860 Census

Jefferson first appears as an independent entity in the 1860 Marion County census, which was conducted by Richard Crump. The original handwritten census counts are available on microfilm and contain a great deal more information than can be found in published census documents. The census is in two parts: an enumeration of free white inhabitants and an enumeration of slaves. In both cases, the county information is arranged in terms of beats, the predecessors to modern census tracts, with separate sections devoted to Jefferson proper (designated City of Jefferson) and nearby areas (designated Jefferson Post Office). The section devoted to Jefferson proper does not constitute a town census in the strict sense, because it apparently includes some persons who lived in Paradise. In any case, the handwritten accounts are compatible with the published census records, which show 722 free white inhabitants and 266 slave inhabitants in Jefferson, for a total population of 988 in 1860.

In the Marion County census of free white inhabitants, Beat 1 is centered on Alleys Mills, Beat 2 on Hickory Hill (now Avinger), Beat 3 on Jefferson, Beat 4 on Smithland, and Beat 5 on Monterey. These are not town censuses, but rather regional censuses in which the town (actually the post office) is used as an identifier. Beat 3 is not concerned with Jefferson proper, but rather with the area to the west and to the north extending up to the county line, which runs from pages 13 through 25 and is designated as Jefferson Post Office. Beat 3 is followed by Beats 4 (Smithland) and 5 (Monterey). The enumeration for the town of Jefferson (designated City of Jefferson) does not actually begin until page 33 and runs to the end of the census on page 51.

The Jefferson portion of the census was taken during August 22–27. The microfilm rendition contains the original census counts and is complete and unblemished. The only textual difficulty is in the interpretation of Crump's handwriting.

The handwritten counts by Crump contain one error. J. M. and J. C. Murphy are listed incorrectly on a single line on page 44 and correctly elsewhere in the census. The counts of males at the bottom of the page was corrected, but the total population count at the bottom of the page should be 35 rather than 36 to produce a final correct count of 722. In addition, there is a problem at the beginning. Page 32 concludes Beat 5 centering on Monterey. At the top of page 33, Charles Merryman, John Ramsey, and John Moseley are listed without a house or family enumeration number. However, these are known to have been Jefferson residents from other records.

The major problem is in determining the geographic area that is covered in the town census. There is no certain delimitation of the antebellum town boundaries. More importantly, even if the boundaries were known, it appears that Crump included in the town census at least a few persons outside of the town boundaries. The most obvious example is Williamson Freeman, whose property was in Paradise outside of the present town boundaries, which are twice as large as the antebellum boundaries. Freeman lived where the Freeman plantation is today.

The census enumerators were not given specific instructions on what to include in a town census, and extension of the census into suburbs was not uncommon. What geographical area Crump included in the 1860 Jefferson census cannot be determined apart from an elaborate analysis of residences in relation to census designations. On the other hand, the town census excludes persons such as John Ligon and Abraham Kohn, who were important Jefferson merchants but are included under "Jefferson Post Office" because they lived too far out in Paradise according to Crump's criteria, whatever they might have been. The town census does not offer a full perspective on Jefferson because most of the people who lived in Paradise were closely connected with the town.

The town census indicates a total population of 722 whites comprised of 456 males and 266 females. Of the total, 287 (40 percent) were under the age of 18, leaving 435 adults. There were only 16 persons aged 50 or older, of whom 15 were in their fifties. The oldest person in Jefferson was Seth Wilcock, a 67-year-old who was born in Canada. Only one person is listed as an illiterate, the 46-year-old city marshal James Moore. There were no deaf, dumb, blind, insane, idiots, paupers, or convicts. Nine persons were married during the year.

Persons shown as having attended school during the year include 114 under the age of 18, three 18-year-olds, and one 19-year old. There were, of course, many children under the age of 18 (approximately one-half) who were too young to attend school, which began at the age of five or six (although there was one child who attended school at the age of four). Of the school-eligible children, approximately three-fourths had attended school during the year.

Females constituted only 37 percent of the population. The vast majority of these were children or spouses. There are only four women listed as heads of families, and only two of these owned the houses in which they lived, with the other two living in houses occupied by others. These were older women with children, indicating that they were widowed or divorced. None are shown with occupations. The two who owned their houses apparently lived on rental income from other families who are listed.

The census enumeration operates on the basis of assigned numbers for houses and families, because more than one family could occupy a house. Some family units within households are not enumerated as such by the census taker. Jefferson contained 102 houses (including at least one hotel), equating to seven persons per household. There were 124 families within these households, equating to six persons per family. The high number of persons per household and persons per family were the result of unrelated, unmarried boarders living in many residences. Only one-third of the houses in Jefferson were single-family residences that did not contain unrelated persons.

Of the 106 heads of families born in the United States, 21 were born in Georgia; 18 each were born in Tennessee and Alabama; 10 were born in Kentucky; eight each were born in Virginia and North Carolina; four each were born in Mississippi and South Carolina; two each were born in New York, Connecticut, New Jersey, Massachusetts, and Ohio; and one each were born in Florida, Arkansas, Iowa, Maine, and New Hampshire. Of the 18 foreign-born heads of families, seven were born in Germany, four were born in Ireland, two each were born in Prussia and England, and one each were born in Bavaria, France, and Europe. No heads of households were born in Texas.

There were 183 persons aged 16 and over who were not family members, of whom nine were females. Of the 133 persons born in the United States aged 16 and older who were not family members, 21 were born in Alabama; 15 were born in Tennessee; 13 were born in Kentucky; 11 each were born in Georgia and North Carolina; nine each were born in New York and South Carolina; eight were born in Pennsylvania; five each were born in Missouri and Louisiana; four each were born in Virginia and Mississippi; three were born in Arkansas; two each were born in Texas, Iowa, Maine, and Massachusetts; and one each were born in Connecticut, Ohio, Illinois, New Hampshire, Delaware, Rhode Island, and Florida. Of the 50 persons born in foreign countries aged 16 and older who were not family members, 15 were born in Germany; 10 were born in Prussia; six were born in England; four were born in France; three were born in Ireland; two each were born in Poland, Switzerland, Austria, Russia, and Scotland; and one each were born in Italy and Canada. Unattached employed males from places other than Texas living as boarders in private residences and hotels were a distinctive feature of Jefferson's demographics, with heavy contributions by persons born in foreign countries.

The total wealth of all persons in Jefferson was $1,157,711 ($484,925 in real estate and $672,786 in personal estate). The richest persons in Jefferson were the merchants Frederick Schluter ($30,000 in real estate and $45,000 in personal estate), James Murphy ($23,500 in real estate and $50,000 in personal estate), John Wallace ($39,000 in real estate and $12,000 in personal estate), and John Speake ($22,000 in real estate and $24,500 in personal estate). The first three of these would qualify as millionaires today, disregarding debts.

Other persons of wealth were Daniel Alley's wife Lucy ($30,000 in real estate and $10,000 in personal estate), the doctor Ithael Eason

($15,000 in real estate and $12,200 in personal estate), the merchant Theophilus Nichols ($5,600 in real estate and $18,300 in personal estate), the druggist James Linn ($16,000 in real estate and $4,500 in personal estate), and the merchant William Nichols ($500 in real estate and $20,000 in personal estate). Williamson Freeman's wife and children (for whom he acted as agent and guardian) had $31,000 in real estate and $5,500 in personal estate; and Jeptha Crawford's wife and son (for whom he acted as agent) had $8,000 in real estate and $17,600 in personal estate. The richest person in the county was the 45-year-old plantation owner Rebecca Hagerty, with $35,000 in real estate and $85,000 in personal estate. Hagerty also owned a plantation in Harrison County.

Occupational listings include: 50 merchants; 49 clerks; 14 mechanics; 12 attorneys and farmers; 10 carpenters; nine laborers; eight tinners, doctors, and painters; six butchers and printers; five bookkeepers and druggists; four shoe and boot makers, saddlers, and blacksmiths; three grocers, teachers, sportsmen, confectioners, tailors, bakers, and coopers; two steamboatmen, machinists, railroad contractors, carriage makers, barbers, millers, agents, brick masons, and dancing masters; and one city marshal, hotel proprietor, fisherman, district clerk, watchmaker, artist, book seller, mayor, sheriff, stock raiser, stage contractor, civil engineer, music teacher, magistrate, dentist, jeweler, musician, postmaster, engineer, milliner, chess player, livery stable operator, harness maker, trader, gunsmith, plasterer, collecting agent, hide buyer, cotton buyer, and drayman.

Only three women are listed with occupations: the 21-year-old milliner (designer, maker, or trimmer of women's hats) Mary Tillus; the 28-year-old teacher M. Marton; and the 18-year-old music teacher Rachael Smither, who was married. Women did not serve as clerks, and two of the four teachers in town were men.

Precision cannot be expected from early censuses, particularly with respect to perspectives that might be drawn from them. The 1860 census for the City of Jefferson contains some persons who lived outside of the town limits and excludes some persons who were integral to the life of the town. The Jefferson Post Office cannot be used for statistical analysis because it included many other persons such as the immensely wealthy planter Rebecca Hagerty (divorced from Spire Hagerty) who played no part in the life of the town. In addition, censuses present a profile only at a point in time. Prominent Jefferson citizens such as William Perry were absent from the town when the census was taken. In spite of these limitations, the 1860 census is the only document that provides insight into the dimensions, complexity, and characteristics of Jefferson's population before the Civil War.

8. Women

Of the 722 free white persons in Jefferson in 1860, 266 (or 37 percent) were female. Of the 266 females, 113 were married, 136 were children of families, and 16 were unattached. Of the 136 children of families, only 15 were aged 15 or greater, with the oldest being 20. This was because the families were young, and women tended to marry early. The vast majority of the females in Jefferson were either married or the young children (under 15) of married women.

Of the 16 unattached, four were heads of families. These were older women with children, indicating that they were widowed or divorced. Of the remaining 12, all lived with other families and ranged in age from infant to 58. These were apparently mostly relations or children of friends located elsewhere, because only two are shown with occupations.

Housewife was not an occupational category in the census. Only three women are shown with occupations. One of these was a married music teacher (Rachael Smither). The other two were the 21-year-old milliner Mary Tillus, who lived in the house of Frederick Stutz, and the 28-year-old teacher M. Marton, who lived in the house of Ephraim Terry. Mary Tillus and M. Marton were the only unattached working females in Jefferson in 1860, and M. Marton was probably the only one who worked away from home.

The dominance of males (63 percent) in the population was common in emerging towns west of the Mississippi. There were 456 males in Jefferson in 1860. Of these, 119 were heads of families and 162 were children of families or, in a few cases, unattached youngsters. The distinctive difference between males and females was the large number of adult males who were not family members. There were 175 persons of this type in Jefferson, ranging in age almost entirely from the late teens to the early forties. All but 21 of these persons are shown with occupations, and it is fairly certain that almost all of them were employed. These unattached males lived with families or in hotels. The unattached males, heads of families, and their older male children constituted Jefferson's employed population.

The only occupations that appear to have been available to women in Jefferson at the time were extensions of domestic activity, including household management and the care of children: hotel operator, educator, making women's apparel, restaurant operator, and postmistress. There are no examples of the latter two categories in Jefferson in antebellum times, and most teachers were male. Women did not clerk in stores. Although there were many bakers and confectioners in Jefferson, none were women. The industrial enterprises in Jefferson such as saw mills and meat packing plants were not suitable for female employment.

The occupations in which women were most distinguished were education and hotel operation. In addition to regular teachers, Mrs. Steel assisted her husband in the Cass County Male and Female Academy, Howard Burnside and his wife Ardelia were in charge of the female department, and Susan Foster was principal of the Jefferson Female Academy. Sardinia Perry assisted her husband in the operation of the Soda Lake Hotel, and Elizabeth Jackson and Caroline Hunt operated the Jefferson Hotel. In addition to operating the hotel, Hunt became its owner. She is the only woman in Jefferson known to have owned and operated a business prior to the Civil War (Fig. 8-1). In August 1860, Joseph McDermott, who had been in the millinery business in Jefferson, established a partnership with Kate Sutton to enter into a new millinery business in rented property. Sutton was to be the primary partner, having put up $5,075 in comparison to McDermott's $1,691.66; but there is nothing to indicate that this business was ever started.

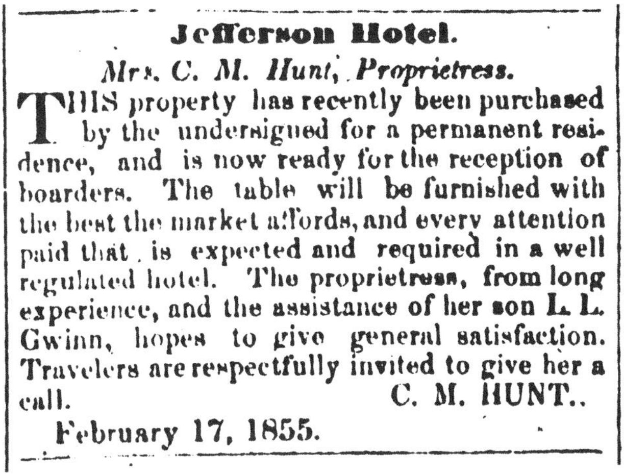

> **Jefferson Hotel.**
> *Mrs. C. M. Hunt, Proprietress.*
> THIS property has recently been purchased by the undersigned for a permanent residence, and is now ready for the reception of boarders. The table will be furnished with the best the market affords, and every attention paid that is expected and required in a well regulated hotel. The proprietress, from long experience, and the assistance of her son L. L. Gwinn, hopes to give general satisfaction. Travelers are respectfully invited to give her a call. C. M. HUNT..
> February 17, 1855.

Fig. 8-1. Caroline Hunt Advertisement. Source: February 17, 1855, *Texas Republican*

There were probably fewer than 50 women in Jefferson in 1850. In 1860, there were only 143 females aged 15 or greater, and only three of these were employed. In contrast, there were 329 males aged 15 or greater, almost all of whom were employed. Adult and young women were scarce, and it is probable that only one (the teacher M. Marton) worked away from home in 1860 at the height of population development in Jefferson. As a group, women can be characterized as married or on the way to marriage, with no intrinsic reason (i.e., employment) for a presence in the business section of town, which was dominated by the merchants and their male employees and slaves.

When Robert Loughery of Marshall attended services in Jefferson in January 1853, he noted that the church was filled to overflowing but that "There were few ladies in the house. This was not owing, however, to any want of interest or devotion on the part of the fair, but from the fact that Jefferson cannot boast of having a large number of the sex. Indeed, I am told that there are only one or two young ladies in the place. As might be supposed, fears are entertained that cobwebs will grow over this portion of the 'moral vineyard.' Nothing better tends to improve the condition of young men than the society of ladies, and if in our abundance any can be shared (which I can scarcely admit,) I know of no place where they are more wanted or will be better entertained."

In December 1854, Charles DeMorse of the Clarksville *Standard* responded to comments by Frank Clark of the *Jefferson Herald* concerning the relative merits of the two towns. Among other things, DeMorse stated that "We do not boast much on our trade in coarse goods—we boast on our feminines—God bless their sweet souls—*all* of them! We have schools, and the prettiest array of bright eyes and blushing faces to be found anywhere. Feminines walking the streets of Jefferson would occasion a Revolution—they don't have them in that healthy place—they live a little out of Town." Although DeMorse was exaggerating to sharpen contrasts, the point would not have been made had it not contained a large element of truth.

From this it can be concluded that women were not often seen on the streets of Jefferson, by which DeMorse meant primarily Dallas and Marshall streets. Part of the reason is given by Loughery, who indicates that there were not many women in Jefferson. DeMorse supplements this observation by indicating that Jefferson's female population was primarily resident in Paradise. He gives as an additional reason for the absence of women on the streets "the wagons in town filling up the business streets, and interrupting the movement of those who would walk them."

Jefferson was the typical town of the day, with dirt streets that were dusty when it was dry and muddy when it rained. Added to the wagons were large numbers of cattle passing through the streets to the meat packing plants and the drays that were in constant movement in the landing area. This traffic, along with the movement of immigrants, assured that the streets were always heavily rutted and normally filled with traffic. Even after a wharf was built in 1854, the area between the wharf and the warehouses was still dirt. The business streets and the landing area were not hospitable to pedestrians and particularly to women. In addition, large numbers of ox-wagon drivers, steamboatmen, and draymen were present, which probably provided a cultural reason for their absence.

Women did not vote or hold political office and therefore did not usually participate in political meetings or rallies unless they were festive. A number of women were present at a Democratic meeting and barbecue in October 1852 and at the Democratic festival in October 1856, both of which included balls. They also did not preach in the churches. Clubs and civic organizations were either restricted to males or else had feminine branches. When women are mentioned in the newspapers as appearing in public, it is usually in connection with balls, dances, cultural events, and weddings. Women were, of course, absolutely essential to balls and dances and were given free tickets or personal invitations to encourage them to attend.

The scope of feminine participation in other aspects of the public life of the town is largely hidden because of the absence of extant local newspapers. In any case, the history of women in Jefferson is largely the history of domestic activities. Women spent most of their time caring for their homes, children, and husbands. Unfortunately, there do not appear to be any journals or sets of letters that would give us an indication of what domestic life was about. The fruits of domestic life, when joined with a high degree of virtue, are indicated in the obituaries, such as that of Eliza Saufley, wife of the mayor, who died at the age of 23 along with her newborn daughter, as reported in the August 27, 1859, *Standard*:

> Mrs. Saufley having been for many years a resident of our city, by her gentle demeanor had endeared herself to all who knew her; with a hand ever open to the poor and needy, she possessed a heart full of sympathy for the afflicted, and her friends found always in her, one to sympathize, to cheer, to praise, to encourage them,— without envy she enjoyed the happiness of others and did all she could to increase it. In disposition she was cheerful, kind and gentle; as a mother loving and devoted; as a wife self-denying and noble. She has left many true friends, who deeply sympathize with her husband in his great affliction; her space will not readily be filled, for the glow of love that has long been burning upon friendship's heart, will not quench, but endure with the altar.

The memory of the noble deed clings to us during life, being awakened afresh in hours of solitude and reflection; thus will this much esteemed deceased lady be constantly recurring to the minds of her living friends, as the foundation of that recollection will be laid in the excellent character and virtues of the departed.

She has gone to that bourne whence no traveller returns, and her remains were laid in the grave, by numerous friends who attended the burial. Let us imitate her virtues, learning to cultivate so excellent a character as she possessed, that we may receive the reward of merit, and live with her in bliss in that world to which we are all tending and where we shall again see her face to face; her friends we encourage to meet her in a better world; her husband, to write her name upon the tablet of his heart as with a pen of iron, and learn her youthful son to love and imitate her virtues.

9. Slaves

Most Texas slaves appear to have been brought by their owners as part of the general emigration from the older southern states. These slaves were the descendants of people who had lived in America for many generations, because slavery was practiced in the American colonies, and the slave trade had come to an end in 1808, at least officially. Slavery throughout the South was based on the labor needs of large-scale agriculture, including tobacco and sugar but primarily cotton. The vast majority of the slaves in Texas were engaged in agricultural operations. Slaves in towns accounted for less than five percent of the population in Texas.

Slaves were persons who were property. They were valued for their labor, and the value of their labor was quite high. Land was cheap in Texas. Slaves were expensive, and their value rose constantly before the war. As property, slaves were sold, hired-out, mortgaged, and included in wills. They were the only form of property readily convertible to cash and the only secure collateral, and they constituted a large portion of the value of estates. They were also taxed like any other property.

During the 1854 annual sales and hiring of property in Marshall, male slaves were sold for $1,500 to $1,800, and females were sold for $1,000 to $1,200. Ordinary male field hands were hired out for $235 to $312 for a year, and females were hired out for $140 to $170. These were considered to be very high prices.

The next year was one of hard times, but the annual sales in Marshall registered high prices. An estate administrator sold at public auction through the sheriff a female aged 10 for $475 in cash, a female aged eight for $452 on twelve months credit, a female aged six for $350 on twelve months credit, a male aged 24 for $1,100 in cash, a male aged 30 for $975 in cash, and a woman with a four-year-old male child for $1,055 on twelve months credit. At the same time, 320 acres of land near Elysian Fields were sold for $4.20 per acre by a private individual, and 320 acres near Benton were sold by the sheriff for 55 cents an acre.

Similar ranges are available from a Jefferson perspective. The Jefferson resident William Logan writing to his brother in January 1856 stated that "The hire for a negro man is $180 to $200, and for a negro woman $150 to $200. They sell high, too. Women from $1,000 to $1,200; men from $1,500 to $2,000, and hard to get at that." This was a time at which business in Jefferson was depressed because of a long period in which navigation had been suspended.

Slaves were sold and rented in Jefferson through public and private transactions. Many of the public transactions were auctions conducted by the sheriff once a month when Jefferson was the county seat for Cass County and later for Marion County. The sheriff had the responsibility of auctioning all properties assigned to him by the court for public sale. Most of the sheriff sales were the result of court judgments against defendants (individuals and businesses) in suits involving debt. Many slaves were sold through succession sales, which occurred when people died without wills. These were public transactions in which slaves often appeared as components of estate properties that were liquidated through the authority of the probate court. The sheriff sales and succession sales were usually conducted by professional auctioneers.

Private transactions could occur at any time between owners and purchasers/renters (Fig. 9-1). However, most private transactions were conducted through the services of auctioneers and commission merchants, both of whom operated on fixed percentages of sales. Auctioneers appear to have been more important throughout the South; and in Shreveport, all of the commission merchants who

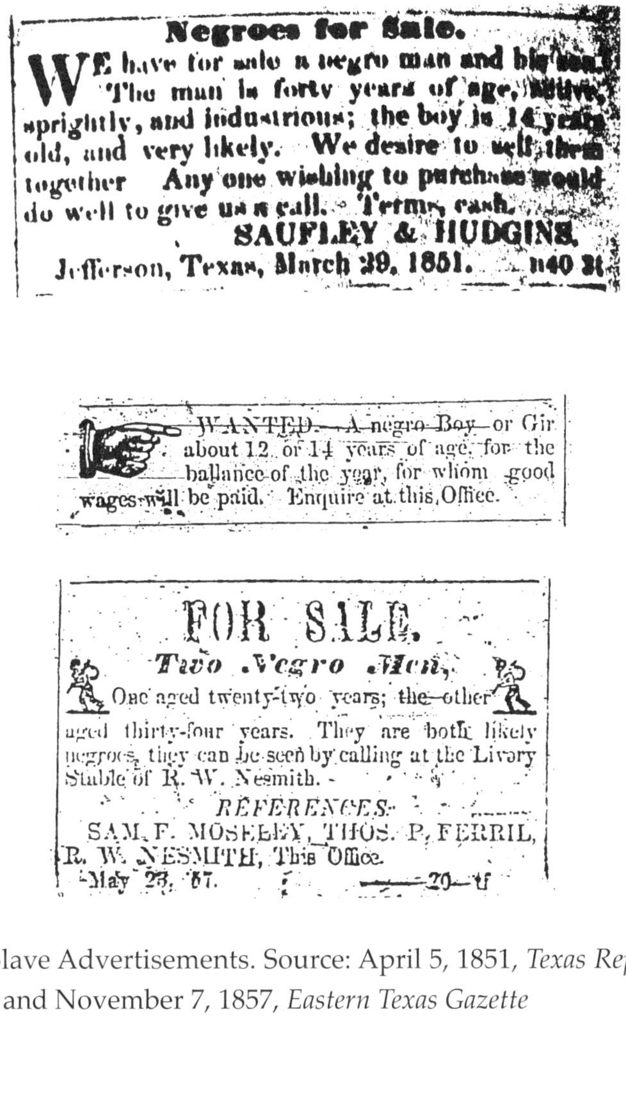

> **Negroes for Sale.**
>
> WE have for sale a negro man and big boy. The man is forty years of age, active, sprightly, and industrious; the boy is 14 years old, and very likely. We desire to sell them together. Any one wishing to purchase would do well to give us a call. Terms, cash.
>
> SAUFLEY & HUDGINS.
>
> Jefferson, Texas, March 29, 1851.   n40 3t

> ☞ WANTED.—A negro Boy or Girl about 12 or 14 years of age, for the ballance of the year, for whom good wages will be paid. Enquire at this Office.

> **FOR SALE.**
>
> Two Negro Men;
>
> One aged twenty-two years; the other aged thirty-four years. They are both likely negroes, they can be seen by calling at the Livary Stable of R. W. Nesmith.
>
> REFERENCES:
> SAM. F. MOSELEY, THOS. P. FERRIL, R. W. NESMITH, This Office.
>
> May 23, '57.   20–tf

Fig. 9-1. Slave Advertisements. Source: April 5, 1851, *Texas Republican*; March 14 and November 7, 1857, *Eastern Texas Gazette*

advertised slave sales were also in the auction business. Auction and commission merchants sold slaves in the same way in which they would sell any commodity. There do not appear to have been any slave traders in Jefferson in the sense that there were no businesses that specialized in the sale of slaves (as was the case in Shreveport). The primary slave sellers in Jefferson were probably the auctioneers Williamson Freeman, James Hosack, and C. D. Morris. Hosack advertised in the October 30, 1874, *Weekly Jimplecute* that he arrived in

Texas in 1840 and became an auctioneer in Jefferson in 1858. He is listed in the 1860 Marion County census as a 26-year-old born in Virginia with a wife and two children.

Slaves were usually hired to others when they were not needed, as a means of generating revenue and avoiding expense. Transactions sometimes involved individual owners. However, many slave hires appear to have emanated from estates under probate. When a person died leaving land and slaves and the farming operation could not be continued, estate administrators hired out the slaves to generate revenue for the beneficiaries of the will. Hires were conducted publicly at the courthouse steps. Slaves were usually hired for a year. Examples from the probate records involving Jefferson residents include the hiring of a boy for $60 by Ithael Eason in 1849 and the hiring of a man for $20 and a woman for $40 by Horatio Walcott in 1852.

Slaves were mortgaged like any other property. James and John Murphy, for example, mortgaged their slaves and other property in the late 1850s when their business ran into difficulties. Slaves were also sold at auction to liquidate mortgaged properties when the terms of the mortgage were not met.

Slaves constituted about 30 percent of the Texas population, 27 percent of the Jefferson population, and about half of the Marion County population. Slaves were enumerated by the census because they contributed to congressional representation. Slave enumerations for 1850 and 1860 are available in the Cass and Marion county census slave schedules. Slaves are enumerated only by owner, age, sex, and color. Names, households, and families are not given. Jefferson was not included as a separate entity in the 1850 census. Slave owners and number of slaves for some of the persons in Precinct 1 who are known to have been Jefferson residents include: Job Baker, 6; Jeptha Crawford, 10; Richard Crump, 1; Eliza Durham, 1; Ithael Eason, 3; Joseph Elliott, 15; Stephen Ellis, 8; Bartholomew Figures, 11; Williamson Freeman, 19; Samuel Garey, 1; August May, 1; William McNeill, 1; Robert Nesmith, 1; Thomas Pugh, 4; Caleb Ragan, 1; Martin Rogers, 1; Robert Rogers, 3; Frederick Schluter, 7; John Speake, 3; Nelson Trawick, 8; Clinton Willard, 5; and Amos Ury, 5. Prominent among these names are merchants, hotel operators, and farmers.

Slaves

The 1860 census lists 67 slave owners (including the double counts for John Murphy and the separate count for the Murphy brothers) and 266 slaves in Jefferson (27 percent of the population), 114 (43 percent) of whom were male and 80 of whom were under the age of 13. Only five slaves were aged 60 or over, with the oldest being 85. The 266 slaves were housed in 73 cabins, which equates to about 3.6 persons per cabin. Because there were 102 households and 124 families in Jefferson in 1860, slightly more than half of the families in Jefferson owned slaves.

The slave owners and number of slaves listed by their order in the slave schedule were as follows: James Moore, guardian for Fannie Fisher, 3; William Brooks, agent of M. Brooks, 8; Anthony Owens, 1; Bob Hughes, 4; L. N. Morris, agent for wife, 4; Edward Jones, agent for wife, 3; James Campbell, 4; Seaborn Wilkinson, 3; S. H. Kirk, agent for M. A. Kirk, 4; Theophilus Nichols, 2; Bass Nichols, 2; Noble Birge, 1; William Hodge, agent for wife, 1; Ithael Eason, 6; Moses McCall, 10; A. D. Tullis, agent for wife, 2; Edward Benners, 10; John Winslow, 6; James Elliott, 1; James Linn, 1; James Brown, 3; William Klyce, 1; Frederick Schluter, 9; Joel Hughes, agent for wife, 4; Thomas Turner, 5; Jeptha Crawford, agent for wife, 9; Samuel Nimmo, 3; Watts Cameron, 2; William Phillips, 1; Orville Yerger, 4; George Terry, 5; John Murphy, 3; John Hobdy, 7; John Murphy, 4; Benjamin Terry, 5; J. H. Faucett, 1; Clinton Willard, 5; Thomas Rogers, 1; William Torrans, 1; Mrs. J. Rush, 2; John Speake, 2; J. M. & J. C. Murphy, 6; R. W. Bullard, agent for wife, 5; Richard Waterhouse, 5; William Mayberry, 2; William Hines, 1; James Durr, 1; James Cole, 5; Williamson Freeman, agent for wife, 8; A. M. Nance, 1; L. A. Jones, 3; Hinche Mabry, 2; Ephraim Terry, 6; Daniel Alley, agent for wife, 10; F. A. Jones, 3; William Todd, 2; Harvey Black, 1; William Saufley, 5; John Dollahite, 1; James Gillean, 12; Lou Harris and sister, Robert Nesmith, guardian, 13; Sam Williams, guardian of minor heirs, 3; Joseph Preston, 2; James Rogers, 3; James Murphy, 7; William Nichols, 3; and Richard Crump, 3.

The slave schedule contains only a category for ownership. However, because slave hiring was common and hired slaves would have been included in the households to which they were attached, it is obvious that the ownership category includes hired slaves. The slave schedule was simply a population census and therefore was not particularly interested in true ownership. An estimate of the number of slave hires living in Jefferson can be made by comparing the slave schedule to the county tax rolls, which were concerned with true ownership. Of the 67 owners listed in the slave schedule, 38 appear with slave ownership in the tax rolls, accounting for 132 slaves. One must conclude that either about half of the slaves in Jefferson were hires or that the tax rolls do not provide an adequate indication of ownership. The tax rolls appear to be valid; for in spite of the fact that there are minor discrepancies for some individuals, the total number of slaves in the tax rolls (132) is almost the same (134) for those persons in the slave schedule.

There may not have been exactly 266 slaves living within the city limits of Jefferson in 1860, just as there may not have been exactly 722 whites living within the city limits in 1860. The census enumerator appears to have included areas outside of the city limits for both the free and slave population. However, because the order of enumeration is the same, it is obvious that the slave schedule was developed at the same time as the schedule of free whites. As a consequence, both enumerations refer to the same geographic area. It is also important to note that all but eight owners listed cabins for their slaves, which must have been adjacent to owner residences because of the concurrent recordation procedures. All but two of the exceptions involved single slaves who obviously lived as in-house servants.

In addition, in attempting to determine the function of slaves in the town economy through the occupations of their owners, it is necessary to take into consideration that many slave owners such as Williamson Freeman and Frederick Schluter engaged in agricultural operations outside of town at the same time they ran businesses in town. Whether their slaves were employed in agricultural or business operations cannot be determined because owners and their respective slaves appear only one place in the census. The county tax rolls do not provide a clarification because the number of slaves taxed for such persons is similar to the census counts, indicating that there were no additional slaves who might have been employed in agricultural operations. Persons other than Freeman and Schluter listed in the tax rolls as owning agricultural property include William Brooks, Edward Benners, John Murphy, John Hobdy, Hinche Mabry, Mrs. F. A. Jones, and William Nichols.

However, owner/renter occupations give a fairly clear idea of what slaves were doing in town. There were 65 individual owners/renters (excluding the multiple counts for James and John Murphy). Clinton Willard was living in the Hickory Hill area as a bookkeeper at the time, but is listed in the slave schedule for Jefferson apparently because he continued in some manner of business in Jefferson. Of the 64 slave owners/renters who are listed as Jefferson residents in the census, occupations are not shown for six. Of the remaining 58, six are listed as farmers (George Terry, Daniel Alley, James Gillean, John Hobdy, S. H. Kirk, and Moses McCall), indicating that their 48 slaves may have been engaged in traditional agricultural operations rather than in town economic functions. However, none of these persons appears in the agricultural census.

The largest owner/renter group was the 23 members of the mercantile class (merchants, clerks, druggists, grocers, a doctor/druggist, and a cotton buyer), who owned/rented 123 slaves. Surprisingly, male slaves constituted only 36 percent of the population, which was lower than the general population ratio, and there were only 33 males over the age of 13. In addition, the rental ratio at 62 percent was larger than the rental ratio for the total slave population.

The second largest group was eight attorneys who owned/rented 32 slaves. Because it is unlikely that attorneys would have a need for a large number of slaves, they may have rented slaves that had been acquired in payment for litigation. The attorney Hinche Mabry's 176 acres in the Gillespie headright are sufficient to account for his two slaves. The attorney Edward Benners owned agricultural property, but his five acres in the Gillespie headright are not sufficient to account for use of his 10 slaves, which may have been rented out. On the other hand, the attorney John Winslow apparently rented his six slaves, because he does not appear as an owner in the tax rolls.

Public officials (the mayor, sheriff, city marshal, and postmaster) each owned one slave; and a miller, brick mason, and stock raiser together owned 12. The stage contractor Robert Nesmith controlled 13, but as guardian of the minor heirs of an estate of a deceased person. Slaves in probate were usually rented out; however, the two slave cabins listed in connection with these slaves indicate that that they were being used by Nesmith. The hotel proprietor William Brooks owned eight (but also owned 210 acres of agricultural land). A dancing master, fisherman, and steamboatman account for the remaining five.

The population of free blacks in Texas was minuscule, and there is no evidence for any free blacks in Jefferson (no slaves are listed as manumitted in the census). The only record that I have found of a free man of color in Cass County is Biddy Lucas' October 1858 district court application for slave status (as required by a state law).

There are no records of slaves who were allowed to live a semi-independent existence in town as craftsmen. The closest to this condition in the records was Williamson Freeman's blacksmith; but he probably returned to the plantation at night. Nevertheless, it was common practice in many areas of Texas for slave owners (particularly agriculturalists) with skilled slaves to allow them to live independently in towns and sell their services as craftsmen on a fee basis, with most of the revenue returned to the owners. Such persons were called self-hires.

That such conditions existed in Jefferson is indicated by the fact that a town ordinance was passed in 1857 providing a fine of $25–$50 for any owner or master who hired a slave to any other slave or free person of color or permitted a slave "to go at large upon a hiring of his or her time for more than one day in the week except in the Christmas holidays to act or deal as a free person within the corporate limits." A supplementary provision stated that "if the town constable shall discover within the corporate limits any slave going at large or living contrary to this ordinance it shall be his duty and it shall be lawful for any other person to arrest any such slave and take him before the mayor without warrant."

It should be noted that the concern was with slaves going at large as free persons through self-hire. The ordinance would not have been passed if slaves had not begun to live semi-independent lives in town. Independent existence was an affront to the institution of slavery because it suggested that slaves could live as free men; and there were obvious concerns with civic order. However, Claudia Goldin in *Urban Slavery in the American South 1820–1860* has demonstrated that the impetus for such ordinances came from free white craftsmen and laborers who were concerned with competition and reduced income.

That the situation was getting out of hand for both hired and self-hired slaves is suggested by the fact that there were additional ordinances indicating that slaves were beginning to act like everyone else. Whites were to be fined ($5 for first offense and not to exceed $25 for each subsequent offense) for renting to free persons of color or slaves such things as buggies or horses for pleasure rides within the town limits, and persons caught in such activities could receive up to 30 lashes. Slaves were prohibited from engaging in balls or similar amusements; and restrictions were placed on remaining in the streets without any apparent business, particularly between Saturday sundown and Monday morning. Hiring a slave or trading with a slave was prohibited unless the slave had written permission from his or her owner. All of these ordinances, with the exception of the self-hire prohibition, were eventually repealed, probably because they were unenforceable.

Independent living was usually a correlate of self-hire, particularly when the slave owner lived distant from the city. There is nothing in the census records to indicate that any slaves lived independently in Jefferson, and all slave residences appear to be accounted for in the cabins attached to the residences or business establishments of owners/renters. If the census is correct, it may be that there were no slaves living independently in Jefferson. On the other hand, the census enumerator may not wish to have dealt with such persons or may have had difficulty finding them (a problem with the census today). Independent living flourished in the larger cities of the South where enclaves were established that were generally avoided by civil authorities. The Five Points area in Jefferson may have afforded such an opportunity; but it may also be that the town population was too small to provide conditions for an enclave.

The Jefferson self-hire ordinance was similar to ordinances in many other southern cities and was a restatement of an 1846 Texas law that was similar to laws in many other southern states. These laws and ordinances were found to be unenforceable because they came into direct conflict with the economic interests of slave owners, who were interested in maximizing the income of their labor. The city records do not provide any indications of enforcement, and it is probable that the ordinance was not enforced in Jefferson, even though it does not appear to have been repealed.

Concrete information on the activities of slaves in town is embarrassingly small. The dry goods and groceries firm of Saufley & Hudgins advertised a 40-year-old male slave and his 17-year-old son for cash sale in 1851. In 1855, one of the slaves belonging to M. Steinlein & Company disappeared along with a horse and a pistol belonging to Ithael Eason, with the disappearance attributed to a band of thieves. A slave acted as oarsman for an 1856 fishing trip by two men to Smithland. In 1857, the *Eastern Texas Gazette* advertised for a boy or girl from 12 to 14 years of age. This may have been for employment at the newspaper, but more probably an instance of the common intermediary service offered by newspapers to persons who wanted to make discrete inquiries. In the same newspaper, two negro men aged 21 and 34 in Nesmith's Livery Stable were advertised for sale. Also in 1857, the livery stable operators Noble Birge and Charles Hynson were sued in the death of a slave they hired and then sublet to Bass Nichols. The slave was guiding a flatboat or barge carrying freight a few miles below Jefferson when he fell overboard and drowned. The October 13, 1858, Shreveport *South-Western* contains a runaway slave advertisement for the dry goods and groceries firm of H. Rhine & Brothers in Jefferson. A male slave was connected with Abraham Kohn's grocery store, and a female slave was connected with James Durr's grocery store, both in 1860.

The nature of the owners and evidence from other towns suggest that the major function of females was as domestics in private residences, and the major function of males was as freight and stock movers for the stores and warehouses. Freight and stock movements were characterized by a large volume of heavy bulk items. The movements by slaves were primarily by hand, wagons, and drays and included movements within the landing area, between establishments, and within establishments. Male slaves probably also operated as skilled independent craftsmen and skilled and semi-skilled subordinates in such places as stables, blacksmith shops, wagon making shops, saw and planing mills, brickyards, tanneries, tin shops, and meat packing plants.

There are no records of any Jefferson slaves ever having been brought before the courts for violent crime. The meager evidence presented in district court records suggests that slaves within the county were dealt with more than fairly in judicial proceedings, which is not surprising because they were of value to their owners. Imprisonment or execution of a slave would be a loss to the owner. Even in cases of rape or murder of white persons, juries were reluctant to decide for execution. There were no lynchings in Jefferson, which would have been incompatible with the soberness of the town.

Whatever the conditions of work in town, it was preferable to fieldwork on plantations because it was not as demanding as agriculture, and town life provided a larger window on the world and greater opportunities for amusement. The town benefitted from the labor and skills of its slave inhabitants, which were essential to its economic and domestic activities. The craft skills acquired by town slaves were important assets during Reconstruction and beyond.

10. Roads and Bridges

Roads

The county commissioners courts were responsible for road maintenance and the licensing of ferries and bridges. Because they did not have staffs for road work, these responsibilities were allocated to the landholders in the vicinity of the road segment that was being created or improved. The actual work was done by slaves. It is possible to gain a fairly precise understanding of old road systems because persons and landmarks are named in connection with road work in the minutes of the commissioners' meetings. Unfortunately, there are no records for Bowie County for the 1840–1845 period. Harrison County records, which cover development south of Cypress Bayou, begin in July 1843, and Cass County records begin in July 1846.

The only roads preceding the development of Jefferson in 1845 were the road from Daingerfield and the Big Cypress Valley Road from Alley's Mills, both of which entered the townsite from the northwest. The former crossed over Cypress Bayou at the foot of Houston Street by ferry, and the latter crossed the bayou by ferry in the proximity of the present-day railroad. The formation of the town in 1845 initiated a flurry of activity in road construction, extension, and repair that is recorded in the minutes of the Cass County commissioners court. The major features of Jefferson's early road system were completed by 1850 (Fig. 10-1). These include:

1. The road south out of Jefferson at Houston Street to Marshall.

Roads and Bridges

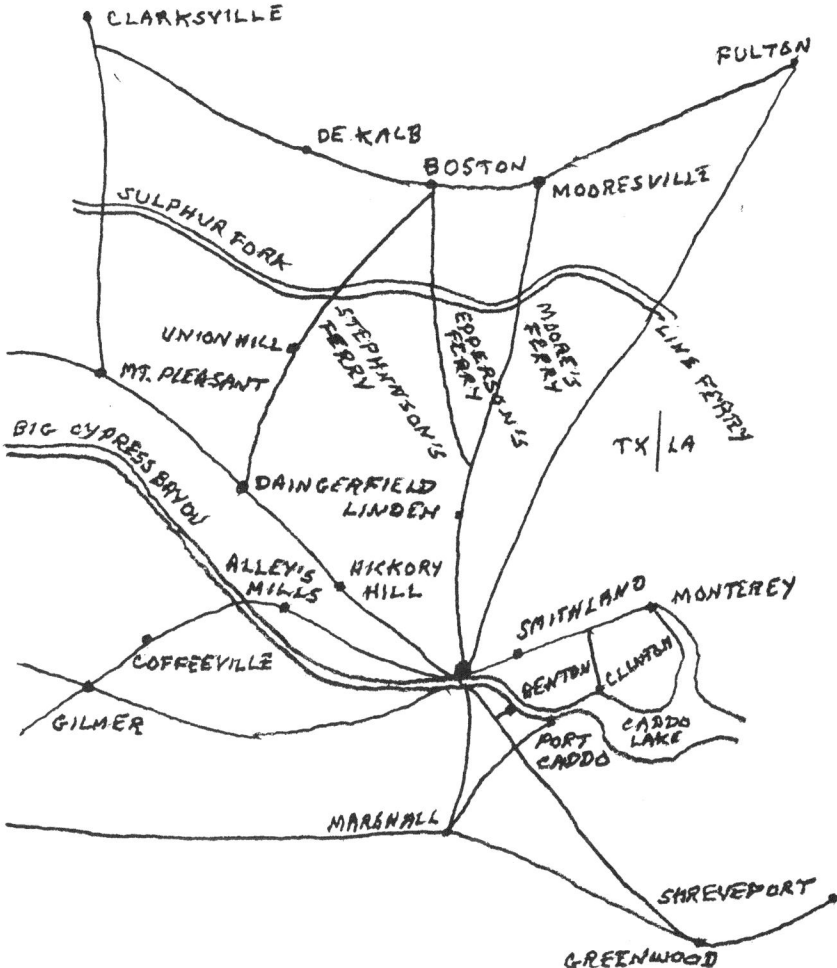

Fig. 10-1. Road System

This road crossed Little Cypress Bayou about three-fourths of a mile west of Highway 59 by ferry and later by bridge.

2. The road southeast out of Jefferson at Houston Street to Greenwood and Shreveport, with linkages along the way to the Big Cypress Bayou ports of Benton and Port Caddo. This road crossed Little Cypress Bayou about three-fourths of a mile east of Highway 49 by ferry and then by bridge, intersected the road from Marshall to Port Caddo, and ran through the Webster plantation southwest of Leigh.

3. The road southwest out of Jefferson branching immediately off the Marshall road and running between Big Cypress Bayou and Little Cypress Bayou to Gilmer, thence west.

4. The road east out of Jefferson to Smithland on Cypress Bayou and continuing on to Clinton and Monterey. There was also a low-water road between Jefferson and Smithland along the bayou that enabled overland transport when steamboats could not reach Jefferson; however, it is unknown when this road came into existence and only begins to be mentioned after the Civil War.

5. The road north out of Jefferson to Boston, which was later complemented by the road to Linden.

6. The road northwest out of Jefferson to Daingerfield and on to Mt. Pleasant and thence north to Clarksville and northwest and west to various points. This road branched off to Alley's Mills and Coffeeville in the vicinity of Hickory Hill (Avinger). In its earliest configuration, it left Jefferson to the north of the present-day road to Daingerfield. A January 1, 1849, bond for title from Martin Rogers to Amos Ury mentions "the new road going west out of Jefferson." This refers to a realignment of the old road to Daingerfield, which was brought closer to the present road to Daingerfield, entered the town at Broadway Street, and can be seen fronting the Freeman Plantation. It is probable that Freeman, who was an important figure in Jefferson and Cass County, played a role in this realignment. After the realignment, the old road to Daingerfield came to be called the Spring Branch and Daingerfield Road and later the Black Cypress Road.

7. The road west out of Jefferson to Alley's Mills and Coffeeville, thence to Gilmer. This road was independent of the earliest alignment of the Daingerfield Road, leaving Jefferson to the south. After the Daingerfield Road was realigned, this road branched off of the Daingerfield Road at the Freeman Plantation and ran south of that road along Cypress Bayou. A part of this road, which was called the Big Cypress Road or the Big Cypress Valley Road, can be seen running towards the bayou at the Freeman Plantation. A much larger portion farther to the west is known locally as the Old Coffeeville Road, which now terminates at Lake O' the Pines.

The roads to the northwest to Daingerfield, to the south to Marshall, and to the southeast to Shreveport were part of a single road system that was joined by the Houston Street ferry. This was the most important road system preceding Jefferson's formation and during its earliest days. This system did not exist in October 1840 when it is not shown on a Harrison County map and did exist by November 1841 when the ferry crossing is shown on Urquhart's survey map. It apparently was created shortly after November 1840 when William Hamilton set the property corners for the Urquhart, Smith, and Gillespie headrights.

A major later addition to the antebellum road system was a road northeast out of Jefferson and directly to Fulton, Arkansas, running east of Linden and crossing the Sulphur Fork by way of Line Ferry.

The primary roads were supplemented by a network of interconnections. This road system provided easy access to and from Jefferson's market area in the north, northwest, and west, as well as to the primary towns on the south, southeast, and east. The roads to the market area were dominated by ox-wagons, whose loads were largely composed of import and export items through Jefferson.

Specifications for a road in 1852 included 20-foot width cleared of all trees, stumps to be cut within six inches of the ground, and causeways at least 12 feet wide (perhaps meaning that stumps were removed from that area). Stumps should not be thought of as an important problem for early road transport. The stumps were widely spaced, such as would occur with the cutting of a managed pine forest today.

The major problem with road transport was surface conditions and the fact that bridges were often washed out by floods. Roads were quickly eroded by rains and rutted by the constant movement of heavy ox-wagons, which was the primary mode of interior transport. The degree to which roadbeds were degraded can be seen in the fact that old roads are heavily indented in the landscape, particularly in the areas where inclines made a chute for rainwater.

Difficulties in road travel for buggies and stage coaches are mentioned quite often; but the major problem was the slowness of ox-wagon transport, which had major economic consequences in the movement of cotton to places like Jefferson; and at times when rains were heavy and streams swollen, fords became impassable and ox-wagons simply had to stop and wait for better conditions, with the capital invested in cotton delayed in the realization of its benefits.

Some of these problems could have been mitigated by aggressive road maintenance. But the allocation of responsibilities for road maintenance to contiguous landholders insured that the road system was universally wretched. The quality of the roads was of particular concern to Robert Loughery of the Marshall *Texas Republican*. In the November 20, 1852, issue, he commented that:

> We understand that the roads leading from Marshall to Shreveport, Henderson, and to Jefferson, need working on. The Shreveport stage driver says that the road from Marshall to the Louisiana line is in a very bad situation. We need an amendment to our road law. It is very defective. We can never expect to have good roads until there is more responsibility created than at present exists. As it is now, it is almost impossible to enforce the requisitions of the road law. We hope there will be an amendment to the law this session of the Legislature.

In the January 29, 1853, issue, Loughery describes a stagecoach ride from Marshall to Jefferson and the types of problems in travel that were endemic to poor road conditions:

> I left Marshall on Sunday morning, in the stage, for Jefferson. After proceeding about a mile and a half, with several disagreeable threatenings of being upset in the road, the body of the vehicle rolled completely to one side, and, on examination, we discovered that the stage was in a fair way to go to pieces, and could not possibly hold together much longer. Our stage driver... immediately drove the carriage to one side of the road, and started back to Marshall for another, leaving the passengers in the road to amuse themselves as they might think best. After waiting a considerable time, he once more made his appearance and we soon found

ourselves under way. The road is none of the best; some parts of it, indeed, sadly need working. We sincerely hope that our Legislature will set themselves to work to reform our road laws; for certainly no country in the world is cursed with worse roads than Texas.

A turnpike from Clarksville to Jefferson was authorized by the Texas Legislature in 1852. A joint-stock company was formed whose primary purpose was to provide adequate bridging, particularly over Sulphur Fork and White Oak Bayou. The initiative came from the north, but the enterprise was enthusiastically endorsed by the *Jefferson Herald*, and Jeffersonians purchased stock in the company. The project was under construction in 1854, but is not reported in the newspapers as having been completed.

Bridges

The ferry that provided passage across Cypress Bayou at the foot of Houston Street since 1841 was insufficient to meet the needs of a growing town. The addition of a bridge was anticipated as early as January 1846 in the purchase of ferry privileges by William Bishop from Allen Urquhart that included the potential for erecting a toll bridge. These privileges were transferred to Asa and James Johnson toward the end of the year. The bridge, like the ferry, was a private venture under government license and therefore required tolls as a correlate to private investment.

The privilege to erect a toll bridge was granted to the Johnsons on October 12, 1847, by the Cass County commissioners, who stipulated that the bridge be built in the same place as the ferry and that tolls remain the same, with the exception of small increases for cattle, hogs, and sheep. The bridge was in existence from at least January 1848, when the Harrison County commissioners court minutes mention that the road from Marshall to Jefferson terminated at the Jefferson bridge. In November 1848, the Cass County commissioners appointed William Perry, William McNeill, James Johnson, Robert Nesmith, and Robert Brownell to determine the best approach route into Jim Johnson's Bridge. It is mentioned in the September 9, 1854, *Texas Republican*

Antebellum Jefferson, Texas

as a point of reference in relation to a bayou improvement project that was being conducted by William Perry.

Johnson's Bridge is shown on Eppinger's 1850 *Map of Jefferson* (Fig. 10-2). The structure, which was made of wood, was not sophisticated and merely ran the short distance from the high banks on both sides

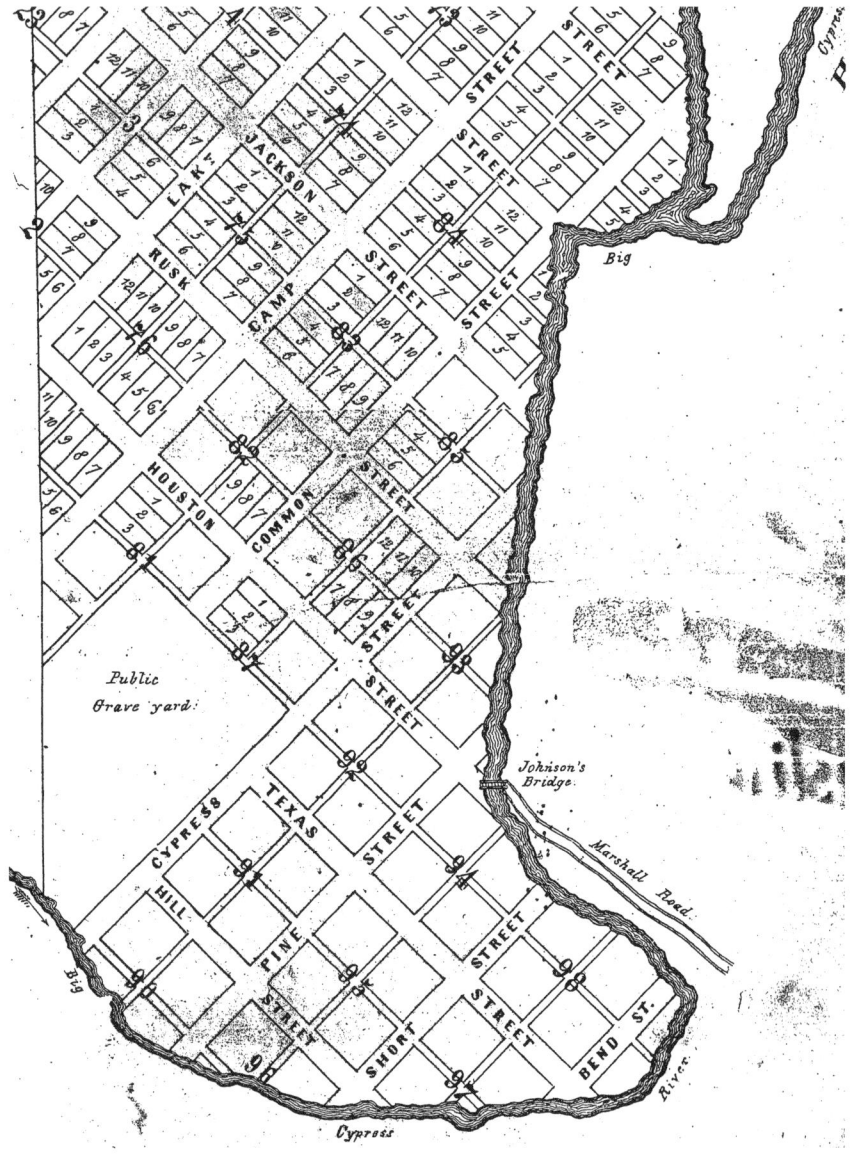

Fig. 10-2. Bridge. Source: Courtesy Texas General Land Office, Austin

of the bayou. The erection of a bridge at Jefferson was not an unusual undertaking. Similar bridges were built shortly thereafter on Little Cypress Bayou and Black Cypress Bayou and even across streams like Kitchens Creek. Larger rivers such as Sulphur Fork presented engineering difficulties that were only to be resolved later.

In November 1850, the Cass County commissioners granted Allen Urquhart a license to operate the toll bridge and ferry previously kept by James and Asa Johnson and to establish the following rates: 10 cents for man and horse and 40 cents in high water; 50 cents for four-horse wagon and $2 in high water; 25 cents for two-horse wagon and $1 in high water; five cents for horses and 10 cents in high water; 5 cents for cattle and 10 cents in high water; 2 ½ cents for sheep and hogs and 5 cents in high water. Similar privileges were granted by the Harrison County commissioners in February 1851. The bridge immediately became known as Urquhart's Bridge. Urquhart's license was renewed by the Cass County commissioners in November 1851 and by the Harrison County commissioners in February 1852.

On February 13, 1852, the Texas Legislature authorized Allen Urquhart to build a toll bridge across Big Cypress Bayou at the town of Jefferson between Cass and Harrison counties. The law stipulated that the bridge must be built within two years, that it must be properly maintained during the 20-year period of the grant, that the commissioners would set the tolls, and that the town had the capacity to build a free bridge at any time. This apparently was to be a replacement for Johnson's Bridge. However, Urquhart's application for renewal of the bridge license in February 1855 was rejected by the Cass County commissioners on the grounds that Urquhart never complied with the provisions of the law.

Tolls were resented and constituted a limitation on commercial activity. In March 1850, for example, Robert Loughery noted that communication between Marshall and Jefferson would be more frequent if the tolls on the bridges could be removed. The articles of incorporation for Jefferson that were enacted by the Texas Legislature on March 28, 1848, provided the mayor and aldermen the power to establish public ferries and to erect public bridges. The town took the former option by establishing a free public ferry on the east side of the landing area at Williamson Freeman's warehouse, as reported in the May 14, 1853, *Jefferson Herald*:

> FREE FERRY.—Our citizens have established a free ferry at this place, across the Big Cypress, opposite Freeman's ware house, for the accommodation of the traveling and trading public. It will be kept up through the entire year, and will be at all times well attended. The outrageously high tolls demanded at Urquhart's bridge have determined the citizens of Jefferson to this course. The press in our neighboring Towns will confer a favor on the public by noticing this fact.

It should be noted that Urquhart was considered an outsider. It is unlikely that the public ferry would have produced substantial cuts in traffic over the bridge, because time was money and people preferred convenience. Urquhart's license to operate the toll bridge and ferry was renewed by the Cass County commissioners in February 1854 with the following rates: 10 cents for man on foot; 20 cents for man and horse; 75 cents for four-horse or ox wagon; $1 for six-horse or mule wagon; 50 cents for two-horse or mule wagon; 10 cents for horses, mules, and cattle; 5 cents for sheep.

The problem of bridge tolls was ultimately resolved through the erection by the town of a free bridge over Big Cypress Bayou. The new bridge is mentioned in the February 23, 1855, Harrison County commissioners court minutes, and its completion is announced in the March 10, 1855, *Texas Republican*. This was shortly after Urquhart's application for a license was rejected. The timeframe suggests that the city simply acquired the old bridge. However, the notices indicate that this was a new structure.

Urquhart continued to operate a ferry, with his license renewed by the Harrison County commissioners on the same day as the mention of the new bridge. Because there is no record of a second bridge, it appears that the new bridge replaced the old one. Only one bridge, at the termination of the road from Marshall to Jefferson, is mentioned each year in the minutes of the Harrison County commissioners court; and a captured Confederate map shows only one bridge leaving Jefferson at the same location as the 1850 Eppinger map.

The free public bridge is described as "large and elegant" in the November 26, 1858, *Texas Republican*. The same article reports a temporary breakdown that was quickly repaired. The only other mention of the bridge prior to the Civil War was in connection with a near-fatal accident involving Judge William Ochiltree, who was at that time living in Marshall and on his way to the Cass County court in Linden. The accident is reported in the April 15, 1859, Marshall *Texas Republican*:

> FEARFUL FALL.—Our whole community were greatly alarmed on Sunday last from the painful intelligence that Hon. W. B. Ochiltree, of this place, was thrown from the bridge at Jefferson, and in all probability killed. Judge O. was crossing the bridge over Big Cypress, just this side of Jefferson, in a buggy, when his horse becoming frightened backed the buggy against the railing. It unfortunately gave way, and horse, buggy, and rider were hurled over the bridge to the ground below, a distance of about twenty-two feet. The fall was a fearful one. We are happy in being able to state, that though severely bruised, the Judge was not seriously injured. It was a moment of imminent peril, and the escape from sudden death seems almost miraculous.

Regarding the accident, the April 15 Marshall *Harrison Flag* remarks that "so fast a town as Jefferson should keep its thoroughfares in a little better repair than hers are. This they will admit."

The bridge continued to be a bone of contention between Urquhart and the town. On September 12, 1860, the town relinquished to Urquhart the bridge and ferry privileges in exchange for a relinquishment by Urquhart of the wharf lots south of Dallas Street from the foot of Polk Street and extending to the northeast. The town was interested in securing full rights to the lands on which the public wharf had been built.

Brosius' 1872 *Bird's Eye View of Jefferson* shows a bridge across Cypress Bayou at the end of Moseley Street, which was known as the

Mayberry Bridge. In May 1861, a partnership was formed between William Mayberry and Augustus Foscue to start a steam saw and grist mill on Mayberry's property on the other side of the bayou from Taylor and Moseley streets. At the end of April, Mayberry had successfully petitioned the aldermen to extend one or more of the town's streets to Mayberry's Mills on Big Cypress. In August, the Marion County commissioners court agreed to lay out a road beginning at Friou Street and running between Moseley and Benners streets to Big Cypress near Foscue and Mayberry's steam saw mill. The area west of Friou was apparently undeveloped at the time.

In November, further action on the proposal mentions that the road would run to Mabry's Bridge, obviously referring to the Mayberry Bridge. Some sort of improvements were probably made as an extension of Moseley Street from Friou, although a full road was not developed until August 1868. The important point is that Mayberry's Bridge was in existence by at least November 1861.

A March 1, 1856, *Texas Republican* advertisement indicates that Frank Clark's tanyard was located "near the bridge on Big Cypress, at the old mill of O'Hara, Richardson, & Hughes." The mill was located in the southeast corner of the Gillespie headright near Big Cypress Bayou. This bridge probably serviced a road that connected with the Big Cypress Valley Road on the north and ran south, later connecting with the Mayberry Bridge to enter the town. Some sort of in-stream covered structure is shown in this area in the 1872 *Bird's Eye View*.

11. County Seat

Cass County

When Cass County was created by the Texas Legislature out of Bowie County on April 25, 1846, Jesse Cherry was designated to survey the county boundaries. A new county seat was needed. This was not accomplished until Linden was created and designated as the county seat by the Texas Legislature in January 1852. In the interim, Jefferson served as the county seat and therefore was the place in which the official county activities were conducted, including those of the commissioners court, clerk's office, surveyor's office, sheriff, justice of the peace, constable, and assessor and tax collector. It was also the place in which the sessions of the 5th district court were held, which drew people from surrounding counties. Political meetings were always a correlate of judicial proceedings, particularly because attorneys then as now were heavily involved in politics. Jefferson benefited not only from prestige and visitation, but also from the rental of facilities and the provision of services.

The legislative act creating Cass County stipulated that courts of the county meet in the tavern house of William Perry in Jefferson until a suitable courthouse could be erected and that they could adjourn to any other place that they deemed suitable. At a minimum, a tavern house was a place where alcoholic beverages were sold and overnight accommodations were provided. However, advertisements in contemporary newspapers such as the Clarksville *Northern Standard* and the

Washington Telegraph published in Arkansas indicate that the term also referred to full-fledged hotels. The location of Perry's tavern house is unknown and probably indeterminable because Perry owned many lots in Jefferson. The first meeting of the commissioners court was held at the tavern house of William Perry on July 23, 1846.

The court moved to the tavern house of William Russell for the January 1847 session, then to Simon Heald's new frame house for the June session. The June session was attended by Charles DeMorse of the Clarksville *Northern Standard*, who provides an account of the district court proceedings and a description of Perry's Soda Lake Hotel in the June 23 issue. DeMorse was impressed by the appearance of the town, the quality of the hotel accommodations, and the sophistication of the people who had assembled in relation to public business:

> The next morning we rode into Jefferson, about eleven o'clock, and were agreeably surprised by the improved appearance of the place, since last summer, and the increased air of comfort which it has, from having a better supply of house room. We found also a much larger number of persons in attendance upon court, than we had expected to see....The attendance of lawyers was quite large, though the bulk of them were from Marshall....
>
> The Hon. David B. Kaufman, Col. A. S. Thurston, and Wm. P. Hill, Esq., of Marshall, were among those whom we had known for many years, in the west, and whom it was pleasant to see again. Judge Roberts of the 5th, Mr. Walker the District Attorney, Col. Burke of Sabine Co., Col. Spearman Holland, James D. Todd, Esq., of Port Caddo, and the members of the Bar in general, from Harrison, were among the new ones, whose company made the hours pass pleasantly....
>
> The court progressed in regular order with its business, and we left it in session, on Friday evening. Of the bearing of his Honor Judge Roberts, upon the bench, we might say much, and still not exceed propriety.— To say that he is dignified and urbane, patient, inves-

tigating, cautious and conscientious, and that he has the full confidence, and the warmest friendship of the people of his district, is not to say too much. In the private circle, the Judge is a modest, and quiet gentleman, highly intelligent, and most agreeable in conversation. Mr. Richard S. Walker, the District Attorney, also comes in for a share of our respect and appreciation, for his capacity, diligence, and gentlemanly propriety. He is young, and promising, and we have no doubt, will attain a rank to his profession highly creditable.

The court moved to Israel Leavitt's frame house (apparently his storehouse on the west half of Lot 9 in Block 4 on Dallas Street) in July 1847. William Perry was paid in January 1848 for boarding court officials at the Soda Lake Hotel during the December 1847 term, and Berry Durham was paid for court advertisements in the *Jefferson Democrat*. In November 1848, Robert Nesmith and Robert Brownell, who had acquired the Soda Lake Hotel from Perry, were paid $8 for keeping prisoners eight days and $4 for boarding a guard during the September term. There was no jail in Jefferson at that time.

Early in 1847, the Texas Legislature appointed a commission to select a location for the county seat and to supervise the erection of public buildings, particularly a courthouse. Members of the commission in its different versions included Henry Mims, Robert Arberry, William Bishop, E. Frazier, Robert Graham, Matthew Mullins, Charles Stanley, John Everett, William Rose, and John Scott.

Locations for a courthouse had been identified for the Urquhart property in Hensey's 1846 plan and for the Alley Addition in Graham's 1847 plan. In March 1847, Urquhart and Durham conveyed to the commissioners the courthouse square shown in the Hensey plan with the stipulation that they retain every second lot other than the site for the courthouse. This offer was apparently not accepted. In April, Alley conveyed to the commissioners for a $10,000 consideration the block bounded by Line, Main, Jefferson, and Taylor with the stipulation that it revert to a public square for the use of Jefferson's citizens should it not be used for a courthouse.

No action was taken to build a courthouse in the Alley Addition, although the commissioners actually sold some of the lots. In mid-1848, the Texas Legislature sought a permanent county seat for Cass County and ordered a survey to determine the center of the county. It was common practice to establish county seats in the geographic center to provide equal access to citizens, but the final determination was made by popular vote. A survey was conducted during the August term of the commissioners court. At that time the county officials were Martin Rogers, chief justice; Richard Crump, sheriff; Perry Graham, clerk; and Jeptha Crawford, treasurer. The survey determined the center of the county, and the commissioners determined that a new town should be created there called Linden. A town plan was later prepared by Alexander Holcomb.

Jefferson was nevertheless hopeful of gaining designation as the county seat and apparently was willing to make a donation of public buildings for the site in the Alley Addition. An election was held in October 1848, and Jefferson lost out to Linden by a vote of 92 to 93. In a long letter to the county commissioners, Daniel Alley and William Perry objected to the results of the election, arguing procedural deficiencies and the fact that Jefferson had been established as the county seat by law in 1846. Alley and Perry made it clear that Jefferson intended to pursue the matter in court. In the district court case of D. N. Alley versus Robert Arberry *et al.*, the jury determined that there had been voting irregularities; and in November the election was overturned.

The county commissioners continued to pursue the Linden option, with Martin Rogers acting as one of their attorneys. In January 1849, the commissioners identified Linden as the new county seat and stipulated sale of lots and the erection of a courthouse, with notification to be provided in the *Spirit of the Age* published in Jefferson. In May, they called for a July sale of lots in Linden and indicated that notification concerning the lowest bidder for courthouse construction would be advertised in the *Independent Monitor* published in Jefferson. Alley sued the county in August 1849; and on December 27, the Texas Legislature called for a new vote on the county seat to be held in March 1850.

Jefferson continued to serve as the temporary county seat throughout this period. Israel Leavitt was paid $62.50 for housing the court in Jackson Hall through October 1848. In November 1849, the hotel owner Bartholomew Figures was paid $18.75 for keeping horses for court officials, Perry Graham was paid $20 for 14 months' rental for accommodating clerk offices, and Richard Peters was paid $50 for rental of his house as a courthouse. Stephen Ellis, who was then proprietor of the Soda Lake Hotel, was given $15 for housing court officials and $5 for housing a prisoner. In 1853, the firm of Speake & Willard was granted $4 for forwarding stationery for the clerk's office in 1850.

The court established itself on a semi-permanent basis at Israel Leavitt's Jackson Hall from sometime in 1848 to the end of 1851 when Leavitt died. This does not appear to have been Leavitt's storehouse that was occupied by the court in 1847. The only other property owned by Leavitt prior to 1848 was Lot 6 in Block 5, which had been purchased by Leavitt from Carey Ragan in December 1847. Leavitt had a building on Marshall Street on the upper portion of this property that may have been Jackson Hall.

Robert Loughery of the Marshall *Texas Republican* was in Jefferson in March and, like DeMorse, was particularly impressed by the quality of the proceedings of the district court:

> The senior editor of this paper returned on Saturday evening last from Jefferson, having spent five days there. Court was in session, and the attendance of the bar was general, embracing many of the most talented lawyers in Eastern Texas. We had the pleasure of hearing several of them speak in an exciting land case in which they were arrayed, and, for legal talent, profundity of thought, and ingenuity, it was a forensic display worthy of any Courthouse in the Union. Hon. L. D. Evans presided, and the business of the Court was dispatched with diligence and celerity.

In the August 1851 term, it was determined that the court would move during the next term to the upper floor of Mayer Dopplemayer's new building in Jefferson, which was then being erected, and that an election for the county seat should be held in September. In the October term, the court announced the results of the election, which was held on September 23. Linden received 256 votes to Jefferson's 156 and was declared the county seat. Loughery was in Jefferson shortly after the election and saw no reason for concern about the results:

> Last week we paid a visit to Jefferson, and remained there a couple of days. The District Court was in session, and quite a number of people were in attendance. Among these we noticed several familiar faces from the neighboring counties, principally lawyers, of which there was a fair delegation from Marshall. The array of legal talent presented, was indeed quite flattering. Among others from a distance, we noticed Gen J. P. Henderson, and Hon. John T. Mills, of Red River....
>
> We learned from the citizens, and afterwards from the Herald, that at the recent election for the county site, LINDEN was chosen as the place. Whether the citizens in favor of Jefferson will acquiesce in the decision we did not learn. There was some talk about the illegality of the election, from which we were led to infer that it would perhaps be contested. We regret very much this unfortunate controversy which has arrayed two parties in this county, and we would rejoice to see it terminated, and the people once more harmonize. Jefferson is now so far ahead, that the removal of the county site can do it but little, if any, injury. On the other hand, the prosperity of the place, will be a decided benefit to the county, and enhance the value of every acre of land within it.

The Texas Legislature officially recognized Linden as the county seat on January 15, 1852. However, the court did not move immediately to Linden, and Dopplemayer was paid $60 for housing the court during its March 1852 term.

A last-ditch effort was made by Jefferson to retain the county seat through a petition to the district court that was made by Daniel Alley, John Speake, Henry Kotho, John Kolster, August Lamprecht, William

Saufley, William Baker, Francis Baker, Thomas Taylor, William McCall, George Tuttle, Clinton Willard, William Robinson, Bartholomew Figures, Frank McKenny, Calvin Bushmiller, Stephen Ellis, Horatio Walcott, William Nichols, William McNeill, James Hatcher, George Slaughter, Wiley Ferrell, George Smith, Daniel Douthit, Richard Johnson, Horatio Geer, Mayer Dopplemayer, Ephraim Beckett, Charles Durgin, Abraham Kohn, August May, Caleb Ragan, Samuel Friou, James Jones, William Brooks, Gideon Baker, John Dollahite, Thomas Cross, John Morgan, Charles Jackson, Jeptha Crawford, and Thomas Crockett.

The petition was unsuccessful, as reported by the *Jefferson Herald* in April:

> On Monday last, after an elaborate argument which was continued from day to day during the District Court, the application for an Injunction against the removal of the seat of Justice from this place to Linden was refused by the Court. With no impediment in the way, it is thought now, that the County Court will proceed to comply with the provisions of the last Act of the Legislature on this subject.

An appeal was made to the Texas Supreme Court, which affirmed the lower court decision. The commissioners court ordered removal of county offices to Linden at the end of May. The *Jefferson Herald* of the 28th described the exodus:

> THE COUNTY SEAT.—Jefferson is no longer the county seat of Cass County. On Monday last, all the papers, records and paraphernalia of the County court, District court, and Surveyor's office were put into a wagon which started *en route* for Linden. As the vehicle rolled off, the welkin rang with shouts and cheers. Some of the boys went so far as to gather our friend Esq. E_____(one of the late Attorneys for Linden,) and put him on the top of the load as a necessary accompaniment.
>
> Our county seat is now at Linden, 20 miles North of Jefferson. We are told that the County Court has let

out the contract for building a large and elegant Court house. Next Monday is Probate court. Go up and take a look at things!

The person unnamed was probably John Everett, who was the county attorney. The *Jefferson Herald* had good reason for the note of sarcasm. A house that was under construction by Henry Collins was used as the courthouse until the permanent structure that was being erected by Thomas Foster was completed in February 1854. Loughery visited the new county seat in September 1852 and reported the following:

We were at Linden, the new county site of Cass, where we spent Tuesday and part of Wednesday. The place is a new one, and of course the accommodations were not so fine as those of older places. It was as good, however, as might have been expected under all the circumstances, and we had the promise of the very best treatment at the next term of the court. Several buildings have been erected at Linden, but they are houses intended for the officers connected with the courts, or for public business. Other houses, however, are going up, and there will be a sufficient number in a short time for convenience and comfort. Among other buildings there is a two story frame Court house, just erected. This building is not complete. The frame is merely up, and the roof on; and the court was held on the ground floor.

Jefferson continued to benefit from the activities of the court because of the lack of facilities in Linden. Of particular importance was the absence of facilities for housing prisoners. A jail for the county seat was proposed in December 1852, with bid specifications to appear in the *Jefferson Herald*. In the meantime, Jefferson provided the requisite services, and prisoners were transported to Linden to appear in court. Robert Nesmith and John Ligon were paid for the boarding of prisoners and guards in Jefferson in 1852 and 1853.

In February 1854, the Texas Legislature directed the county commissioners to reconvey to Alley all unsold lots donated for building the courthouse. This was not accomplished until February 1855. The commissioners had selected 24 lots and sold 15, some of which were to buyers not remembered. The land was returned to Alley because he had not actually sold it to the commissioners. In the 1852 petition, Alley testified that the consideration mentioned in the deed that transferred the property was purely formal, that he had not received any money, and that the $10,000 was an estimate of increased property values in the Alley Addition that would result from the donation.

Marion County

Marion County was created out of Cass County by the Texas Legislature on February 8, 1860. The name "Marion" has traditionally been assumed to have been derived from Francis Marion of Revolutionary War fame. In 1780, the British captured Charleston and overran South Carolina. Francis Marion was appointed brigadier-general by the governor and organized a band of guerrilla volunteers that became widely known for its exploits against the British. The British Colonel Tarleton was sent to capture him but was unsuccessful, designating Marion "the old swamp fox" because he eluded capture by following swamp paths.

The traditional interpretation was challenged by Lucille Bullard in her *Marion County, Texas, 1860–1870*, pointing out that Marion DeKalb Taylor was a better possibility. Taylor, who was the son of Ward Taylor and the brother of Ward Taylor, Jr., was a highly respected resident of the county and was instrumental in its organization while serving in the Texas House of Representatives in 1860. Both interpretations were carried forward by Fred Tarpley in his *Jefferson: Riverport to the Southwest*.

The "Swamp Fox" interpretation is supported by a contemporary source that appeared in the correspondence column of the March 3, 1860, Clarksville *Standard*. The letter was dated February 12 and was written to the newspaper's editor Charles DeMorse by A. J. E., a Jefferson resident:

> While I write I hear the shrill whistle of some steamer, plying for our port. Navigation is very good now,

and if reports be true, we are destined ere long to have a full "Bayou." The largest size "Red River Packets" visit this place very regularly now, but the freights are yet high, owning mainly to the fact that the water is not yet at the middling fair point.

The "Trio" reached here between 7 and 8 o'clock P.M. yesterday, and left for upper "Red River" about 3 P.M. Latest news from the city—notes the cotton market depressed, extremes ruling from 5 to 7 to 12 ½ and 12 ¾. Cotton still continues to come in here at the rates of 1000 and 1500 bales per week. Some selling at 7 ¾ to 10c. None can be shipped at lower marks than $2.50. We are enjoying very pleasant weather now, and it seems the citizens are improving the opportunity, as every street and corner are alive with business.

Jefferson was improving very rapidly. In every part of town new buildings are being erected. Several new stores have been opened this season, which clearly evidences an increase in her trade.

The news of the division of this county, was received here by every citizen, with the strongest demonstrations of joy—and approval of the step. It will be a great help as well as convenience to the people of Jefferson.

The name given them is appropriate, if for no other than to retain fresh and verdant in the memory of the people, the name and acts of the noble and patriotic "Marion" the "Wily Fox of the Swamps," whose blood flowed freely in the cause of freedom, and whose strong arm and bold heart, wielded a mighty influence in establishing permanently upon American soil the liberty which we all enjoy.

And with his name are associated others, the memory of whom can never fail, to endear to the hearts of every American, the soil which holds their ashes, and the institutions fostered upon it, under the guidance of their wise admonitions.

On the other hand, the Rev. John McLean, who was well acquainted with Jefferson and Marion County when the county was formed, reports in his reminiscences that "Dr. Marion Taylor was prominent in politics. Under his manipulation, Marion County was created from Cass, Upshur and Harrison and named in his honor—instead of Marion, the Swamp-fox, as some others hold." Given the alternate interpretations from persons close to the event, it is possible that the name was meant to serve a dual purpose.

When Marion County was created out of Cass County by the Texas Legislature in February 1860, Jefferson was designated the county seat, making it the location of the county commissioners court and the 8th judicial district court. The commissioners court held its first meeting in March, with Shadrach Eggers as chief justice, Noble Birge as sheriff, Labon Bayless as clerk, and Perry Graham as surveyor. The initial meetings were held at Birge's Hall, with the clerk's office in John and Samuel Smith's store. In August, James Durr was elected chief justice and Noble Birge continued as sheriff and is listed as such in the census. In November, the commissioners court moved to Freeman's Hall, which was already occupied by the district and county clerks.

Activities of the commissioners court were similar to those when Jefferson was the Cass County seat, with construction and maintenance of county roads and bridges as the primary concern. Works of interest to Jefferson included the Daingerfield road, the road to Linden, the Big Cypress Valley Road, the road to Smithland and Monterey, and the road to Line Ferry from the Black Cypress Bayou crossing of the Linden road. Roads were to be cleared 20 feet. Repairs were to be made to the bridges over Black Cypress Bayou on the roads to Linden and Monterey. An extension was made from the Daingerfield road past the Big Cypress Valley Road down to Bushong's Crossing at Big Cypress near Mill Creek. The extension left the Daingerfield road west of Freeman's property at Porter's Mill, apparently providing the present alignment of the county road that is partly equivalent to the Big Cypress Valley Road.

Private individuals were paid for recovery of a body from the bayou, for housing and guarding prisoners, and for the care of paupers, including pauper coffins. Licenses to sell liquor in quantities less than a quart were issued to George Prewitt, Waterhouse & Company, James Henderson, Richard Crump, J. W. Gardner (in a house adjoining the livery stable), and John Neff (in the Horse Shoe Saloon in Jefferson). A decision to build a jail was made in August 1860, with proposals to be submitted in November; and a jail was apparently completed late during that year. In May 1861, the commissioners appropriated $8,000 for arms and ammunition, and a mass meeting of the citizens of the county was called for June 1.

12. Municipal Affairs

Incorporation

Jefferson was incorporated on March 20, 1848, by the Texas Legislature. Free white citizens constituted the corporate body, and a mayor and five aldermen constituted the legal body, capable of suing and being sued and holding and conveying real and personal property. The aldermen were to be elected from five wards. The mayor and aldermen had the capacity to create ordinances, which were enforced by the mayor as justice of the peace and by a town constable (marshal). The mayor and aldermen were to appoint a recorder and treasurer from among themselves and a constable from among the citizens of the town. Taxes required a two-thirds vote of the citizens, and citizens who paid taxes were exempt from county road duties. The scope allowed for the ordinances was typical of the period, with the exception of provisions concerning Jefferson's status as a port:

> To maintain the cleanliness and salubrity of said town; to secure the safety and convenience of passing in the streets and squares, ways, lanes and other public streets and alleys; to fix the squaring and to prevent any encroachment or other undertaking on the said streets; to determine the completion and dimensions, the maintenance and repair of pavements in said streets, at the cost of the proprietors of houses, lands or neighboring lots; to fix the place or places of landing and anchoring

for all water crafts, in the stream adjacent thereto; to establish an active system of inspection over the slaves of said town; and those employed in any water craft, that may be at such landing; to establish a town guard or patrols; to provide for the lighting the streets; to determine in what part of the town, wooden chimneys shall be allowed to be erected; to prevent gunpowder to be stowed within the town and suburbs, in such quantity as to endanger the public safety; to determine on the means to be resorted to extinguish conflagration and to prevent the same; to regulate the service of persons employed in working fire engines; to permit or forbid all public amusements, whenever the preservation of order, tranquility or public safety may require it; to establish market places; to erect all public buildings; to determine the mode of inspection for all marketable commodities sold publicly in said town; to regulate every thing which relates to bakers, butchers, tavern keepers, and in all establishments in which liquors or food of any kind are sold, or persons keeping any public house whatever; to regulate the prices of draymen and teamsters, water carriers; to erect bridges whenever the public convenience of the citizens of said town may require it; and to make all other regulations which may contribute to the better administration of the affairs of said corporation, as for the maintenance of the tranquility and safety of the same.

Although incorporation took place in March 1848, a charter was not obtained until 1850, with a municipal government established in late 1850 through the election of Stephen Ellis as mayor, according to the September 1, 1876, *Daily Jimplecute*. This lateness may have been related to the fact that there were problems with the Urquhart survey that were not resolved until November 1849; but it apparently was the result of a problem in the Act of Incorporation, which stated that the first mayor and aldermen were to be elected by citizens who had resided within the corporate limits for three months and that the corporate limits were to include the headrights of Urquhart and Alley and were to be laid off after the election of the mayor and aldermen. Persons who qualified as electors obviously could not be identified until the corporate limits were established. This was done by a September 20, 1850, amendment to the Act, which established the corporate limits as "commencing at the point where the east boundary line of Allen Urquhart's survey, leaves the Big Cypress Bayou, and running from thence in a north-west course one mile, and thence on a south-west line, or to a point where the said line may strike the Big Cypress Bayou, thence down said Bayou, with its meanders, to the place of beginning."

There is a problem with this delineation, because it describes a triangle that would encompass a portion of the Gillespie headright on the west. Nevertheless, the delineation was carried forward in 1854 in the *Charter, By-Laws and Ordinances of the Town of Jefferson* and in 1866 when a new charter was obtained for the City of Jefferson. The delineation is incompatible with John Eppinger's 1850 *Map of Jefferson As owned by Allen Urquhart*. The northern boundary of this map runs straight west, as was common practice in corporate boundaries. This map was obviously correlated with the formal organization of the town because it was prepared in 1850 when Urquhart had no other apparent reason to delineate his properties.

The only useful piece of information in the delineation is the mention of a boundary running one mile. A one-mile northern boundary encompassing the top of the Eppinger map and running for another half mile to the west through Alley's property is compatible with later maps, such as Graham's May 1869 *Plan of the City of Jefferson, Texas* (Fig. 12-1). In terms of formal boundaries, Jefferson was much smaller in 1850 than the two-mile square that forms the city today, being restricted to the area north of Cypress Bayou and running only one mile from east to west at its northern perimeter, with the northern boundary a few blocks north of Broadway and the western boundary slightly to the west of Crawford (Fig. 12-2). Paradise, which was integral to the life of the town, was not included within the corporate limits.

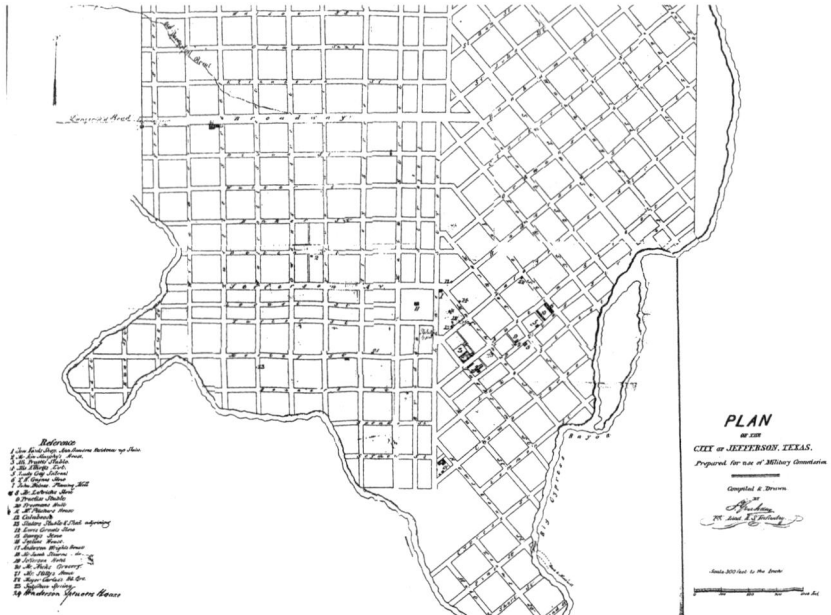

Fig. 12-1. Graham's 1869 City Plan. Source: Courtesy Historic Jefferson Foundation

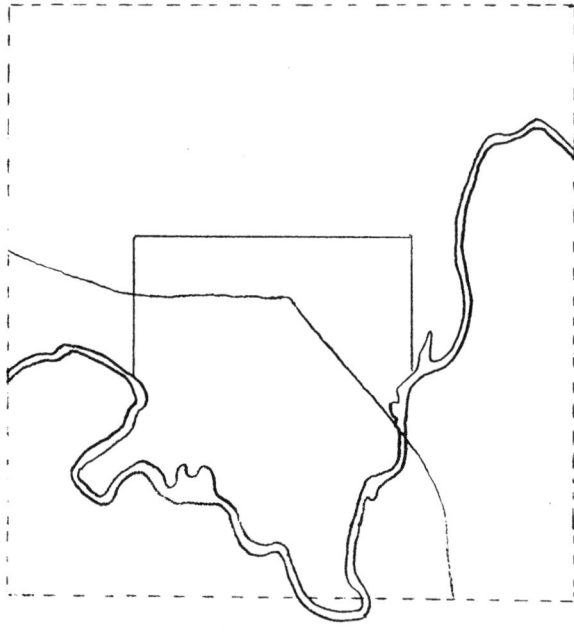

Fig. 12-2. Corporate Boundaries

- - - - Present City Limits
———— Probable 1850 City Limits

Unfortunately, there is no precise description or representation of the antebellum city limits. Although a town plan was supposed to be prepared, this appears only to have been done for the Urquhart Addition through the Eppinger map. This may be because the Alley Addition did not receive its definitive survey until January 1851; and the new survey did not result in a new map for that portion of the town showing street delineations. A unified town plan is not mentioned in the deed records, which continue to use the Hensey's 1846 and Eppinger's 1850 maps for the Urquhart Addition and Baker's 1848 map for the Alley Addition. In any case, as a practical matter, the town was not thought of as restricted to the corporate limits; as today, persons living outside of the corporate limits on the road to Daingerfield would have said that they lived in Jefferson.

The corporate limits were expanded in 1870 to include the Archer and Gillespie headrights on the west, the western portion of the Humphries headright on the east (from Moseley's Bridge on Black Cypress Bayou to McFarland's mill on Big Cypress Bayou), and a vast area between Big and Little Cypress bayous running from the east boundary of the Elias Hamilton headright on the east to the west boundary of the Reddick Overton headright on the west. This delineation did not appear on any maps and is incompatible with Graham's 1869 maps.

Although the city limits now extend a short distance south of Big Cypress Bayou, persons living south of the bayou in antebellum times were generally thought of as living outside of town, which was reasonable because it was part of Harrison County. However, the expanded corporate limits north of the bayou in 1870 were generally expressive of what people meant when they spoke of Jefferson.

Civic Order

"By the way, Jefferson is one of the most orderly towns in Texas; and the reason is that the corporation laws are rigidly enforced." This observation was made by Robert Loughery of the Marshall *Texas Republican* in April 1855, and Loughery knew Jefferson well. Although Jefferson was a port town frequented by steamboat crews and ox-wagon drivers, civic order appears to have been the norm, apart from an occasional killing. The only mention of disorderly conduct in Jefferson appears in the *Jefferson Herald*, as quoted by the June 16, 1855, *Texas Republican*: "The Summer fights opened on Marshall street on Tuesday. There was some clubbing, shooting, and stampeding." Loughery's comment on Jefferson was made in the context of his continuous concern about problems in Marshall, an example of which appears in the February 18, 1854, *Texas Republican*:

> It would seem as if the rowdies have again taken possession of our streets, making night hideous with their orgies. On Monday night we saw two or three youths whooping and hallowing on the public square, and pouring forth a strain of blasphemy and blackguardism, perfectly disgraceful; firing off pistols, and running to and fro, snapping caps at each other. From the number of fire-arms discharged during the last week, at night, a stranger would have supposed that our town was in a state of siege. Have we no town corporation? Or are our quiet and order loving citizens content to put up with such a state of affairs.

The Texas Act that incorporated Jefferson in 1850 gave the town the capacity to create ordinances, whose enforcement was in the hands of the mayor and the town constable or marshal. A set of town ordinances was adopted by the aldermen and the mayor on March 15, 1854, and published as a small booklet titled *Charter, By-Laws and Ordinances of the Town of Jefferson* by the *Jefferson Herald* in that month under the signature of the mayor, William Saufley, and the recorder, John Waskom. The ordinances are largely concerned with prohibited activities and attendant fines.

The first ordinance delineates the corporate limits.

The second ordinance is concerned with the quiet and good order of the town and prohibits: 1) lying in streets, alleys, or public places in a state of intoxication; 2) breaches of the peace, affray, or riot; 3) quarreling or using threatening, violent, or abusive language in public places; 4) getting drunk and using loud, noisy, and boisterous language; 5) behaving in a rude, riotous, and turbulent manner; 6) indecent conduct or any mischief or any kind of disturbance; 7) firing a pistol or other firearms, with the exception of heads of families slaughtering cattle or hogs for food on their own property; and 8) riding or driving in a furious or disorderly manner through the streets or passways.

The third ordinance is concerned with the Sabbath and prohibits business activities, with the exception of doctors, druggists, and hotel keepers. Fines ranged from $5 to $10.

The fourth ordinance is concerned with town cleanliness and prohibits: 1) disposal of dead animals, filth, or other nuisances into streets, alleys, or open lots or enclosures; and 2) allowing a dead animal to remain on private property more than 24 hours. Owners of animals that died any place within the corporate limits were required to remove the same within 24 hours. Removals by the town marshal cost $1.50.

The fifth ordinance is largely concerned with establishing the following tax rates: 1) 15 cents per $100 on value of real and personal property within the corporate limits; 2) 20 cents per $100 on all goods, wares, and merchandise imported into the town, with assessment and collection to be made every three months beginning on January 1; 3) $50 annual license tax on retailers of spiritous liquors in quantities less than a quart; 4) $10 annual license tax on taverns and houses of entertainment; 5) $10 annual license tax on wagons, carts, drays, and other vehicles employed within the corporate limits in transporting goods, wares, merchandise, timber, lumber, firewood or anything else for pay, with the license number to be posted on the vehicle by tin or painted sign; 6) $50 annual license tax on billiard tables and $20 annual license tax on nine and ten pin alleys, with fines from $20 to $50 for operating on Sundays; 7) $25 license tax on circuses, exhibitions, and shows taxed by the state and $5 for each event on those not taxed by the state; 8) $1 poll tax on white males over 21; 9) $10 per year on livery stables; 10) wharfage tax of $20 for every steamboat landing; and 11) $15 per year on toll bridges and ferries. This ordinance also establishes a fine of from $1 to $10 for using fire within 100 yards of cotton sheds at the landing, except lights by steamboats or for the purpose of recovering or discharging freight.

The sixth ordinance is concerned with the formation of patrols, which were civilian surveillance units with a military cast that patrolled the streets of the town from 9 to 12 from Monday through Saturday, functioning much like policemen on walking beats, but apparently without the capacity to engage in arrests. One captain and two privates from each of two companies were assigned responsibilities by the mayor for one month. This apparently was an uncompensated activity, because there were fines for noncompliance. The marshal patrolled for one hour in the afternoon on Sundays.

The seventh ordinance establishes an annual license tax of $15 for bakeries, candy shops, eating houses, and beer shops.

The eighth ordinance concerns the method by which the town marshal is to collect taxes on citizens and property holders, which are to be similar to those of the county assessor and tax collector.

The ninth ordinance prohibits the explosion of firecrackers and riding, driving, or leading any horse, mule, or oxen on any sidewalk or pavement.

The tenth ordinance prohibits the keeping of more than 12 pounds of gunpowder in tin canisters in stores, shops, and offices.

The eleventh ordinance prohibits steamboats from discharging freights on Sundays, with a fine of $50 and elimination of consignee responsibilities for picking up discharged freight.

Almost all of the 1854 ordinances are concerned with civic order, including the Sunday prohibitions, which were concerned with civic order in a larger sense. The exceptions are the provisions concerning taxation and the obvious concern for fires, particularly in the warehouse district. The exemption for steamboat firebaskets was necessary because they provided the only illumination for nighttime discharge and receipt of freight, which was common. It is notable that provisions "Concerning the Quiet and Good Order of the Town" should immediately follow the delineation of the town boundaries, which was not the case with the 1870 *Digest of the Laws of the City of Jefferson, Texas*, where they are given much less prominence. It is also notable that citizens were assigned formal responsibilities for civil order through the formation of patrols, a town citizen responsibility that paralleled county citizen responsibilities for road maintenance. This was a period in which citizens played a more active role in what are now considered governmental functions.

One ordinance that was probably disregarded was the Sunday prohibition on the discharge of steamboat freights. It is known that similar prohibitions were disregarded by everyone in Shreveport, including the civil authorities who promulgated the ordinances. This was because steamboats could not devise schedules to assure that they would not arrive at a port on Sunday, and it was much too expensive to pay a day's wages to steamboat crews and officers when the vessel was idle. The ordinance would either have been disregarded in Jefferson, or fines would have been paid, or steamboats would have discharged freight downstream of the town.

The enforcement of ordinances was not simply a matter of political action. Civic disorder was incompatible with the smooth flow of economic activity, which was a complex interrelated system in Jefferson. Although there is no direct evidence, it can be assumed that the business class, which was heavily involved in the political affairs of the town, was instrumental in the rigid enforcement of the corporation laws. The town also benefited from compactness, which made enforcement of ordinances both necessary and possible. It should be noted that the "summer fights" occurred during the season when business activity was at a minimum.

It is a sociological truism that unmarried young males are the primary source of disorder in communities. There were many unmarried young males in Jefferson (exceeding the number of married males), and the number of young males far exceeded the number of young females. This would seem to provide ideal conditions for social disorder, but Jefferson was a fairly peaceful town. In addition to the enforcement of ordinances, this was due to the fact that all young males appear to have been employed, and much of the employment consumed a large part of the day and night or was hard physical labor that necessitated rest. Most young males lived in private residences, often the residence of their employer, and the rest lived in hotels that did not allow entrance late at night. Opportunities for mischief were few, the town was not large enough to provide anonymity, and businessmen exercised a great deal of control over their employees.

City Records

The city records describe the decisions of the mayor and aldermen concerning the governance of the town. The mayor and aldermen were normally elected annually at the end of October by free white male adult residents. Aldermen were elected at large until October 1860, when the wards were delineated. The city records also cover the activities of the marshal and, to a lesser extent, the treasurer, both of whom were appointed. The marshal, as constable, was responsible for enforcement of the city ordinances and, as administrator, for the conduct of public works. The marshal was appointed from among the citizens, and the treasurer was appointed from among the aldermen. A recorder, who was usually the treasurer, kept the city minutes.

Meetings do not appear to have taken place in a separate public building. Meetings prior to November 1859 were held at the mayor's office, after which they are recorded as occurring in the Corporation Hall or the Council Hall. Williamson Freeman was paid $60 for 14 months' rental of the meeting room in December 1861. This was obviously for Freeman's Hall, which was completed in July 1860.

The decisions of the mayor and aldermen were largely restricted to the corporation limits, although they sometimes extended outward to include things like the city cemetery. Unfortunately, there is no precise delineation of the corporate limits. A committee was supposed to be established in December 1857 to draw up and obtain signatures for a petition to the Texas Legislature to change the town boundaries, but this does not appear to have been done. In May 1860, the mayor was to request the county surveyor to lay out the town boundaries and the marshal to establish a list of taxable properties. This was probably done and served as the basis for the ward delineations in October. The survey has been lost, and the ward delineations indicate nothing about the outward boundaries.

The extant city records, which are contained in a vault in the city hall, begin on November 4, 1857. The September 1, 1876, *Daily Jimplecute* says that many of the early records of the town burned during James Elliott's administration after the Civil War, that Stephen Ellis was elected the first mayor in 1850, and that he was succeeded by James Brickell in 1851. Brickell was probably reelected in October 1852. He was succeeded by William Saufley in October 1853, because Saufley is mentioned as mayor in March 1854 district court minutes. It was under Saufley's name that the 1854 ordinances were published. He probably remained mayor until October 1857, when he was succeeded by Ward Taylor, Jr., who was mayor when the city records begin.

Little is known about municipal affairs from 1851 until the end of 1857, other than the publication of the 1854 ordinances and the establishment of a public ferry in 1853, a wharf in 1854, and a bridge in 1855. Caroline Leavitt, as administratrix of the estate of Israel Leavitt, brought suit against the former mayor, Brickell, and aldermen in March 1854. The suit was joined by the then-mayor Saufley. A judgment was made in favor of Leavitt in September. In March 1856, Allen Urquhart took legal action against Mayor Saufley in connection with his long-standing dispute with the town over rights to the bridge. A notice signed by Mayor Saufley dated July 6, 1857, and appearing in the November 7 *Eastern Texas Gazette* stated that the proceedings of the mayor's court would appear in the newspapers.

In November 1857, Taylor was mayor, Thomas Owens was marshal, and the aldermen were Benjamin Terry, Anselm Prewitt, William Mayberry, and John Stewart. An election was held at the end of the month to fill the fifth alderman seat, which had been vacated by John Speake, who had also served as treasurer. Noble Birge was elected with 45 votes, surpassing John Cocke's 23 and William Perry's 20. The total votes cast (88) provide a sense of the dimensions of the electorate in late 1857.

Thomas Swanson was appointed marshal in February 1858 to replace Owens, who had resigned. Taylor resigned as mayor in March 1858, and Saufley was overwhelmingly elected for another term. Swanson resigned in April because of bad health (and was soon to die) and was replaced by Jesse Veal. In October, Saufley was reelected, and Benjamin Terry, Charles Stanley, William Mayberry, John Speake, and William Brooks were elected aldermen. In October 1859, William Hodge was elected mayor and is listed as such in the census, and Charles Stanley, William Torrans, Noble Birge, Bass Nichols, and James Murphy were elected aldermen. James Moore was appointed marshal.

Wards were established in October 1860. Ward 1 was northeast of Vale Street and Line Street; Ward 2 was southwest of Vale Street to Jackson Street and Line Street; Ward 3 was southwest of Jackson Street and Jefferson Avenue; Ward 4 was southwest of Baker Street to Jefferson Avenue; and Ward 5 was northeast of Baker Street. In late October, William Mayberry was elected alderman from Ward 1; John Smith was elected alderman from Ward 2; Samuel Nimmo was elected alderman from Ward 3; Richard Crump was elected alderman from Ward 4; and Bass Nichols was elected alderman from Ward 5. Crump did not take the oath of office (for reasons not explained), and James Murphy was elected in November to fill the vacant seat from Ward 4. James Eldridge was appointed marshal.

Nimmo resigned from the Ward 3 seat in January 1861 because of ill health (and was soon to die) and was replaced by W. J. C. Rogers in April, who was replaced by Thomas Sedberry in June. Mayberry resigned from the Ward 1 seat in February and was replaced by Benjamin Terry in April. Bass Nichols resigned in April because he had moved from Ward 5 and was replaced by James Campbell in June.

Benjamin Terry was elected mayor in October 1861 with 97 votes over John Penman with 39. George Terry was elected in Ward 1 over E. W. Taylor with 22 total votes cast; John Smith was elected in Ward 2 over William Perry and G. Wacker with 49 total votes cast; Thomas Sedberry was elected unopposed in Ward 3 with 23 votes; James Murphy was elected unopposed in Ward 4 with 13 votes; and A. D. Tullis was elected in Ward 5 over James Campbell with 19 total votes cast. The distribution of the votes by ward gives some idea of residential locations.

The first major act of the aldermen in the extant city records was to establish a new set of ordinances. These were essentially a repetition of the 1854 ordinances. The only substantive changes were in tax rates and the inclusion of restrictions on the activities of slaves. These were later supplemented by ordinances concerning sidewalk obstructions, prostitutes, and taxes.

Towns cannot function without revenue, which means taxes. The treasurer kept books on revenues and expenditures, but all of these have disappeared. Robert Loughery of the Marshall *Texas Republican* commended Jefferson in October 1854 for publishing in the *Jefferson Herald* an "Annual Report of the Corporation" showing the amounts collected and disbursed within the past year (which Marshall did not do). Similar reports and other public notices appeared in the *Eastern Texas Gazette* (later *Jefferson Gazette*) in 1859 and in the *Herald and Gazette* in 1860, but all of these have disappeared. As a consequence, other than the fact that the town was $1,252.02 in the black in April 1860, the only perspective that can be obtained on revenues is in the tax structure outlined in the ordinances, and the only perspective that can be obtained on expenditures is in the disbursements that would have been entailed by the public works described in the city records.

State taxes on personal property and real estate, including city lots, were collected at the county level and appear in the tax rolls. The 1854 ordinances contain a city tax of 15 cents on every $100 of real and personal property, which was reduced to 10 cents in 1857. The reason for the May 1860 request for the county surveyor to lay out the city boundaries was so that the marshal could prepare a list of taxable properties. In addition, a January 1860 ordinance required property holders to pay a $2.50 street tax. However, this was a uniform tax that bore no relation to property values.

The 1854 ordinances contain a poll tax of $1 on all white males over 21, which was replaced in 1857 by a $1 street tax on white males over 18 and under 45. This was either replaced or supplemented by a May 1858 ordinance requiring all white males subject to road duty to pay a tax of $5, which was to be put into a special fund for street improvements.

The 1854 ordinances contain a tax of 20 cents on every $100 of goods and merchandise imported into the town, with assessments and collections to be made every three months. This probably refers to export as well as import commodities. The rate was reduced to 15 cents in 1857. This would have been a lucrative source of revenue if rigidly enforced because of the high volume of trade passing through the town. This was in addition to the merchandise tax collected by the state.

The 1854 ordinances contain a wharfage tax of $20 per steamboat landing. This tax was in existence before the wharf was built in 1854 and referred to use of the landing rather than use of a wooden structure. This was replaced in 1857 by a wharfage tax of five cents per ton, referring to the tonnage capacity of the boat rather than what it was carrying. The rate was increased to eight cents per ton in December 1858. Similar language was used in January 1861 with "repealed" marked next to it. The wharfage tax may have been repealed to discourage docking downstream of the town.

The largest class of taxes were annual licenses to operate various businesses, which were similar to the county occupational taxes:

1. Saloons—$50 in 1854, $250 in 1857
2. Taverns, houses of entertainment—$10 in 1854, $25 in 1857
3. Local wagons, carts, drays—$10 in 1854, $25 in 1857, $2 in 1859 and $5 for wood haulers
4. Billiard tables—$50 in 1854 and 1857
5. Ten-pin alleys—$20 in 1854 and 1857
6. Circuses, menageries—$25 in 1854, $20 in 1857
7. Other performances—$5 in 1854 and 1857
8. Livery stables—$10 in 1854, $20 in 1857
9. Toll bridges, ferries—$15 in 1854, $50 in 1857
10. Confectionaries—$15 in 1854, $25 in 1857
11. Beer shops, candy shops—$15 in 1854, $20 in 1857
12. Eating houses, restaurants—$15 in 1854, $20 in 1857
13. Shooting pistol galleries—$25 in 1859

The primary function of city government was street maintenance, and a standing committee on streets was appointed in November 1857. There are no descriptions of Jefferson's antebellum streets. It is not even known how many of the streets on town maps were laid out and functional. This should not be surprising given the fact that some streets on present city maps do not exist or terminate in wooded areas.

The earliest description of Jefferson's streets is provided by the editor of the Shreveport *South-Western* in 1867: "Who ever laid off the streets evidently had no idea of the future of the place. The main street is about as wide as a common alley, both sides of which are built up with one-story wooden buildings.... The streets are in almost the same condition as when they came from the hands of the maker, except perhaps here and there, where some enterprising swine has improvised a wallow. And the sidewalks—what a burlesque!" The main street referred to was Dallas. It can be assumed that the conditions described were no better before the war.

The streets were of dirt, soggy when it rained and dusty when it was hot. They were constantly disturbed by ox-wagons hauling merchandise to and from town; by the numerous wagons, carts, and drays operating in town; by cattle passing through town on their way to local meat markets and the meat packing plants or to steamboats for live transport to the New Orleans fresh meat markets; by immigrants and businessmen passing through town and using various modes of transport; by stagecoaches; and by the numerous horses that were used for personal conveyance. As a consequence, they needed to be constantly graded. As with all public works at the time, the grading was done by contractors.

The sidewalks were raised planking over timber supports. The extent of sidewalks is unknown, but they were probably limited to the major mercantile streets such as Dallas and Marshall. Sidewalks appear to have been privately financed by property owners but publicly constructed and maintained, because timber and lumber are mentioned in contracts for street repair. The 1857 ordinances provide a fine for riding, driving, or leading horses, mules, and oxen on sidewalks and for obstructing passage by leaving merchandise on sidewalks (for more than one hour in 1858, increased to more than 24 hours in 1859).

In November 1857, the marshal was authorized to have six racks put up for hitching horses on the major streets, beginning with Marshall. In June 1861, an ordinance required property holders to keep the gutters in front of their premises cleared out. This probably referred to ditches and may have been largely confined to residential areas. In addition, mention is made of wooden box drains, which appear to be street related. In August 1862, Richard Figures was paid $10.50 for brick used in streets. The number of bricks was small, and what they were used for is unknown. The first mention of a brick sidewalk was after the Civil War in connection with Hinche Mabry's hotel and the sidewalk may have been built by Mabry as part of the hotel premises.

With respect to health and sanitation, various ordinances prohibited the disposal of animal carcasses and other refuse in streets, alleys, and open lots and required the removal of dead animals within 24 hours. Jesse Veal was paid $2.50 for removing a dead horse from the bayou in July 1858. A September 1861 ordinance required that privies be at least 10 feet deep and that lime be thrown in at least every two weeks. Modest efforts along these lines probably did little to affect the overall conditions of sanitation, which were dominated by the discharge of animal wastes from the Stanley & Nimmo meatpacking plant above the landing area and by the feces and urine of horses, oxen, cattle, and domestic animals that must have been a permanent feature of the city streets.

City government was active in the fight against the smallpox epidemic in February 1859, ordering that houses with smallpox be barricaded, with a fine of $50 and imprisonment at the discretion of the mayor. Corporation script was issued to defray the expense of waiting on the sick. Doctors such as W. J. C. Rogers were paid for medical services. Saufley was paid $200 in October 1859 by the incoming Hodge administration, apparently for extraordinary efforts during the epidemic. The epidemic precipitated a report on the sanitary conditions of the town in May 1859.

There was no fire department or fire engine. Ordinances prohibited setting off firecrackers, restricted the amounts in which gun powder could be stored, and prohibited the lighting of fires near cotton sheds at the landing, except for lights needed by steamboats or for receiving and discharging freight. Firefighting was the responsibility of citizens, and water to quench fires was obtained from the bayou and from private wells. In December 1858, Charles Stanley was paid $38 for building a public well; and in February 1862, A. D. Tullis was paid $3.25 for new buckets and chains for the public well. The well was probably built primarily for firefighting, although it may also have been used for public water supply, particularly for horses.

With respect to law enforcement and safety, there was no police department. The mayor acted as chief magistrate and the marshal as constable. The marshal and private citizens had patrol duties, which appear to have concentrated more heavily on the activities of slaves as events elsewhere in the nation raised public concerns. There was a near-prohibition on the firing of pistols in town and fines for riotous

Municipal Affairs

behavior and reckless driving. In March 1860, James Hosack was paid $1 for putting a lock in the jail. The town apparently had its own jail, which was supplemented by a county jail sometime after November 1860.

Paupers were cared for at the city level as well as the county level. In April 1860, Mrs. Lynch, the wife of an Irish laborer with six children, was paid $84 for the care of paupers, with the stipulation that services to one of them be discontinued. H. L. Erwin was paid for a pauper coffin in September 1859.

Jefferson's original graveyard was located in the southwest portion of the Urquhart Addition, as shown on the 1846 Hensey and 1850 Eppinger maps in an area that came to be known as Sandtown (Fig. 12-3). Although marked "Public Grave Yard" on the maps, this was a site designation rather than an indication of ownership, and the land was never conveyed to the city. People were buried in this cemetery; but as the name Sandtown suggests, the soil conditions were inappropriate, and the cemetery was moved to the northeast where it now is before

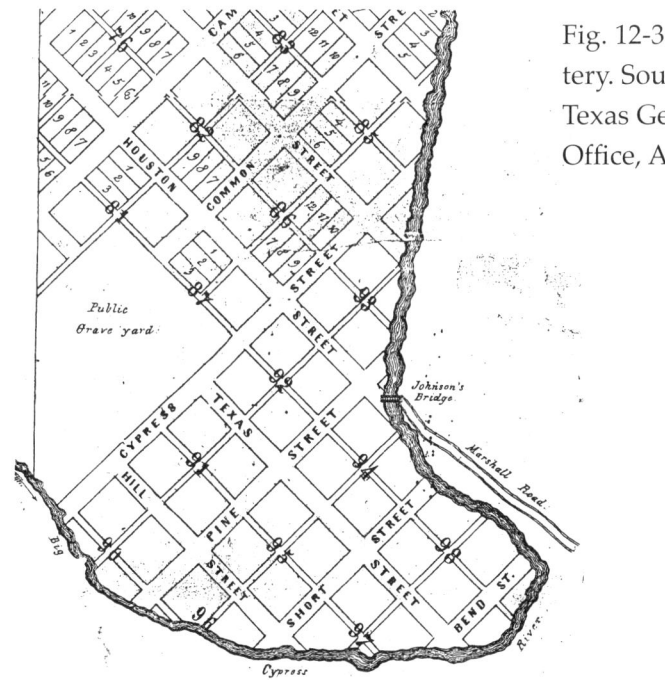

Fig. 12-3. Early Cemetery. Source: Courtesy Texas General Land Office, Austin

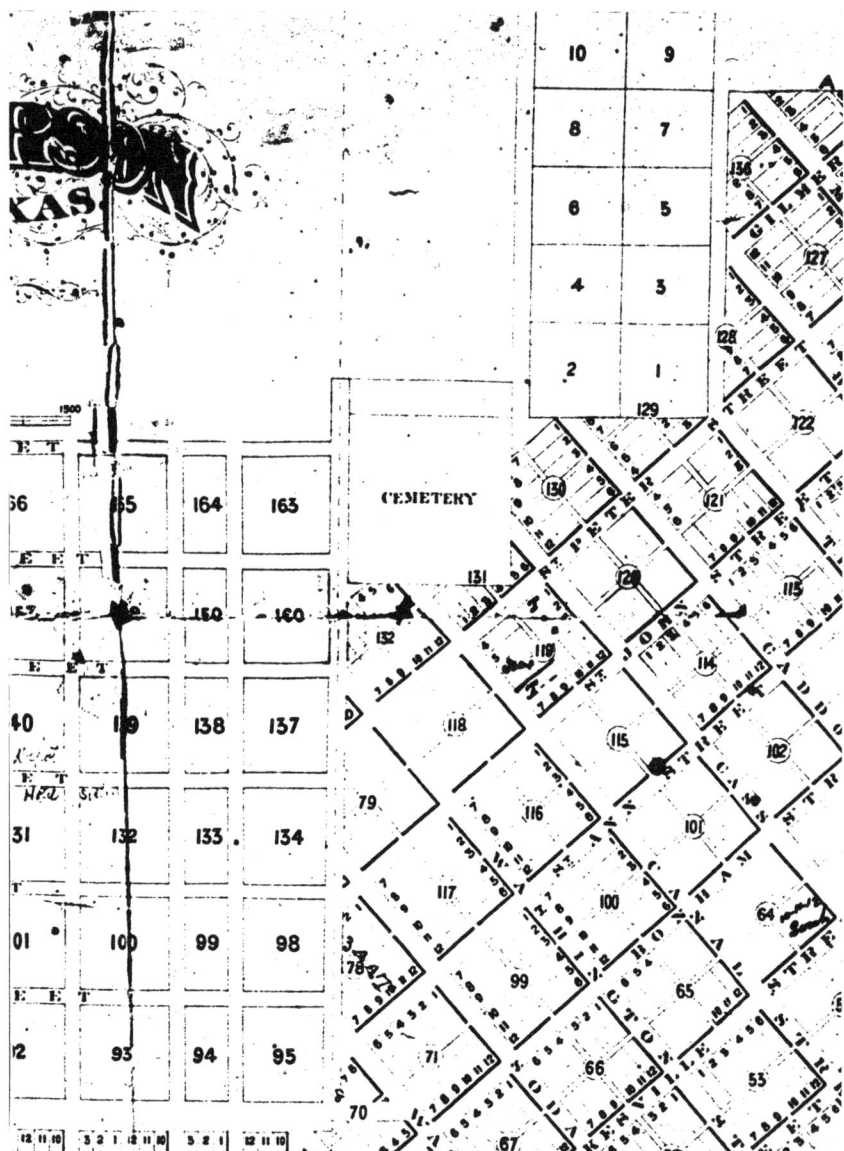

Fig. 12-4. Present Cemetery

the Civil War on land owned by Urquhart that was probably outside the city limits at that time (Fig. 12-4).

When this happened is not known. The earliest extant gravestone is that of the Rev. Benjamin Foscue, who died on January 4, 1850. This may have been a reburial from the old graveyard, which is still shown on Eppinger's 1850 map. However, there is another gravestone for 1850, four for 1852, and burials for each year thereafter. This strongly suggests that the changeover to the new graveyard took place in late 1849, with a few years of burials leading to dissatisfaction with conditions in the old graveyard. The two earliest extant gravestones are in sections F and G; and all of the gravestones through 1860 are in sections A–G, T, and Y.

The first clear evidence of the existence of the new graveyard is a contract made by the aldermen with William Perry in November 1857 to clear off and fence an additional three acres of graveyard. However, this transaction indicates that the graveyard was already in existence. In April 1858, the portion of the graveyard west of the north and south gates was reserved, with no one to be buried until it was laid out. A committee was formed to present a plan for laying out the graveyard, and a plan was adopted toward the end of April. A decision was made in November 1858 to open Line Street to the graveyard, with a stipulation in September 1859 that the road be 40 feet wide.

In December 1857, Mayor Taylor was given the duty of looking into an appropriate lot for establishing a public market house. In June 1859, provisions were made for the preparation of a draft plan for the market house. Specifications were prepared in June 1861, bid requests were solicited, and Richard Crump submitted the only bid, which was accepted in July. Crump's contract, which was described in February 1862, called for a 40-foot by 84-foot two-story structure with brick floor and columns. Crump was to have rental rights to market privileges for 20 years, after which the building would revert to the city. The city would provide ordinances prohibiting street competition from street peddlers and hawkers, and the mayor and aldermen would have the use of a room in the upper story for their meetings. It does not appear that a public market house was completed until after the Civil War.

William Perry received a state contract for clearing out Cypress Bayou and Caddo Lake down to the state boundary in August 1857. The contract was for $21,298, of which one-fifth was a local subscription match whose source is uncertain. In September 1859, Perry and Ward Taylor, Sr., were invited by a committee composed by Williamson Freeman, John Murphy, Richard Crump, R. A. Smiley, and Bass Nichols to accompany them on an examination of Perry's work. In November 1859, Perry was paid $500 by the city for the balance of the first, all of the second, and part of the third installments of the city's bayou and lake improvement efforts. However, when Perry submitted a final bill of $1,150, a committee of James Murphy, Thomas Sedberry, and John Smith went back through the city records, found that the aldermen had never authorized subscriptions, and determined that the payments made to Perry in the past were a mistake.

The Memphis, El Paso & Pacific was intended as a transcontinental railroad that would be built west from Clarksville, with iron to be brought in by a branch line from Moore's Landing on the Sulphur Fork. However, low water on the upper Red River subverted this plan, and it was decided to build a branch line out of Jefferson, only six miles of which were completed before the war. In July 1860, the aldermen passed a motion to take $6,000 in stock in the railroad with a specified payment schedule if acceptable to the company. A meeting was held at the Cumberland Presbyterian Church in late July to discuss the proposal, which was amended in September to $5,000 with six installments over two years. Whether any action was taken on this proposal is unknown.

Allen Urquhart had been in a long-standing dispute with the city over ferry, bridge, and wharf privileges. In November 1850, Urquhart was operating a toll ferry and bridge at the foot of Houston Street. The city established a free public ferry to the east in May 1853 and took control of the bridge in February 1855. Urquhart owned part of the land south of Dallas and between Polk and the Perry Claim. The exceptions on the east side of the landing area were most of Fractional Block 10, which Williamson Freeman sold to John Hobdy in February 1859, a 50-foot lot in Fractional Block 10 purchased by Freeman as guardian for his son Hugh in 1852, and a triangular piece of land adjacent to the Perry Claim purchased by William Perry from Urquhart in January

1860. The city built a public wharf in the landing area in early 1854 that charged a wharfage fee. In June 1860, William Mayberry entered into an agreement with Urquhart, Perry, and Freeman as agent for Hobdy to build a wharf for them that would extend to the east from the public wharf and for which they would charge a wharfage fee equivalent to the city fee.

In March 1856, Urquhart sued the city for bridge privileges. In November 1858, the mayor conferred with Urquhart's attorneys to see whether resolution could be reached with respect to the bridge and ferry privileges. The city was concerned with gaining full control of the wharf, including its public and private components and the land on which they were built. A resolution was reached in September 1860 in which the city relinquished its claim to bridge and ferry privileges to Urquhart in exchange for wharves and wharf privileges from Polk Street to the Perry Claim, with the exception of Hugh Freeman's 50-foot lot. Urquhart was also paid $1,150 for excavations and other expenses in connection with the construction of his portion of the private wharf.

In January 1861, Mayberry, who was an alderman at the time, was paid by the city for his work on the wharf. During the same month, an ordinance was passed prohibiting steamboats from tying to wharf timbers. Also during the same month, Freeman presented a claim for Hobdy and his son Hugh to 320 feet of the wharf in front of Lots 1–6 in Block 10 on the north side of Dallas. In the next month, the city agreed to pay Freeman as agent for Hobdy one-third of the wharf revenues. Freeman was said to pretend to own a portion of the wharf in February 1862 when the city was making repairs. He objected to some of the timber work that was being done, but was disregarded, in spite of the fact that he was acting as an agent for Hobdy and as a guardian for his son Hugh. In June 1862, the treasurer reported that $2,200 had been issued in script for wharf improvements (probably in addition to what had been spent through wharfage fees). In April 1863 the city agreed to pay Freeman as agent for Hobdy $3,300 for the wharf portion and the land on which it was built. This agreement was consummated by separate transactions between Hobdy and the city and Hugh Freeman and the city in 1863. By these actions the city gained clear title to Jefferson's most important infrastructure feature.

18. Wharves

Wharves were uncommon because they were costly; and the great disparity between high-water and low-water levels on the waters of the Mississippi River and its tributaries presented special design problems. The vast majority of landings were of dirt and were accessed by steamboats through the simple procedure of running the bow into the shore and placing a plank between the boat and the shore. Jefferson was unusual in that it invested heavily in public and private wharves. The only other wharf in the vicinity of Jefferson was at Swanson's Landing on Caddo Lake, but this was built specifically for the unloading of railroad iron for the Southern Pacific.

Wharves are not mentioned in Jefferson's articles of incorporation, which gave the town power to create ordinances to fix the place or places of landing and anchoring for all watercraft, to establish a system of inspection over persons employed by watercraft at the landing, to regulate the prices of draymen, and to "make all other regulations which may contribute to the better administration of the affairs of said corporation." The ordinances that were published in March 1854 established license fees for draymen, prohibited fires within 100 yards of cotton sheds with the exception of recovering or discharging freight, established a Sabbath prohibition on the discharge of steamboat freights, and established a wharfage tax of $20 for every steamboat that arrived at the landing.

In the terminology of the day, a wharfage tax did not necessarily refer to the existence of a wooden wharf, because such fees were also charged for dirt landings. Although Jefferson had a wooden wharf by the time the ordinances were published, the tax probably went back to early 1851—the 1854 ordinances were simply the published form of decisions that had previously been made by the town aldermen. Because bridges and ferries are mentioned in these documents, it is apparent that wharves were not topical when the town achieved and implemented its legal status, which was a surprising oversight.

Prior to the erection of the first public wharf in 1854, the landing area was of sloped dirt. Because the main deck of steamboats ran only slightly above the water even when they were without freight, it was necessary to excavate perpendicular natural banks at an angle down to the low-water level. Otherwise, a boat arriving at a dirt landing during low water would have to extend a plank upward to reach the shore, which would have made it difficult to offload or onload freight. Consequently, graded banks sloping gradually down to the point of low water were standard for dirt landings. Grading of the dirt landing would have been the first public contribution to the improvement of the landing area.

The landing area was composed of the warehouses surrounding the turning basin and the landing proper, which was referred to as the levee. Steamboats pushed as close to shore as possible at a 45-degree angle and ran a plank to the shore. Items were transported up and down the sloping bank by hand and were placed on a relatively flat area below Dallas, where they were picked up and deposited by drays that ran between the levee and the warehouses. Constant movement of deckhands, drays, and passengers on the levee produced highly eroded conditions that were dusty when it was dry and muddy when it was wet. Heavy rains produced deep mud that was nearly impassable.

When a town decided to invest in greater efficiencies in freight movements, the choice was between cobblestones and wood. Cobblestones, for obvious reasons, had to follow the slope of the preexisting graded dirt landing. However, this was also the case for most wooden wharves because sloped wooden wharves avoided the problems of water-level fluctuations encountered by horizontal wharves. All of Jefferson's wharves where of the sloped wooden variety, following the contour of the preexisting graded dirt landing. Pilings were driven to the land surface, and planks were secured to timber undersupports that ran from the water's edge uphill. This design enabled wharf access during low-water periods and during higher-water periods when the lower portion of the wharf was inundated.

Public Wharf

Jefferson's first public wooden wharf was completed in early 1854, with construction probably begun in the summer of 1853. It is first mentioned as functional in the March 18, 1854, Clarksville *Standard*: "The Lake is now navigable, and boats have doubtless arrived at Jefferson before this. Jefferson is still improving with the constant pace which it has kept for three years past. A fine wharf has been erected, giving facility for the loading and unloading of boats." There is no documentation concerning the placement or composition of this structure. However, it almost certainly followed the delineation of the bayou and

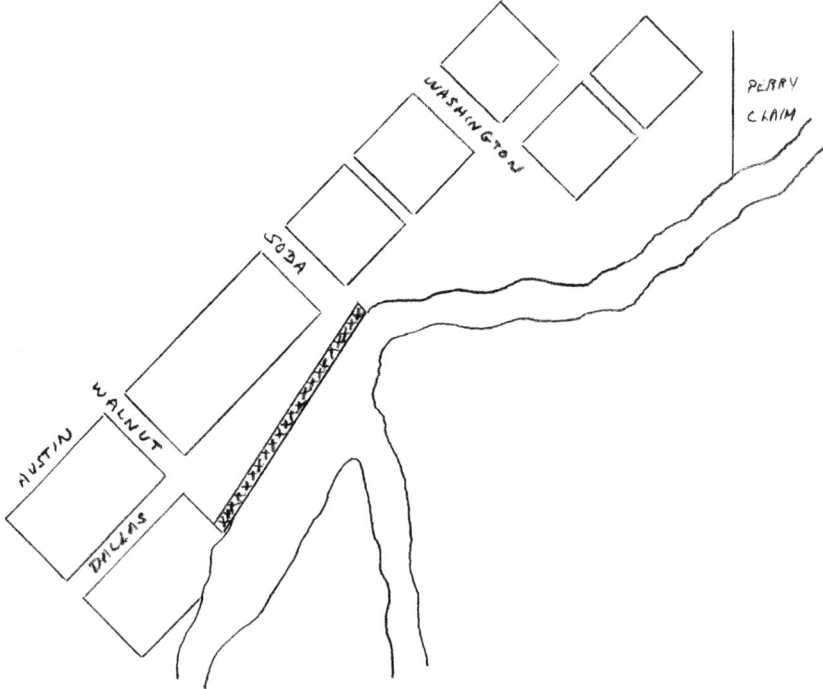

Fig. 13-1. 1854 Public Wharf

ran in a straight line between the west side of Walnut Street and the east side of Soda Street, fronting the Block 9 warehouses and including the public streets (Fig. 13-1).

That this wharf did not proceed east past Soda Street is known because a private wharf was built in that area in 1860. That it did not proceed west past Walnut Street is likely because that area included private land that was occupied by facilities beginning in 1845. The fate of this wharf is unknown. It apparently fell into disrepair during the latter years of the Civil War and the immediate postwar period, because the editor of the Shreveport newspaper, on a visit to Jefferson in January 1867, noted that Jefferson's landing was in worse condition than Shreveport's, which had only a dirt landing. A new public wharf was built by Asa Wright under contract in 1867.

Packery Wharf

Charles Stanley began advertising in January 1855 as a commission and forwarding merchant with a cotton warehouse on the east side of the foot of Houston Street. The frame warehouse was 15 feet above the water's edge because it was located in the floodplain, and it had a large door opening out onto the water. Because it was a cotton warehouse, it is obvious that Stanley expected navigation on Cypress Bayou to be extended above the landing area to at least the foot of Houston Street. The warehouse was converted into a furniture storeroom in March 1856 when Stanley was joined by Samuel Nimmo to form the firm of Stanley & Nimmo. The storeroom was modified in 1858 and an addition was constructed. These were the facilities for the Stanley & Nimmo packery, which opened in the winter of 1858. The facilities and stockyards covered the whole of Block 93 and fractional Block O on the bayou east of Houston Street and south of Cypress Street.

In conjunction with the establishment of the packery, Stanley and Chester Bulkley cleared Cypress Bayou of obstructions from J. M. & J. C. Murphy's warehouse in the landing area up to the packery. Bulkley participated in this project because he owned St. Catherine's Island. The editor of the *Jefferson Gazette*, who reported on these events in early October, indicated that the bank of the bayou from Marshall Street to the packery was above high water and expected to see the entire area occupied by warehouses within the next two years. In addition to the bayou clearing effort, construction had begun on a wharf at the foot of Marshall Street that was expected to be completed in a few weeks. Marshall Street ended at an embayment formed by the upstream split of the bayou at St. Catherine's Island and therefore offered room for a turning basin. Robert Loughery of the *Texas Republican* noted at the same time that the packery was "situated immediately on the bayou, and they have nothing to do but to roll the beef when packed from the warehouse on board of a steamboat," suggesting that the wharf was to extend somewhat upstream of Marshall Street.

Although Stanley & Nimmo went out of business in 1860, the facility and wharf continued to be used during the early years of the Civil War under other ownership. The wharf probably fell into disrepair thereafter, because the facility was abandoned during the latter part of the war.

Private Wharf

On June 6, 1860, William Mayberry signed an agreement with William Perry, Allen Urquhart, and Williamson Freeman as agent for John Hobdy to build a 650-foot wharf in the landing area. Freeman was acting as agent for his business partner Hobdy under a power of attorney granted in May:

> This is an agreement made and entered into this the 6th day of June 1860 between William Perry, Allen Urquhart, and W. M. Freeman for John M. Hobdy of the first part and W. K. Mayberry of the second part. Witnesseth that the party of the second part have this day and date bargained and agreed with the parties of the first part to build for them a wharf at the Steam Boat Landing at Jefferson, Marion County, Texas, six hundred and fifty feet in extent, for the sum of one dollar and seventy-five cents per running foot, in the following manner and materials herein described. Said materials are to be of post and white oak throughout, except the mud sills which may be of any other sound

lumber. The mud sills are to be no less than one foot in thickness after hewed. All the posts are to be ten feet long one foot square. Cap sills at convenient length and one foot square. This is to be a tie framed on the top of each said post of the same size and run back into the bank not less than 16 feet, to be square one foot at the end framed in the post. And to be framed into the mud sill with a dovetail and head. The top plate is to shouldered on and pinced (?) secure. All digging for the reception of work is to be done by the parties of the first part. And the party of the second part hereby binds himself to complete said work by the first day of October next. The said posts are to be placed eight feet apart from center to center. And all work to be done in workmanlike manner. Said party of the second part is to receive pay of the parties of the first part as the work progresses, not to exceed the amount of work done, and at the completion of the work the full amount may be considered due.

This agreement was clarified on June 26:

> Know all men by these present that we William Perry, Allen Urquhart and W. M. Freeman for John M. Hobdy have agreed with each other to build a wharf on the bayou in the City of Jefferson and have made and entered into a contract with William K. Mayberry to build the same as for contract entered into and on record. William Perry agrees to commence near his old shed and to build up to Allen Urquhart's line at his own expense. Then the above named Allen Urquhart builds from where William Perry stops at his own expense up to W. M. Freeman's or John M. Hobdy's line to Block Ten the east line. And then the above named W. M. Freeman for John M. Hobdy agrees to build from where A. Urquhart stops across from his lots on Block Ten at his own expense. And when the season com-

mences for wharfage, we agree to charge the same rate of wharfage of said Incorporation, and the same to be equally divided between us three. It is further agreed that this shall be our agreement for the term of five years, and longer if the above named parties think it to their interest. The season to commence the first October next, and the money to be divided every sixty days. Which we have signed our names and affixed our seals this 26th day June AD 1860.

The agreement and its clarification indicate that all necessary grading was to be done by Perry, Urquhart, and Freeman/Hobdy and that the wharf was to be constructed by Mayberry at $1.75 per running foot, with payment made to Mayberry by the three parties in terms of the distance that the wharf passed through their respective lands. Perry was to build from his old cotton shed to Urquhart's property, Urquhart was to build from where Perry left off to the east line of Block 10, and Freeman/Hobdy was to build from the east line of Block 10 to the western end of the wharf.

William Perry's land included the Perry Claim, which at that time was outside of the city limits and apparently contained Perry's old cotton shed. The Perry Claim line ran north from the point where the alley between Washington and Canal struck the bayou. Perry had also acquired from Urquhart in January 1860 a triangle of land immediately west of the Perry Claim that was south of Dallas and east of the alley that ran between Washington and Canal. This triangle was the location of new cotton sheds erected by Perry in August 1860.

Allen Urquhart owned the land from the triangle he sold to Perry to the east edge of Fractional Block 10 (the undivided southeast quadrant of Block 10 south of Dallas). Williamson Freeman had acquired from Urquhart a lot in Fractional Block 10 as guardian for his son Hugh in 1852 and the rest of Fractional Block 10 from Urquhart in 1858. Freeman transferred Fractional Block 10, with the exception of Hugh Freeman's lot, to his business partner John Hobdy in 1859.

Freeman had acquired all of the lots in Block 10 north of Dallas and operated as a receiving, forwarding, and commission merchant

Wharves

in a large warehouse on Lots 5 and 6 at the northeast corner of Dallas and Soda. Freeman transferred Lots 1–3 to Hobdy in 1859, and Freeman and Hobdy leased Lots 1–6 to Hiram Cutrer in May 1860; thus, neither was in business when the wharf was built but were obviously interested in increasing the value of their property as well as in securing wharfage fees.

The private wharf was apparently intended to tie into the public wharf, which probably ended at Soda on the west end of Block 10. It must have followed the delineation of the bayou and extended at least to the Perry Claim, which meant that it formed a slight V, with the west arm running about 320 feet and fronting the whole of Block 10 at an angle (Fig. 13-2). The private wharf was obviously built, or at least was in the process of being built, because it was part of subsequent transactions in which the city gained control of the entire wharf (including its private component) and all of the wharf lands south of Dallas to the bayou and from Polk to the Perry Claim. These transactions were

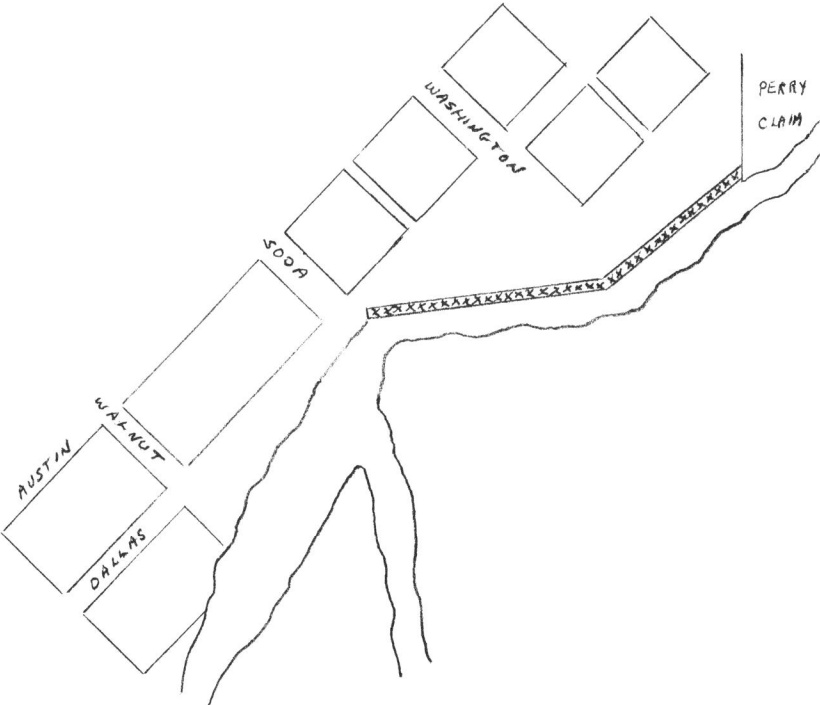

Fig. 13-2. 1860 Private Wharf

complex because they involved a private wharf with multiple owners and the land on which the public and private wharves had been constructed.

Combined Wharf

Urquhart through his headright was the original owner of all of the wharf lands south of Dallas in the landing area from Polk on the west to the Perry Claim on the east. The developable land in Block 8 south of Dallas had been sold early on, and part of the land east of Polk had been sold to Freeman and Perry. Ownership of the unplatted land south of Block 9 on which the public wharf had been built was apparently contestable, in spite of the fact that it had always been intended for a public landing.

Urquhart had a long-standing dispute with the city over control of the bridge and ferry at the foot of Houston and was anxious to have clear title to the privilege of operation. The city was anxious to have clear title to the public wharf and the lands on which it stood and to extinguish competition for wharfage fees from the private wharf. On September 12, 1860, Urquhart and the city reached a compromise. The city quit its claims to bridge and ferry privileges. In exchange, Urquhart quit his claims to all wharf lands south of Dallas from Polk to the Perry Claim, with the exception of Hugh Freeman's lot, but including the east 35 feet of Lot 10 in Block 8. The city also paid Urquhart $1,150 out of the wharf revenues for excavations and other expenses that he had incurred.

Although Perry appears to have been a participant in the building of the private wharf, there is nothing in the subsequent transactions to indicate that this was the case. The final resolution of the transactions was the establishment of public control over the wharf and wharf lands up to the Perry Claim. It is unlikely that the city would have neglected to include a portion of the private wharf if it had actually been built by Perry. A 650-foot wharf would not have extended into the Perry Claim, and the triangle that was purchased by Perry from Urquhart would not account for a third of the wharf. Freeman/Hobdy claimed 320 feet of the wharf, which was nearly half of the 650 feet; and Urquhart was the only other claimant before the city, suggesting that Perry never built his portion of the wharf.

In October 1860, Hobdy sold to Mary Geer one-half interest in Fractional Block 10 south of Dallas, with the exception of Hugh Freeman's lot. To enforce the September agreement with Urquhart, the city secured a court judgment against him in November. The land south of Blocks 10 and 11 from the east side of Soda to the Perry Claim and from Dallas to the water's edge was sold by the sheriff to Hobdy and Geer for $95.50 in October 1861. The tract delineations mention a wharf and wharf timbers that ran along the low-water line as the southern boundary of the property.

In January 1861, Mayberry was paid by the city for work that he had done on the wharf. In February, the city began paying Freeman/Hobdy one-third of the wharfage fees. Improvements were made to both portions of the wharf in 1861 and 1862. In April 1863, the city decided to pay Freeman/Hobdy $3,300 for their portion of the levee (apparently meaning the wharf and the land on which it was situated). During the same month, Hobdy and Geer sold the land south of Dallas with the exception of Hugh Freeman's lot to the city for $3,000. Hugh sold his lot to the city for $300 in July. By late 1863 the city had established clear public title and control over Jefferson's most important infrastructure feature.

14. Navigation

Navigation in its dual features of a navigable waterway and the use of that waterway by boats was the most important factor in Jefferson's creation and success. Jefferson was founded as a port, with the site chosen because it was the highest feasible point for steamboat navigation on Cypress Bayou. There were many landings that never developed into towns. Jefferson was able to grow commercially because it commanded a market area that was geographically large and continuously expanding in terms of population and production. The market area grew because navigation provided the opportunity for interior merchants and planters to import and export commodities. In this sense, navigation and location were the necessary and sufficient conditions for Jefferson's success.

Navigable waterways were useless without boats. The older forms of water carriage (pirogues, flatboats, and keelboats) would have allowed for the emergence of a modest settlement on Cypress Bayou; but it was the steamboat, and particularly the shallow-draft western river version developed by Capt. Henry Shreve, that provided the conditions for the emergence of a flourishing town. Unlike their predecessors, steamboats operated on the basis of steam power rather than manpower. They were ideal bulk freight carriers, moved quickly by the standards of the day, and had the capacity to move quickly upstream. Most of the people who arrived in northeast Texas and beyond came overland. Steamboats were an important factor in Jefferson's success because they were freight carriers, particularly suited to the transport of large quantities of cotton.

Steamboats were largely passive to freight opportunities—that is, they went to places that afforded opportunities for freight carriage rather than creating those opportunities themselves. On the other hand, cotton agriculture would not have developed throughout the South without navigation and would not have developed to the extent that it did without the efficiencies afforded by steamboat navigation. This was because cotton was an export commodity throughout the South (it was not grown for processing in local mills) and could not be sent to distant markets at a profit without water transportation. Overland transport, which was carried out by ox-wagons, was slow and expensive. Cotton agriculture developed throughout the South only in areas that were fairly close to navigable streams.

Conversely, navigation was of little use without overland transport because freight needed to be carried from its inland points of production and to its inland points of consumption. Ox-wagons were efficient freight carriers in relation to alternative overland transport modes where, as was the case throughout the lower South, there were practically no railroads. Navigation was ox-wagon dependent. Places like Jefferson should be thought of as steamboat and ox-wagon destinations and points of departure, with the two transport modes dependent on each other for the volume of traffic.

Jefferson would not have been possible were it not for the Great Raft on Red River, which provided sufficient diversion of water to make the Cypress Bayou and the Lakes route navigable. It would not have come into existence if there had been a well-developed rail system in the lower South, which would have made a port at that point unnecessary. The existence of the Great Raft also contributed to Jefferson's prosperity by diverting some of the upper Red River trade to Jefferson that would otherwise have been carried on the Red River. This diverted trade was of sufficient dimensions to cause Jefferson to be opposed to raft removal, apart from any concerns about possible implications for the navigability of the route.

The route was composed of Cypress Bayou, Caddo Lake, Soda Lake (now extinct), and Twelvemile Bayou, which emptied into the

Red River. It was generally navigable when the Red River was navigable, but required improvements to make it efficient. If there was sufficient water in Soda Lake, boats could usually get to Jefferson. Between the foot of Caddo Lake and Black Cypress Bayou (which emptied into Big Cypress Bayou six miles below Jefferson where Smithland was located), the backwater effects of the raft created a slackwater (or lake-like) condition that provided ease of navigation. Above the confluence with Black Cypress Bayou, Big Cypress Bayou was much more shallow, which during low-water periods necessitated the pulling of boats over mud or the diversion of commodities to a low-water road that ran along the bayou.

A navigable route would have been of little use unless it led to someplace of importance. The route was connected with the Red River, which emptied into the Mississippi, which ran past New Orleans. New Orleans had a fleet of seagoing vessels that ran to the East Coast, where cotton was shipped to Europe and where most of the commodities that were sent into Jefferson's market area were produced. It was this extended navigation system that enabled the route to function in the national and international economy.

Navigation Record

Boats known to have traveled to Jefferson prior to 1861 include the *Afton, Jr., Alabama, Alida, Allen Glover, Alligator, Amanda, Andy Fulton, Archer, Ariel, Arkansaw, Augusta, B. E. Clark, Banjo, Belle Gates, Bloomer, Caddo, Caddo Belle, Caddo No. 2, Camden, Caspian, Cleona, Col. Edwards, Comet, Corinne, Creole, D. R. Carroll, De De, Dick Nash, Duck River, E. M. Bicknell, Echo, Effort, Eleanor, Ellen, Era No. 1, Era No. 3, Era No. 4, Financier, Fleta, Frances Jones, Gazelle, Gossamer, Grenada, Ham Howell, Homer, Hope, J. D. Swaim, J. E. Roberts, J. M. Sharp, John Ray, John Strader, Joseph Holden, Julia, Lafitte, Lama, Larkin Edwards, Latona, Lecompte, Linda, Lizzie Lee, Lone Star, Martin Walt, Mary L. Dougherty, Monterey, Morgan Nelson, Morning Light, Music, Osceola, Osprey, Picayune No. 3, Pitser Miller, Planter, Post Boy, R. C. Oglesby, R. M. Jones, R. W. Powell, Red River, Rescue, Reub White, Robert Watson, Rosa, S. W. Downs, Sallie Robinson, Shamrock, Silver Moon, Sodo, Southern, St. Charles, Starlight, Storm, Sunbeam, Swan, Telegram, Texas Ranger, Trio, Venture, Victress, Vigo, Vio-*

EXPRESS MAIL,

John Smoker, Master.

This substantial and elegant steamboat will run as a regular packet between New Orleans and Shreveport and as high up as Port Caddo and Jefferson in Texas, commencing her trips as soon as Red River becomes navigable for boats of her class.

The *Express Mail* has been purchased by the old proprietors of the Bois d'Arc, and they bespeak for the former the same liberal patronage which was bestowed upon the latter, pledging themselves to use every exertion to merit its continuance.

The *Express Mail* will not be surpassed by any boat in the Red River trade in point of capacity for carrying freight and passengers. She will stow about 1800 bales of cotton, and has thirty-eight large state rooms.

She may be expected as soon as the water will permit.   LEWIS & HOWELL, Agents

Shreveport, December 17, 1845.—12tf

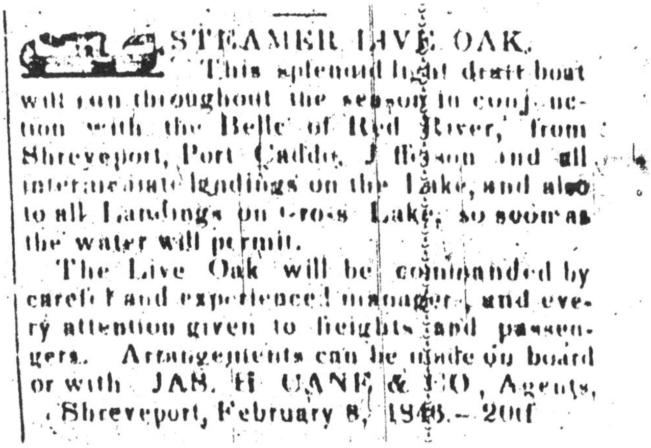

STEAMER LIVE OAK.

This splendid light draft boat will run throughout the season in conjunction with the 'Belle of Red River,' from Shreveport, Port Caddo, Jefferson and all intermediate landings on the Lake, and also to all Landings on Cross Lake, so soon as the water will permit.

The Live Oak will be commanded by careful and experienced managers, and every attention given to freights and passengers. Arrangements can be made on board or with JAS. H. CANE & CO, Agents.

Shreveport, February 8, 1846.—20tf

Fig. 14-1. First Steamboat Advertisements for Jefferson. Source: February 11, 1846, *Caddo Gazette*

lett, W. A. Andrew, W. A. Violett, Wabash Valley, White Cliff, William C. Young, William Campbell, William N. Sherman, William R. Douglass, and Yazoo Belle.

These 109 boats were mid-sized to small. Of the 90 boats whose dimensions are known, the average length was 132 feet. The average is upwardly biased because dimensions are unknown for many of the smallest boats. Only five boats were longer than 170 feet; of these, the *D. R. Carroll* and the *R. W. Powell*, both at 175 feet, were the longest. The smallest boats whose dimensions are known were the *Financier* and the *Julia,* both at 93 feet. Only 26 of the 108 boats were sternwheelers. Sternwheelers exceeded sidewheelers only in 1855 and 1859. In 1855, only four boats were operative because of extreme low water, and three of these were sternwheelers. In 1859, 18 boats were operative, of which nine were sternwheelers, eight were sidewheelers, and one was unknown.

The record of boat movements in the newspapers is not of sufficient quality to establish trends from year to year. The primary deficiency is the Shreveport newspapers, most of which have disappeared. Many of the trips to Jefferson were made by boats that ran from Shreveport, where freight was offloaded and onloaded to boats that ran between Shreveport and New Orleans. The incompleteness of the Shreveport record produces undercounts in the number of boat trips to Jefferson.

The available record produces the following numbers for boats and trips to Jefferson by year: 1845 (2 boats, 2 trips); 1846 (1 boat, 1 trip); 1847 (3 boats, 4 trips); 1848 (2 boats, 3 trips); 1849 (5 boats, 17 trips); 1850 (3 boats, 11 trips); 1851 (6 boats, 21 trips); 1852 (9 boats, 26 trips); 1853 (8 boats, 27 trips); 1854 (7 boats, 23 trips); 1855 (4 boats, 4 trips); 1856 (24 boats, 52 trips); 1857 (26 boats, 67 trips); 1858 (17 boats, 60 trips); 1859 (18 boats, 87 trips); 1860 (28 boats, 53 trips).

The available record indicates that by 1850 the number of boats running to Jefferson exceeded the number of boats running to Port Caddo and that no boats stopped at Port Caddo without going on to Jefferson after 1854. The record also indicates that there was a gradual increase, with one major exception, in the number of boats and trips to Jefferson, beginning with two boats making two trips in 1845 and ending with 18 boats making 87 trips in 1859 and 28 boats making 53 trips in 1860. It is probable that on the eve of the Civil War 30 boats were making 90–120 trips to Jefferson annually, including mail runs by the *Fleta*.

The exception to the trend of increase was in 1855, when only four boats made four trips to Jefferson, after reaching seven boats and 23 trips in 1854. This was the result of a period of extreme low water on the Red River that lasted from the second half of 1854 to the end of 1855. The consequences for Jefferson and the regional economy were devastating because import and export of freights was brought to a near halt. Some cotton was hauled overland to Shreveport. A tremendous amount of capital was tied up in cotton that was unable to move to market; merchandise prices skyrocketed; and there were large declines in the commercial activities of Jefferson merchants. In early 1856, at the end of the low-water period, there were 25,000–30,000 bales of cotton in Jefferson's warehouses, representing the unshipped portions of two cotton production seasons. Merchants had immense difficulties in obtaining commodities sufficient to meet demand even at high prices. The effect on Jefferson's merchants was partly mitigated by the sustaining loans they were able to obtain from the cotton factors in New Orleans with whom they had business arrangements.

Jeffersonians known to have captained steamboats include William Brooks, who operated the *Belle Gates* in 1854; Richard Crump, who operated the *Grenada* from 1854 to 1856; and William Perry, who operated the *Bloomer* in 1856 and 1857 and the *Homer* in 1860 and 1861 (Fig. 14-2). The 1860 census lists Sidney Smith and Edward Jones as steamboatmen, but the meaning of the occupational designation is unclear. Smith was a Red River captain. Jones does not appear to have been a captain and was probably a clerk. Many Jeffersonians owned shares in steamboats, which usually provided good returns on investments. The *Alligator*, for example, was owned by Harvey Black and made at least one trip to Jefferson in 1860. There is no evidence of boat building in Jefferson prior to the Civil War. Capt. J. S. Smith and his partners in Jefferson had the *Lone Star* built in Kentucky in 1854, which ran to Jefferson in 1856. The Jefferson merchant Charles Peele had a steamboat built in 1855 for operation on the Sulphur Fork.

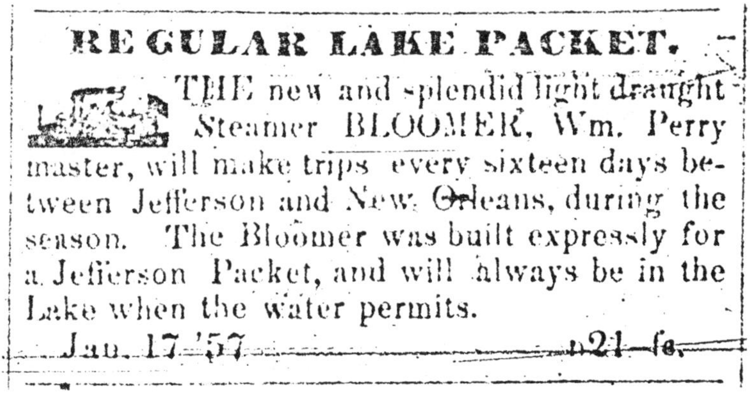

> **REGULAR LAKE PACKET.**
>
> THE new and splendid light draught Steamer BLOOMER, Wm. Perry master, will make trips every sixteen days between Jefferson and New Orleans, during the season. The Bloomer was built expressly for a Jefferson Packet, and will always be in the Lake when the water permits.
>
> Jan. 17–'57   n21—ta.

> **NEW ORLEANS & JEFFERSON PACKET.**
>
> The new, substantial, and fast running steamer HOMER, WILLIAM PERRY, master, will run during the entire season as a regular packet between New Orleans and Jefferson, touching at all the landings and plantations on the river, lake and bayou. In point of speed, safety and superior accommodations, the Homer is unsurpassed by any boat in the trade.
>
> Captain Bateman, thankful for the liberal patronage heretofore bestowed upon him, solicits a continuance of the same. Particular attention will be paid to all orders entrusted to the boat.
>
> dec13.

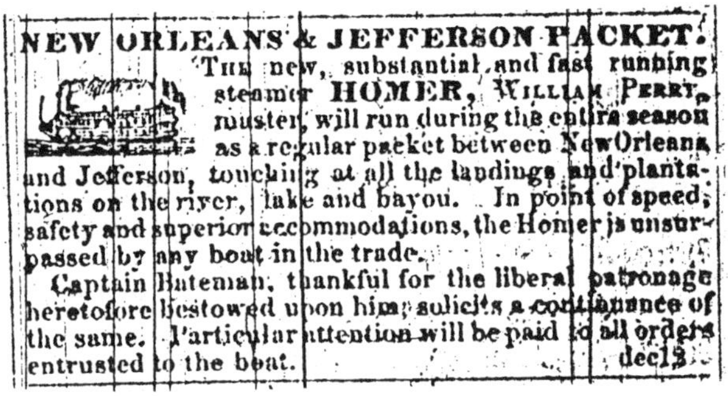

Fig. 14-2. *Bloomer* and *Homer* Advertisements. Source: January 17, 1857, *Texas Republican* and December 28, 1860, *Daily Picayune*

Navigation Improvements

Jefferson owed its existence to the 1844 bayou clearing effort upstream of Smithland. Jeffersonians, along with the other citizens of Cass and Harrison counties, were continuously interested in improvements to the route, which were directed to extending the navigation season and securing lower freight rates (resulting from reduced insurance because of greater safety, reduced travel time, heavier loads, larger boats, and increased competition). Projects were initiated in 1849, 1854, and 1857. None of these involved the federal government or the City of Jefferson, although the city accidently paid out some money for the 1857 project. The first two were conducted under contract through private subscriptions, and the third was state sponsored with a local subscription match. William Perry was the contractor for all three projects. The work was conducted by hand and involved tree and debris removal, stump cutting down to the low-water level, and some channel straightening and construction.

When Charles DeMorse of Clarksville made his first trip to Jefferson in June 1847, a meeting was being held to nominate a candidate for governor. The meeting included consideration and adoption of a plan to clear out the lake (that is, the navigation route between Jefferson and Shreveport), which appeared to DeMorse to be of more interest to those assembled than the nomination. Speeches in relation to the plan were given by Bennett Martin of Clarksville and Simon Heald and Berry Durham of Jefferson. The December 16, 1848, issue of the Jefferson newspaper *Spirit of the Age* appears to contain an article on proposed bayou clearing down to Benton.

The first issue of the *Texas Republican*, which appeared on May 26, 1849, contains a long article on the advantages of navigation improvements to Harrison County. Subscriptions were taken in Harrison and neighboring counties beginning in June, and Perry was chosen to do the work for $3,000. The provisional subscription list does not contain the names of any Jefferson merchants, but it is highly unlikely that they did not participate. The geographic scope of the project is unknown. Perry was to cut stumps down to the low-water level of 1848, producing four feet of navigable depth throughout the extent of the project. The full amount required for the contract was not raised, and assistance was sought unsuccessfully from the district court. This project was either not begun or not completed. It is probable that it was not begun because the low-water level of 1848 was not achieved.

Interest in clearing out Cypress Bayou and the lakes was revived in early 1853 when a correspondent to the *Jefferson Herald* pointed out that there was sufficient water for boats to bring out full loads of cotton if the stumps were cut down to the low-water level and proposed that the work be financed by planters and merchants in Harrison and Cass counties who would contribute 50 cents on each bale of cotton produced in 1853, with the proceeds collected by the port warehousemen. The editor agreed that something along these lines needed to be done, pointing out that the 50 cents per bale was presently being lost through higher freight rates and that an improved channel would increase trade and the value of property.

A meeting of the citizens of Cass and adjoining counties was held in Jefferson in May 1854 to initiate a process for clearing out the navigation channel to Shreveport. Mayor William Saufley chaired the meeting, and W. P. Ward acted as secretary. Justice Ferris, John Speake, Willis Whittaker, Hiram Grinsted, and Fleming Jones drafted a resolution expressing the sense of the meeting, which stated that the commerce of the ports had increased substantially and that expenditure of a modest amount on navigation improvements would significantly increase the navigation season and significantly reduce freight and insurance costs. District agents were appointed to solicit subscriptions, which were to be reported back on July 4, at which time a barbecue would be held and the subscribers would determine how the money would be spent.

Speeches in support of the effort were given by Marion Taylor, Justice Ferris, Hiram Grinsted, and Duncan McNab. Marion Taylor, William Perry, William Baker, James Murphy, Daniel McKay, Fleming Jones, Willis Whitaker, Daniel Roberts, James Maddox, and Jackson Morgan were appointed to the barbecue committee. Hiram Grinsted, Duncan McNab, John Wascom, John Speake, and Dr. Frank Baker were appointed to a committee to draft an address to the citizens of the region on the importance of navigation, of which 1,000 copies were to be distributed.

A complementary meeting was held in Marshall in June. The July 4 celebration and lake barbecue was held in Jefferson as scheduled, with a ball and supper at the Alhambra Hall. Subscriptions reached $8,000, including major contributions from New Orleans merchants. In August, the *Jefferson Herald* advertised for 100 hands to clear out the lake. William Perry had the contract for improvements between Jefferson and Port Caddo, and Capt. Robert Martin had the contract for improvements between Port Caddo and Albany (on Soda Lake). Perry constructed a dam above the bridge at Jefferson to divert water from the channel as far as Smithland into the floodplain in Harrison

County so that his 20 hands could work in a dry bed. Martin's portion of the project, which was conducted almost entirely at his own expense, included cutroads in Caddo Lake and Soda Lake. The efforts of Perry and Martin appear to have been restricted to debris removal and stump cutting and tree removal down to the low-water level.

Even before the 1854 project began, the Texas Legislature was contemplating an internal improvements program, which was implemented in August 1856. The program provided $4,000 in state funds for every $1,000 in private subscriptions for improvement projects up to $50,000, with $25,000 appropriated for Cypress Bayou and the lakes to the Louisiana line. Interested citizens elected Fleming Jones as collector and treasurer for the project, and he posted a bond (filed with the Cass County deed records) with the state in August with Caleb Ragan, John Murphy, John Speake, and William Saufley as sureties.

The needed subscriptions were secured. Jefferson recommended to the state that William Perry conduct the work, and Perry received a contract for $21,298 in July 1857. The contract called for the provision of 40 inches of navigable depth from Jefferson to the state line, a channel 50 feet wide from Jefferson to Benton, and a channel 150 feet wide from Benton to the state line. Perry's effort involved debris removal, stump cutting (apparently with power saws), and bend straightening and construction of two cutoffs at Benton (apparently by hand labor).

Matt Ward was instrumental in securing the acquiescence of the Louisiana Legislature for improvements to the route downstream of the state line, which involved debris removal, stump cutting, and the construction of one cutoff. However, the major problem with the route in Louisiana was sedimentation at Albany Flats and at the foot of Caddo Lake. Perry proposed for an additional $20,000 to secure dredges and remove these sediments from the channel, but his proposal was not accepted.

Although these projects obviously improved the route, there is no indication that the desired reduction in freight costs was achieved. The improvements enabled a larger class of boats to operate for longer periods and for all boats to operate more efficiently in terms of time and freight loads. Because the amount of water that entered the lakes from the Red River was the dominant factor in the navigability of the route, improvements could not radically extend the navigation season. However, the improvements significantly extended the navigation season for both small and large boats, contributing to Jefferson's primacy as a center of commerce, as reported by the editor of the Marshall *Harrison Flag* in March 1860:

> We visited the flourishing commercial town of Jefferson in the early part of the week. In a business point of view, if it has an equal with no greater population, we have not seen it. Although the bulk of the cotton has been shipped, up freights employ several steamers, two or three of which were at the wharf at the time of our visit. Several large buildings are going up. The water is comparatively low, indeed so low that the smallest boats could not have reached there two years ago; and yet, the largest class boats that ever ascended that high are plying regularly. The seems strange, but it is nevertheless true. As a place of commerce, Jefferson is a fixed fact.

15. Navigation Controversies

There were three navigation-related measures proposed by entities external to Jefferson that would have damaged its commercial activity. These were an attempt by steamboatmen in the Cypress Bayou and the Lakes trade to establish a monopoly, an attempt by Louisiana strongly supported by Shreveport to drain Cross Lake, and an attempt by private interests strongly supported by the Arkansas Territory and Clarksville to remove the Great Raft on the Red River. Jefferson was a primary factor in blocking these efforts because of its mercantile importance and political clout.

Steamboat Combination

Steamboats operated in a free enterprise open-entry system. Any steamboat could enter any trade, although they generally restricted themselves to a primary trade, with other boats referred to as "transients." Freight transport costs were on-the-spot determinations by shippers and carriers, although generally operating in the context of prevailing freight rates. The more boats in any trade, the greater the competition and the lower the freight rates and consequently profitability. With an open-entry system and competition in establishing freight costs for particular trips, steamboats usually operated on small profit margins. Steamboats that dominated primary trades had an interest in restricting entry because this reduced their profitability. They sometimes attempted to create monopolies by entering into combinations. The boats involved in combinations established uniform rates so that they would not compete with each other and provided rate flexibility to drive out competition from non-members.

Eighteen New Orleans boats in the Cypress Bayou and the Lakes trade established a combination in November 1853 called the Red River Association. Uniform rates were established for all boats, and every boat was given the authority to reduce freight costs 25 percent below the costs that might be offered by any non-member boat on a particular trip. The intent was to establish a monopoly that would be able to demand freight rates higher than would prevail under normal competitive circumstances.

Marshall, Clarksville, Greenwood, and all of the ports and landings along the Cypress Bayou and the Lakes route entered immediately into efforts to break the combination before it was implemented. Marshall and nearby Harrison County merchants agreed to not use combination boats and to provide generous rates for transient boats. Participation in this agreement was sought from the merchants of Jefferson, Port Caddo, Benton, Smithland, Clinton, Monterey, and Swanson's Landing. A Jefferson merchant published a letter in the December 10 *Jefferson Herald* that was abstracted by the *Texas Republican* as representative of sentiments with respect to the monopoly:

> It becomes us a people who claim to be free, to protest against the tariff enacted by the Lake boats—more particularly that clause in their proceedings which says that they will work or carry freight for 25 cts. less than any transient boat that may come in and offer to carry freight for a less rate than they themselves have established, in the city of New Orleans, in Nov. 1853; and the merchants, planters, and people, upon Red River and the Lakes, should pledge themselves in convention, that they will sustain any transient boat or boats that may come into our trade, and work for last season prices, and invite transient boats to come, under a guaranty that we would give them the preference, at those prices, in all our freights, both up and down, and that we would instruct our several

Commission Merchants in New Orleans to ship only by these transient boats, and in this way break up the odious monopoly that the Red River steamboat owners and Captains are endeavoring to fix upon us, and that we will carry out these views without fear or affectation. Will the people speak out now upon this matter?

A meeting was held in Marshall on January 4, 1854, in which Capt. E. Alexander proposed to establish a line of independent boats that would operate in opposition to the combination. Captains Sweeney and Withenbury agreed to bring their boats into the trade. A meeting was held in Jefferson the next day, with resolutions adopted to condemn the combination and to support a line of boats formed by Captain Alexander, Richard Crump of Jefferson, and their associates, as reported in the January 7 *Jefferson Herald*:

> A large and enthusiastic meeting of the citizens of Jefferson and surrounding country was held at the Alhambra Hall on Thursday evening the 5th inst.; Wm. P. Saufley was called to the chair and Frank H. Clark appointed Secretary. H. L. Grinsted explained the object of the meeting to be for the purpose of devising ways and means to protect shippers on the Red River and Lake from the ruinous, unjust, exorbitant tariff of charges on freight, established by the Red River and lake Steam Boatmen at their meeting in New Orleans last November, which said meeting is styled and known by the odious appellation of the "Red River Association." Resolutions were then adopted condemning the course of the Red River Association—refusing those engaged in it support, and pledging support to a line of independent boats to be brought into the trade by Captain E. Alexander, formerly of the Pitser Miller, and Richard P. Crump and their associates. Articles to this effect were drawn up and numerously signed.

In keeping with the effort to introduce boats in opposition to the combination, the Jefferson merchant William Brooks purchased the *Belle Gates*, established himself as captain, and began advertising the boat as a lake and Jefferson packet in March. The *Belle Gates* made one trip to Jefferson and one to Benton under Captain Brooks and two trips to Jefferson under other captains. Also during March, Richard Crump and his associates purchased the *Grenada*, which Crump ran as captain to Jefferson from March 1854 to May 1856. The *Belle Gates* and *Grenada* advertised jointly in the New Orleans newspapers as an independent line that would make two monthly trips each to Jefferson (Fig. 15-1). These various initiatives led to the dissolution of the combination in early 1854.

Draining Cross Lake

Cross Lake west of Shreveport was one of the five shallow lakes in the Sodo Lake complex that had been created by the actions of the Great Raft. Cross Lake was connected on its northern perimeter with Soda Lake through a floodway, and Soda Lake was the passage for steamboats to Jefferson. As a consequence of this connection, Jefferson was concerned with any actions that might be taken with respect to Cross Lake.

In late 1858, the Louisiana Board of Swamp Land Commissioners developed a proposal to drain Cross Lake so that it could be used for cotton production. The Commissioners justified their proposal by claiming that Cross Lake was a transient submerged lowland that owed its contingent existence to the Great Raft. Although there are no technical descriptions of the proposed project, its general features were presented in the local newspapers.

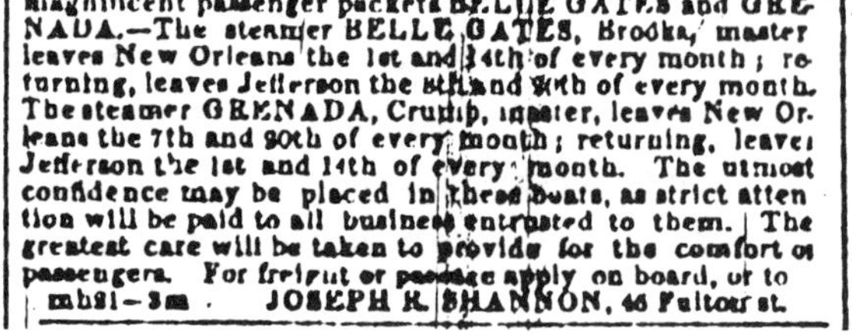
INDEPENDENT LINE—New Orleans, Jefferson, Port Caddo, Shreveport, and all intermediate landings on Red River.—The magnificent passenger packets BELLE GATES and GRENADA.—The steamer BELLE GATES, Brooks, master leaves New Orleans the 1st and 14th of every month; returning, leaves Jefferson the [illegible] and [illegible] of every month. The steamer GRENADA, Crump, master, leaves New Orleans the 7th and 20th of every month; returning, leaves Jefferson the 1st and 14th of every month. The utmost confidence may be placed in these boats, as strict attention will be paid to all business entrusted to them. The greatest care will be taken to provide for the comfort of passengers. For freight or passage apply on board, or to
mh31—3m JOSEPH K. SHANNON, 46 Fulton st.

Fig. 15-1. Independent Line Advertisement. Source: June 29, 1854, *Daily Picayune*

Cross Lake received water at its northern perimeter from the Red River by way of Soda Lake through the floodway. The surveys conducted in conjunction with the proposed project found that there was only three feet of water in Cross Lake and that there was only six inches of water in the floodway, which had been subject to sediment deposition from the Red River for nearly 60 years.

Cross Lake was connected at its eastern end to the Red River through Cross Bayou. When the lake was in the initial stages of formation in the late 1700s, sediments were deposited at its eastern end by the actions of the Great Raft; and these sediments were added to over time by Red River water that came from the north. This enabled Cross Lake to continue to exist even with perceived declining inputs of Red River water.

The proposed project for draining Cross Lake envisioned the cutting of a canal one mile long, 15 feet wide, and six feet deep through the deposited sediments at the eastern end of the lake and into the Red River. This action was strongly supported by Shreveport and strongly opposed by Jefferson, which assumed that the purpose was to destroy its navigation so that commerce would be diverted to Shreveport.

The merits of the various arguments cannot be determined because of a lack of technical information on the project. Shreveport maintained that the project would take some water out of Soda Lake, but without consequences to Jefferson's navigation because the submerged channel of Cypress Bayou, which ran through Soda Lake, would still be useful. However, the early federal surveys of Cypress Bayou indicated that it was not navigable in the vicinity of Caddo and Soda lakes before the lakes were formed. In any case, Shreveport would only be able to capture a portion of Jefferson's market area because of the high cost of overland transport.

Shreveport did not help its case by indicating through the *Caddo Gazette* that the project was the first step in draining all Red River bottomlands, including Soda Lake, and that in accomplishing this reclamation, "the pretensions of an obscure Texas village cannot be considered." Indelicate language of this type led Robert Loughery of the Marshall *Texas Republican* to finally conclude that the purpose of the project was to destroy Jefferson.

In September 1858, the merchants of northeast Texas, including the merchants of Jefferson, sent a letter to Governor Runnels of Texas complaining about the project. Runnels forwarded the letter to Governor Wickliffe of Louisiana along with his own protest, and the project was dropped. Although the local newspapers do not indicate what happened, it is apparent that New Orleans feared that the project might diminish the value of one of its most lucrative trade areas.

Raft Removal

The Great Raft was an impediment to navigation on the Red River. Bypasses to reach the upper Red River were developed to the west through the distributary system that fed the lakes west of Shreveport that provided navigation to Jefferson. These bypasses were dangerous and inefficient, resulting in high transport costs. At many times, they could not be used, which resulted in a diversion to Jefferson of the trade of the northeast corner of Texas and the southwest corner of Arkansas that would proceed directly to New Orleans by way of Red River if the raft had not been in existence. Jefferson was opposed to raft removal because it wished to maintain the viability of its navigation and to continue to capture a large portion of the upper Red River trade.

Federal efforts to do something about the raft had been ineffectual after Henry Shreve temporarily removed the raft in the late 1830s. Early in 1859, the Louisiana, Arkansas and Texas Navigation Company was organized as a private enterprise to remove the raft, with C. M. Hervey as president. This company was financed by stocks and had no federal or state monetary support. It intended to recoup the cost of raft removal by charging tolls on steamboats moving through the cleared channel. This effort was strongly supported by the people of the northeast corner of Texas—particularly Clarksville—and the people of the southwest corner of Arkansas, and it was strongly opposed by Jefferson. Shreveport played a secondary role in the controversy, but was again accused by Jefferson of trying to capture her commerce by destroying her navigation. This was essentially an intra-Texas controversy, pitting Jefferson against Clarksville.

Although the raft was totally within Louisiana, the company thought that it was necessary to secure approval for incorporation from Arkansas, Louisiana, and Texas. Arkansas and Louisiana provided immediate approval. In Texas, the bill authorizing the company was reported on favorably by two committees, but was defeated in the House of Representatives, apparently through the influence of Marion Taylor, who lived near Jefferson and was a representative of Cass and Titus counties and Speaker of the House. Clarksville was understandably infuriated, because it was a Texas town whose legitimate interests had been subverted by its own legislature through backroom dealings.

The merits of the arguments in this case were clearer, because the same arguments were addressed in the early 1870s through surveys that gave rise to the removal of the raft in 1873. Jefferson did not mention its pecuniary interest in holding on to a portion of the upper Red River trade. It argued that raft removal would destroy its navigation and navigation on the Red River. The latter argument was bogus and introduced to undermine support for raft removal in the areas where the idea was popular. The argument about destruction of navigation to Jefferson was more complicated. Clarksville pointed out that the distributary system was strong and would continue to capture Red River water and carry it into the lake area long after the raft was removed. This position was confirmed by the surveys of the early 1870s. However, it was obvious in the 1850s and the 1870s that Jefferson's navigation would eventually be harmed by raft removal. Clarksville argued that there was no legal or moral impediment to removal of obstructions on a waterway, particularly because it did not involve any public monies.

In early 1861, the Louisiana Legislature decided that approval of the organization's efforts fell solely within its purview because the raft was in Louisiana. The company was authorized to remove the raft and to levy tolls for a number of years. Work never got underway because of the advent of the war.

16. Market Area

Jefferson's market area was the geographic region that exported agricultural commodities and imported merchandise through Jefferson. Exports through Jefferson were based on supply factors in the market area and particularly on the production of cotton and cattle and cattle products. Imports through Jefferson were based on demand factors in the market area that were constituted by the needs of interior merchants, planters, and citizens. The geographic extent of Jefferson's market area did not change over time. The town grew because of population and production increases in its market area, which were driven by cotton agriculture.

Jefferson's commercial primacy was determined by its geographic location, a fact recognized by Josiah Gregg in 1841, before the town came into existence. Gregg was at the emerging town of Smithland six miles downstream of the townsite of Jefferson and noted that if the bayou could be cleared of obstructions above Smithland, "Jefferson would take all of the western business." As the highest port on Cypress Bayou, Jefferson was positioned to capture all of the trade to the west. This was not because of any unique services offered by the town or the acumen of its businessmen, but rather because of the high cost of overland transport compared to water transport. Exporters in the region sought the nearest water outlet, and importers sought the nearest water inlet. Cypress Bayou extended far into the interior, and Jefferson was well upstream at the head of potential steamboat navigation. It had a captive market area.

Geographic determination in commercial activity implies an absence of competition. A new town like Jefferson could secure business that had previously gone to another port town like Shreveport; but after its establishment it could do very little to take more business away, and there was very little that Shreveport could do to recapture what it had lost. There was, of course, merchandise price competition among merchants in different towns as well as within towns such as Jefferson. But if an interior buyer was able to get a better price at Shreveport than at Jefferson, the savings were generally obviated by the difference between overland and waterborne transport costs. The absence of competition between these two towns was stated forcefully by the October 15, 1858, Marshall *Texas Republican*:

> Now we have no idle prejudices against Shreveport, nor are we at all interested in the spirit of hostility engendered between that place and Jefferson. There is really no rivalry between the two towns. Each has its appropriate commercial sphere, which personal bickerings or invidious editorials cannot disturb. Jefferson commands the trade of a country extending from 150 to 200 miles into the interior, and which cannot be diverted to Shreveport; while the latter place, in like manner, possesses the trade of a thickly settled and wealthy section that would continue to trade there if Jefferson were ten times its present size.

Cotton was the most important export commodity and was handled by receiving and forwarding merchants. These merchants operated on the basis of prevailing commission rates and did not engage in price competition with respect to their services. Their advertisements emphasized the quality of their services (e.g., ability to advance cash on cotton brought to them) and never mentioned service costs. Cost elements in their advertisements always relate to their collateral activities as wholesale and retail dealers in merchandise.

The ports and landings along the steamboat route from Shreveport to Jefferson commanded specific market areas depending on their geographic locations. Shreveport's primary market area was to the east, north, south, and southwest. Swanson's Landing, Port Caddo, and Benton were primary centers for Harrison County imports and exports. Monterey and Smithland captured a portion of the trade to the north. Jefferson's market area was primarily to the north, west, and northwest.

Jefferson's market area to the north reached up to and beyond the Red River. Jefferson's ability to participate in the export trade of this area was dependent on water conditions on the upper Red River. When steamboats were able to reach the upper Red River, this trade was carried out between the upper Red River ports and New Orleans. When the upper Red River was not navigable, which was often the case, the export trade of the area to the north proceeded largely through Jefferson. Because the upper Red River counties were among the largest cotton producers in the state, this provided a large element of contingency in the volume of trade through Jefferson. Import trade was probably not as variable, because upper Red River merchants often found it more convenient to do business in Jefferson than in New Orleans

Jefferson's market area to the west and northwest did not extend much beyond Dallas. This was partly because there was little beyond Dallas; but even if there had been significant development, the trade would have gone to Houston, which provided immediate access to seagoing vessels at Galveston. The farthest point that I have been able to document for trade relations with Jefferson is Gainesville in Cooke County, which is 175 straightline miles to the northwest. Although the documentation is for 1867, it is probable that at least some trade activity extended slightly beyond Dallas prior to the Civil War.

There are a few descriptions of Jefferson's market area prior to the Civil War. A prospectus for a commercial newspaper published in the August 20, 1850, *Texas Republican* states that Jefferson, "extending further than any other into the heart of the rich Cypress Bayou and Sulphur Fork country, will of course concentrate the trade of those regions, which extend in some directions upwards of 150 miles. Indeed, this is naturally the principal Port for a great portion of the vast Red River, Upper Trinity, and 'Cross Timbers' regions of Texas. Goods shipped to Jefferson already find their way as far west as the town of Dallas on Trinity River."

Another description of the market area appears in a September 11, 1852, *Northern Standard* advertisement for the receiving, forwarding, and commission firm of Speake, Saufley & Nimmo, which states that Jefferson "offers many advantages as a *Shipping point*, as it is the nearest depot for the counties of Smith, Wood, Upshur, Titus, Hopkins, Hunt, Kaufman, Van Zandt, Dallas, Henderson, Anderson, Navarro, Collin, Ellis, Denton, Cook, Grayson, Fannin, Lamar, &c." The inclusion of the southern tier of counties (Ellis, Navarro, Henderson, and particularly Anderson) was probably more of an appeal for business than an indication of a realized market because the overall cost of shipments from that area would probably have been more expensive through Jefferson than through Shreveport.

A third description appears in the May 20, 1854, *Texas Republican*: "When we consider the large district of country dependent upon Jefferson for trade and commercial facilities, a great portion of which cannot be diverted from it; when we reflect that not one acre in five hundred of the land in this large district is in a state of cultivation, it is evident that our sister town is necessarily bound to become eventually a large commercial place. This territory dependent upon Jefferson reaches back into the interior two hundred and fifty miles, the citizens of which are actively engaged every year in the business of buying and exporting."

The last description before the Civil War is from an article on "Texas Progress and Prospects" that cites the *Jefferson Gazette* with respect to the growth of the town and states: "One of the principal reasons of this progress is that Jefferson, whence New Orleans receives so much cotton, is the shipping point for a belt of fertile country two hundred miles wide, stretching back a distance of three hundred miles, which though only partially settled, already gives constant occupation to forty large business houses in Jefferson to purchase and forward its cotton, wool, cattle, horses, sheep, beef, pork, hides, peltries, iron, castings, pecans, tallow, beeswax, and many valuable medicinal roots—all coming to New Orleans."

The difference between these accounts suggests a geographic expansion of the market area over time; but this was not the case. The latter estimates of 250 and 300 miles are not supported by any evidence and contradict later accounts that appeared after the market area was more extensively developed. The previously cited October 15, 1858, *Texas Republican* states that Jefferson's market area extended 150 to 200 miles. The 1870 *Digest of the Laws of the City of Jefferson* states that "Jefferson enjoys the trade of at least twenty counties in Texas, a portion from Arkansas, and a valuable trade from the Indian Nation"; and the September 1, 1881, *Galveston News* states that "Jefferson was once the trade center, the metropolis of Eastern Texas, and the point of distribution for a region 200 miles in extent to the west and northwest. Fifteen years ago... Jefferson sold her goods as far west as Dallas and Sherman, and points far in the interior of the Indian Territory, whence she drew the products of the country."

The various mileage figures are obviously estimates and refer more to travel distances than to straightline miles (Dallas and Sherman, for example, are not 200 miles from Jefferson). The Indian Territory referred to was Oklahoma, with cotton production largely restricted to the Red River Valley. This trade did not go through Jefferson when the upper Red River was navigable. The Arkansas trade was probably restricted to the extreme southwestern part of the state, with most of the southwest Arkansas trade going through Shreveport. The Arkansas trade did not pass through Jefferson when the upper Red River was navigable. The probable boundaries of Jefferson's market area are shown in the accompanying map, which uses the documented Gainesville in Cooke County as the northwestern limit (Fig. 16-1).

Clark Ward was a freighter and stagecoach driver. His family was one of the earliest to settle in Rocky Comfort, Arkansas, in the southwest corner of Little River County near the Red River. Ward provided his reminiscences to H. M. McIver in 1890, which appear in the Spring 1958 *Arkansas Historical Quarterly*. Ward says that he drove a freight wagon for Capt. John Hunter's Hunter Transfer from Jefferson to Rocky Comfort about 1838 or 1840. He briefly worked for another company freighting from Jefferson to Black Jack Grove (now Cumby) in western Hopkins County on the road to Dallas, but quit because Black Jack Grove was too dangerous. He went back to work for Hunter Transfer on and off until the war. Hunter Transfer hauled cotton from the river plantations of Benjamin and Henry Hawkins and David

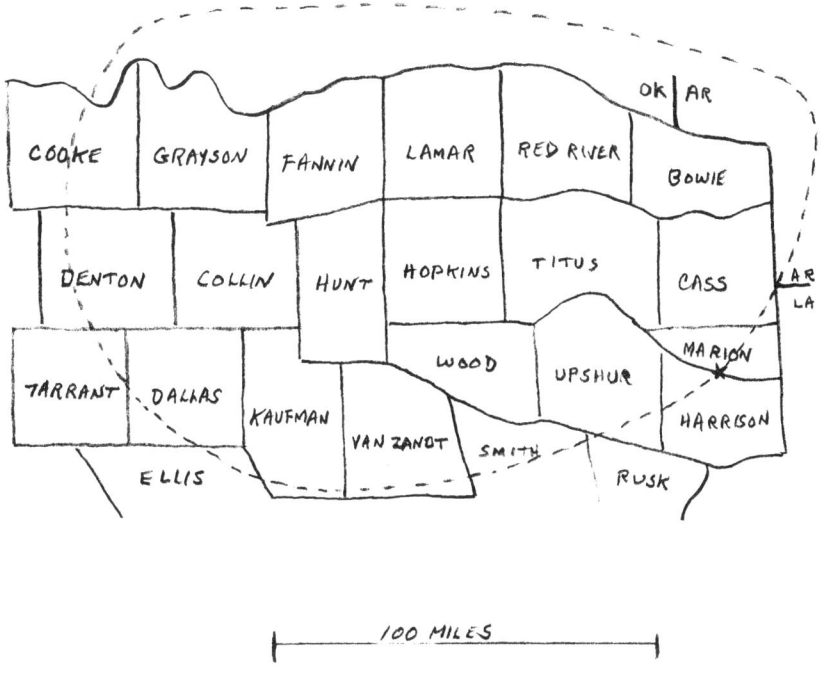

Fig. 16-1. Market Area

Hamiter in Little River County and Robert Jones in the southeast corner of the Indian Territory (now Oklahoma). According to Ward, this cotton was sold at Jefferson or shipped from Jefferson.

After the war, Ward went back to Rocky Comfort where he found Captain Hunter, all of whose property had been confiscated. Hunter went to Jefferson, where his old friend Erastus Jones helped him get more wagons and mules, which put him back in business. Ward worked for Hunter until Hunter moved to Texarkana about 1882. McIver provided a personal set of reminiscences in the Summer 1955 *Arkansas Historical Quarterly*, including information on John Hunter obtained from Benjamin Hawkins, mentioning that Erastus Jones was a cotton buyer at Jefferson who shipped to Kinsworthy Brothers of London,

England. I have not been able to find any relationship between Erastus Jones and Jefferson prior to the Civil War; however, in 1870 he was associated with Norsworthy & Clopton, Bankers and Exchange Dealers.

The establishment of this market area was coincident with the formation of the town in the sense that whatever trade was to be had in the region was destined to eventually pass through Jefferson. There was an initial problem noted by Edward Smith in 1849 that the high cost of waterborne transport between Jefferson and Shreveport, which was produced by the low volume of transport during Jefferson's earliest years, led some potential customers to deal directly with Shreveport. The consolidation of the trade of the market area through Jefferson was probably achieved by the latter part of 1849, as suggested by the March 14, 1850, Marshall *Texas Republican*:

> We are gratified at the accounts we receive of the increasing prosperity of our sister town. There are now, we understand, nine or ten large mercantile establishments at Jefferson, that are doing an excellent business. Not a bale of cotton, it is said, has, during the last year, passed by there, and the lake navigation has been uninterrupted during the business seasons. Merchants from the interior, and particularly from the Red River counties, as well as the planters, now go there for supplies, and are accommodated on the best terms. The lands surrounding it are rapidly filling up with that kind of population most desirable.

Trade volume within this area was not homogeneous. The primary export commodities were cotton and cattle and cattle products, including hides and, in the years immediately before the Civil War, pickled beef, which was produced in Jefferson's meat packeries. Cattle for export and processing were obtained from the plains of Fannin, Hopkins, Hunt, Lamar, Red River, and Titus counties in the north-central portion of the market area. The most significant minor export commodity was bois d'arc seed, which was used to grow fences.

Cotton was the most important export commodity. Cotton could have been produced in a fairly uniform fashion throughout Jefferson's market area, but it was not. Proximity to waterborne transport was the limiting factor with respect to cotton production throughout Texas prior to the Civil War. The ability to produce cotton at a profit diminished rapidly more than 100 miles from a water outlet because of the high cost of overland transport. With cotton selling at 10 cents a pound in New Orleans, a 500-pound bale was worth $50. Overland transport was one cent per mile per hundred pounds. A 100-mile trip to a water outlet like Jefferson consumed one-tenth of the value of a bale, and a 200-mile trip consumed one-fifth. With high production costs and further transport and handling costs downstream of Jefferson, overland transport costs were the primary factor in profitability.

Cotton production in Jefferson's market area (excluding Harrison County, which had outlets such as Port Caddo) was concentrated in the upper Red River counties (Fannin, Lamar, Red River, and Bowie) and in the counties within 100 miles (Marion, Cass, Titus, Upshur, Hopkins, and Wood), which collectively in 1859 produced 49,208 bales. The nine counties that constituted the western half of the market area (Cooke, Grayson, Denton, Collin, Hunt, Tarrant, Dallas, Kaufman, and Van Zandt) produced only 1,353 bales in 1859. Trade between Jefferson and these western counties was largely an import trade.

The primary import commodities were food, clothing, and supplies that were ultimately destined for the people of the area, although often transmitted to them by interior merchants. Population was not evenly distributed throughout the market area. Of the 19 full counties shown on the market area map (excluding Harrison), Van Zandt's 1860 population of 3,777 was approximately one-third of Upshur's 10,645. Upshur ranked first in population and third in cotton production; but Cass ranked first in cotton production and only eighth in population, preceded by the negligible cotton producers of Collin and Dallas counties, which ranked fourth and sixth, respectively, in population. Thus, there was a degree of discontinuity in the market area between the supply (as measured by cotton production) and demand centers (as measured by population) for Jefferson's export and import trade.

Population within the counties was not concentrated in towns. Recent issues of the *Texas Almanac* contain data from an 1858 census of incorporated towns conducted by the county tax assessors and collectors. The population figures for the towns of northeast Texas in 1858 were as follows: Paris, Lamar County, 1,003; McKinney, Collin County, 523; Bonham, Fannin County, 477; Sulphur Springs, Hopkins County, 441; Dallas, Dallas County, 430; Clarksville, Red River County, 400; Greenville, Hunt County, 246; Mt. Pleasant, Titus County, 227. Jefferson does not appear in the 1858 census, but does appear in the 1860 federal census with a population of 988. Marion County, with a population of 3,977 in 1860 and a small geographic area, appears to have been the most urbanized of the northeast Texas counties. In considering the size of these towns, it should be kept in mind that the largest town in Texas in 1860 was San Antonio, with a population of 8,235, and that Austin had a population of 3,494, approximately the size of Jefferson today.

Jefferson's newspapers contained a consignments column showing the destination of merchandise stored in the warehouses of the receiving and forwarding merchants. Unfortunately, listings are available for only one firm, for March 1857. Among the destinations listed are: Sulphur Springs (Hopkins County); Greenville (Hunt County); Linden (Cass County); Paris (Lamar County); Honey Grove (Fannin County); Douglassville (Cass County); Daingerfield (Titus County); Quitman (Wood County); Boston (Bowie County); Pittsburg (Titus County); Mt. Carmel (northeast Smith County).

The supply factors for Jefferson's export trade and the demand factors for Jefferson's import trade increased over time. Cattle production in the six north-central counties increased from 25,069 head in 1849 to 118,361 in 1859. Cotton production in the 19 Texas counties of the market area increased from 5,785 bales in 1849 to 50,561 bales in 1859. The population of the Texas counties of the market area increased from 41,369 in 1850 to 124,859 in 1860. These changes produced increases in the number of ox-wagons that traveled to Jefferson, in the number of steamboat landings at Jefferson, and in the growth of the number and size of Jefferson's commercial enterprises.

In the absence of import and export statistics, there is no way to determine the volume of trade that passed through Jefferson. The volume obviously increased over time as cotton production and population expanded. The only reliable statistic for cotton through Jefferson is 25,000 bales during the 1857–58 commercial season (September through

August), which is reported in the 1859 *Texas Almanac* and confirmed by the April 17, 1858, *Texas Republican*. Given the cotton production trends, it can be assumed that Jefferson was exporting about 30,000 bales of cotton on the eve of the Civil War. The other significant export factor was the emergence of large meat packing facilities in Jefferson in the late 1850s, which would have increased the exports of hides and added a new export commodity in the form of pickled beef in barrels. However, there are no statistics that would indicate the volume of this trade.

The relationship between Jefferson and its market area was reciprocal. The town grew because of a growing market area, and the market area grew because it had the ability to import and export commodities through a port. With locational advantages in relation to a geographically large and economically growing market area and merchants who knew how to capitalize on the afforded opportunities, it was apparent by early 1850 that Jefferson had the capacity to become one of the largest towns in the state, as expressed by a letter in the March 28 *Texas Republican*:

> I was much pleased with the improvement which Jefferson has made in the last six months, both in appearance and commerce. She commands the highest navigation for an extensive section of new and fertile country, which is settling and improving rapidly. Her houses are filled with goods and groceries sufficient in quality and quantity for the entire demand of her extensive patronage, and her merchants are liberal….
>
> Her position gives her a double advantage over any other point in Eastern Texas. She has the benefit of being interior, and at the same time at the head of navigation. This may safely be accorded to her without detracting in the least from any of her neighboring commercial points. Artificial help may give her a rival, but not a competitor. She alone will command almost the entire trade of a territory sufficient in extent and agricultural resources to make her one of the first towns in the State.

These things are now becoming known to the public, and they will be duly appreciated. The time is at hand when commercial advantages like those of Jefferson will not be ignorantly passed over by emigrants—such at least as are now pouring into Eastern Texas. The husbandman and the merchant are both alike invited. The success of the one promotes the interest of the other, and the way to the ultimate prosperity of both seems to be well understood—the exercise of liberality, production of reciprocity between them.

COTTON AND POPULATION

County	Cotton (in bales)		Population	
	1849	1859	1850	1860
Bowie	1,113	6,874	2,912	5,052
Cass	1,537	9,968	4,991	8,411
Collin	1	16	1,950	9,264
Cooke	0	58	220	3,760
Dallas	44	0	2,743	8,665
Denton	0	2	641	5,031
Fannin	374	1,499	3,788	9,217
Grayson	5	220	2,008	8,184
Hopkins	8	856	2,623	7,745
Hunt	5	22	1,520	6,630
Kaufman	6	381	1,047	3,936
Lamar	1,055	4,191	3,978	10,136
Marion	NA	3,708	NA	3,977
Red River	579	7,970	3,906	8,535
Titus	292	5,129	3,636	9,648
Tarrant	0	0	664	6,020
Upshur	673	7,965	3,394	10,645
Van Zandt	57	654	1,348	3,777
Wood	NA	1,108	NA	4,968
Total	5,785	50,561	41,369	124,859

NA = Not Applicable (formed by county subdivisions after 1850).

17. Primary Business Types

Jefferson possessed a large number of two types of businesses that made it distinctive among most of the towns of Texas prior to the war. These were the wholesale operations and the receiving, forwarding, and commission operations. Wholesaling is better known because it has continued into the present. Receiving, forwarding, and commission operations have disappeared as a business type and do not appear to have ever been specifically addressed in any publication. Both of these business types were directly related to Jefferson's status as a port with a large market area.

Wholesale Operations

Most of the early towns of Texas were oriented on retail services to residents and nearby farmers and planters and were occupied by small mercantile establishments that have been described to perfection by Lewis Atherton in *The Southern Country Store*. Jefferson, on the other hand, was oriented on wholesale services to retail merchants and planters in its market area, and it was occupied by large mercantile establishments that had the capacity to handle the immense quantities of goods that were demanded in its market area.

There were a few Jefferson merchants who engaged solely in wholesaling, and there were some Jefferson merchants who engaged only in retail trade. However, most of Jefferson's merchants engaged in wholesale and retail operations. Wholesalers were able to obtain large quantities of goods because of the availability of waterborne transport and because steamboats were ideal carriers of bulk merchandise. Large-volume purchases of groceries, dry goods, and other manufactured articles were made by Jefferson merchants in cities like New Orleans, Boston, and New York and transported to Jefferson by steamboat. These purchases were made on credit. Jefferson merchants then sold these commodities wholesale to merchants and planters within its market area. Planters were extended wholesale prices because they were essentially small towns that purchased goods in large amounts. Wholesale sales to planters and merchants were also on credit. The merchants within Jefferson's market area then sold these commodities on a retail basis to residents and the smaller planters and farmers in their immediate vicinity. These transactions were also usually on credit. The various credits were generally resolved when the cotton crop was produced.

Wholesale houses were unusual in northeast Texas. During 1857, only one Clarksville merchant advertised as a wholesaler in the Clarksville *Standard*, and no Marshall merchant advertised as a wholesaler in the Marshall *Texas Republican*. Jefferson merchants advertising as wholesalers during the same year were as follows:

Stanley & Nimmo—furniture and jewelry
C. A. Bulkley—groceries
Bryan & Clark—staple and fancy groceries
Reece Hughes—dry goods and groceries
W. M. Freeman—groceries and plantation supplies
R. W. Walker—staple and fancy drugs
B. J. Terry—groceries and plantation supplies
J. W. Pitkin & Company—staple and fancy dry goods
L. J. Graham & Company—medicines, paints, books, stationery
H. Jolly—tinware
H. Rhine & Brothers—dry goods and groceries
D. N. Alley—staple and fancy dry goods and groceries

The only place in the general area in which Jefferson was located that published a similar set of advertisements was Shreveport, which was also a port with a large market area.

A "Price Current" column was published in the newspapers of towns with substantial wholesaling activities. The prices shown were primarily the prevailing sales prices for wholesale merchandise during the previous week, if published in a weekly newspaper, or on the previous day, if published in a daily newspaper. The columns also included the prevailing prices for agricultural commodities that were produced in the town's market area and sold in the town. These columns were sometimes picked up by other newspapers. The only ones that appeared in the general area were for Jefferson, Shreveport, and New Orleans, again indicating how unusual the circumstances were in Jefferson.

The only complete copy of an early Jefferson newspaper (May 14, 1853) does not contain a "Price Current" column. Columns for Jefferson dating from the late 1850s (Fig. 17-1) include the following wholesale merchandise types: sugar, molasses, flour, pork, bacon sides, bacon shoulders, hams, lard, coffee, salt, whiskey, lard oil, candles, corn, bagging, rope, twine, nails, shot, lime, lowels (a type of slave clothing produced in Lowell, Massachusetts), linsey, potatoes, iron, and tobacco. The wholesale merchandise types were sold to interior merchants and planters. The cotton, hides, pelts, and wool in the listing were agricultural commodities sold in Jefferson and destined for downstream mar-

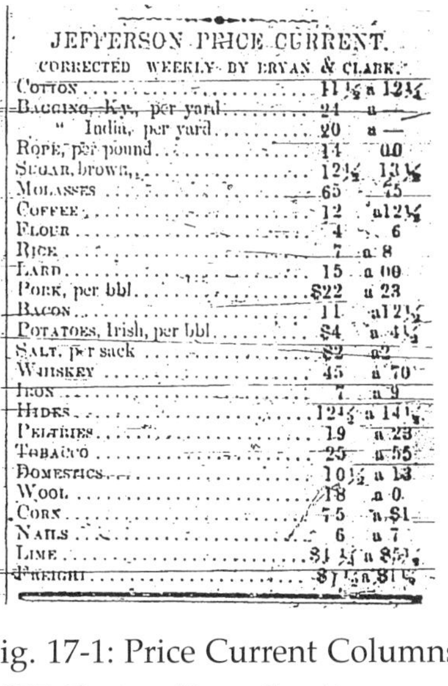

JEFFERSON PRICE CURRENT.

CORRECTED WEEKLY BY BRYAN & CLARK.

Cotton	11½	a 12¼
Bagging, Ky., per yard	24	a —
" India, per yard	20	a —
Rope, per pound	14	00
Sugar, brown	12½	13½
Molasses	65	75
Coffee	12	a 12½
Flour	4	6
Rice	7	a 8
Lard	15	a 00
Pork, per bbl	$22	a 23
Bacon	11	a 12½
Potatoes, Irish, per bbl	$4	a 4½
Salt, per sack	$2	a 2
Whiskey	45	a 70
Iron	7	a 9
Hides	12½	a 14½
Peltries	19	a 23
Tobacco	25	a 55
Domestics	10½	a 13
Wool	18	a 0
Corn	75	a $1
Nails	6	a 7
Lime	$1 ¼	a $5½
Freight	$1 ½	a $1½

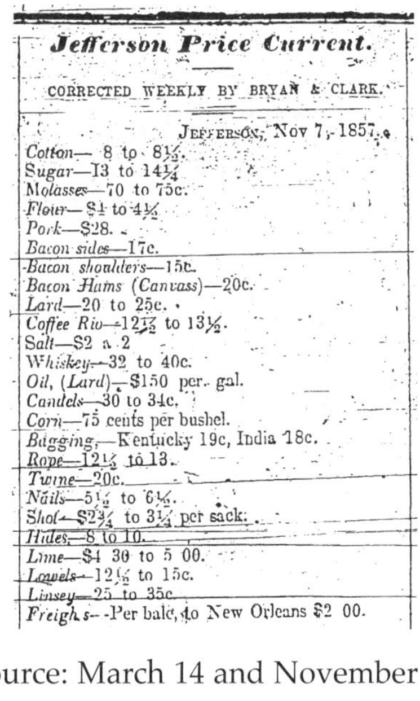

Jefferson Price Current.

CORRECTED WEEKLY BY BRYAN & CLARK.

Jefferson, Nov 7, 1857.

Cotton— 8 to 8½.
Sugar—13 to 14¼
Molasses—70 to 75c.
Flour—$4 to 4½
Pork—$28.
Bacon sides—17c.
Bacon shoulders—15c.
Bacon Hams (Canvass)—20c.
Lard—20 to 25c.
Coffee Rio—12½ to 13½.
Salt—$2 a 2
Whiskey—32 to 40c.
Oil, (Lard)—$150 per gal.
Candels—30 to 34c.
Corn—75 cents per bushel.
Bagging,—Kentucky 19c, India 18c.
Rope—12½ to 13.
Twine—20c.
Nails—5½ to 6½.
Shot—$2¾ to 3¼ per sack.
Hides—8 to 10.
Lime—$4 30 to 5 00.
Lowels—12½ to 15c.
Linsey—25 to 35c.
Freights—Per bale, to New Orleans $2 00.

Fig. 17-1: Price Current Columns. Source: March 14 and November 7, 1857, *Eastern Texas Gazette* kets such as New Orleans. These listings are only indicative of some of the major wholesale merchandise types. Jefferson merchants supplied at wholesale an extraordinary variety of merchandise, essentially anything that might be found in a Jefferson store other than large manufactured items such as cotton gins and carriages and smaller items such as saddles that were not suitable for sale in bulk quantities.

The first Jefferson advertisement mentioning wholesaling was for May & Company, wholesale and retail dealers in dry goods and groceries, in the April 5, 1851, *Texas Republican* (Fig. 17-2). However, Samuel Garey's April 8, 1847, drugstore advertisement in the *Northern*

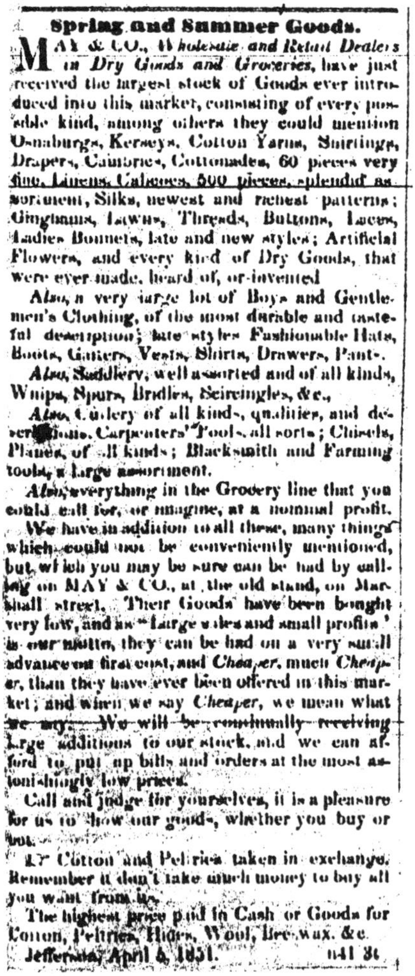

Spring and Summer Goods.

MAY & CO., *Wholesale and Retail Dealers in Dry Goods and Groceries*, have just received the largest stock of Goods ever introduced into this market, consisting of every possible kind, among others they could mention Osnaburgs, Kerseys, Cotton Yarns, Shirtings, Drapers, Cambrics, Cottonades, 60 pieces very fine, Linens, Calicoes, 500 pieces, splendid assortment, Silks, newest and richest patterns; Ginghams, Lawns, Threads, Buttons, Laces, Ladies Bonnets, late and new styles; Artificial Flowers, and every kind of Dry Goods, that were ever made, heard of, or invented

Also, a very large lot of Boys and Gentlemen's Clothing, of the most durable and tasteful description; late styles Fashionable Hats, Boots, Gaiters, Vests, Shirts, Drawers, Pants.

Also, Saddlery, well assorted and of all kinds, Whips, Spurs, Bridles, Seircingles, &c.,

Also, Cutlery of all kinds, qualities, and descriptions. Carpenters' Tools, all sorts; Chisels, Planes, of all kinds; Blacksmith and Farming tools, a large assortment.

Also, everything in the Grocery line that you could call for, or imagine, at a nominal profit.

We have in addition to all these, many things which could not be conveniently mentioned, but which you may be sure can be had by calling on MAY & CO., at the old stand, on Marshall street. Their Goods have been bought very low, and as "Large sales and small profits" is our motto, they can be had on a very small advance on first cost, and *Cheaper*, much *Cheaper*, than they have ever been offered in this market; and when we say *Cheaper*, we mean what we say. We will be continually receiving large additions to our stock, and we can afford to put up bills and orders at the most astonishingly low prices.

Call and judge for yourselves, it is a pleasure for us to show our goods, whether you buy or not.

☞ Cotton and Peltries taken in exchange. Remember it don't take much money to buy all you want from us.

The highest price paid in Cash or Goods for Cotton, Peltries, Hides, Wool, Beeswax, &c.

Jefferson, April 5, 1851. n41 3t

Fig. 17-2. May & Company Advertisement. Source: April 5, 1851, *Texas Republican*

Fig. 17-3. Samuel Garey Advertisement. Source: April 8, 1847, *Northern Standard*

Standard mentions dealers in drugs and medicines as his clientele and that fresh supplies would be received every three months, indicating that he was primarily in the wholesale business (Fig. 17-3). In addition, the high dollar values of merchandise on hand mentioned in the tax rolls for Jefferson merchants during the 1840s indicate that wholesaling was an important component of Jefferson's business activities from the earliest years.

Jefferson's merchants usually obtained their supplies in the summer and spring by travel to New Orleans and the East Coast, with arrangements made for immediate, delayed, or staged shipment. The buying function was sometimes carried out by family relations who were with firms in supply cities. New supplies of staple goods were generally opened in the fall and winter, which was the period in which most sales were made. New lines of fancy dry goods, primarily for female retail customers sensitive to changing styles, were introduced in the spring and summer with their appearance in national markets. Purchased merchandise was generally bulk packaged (such as in sacks, barrels, or crates), because brand naming and packaging for retail sales were uncommon, except for patent medicines. Merchandise was usually transported to Jefferson by steamboat in large shipments of bulk packages. Bulk packages were conveyed to interior merchants and planters in smaller shipments by ox-wagon. Retail sales usually involved the packaging of small quantities from the bulk packages at the time of sale (e.g., the sale of a pound of coffee from a sack of coffee to a retail customer).

Wholesalers maintained large inventories because of the nature of their business and because of the uncertainties and slowness of waterborne transport from the places where merchandise had been purchased. Large inventories required large storage capacities in the storehouse or a contiguous warehouse. The large quantities of stock on hand were often emphasized in advertisements. In the November 7, 1857, *Eastern Texas Gazette*, Reece Hughes announced that he had just received $100,000 in goods purchased in eastern cities expressly for the Texas trade; and H. Rhine & Brothers listed (among other items) 250 dozen pocket knives, 100 cases of shoes and boots, and 80 boxes of chewing and smoking tobacco (Fig. 17-4). In the August 13, 1853, Clarksville *Standard*, John Pitkin claimed that he kept constantly on hand (among other items) 200 sacks of Rio, Havana, and Java coffee; 20 barrels of pulverized and loaf sugar; 20 casks of bacon sides; 25 kegs of lard; 200 barrels of whiskey; 100 barrels of brandies, wine, and gin; 75 boxes of lemon syrup; 100 boxes of candles; 25 boxes of bar soap; 100 kegs of nails; and 80,000 cigars, from Cuba Sixes up to the finest.

In comparing the mercantile activities of Jefferson and Clarksville, Charles DeMorse maintained that the stocks of stores in Clarksville were as large as those in Jefferson, but that Jefferson did more business because of the high turnover of bulk commodities. Characteristic of the (obviously retail) establishments in Clarksville was the provision of "Dainty little articles for the feminines; delicate laces, the neatest little gaiters, kid gloves, Merinos, Silks, and all the catalogue of summer gossamers." Characteristic of the (obviously wholesale) establishments in Jefferson was the provision of "rough articles as suit their trade; Russet shoes, Lowells, Sugar and Coffee and Nails." The individual items were available in Jefferson's retail establishments and through the wholesalers who also sold retail, but the distinctive feature of Jefferson's mercantile activity was the movement of high vol-

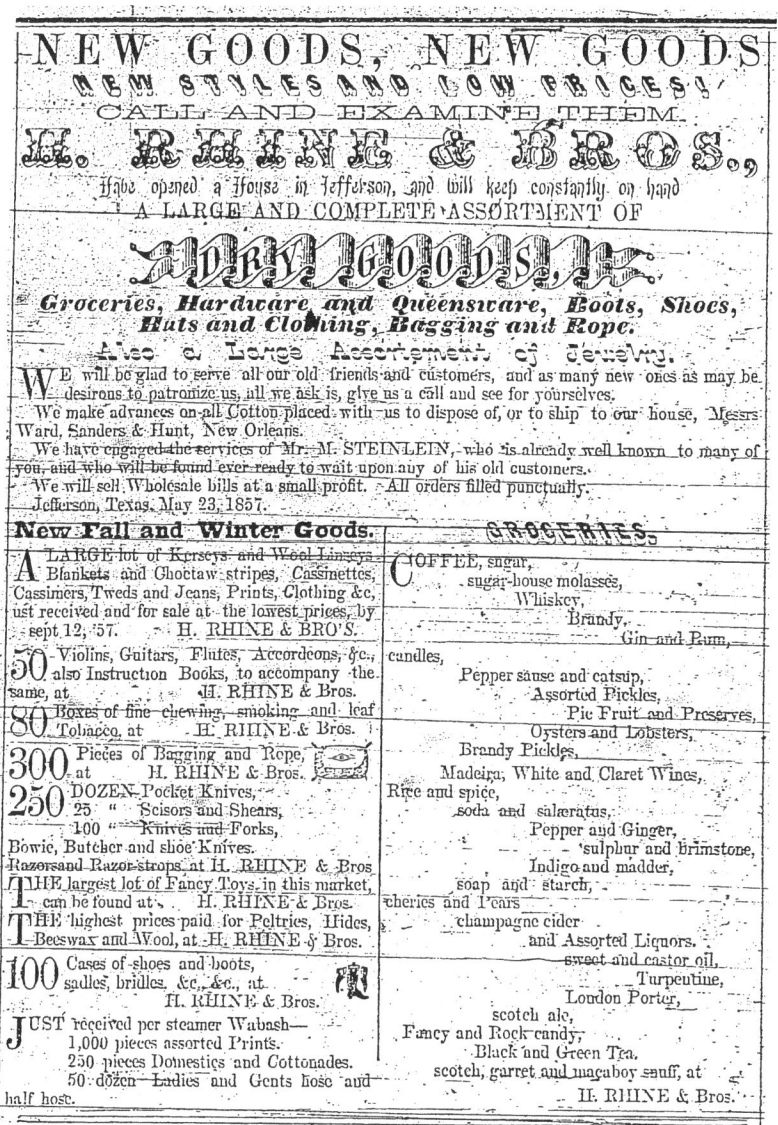

Fig. 17-4. H. Rhine & Brothers Advertisement. Source: November 7, 1857, *Eastern Texas Gazette*

umes of bulk commodities such as salt and whiskey in barrels through the wholesale establishments to interior merchants and planters.

Receiving, Forwarding, and Commission Operations

Receiving and forwarding operations existed throughout the United States wherever goods were transferred from one transportation mode to another. Goods traveling over long distances were usually not accompanied by their owners. Transporters were responsible for the goods they carried, but that responsibility ended at transfer points. The transfer of goods from one transport mode to another was not immediate. Storage in warehouses or sheds was required, with some entity acting as an intermediate between the two transport modes and responsible for the goods while they were in storage. This was where receiving and forwarding services were required. Such services should initially be thought of as a function rather than as a business type, because any merchant with storage capacity could provide the service. However, wherever large quantities of goods were transferred, firms specializing in such activities emerged. The services were usually provided in both directions, with the merchant responsible for import and export items. The receiving and forwarding merchant was an agent of safe passage between the two transport modes, with particular responsibility for arranging the transport of forwarded goods.

Most transfers were from land to water and from water to land, but there were also transfers from land to land (e.g., ox-wagons to railheads) and from water to water (e.g., steamboats to sailing ships). In Texas, most goods were transferred from ox-wagons to steamboats and vice versa; but in the larger coastal ports such as Galveston, there were transfers from oceangoing vessels to steamboats that ran to Houston, where goods were transferred to ox-wagons for transport to the interior. The services of receiving and forwarding merchants were required at each of these points and were concentrated in the ports with large market areas because of the large volumes of goods that were moved.

The function was much more widespread than the facility type. Even small landings with small market areas required these services, but they were usually provided by merchants who were in other businesses and had storage space. Retail merchants distant from waterborne transport acted as collecting points for outgoing agricultural commodities and incoming merchandise and therefore served as receiving and forwarding merchants. At such points, the transfer was between ox-wagons and farm vehicles such as carts. Specialization in such services, which was manifest in the business type, usually occurred only in the larger ports. Because there were not many ports in Texas, the receiving and forwarding operation as a business type was not common.

Receiving and forwarding merchants in an interior port like Jefferson (Fig. 17-5) were transfer agents for goods moving from ox-wagons to steamboats and vice versa. Export goods from Jefferson's market area were carried out by ox-wagons, handled by receiving and forwarding merchants in Jefferson, and shipped to New Orleans by steamboat. Import goods from New Orleans were shipped to Jefferson by steamboat, handled by receiving and forwarding merchants, and sent into Jefferson's market area by ox-wagon. Receiving and forwarding thus operated in both directions. The warehouses for the receiving and forwarding operations were concentrated in the landing area. Goods were consigned to the receiving and forwarding merchants, which means that they were placed in their care. Incoming goods and their destinations were listed in Jefferson's newspapers in a consignments column. Outgoing goods were not listed in this column, but rather in a similar column in New Orleans when they were received at that port.

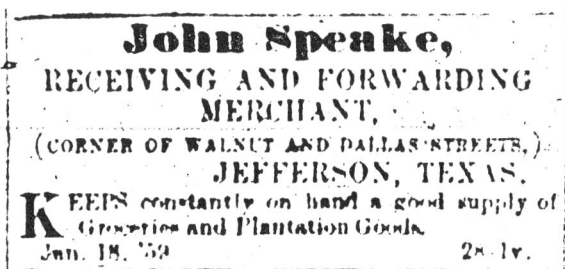

Fig. 17-5. John Speake Advertisement. Source: January 28, 1859, *Harrison Flag*

Cotton factors were agents for the sale of cotton. There were no cotton factors in Jefferson prior to the war. However, there were many cotton factors in New Orleans who had long-term business relations with planters in Jefferson's market area. The planter agreed to send the cotton that he produced to a factor who would sell the cotton for him on a commission basis. In exchange, the factor acted as a purchasing agent for the supplies needed by the planter and extended the planter lines of credit, essentially serving as a banker. Accounts were generally balanced when the factor sold the cotton for the planter. Cotton factors were, of course, interested in obtaining the business of cotton growers other than their regular customers.

Receiving and forwarding merchants in Jefferson shipped cotton for everyone and to a number of different factors in New Orleans. However, many of these merchants had special working relationships with particular cotton factors, who are sometimes mentioned by name in advertisements or referred to as "our friends in New Orleans." These relationships enabled the Jefferson merchant to provide advances in cash and goods to cotton producers who shipped through their facility to the designated factor in New Orleans (Fig. 17-6). The goods advanced were plantation supplies of all types, but particularly rope and bagging that were used to form cotton bales.

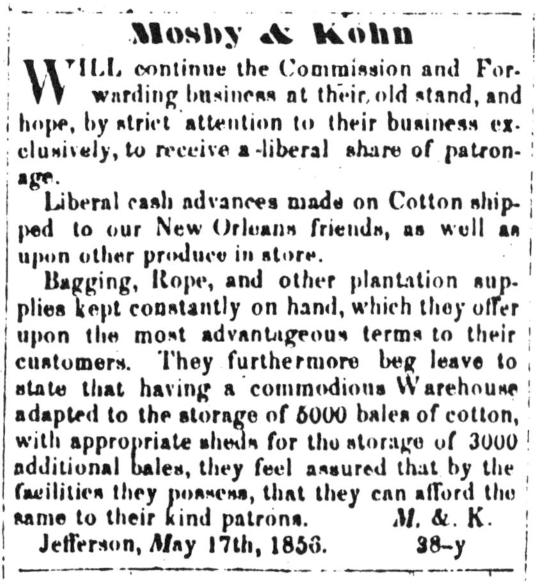

Fig. 17-6. Mosby & Kohn Advertisement. Source: May 17, 1856, *Texas Republican*

Mosby & Kohn

WILL continue the Commission and Forwarding business at their old stand, and hope, by strict attention to their business exclusively, to receive a liberal share of patronage.

Liberal cash advances made on Cotton shipped to our New Orleans friends, as well as upon other produce in store.

Bagging, Rope, and other plantation supplies kept constantly on hand, which they offer upon the most advantageous terms to their customers. They furthermore beg leave to state that having a commodious Warehouse adapted to the storage of 5000 bales of cotton, with appropriate sheds for the storage of 3000 additional bales, they feel assured that by the facilities they possess, that they can afford the same to their kind patrons.   M. & K.

Jefferson, May 17th, 1856.   38–y

This meant that the Jefferson merchants carried large stocks of goods in their warehouses in addition to those that were in transit. This was a mutually beneficial arrangement. Advances acted as an enticement for producers to ship through a particular receiving and forwarding facility and to a particular factor. The producer also benefited because he was able to obtain a return on his crop before it was actually sold. The goods advanced apparently belonged to the factor rather than to the receiving and forwarding merchant and were placed with him on consignment, which is why they do not appear in the tax rolls. The producer ultimately paid for the goods and compensated for the cash by having these amounts debited to his account with the factor after his cotton was sold. The factor, of course, made a profit on these goods in addition to his charges for his services.

Receiving and forwarding merchants generally engaged in or expanded into related business activities. Because they were handlers of goods with large storage capacities, it was easy to include sales of goods as an additional service. One form of sales was commission sales, in which the receiving and forwarding merchant sold agricultural commodities (of which cotton was the most important) for others on a commission basis. This transformed the receiving and forwarding operation into a receiving, forwarding, and commission operation and its owner into a merchant in the strict sense as one who sells goods (Fig. 17-7). There were, of course, receiving and forwarding operations that were not in the commission business and commission operations that were not in the receiving and forwarding business; however, most Jefferson merchants who engaged in these activities were in the receiving, forwarding, and commission business. Commission merchants sold anything that anyone was interested in having sold. They received goods on consignment, meaning that they were placed in the merchant's care for sale, with the option of returning unsold items. Some merchants who offered commission services advanced cash and merchandise on consignments as a means of soliciting business. Commission merchants sometimes provided auctioning services, which was a collateral form of sales.

Many receiving, forwarding, and commission merchants expanded into wholesale and retail sales of dry goods and groceries. Sales

> **B. J. TERRY,**   **T. J. ROGERS.**
> ## TERRY & ROGERS,
> ### RECEIVING, FORWARDING AND COMMISSION MERCHANTS,
> (Successors to W. M. Freeman.)
>
> Dallas Street, Jefferson, Texas.
>
> THE undersigned having leased the Ware House of W. M. Freeman, well known for its proximity to the water's edge, and convenience in receiving freight, are now prepared to receive and store Cotton or other goods, committed to their care.
>
> We solicit a liberal share of patronage, and promise that no reasonable man shall go away dissatisfied.
>
> All kinds of articles sold on commission.
>
> Bagging and Rope and Liberal Cash advances made on cotton.
>
>   TERRY & ROGERS.
> Feb 14, '57   25–1y

Fig. 17-7. Terry & Rogers Advertisement. Source: February 14, 1857, *Texas Republican*

by receiving, forwarding, and commission merchants on their own accounts rather than for others was always wholesale as well as retail. This was in part because the receiving and forwarding merchants were used to handling large volumes of goods and had little reason to enter solely into retail operations. This transformed the receiving, forwarding, and commission merchants into receiving, forwarding, and commission merchants and wholesale and retail dealers in dry goods and groceries, as they generally characterized themselves in newspaper advertisements (Fig. 17-8). The wholesale and retail component operated in the same way as any other business that devoted itself to those activities.

There were many receiving and forwarding merchants in Jefferson because Jefferson's market area was large and productive and there was a high demand for merchandise. This produced a high-volume flow of agricultural commodities and merchandise through Jefferson that required receiving and forwarding services, and, for persons wishing to sell agricultural commodities in Jefferson without actually going to town, the services of a commission agent. The level of these services was much higher than is indicated by the number of businesses that were specifically devoted to these services. It is likely that all of Jefferson's wholesaling establishments provided receiving and for-

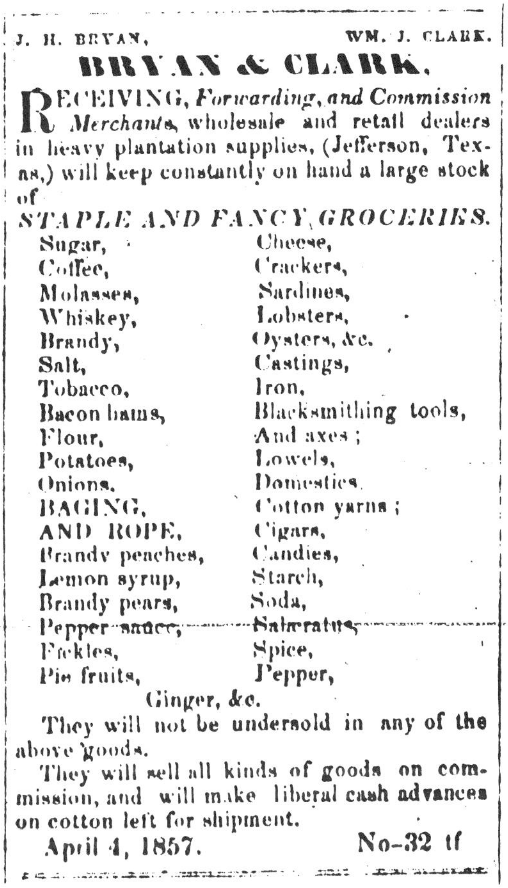

Fig. 17-8. Bryan & Clark Advertisement. Source: April 4, 1857, *Texas Republican*

> J. H. BRYAN,   WM. J. CLARK.
> ## BRYAN & CLARK.
> RECEIVING, *Forwarding, and Commission Merchants*, wholesale and retail dealers in heavy plantation supplies, (Jefferson, Texas,) will keep constantly on hand a large stock of
> ### STAPLE AND FANCY GROCERIES.
>
> | | |
> |---|---|
> | Sugar, | Cheese, |
> | Coffee, | Crackers, |
> | Molasses, | Sardines, |
> | Whiskey, | Lobsters, |
> | Brandy, | Oysters, &c. |
> | Salt, | Castings, |
> | Tobacco, | Iron, |
> | Bacon hams, | Blacksmithing tools, |
> | Flour, | And axes; |
> | Potatoes, | Lowels, |
> | Onions, | Domestics, |
> | BAGING, | Cotton yarns; |
> | AND ROPE, | Cigars, |
> | Brandy peaches, | Candies, |
> | Lemon syrup, | Starch, |
> | Brandy pears, | Soda, |
> | Pepper sauce, | Saleratus, |
> | Pickles, | Spice, |
> | Pie fruits, | Pepper, |
>
> Ginger, &c.
> They will not be undersold in any of the above goods.
> They will sell all kinds of goods on commission, and will make liberal cash advances on cotton left for shipment.
>
> April 4, 1857.   No-32 tf

warding services to one degree or another because they all had large storage capacity. For example, May & Company, wholesale and retail dealers in dry goods and groceries, advertised in the May 14, 1853, *Jefferson Herald* "Liberal advances made in cash or goods, for Cotton shipped through us to J. H. Heald, New Orleans." This advertisement illustrates that receiving and forwarding was a function as well as a specific business type and that firms other than receiving and forwarding merchants made advances on cotton shipped to designated factors. In addition, H. Rhine & Brothers, wholesale and retail dealers in dry goods and groceries, advertised in the November 7, 1857, *Eastern Texas Gazette* "We make advances on all Cotton placed with us to dispose of, or to ship to our house, Messrs. Ward, Sanders & Hunt, New Orleans," indicating that it made advances, received and forwarded, and even served as a commission merchant (the apparent meaning of the words "dispose of").

The availability of merchandise supplies in Jefferson through the receiving, forwarding, and commission merchants and the wholesalers of dry goods and groceries as well as their close working relationship with New Orleans factors probably enabled factors to meet the everyday needs of their regular customers long before cotton shipments were made. Continuous service appears to be suggested in advertisements such as those of the receiving, forwarding, and commission merchants and wholesale and retail dealers in dry goods and groceries J. M. & J. C. Murphy in the July 5, 1851, *Texas Republican* that references the New Orleans factor Wright, Williams, & Company and states: "Cash advances made, Bagging and Rope, and plantation supplies furnished to planters, who may wish to consign their Cotton to the above House." A similar advertisement appears in the May 14, 1853, *Jefferson Herald* by the wholesale and retail dealer in dry goods and groceries John Sabine that references the New Orleans factor Farley Jurey & Company and states: "Cash advances made. Bagging, Rope and Plantation supplies furnished to planters who may wish to consign their cotton to the above house." The meaning of these statements is clarified by an advertisement in the November 7, 1857, *Eastern Texas Gazette* by the wholesale and retail dry goods and groceries merchant Chester Bulkley referencing the New Orleans factor Ward, Saunders & Hunt: "Referring to the above Card, the subscriber will furnish or order for Planters of known responsibility, their Plantation Supplies; and at all times will make Cash Advances on Cotton delivered for shipment." Jefferson merchants even appear to have been able to participate in the financial services offered by factors, as indicated by the advertisement by the wholesale and retail dealer in dry goods and groceries May & Company that appeared in the May 14, 1853, *Jefferson Herald*: "The undersigned will make cash advances, Bagging and Rope and Plantation Supplies, to those who may feel it their interest to consign their Cotton to the above house J. H. Heald. For convenience and safety, all cash balances due planters paid by us free of charge."

Receiving and forwarding services must have been present in some form when Jefferson was a townsite, because cotton was transported to the townsite by ox-wagon and from the townsite by water. After the town came into existence, the earliest services (i.e., in the 1840s) appear to have been restricted to receiving and forwarding. However, the commission and forwarding firm of J. M. & J. C. Murphy appeared in June 1851 and was followed in October by the auction, commission, and forwarding firm of W. M. Freeman. J. M. & J. C. Murphy expanded into wholesale and retail dry goods and groceries in October, becoming the first of Jefferson's fully integrated operations.

Debt, Credit, and Loans

The chartering of banks and the issuing of currency were prohibited by the Texas Constitution. There were no banks in Jefferson prior to the Civil War, the stock of currency and gold was small, and most things were purchased on time. As a consequence, financial transactions were highly personal and largely paper-based, and most people and businesses were usually in debt even if they were wealthy. Much of the debt burden was incurred against the future cotton crop and included not only the farmers and planters, but also the merchants who supplied them and the merchants who supplied those merchants. Debt clearance was a function of the harvest; and when the harvest was poor, all that were involved in the web of debt suffered.

Personal loans were quite common. These were loans from one person to another and were usually secured by promissory notes identifying the parties, stating the amounts, and stipulating the terms of payment, including time and interest. Probate records that list debtors and creditors to estates indicate that many individuals engaged in a great deal of simultaneous borrowing and lending, suggesting that personal loans were not secured strictly on the basis of financial need.

When a note became due, it was either paid, renegotiated, or disregarded. One method of debt payment was to secure a loan from another person. In some cases, notes contained stipulations for interest increases after maturity. Creditors could sue for nonpayment of debt, and a person's property could be seized and sold by the sheriff for debt payment. Court records indicate that suits regarding personal loans were common, but uncommon if considered in terms of the number of loans that were outstanding. Mortgages were often used to cover difficulties in the payment of large loans. It appears from probate records that people were not diligent in paying loans or in calling them in.

Notes were usually signed by sureties, who were legally responsible for the debt if the debtor was unable to pay. Sureties apparently had nothing to gain financially from signing a note and acted out of friendship and honor and probably also out of the expectation that similar services would be rendered to them. Suits against securities appear to have been uncommon. The May 14, 1853, *Jefferson Herald* states: "There is only one thing less profitable than sueing people, and that is going security for them." Robert Nesmith violated both of these strictures in 1858 when he sued a debtor for the amount he had paid to a creditor as surety on four notes.

Notes were not secured by collateral, but rather by the credit power of the issuer and his securities. Because notes had value, they could be used as currency. When they were transferred to another person, they were discounted for any value decreases incurred through capital or interest payment. The acceptability of a note was determined by the credit-worthiness of the issuer and his securities, which was usually based on wealth and records of repayment. Slaves and town lots were usually purchased for cash, which included currency, gold, and notes that had entered into the currency stream. Large tracts of land outside of town were usually purchased with a mixture of cash and promissory notes, the latter enabling the purchase to be paid off over time.

Most Jefferson merchants extended credit to their customers, whether those customers were individuals or interior merchants. Even the relatively few "cash only" stores usually provided credit to preferred customers. Although interest was charged on accounts, people who could afford to pay cash apparently preferred to have credit lines with various businesses and to charge even items of minor value. Notes were apparently used for large purchases. Accounts were cleared incrementally and with larger sums when the cotton crop came in. These clearances were usually not final, because they were embedded in additional credit transactions. The relationship between the merchant and his credit customers was personal and long lasting.

Jefferson merchants purchased from their suppliers on credit. These relationships were also personal and long lasting. Because merchants were lenient with their customers, they often found themselves in financial difficulties with their suppliers. Cajoling was probably the primary means of securing debt payment from customers. If a merchant found himself in financial straits or if a company in which he was involved was dissolved, he might place an advertisement in the newspaper appealing for his customers to pay up and, if the situation was critical, threatening suit (Fig 17-9).

Fig. 17-9. Debt Payment Requests. Source: May 14, 1853, *Jefferson Herald*; March 14 and November 7, 1857, *Eastern Texas Gazette*

> **The First and Last Call!**
> ALL THOSE INDEBTED to the undersigned, by notes or accounts, for the year 1852, will please make settlements by the 1st of February or [...] of *Legal Gentlemen*, as longer indulgence is impossible.
> MORGAN & TOMLIN.
> Jefferson, Jan. 15. n3–tf

> **Pay up and Commence Anew.**
> ALL those indebted to the firm of Saufley & Batte, also the old firm Saufley & Nimmo, will please come forward and settle; not by note but *Cash*.
> We have been very liberal with our friends for the last five years, and have allowed ourselves pressed to save them; and we shall now expect in return for our indulgence to them, they will come forward and assist us.
> With everything going out, and nothing coming in, we would be forced to stop business.
> We therefore have determined to refuse credit to those who do not pay up for their past liabilities.
> SAUFLEY & BATTE
> SAUFLEY & NIMMO.
> January 10, 1857. 1–tf

> **I Will Sue.**
> ALL Persons that are indebted to Morris & Rush or Morris & Co., if immediate payment is not made to me.
> C. D. MORRIS.
> Jefferson, August 29th 1857. tf.

Attorneys served as collection agents because threat of suit usually brought an immediate response. Collection agencies were also used, and there was probably at least one person in Jefferson who specialized in such activities from the earliest years. In March 1857, T. J. Clayton advertised as a general collecting agent, offering his services to the public with the promise that "Any business entrusted to him will receive prompt attention; and money collected will be paid to the owner immediately thereafter." James Hosack, who was also an auctioneer, advertised as a general collecting agent in March 1860 and was joined by a partner in 1861.

Suppliers of Jefferson merchants often found themselves in the same difficulties as the Jefferson merchants with respect to their customers. Suppliers could sue and have the courts order liquidation of properties. This appears to have been uncommon. Suppliers had no interest in eliminating their customers, particularly when the relationship was personal and court-ordered sales did not secure full debt payment. Mortgages appear to be the preferred course of action for all concerned, with land, buildings, stock, and slaves put up as collateral to suppliers in places like New Orleans and New York. Mortgages usually involved debt consolidation, with the primary creditor paying off other creditors on the security of the mortgaged properties. Nevertheless, mortgages often resulted in foreclosures, with liquidation of properties and termination of businesses.

18. Commodity Markets

Much of the agricultural produce emanating from Jefferson's market area passed through receiving and forwarding merchants for sale in New Orleans. However, a substantial portion of this produce was sold in Jefferson through commodity markets, which were the activities associated with the selling and buying of specific commodity types. The major commodity types that were purchased in Jefferson were cotton and hides. The available "Price Current" columns add pelts and wool. However, it is evident from merchant advertisements indicating cash purchases that all of the commodity types produced in Jefferson's market area were sold in Jefferson, including cotton, hides, cattle, pelts, wool, skins, furs, beeswax, tallow, bois d'arc seed, honey, and snakeroot.

Speculation was integral to most commodity market activities because buyers were guessing as to the price that various commodities could obtain at the next point of sale. The speculator hoped to realize a profit by the purchase of a commodity below the price that it would obtain when it was resold, taking interim handling and transport costs into account. Sellers risked selling lower than they might obtain later at another place; the incentive was to have money in hand sooner. Buyer decisions were reached in the context of intense competition from other buyers, which tended to move prices upward, and in ignorance of the prices that were currently being obtained at downstream points of sale—a problem that could only be resolved by the telegraph, which was not available in Jefferson before the war.

Although commodity markets were not businesses, they joined the wholesaling operations and the receiving, forwarding, and commission operations as key features in the commercial life of the town. The unusualness of these markets is again indicated by the "Price Current" columns that appeared in area newspapers, which indicate the existence of such activities only in Jefferson, Shreveport, and New Orleans.

The only information on Jefferson's commodity markets is for cotton and hides (and related commodities such as pelts). Robert Loughery visited Jefferson in 1850 and reports in the June 20 *Texas Republican* that "speculation in beef cattle has almost become a mania." Loughery's comment indicates that there was a market for cattle, that this was a speculative market, and that competitive bidding occurred on the streets of Jefferson. This was in addition to whatever cattle were sent to Jefferson with the intent of placing them on steamboats for sale in New Orleans. The street market for cattle in Jefferson was composed of speculators who purchased cattle in Jefferson for resale in New Orleans, hopefully at a higher price. This was also in addition to whatever cattle were sent to the meatpacking facilities in Jefferson. Meatpackers needed a steady supply and therefore operated on the basis of contracts for delivery of specific quantities at specific times and at a set price. As with the other commodity types, the flow of cattle through Jefferson was much larger than the volume of sales in the cattle market.

Cotton Market

A cotton market existed wherever there was a concentration of transactions in which cotton was sold. Sales did not necessarily involve cash transactions. Change of ownership in the Jefferson cotton market involved cash transactions, but also barter transactions in which cotton was exchanged in whole or in part for merchandise (farm and plantation supplies). Sales of cotton tended to concentrate in places where a large volume of cotton was transferred from one transport mode to another. This tendency is readily observable in the proliferation of cotton markets after the Civil War in places like Marshall that were serviced by rails. However, before the Civil War competitors to Jefferson's cotton market were found only in Shreveport and New Orleans.

Cotton entered the Jefferson market directly from producers and indirectly from merchants in Jefferson's market area. Interior merchants purchased cotton in small amounts speculatively and accepted cotton from producers as barter in exchange for merchandise and in payment of debts owed by producers from credit transactions. The flow of cotton through Jefferson prior to the Civil War was generally through receiving and forwarding merchants for sale in New Orleans, with these merchants usually providing cash and merchandise advances on cotton left for shipment. An indeterminate, but obviously significant, portion of this flow was sold on the streets and in the warehouses of Jefferson, usually with the intent of resale in New Orleans. This portion constituted Jefferson's cotton market.

There were two types of ownership transfer that were not part of the formal cotton market. Jefferson merchants accepted cotton in payment of debts owed by producers from credit transactions. More importantly, all Jefferson merchants that were in the receiving and forwarding business provided cash and merchandise advances on cotton placed in storage and intended for sale in New Orleans. The advances were usually made in the name of a cotton factor or factors in New Orleans that would sell the cotton. J. M. & J. C. Murphy, for example, advertised in the July 5, 1851, *Texas Republican*: "Cash advances made, Bagging and Rope, and plantation supplies furnished to planters, who may wish to consign their Cotton To the above named House," with the house identified as Wright, Williams, & Company, Cotton Factors and Commission Merchants on Carondelet Street in New Orleans. These advances usually represented a significant percentage of the value of the cotton. However, the cotton that was received in debt payment and the cotton on which advances were made did not enter into official records of number of bales sold.

There is little information on Jefferson's cotton market, primarily because of the near absence of extant antebellum newspapers. There do not appear to be any analyses of how local cotton markets functioned in the antebellum South or any descriptions of market mechanisms (players and procedures) in a particular town. Shreveport was one of the largest interior cotton markets in the antebellum South. Shreveport's newspapers contained a commercial column after the Civil War that provides detailed information on cotton transactions first on a weekly and then on a daily basis. Although there are obvious dangers in inferring antebellum conditions in Jefferson from postbellum conditions in Shreveport, Jefferson and Shreveport had similar markets, and there is sufficient information in the antebellum Shreveport newspapers to make a backward projection for Jefferson.

Shreveport's cotton market after the Civil War was composed of a street component and a facility component constituted by Shreveport's cotton factors. The Shreveport factors displayed on tables in their business offices samples of the cotton that had been placed for sale by producers (farmers and planters), usually with cash and merchandise advances from the factor to the producer. Factors attempted to obtain the best price for their clients and charged a percentage commission for their services. They were highly sensitive to downstream (primarily New Orleans, New York, and England) market conditions that were continuously conveyed by telegraph. The primary buyers from factors were speculators and brokers, both of whom purchased for cash. Speculators were gamblers. Brokers (also called spinners' agents) were buyers for the mills, at first in New England and then in Europe. They operated on the basis of orders for specific amounts of cotton at specific grades and at price limits and therefore did not incur any personal risk. In Shreveport, they were all members of brokerage houses (firms that specialized in the purchase of cotton for more than one mill).

In the street component, producers and, to a lesser extent, interior merchants sold their cotton off of their wagons as they came into town. Producers could, of course, send their cotton to Shreveport through commercial ox-wagons for sale by factors, usually with prior mail transmissions indicating desired prices. However, if a producer wanted to avoid a factor's commission charge and sell his own cotton, it was necessary to physically transport his cotton to Shreveport on his own wagons. Commercial ox-wagon drivers obviously could not serve as agents in a competitive bidding process. The primary buyers in the street component were speculators, brokers, and merchants who sold dry goods and groceries.

Dry goods and groceries merchants were automatically in the cotton market insofar as they accepted cotton as barter (the exchange of one good for another without any cash passing hands), a near necessity in a cash-poor economy. There was no greater risk in barter transactions than in cash transactions because it was necessary for the merchant to value the cotton, keeping an eye on downstream prices. Dry goods and groceries merchants sometimes purchased cotton in the street market for cash, sometimes through exchange of merchandise, but usually through mixed cash/merchandise transactions. They were able to offer slightly higher prices than their competitors because they avoided to some degree the cost of money (purchases for cash were usually conducted through bank loans). They did not purchase from factors.

The street component was also highly sensitive to market information conveyed by telegraph and often affected by weather conditions. It was characterized by frenetic competitive bidding by multiple buyers for the offerings of multiple sellers. The same lot of cotton could be sold more than once on the street. If a producer was not satisfied with offerings, he could always place his cotton in the hands of a factor for sale in Shreveport or in the hands of a receiving and forwarding merchant for transport and sale in New Orleans.

To apply this description of Shreveport's postbellum cotton market to Jefferson's antebellum cotton market, the telegraph needs to be eliminated. The basic structures of a street component and a facility component need to be retained, along with speculators and dry goods and groceries merchants as primary buyers in their respective market components. There do not appear to have been any brokerage houses in Jefferson. However, it is likely given the amount of cotton passing through Jefferson that there were agents for brokerage houses in New Orleans. Finally, cotton factors need to be replaced by commission merchants in the facility component.

There were no cotton factors in antebellum Jefferson. However, commission merchants acted as sales agents for cotton in exactly the same way as did factors. What they did not provide was the robust supply and banking services that factors offered to planters. As sales agents, commission merchants were functionally equivalent to factors in the cotton market. The close relationship between these two types of firms is evident from the fact that many of the postbellum cotton factors in Jefferson developed out of antebellum commission merchants in Jefferson.

Jefferson's antebellum commission merchants and receiving, forwarding, and commission merchants sold everything consigned to them, including cotton, at a specific commission rate (usually 2.5 percent of the amount obtained from the sale). They also usually extended cash and merchandise on cotton in store for sale or shipment. Advertisements mentioning cotton as a sales item were fairly common, but it can be assumed that every commission merchant was in the business of selling cotton. Some commission merchants also bought cotton on their own account or on the account of New Orleans firms with which they had business relations, thereby entering the speculative realm.

The auction, commission, and forwarding merchant Williamson Freeman advertised in the November 1, 1851, *Northern Standard*: "The subscriber offers his services to his friends, planters, merchants, and traders, generally for the storage and sale or shipping of their cotton, peltries and stock of any kind," with "Cash advanced on cotton in store." Freeman also advertised (as a receiving, auction, forwarding, and commission merchant) in the October 5, 1852, *Northern Standard*: "Cash advanced on cotton and merchandise in store for shipment or sale." The receiving, forwarding, and commission merchant John Waskom advertised in the May 14, 1853, *Jefferson Herald*: "I am prepared to advance liberally in cash, groceries or produce, on cotton in store for shipment; and promise that every man's cotton shall be sold on its own merits." The receiving, forwarding , and commission merchant and wholesale and retail dealer in dry goods and groceries J. M. & J. C. Murphy advertised in the February 10, 1855, *Texas Republican*: "Liberal Advances made in Cash and Supplies upon Cotton and Produce left with them for shipment or sale. All kinds of Produce and Manufactured articles received to sell on Commission."

There are no descriptions of the activities of commission merchants in Jefferson. It can be assumed that they sold out of business offices connected with warehouses, with samples on display, to speculators and broker agents for cash. Likewise, there are no descriptions of street activities with respect to cotton sales. It can be assumed that sales on the streets were made by planters and farmers and, to a lesser extent, by interior merchants. The buyers were speculators, broker agents, and dry goods and groceries merchants.

There were many dry goods and groceries merchants that advertised an interest in purchasing cotton for cash and/or merchandise, with the terms "highest cash prices" and "highest market prices" used to cover the mix. This included the so-called "cash only" merchants such as H. N. Walcott, who advertised in the May 14, 1853, *Jefferson Herald* (Fig. 18-1) dry goods at wholesale and retail "which he is selling at reduced prices for cash, cotton, beeswax or peltries." All of the advertisements were by wholesalers, apparently because producers demanded wholesale rates for valuations of their cotton in the context of merchandise exchanges. The advertisements suggest that merchants simply waited for cotton to be brought to their doorstep for private transactions. However, this was not the case. Producers desired the highest prices for their cotton, which could be obtained only in a competitive bidding setting. This forced merchants who wished to participate in the cotton market to go out into the streets and bid competitively against speculators and spinners' agents.

The first firm to advertise that it wished to purchase cotton was May & Company, wholesale and retail dealers in dry goods and groceries, which offered in the April 5, 1851, *Texas Republican* "The highest price paid in Cash or Goods for Cotton, Peltries, Hides, Wool, Beeswax, &c." May & Company also advertised in the May 14, 1853, *Jeffer-*

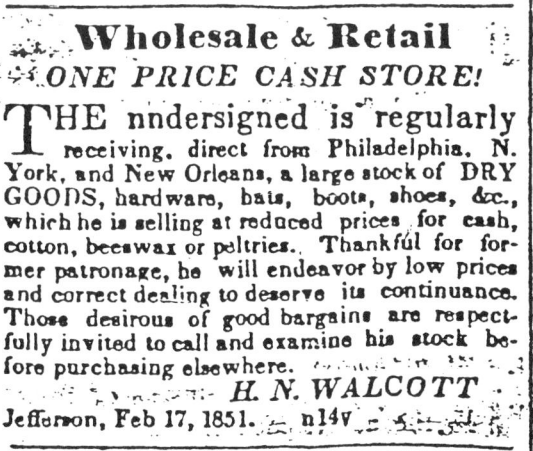

Fig. 18-1. H. N. Walcott Advertisement. Source: May 14, 1853, *Jefferson Herald*

son Herald, offering "The highest prices paid for Cotton, Hides, Peltries and Beeswax, in Cash or Goods," with "Liberal advances made in cash or goods, for Cotton shipped through us to J. H. Heald, New Orleans."

In the May 1, 1852, Marshall *Star State Patriot*, M. Steinlein & Company, wholesale and retail dealer in dry goods and groceries, indicated that "we will give the highest market prices for Cotton, Peltries, Hides, Beeswax, &c." The same advertisement appears in the May 14, 1853, *Jefferson Herald*, but with a larger companion advertisement (Fig. 18-2) stating that "We will pay the highest market prices for cotton, hides, peltries, beeswax, tallow, &c., &c. And to those who desire to ship their produce to the house of Ward & Jonas, New Orleans, we will make liberal advances in money or groceries." In the same issue, Veal & Jennings, wholesale and retail merchants in dry goods and groceries, stated that they would "receive in exchange for goods, at the *highest cash prices*, all the products of the country generally sold in Eastern Texas, such as *Hides, Peltries, Beeswax, Tallow, &c., &c.*" Spilker & Company, wholesale and retail dealers in dry goods and groceries, advertised in the March 14, 1857, *Eastern Texas Gazette* "The highest prices paid for Cotton and Peltries." Manwaring & Company, wholesale and retail dealer in dry goods and groceries, advertised in the February 18, 1860, *Texas Republican* that "They buy Cotton, Hides, Peltries, Wool, &c., on which they pay the highest market price."

There are no mentions of speculators or broker agents in the extant Jefferson newspapers, and the level of buying activity on the part of dry goods and groceries merchants can only be inferred from their advertisements. However, R. W. Bullard is listed in the 1860 Marion County Census as a 38-year-old cotton buyer born in Georgia with a wife and child and living in the house of John Speake. Bullard probably acted as a buyer for one of the New Orleans brokerage houses.

The first mention of an actual sale in the limited newspaper sources is in the August 27, 1853, *Jefferson Herald*, as quoted in the September 3 Clarksville *Standard*:

> THE FIRST BALE OF COTTON OF THE SEASON.—On Monday last, the 22nd inst., Mr. J. M. Lasater, whose plantation is eight miles south of Jefferson, in Harrison county, sent to Jefferson the first bale

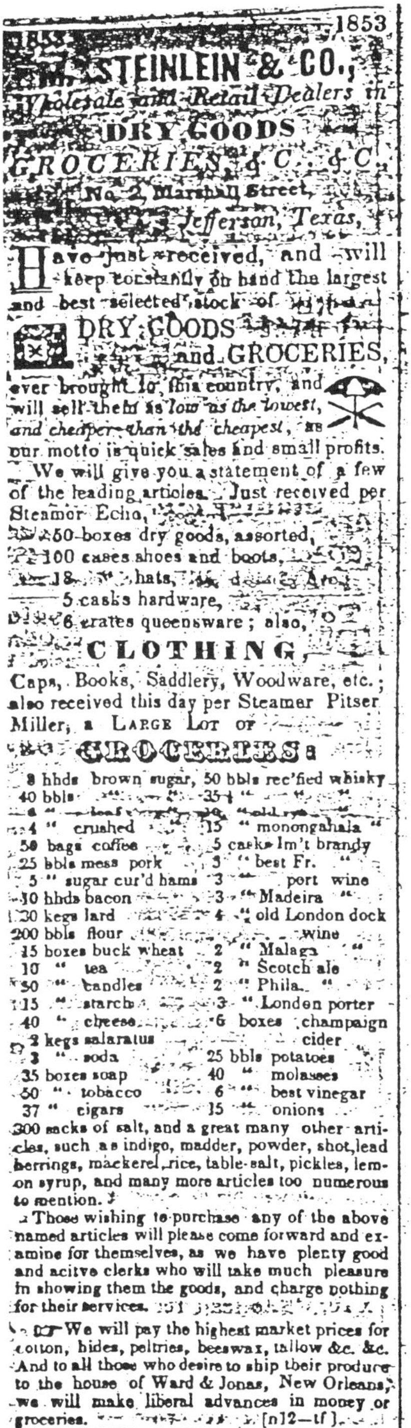

fig. 18-2. M. Steinlein & Company. Source: May 14, 1853, *Jefferson Herald*

of new cotton received here this season. The cotton was of superior quality and staple, and was purchased by those clever, accommodating and enterprising Merchants, M. Steinlein & Co., at ten cents per pound. The weight of the bale was 570 pounds, and the amount paid for it was $57. Send in your cotton; now is the time for good prices, and our Merchants are the very men to give them.

M. Steinlein & Company was in the wholesale and retail dry goods and groceries business. The transaction might have included merchandise exchange as well as cash. This notification is important for the specific sale, but also for the appended comment, which indicates that many Jefferson merchants were purchasing cotton.

The degree of regional interest about events in Jefferson is reflected in the fact that the May 29, 1858, Marshall *Texas Republican* republished a "Price Current" column from the *Jefferson Gazette* (Fig. 18-3), introducing it with the comment that "A very large number of our subscribers are interested in the Jefferson market," and citing the prevailing price at from nine to 10½ cents per pound. And indeed, important things were happening in Jefferson, as witnessed by the September 10, 1858, Marshall *Harrison Flag*:

> The Jefferson Gazette wishes it distinctly understood that the house of Messrs. Murphy of Jefferson has paid the highest price for new cotton that has been paid at any point in the United States; and that the cotton was well worth the money it brought. Jefferson is truly a flourishing commercial point, and we have no disposition to controvert either position. In agriculture old Harrison claims a high position, if she is willing to concede that cities of neighboring counties rival her commercial marts. These reflections lead us to inquire of the Gazette where this superior cotton was raised, to which the editor will please reply.

Fig. 18-3. Price Current Column. Source: May 29, 1858, *Texas Republican*

JEFFERSON MARKET.

A very large number of our subscribers are interested in the Jefferson market. For their benefit we publish the following:

The last Jefferson Gazette quotes the sales of cotton at that place at from 9 to 10¼. Other articles are quoted as follows:

	From	To
SUGAR, per pound	7	9¼
MOLASSES, per gallon	40	45
FLOUR, per bbl	5 50	7 00
PORK, per bbl	20 00	23 00
BACON SIDES, per pound	12	13
SHOULDERS, per pound	10	
HAMS, per pound	12	16
Canvas, per pound	18	
LARD, per pound	15	17
COFFEE, Rio, per pound	13½	14
SALT, per sack	1 75	2 00
WHISKEY, per gallon	28	35
LARD OIL, per gallon	1 50	
CANDLES, per pound	24	31
CORN, per bushel	90	1 00
BAGGING, Kentucky, per yard	18	
India, per yard	16	
ROPE, per pound	12	12½
TWINE, per bunch	18	
NAILS, per pound	5	6
SHOT, per sack	2 50	2 75
HIDES, per pound	9	10
LIME, per bbl	1 00	
LOWELS, per yard	12½	15
LINSEYS, per yard	25	35
FREIGHTS to New Orleans, per bale	1 00	

The purchasing firm was J. M. & J. C. Murphy, receiving, forwarding, and commission merchants and wholesale and retail dealers in dry goods and groceries. Additional information on this transaction was presented in the August 14, 1858, *Jefferson Herald*, as quoted in the August 24 *Daily Picayune*: "The first bale of new cotton was brought in our town on the 10th inst., by Mr. John G. Morris of Harrison county, and was purchased by the commission house of J. M. & J. C. Murphy, of this city, at 16½ cents. P. lb." This indicates that commission merchants bought cotton while engaged in the business of selling cotton. Because J. M. & J. C. Murphy were also in the dry goods and groceries business, the transaction could indicate normal business operations.

However, the emphasis in the *Jefferson Herald* is on the commission dimension of the business; and similar transactions in the Shreveport newspapers indicate that cotton purchases by commission merchants were not uncommon.

Williamson Freeman was a receiving, forwarding, and commission merchant and wholesale and retail dealer in dry goods and groceries. He advertised in the January 7, 1859, *Harrison Flag*: "1000 BALES OF COTTON WANTED, for which a liberal price in cash will be paid." This is another example of a commission merchant who was also in the business of buying cotton. If cotton was selling at 10 cents a pound and the average bale weighed 500 pounds, Freeman's 1,000 bales would have been purchased for a million dollars (in current dollars).

The volume of sales of cotton in Jefferson may never be known because of the near absence of period newspapers. The only evidence with respect to the relative weight of sales versus shipment through Jefferson for sale in New Orleans is in a "Price Current" column in the February 18, 1859, *Harrison Flag*, which states that 621 bales had been received and 227 sold in the week previous to February 14, and that under depressed market conditions (Fig. 18-4). Similar numbers in the Shreveport newspapers make it clear that the "sales" figures included merchandise and/or cash transactions. However, it appears that large amounts of cash were changing hands during the late antebellum period, as reported by the editor of the *Harrison Flag* in the January 7, 1859, issue based on a visit to Jefferson at the height of the cotton season:

> But our purpose is more particularly to speak of the commerce of Jefferson, and of her enterprizing citizens and of her prospects in the future. From what we witnessed when there on our recent visit, we very much doubt whether there is a place on the face of the green earth, with less than twenty-five hundred inhabitants, which does a like amount of business. Two thousand bales of cotton have been sold for cash alone within a week the present season, to say nothing of the amount obtained in barter. And there is plenty of money to pay for all that may arrive. This is no idle boast, as our readers may see by reference to Mr. Freeman's adver-

tisement. He has the money now in his safe to pay for one thousand bales, for which he will give a fair price.

Commercial.

Jefferson Wholesale Market—Corrected.

COTTON.—This week Cotton has come in slowly, the receipts for the week ending February 14th, barely reached 621 bales, and sales for the week were only 227 bales. The adverse news from Europe, has had quite an effect on our market, coupled with the unprecedented receipts at the ports has lowered our market a full cent ℔. We now quote Middlings 9¢a9¼. The lower grades are nominal.—*Jefferson Herald.*

SUGAR, ℔	8 @ 11
MOLASSES, ℔ gal.	45 @ 50
FLOUR, ℔ bbl Western	6 @ 8
" Texas, ℔ hundred	$2@ 2¼
PORK, ℔ bbl	$22 @ —
BACON, Sides, ℔ ℔	12 @ 14
" Shoulders, ℔ ℔	10 @ 8?
HAMS, Plain, ℔ ℔	12 @ 14
" Canvass, ℔ ℔	18 @ —
LARD, ℔ ℔	15 @ 16
COFFEE, Rio, ℔ ℔	13 @ 13½
SALT, ℔ sack	$2 @ 2.25
WHISKEY, ℔ gal	35 @ 50
OIL, lard, ℔ gal	$1.50
CANDLES, ℔ ℔	25 @ 30
CORN, ℔ bushel	75 @ —
BAGGING, Ky. ℔ yd	15 @ 17
" India ℔ yd	14 @ —
ROPE, ℔ ℔	10 @ 11
TWINE, ℔ bunch	5 @ 6
HIDES, ℔ ℔	14 @ 15
LOWELS, ℔ yd	12 @ 14
LINSEY, ℔ yd	25 @ 30

Shreveport Market.

Cotton—Middling 9½ @ 10¼.

New Orleans Market.

Inferior	nominal	Middling	10½ @ 11
Ordinary	nominal	Good "	11½ @ 12
Low middling	10¼ @ 10½	Middling fair	12½ @ 12¾

Fig. 18-4. Price Current Column. Source: February 18, 1859, *Harrison Flag*

Jefferson's cotton market was not institutionalized. It was composed of a street component and a facility component constituted by the commission merchants. Producers did not need to come to town to sell through commission merchants. Commission sales usually did not interrupt the normal pattern of commercial ox-wagon transport, which was directed towards receiving and forwarding merchants for placement on steamboats for sale in New Orleans. The street component was a different matter because it required producers to come to town, probably using smaller wagons. There was a lot more activity on Jefferson's streets than would be suggested by the circular movement of commercial ox-wagons, particularly if commodities other than cotton are taken into consideration.

It can be assumed that there were transactions from Jefferson's earliest years in which ownership of cotton changed hands and that these transactions involved speculators and dry goods and groceries merchants at a minimum, with receiving and forwarding merchants definitely providing cash and merchandise advances and probably engaging in commission sales even if they did not advertise as such. As a consequence, the basic features of a cotton market were in existence from the earliest years. The expansion of these activities was directly proportional to the expansion of cotton production in Jefferson's market area, which increased sevenfold from 1849 to 1859; and the relative proportion of the cotton that passed through Jefferson that was sold in Jefferson increased over time.

As with any developing phenomenon, it is difficult to designate a particular point at which a full-fledged cotton market emerged. Mention of cotton in a "Jefferson Price Current" column is a strong indicator because these columns announced to regional buyers and sellers the prevailing prices for wholesale merchandise and agricultural commodities and usually included columns for the competitive markets in Shreveport and New Orleans. Unfortunately, only three complete antebellum Jefferson newspapers have survived. There is no "Price Current" column in the May 14, 1853, *Jefferson Herald*. The March 14 and November 7, 1857, issues of the *Eastern Texas Gazette* contain "Price Current" columns that list the sales ranges during the preceding week for the export commodities of cotton, wool, hides, and pelts.

When this column came into existence in Jefferson newspapers cannot be determined; and in any case, it recognized existing activities rather than introducing a formal market. Advertisements and the operations of various firms suggest that a full-fledged cotton market existed in Jefferson by 1851. When May & Company advertised in the regionally distributed Marshall *Texas Republican* "The highest price paid in Cash or Goods for Cotton, Peltries, Hides, Wool, Beeswax, &c.," the advertisement indicates competition within a Jefferson market as well as in relation to other markets. The formation of the commission operations of J. M. & J. C. Murphy in June and W. M. Freeman in October confirms that cotton and other agricultural commodities were being sold in Jefferson in substantial quantities by at least 1851.

The extent of this market should not be exaggerated, particularly given the paucity of sales accounts. The editor of the Shreveport *South-Western* did not recognize until the November 5, 1856, issue an emerging desire to sell in the Shreveport market: "Cotton is arriving briskly from the interior, and our town begins to wear a lively aspect.—We are pleased to find a growing disposition among planters to sell at this place, instead of shipping to New Orleans." Moreover, the dominance of traditional transport modes for Shreveport and Jefferson during the antebellum period as well as a significantly changed balance in relation to the New Orleans market was not expressed until the July 13, 1870, issue in the words of Capt. E. W. Gould of St. Louis, agent for the Star Line of steamboats, who had visited Shreveport and intended to visit Jefferson: "The trade of this country… has always been monopolized by New Orleans. But the former mode of doing business is undergoing a change; and instead of cotton being shipped to New Orleans to be sold on account of the planter, to cover advances, it is now sold to merchants and speculators in Shreveport and Jefferson, to a great measure."

Hide Market

In addition to the cotton market, there were separate markets in Jefferson for other agricultural commodities such as cattle, hides, skins, pelts, furs, wool, beeswax, tallow, bois d'arc seed, honey, and snakeroot. All of these commodities were purchased speculatively on the streets of Jefferson, sold by commission houses, and purchased or received as barter or in debt payment by mercantile establishments.

The hide market was probably the market second in importance to cotton. Cattle hides were produced in abundance in Jefferson's market area and became increasingly important through the formation of meat packeries and attendant tanning operations in the vicinity of Jefferson in the late 1850s. There was one important feature of the hide market that did not pertain to the cotton market. No Jefferson merchant advertised as solely in the business of buying cotton, but there was one such merchant for hides.

N. G. Tryon was a Shreveport dealer in hides, skins, wool, and related commodities who established a branch on Dallas Street in Jefferson in early 1860, with H. B. Orton as agent. Tryon began advertising in the March 17, 1860, *Texas Republican* (Fig. 18-5) "Cash and the highest market prices paid for all articles in my line of business, at all seasons of the year." The location is given as one door below James Durr's grocery store, which would place it on the west half of Lot 1 in Block 6. Harry Orton acquired both operations from Tryon in September 1865, operating under the name of H. B. Orton & Company (with E. M. Van Nostrand as partner) and advertising cash payments for hides, wool, peltries, furs, tallow, beeswax, and related commodities. Orton is shown in the 1860 census as an unmarried 33-year-old hide buyer born in New York and living in the house of John Speake.

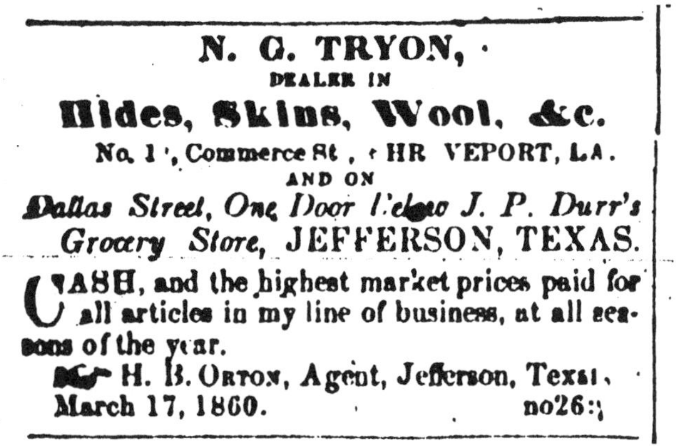

N. G. TRYON,
DEALER IN
Hides, Skins, Wool, &c.
No. 1 ', Commerce St , r HR VEPORT, LA.
AND ON
Dallas Street, One Door below J. P. Durr's Grocery Store, JEFFERSON, TEXAS.

CASH, and the highest market prices paid for all articles in my line of business, at all seasons of the year.
☞ H. B. Orton, Agent, Jefferson, Texas.
March 17, 1860.   no26:j

Fig. 18-5. N. G. Tryon Advertisement. Source: March 17, 1860, *Texas Republican*

19. Warehouse District

The warehouse district encompassed all of the land south of Austin, east of Polk, and west of the alley that runs through the block bounded by Washington and Soda. This was the land immediately contiguous to the steamboat landing. It included land south of Dallas that is presently unoccupied by structures. It was not the only area devoted to warehouses, which were common throughout the business section of town. The warehouse district was the area in which the warehouses of the specialists in receiving and forwarding were concentrated.

The warehouse district was a separate area in the original concept of the town. Warehouse lots were not numbered consecutively with the rest of the lots in the Jesse Cherry town plan, but received their own set of designations. The only warehouse lots that are mentioned by name in the deed records are Lots 1–8 in Block 9 and Lot 13 in Block 8. Lots 1–8 occupied the block bounded by Dallas, Austin, Walnut, and Soda. This was the center of the landing area. The eighth lot, which is no longer in existence, extended out into Walnut Street. Lots 9–13 corresponded to present-day Lots 1–5 in Block 8. The lots south of Dallas in Block 8 and east of Soda in Block 10 were originally not numbered and are referred to as unnumbered warehouse lots in the early deed records, with locations given by reference to other points. These lots were eventually numbered. Lots east of Soda and south of Dallas in Block 10 were never numbered.

Warehouses are storage facilities; but to think of them in this manner misses the point of their purpose in the landing area. The warehouses in this district were devoted to the storage of cotton and other commodities to be sent out by steamboat and the reception of commodities from steamboats to be sent out to Jefferson residents and merchants and to interior merchants, planters, and residents. They should be thought of not so much as places to keep things as places to temporarily store things that were in transit.

The warehouse district was of mixed use during the early years and probably contained a number of vacant lots. William Bishop purchased Lot 4 in Block 8 fronting Polk, Dallas, and Austin in January 1846, where he soon established a residence with a garden. Bishop became postmaster in May 1846, served until January 1847, was reappointed in June, and served until February 1849. The lot and residence, which probably also served as the post office, was sold by Bishop in December 1848.

A July 10, 1845, bond for title from Berry Durham to Pertle and Manker mentions Lot 5 in Block 8 as "adjoining Russell's bottom shed." This was an apparently unenclosed livery stable operated by William Russell. The stable was probably located on Lot 1 in Block 8, because Russell quit claimed this lot to John Speake in 1852. Apparently there was nothing on Lots 3 and 4 in 1845. A January 12, 1847, bond for title from Durham and Russell to Alford and Hotchkiss indicates that Russell's upper (i.e., upstream) and larger stable was located on Lot 7 in Block 74 on Jackson Street. A February 25, 1853, deed of conveyance from Thomas Hotchkiss to Speake and Willard mentions a stable operated by Russell on Lot 2 in Block 9. It appears that Russell's upper stable serviced travelers on the road to Marshall, and the lower stables serviced the wagons, drays, and buggies that operated in the landing area. The move from Block 8 to Block 9 was for the sake of making way for the erection of a warehouse on Lot 1 in Block 8 that was occupied by Speake, Saufley & Nimmo in 1852.

There is not much information on what was happening in the warehouse district during the earliest years. Lot transactions appear in the deed records, but owners and users were not necessarily the same. The tax rolls, which value merchandise on hand as of January 1, extend through 1857, with 1852 unreadable. However, because many of the warehouses were occupied by merchants who did not sell goods out of those facilities, they do not appear in the tax rolls or the newspapers and are seldom mentioned in the deed records.

All of the lots in Block 9 were purchased by the end of 1845. Lot 1 was purchased by William Perry in April 1845, Lot 2 by Alford & Company in November 1845, Lot 3 by William Perry in October 1845, Lot 4 by William Perry in December 1844, Lot 5 by John Speake in October 1844, Lot 6 by Joseph Prewitt in March 1845, and Lots 7 and 8 by Ephraim Hart in August 1845. In addition, in May 1844, Durham sold to William Brown "one warehouse lot not numbered to be the usual size of warehouse lots in other places," with the lot situated "on the Lake stream below the island and the fourth lot from Allen Urquhart's line and third lot from John Wm. Withie's lot, running almost a south course from said Withie's." This lot was obviously in Block 10 south of Dallas.

There is no concrete evidence for the existence of warehouses on any of these lots. Alford & Company and Ephraim Hart were Shreveport merchants. In March 1850, Hart acquired C. Lewis & Company in Shreveport, which had advertised in December 1848 in the *Spirit of the Age*. It may be that the Shreveport firms maintained warehouses in Jefferson during the early years because they had the capacity to be competitive with Jefferson merchants in servicing Jefferson's market area.

Perry sold Lot 1 back to Durham in October 1845, and this lot was purchased by Stanley & Ward in March 1847. Speake & Willard secured Lot 2 from Alford & Company at auction in 1850. It may be that these lots contained warehouses that were used by these firms in connection with their own mercantile operations rather than for receiving and forwarding services. Perry may also have been in this situation if he was a merchant, but his purchases appear to simply be investments. Perry had at least one warehouse on Lot 1 in Block 4 in June 1846, but the only evidence that he operated a store is the listing of a small amount of merchandise in the 1847 tax rolls.

When Buck Barry arrived at Jefferson in April 1845, he did not mention any warehouses. The first mention of a warehouse in the landing area is in an October 8, 1845, bond for title from Berry Durham to William Perry that refers to "a certain lot lying at the Lake on the South East side of Dallas fronting said Street fifty five feet running back one hundred feet to the waters edge fronting Colonel Urys warehouse on the South west." Amos Ury's warehouse was on the west side of the landing area in the floodplain, occupying Lot 10 in Block 8. This was an 80-foot lot on the south side of Dallas Street and running to the water's edge that had been purchased by Ennis Ury in late May 1845. The warehouse was probably of raised frame construction, was obviously built between June and September 1845, offered direct loading from and to steamboats, and was probably used by Ury primarily in connection with his store.

The second mention of a warehouse in the landing area is in a June 1846 filing of a schedule of separate property by Eliza Durham in which she mentions two warehouse lots owned by her east of the Alford lots and east of the warehouse built by Jesse Nave. Alford & Company of Shreveport owned Lot 2 in Block 9. Eliza Durham's warehouse lots were thus in Block 10, and Nave's warehouse was thus on Lot 1 in Block 9 at the corner of Dallas and Soda or Lot 6 in Block 10 across the street, with the latter confirmed by other records. Nave was a resident of Harrison County and did not own either of these lots, and the warehouse could have been constructed at any time prior to June 1846. This was also a frame structure.

An article on warehouses in the landing area in the December 16, 1848, *Sprit of the Age* mentions two that had just been completed, one of which was 40 feet by 70 feet and the other 75 feet long. These are mentioned as additions to the present warehouses, which means there must have been at least four by the end of 1848. These four would have been the two newly completed, Amos Ury's warehouse, and Jesse Nave's warehouse. The article also states that the warehouses were "amply sufficient to accommodate the merchants and planters who ship at this place." However, when Edward Smith visited Jefferson in May 1849, he mentions only one warehouse for the shipment of merchandise. Smith could not have been wrong, because he was an acute observer and had been commissioned to report on such matters. The only possible explanation is that the other warehouses, of which there were at least three, were operated by Jefferson merchants in connection with their own mercantile establishments, with receiving and forwarding services as a secondary consideration.

The warehouse devoted to shipping and receiving that was seen by Smith was the one owned by Jesse Nave and soon to be acquired by William McNeill. McNeill was a lawyer, acted as agent for Urquhart in 1847, owned 11 lots in Jefferson in 1847, and is listed in the 1850 census as a married 38-year-old clerk born in North Carolina with real estate valued at $1,200. McNeill purchased Lot 6 in Block 10 from Urquhart in August 1849. This lot apparently contained the warehouse built by Nave. Half ownership of the lot with a frame warehouse on it was acquired by the merchant Horatio Walcott in June 1850.

When this property was sold by McNeill's estate in September 1857, the transaction mentions that Walcott & McNeill had been in the receiving and forwarding business. Walcott & McNeill were restricted to receiving and forwarding services, appearing in the 1851 tax rolls as owning one lot valued at $800 but no merchandise. Walcott continued to maintain a mercantile operation on Marshall Street and is listed separately with merchandise in the 1851 tax rolls. The firm of Walcott & McNeill did not last very long and is last mentioned in November 1851, with McNeill dying in May 1852. Separate advertisements dated 1851 for H. N. Walcott as a merchant and as a receiver and forwarder appeared in the May 14, 1853, *Jefferson Herald*, with the latter advertisement mentioning a large warehouse and cotton shed.

Because McNeill did not acquire Lot 6 in Block 10 until August 1849, the warehouse mentioned by Smith in May was the one owned by Jesse Nave and subsequently acquired by McNeill. This means that the first warehouse to be devoted solely to receiving and forwarding operations was the warehouse on Lot 6 in Block 10 owned by Jesse Nave, which was erected before June 1846. Because Nave was not a Jefferson resident, it is probable that Joseph Mosby, who is listed in the 1850 census as a warehouse keeper, ran the warehouse for him. This also means that William McNeill was the proprietor in August 1849 of the first Jefferson firm specializing in receiving and forwarding services, which became Walcott & McNeill in June 1850 and H. N. Walcott in late 1851. Walcott continued in the receiving and forwarding business until September 1853, when the warehouse was acquired by W. Brooks & Brother.

Jesse Nave's warehouse and Walcott & McNeill were restricted to receiving and forwarding services. The firm of J. M. & J. C. Murphy, formed by the brothers James and John in 1851, has the distinction of being the first advertised receiving, forwarding, and commission operation, the first receiving, forwarding, and commission operation to also be involved in wholesale and retail sales, and the constructor of the first brick building in Jefferson.

James and John Murphy first appear in the deed records in a May 19, 1851, sale by John Speake to them of Lot 4 in Block 7. The firm advertised in the July 5, 1851, *Texas Republican* as a new house in town in the commission and forwarding business, that it would be located on Dallas Street near the steamboat landing but above the high-water mark, and that it was constructing a warehouse that would be completed with most of the stock in store by September 1, at which time it would be ready to receive customers. This was the first advertisement for a receiving and forwarding business in Jefferson, with receiving

Fig. 19-1. J. M. & J. C. Murphy Initial Advertisement. Source: July 5, 1851, *Texas Republican*

> **A New House In Jefferson, Texas,**
> *Dallas Street, Near the Steam Boat Landing, above high water mark.*
>
> J. M. & J. C. MURPHY, commission and forwarding merchants. Particular attention given to storing and shipping cotton and to receiving and forwarding all kinds of merchandise, &c.
>
> Dry goods and groceries of all kinds; bagging, rope, and plantation supplies, kept constantly on hand.
>
> Also cash advances made on cotton to be shipped to our friends in New Orleans.
>
> Our warehouse will be completed and the most of our stock in store on or before the 1st September next. At which time and place, we will be pleased to meet and serve our friends and the public generally, and hope by strict attention to business, with low prices and liberal accommodations to merit and receive a liberal share of public patronage.
>
> J. M & J. C. MURPHY.
>
> Jefferson, Texas, June 21. 1851.   n52 y.

understood as a correlate to forwarding (Fig. 19-1). The firm is first mentioned in operation in a January 1, 1852, conveyance from Bennett Martin.

Lot 4 in Block 7 fronting Dallas Street, which was slightly to the west of the warehouse district, was the location of the Murphys' storehouse according to a September 24, 1855, conveyance from Harper and Waddill to Dickinson and Churchill. The erection of this frame structure was noted in the September 27, 1851, Marshall *Texas Republican* by Robert Loughery reporting on one of his many visits to Jefferson: "Among the new houses going up, we noticed a large building in progress owned by Messrs. J. M. & J. C. MURPHY, who intend opening a large store in that place." The use of the term "store" was appropriate because the firm sold merchandise in addition to its receiving and forwarding operations.

The firm noted in its initial advertisement that it would receive and forward all kinds of merchandise, that it would keep in stock a large supply of dry goods and groceries, including bagging, rope, and other plantation supplies, and that it would make cash advances on cotton to be shipped to the firm's friends in New Orleans. A companion advertisement indicates that the companion firm was Wright, Williams & Company, Cotton Factors and Commission Merchants, New Orleans (Fig. 19-2). In October 1851, the firm advertised in the *Texas Republican* as wholesale and retail dealers in all kinds of merchandise and groceries, which was the first time that a receiving and forwarding operation entered into this supplemental line of business (Fig. 19-3). The firm is listed in the 1853 tax rolls as owning three lots valued at $3,000 with $7,000 in merchandise.

The warehouse facilities connected with the storehouse on Lot 4 in Block 7 were soon found to be insufficient, perhaps in location as well as in size. Lots 3 and 4 in Block 9 were acquired by the firm on January 6, 1854. This became the location of the Murphys' fireproof brick warehouse in early 1855. This was the first recorded brick structure in Jefferson. Its location is given in three deed records, the first of which is a March 10, 1855, mortgage from J. M. & J. C. Murphy to Wright, Davenport & Company in New Orleans. Its existence is first mentioned in a February 10, 1855, advertisement for the firm in the *Texas Republican*,

> **WRIGHT, WILLIAMS, & Co.,** *Cotton Factors and Commission Merchants,* Union Row, 61, Carondalet Street, New Orleans.
>
> Cash advances made, Bagging and Rope, and plantation supplies furnished to planters, who may wish to consign their Cotton to the above House.
>
> **J. M. & J. C. MURPHY**
> Jefferson, Texas. v3n2y

Fig. 19-2. J. M. & J. C. Murphy Companion Advertisement. Source: July 5, 1851, *Texas Republican*

> **J. M. & J. C. MURPHY,** Wholesale and Retail dealers in all kinds of Merchandise and Groceries, Iron, Salt, &c. &c.
> Dallas Street, near the Steam Boat Landing, Jefferson, Texas.
> November 15th, 1851. n. 1 tf.
>
> **75** Pieces Bagging; 75 coils Rope, and some Twine for sale.
> J. M. & J. C. MURPHY.
> Jefferson, Nov. 15, 1851. n21 tf.

Fig. 19-3. J. M. & J. C. Murphy Wholesale Advertisement. Source: November 15, 1851, *Texas Republican*

> **NEW ADVERTISEMENTS.**
>
> **J. M. & J. C. MURPHY:** Fire-proof Brick Warehouse, Receiving, Forwarding and Commission Merchants. Dallas street, Steamboat Landing, Jefferson, Texas.
>
> Liberal Advances made in Cash and Supplies upon Cotton and Produce left with them for shipment or sale. All kinds of Produce and Manufactured articles received to sell on Commission. Feb 10, 1855. 27 ly

Fig. 19-4. J. M. & J. C. Murphy Brick Warehouse Advertisement. Source: February 10, 1855, *Texas Republican*

which indicates that the receiving, forwarding, and commission operations were provided out of this facility (Fig. 19-4). A note by Loughery in the next issue indicates that the structure was two stories high with a front of 80 feet and running back 180 feet. The firm appears in the 1855 tax rolls with $7,000 in merchandise.

This was a bad year for a new business initiative. Navigation had been poor in 1854 and declined to practically nothing in 1855, with a devastating effect on most commercial operations in Jefferson. The Murphys sold various properties on March 10, including their slaves and the storehouse on Lot 4 in Block 7, to William Harper and Daniel Waddell of Caddo Parish. This was the same day on which they mortgaged to Wright, Davenport & Company the recently completed brick warehouse. The firm was reorganized in January 1856 as J. C. Murphy & Company, composed of John Murphy, Perry Graham, and Henry Yell. James Murphy replaced Perry Graham in March 1856, and the firm reverted to its old name. J. M. & J. C. Murphy advertised from March through September 1857 in the Jefferson *Eastern Texas Gazette* as receiving, forwarding, grocery, and commission merchants in the large brick warehouse at the steamboat landing. The firm appears in the 1857 tax roles with one lot valued at $10,000, but only $500 in merchandise. It appears to have maintained a continuous existence through at least 1861, and both brothers were in various receiving and forwarding firms in Jefferson after the Civil War.

W. M. Freeman, which was started by Williamson Freeman, was the second receiving, forwarding, and commission operation to advertise, and the first to advertise and also be located within the boundaries of the warehouse district. Freeman did not add a wholesale component until January 1858. In the November 1, 1851, Clarksville *Northern Standard*, Freeman advertised as a new warehouse and as an auction, commission, and forwarding merchant offering services to planters, merchants, and traders in the storage and sale or shipping of their cotton, pelts, and stock of any kind, with cash advances on cotton in store. The advertisement indicates that the warehouse was above the highwater mark, that contiguous lots were available for keeping stock designed for shipment, and that Freeman's business office was at Samuel Friou's store on Dallas Street (Fig. 19-5).

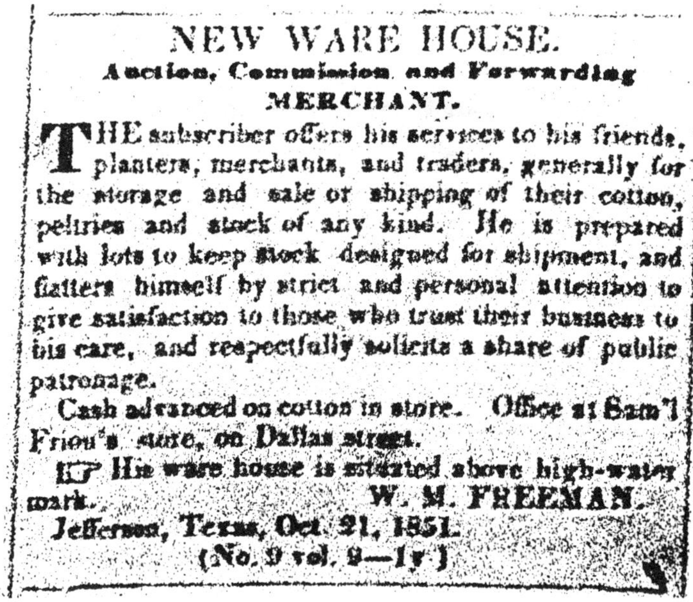

> **NEW WARE HOUSE.**
> **Auction, Commission and Forwarding MERCHANT.**
>
> THE subscriber offers his services to his friends, planters, merchants, and traders, generally for the storage and sale or shipping of their cotton, peltries and stock of any kind. He is prepared with lots to keep stock designed for shipment, and flatters himself by strict and personal attention to give satisfaction to those who trust their business to his care, and respectfully solicits a share of public patronage.
>
> Cash advanced on cotton in store. Office at Sam'l Friou's store, on Dallas street.
>
> ☞ His ware house is situated above high-water mark. **W. M. FREEMAN.**
> Jefferson, Texas, Oct. 21, 1851.
> (No. 9 vol. 9—1y.)

Fig. 19-5. W. M. Freeman Advertisement. Source: November 1, 1851, *Northern Standard*

Freeman referred to himself as a receiving, auction, forwarding, and commission merchant in the October 5, 1852, *Northern Standard*. The advertisement emphasized that the warehouse was located above the high-water mark and close enough to the landing that goods could be received directly from the boats, thereby avoiding drayage costs. The office had been relocated to the warehouse. Freeman's warehouse was said to be new and apparently was located on Lot 4 in Block 10, which had been acquired from Urquhart on November 9, 1852, as a correction to a previous transaction that went back to January 1851. Freeman was able to advertise direct offloading from boats because the bayou impinged on Dallas in front of his warehouse. Lot 4 in Block 10 was apparently Freeman's location in 1851 and 1852.

Freeman advertised in May 1853 in the *Jefferson Herald* as a receiving, auction, forwarding, and commission merchant with a large and commodious warehouse. Benjamin Terry and Thomas Rogers formed the firm of Terry & Rogers and advertised in February 1857 that they were in the receiving, forwarding, and commission business and had leased Freeman's warehouse. Freeman, Terry, and Rogers formed the firm of Wm. M. Freeman & Company, advertising in March 1857 in the *Eastern Texas Gazette* as receiving, forwarding, and commission merchants at Freeman's old stand on Dallas Street. B. J. Terry ran an advertisement in the same issue as a wholesale and retail dealer in groceries and plantation supplies and gave as his location Freeman's old stand. Both of these advertisements continued to run in the *Eastern Texas Gazette* through November 1857.

Terry ran an independent operation at Freeman's old stand because Wm. M. Freeman & Company was not in the business of selling goods. The partnership with Freeman and Rogers in the receiving and forwarding business ended in late 1857. B. J. Terry & Company, composed of Benjamin Terry, James Gardner, and David Culberson, purchased Lot 7 (and 10 feet of Lot 8) in Block 9 from William Torrans in October 1858; and in February 1860, William Perry sold to William Torrans Lot 6 in Block 9 with one-half of a brick wall that he had built jointly with David Culberson. Although there are no advertisements for B. J. Terry & Company, it apparently was a continuation of B. J. Terry and therefore in the groceries and plantation supplies business. It was located at Freeman's old stand on Lot 4 in Block 10 or else in the newly acquired Lot 7 in Block 9, with the latter being the most probable.

It should be noted that there were brick structures on Lots 6 and 7 in Block 9 in 1860, probably going back to late 1858, with simultaneous construction by Perry and B. J. Terry & Company. Perry's use of the facility on Lot 6 is unknown. He may have been a renter, with the occupant also unknown. Torrans had been in the grocery business on Lot 9 in Block 5 from 1855 until March 1860, when the property was sold to William Prewitt. It is probable that he moved to Lot 6 in Block 9 during March, with the property having been purchased from Perry in February, and continued in the wholesale and retail grocery business.

Freeman found it necessary in October 1857 to advertise in the Clarksville *Standard* that he had not sold out and left Jefferson and that he was constructing a new fireproof brick warehouse next to his old warehouse that would be 100 feet by 140 feet. The new warehouse was apparently on Lots 5 and 6 in Block 10 at the corner of Dallas and Soda.

Freeman acquired Lot 5 from William Perry in April 1855 and Lot 6 containing the old Nave warehouse from Horatio Walcott in September 1857. This new facility was the second brick structure in Jefferson. The inception of this new building was noted by the *Jefferson Gazette*, as quoted by the January 9, 1858, *Standard*:

> Messrs. W. M. Freeman & Co.'s card appears in our columns to day, to which we refer you for particulars. We will not say anything by way of recommendation of Mr. F., as a business man, his experience in business for thirty years, the last seven of which were spent in Jefferson, has given satisfaction to his patrons and made him many warm and strong friends. By his industry and energy he has nearly completed his Mammoth Fire proof Warehouse, and will be ready to receive produce and merchandise by the 15th inst. He has already a large and commodious Frame House, where he has been doing business for the past seven years. When his mammoth ware house is completed, it would honor any city. As Mr. Freeman is a native Georgian, the house is constructed on the plan of the Georgia and Alabama warehouses.

The new facility was advertised in the January 16, 1858, *Standard*, under the name W. M. Freeman & Company, with Thomas Rogers as the other partner, as receiving, forwarding, and commission merchants and wholesale dealers in groceries and plantation supplies. The firm became Freeman, Clark & Bryan (with William Clark and John Bryan) in April 1858 and was dissolved in July according to an October notification in the *Standard*, with an indication that Freeman would continue in the commission and forwarding business under his own name. Freeman advertised briefly in January 1859 as a dealer in groceries, boat and bar stores, and plantation supplies and emphasized that he paid cash for cotton. An accompanying article indicates that he had sufficient cash in his safe to purchase 1,000 bales. In February 1859, Freeman advertised as a receiving, forwarding, and commission merchant and wholesale and retail dealer in groceries and plantation supplies. Also in February 1859, Freeman transferred Lots 1–3 in Block 10 to John Hobdy; and in May 1860, Freeman and Hobdy leased Lots 1–6 along with the warehouse, store, and sheds to Hiram Cutrer, who entered into the receiving, forwarding, and commission business in September 1860 under the name H. A. Cutrer & Company, with Benjamin Terry and David Culberson as partners.

Speake, Saufley & Nimmo advertised as receiving, forwarding, and commission merchants in the September 11, 1852, *Northern Standard*, with cash advanced on all consignments. This firm, which was composed of John Speake, William Saufley, and Samuel Nimmo, was the third to advertise in the receiving and forwarding business. The advertisement stresses to immigrants that Jefferson is the nearest shipping point for the counties of Smith, Wood, Upshur, Titus, Hopkins, Hunt, Kaufman, Van Zandt, Dallas, Henderson, Anderson, Navarro, Collin, Ellis, Denton, Cook, Grayson, Fannin, Lamar, and others. Speake was one of Jefferson's earliest merchants. He acquired Lot 5 in Block 9 in 1844, which is a possible location for the warehouse. Another possibility is Lot 1 in Block 8, which Speake acquired along with Lot 2 from Urquhart in July 1852. Speake, Saufley & Nimmo did not last very long, with Saufley and Nimmo entering into a dry goods and groceries business in February 1853. John Speake advertised in the January 28, 1859, *Harrison Flag* as a receiving and forwarding merchant located on the corner of Dallas and Walnut streets, which apparently was on Lot 1 in Block 8.

In the May 14, 1853, *Jefferson Herald*, John Waskom advertised that he had leased the large, new, and commodious warehouse formerly occupied by Speake, Saufley & Nimmo and that he was operating as a warehouseman, with particular attention to the care of cotton and a footnote indicating that he was "prepared to advance liberally in cash, groceries or produce, on cotton in store for shipment; and promise that every man's cotton shall be sold on its own merits." Although he did not advertise as such, Waskom obviously was in the receiving, forwarding, and commission business.

Stanley & Seymour advertised as receiving, forwarding, and commission merchants in the May 14, 1853, *Jefferson Herald*. This firm, which was composed of Charles Stanley and Daniel Seymour, was the fourth to advertise in the receiving and forwarding business. Stanley was one of Jefferson's earliest merchants. Seymour was a resident of Hartford, Connecticut. Lot 1 in Block 9 was sold to Stanley & Seymour by Gad Stanley and James Moore of Connecticut in September 1851, which marks the beginning of the firm and the probable location of the warehouse. C. N. Stanley advertised in the January 13, 1855, *Texas Republican* as a commission and forwarding merchant, with a large and well-finished warehouse entirely above overflow. Heald, Massie & Company and McKleroy & Bradford of New Orleans are given as references. Stanley's warehouse was located at the foot of Houston Street at the bridge. The remoteness of this location from the landing area suggests that C. N. Stanley was primarily in the commission business, as its advertisement indicates. Stanley joined with Samuel Nimmo in early 1856 to establish a furniture store in the warehouse.

W. Brooks & Brother, composed of William and John, was the fifth firm to advertise in the receiving and forwarding business and the second to enter the wholesale and retail business, having done so before Freeman. W. Brooks & Brother had been in the dry goods and groceries business in Jefferson since 1851 on Dallas Street on the west half of Lot 8 in Block 5. The firm advertised in the September 17, 1853, *Standard* that it had entered into the receiving and forwarding business and that it had acquired the warehouse formerly occupied by H. N. Walcott at the landing. Listed as references in northeast Texas are merchants and individuals in Clarksville, Dallas, McKinney, Boston, Daingerfield, Tyler, Gilmer, Coffeeville, Linden, Mt. Pleasant, Paris, and Bonham. Cash, groceries, dry goods, and plantation supplies were kept on hand for advancement to anyone consigning their shipments to the firm, with a particular desire for cotton, pelts, hides, and wool.

W. Brooks & Brother expanded into the commission business and into the wholesale and retail sale of dry goods and groceries in January 1854. The brothers dissolved this firm in February 1854 and entered a new partnership at the same location with Hinche Mabry under the name Brooks, Brother & Mabry. This firm lasted less than a year, and the Brooks brothers were apparently out of the receiving and forwarding business by February 1855, when they advertised as in the wholesale and retail dry goods business on Dallas Street, apparently having maintained this business during the years when they were in the receiving and forwarding business in the landing area.

W. C. Baker & Company advertised in the February 18, 1854, *Texas Republican* as general dealers in dry goods and groceries and also as receiving, forwarding, and commission merchants on Dallas Street. This firm, which was composed of William and Francis Baker, had advertised in May 1853 as in the general mercantile business. The location in 1853 was apparently on the east half of Lot 10 in Block 5 on Dallas Street. There is nothing to indicate that the Bakers were ever located in the landing area. It appears that the receiving and forwarding services were provided through the Bakers' mercantile business.

J. Mosby & Company, composed of Joseph Mosby and Labon Bayless, advertised in the April 3, 1852, *Texas Republican* as commission merchants featuring groceries, produce, cotton gins, and horse mills sold for cash. There is nothing in the advertisement to indicate that the firm provided receiving and forwarding services. This firm became Mosby, Schluter & Company, commission merchants, in March 1856, with Henry Schluter as a primary partner, with the advertisement in the *Texas Republican* indicating that they were also in the receiving and forwarding business. Abraham Kohn, who had been in the dry goods and groceries business in 1855, was apparently a member of this firm. Mosby, Schluter & Company became Mosby & Kohn, with Abraham Kohn as the only partner, in May 1856, with the advertisement in the *Texas Republican* indicating that they would continue in the commission and forwarding business at their old stand on Dallas Street and that they had a warehouse that could store 5,000 bales of cotton and sheds that could store an additional 3,000 bales. Mosby was probably on Lot 1 in Block 7, which was acquired from John Speake in January 1852 and mortgaged to John Withee in September 1852 and to J. M. & J. C. Murphy in January 1853. The firm was out of business by March 1857, when the facility was occupied by the dry goods and groceries merchants Spilker & Company.

Bryan & Clark, composed of John Bryan and William Clark, advertised in the March 14, 1857, *Eastern Texas Gazette* as receiving, forwarding, and commission merchants on Dallas Street, keeping on hand a large stock of sugar, coffee, molasses, whiskey, brandy, salt, tobacco, bacon hams, flour, potatoes, onions, bagging, rope, brandy peaches, lemon syrup, brandy pears, pepper sauce, pickles, cheese, crackers, sardines, lobsters, oysters, castings, iron, blacksmithing tools, axes, lowels, domestics, cotton yarns, cigars, candies, starch, soda, saleratus, spice, pepper, ginger, etc. A similar advertisement in the April 4, 1857, *Texas Republican* indicates that they were also wholesale and retail dealers in heavy plantation supplies. This was the third receiving and forwarding firm to be engaged in wholesaling and retailing, having done so before Freeman.

Bryan & Clark is listed in the 1857 tax rolls as having $2,000 in merchandise and no town lots. The only transaction concerning this firm is a May 4, 1858, conveyance of Lots 1 and 2 in Block 6 from George Clapp to Bryan & Clark. Clapp had given Sam Moseley power of attorney in March 1858 to dispose of this property. The sales price of $1,000 indicates that there was a structure on the property, but it appears to have been too far from the landing area to have been the location of a major cotton warehouse. Bryan and Clark joined Freeman in his new brick warehouse on April 10, 1858, in the firm of Freeman, Clark & Bryan; but this firm was dissolved on July 27, and there is no evidence that Bryan and Clark continued in the receiving and forwarding business after that time.

The amount of commerce that passed through these facilities is unknown. Import quantities can only be inferred from the information about wholesaler activities, and export quantity information is limited to the estimated 25,000 bales of cotton shipped during the 1857–58 commercial season (September through August). There were three receiving and forwarding firms in the landing area in 1857. The consignees of imported merchandise are listed for these three firms in the March 14 and November 17 *Eastern Texas Gazette*, but only the former has information on the geographic distribution of the consignees for one firm (Fig. 19–6), and neither shows number of packages (as happened after the war). The latter issue lists the number of bales received during the previous week (224), but does not indicate anything about shipments (which nevertheless closely tracked receipts). The only other information on receipts is the 621 bales for the week ending February 14, 1859, as recorded in the February 18 *Harrison Flag*. A letter from a Jefferson resident published in the March 3, 1860, *Standard* says

"Cotton still continues to come in here at the rates of 1000 and 1500 bales per week. Some selling at 7¾ to 10c."

Fig. 19-6. Consignments and Cotton Receipts. Source: March 14 and November 7, 1857, *Eastern Texas Gazette*

Consignees of Merchandise

FOR THE WEEK ENDING MARCH 14.

AT BRYAN & CLARK'S.

Buford & Thomas, Sulphur Springs; O H King, Greenville; William Clark; Murry Institute; J W Moor, Linden; Miller & Floyd, Cuseta; A S Kottwitz, Paris; S & W Evans Honey Grove; W M Hewitt, Douglassville, J C Moon, Bowie co.; Pouns & Morris, Daingerfield; J M Wiggins, Mt. Carmell; J W Clinton, Mt. Carmell; O Donner Daingerfield; Willis & Wells, Quitman; C H Jennings, Pittsburg; J Bruce, Upshur co.; J K & R K Black Cass co., Samuel Morris, Unionville; Bullen & Connally, Sulphur Springs; S Sherwood, Melwood; James Williams, not known; A D Taylor & Co. Jefferson; Ellis & Carter, Boston.

AT W. M. FREEMAN & CO'S.

Mrs. Roggens, D W H Taylor, W B Willis, Sanders & King; J H Black, L S Wright, D C Chavis, A V Dashy, P M McCown, Richards & Brothers, F Richards, Taylor & Darby, Dagley & Spencer, G W Cox, B J Terry, Robt Hughes, W M Freeman, T J Logwood & Co., Donelson & Caffery, A S Kottwitz.

AT J. M. & J. C. MURPHEYS.

G W & J T Connalley, O Ashworth, J D Digon, S E Clements, P W B, P H Flemming, A E Pace, A G Wright, Xemenes & Eude, L in a diamond, Davis & Brother, M. in a diamond, J L Bowen, P B Smith, J W Moore, Thos. Scott, L S Wells & Bro., Rev. C L Hamill, Chas. Hamill, G W & J T Connaley, Wilson & Taylor, H H Veal, L A Lollar, Winston Banks, W J Henderson, N Smith, Lockett & Stewart, P R Houghton, Hirsh & Shirek, Dan Garrison, J D Newsom.

Cotton

RECEIVED FOR THE WEEK, ENDING NOV 7, '57

At Bryan & Clark's................96 bales
At J. M. & J. C. Murphey's....103 "
At Wm. M. Freeman Co.'s......25 "

The consignments column and the cotton receipt statistics in the *Eastern Texas Gazette* suggest that there were only three firms receiving merchandise and shipping cotton in 1857: Bryan & Clark, W. M. Freeman & Company, and J. M. & J. C. Murphy. This can be assumed because there are similar listings in the Shreveport newspapers, usually with information on cotton shipments as well as receipts. The commercial data in the Shreveport newspapers constituted the city's official statistics and were used at the end of the commercial year to provide yearly totals for cotton receipts and shipments, usually representing the weekly transactions in a table. If the receipt numbers in the *Eastern Texas Gazette* are merely intended to represent the largest shippers, they obviously are not indicative of the total receipts during that week. If they are representative of the total receipts during that week, it is apparent that wholesalers who purchased or received cotton for shipment did not deal directly with steamboats, but rather transferred or directed their cotton to shippers in the landing area.

The scarcity of records should not lead to an incorrect impression about the development of the warehouse district. It is highly unlikely, for example, that the prime commercial locations on Lots 5–8 in Block 9 would have been unoccupied, and it is almost certain that Bryan & Clark, whose location is unknown, would have occupied one of these lots. The available records indicate that there were three cotton shippers in 1857, confirming Smith's observation that there was only one in 1849 (Jesse Nave's frame structure, which was constructed prior to June 1846). The warehouse district was dominated by receiving, forwarding, and commission merchants, but included mercantile establishments, a stable, and at least one residence. There was significant development on the northwest quadrant of Block 10 that had not been anticipated in the Jesse Cherry town plan. Receiving and forwarding functions extended west of the formal boundaries of the warehouse district.

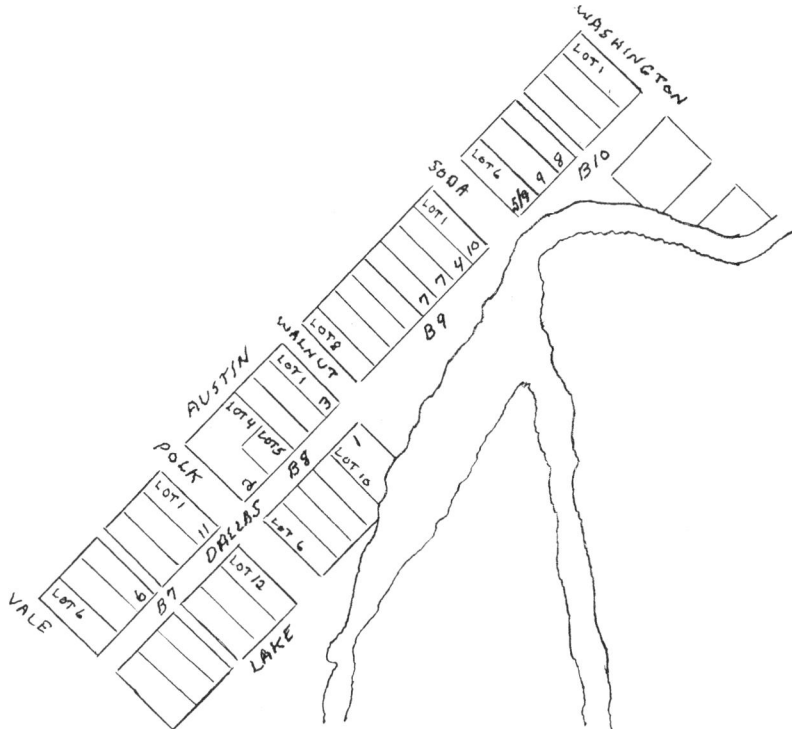

Fig. 19-7. Warehouse District
KEY:
1. Amos Ury's warehouse (1845)
2. William Bishop's residence and post office (1846)
3. William Russell's stable (1845); Speake, Saufley & Nimmo's warehouse (1852); John Waskom (1853); John Speake (1859)
4. William Russell's stable (1853)
5. Jesse Nave's warehouse (1846); William McNeill (1849); Wallcott & McNeill (1850); H. N. Walcott (1851); W. Brooks & Brother (1853); Brooks, Brother & Mabry (1854)
6. J. M. & J. C. Murphy's frame warehouse (1851)
7. J. M. & J. C. Murphy's brick warehouse (1855)
8. Williamson Freeman's frame warehouse (1851); Terry & Rogers (1857); Wm. M. Freeman & Company (1857)
9. W. M. Freeman & Company's brick warehouse (1858); Freeman, Clark & Bryan (1858); W. M. Freeman (1859); H. A. Cutrer & Company (1860)
10. Stanley & Seymour (1853)
11. J. Mosby & Company (1852); Mosby, Schluter & Company (1856); Mosby & Kohn (1856); Spilker & Company (1857)
12. B. J. Terry & Company (1858)

20. Earliest Merchants

Merchants were people who sold goods and therefore included the wholesalers and retailers and the receiving, forwarding, and commission merchants insofar as they expanded into such operations. Merchants and their employee clerks constituted by far the largest occupational listings in the 1860 census, indicating the degree to which Jefferson was a mercantile town. All merchants sold retail to the local population and people who came to town. Many sold wholesale to interior merchants and planters, providing one of the features that was integral to Jefferson's unusual status as a commercial center.

First Advertisement

The first extant advertisement for a Jefferson business is for the druggists Alexander & Chrisman and appears in the June 17, 1846, Clarksville *Northern Standard* (Fig. 20-1). The firm was composed of the partners Alexander Alexander (his name according to the deed records) and John Chrisman. The advertisement announces a desire to close the business and to sell the small stock of drugs and medicines along with equipment such as specie jars, tincture bottles, and drawers. That Jefferson had a drugstore at such an early date is not surprising because drugs and medicines were imported and sold to interior druggists. What is surprising is the dissolution of this firm shortly after it was started. The reasons remain unknown.

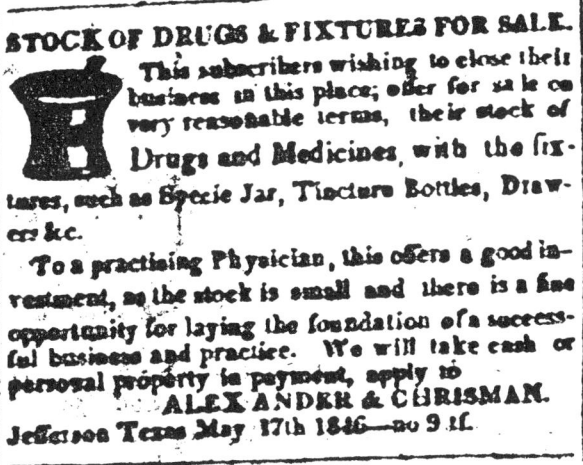

Fig. 20-1. Alexander & Chrisman Advertisement. Source: June 17, 1847, *Northern Standard*

Alexander & Chrisman began purchasing lots in Jefferson along with the firm of Stanley & Ward (composed of Charles Stanley and Mortimer Ward) from Berry Durham in January 1846. They also independently purchased from Durham Lot 4 in Block 5 on Dallas Street between Marshall and Market for $225 in January. If this firm owned their place of business, it was probably located on this lot. However, the advertisement does not mention a location. The 1846 Cass County tax rolls list the firm as owners of three lots in Jefferson along with a $500 stock in drugs.

In November 1846, Alexander relinquished to Chrisman his interest in three unidentified lots owned by the firm. Chrisman purchased a lot from James Durham in March 1847 and another from Berry Durham and Urquhart in May 1847 and gave power of attorney concerning his properties to Stanley & Ward during the same month until his return to Texas. Chrisman purchased two half lots from Mortimer Ward in January 1849. This was the last time that he appears in the deed records, and neither man is in the 1850 census.

The Alexander & Chrisman stock was purchased by Samuel Garey, as stated in an April 4, 1847, *Northern Standard* advertisement. This was the third advertisement for a Jefferson business, having been preceded by William Perry's advertisement for the Soda Lake Hotel in

December 1846. Garey operated under the sign of the Golden Mortar and advertised fresh supplies of drugs and medicines in addition to those obtained from Alexander & Chrisman. Fresh supplies would be received every three months, and the advertisement was directed to interior dealers in drugs and medicines. Garey is shown in the 1847 Cass County tax rolls as owner of seven lots in Jefferson and stock in trade valued at $1,300.

Merchants through 1850

The Rev. John McLean visited Jefferson as a boy in 1846 (or perhaps 1847) and remembered "two or three stores" and "three or four stores and shops of different kinds." Among the earliest merchants, McLean remembered Speake & Willard, Perry Graham, and Jeptha Crawford. In June 1847, the *Houston Telegraph* reported 13 stores in Jefferson. Edward Smith visited Jefferson in May 1849 and reports "several large well supplied stores." The March 14, 1850, Marshall *Texas Republican* reports "nine or ten large mercantile establishments at Jefferson."

The best source of information on Jefferson's earliest merchants is the county tax rolls. Bowie County taxes are included in the Red River County tax rolls, but they contain nothing of interest. The Cass County tax rolls begin in 1846. The taxes were on a wide range of properties for people throughout the county who owned property. Property owners are not shown by location; but if a person owned lots in Jefferson, the number is indicated along with the value. Merchants are not identified as such, but are indicated through a column showing value of merchandise on hand as of January 1 of the tax year. Some known merchants in Jefferson do not appear as lot owners in the tax rolls, which is not surprising because merchants did not need to own the land on which they operated; but some of these are known to have purchased lots in Jefferson from the deed records.

Persons who owned town lots and carried merchandise from 1846 to 1850 include: Alexander & Chrisman (1846); Josiah Hill (1847–49); Samuel Garey (1847); John Speake (1847); Israel Leavitt (1847–48, 1850); William Perry (1847); W. C. Baker & Company (1847); Jeptha Crawford (1847–50); Caleb Ragan (1848–50); Perry Graham (1848–50); Speake & Willard (1849–50); Ithael Eason (1850); Thomas Pugh (1850); and Horatio Walcott (1850). Persons with merchandise and without lots but known to have operated in Jefferson include: Stanley & Ward (1847); Reuben Drake (1847); Ury & Ward (1847, 1849–50); Richard Crump (1848–50); Charles Dunn (1848); and August May (1850). In addition, the firm of G. N. Butt & Company is listed as a multiple lot owner in 1846.

Listed as merchants in Precinct 1 in the 1850 census and known to have been Jefferson residents are: John Speake; Caleb Ragan (grocery merchant); August May; George Tuttle (in Soda Lake Hotel); Moses Ambros (in Soda Lake Hotel); William Falk (in Soda Lake Hotel); Perry Graham (in Soda Lake Hotel); S. F. Moley (probably Samuel F. Moseley, in Soda Lake Hotel); Clinton Willard; Anthony Owens (and S. N. Owens in house); Jeptha Crawford (and Thomas Ferrell in house); William Nichols; Horatio Walcott (in house of William McNeill, clerk); Amos Ury (and Matt Ward in house). No occupation is listed for Israel Leavitt. Josiah Hill is listed as a minister, Richard Crump as sheriff, Mortimer Ward as a clerk living in Robert Rogers' Star Hotel, and Ithael Eason, Thomas Pugh, and Samuel Garey as physicians. Occupational listings in the census do not necessarily indicate current practice.

Clerks listed in the 1850 census are: J. W. Fleming (in house of John Speake); M. N. Pugh (in house of Thomas Pugh); George Ury; Joseph Elliott; A. Bussineber (in house of August May); James Brickell (in Soda Lake Hotel); Willis Childress (in Soda Lake Hotel); T. B. Grogin (probably Thomas Goyne, in Soda Lake Hotel); George Morgan (in house of Clinton Willard); J. N. Mabane (in house of Clinton Willard); Abraham Kohn; Wiley Ferrell (in house of Jeptha Crawford); J. J. Hatcher (in house of William Nichols); Hiram Tomlin (in house of Amos Ury); A. M. Ward (in house of Amos Ury); Jacob Green (in Star Hotel); Mortimer Ward (in Star Hotel); Richard Bailey (in Star Hotel).

Although it is obvious that Amos Ury was operating as a merchant in 1845, the first actual mention of a mercantile facility in Jefferson occurs in a January 12, 1846, bond for title from Berry Durham to Jeptha and Merriweather Crawford concerning a portion of Lot 11 in Block 5, "being a portion of the lot on which the house stands occupied by Messrs. Butt & Speak." There is no other evidence that George Butt and John Speake were ever in business together, although they did jointly purchase Lot 4 in Block 27 at auction on October 4, 1845. It may be that the firm of G. N. Butt & Company was already in existence, with Butt as the senior and Speake as the junior partner.

Butt had been in business with William Waddey in Shreveport until late 1842. He swore in March 1845 to having witnessed a land transaction between Berry Durham and Richard Peters in January. The firm of G. N. Butt & Company appears in the 1846 tax rolls as owner of 10 lots in Jefferson valued at $440, but no mention is made of merchandise. The company is mentioned in a June 6, 1846, bond for title from Jesse Nave to Jeptha Crawford. A March 5, 1847, conveyance mentions the house of George N. Butt & Company as located east of Lot 10 in Block 5. A December 13, 1847, bond for title mentions Lot 11 in Block 5 "whereon the store house of Speak, Willard & Co. now stands, it being the house formerly occupied by G. N. Butt and Company." This is the last mention of George Butt in connection with Jefferson. He is mentioned as a resident of Fannin County in the December 22, 1847, *Washington Telegraph*. The company was located on Dallas on the west part of Lot 11 in Block 5, one lot over and to the east of Amos Ury's store on Lot 9.

John Speake had a headright north of Clinton Lake and slightly to the northwest of Clinton Willard's headright. Speake went to New Orleans in late February 1845 to arrange for the trip of the *Lama* to Jefferson. He was the brother of the New Orleans wholesale grocer James Speake. John Speake was probably operating as a merchant in the Caddo Lake area at least by February 1842. He began purchasing lots in Jefferson from Berry Durham in October 1844, including Warehouse Lot 5 in Block 9. He appears to have been in business with George Butt in 1846. He is listed in the 1847 Cass County tax rolls as an owner of 10 lots valued at $500, with $4,000 in merchandise, probably continuing to occupy the storehouse on Lot 11 in Block 5 under the name John Speake after the partnership with Butt ended sometime between March and December.

Clinton Willard was the founder of Clinton, which was a steamboat landing on the north shore of Clinton Lake immediately below his headright. It is probable that he operated some sort of mercantile establishment at that point from the early 1840s, with commodities transported to and from Port Caddo, because steamboats did not begin to penetrate Clinton Lake until after 1845. The landing contained a storehouse and warehouse until early 1855, which was operated at least in 1847 by Willard, Browning & Company, with William Browning of Monterey as a partner; but Willard moved permanently to Jefferson in 1847 to join Speake in business.

The firm of C. J. Willard & Company, composed of Willard and Speake, is mentioned in a September 11, 1849, deed of trust from William Maury to Sam Moseley. Accounts submitted by William Browning to the November 1850 probate court indicate that C. J. Willard & Company was in existence in 1847 and was replaced by Speake & Willard in 1848. The firm of Speake, Willard & Company was in existence by December 1847, occupying the storehouse formerly occupied by Butt on Lot 11 in Block 5. The other partner was William Browning of Monterey. C. J. Willard & Company was a short-lived predecessor to Speake, Willard & Company, which was soon succeeded by Speake & Willard.

In March 1848, Speake, Willard & Company purchased from William Perry parts of Lots 1 and 2 in Block 4 containing a house and fronting 47 ½ feet on Marshall and running back 66 feet on Dallas, which was their second location. The firm is listed in the 1848 tax rolls with $3,000 in merchandise but no lots, and Speake is listed separately as owner of eight lots valued at $400. The firm changed its name to Speake & Willard in 1848, owning one lot valued at $1,500 with $1,500 in merchandise in 1849, five lots valued at $2,000 with $5,000 in merchandise in 1850, and two lots valued at $200 with $7,700 in merchandise in 1851. In August 1850, the firm acquired Warehouse Lot 2 in Block 9 from Alford & Company of Shreveport at auction for nonpayment of taxes.

Speake appears in the 1850 census as a 34-year-old merchant born in Kentucky with $6,000 in real estate, a wife, two children, and adults Jesse Parker and J. W. Fleming, a clerk, living in the house. Willard is listed in the 1850 census as a 33-year-old merchant born in New York with $8,120 in real estate, a wife, two children, and the clerks George Morgan and J. N. Mabane living in the house. The firm of Speake & Willard was still in existence in 1851. The 1852 tax rolls are unreadable, and the firm does not appear in 1853. The firm apparently went out of existence in late 1851. In 1852, Speake joined with William Saufley and Samuel Nimmo to establish the receiving and forwarding firm of Speake, Saufley & Nimmo. Willard entered into a business relationship with George Tuttle.

George Tuttle is listed in the 1850 census as a 23-year-old merchant born in New York and living in the Soda Lake Hotel. The 1849 tax rolls indicate that he had $1,000 in merchandise but no town lots. The location of the facility he operated out of in 1850 is unknown. He did not begin to purchase town lots until April 1851, when he joined with Clinton Willard in purchasing Lot 10 in Block 4. He was operating as a merchant in 1851 with $3,000 in merchandise but no town lots. He purchased independently part of Lot 7 in Block 4 in May 1852.

The firm of Willard & Tuttle was signatory to a November 4, 1851, deed of conveyance from John Speake and Clinton Willard to Memucan Horton concerning a debt of $3,000 owed by them to Horton. By early 1853, Willard and Tuttle were in debt to the New Orleans firm of Cherry, Henderson & Company for more than $6,000. In February 1853, Tuttle sold Willard his half interest in Lot 10 and parts of Lots 1 and 2 in Block 4, and Willard sold John Speake his half interest in parts of Lots 1 and 2 in Block 4. Speake became the owner of the south half of these parts of lots. The firm of Veal & Jennings advertised in the *Jefferson Herald* in May 1853 that it was operating at Willard & Tuttle's old stand at the corner of Dallas and Marshall streets. Willard & Tuttle's store was thus on the northwest corner of Dallas and Marshall on Lots 1 and 2 in Block 4. This was the lot purchased by Speake, Willard & Company from William Perry in March 1848.

In March 1853, Willard mortgaged the properties in Block 4 (including portions of Lots 1 and 2 containing a storehouse occupied by M. Steinlein & Company and Lot 10 containing two two-story storehouses with the upper stories occupied by the *Jefferson Herald* and the Odd Fellows Hall) to Cherry, Henderson & Company and in May 1853 authorized J. W. Fleming to act as agent in his absence. Most of Willard's Jefferson properties were sold by court order at auction to Jesse Veal in September 1853 to satisfy debts. Neither Willard nor Tuttle appears in the 1853 tax rolls.

The firm of Stanley & Ward was composed of Charles Stanley and Mortimer Ward. Stanley, Ward, Alexander, and Chrisman purchased four lots from Berry Durham in January 1846, and the firm of Stanley & Ward is shown in the 1846 tax rolls as owner of two lots valued at $150 but without any merchandise. Stanley & Ward purchased Warehouse Lot 1 from Durham and Urquhart in March 1847 and is listed in the 1847 tax rolls as owning 3 ½ lots valued at $250 and $2,500 in merchandise. The firm was still in existence in May 1847 but out of existence by February 1848, when Ward provided a quit claim deed to Stanley that included the warehouse lot and a 50-foot-square lot on the southwest corner of Marshall and Austin where their storehouse was located. The corner lot had been sold by William Perry to William Johnson in January 1846.

The dissolution of the firm is recorded in the December 16, 1848, *Spirit of the Age*, where Stanley calls for immediate payment of debts, with Josiah Hill acting as agent in Stanley's absence. Within the 50-foot-square corner lot, Stanley erected a new storehouse on the north 20 feet in 1849 that was occupied by the firm of Owens & McElroy in January 1850 and another on the south 30 feet in 1853 that was occupied by Thomas Pugh's drugstore in 1853. The 30-foot lot came to be known as Stanley's drugstore property. Although Stanley appears in the 1850 tax rolls as owner of one lot valued at $500, he is not listed in the 1850 census. Ward appears in the census as a 40-year-old clerk born in New York and residing in the Star Hotel. Stanley was later to continue as an important merchant in Jefferson, including owner of the first meat packery within the city limits.

Perry Graham appears in the 1846 and 1847 tax rolls, but without town lots or merchandise. He is listed as having $300 in merchandise and no town lots in 1848 and 1849 and $500 in merchandise and no town lots in 1850. In December 1849, Graham purchased from Jeptha Crawford Lot 7 in Block 4 fronting 50 feet on Dallas Street and 67 feet on Jackson Street, with the storehouse occupied by Graham. This lot is referred to in the deed records as Graham's old storehouse. Graham is shown in the 1850 census as a 23-year-old merchant born in Tennessee and living in the Soda Lake Hotel.

Graham appears in the 1851 tax rolls as owner of one lot valued at $1,000 but no merchandise. He advertised in March 1851 in the Marshall *Texas Republican* as selling the types of goods normally found in a country store (Fig. 20-2), in May 1853 in the *Jefferson Herald* as a dry goods merchant catering especially to women, and in January 1854 as a dry goods merchant who would soon have an additional stock of groceries. He is listed in the 1853 tax rolls as owner of 2 ½ lots valued at $3,000 with $2,000 in merchandise and in the 1854 tax rolls as owner of a half lot valued at $2,000 with $1,500 in merchandise.

By April 1854, Graham was in business with his brother Charles in the firm of P. M. Graham & Brother, advertising in the *Texas Republican* as merchants in dry goods and groceries. P. M. Graham & Brother was located on Dallas Street on the west half of Lot 10 in Block 5, according to an October 23, 1854, mortgage by William and Francis Baker to J. Burnsides & Company concerning the east half of Lot 10. The advertisement indicates that Perry Graham had been operating out of this store before the firm was formed. A January 31, 1852, transaction between Urquhart and W. Brooks & Brother mentions that P. M. Graham's new building was under construction at that site. A December 10, 1851, transaction between John Waskom and Francis and William Baker concerning the east half of Lot 10 mentions that the other half of the lot had been recently sold by Waskom to Graham. P. M. Graham & Brother is not listed in the 1855 tax rolls, but reappears in the 1856 tax rolls as owner of $5,000 in merchandise on Jim's Bayou.

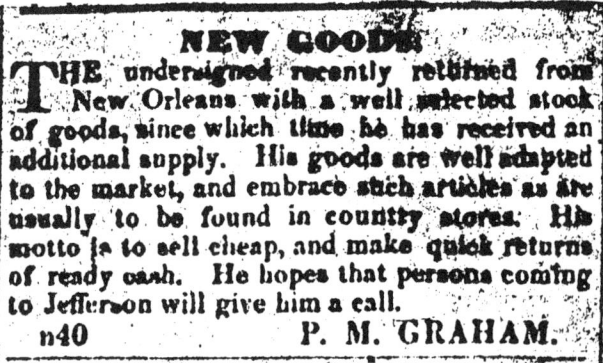

Fig. 20-2. P. M. Graham Advertisement. Source: March 29, 1851, *Texas Republican*

Earliest Merchants

On February 5, 1853, Jeptha Crawford of Harrison County sold to Samuel Nimmo and William Saufley a lot fronting 30 feet on Marshall Street and running back 70 feet on Austin known as Crawford's corner and containing a storehouse and barber shop. This appears to be portions of Lots 11 and 12 and was probably the location of Crawford's mercantile establishment from the earliest days. Jeptha and Merriweather Crawford owned lots in Jefferson in 1844. Jeptha Crawford is shown in the 1846 tax rolls as owner of five lots valued at $1,350 but no merchandise and in 1847 as owner of five lots valued at $1,500 with $3,000 in merchandise. No lots and only $300 in merchandise are listed for 1848 and 1849, but the five lots reappear in 1850 with $3,650 in merchandise.

Crawford appears in the 1850 census as a 37-year-old merchant born in Kentucky with real estate valued at $10,000, a wife, and five children. Living in the house were Thomas Ferrell, a 33-year-old merchant born in Alabama; his 35-year-old brother Wiley, who is listed as a clerk; the 17-year-old clerk Samuel Nimmo born in Mississippi; and H. Hollingsworth, a 15-year-old female from England. In 1851, Crawford joined with Thomas Ferrell in the firm of Crawford & Ferrell. The firm is shown in the 1851 tax rolls as having $4,000 in merchandise but no town lots. The firm is not listed in 1853, but reappears in 1854 without town lots or merchandise. Crawford appears as an individual in 1855 owning town lots but without merchandise. The firm apparently dissolved in 1854, and Crawford moved to Harrison County but continued to own lots in Jefferson.

Reuben Drake is listed in the 1847 tax rolls as having $7,000 in merchandise, second only to Ury & Ward among the early merchants. Drake purchased lots in February 1848 from Urquhart and was owed money in June by the owners of the Steam Mill Company. According to a June 16, 1848, deed of conveyance from Simon Heald to Enoch Ordway, Drake's mercantile house was located on Lot 6 in Block 5 at the corner of Marshall and Austin, with the lot occupying 50 feet on Austin and 40 feet on Marshall. Drake did not own the lot and apparently died at the end of 1848.

Horatio Walcott advertised dry goods for sale in the December 16, 1848, *Spirit of the Age*. An April 3, 1849, conveyance from Samuel

Mosely to Enoch Ordway mentions the lot on the corner of Marshall and Austin that had been occupied by Drake, but was then occupied by Walcott. Walcott apparently began to operate out of the storehouse on Lot 6 in Block 5 sometime between June and December 1848. He is listed in the tax rolls as owner of $5,000 in merchandise but no town lots in 1849, $4,000 in merchandise and a half lot valued at $300 in 1850, $3,000 in merchandise and one lot valued at $100 in 1851, and $4,000 in merchandise and 5 ½ lots valued at $1,700 in 1853. He is listed in the 1850 census as a 40-year-old merchant born in Rhode Island with real estate valued at $700 and living in the house of William McNeill.

Walcott went into a receiving and forwarding business in the landing area with McNeill under the name of Walcott & McNeill in June 1850 and operated by himself in the business under the name H. N. Walcott from late 1851 to late 1853. During this time he remained in the mercantile business. In an advertisement dated February 17, 1851, in the May 14, 1853, *Jefferson Herald*, Walcott indicated that he was a wholesale and retail dealer in dry goods, accepting cash, cotton, beeswax, and pelts. A June 16, 1856, conveyance from William C. and Francis Baker to Fleming Jones mentions that Walcott had a house on Lots 11 and 12 in Block 74 in 1854, but this appears to have been a residence. There is no evidence that Walcott operated as a merchant after 1853. When he sold his storehouse on the corner of Marshall and Austin to John and Samuel Smith on October 24, 1857, the transaction indicates that the storehouse was occupied by J. L. & S. C. Smith, which had been in operation since 1854. The transaction also indicates that the property included portions of Lots 5 and 6 in Block 5, fronting 38 feet on Marshall and running back 100 feet.

Josiah Hill lived in Paradise and owned one town lot in Jefferson from 1847 to 1849 valued at $150. This was fractional Lot 7 in Block 47 fronting 50 feet on Marshall and running back to the Urquhart line. It was acquired by Hill and William Crawford from Durham and Urquhart on May 29, 1847, for $50. According to the 1848 district court case of Hill and Crawford versus Samuel Garey, Crawford was a resident of Shelby County, and the firm in Jefferson, which carried dry goods and groceries, was known as Hill & Crawford. This was not a remote location because it was contiguous to Jefferson's first hotel and the earliest residences in the Alley Addition. Hill had $2,000 in merchandise in 1847, $1,400 in 1848, and $600 in 1849. The lot, with storehouse, was sold to Samuel Garey on February 27, 1849. Hill is listed in the 1850 census as a 40-year-old minister born in South Carolina with real estate valued at $3,000, a wife, and six children.

Charles Dunn was living in Jefferson in 1846 and had merchandise valued at $900 in 1848. His mercantile establishment was located on Lot 6 in Block 5 at the corner of Dallas and Marshall. The lot and storehouse were not owned by him. The property was sold by Gilbert Ragan, administrator for Carey Ragan, to Israel Leavitt in December 1847, with the transaction indicating that Dunn lived in the storehouse. Caleb Ragan operated out of the same store as Dunn in 1848. The Steam Mill Company owed Dunn money in June 1848. The storehouse was occupied by Ragan alone in April 1849, the year in which Dunn died.

In the May 13, 1846, *Northern Standard*, Gilbert Ragan published a notification that he had been appointed by the Bowie County probate court in February to act as administrator of the estate of Carey Ragan, whose property included two storehouses and a log cabin in Jefferson. There is no evidence that Carey Ragan was a Jefferson resident, although the log cabin was apparently a residential structure. Carey Ragan had purchased Lot 6 in Block 5 in October 1844 and Lot 6 in Block 21 in December 1845. It is obvious that both of the storehouses went back to 1845 and that one of them was the storehouse on the corner of Dallas and Marshall that was occupied by Charles Dunn.

Caleb Ragan is listed in the 1850 census as a 38-year-old grocery merchant born in South Carolina with a wife but no children. Ragan purchased the southwest half of Lot 11 in Block 22 fronting 25 feet on Austin Street from Daniel Biddlecome in February 1846, but sold it in April. Ragan is listed in the 1847 tax rolls with $375 in merchandise, but no lot ownership. Ragan operated out of the same store as Charles Dunn on Lot 6 in Block 5 in 1848. He is listed in the 1848 tax rolls as an owner of one lot valued at $200 with merchandise of $500. He continued to operate out of the same store in 1849, when he owned two lots valued at $300 with $400 in merchandise. He is listed in the 1850 tax rolls as owner of two lots valued at $750 with $500 in merchandise, in the 1851 tax rolls as owner of two lots valued at $750 with $750 in merchandise, and in the 1853 tax rolls as owner of five lots valued at $10,000 but without merchandise. Ragan was joined by Hiram Tomlin by at least February 1852, operating under the name C. Ragan & Company. This partnership was dissolved in January 1853 when Tomlin sold to Ragan his interest in the properties owned jointly by them, including parts of Lots 5 and 6 in Block 5 and Lot 4 in Block 73. The storehouse was located on a 50-foot-square lot on the corner of Dallas and Marshall.

Israel Leavitt is listed in the 1850 census as a 42-year-old born in Maine with a wife and child and real estate valued at $5,000. He purchased the east half (the transaction says west, but this is incorrect) of Lot 8 in Block 4 on Dallas Street from Berry Durham in September 1845 and half of Lot 9 in Block 4 from Durham in November. Leavitt's residence was on the east half of Lot 8 in Block 4, and his store was probably on the adjoining half lot. The commissioners court met at this store in July 1847. Leavitt is shown in the 1846 tax rolls as owner of 1 ½ lots valued at $1,040 but no merchandise and in the 1847 tax rolls as owner of three lots valued at $1,550 with $1,500 in merchandise.

The property on Lot 6 in Block 5 was not purchased from Carey Ragan until December 1847, after the tax rolls were prepared. Leavitt owned four lots valued at $2,050 with $150 in merchandise in 1848, 1 ½ lots valued at $2,500 but no merchandise in 1849, and 1 ½ lots valued at $2,250 with $150 in merchandise in 1850. Leavitt died in 1851. An October 1859 conveyance from Gustavus Leavitt to Israel's widow Caroline indicates that Leavitt owned a building on Lot 6 in Block 5 that fronted 24 feet on Marshall, was 38 feet from Austin, and was occupied by May & Company. This building may have been occupied by Leavitt as a storehouse from 1848 through 1850 and/or may have been the Jackson Hall used by the commissioners court during the same period, particularly if it was two stories tall.

Richard Crump appears in the 1847 tax rolls as an owner of one town lot valued at $100 but no merchandise, in the 1848 tax rolls as having $4,000 in merchandise but no town lots, and in the 1849 tax rolls as having $1,800 in merchandise but no town lots. The 1850 census shows Crump as the Cass County sheriff, 34 years old, born in Virginia, with a wife and two children. Crump purchased Lot 8 in Block 5 from Berry Durham in January 1845, but there is no evidence that he operated at this location. A January 7, 1846, indenture from Urquhart to Bishop indicates that Lot 2 in Block 8 had previously been sold to Crump, but there is nothing to indicate that he might have operated a store out of that location. This lot was quit claimed to John Speake in July 1852. It is highly probable that the merchandise mentioned in the 1848 and 1849 tax rolls was in an establishment near Crump's house, which was two miles east of Jefferson.

William Perry may have operated a grocery house in early 1845, because he sold a lot in Block 23 containing a grocery house to John Withee on April 30. However, there are no records indicating the operation of a grocery house in that area at any time, and it may be that the structure was simply intended as a grocery house. In addition, the city records suggest that grocery houses were sellers of ardent spirits, which may be a better indicator of the nature of the operation. The term was used to characterize bulk sellers of liquor as opposed to saloons, which sold by the drink. Perry appears in the 1847 tax rolls with 14 lots valued at $5,000, $500 in stock, three slaves, two horses, five cattle, hogs, and a wagon. Perry is known to have been operating the Soda Lake Hotel in 1847, and the stock may have been in connection with the hotel, particularly because it is not referred to in the tax rolls as stock in trade. Another possibility is Perry's tavern house, which may not have been related to the hotel. However, neither of these possibilities is compelling.

Perry purchased Lot 1 in Block 4 from William Brown in 1845 and sold the corner portion of this lot at Marshall and Austin to William Johnson in January 1846, which was occupied by Stanley & Ward in 1846. Perry sold the middle portion of this lot to Williams and Webster in June 1846. The transaction mentions Perry's warehouses on the remaining portion, which was on the corner of Dallas and Marshall. Perry sold this corner lot, fronting 47 ½ feet on Marshall and 66 feet on Dallas, to Speake, Willard & Company in March 1848. The transaction mentions a house on this corner lot. The corner lot at Dallas and Marshall offers the best possibility for where Perry was operating as a merchant in 1847.

William Nichols is listed in the 1850 census as a 45-year-old merchant born in Georgia with real estate valued at $250, a wife and child, and a clerk living on the premises. In late 1849, he joined with Duncan McNab to establish the firm of Nichols & McNab, which operated a grocery store. In January 1850, John Speake sold to McNab parts of lots 11 and 12 in Block 22 fronting 30 feet on Marshall Street and running back 75 feet in which the grocery store was already operating. Nichols & McNab appears in the tax rolls with $600 in merchandise and no town lots in 1851, $8,000 in merchandise and no town lots in 1853, and $6,500 and three town lots valued at $600 in 1854. Nichols & McNab advertised in the *Jefferson Herald* in May 1853 as dealers in dry goods and groceries sold for cash or on credit to responsible customers.

In June 1854, Duncan McNab purchased from Mayer Dopplemayer for $2,000 a 45-foot by 75-foot lot on Marshall. Later transactions indicate that this property was adjacent to the 30-foot lot and contained a two-story structure that was referred to as the McNab building. The McNab building became the location of Nichols & McNab in 1854, and the earlier location of Nichols & McNab came to be occupied by Theophilus Nichols, who was either a brother or cousin of William.

Anthony Owens appears in the 1850 census as a 28-year-old merchant born in South Carolina. Also listed in the household is S. N. Owens, a 23-year-old merchant born in South Carolina, obviously his brother. Anthony joined with William McElroy in late 1849 to establish the firm of Owens & McElroy. The firm first appears in a January 24, 1850, deed from Charles Stanley to Samuel Seymour for a 50-foot square corner lot on Marshall and Austin in Block 4 with a storehouse recently built by Stanley and occupied by Owens & McElroy. Owens & McElroy was actually located immediately on the corner of Marshall and Austin on the upper 20 feet of the 50-foot lot. The firm appears in the tax rolls as owning $3,000 in merchandise and no town lots in 1851, $6,000 in merchandise and no town lots in 1853, and $5,000 in merchandise and one town lot valued at $20 in 1854. Nichols & McNab advertised in the *Jefferson Herald* in May 1853 as retail dealers in dry goods on Marshall Street providing cash advances on cotton and other produce shipped to McElroy & Bradford, General Factors and Commission Merchants in New Orleans.

Earliest Merchants

August May appears in the 1850 census as a 32-year-old merchant born in Germany with a wife and three children. Also living in the house were the 22-year-old clerk A. Bussineber and the females L. and M. Kohn, all from Germany. May appears in the 1850 tax rolls with $1,000 in merchandise but no town lots. He joined with G. S. Oliver in 1851 to form May & Company, which is shown in the 1851 tax rolls as having $1,800 in merchandise but no town lots and in the 1853 tax rolls as having $6,000 in merchandise but no town lots.

May & Company advertised in April 1851 in the *Texas Republican* as wholesale and retail dealers in dry goods and groceries, with the largest stock of goods ever introduced into the Jefferson market (a valid claim). Cotton and pelts were taken in exchange, and cash and goods were paid for cotton, pelts, hides, wool, beeswax, etc. The advertisement indicates that May & Company were continuing at the location on Marshall previously occupied by May alone. May 1853 advertisements in the *Jefferson Herald* indicate that the firm had adopted the cash system, that merchandise was brought in directly from eastern and northern cities, that one of the partners had a brother in the clothing manufacturing business in New York, that prices were as low as any that could be found in New Orleans with freight and expenses added, and that advances would be made in cash or plantation supplies for cotton shipped through the firm to J. H. Heald of New Orleans.

When Oliver retired in January 1854, the firm was joined by Abraham Kohn. May & Company began operating in March 1854 out of a storehouse built by Caleb Ragan fronting Marshall Street on Lots 5 and 6 in Block 5 and sold to them by Ragan. May & Company is shown as having $10,000 in merchandise and no town lots in the 1854 tax rolls. The firm was reorganized in 1855 under the name of Kohn & May with $20,000 in merchandise, but does not appear in the 1856 and 1857 tax rolls. The storehouse property was assigned in September 1855 to firms in New York and New Orleans to which May & Company was in debt for $9,000. August May and Abraham Kohn are referred to in the transaction as late merchants in Jefferson but still living in town. May & Company reappeared in 1859, but at a different location.

William Falk is listed in the 1850 census as a 35-year old merchant born in Prussia and residing in the Soda Lake Hotel. He appears in the

1851 tax rolls with $800 in merchandise and no town lots. Falk's store was located on Marshall Street in Block 21 about 25 feet south of the alley. The property fronted 25 feet on Marshall and ran back 150 feet, occupying portions of Lots 7–9. There is no record of when Falk acquired the property, but he was definitely part owner, because he and August Lamprecht sold the storehouse and land to David Douthit in August 1851. Ownership was transferred to R. C. Armistead and P. A. Mallard in August 1852 and to M. Steinlein & Company in December 1853.

William Baker is shown in the 1850 census as a 24-year-old with $3,147 in real estate and living in the house of the physician Job Baker (apparently his father). The firm of William C. Baker & Company is first mentioned in January 1847, with William and Job as partners, and was extended in August 1847 to include Francis Baker. William and Job participated in the formation of the Steam Mill Company in 1845, which was in operation at least by 1847. W. C. Baker & Company published the *Spirit of the Age* from August 1848 to March 1849. The firm is shown in the 1847 tax rolls as owning two lots valued at $350 with $1,000 stock in trade and in the 1848 tax rolls as owning two lots valued at $800 and a printing press and fixtures valued at $800. The stock in trade was apparently merchandise, and the nature of this operation is unknown. The firm of W. C. Baker & Company disappears from the records after 1848, until it was recreated in 1853 with William and Francis Baker as partners. An October 23, 1854, mortgage from William and Job Baker to J. Burnsides & Company of New Orleans suggests that the early mercantile operations were on Lot 1 in Block 74, which was across Marshall Street slightly north of the Steam Mill Company property. The transaction mentions storehouses on the lot, indicating that the Bakers continued in some sort of mercantile operation in spite of the fact that the company does not appear in the tax rolls.

Samuel Garey is listed in the 1850 census as a 41-year-old physician born in Missouri with real estate valued at $4,000, a wife, and two children. It was common for physicians and surgeons to operate drugstores, which provided the designation of merchant, and it was common for drugstores at import points like Jefferson to sell drugs and medicines on a wholesale basis to interior druggists as well as on a retail basis. Garey purchased the stock of Alexander & Chrisman in

March 1847 and may already have been in business as a druggist. He is shown in the 1847 tax rolls as owning seven lots valued at $700 and $1,300 in merchandise. The tax rolls show $200 in drugs and a library but no lots in 1848 and one lot valued at $50 but no drugs in 1849.

Edward Smith in an *Account of a Journey through Northeastern Texas* reports that Garey had moved from Jefferson and was practicing on Sulphur Prairie in 1849. Back in Jefferson, Garey advertised the water cure as an alternative treatment method in October 1850 in the *Texas Republican*. He ran into financial difficulties in 1851, and Perry Graham and Horatio Walcott acted as securities. Sued by many people, he left town in 1853. A trust sale advertised in the *Jefferson Herald* in May 1853 indicates that his storehouse, which also contained the post office, was located on the east half of Lot 2 in Block 74.

Thomas Pugh is listed in the 1850 census as a 27-year-old physician born in Alabama with $3,000 in real estate, a wife, and a 20-year-old brother (M. N.) who served as a clerk. Also shown in the household is the carpenter Prentiss Stetson. Pugh is shown in the tax rolls as owner of one lot valued at $750 with $500 in merchandise in 1850, as owner of 15 lots valued at $2,000 with $1,000 in merchandise in 1851, and as owner of 16 lots valued at $4,000 and $2,000 in merchandise in 1853. In May 1853, Pugh advertised in the *Jefferson Herald* as a wholesale and retail dealer in medicines, drugs, chemicals, patent medicines, surgical instruments, and fine wines for medicinal purposes, indicating that he had just moved to the new building erected by Stanley two doors north of Willard & Tuttle's old stand on Marshall Street.

Pugh's new location was near the southwest corner of Marshall and Austin on Stanley's drugstore property (i.e., on the south 30 feet of the original 50-foot square lot). In 1853, Owens & McElroy occupied the building on the north lot, and Pugh occupied the building on the south lot. With respect to the prior location, John Pitkin advertised in August 1852 in the Clarksville *Northern Standard* that his store was on Dallas Street next door to Pugh's drugstore and in March 1857 in the *Eastern Texas Gazette* that his store was on the southwest corner of Dallas and Marshall. Because Pitkin was located on the west half of Lot 12 in Block 4, Pugh was located on the east half. Pugh purchased an undivided half interest in the full lot from the estate of Enoch Crow in late 1852. Pugh sold the west half of the lot to Pitkin on May 23, 1853, and the full lot to Pitkin on November 22 of the same year.

Ithael Eason is listed in the 1850 census as a 33-year-old physician born in Georgia with real estate valued at $4,000, a wife, and four children. He is listed in the 1849 tax rolls as having $500 in merchandise and a library and in the 1850 tax rolls as having two lots valued at $800 and $500 in merchandise. He advertised in December 1848 in the *Spirit of the Age* as a physician, surgeon, and pharmacist. The drugstore and medical office was apparently one door above the printing office. Eason carried a large stock of drugs and medicines and patent and botanic concoctions that were sold for cash or on credit to select customers. George Loy and James Smith apparently built a new storehouse for Eason in November 1851, but it is unknown if it was ever occupied by him.

The original location of Eason's drugstore was probably on part of Lot 12 in Block 22 fronting 22 feet on Marshall and running back 50 feet. Eason placed this property with the drugstore then occupied by Frith & Robinson in trust in October 1851 in conjunction with a $400 debt to Wiley Ferrell. Eason was not operating as a druggist in 1851. Eason later operated a drugstore with his son Hanibal under the name I. G. Eason & Son, which was sold to John Cocke in August 1861. Eason had a long and distinguished career as a physician in Jefferson and was still living there in 1876.

There is no information on Moses Ambros. S. F. Moley in the census is undoubtedly Samuel F. Moseley, who is known to have been living in Jefferson in 1850 but is not otherwise in the census. Moseley was always a lawyer, and there is no evidence that he was a merchant until 1860. In April 1847, Urquhart and Durham sold to Jeptha Crawford Lot 7 in Block 4 running south on Jackson Street to the house of Solomon Garner. Garner apparently operated a store on the northeast corner of Lake and Jackson streets. An unnamed storehouse is mentioned in an 1849 conveyance from Sam Moseley to Enoch Ordway concerning half of Lot 7 in Block 3 on the corner of Jackson and Lake. Although Frederick Schluter is listed as a farmer in the 1850 census and does not appear in the tax rolls with merchandise until 1853, it is probable that he operated this store because he was required by the Town of Jefferson in April 1847 to reposition Jackson Street, which was being obstructed by his fence.

It is apparent from these records that there was a substantial number of large mercantile establishments in Jefferson from the earliest years and that these establishments were wholesalers as well as retailers, with the wholesale component providing the bulk of the business. It is inconceivable, for example, that Reuben Drake would have carried $7,000 in merchandise for Jefferson's minuscule resident population in 1847. The primary customers were interior merchants and planters who purchased at wholesale prices. This is reasonable because Jefferson was an import point for commodities needed in its extensive market area. Strictly retail establishments did not emerge until much later and were never as important to the commercial life of the town as the wholesalers who also sold retail.

Druggists were a special class of merchants because they were practicing physicians, with sales of drugs and medicines complementing their professional activities. They also were primarily wholesalers. The rest of the merchants apparently carried dry goods and groceries, with some degree of specialization, particularly in the case of grocery stores like that of Caleb Ragan. However, pressures for specialization were not great. Nichols & McNab sold dry goods and groceries, but they were also major sellers of school books.

The early merchants were young and fairly wealthy, and the business community was obviously closely knit. Partnerships formed and dissolved, and new partnerships were formed. Businesses changed hands through the purchase of existing stocks of merchandise at the same location. Merchants often found themselves heavily in debt because of the prevailing credit system and the uncertainties of cotton production. They bought on credit from New Orleans and the East Coast and were often unable to pay their debts when interior merchants and planters indebted to them were unable to pay their debts. Appeals to the interior for payment of debts were quite common in the newspapers, with the merchant often mentioning his own financial difficulties.

Storehouses tended to be used by more than one business over time. The distribution of these early structures confirms the statement in the September 1, 1876, *Daily Jimplecute* that before the Civil War most of the businesses were located on Dallas and Marshall streets. It also indicates that merchants favored the higher land west of Market Street where their merchandise would not be subject to flooding even in the highest waters.

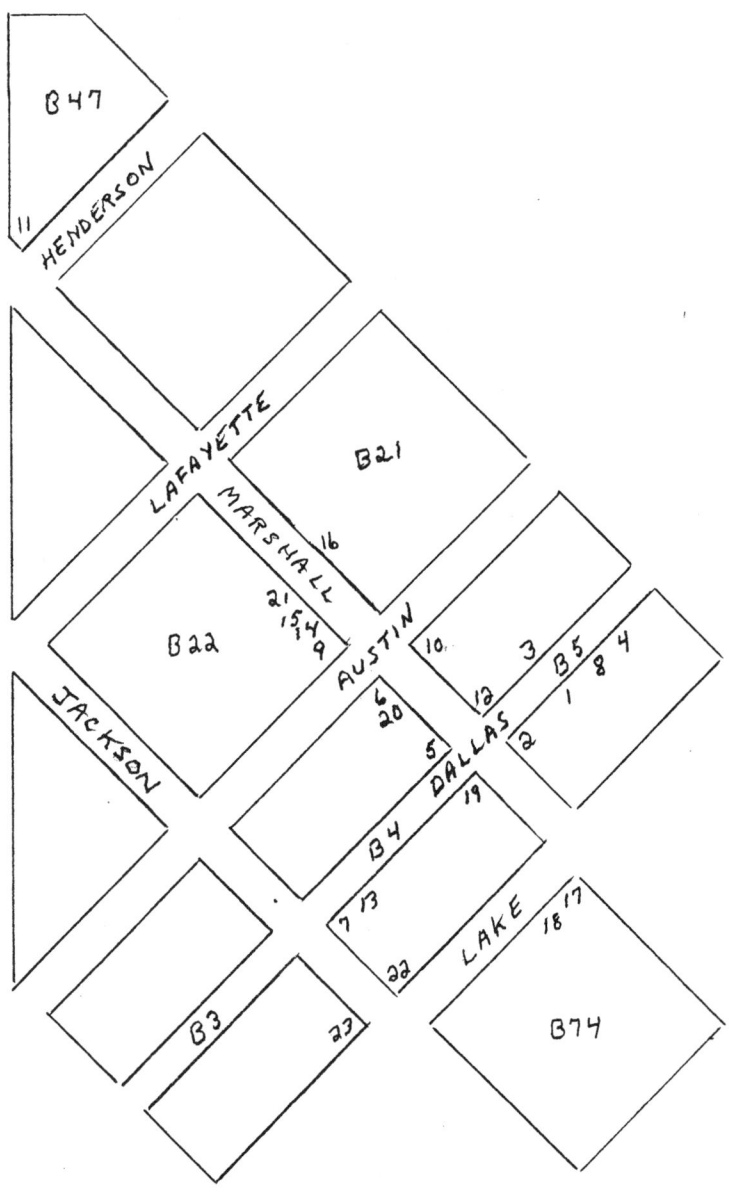

(opposite page) Fig. 20-3. Earliest Merchants
KEY:
1. Amos Ury (1845); Ury & Ward (1847)
2. Ury & Ward (1851)
3. Alexander & Chrisman (1846)
4. G. N Butt & Company (1846); John Speake (1847); C. J. Willard & Company (1847) Speake, Willard & Company (1847)
5. William Perry (1847); Speake, Willard & Company (1848); Speake & Willard (1848); Willard & Tuttle (1851); Veal & Jennings (1853)
6. Stanley & Ward (1846); Owens & McElroy (1850)
7. Perry Graham (1847)
8. Perry Graham (1852); P. M. Graham & Brother (1854)
9. Jeptha Crawford (1847); Crawford & Ferrell (1851)
10. Reuben Drake (1846); Horatio Walcott (1848)
11. Hill & Crawford (1847)
12. Charles Dunn (1847); Caleb Ragan (1848); C. Ragan & Company (1852); May & Company (1854); Kohn & May (1855)
13. Israel Leavitt (1846)
14. Nichols & McNab (1849)
15. Nichols & McNab (1854)
16. William Falk (1850); David Douthit (1851); M. Steinlein & Company (1853)
17. W. C. Baker & Company (1847)
18. Samuel Garey (1853)
19. Thomas Pugh (1850)
20. Thomas Pugh (1853)
21. Ithael Eason (1848); Frith & Robinson (1851)
22. Solomon Garner (1847)
23. Frederick Schluter (1847)

21. EARLY 1850S MERCHANTS

The Cass County tax rolls indicate ownership of town lots and value of merchandise in stock as of January 1 for the years 1851 through 1853; however, the year 1852 is unreadable. Persons with town lots and merchandise from 1851 through 1853 include: M. J. Jones (1851–1856); Brooks & Brother (1853–1855); Hugo Fox (1853–1857); Morgan & Tomlin (1853–1855); John Pitkin (1853–1857); Frederick Schluter (1853–1857); Steinlein & Company (1853 and 1855); and John Waskom (1853–1855). Persons listed without town lots but with merchandise and known to have been Jefferson merchants include Saufley & Hudgins (1851) and Veal & Jennings (1853–1854).

Merchants appearing in various newspaper advertisements from 1851 through early 1853 include: Saufley & Hudgins (April 1851); Beckett & Company, dry goods and groceries (April 1851); William P. Saufley, dry goods and groceries (May 1851); J. Mosby & Company, commission merchants (April 1852); D. W. Douthit, dry goods and groceries (April 1852); Norris & Tackett, drugs (May 1852); M. Steinlein, dry goods (May 1852); J. W. Pitkin (August 1852); Speake, Saufley & Nimmo, receiving, forwarding, and commission merchants (September 1852); John Sabine, dry goods and groceries (February 1853); Veal & Jennings, dry goods and groceries (February 1853); and Elliott & Frith, drugs (March 1853).

Merchants advertising in the May 14, 1853, *Jefferson Herald* include: J. W. Pitkin, dry goods and groceries; F. A. Schluter, groceries;

W. Brooks & Brother, dry goods and groceries; M. Steinlein, dry goods and groceries; Elliott & Frith, drugstore; Veal & Jennings, dry goods and groceries; Morgan & Tomlin, general mercantile business; J. M. Waskom, dry goods; W. C. Baker & Company, general mercantile business; Hugo Fox, candies and confectionaries; John Sabine, dry goods and groceries; and Stanley & Seymour, receiving, forwarding, and commission merchants.

The September 1, 1876, *Jefferson Jimplecute* lists Frederick Schluter as one of the persons who arrived prior to 1848 and was still in the city. Schluter is listed in Precinct 1 in the 1850 census as a 31-year-old farmer born in Tennessee with a wife, Ann, and two children and real estate valued at $6,350 and in the 1860 census as a merchant living in town with two more children, real estate valued at $30,000, and personal estate valued at $45,000. The reason for the 1850 occupational designation is that Schluter maintained a 320-acre farm in the Greenleaf Perry headright west of Jefferson. The Schluters were also long-term residents on Lots 7–9 in Block B of the Alley Addition, with the January 1847 sale of this property by the Alleys to the Schluters indicating that it already contained improvements of some sort.

Schluter also appears to have been one of the earliest merchants. Although there are no specific indicators of business operations before 1853, an April 3, 1849, conveyance from Samuel Moseley, trustee for the estate of Simon Heald, to Enoch Ordway included half of Lot 7 in Block 3 on the corner of Jackson and Lake containing a storehouse and other improvements. Although it is known that Heald was part-owner of a blacksmith shop on an adjacent lot, it is uncertain who operated the store. However, in April 1847 Schluter reached an agreement with the Town of Jefferson to reposition Jackson Street, which was being obstructed by his fence. Because Schluter resided in the Alley Addition, it is probable that the storehouse on Lot 7 in Block 3 was operated by him.

Schluter appears in the tax rolls from 1853 through 1857, with 4 ½ town lots valued at $800 and $3,000 in merchandise in 1853 and four lots valued at $400 and $2,500 in merchandise in 1857. Schluter did not advertise in the newspapers external to Jefferson. However, he advertised as a grocer in the May 14, 1853, *Jefferson Herald*, with the advertisement dated March 12, 1852. A March 4, 1858, sale of the west half of Lot 11 in Block 6 on Dallas Street by William and Isaac Hines to Henry Bilger mentions that Schluter's old storehouse was adjacent, apparently on the east half of the lot. Schluter had apparently moved to the west half of Lot 10 in Block 5, which he purchased for $1,300 on February 3, 1858, from the New Orleans firm of Thomas C. Payne & Company, with the purchase price indicating that the property contained a storehouse. Schluter did not advertise in the March 14, 1857, *Eastern Texas Gazette*. Schluter sold his entire stock of goods to Lewis Moody in December 1861 for 150 bales of cotton.

M. J. Jones appears in the tax rolls from 1851 through 1856, purchasing his first lot (Lot 4 in Block 74) from Urquhart in January 1851. Nothing is known about the nature of this operation, but apparently it was quite small, reaching a maximum value of $800 in merchandise in 1855. The tax rolls indicate that Jones owned Lots 8 and 9 in Block 3 and Lots 3, 4, 5, 7, and 8 in Block 74. The values given for the lots do not suggest any improvements.

The firm of Saufley & Hudgins appears in the 1851 tax rolls as owner of $4,000 in merchandise and no town lots. They did not advertise in the Marshall or Clarksville newspapers, although they offered a slave for sale in the April 5, 1851, *Texas Republican*. Neither Saufley nor Hudgins is listed in the 1850 census. The firm did not last very long and was succeeded by the dry goods and groceries firm of William P. Saufley in May 1851. His advertisement in the May 17, 1851, *Northern Standard* stressed that "He is constantly receiving by the boats, which ply regularly to Jefferson during the season for navigation; and will feel especial pleasure in serving his friends in the upper Red River Counties." The location is unknown. Saufley was probably a renter, having purchased only low-value properties in Blocks 76 and 77 in 1851. Saufley entered into a receiving, forwarding, and commission business with John Speake and Samuel Nimmo in September 1852 and was later involved in the firms of Saufley & Nimmo and Saufley & Batte. Saufley was Jefferson's long-term mayor and is listed in the 1860 census as a 37-year-old merchant born in Kentucky with $14,000 in real estate, $3,000 in personal estate, and a four-year-old son (his wife had died).

Beckett & Company advertised as wholesale dealers in dry goods and groceries on Marshall Street in the April 12, 1851, *Texas Republican*. The advertisement indicates that the firm had been selling dry goods at wholesale in New Orleans for the past seven years to merchants in Texas, Arkansas, and throughout the South and that at its new location it would pay particular attention to the needs of interior merchants. One of the members of the firm would be constantly buying in the New Orleans and northern markets, from which the store would receive fresh supplies by every steamboat during the boating season. The principal in this firm was Ephraim Beckett, who purchased properties in Blocks 7 and 19 from Urquhart and Sidney Neal in July 1851. Beckett was obviously a renter, but his exact location is unknown. On June 29, 1854, Hannah Beckett provided William Arrington power of attorney to deal with the properties of her deceased husband's estate.

David Douthit advertised in the April 3, 1852, *Texas Republican* as a dry goods and groceries merchant located on Marshall Street in Jefferson. The advertisement says that Douthit would be "constantly receiving Goods of every description during the boating season." Douthit had purchased William Falk's storehouse and lot on Marshall at the northern end of Lot 7 in Block 21 in August 1851, which was obviously Douthit's first location. However, he sold this property to R. C. Armistead and P. A. Mallard in August 1852, and his subsequent location is uncertain. Douthit killed (apparently accidently) an orphan boy working in a stable in January 1853, was brought to trial, and disappeared from the records.

Douthit's storehouse, stock, and accounts were acquired by W. C. Baker & Company (composed of William and Francis Baker) by May 1853, which entered into a general mercantile business, as indicated by an advertisement in the *Jefferson Herald*. There is no deed record concerning any property transfers from Douthit to the Bakers. Douthit's second location may have been on Lot 1 in Block 74 containing storehouses, which was mortgaged by William and Job Baker to J. Burnsides & Company in October 1854. A better possibility is the east half of Lot 10 in Block 5, which was mortgaged at the same time to the same firm by William and Francis Baker comprising the firm of W. C. Baker &

Company. However, no storehouses or improvements are mentioned in connection with the second transaction.

W. C. Baker & Company (composed of William, Job, and Francis Baker) was one of the oldest mercantile operations in Jefferson, originating in 1847. It disappears from the records after 1848, although some sort of mercantile operation apparently continued on Lot 1 in Block 74. A new W. C. Baker & Company composed of William and Francis Baker appeared in 1853, advertising in May 1853 in the *Jefferson Gazette* as in the general mercantile business, having assumed David Douthit's accounts, purchased his stock, and located in his old stand. The new firm is listed in the 1854 tax rolls as owning two lots valued at $2,000 with $3,500 in merchandise. It appears to have been located on Dallas Street on the east half of Lot 10 in Block 5, bounded on the west (i.e., on the west half of Lot 10) by P. M. Graham & Brother and on the east (i.e., on the west half of Lot 11) by William Torrans' grocery house. This half lot had been sold to the Bakers by John Waskom on December 10, 1851. According to an advertisement that appeared in the February 18, 1854, *Texas Republican*, W. C. Baker & Company expanded its dry goods and groceries business into receiving, forwarding, and commission operations. The company does not appear in the 1855 tax rolls; however, William Baker is listed with $3,200 in merchandise and Lots 1 and 6 in Block 73. An April 19, 1859, sale of the old steam mill property (on Lots 7–9 in Block 23) by Francis Baker to Charles Stanley and Samuel Nimmo mentions that the property contained Baker's warehouse.

According to the May 1, 1852, Marshall *Star State Patriot*, Moses Steinlein was a longtime Marshall merchant who had opened a new and elegant establishment in Jefferson. The same issue contains an advertisement (dated May 1, under "New Advertisements") for M. Steinlein & Company located at No. 6 Marshall Street in Jefferson. The advertisement indicates that Steinlein was in the wholesale and retail dry goods and grocery business, that he maintained a cash store, that he purchased in the eastern cities, and that he offered the highest market prices for cotton, pelts, hides, and beeswax. Steinlein may have continued as a Marshall merchant, because an advertisement in the March 19, 1853, *Star State Patriot* shows Steinlein (under the firm name of Moses Steinlein rather than Steinlein & Company) as recently established in the grocery business in Marshall on the east side of the public square.

The same advertisement that appeared on May 1 in the Marshall newspaper can be found in the May 14, 1853, *Jefferson Herald*, but dated April 3, 1852. (Advertisements were usually dated with the first date of appearance, which is important in determining when a company started, especially when extant issues are scarce.) A companion advertisement dated March 1853 gives No. 2 Marshall Street as the location and lists various goods received through the steamboats *Echo* and *Pitser Miller*. A large number of clerks were on hand to service customers. Liberal advances in money or groceries were made to persons willing to ship their produce to the house of Ward & Jonas in New Orleans.

Steinlein & Company's first facility was on the old property of Willard & Tuttle in Block 4 at the corner of Dallas and Marshall. When Willard mortgaged 22 feet of the property on Marshall to the New Orleans firm of Cherry, Henderson & Company on March 19, 1853, the transaction mentions this as the lot "in which is built the new store house now occupied as such by M. Steinlein & Co." This was the northern half of the original Willard & Tuttle lot that ran 47 ½ feet on Marshall and 66 feet on Dallas. The storehouse was not owned by Steinlein, but rather by Mayer Dopplemayer, who offered it for sale in November 1852 according to the May 14, 1853, *Jefferson Herald*. Because Dopplemayer did not own the land and lived in Harrison County (deed records indicate that he lived in that county in 1851 and 1854), he apparently built speculative buildings, as indicated by his advertisement. This appears to have been the two-story structure under construction in August 1851 that was chosen by the commissioners court for the location of its next term. The firm of Veal & Jennings occupied the old store of Willard & Tuttle immediately on the corner, which appears to have been owned by John Speake; Steinlein's store was one door above. The designation No. 2 Marshall appears to refer to the second house north of Dallas. This is the only street number given for any facility in Jefferson before the war.

Steinlein & Company was composed of Moses Steinlein and Mark Dorn. On December 23, 1853, Steinlein & Company purchased from R. C. Armistead and P. A. Mallard the lot and storehouse previously owned by David Douthit and before him by William Falk, as indicated in a February 25, 1856, transaction in which Dorn sold his half interest in the property to Steinlein. Steinlein & Company's second facility was thus on Marshall at the northern end of Lot 7 in Block 21. Steinlein & Company is listed in the 1853 and 1855 tax rolls, and Steinlein does not appear as an individual in the 1854 tax rolls. In 1855, Steinlein & Company owned one lot in Jefferson valued at $3,000 and had $15,000 in stock, second only to Kohn & May in size of operation. Dorn does not appear in the 1860 census. Steinlein is listed as an unmarried 31-year-old merchant born in Germany, without assets, and living in the home of Orville Yerger.

Nelson Trawick is listed as a physician in the 1850 census, owned the Jefferson Hotel and attendant stables for a few months in late 1852, and was practicing medicine in Shreveport by December 1853. He was also a Jefferson merchant. Although the nature of his business is uncertain because of an absence of advertisements, he probably operated a drugstore, which was the common mercantile operation for doctors.

Trawick purchased the east half of Lot 8 in Block 5 from Samuel McFarland in November 1850 and sold it to Eliza Smith in December, with the latter transaction indicating that Trawick was located on the east (i.e., on the west half of Lot 9 in Block 5). A schedule of separate property prepared by Eliza in May 1851 indicates that she and her husband George were living on their property and that it contained a storehouse. On January 31, 1852, Urquhart sold to W. Brooks & Brother Lot 4 in Block 73 fronting 50 feet on Lake and opposite (apparently across Lake) the storehouse then occupied by N. Trawick & Company and the half lot on the side next to the new building being erected by Perry Graham. Trawick did not own the properties mentioned by Smith and Urquhart.

On September 30, 1852, Trawick purchased from Amos Ury the west half of Lot 9 in Block 5 fronting 25 feet on Dallas. Trawick sold this property to a New York firm on December 8. The latter transaction indicates that the storehouse and warehouse on the property were formerly occupied by Ury & Ward and subsequently by Trawick. This was Ury's original storehouse, which later was occupied by Ury & Ward before they moved to their new store on Lot 7. On February 25,

1853, John Frith sold to Trawick the north half of Lot 11 in Block 22 fronting 25 feet on Marshall and running back 50 feet, including the improvements formerly occupied by Frith as a drugstore. Trawick sold his house in the Alley Addition on April 23 and the Frith property to another New York firm on July 30. The Frith property transactions do not make sense, because Lot 11 does not border on Marshall. This was obviously part of Lot 12 in Block 22 running 25 feet on Marshall and 50 feet along the alley purchased by Amanda Frith from Charles Westmoreland on December 9, 1851.

From these transactions, it can be concluded that N. Trawick & Company was located by at least January 1852 at the old Ury & Ward storehouse on the west half of Lot 9 in Block 5 and during early 1853 on the northern 25 feet of Lot 12 in Block 22. Ury & Ward built a new store on Lot 7 in Block 5 in November 1850. The old store on the west half of Lot 6 was apparently rented to Trawick in December 1850, which would account for Eliza Smith's mention of Trawick's location during that month. N. Trawick & Company was thus located in the old Ury & Ward storehouse from December 1850 to December 1852 and in the old Frith drugstore in the first few months of 1853. April 1853 district court minutes indicate that the partner in N. Trawick & Company was John Hendrick, that the firm was no longer in existence by that time, and that Hendrick was living in Titus County.

Amos Ury purchased the west half of Lot 9 in Block 5 from Urquhart and Durham in January 1846 and sold it to Nelson Trawick in September 1852, who sold it to Grant & Barton in December 1852, who sold it to William Torrans in January 1855. There is another set of deeds concerning the west half of Lot 9 in Block 5, which was sold by James McCown to John Waskom in December 1851, who sold it to William Towers in February 1852. The latter set of transactions, which mention the firm of Waskom & Crockett, was in error. This error was not corrected until June 18, 1856, in a conveyance from John Waskom to Caroline Crockett, which identifies the west half of Lot 11 in Block 5 as the former location of Waskom & Crockett's store and later William Towers' store. This property was purchased (in the set of incorrect transactions) by Waskom from James McCown on December 8, 1851, and sold by Waskom to William Towers on February 27, 1852, with the latter transaction mentioning that this was the house and lot formerly occupied by Waskom & Crockett. Waskom & Crockett apparently extended only from December 1851 to February 1852 and was terminated with Thomas Crockett's death.

Waskom is listed in the tax rolls as owner of two town lots valued at $1,000 and $1,000 in merchandise in 1853, as owner of one lot valued at $800 and $400 in merchandise in 1854, and as owner of two lots valued at $800 and $400 in merchandise in 1855. Waskom did not advertise in newspapers external to Jefferson. In the May 14, 1853, *Jefferson Herald*, Waskom advertised that he had leased the warehouse formerly occupied by Speake, Saufley & Nimmo, with the advertisement suggesting that he was in the receiving, forwarding, and commission business. Waskom does not appear in the 1860 census.

W. Brooks & Brother is listed in the tax rolls as owning four town lots valued at $2,200 and $3,000 in merchandise in 1853, four town lots valued at $2,800 and $5,000 in merchandise in 1854, and two town lots valued at $200 and $8,759 in merchandise in 1855. This firm was composed of William and Joseph Brooks and advertised in the May 14, 1853, *Jefferson Herald* as in the dry goods and groceries business. It went back to at least 1851, because William Wynn sold a lot to the firm in December 1851; and Urquhart sold a lot to the firm in January 1852, with the transaction mentioning that they were operating in Jefferson as merchants. When George Smith sold to Samuel Friou the east half of Lot 8 in Block 5 fronting Dallas Street in December 1851, the transaction mentions Brooks' lot on the west (i.e., the west half of Lot 8). Although no mention is made of a storehouse, this is the probable location of W. Brooks & Brother in 1851.

W. Brooks & Brother entered into the receiving, forwarding, and commission business in September 1853, occupying Horatio Walcott's warehouse in the landing area. The firm became Brooks, Brother & Mabry, with the inclusion of Hinche Mabry in February 1854. However, in February 1855, William and Joseph advertised that they were in the dry goods and groceries business on Dallas Street under the name W. & J. W. Brooks. It is probable that the dry goods and groceries business was never abandoned, because Brooks & Brother are listed in the tax rolls with merchandise from 1853 to 1855. On July 1, 1856, William

Brooks sold for $2,000 to Seaman, Peck & Company of New Orleans the west half of Lot 8 in Block 5 containing a storehouse, which obviously was their location in 1855 and probably was their location back to 1851. Joseph sold his interest in the business to William in November 1855 and is not listed in the 1860 census. William sold his residence in December 1856, became the operator of the City Hotel in early 1858, and is listed as a hotel proprietor in the 1860 census.

The old Eason drugstore property was located on Lot 12 in Block 22, fronting 25 feet on Marshall and running back 50 feet along the alley. When Eason mortgaged this property to George Ury in October 1851, the transaction mentions that it was then occupied by Drs. Frith and Robinson as a drugstore. Amanda Frith purchased this property from Charles Westmoreland in December 1851. John Frith sold this property to Nelson Trawick in February 1853, with the transaction mentioning improvements formerly occupied by Frith as a drugstore. Frith joined with James Elliott to establish a new drugstore on Marshall, with the firm of Elliott & Frith advertising in the March 5, 1853, *Texas Republican*. A May 14, 1853, *Jefferson Herald* advertisement indicates that the firm had purchased the entire stock of Norris & Tackett in addition to its own stock. Because the advertisement was dated February, Frith's transition to the new business was immediate. In addition to drugs and medicines, Elliott & Frith sold chemicals, paints, oils, dyestuffs, books, stationery, perfume, window glass, fine cutlery, and surgical instruments. Sales were wholesale and retail, for cash or on time to responsible men, with particular attention paid to physicians and country merchants. On February 15, 1853, Elliott mortgaged Lot 3 in Block 83 and Lot 9 in Block 22 to cover the debt incurred by Elliott & Frith on the same day. Because neither of these lots was on Marshall, it appears that Elliott & Frith were renters and that they occupied the establishment previously occupied by Norris & Tackett. Frith is listed in the 1860 census as a farmer living near Jefferson.

The January 10, 1852, *Texas Republican* reports that Dr. Samuel Norris had removed the drugstore of Norris & Tackett from Marshall to Jefferson. Loughery received a present from the new firm, which he reports on in the April 24, 1852, *Texas Republican*:

> We received on Thursday evening a very handsome present from our friend NORRIS, of the firm of Norris & Tackett, Jefferson. It consisted of a fine razor, (one of Wade & Butcher's best,) a bottle of hair oil, a ball of superb shaving soap, a box of shaving powder, a tooth brush, and a bottle of perfume. We were very "happy" to be thus kindly remembered, and can say that the trial of these articles fully warrant us in recommending the establishment from which they come. They are of a superior character. It will be seen that Messrs. Norris & Tackett have recently received a large stock of Drugs, and "pretty things," which they propose to sell out at cash, at a small profit. Give the "Doctor" a call, and examine his fine stock and his prices.

Norris & Tackett advertised in the May 1, 1852, *Texas Republican* that they were opening one of the largest and most general stocks of drugs and medicines ever brought into East Texas, with competitive prices afforded by location at the head of navigation. There are no property transactions for Norris or Tackett, indicating that they were renters. This was a two-story structure, because the attorney Hiram Grinsted advertised in 1853 that he was located over the Norris & Tackett drugstore. The drugstore was in operation for only a little over a year. The stock of Norris & Tackett was acquired by Elliott & Frith according to their May 14, 1853, *Jefferson Herald* advertisement, which was dated February.

James Todd was Smithland's primary merchant, having moved there from Port Caddo. He advertised in the May 14, 1853, *Jefferson Herald* that he desired to close his business in Smithland and move to Jefferson. On June 15, 1853, Todd mortgaged to S. O. Nelson & Company of New Orleans his Smithland properties (including a storehouse, warehouse, residence, ferry, and saw and grist mill) and a lot and house in Jefferson fronting Austin and Dallas that had been purchased from John Waskom. This was the west half of Lot 2 in Block 5, which had been purchased for $400 on March 8, 1852. Todd sold the lot, which contained a storehouse, to Anthony Owens on

July 3, 1854, for $2,500 to satisfy part of the debt owed to Nelson & Company. However, this transaction does not appear to have been consummated.

A February 12, 1856, release by Henderson & Gaines and other creditors indicates that Todd had run into financial difficulties and that he still owned the lot in Jefferson. On June 15, 1858, Todd mortgaged the lot and storehouse to Nelson & Company. On August 11 of the same year, the district court ruled against Todd and in favor of Nelson & Company in connection with a debt of over $15,000. Todd sold the lot and storehouse to Nelson & Company for $2,500 on the same day and the Smithland properties to Nelson & Company on December 28, with the latter transaction indicating that the storehouse in Jefferson was being rented. Todd appears in the 1860 census as a 47-year-old farmer born in Georgia with a wife (Susan) and eight children and living in Beat 3, which was part of the Jefferson Post Office area. He does not appear in the tax rolls with merchandise, but is shown as owning one town lot in Jefferson in 1854 and 1857. The announcement of Ada Todd's marriage in October 1854 indicates that James Todd was living in Smithland. There is no concrete evidence that he was ever a Jefferson merchant; if he was, it may have been only during late 1853 and early 1854.

John Pitkin is listed in the 1850 census as a 40-year-old clerk born in Connecticut and living with Todd in Smithland. A November 8, 1850, sale by Todd to Martha Horner of a lot in Smithland mentions that it was located on Common Street at the corner of Pitkin Street immediately opposite Todd's storehouse. Pitkin is listed in the 1860 census as a 40-year-old merchant born in Alabama and living in Jefferson with his wife Adaline. In spite of the discrepancies between the two censuses, it is unlikely that the J. W. Pitkin living in Smithland in 1850 was not the J. W. Pitkin living in Jefferson in 1860. The "Pitkin Geneaology" indicates that John Pitkin was born in 1808 and moved from Hartford, Connecticut, to New Orleans, where he operated as a merchant. Prior to moving to Smithland, Pitkin lived in Houston, where he participated in 1840 in efforts to establish a railroad and in the Republic's war with Mexico. DeMorse commented briefly on Pitkin's career and character in the August 21, 1852, *Northern Standard*:

We call attention to the card of J. W. Pitkin of Jefferson, in this number. Pitkin is an old Texan, and in former days, poured out his money in the cause of the Republic of Texas, when it had no money, and little credit; for which he got in return,—only glory. "The Pitkin Guards," we remember them. Just now however, we have no doubt he would rather we would call attention to his goods. The gentleman who handed us his card, says he has a large and superb stock of goods, and we say, that any body who deals at Jefferson, and would like to deal with one of the pleasantest humored and most accommodating gentlemen he ever met with, can call on Pitkin and find the man. "He'll do to tie to."

Pitkin advertised in August 1852 that he was located on Dallas Street next to Pugh's drugstore and in March 1857 that he was located on the southwest corner of Dallas and Marshall. Pugh's drugstore in 1850 was on the east half of Lot 12 in Block 4, immediately on the corner. Pitkin was located next door on the west half of Lot 12 according to numerous transactions, such as the May 6, 1857, sale by Pitkin of the east half of the lot to his wife Adaline. Thomas Pugh sold the west half of Lot 12 to Pitkin on May 23, 1853, and the full lot to Pitkin on November 22. When the full lot was mortgaged by Pitkin to Robert Pitkin (his brother, who advertised as a New Orleans clothing merchant in the April 19, 1856, *Texas Republican*) and Charles Fonda on September 5, 1854, mention is made of a two-story frame house on the property, apparently referring to Pitkin's storehouse. The building formerly occupied by Pugh does not appear to have been in existence by that time, because no other storehouse is mentioned on the property.

Pitkin began operating in August 1852 in the storehouse purchased from Pugh in May 1853. He is listed in the 1853 tax rolls as owning no town lots in Jefferson and $4,000 in merchandise and in the 1854 tax rolls as owning one town lot in Jefferson valued at $1,600 and $9,000 in merchandise. He appears in the 1855 and 1857 tax rolls under the name J. W. Pitkin and in the 1856 tax rolls under the name J. W. Pitkin & Company. Pitkin was a wholesale and retail dealer in dry goods and groceries, buying from the northern and eastern cities and selling primarily to country merchants and planters. He advertised in the Jefferson, Marshall, and Clarksville newspapers, favoring the "Just Received" type of advertisement (Fig. 21-1), which often ran for more than a year. His February 5, 1859, advertisement in the Clarksville *Standard* suggests that he had moved away from credit sales toward sales for cash or produce.

Fig. 21-1. J. W. Pitkin Advertisement. Source: March 25, 1854, *Texas Republican*

```
JUST RECEIVED,
            BY
     J. W. PITKIN,
              Jefferson, Texas,
WHOLESALE and Retail Dealer in Iron,
    Nails, Castings,
    Groceries and Staple Dry Goods.
A large stock of every description of sup-
plies for
    Country Merchants and Farmers,
The following is a list of some of the leading
articles always kept on hand:
  300 sacks Rio, Havana, and Java coffee;
   20 bbls brown sugar.
   10 hogsheads  do
   20 bbls pulverized and 15 tons Tenn Iron:
      Loaf Sugar;
  100 kegs of nails;
   20 casks bacon sides;
   25 kegs lard;
  200 bbls whisky; 100 bbls brandies—va-
      rious brands; gin, etc
   75 boxes of brandy cherries;
   75 boxes lemon syrup;
  100  do   claret wine;
  100  do   champagne cider;
   50  do   muscat wine;
   50  do   assorted cordials;
   50  do   essence of peppermint;
   50  do   stoughton's bitters;
  100  do   star candles;
  100  do   tobacco, of every description;
   25  do bar soap;
80000 segars, from Cuba sixes up to the finest:
   Cedar buckets, counter brushes, counter
scales, brooms, bottles, flasks, decanters, corks
and cork screws,
   And a complete assortment of Bar Stores,
&c., &c.
   Also a large supply of Staple and Fancy
Dry Goods, Bonnets, Hats, Boots, and
Shoes, Saddlery, &c., &c.
   Jefferson, March 25, 1854.        35–1y
```

Pitkin established a partnership with Labon Bayless in early 1855, forming the firm of J. W. Pitkin & Company according to the April 14, 1855, *Texas Republican*. The firm advertised under this name in the March 14, 1857, *Eastern Texas Gazette*. The firm went heavily in debt to Taylor, Knapp & Co. in New Orleans. After the partnership with Bayless ended, Pitkin mortgaged the storehouse and half lot to Taylor, Knapp on April 15, 1859.

John Sabine is not listed in the 1850 or 1860 censuses. He appears in the 1854 tax rolls as owner of one town lot in Jefferson valued at $1,600 and $4,000 in merchandise, in the 1855 tax rolls as owner of one lot valued at $2,000 and $5,000 in merchandise, and in the 1856 tax rolls under the name Sabine, Gillian & Company as owning $5,000 in merchandise but no town lots. He advertised in the February 12, 1853, *Texas Republican* as a new store in Jefferson on Marshall Street. The advertisement suggests that Sabine had been a merchant elsewhere and had recently located in Jefferson. Sabine was in the dry goods and groceries business, purchasing in New York and New Orleans and selling primarily to planters and interior merchants. Bagging and rope for cotton bales was advanced to planters who would send their cotton to him. A May 14, 1853, *Jefferson Herald* advertisement indicates that he was in the wholesale and retail business, selling cheap for cash. Consider Sabine, who is mentioned in the newspapers, was apparently a member of this firm.

T. D. Frazor joined Sabine to form the firm of John Sabine & Company in early 1855 according to the April 14, 1855, *Texas Republican*. They were joined by James Gillian (previously a farmer on Jim's Bayou) in early 1856 according to the March 22, 1856, *Standard*, and the three men advertised under the name Sabine, Gillian & Company in that issue. Advertisements indicate that the firm became Sabine & Frazor in September 1856 and that the stock was acquired by a new business, Frazor & Company, in January 1857. Frazor & Company was composed of Thomas and O. C. Frazor, who continued to operate at the old location of Sabine & Frazor, renting from Sabine.

On July 17, 1857, Sabine mortgaged to Robert Walker the south half of Lot 6 in Block 21 fronting 25 feet on Marshall and running back 150 feet along the alley and containing Sabine's storehouse, then occupied by Thomas and O. C. Frazor. This lot had been bonded to Sabine for $400 by Caleb Ragan in January 1852 and conveyed to him in December. An October 1, 1857, transaction between Sabine and James Rogers concerns a debt owed by Sabine & Frazor, successors to Sabine, Gillian & Company, to a New York firm. Sabine describes himself as the surviving partner of that firm, indicating that Thomas Frazor had died by that time. Sabine and his wife Victoria sold their residence in the Alley Addition to John Ligon in November 1858.

The firm of Veal & Jennings is listed in the 1853 tax rolls with $10,000 in merchandise and in the 1854 tax rolls with $2,000 in merchandise. The firm is not shown as owning any town lots. They advertised in the February 12, 1853, *Texas Republican* as being in the dry goods and groceries business and located at Willard & Tuttle's corner, which was on Lot 1 in Block 4 at the northwest corner of Dallas and Marshall. They advertised in the May 14, 1853, *Jefferson Herald* as wholesale and retail merchants in dry goods and groceries, with $25,000 in stock, located in the old stand of Willard & Tuttle, and providing the highest cash prices for hides, pelts, beeswax, and tallow exchanged for goods. Most of Clinton Willard's Jefferson properties were seized by the sheriff (George Ury) and sold at auction to Jesse Veal for $2,000 on September 8, 1853. These properties included Lot 10 in Block 4 and parts of Lots 1 and 2 in Block 4 fronting 22 ½ feet on Marshall Street. The latter appears to have been the property formerly occupied by M. Steinlein & Company rather than Willard & Tuttle's corner immediately to the south in which Veal & Jennings was located. Veal & Jennings was renting the old Willard & Tuttle storehouse from John Speake. When Speake sold the property on Lots 1 and 2 in Block 4 (described as fronting 47 ½ feet on Marshall and running back 100 feet) to Henry Bilger and Alexander McKimens in December 1862, the transaction mentions the storehouse formerly occupied by Veal & Jennings.

Neither Veal nor Jennings appears in the 1860 census. Veal sold Lot 10 in Block 4 to a New York firm for $5,787.30 in May 1854. The reason for the high sales price was that this lot contained two two-story storehouses (apparently side-by-side on Dallas), the upper stories of which had been occupied in March 1853 by the *Jefferson Herald* and the Odd Fellows Hall. Veal's other property in Lot 4 (the north half of the original Willard & Tuttle property) was sold by the sheriff (W. H. Crow) to Cherry, Henderson & Company on March 6, 1855, in connection with a March 1854 district court judgment against Veal and in favor of another firm. The transaction mentions that this property was formerly occupied by the firm of Morgan & Tomlin.

Hiram Tomlin had been in the grocery business with Caleb Ragan from February 1852 to December 1853. He apparently immediately went into business with John Morgan to establish the firm of Morgan & Tomlin on Marshall Street one door above Willard & Tuttle's corner in the storehouse that was owned by Jesse Veal and had been vacated by M. Steinlein & Company in December. Tomlin's brother John was the author of the 1849 *Tales of the Caddo*, which had been prepared on the basis of an 1848 visit. Hiram Tomlin appears in the 1850 census as a 23-year-old clerk born in Tennessee and living in the house of Amos Ury.

Morgan & Tomlin is listed in the 1853 and 1854 tax rolls with $3,000 in merchandise and no town lots and in the 1855 tax rolls with $5,000 in merchandise and two town lots. An advertisement in the May 14, 1853, *Jefferson Herald* indicates that they were in the general mercantile business, probably meaning dry goods and groceries. Bagging and rope were furnished and liberal cash advances made on cotton for shipment. On March 1, 1855, Morgan & Tomlin mortgaged to Jackson Morgan various properties, including Tomlin's residence in the Alley Addition, Tomlin's tract of land eight miles from Jefferson in the Richardson headright, three lots in the Alley Addition, a slave, and a lot and house in the Urquhart Addition purchased from Job Baker.

Morgan shot Henry Parsons of the *Tyler Telegraph* in Jefferson in January 1854 in connection with an affair of honor and was fined one cent after having been judged guilty of assault with intent to kill. Morgan was killed in an unrelated incident after he left Jefferson according to a report in the November 10, 1857, *Texas Republican*: "ANOTHER MURDER.—We learn that Mr. JOHN F. MORGAN, formerly of the firm of Morgan & Tomlin, Jefferson, was killed recently in Jonesville, Angelina county, by a young man by the name of Wm. Burks. Mr. Morgan had removed to Jonesville, where he was living at the time of his death. He was shot down in front of his store. We have not learned the circumstances which led to the commision of the deed, or anything further in relation to it. Mr. Morgan has many friends in Jefferson who will lament his tragical end."

In September 1853, Charles DeMorse of the Clarksville *Standard* characterized the larger merchants in Jefferson as advertisers with large stocks and rapid turnovers at low prices that produced benefits to themselves and their customers:

> We insert this week, the cards of John Sabine, and M. Steinlein & Co., Merchants at Jefferson. We have noticed for a long time past that these gentlemen advertise large stocks of goods, and propose to do business for moderate profits. We commend these to the attention of the very considerable portion of our readers who trade at that place.
>
> It may be always set down as unquestionable, that Merchants who advertise largely and by calling the attention of the people endeavor to get rid of their wares speedily, are the best for the purchaser to deal with. They call everybody's attention; they sell their goods as rapidly as possible at small advances on cost and charges; then renew and go through the same routine as frequently as possible. Of course if they can turn over their capital four or five times a year instead of once or twice, they can sell at less profit on each article and still accumulate more within the year. Furthermore a liberal man in expenditure for business purposes, is a liberal and accommodating man to deal with—it cannot be otherwise. So you who deal at Jefferson, go and see Sabine and Steinlein, and Pitkin, and you who have cotton to store, call on Freeman, and you may profit by it.

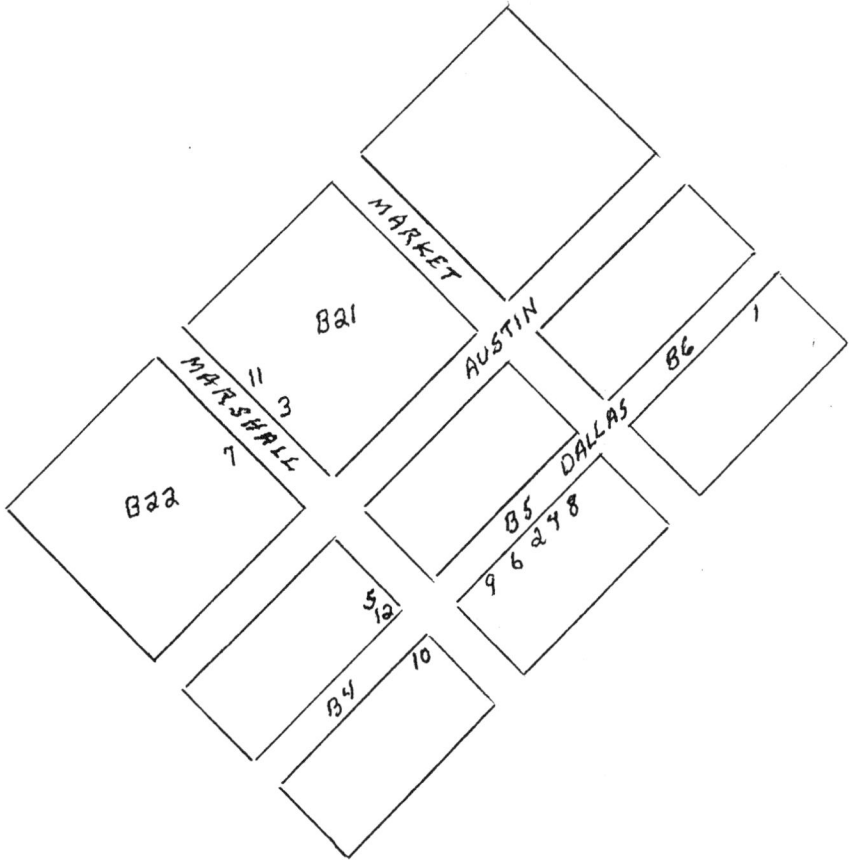

Fig. 21-2. Early 1850s Merchants
KEY:
1. Frederick Schluter (1852)
2. Frederick Schluter (1858)
3. David Douthit (1851); M. Steinlein & Company (1853)
4. David Douthit (1852); W. C. Baker & Company (1853)
5. M. Steinlein & Company (1852); Morgan & Tomlin (1853)
6. N. Trawick & Company (1850)
7. Frith & Robinson (1851); N. Trawick & Company (1853)
8. Waskom & Crockett (1851)
9. W. Brooks & Brother (1851)
10. John Pitkin (1852); J. W. Pitkin & Company (1855)
11. John Sabine (1853); John Sabine & Company (1855); Sabine, Gillian & Company (1856); Sabine & Frazor (1856); Frazor & Company (1857)
12. Veal & Jennings (1853)

22. Middle 1850s Merchants

The Cass County tax rolls indicate ownership of town lots and value of merchandise as of January 1 for the years 1854 through 1856. Persons with town lots and merchandise from 1854 through 1856 include: W. C. Baker & Company (1854–1855); J. T. Prewitt & Company (1854–1855); John Sabine (1854–1855); W. P. Torrans (1855–1857); C. G. Peele (1855–1856); and Sabine, Gillian & Company (1856). Persons without town lots but with merchandise and known to have been Jefferson merchants include: Walker & Sayre (1854); J. C. Preston & Company (1855); J. L & S. C. Smith (1854–1857); Henry Schluter (1855); Turner & Jenkins (1855–1856); and J. W. Kemp (1856). William Hodge, who was mayor of Jefferson in 1860, appears in the tax rolls without town lots but with merchandise in 1854–1855; however, this facility appears to have been located on Black Cypress Bayou.

Merchants appearing in various newspaper advertisements from late 1853 through early 1857 include: W. Brooks & Brother, receiving, forwarding, and commission merchants (September 1853); Brooks, Brother & Mabry, receiving, forwarding, and commission merchants (February 1854); W. C. Baker & Company, dry goods and groceries (February 1854); Joseph T. Prewitt, dry goods and groceries (May 1854); C. N. Stanley, commission and forwarding merchant (January 1855); W. & J. W. Brooks, dry goods (February 1855); J. C. Preston & Company, drugs (February 1855); Stanley & Nimmo, furniture (March 1856); Mosby, Schluter & Company, receiving, forwarding, and commission merchants (March 1856); Sabine, Gillian & Company, dry goods and groceries (March 1856); Mosby & Kohn, receiving, forwarding, and commission merchants (May 1856); Sabine & Frazor, dry goods and groceries (September 1856); Frazor & Company, dry goods and groceries (January 1857); Terry & Rogers, receiving, forwarding, and commission merchants (February 1857); and C. A. Bulkley, groceries (February 1857).

Merchants advertising in the March 14, 1857, *Eastern Texas Gazette* include: J. W. Pitkin & Company, dry goods; R. W. Walker, drugs; L. J. Graham & Company, drugs; C. A. Bulkley, dry goods; Morris & Company, dry goods and groceries; Bryan & Clark, receiving, forwarding, and commission merchants; Stanley & Nimmo, furniture; B. J. Terry, groceries; Hugo Fox, groceries and candy; J. L. and S. C. Smith, staple and fancy goods; and Spilker & Company, dry goods and groceries.

When John Sabine mortgaged his property in Lot 6 of Block 21 containing his storehouse in July 1857, he mentions that the storehouse was then occupied by Thomas and O. C. Frazor. Thomas had been in the dry goods and groceries business with Sabine. He joined with his brother O. C. in January 1857 to establish the dry goods and groceries business Frazor & Company. The Frazors purchased the stock of Sabine & Frazor and continued to operate out of the same storehouse, renting from Sabine. Frazor & Company's advertisement in the January 24, 1857, *Texas Republican* mentions that the stock included "French and American prints, muslins, delaines, barazes [a striped cloth], silk goods, trimmings, brown and bleached domestic, osnaburgs, kerseys, linseys, fine black and blue cloths, cassimeres, and ready made clothing. Boots and shoes from the common brogan to the finest French calf skin. Hardware, cutlery, china and glass ware. Fine wines, Brandies and imported cigars of favorite brands." Bagging and rope were on hand at all times and furnished to planters on the usual terms.

Frazor & Company advertised in the November 7, 1857, *Eastern Texas* Gazette as "having just received a large and well selected stock of fashionable fall and winter goods which for beauty and elegance cannot be surpassed by any house in Jefferson," with liberal deductions for cash sales. Thomas was dead by October 1857. O. C. Frazor is listed in the 1857 tax rolls as owning $7,000 in merchandise and no town lots.

He is shown in the 1860 census as a 30-year-old clerk born in Tennessee with real and personal estate valued at $4,200. The clerk designation indicates that he was working for someone else.

William Torrans is listed in the 1855 tax rolls as owner of half a town lot valued at $800 and $350 in merchandise, in the 1856 tax rolls as owner of half a town lot valued at $800 and $600 in merchandise, and in the 1857 tax rolls as owner of one town lot valued at $500 and $500 in merchandise. An October 23, 1854, mortgage from W. C. Baker & Company to J. Burnsides & Company concerning the east half of Lot 10 in Block 5 mentions that Torrans' grocery house was on the west half of Lot 11 in Block 5, which was the old Waskom & Crockett storehouse. On January 10, 1855, Torrans purchased from the New York firm of Grant & Barton the west half of Lot 9 in Block 5, which was the storehouse originally owned by Amos Ury and later occupied by Nelson Trawick, who sold the property to Grant & Barton in December 1852. The west half of Lot 9 in Block 5 was Torrans' location from January 1855 to March 1860, when the property was sold to William Prewitt.

Torrans advertised in the April 10, 1858, Clarksville *Standard* who as a "Dealer in staple groceries, Sugar, Coffee, Tobacco, Liquors, Molasses, Salt, Rice, etc., invites the attention of the citizens of the Northern counties of Texas, to the full and complete stock which he keeps up in his line, and offers for sale at the lowest rates." Because of the low value of merchandise in stock, this may have been a retail operation, although the appeal to interior customers suggests that it was wholesale. Torrans apparently did not go out of the grocery business after the March 1860 sale to William Prewitt, because he had purchased Lot 6 in Block 9 with a brick structure on it from William Perry in February 1860. However, he is not listed in the 1860 census as a merchant, but rather as a 40-year-old bookkeeper born in North Carolina with a wife and two children and real and personal estate valued at $9,000.

Charles Peele is listed in the tax rolls as owning $4,500 in merchandise in 1855 and $1,800 in merchandise in 1856. The nature of this firm is unknown. On August 12, 1852, Peele purchased from Caleb Ragan what is described as the south halves of Lots 5 and 6 in Block 21, both fronting 25 feet on Marshall and running back 150 feet to an alley. On

May 11, 1853, Peele purchased from John Speake the west half of Lots 1–6 in Block O of the Alley Addition, which was the location of his residence. On December 8, 1857, Peele sold to Thomas Smith the north half of Lot 6 in Block 21 containing a storehouse; and on February 27, 1858, Peele sold to Saufley & Batte the south half of Lot 5 in Block 21. It can be assumed that the original transaction was scrambled and that Peele's storehouse was located on the north half of Lot 6 in Block 21. The October 31, 1855, Shreveport *South-Western* reports that Peele was building a steamboat for operation on the Sulphur Fork. He is not listed in the 1860 census.

Joseph T. Prewitt & Company advertised in the May 20, 1854, *Texas Republican* as in the dry goods, groceries, and jewelry business, obtaining stocks from New York, and featuring the latest fashions in ready-made clothing from France, the prettiest and neatest ladies' bonnets, fine ventilated hats, and breast pins emblematic of Masonry and Odd Fellowship. The tax rolls show Joseph T. Prewitt & Company with one lot valued at $3,000 and $2,000 in merchandise in 1854 and one lot valued at $400 and $2,000 in merchandise in 1855. In April 1855, Prewitt was in debt to J. Burnsides & Company and mortgaged to S. K. Fowler various properties, including Lot 6 in Block 12 on the east side of the landing area. On January 13, 1858, John Shaw sold to Ligon & Bulkley Lot 12 in Block 7, formerly occupied by Joseph T. Prewitt & Company. The same lot designation is given in an August 12, 1858, conveyance from John Ligon to Chester Bulkley. However, on April 12, 1859, when Bulkley transferred the property (then occupied by R. Manwaring & Company) to Richard Manwaring, the designation is given as Lot 12 in Block 6.

Walker & Sayre is shown in the 1854 tax rolls with $2,000 in merchandise and no town lots. Dr. R. W. Walker began practicing in Jefferson in 1852. Walker & Sayre was the predecessor to the wholesale and retail druggists J. C. Preston & Company, which was established in February 1855. J. L. & S. C. Smith advertised in the March 14, 1857, *Eastern Texas Gazette* that they were located on Marshall opposite the drugstore formerly occupied by J. C. Preston & Company. In a June 20, 1860, transaction, Horatio Walcott indicated that he sold his lot and storehouse at the southeast corner of Marshall and Austin (occupying

38 feet on Marshall and 100 feet on Austin) on October 27, 1857, to John and Samuel Smith, with the transaction indicating that the Smiths had been occupying the store. Thus, J. C. Preston & Company and its predecessor Walker & Sayre were located on Marshall near the southwest corner of Marshall and Austin in the drugstore operated by Thomas Pugh in 1853 (i.e., on the lower 30 feet of the original 50-foot lot).

Walker reemerged as a wholesale and retail dealer in staple and fancy drugs in the March 14, 1857, *Eastern Texas Gazette*, advertising as located on Marshall Street one door above Frazor & Company. Because Frazor & Company was located on the south half of Lot 6 in Block 21, Walker was located on the north half. This half lot with a storehouse was purchased by Walker from Thomas Smith in December 1858. The May 20, 1854, *Texas Republican* says that an advertisement for the Jefferson merchants T. and W. F. Smith, who were said to have a fine store, would appear in the next issue. Although this did not happen, the Smiths obviously operated a store of some sort in 1854 at the location that came to be occupied by Charles Peele in 1855 and R. W. Walker in 1857. Neither the Smiths nor Walker appear in the 1860 census.

J. C. Preston & Company is shown in the 1855 tax rolls with $3,200 in merchandise and no town lots because the facility on the southwest corner of Marshall and Austin was rented. The company's advertisement in the February 17, 1855, *Texas Republican* (Fig. 22-1) indicates that it was composed of Joseph Preston and Francis Clark, that they were successors to Walker & Sayre, and that they were in the wholesale and retail drug business, selling for cash or to responsible men on credit. An endorsement was supplied by R. W. Walker. An advertisement in the March 14, 1857, *Eastern Texas Gazette* says that J. C. Preston & Company had sold its stock to Dr. Anselm Prewitt and was going out of business. Preston appears in the 1860 census as a 25-year-old druggist born in Georgia with a wife and two children and real and personal estate valued at $2,200.

J. L. & S. C. Smith was composed of the brothers John and Samuel Smith. The Smiths are listed in the 1860 census as merchants born in South Carolina and living in the house of L. W. Morris, with John aged 42 and having $19,500 in assets and Samuel aged 40 and having $100 in assets. J. L. & S. C. Smith appears in the tax rolls without town lots and

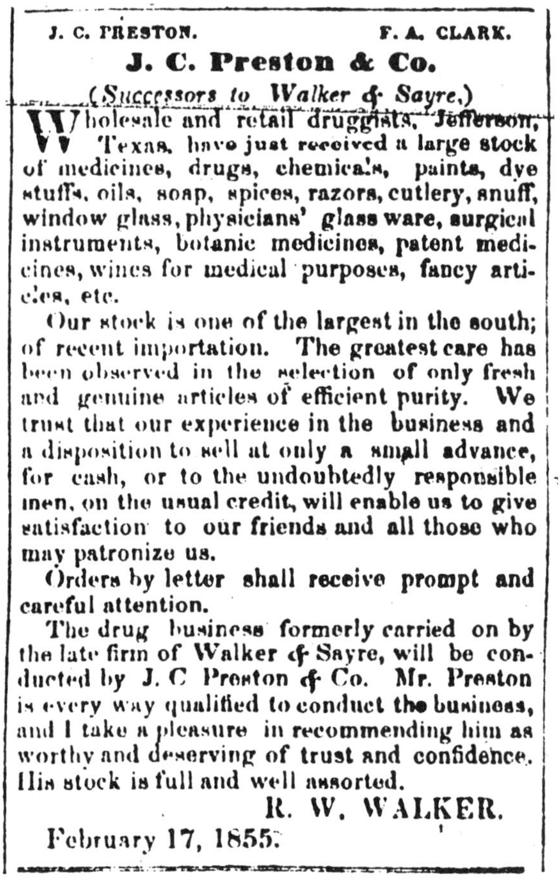

Fig. 22-1. J. C. Preston & Company. Source: February 17, 1855, *Texas Republican*

> J. C. PRESTON.   F. A. CLARK.
> ## J. C. Preston & Co.
> *(Successors to Walker & Sayre.)*
>
> Wholesale and retail druggists, Jefferson, Texas, have just received a large stock of medicines, drugs, chemicals, paints, dye stuffs, oils, soap, spices, razors, cutlery, snuff, window glass, physicians' glass ware, surgical instruments, botanic medicines, patent medicines, wines for medical purposes, fancy articles, etc.
>
> Our stock is one of the largest in the south; of recent importation. The greatest care has been observed in the selection of only fresh and genuine articles of efficient purity. We trust that our experience in the business and a disposition to sell at only a small advance, for cash, or to the undoubtedly responsible men, on the usual credit, will enable us to give satisfaction to our friends and all those who may patronize us.
>
> Orders by letter shall receive prompt and careful attention.
>
> The drug business formerly carried on by the late firm of Walker & Sayre, will be conducted by J. C Preston & Co. Mr. Preston is every way qualified to conduct the business, and I take a pleasure in recommending him as worthy and deserving of trust and confidence. His stock is full and well assorted.
>
> R. W. WALKER.
> February 17, 1855.

$3,000 in merchandise in 1854, $2,000 in merchandise in 1855, $2,000 in merchandise in 1856, and $3,000 in merchandise in 1857. When the Smiths acquired the property on the southeast corner of Marshall and Austin in October 1857, the transaction indicates they were already operating in the storehouse, which means that they probably had been renting from Walcott back to 1854. The Smiths advertised in the March 14, 1857, *Eastern Texas Gazette* that they dealt in staple and fancy goods. The Smiths built a brick storehouse on this property in 1858.

Henry Schluter appears only in the 1855 tax rolls with no town lots and $1,000 in merchandise. The nature and location of his business are unknown. In November 1855, he purchased the home of August May on Lots 9 and 10 in Block I of the Alley Addition. In March 1856, Schluter joined Joseph Mosby and Abraham Kohn in the receiving, forwarding, and commission business of Mosby, Schluter & Company, which lasted only two months. He was still in Jefferson in October, when he attended a Democratic meeting. Loughery of the *Texas Republican* commented on Schluter in September 1860 after he had moved to New Orleans:

> Our friend Mr. H. L. Schluter, formerly of Jefferson, who has a business connection with the wholesale grocery establishment of Messrs. Pinkard, Steele & Co., New Orleans, had been in this section of the State for several weeks. Mr. Schluter is an active, prompt, popular business man. We know of no man in the "Crescent City" who exhibits more gratification in the society of his Texas friends, or a readier disposition to serve them. Hence they never fail to call on him. The house with which he is connected, is one of the largest, if not the very largest, wholesale grocery establishment in New Orleans. Its immense stock has to be seen to be appreciated. It did a very large business with Texas last year, and we have no doubt its trade will be greatly increased this year. If you visit the city, reader, don't fail to call on Schluter.

Turner & Jenkins appear in the 1855 tax rolls with $5,000 in merchandise and no town lots and in the 1856 tax rolls with $300 in merchandise and no town lots. The partners were J. W. Turner and E. M. Jenkins. The firm split in 1857, with Turner shown as having three lots valued at $300 and $2,500 in merchandise and Jenkins shown as having two lots valued at $600 and $2,200 in merchandise. Nothing is known about these firms. Jenkins is not listed in the 1860 census, and Turner is shown as a farmer living outside of Jefferson.

J. W. Kemp appears in the 1856 tax rolls with $400 in merchandise and owning Lots 3–5, 7, and 8 in Block 74 valued at $600. Nothing is known about the nature of this firm, and the low value of its stock and its remote location indicate that it was a very small operation. This was the J. W. Kemp who was associated with the Jefferson Hotel in 1853. He does not appear in the 1860 census.

Spilker & Company advertised in the March 14, 1857, *Eastern Texas Gazette* as dealers in groceries, dry goods, and general plantation supplies located on Dallas Street at the old stand of Mosby & Schluter and offering the highest prices for cotton and pelts. The principal in this firm was Charles Spilker, who attended the Democratic meeting in Jefferson in late 1856. Spilker is not listed in the 1860 census. Mosby, Schluter & Company was in the receiving and forwarding business through 1856 on Lot 1 in Block 7 on the corner of Dallas and Polk.

L. J. Graham & Company advertised in the March 14, 1857, *Eastern Texas Gazette* as a wholesale and retail dealer in drugs, medicines, paints, oils, dye stuffs, books, stationery—anything that might be found in a drugstore. The location is given as Marshall Street. L. J. Graham & Company does not appear in the tax rolls, and Graham does not appear in the 1860 census. A companion advertisement shows Dr. L. J. Graham as a practicing physician with an office at the drugstore.

B. J. Terry advertised in the March 14, 1857, *Eastern Texas Gazette* as a wholesale and retail dealer in groceries and plantation supplies, with everything normally found in a grocery store, and featuring "polite and obliging young men, who will always take pleasure in showing my goods." The location is given as Freeman's old stand, which was on Dallas Street on Lot 4 in Block 10 in the landing area. Benjamin Terry had formed a receiving, forwarding, and commission business at that location in February 1857 with Thomas Rogers under the name Terry & Rogers, and Terry and Rogers established a partnership with Williamson Freeman in March, operating under the name Wm. Freeman & Company. The reason that Terry continued an independent operation is that neither Terry & Rogers nor Wm. Freeman & Company were wholesalers or retailers. B. J. Terry & Company, with James Gardner and David Culberson, purchased Lot 7 in Block 9 and ten feet of Lot 8 from William Torrans in October 1858 after the dissolution of the partnership with Freeman and may have moved to that location or else continued to occupy Freeman's old stand.

Morris & Company advertised in the March 14, 1857, *Eastern Texas Gazette* as a wholesale dealer in dry goods, groceries, jewelry, books, and stationery. A companion advertisement indicates that Morris & Company was also in the auction business. In an advertisement in the

November 7, 1857, *Eastern Texas Gazette*, C. D. Morris indicated that he would sue persons indebted to Morris & Company and Morris & Rush, with the latter obviously a predecessor to the former. Morris & Company was out of business by December 1858 when their stand was occupied by Chester Bulkley.

On February 23, 1860, C. D. Morris and his wife sold Lot 12 in Block 21 to R. H. Keen for $900, but no mention is made of a storehouse. On July 1, 1856, William Brooks sold to Seaman, Peck & Company of New Orleans the west half of Lot 8 in Block 5 (22 ½ feet on Dallas and running back to Lake) containing his storehouse. This property was transferred to William Prewitt in February 1860 and by Prewitt to Adolph Lewis in November 1860 (deed corrected in December 1860). The latter transaction indicates that the storehouse was then occupied by an E. Morris. C. D. and E. Morris do not appear in the 1860 census; however, the merchants A. B. and Peter Morris do.

Chester Bulkley was from Galveston. C. A. Bulkley was advertised as a new grocery store in Jefferson early in 1857 in the *Eastern Texas Gazette*, Marshall *Texas Republican*, Clarksville *Standard*, and *Dallas Herald*. The advertisement that appeared in the March 14, 1857, *Eastern Texas Gazette* is dated February 21 and indicated that the firm employed Clinton Willard, sold staple plantation goods to interior merchants and planters on a cash basis, and had purchased the stock of Speake & Smoker and was located at their old stand. The firm of Speake & Smoker was composed of John Speake and John Smoker, the famous Red River captain. That Smoker was a Jefferson merchant for a year or two is mentioned in the September 22, 1880, *New Orleans Daily Democrat*. The only evidence with respect to the location of Speake & Smoker is that the confectioner Hugo Fox was located on Marshall Street one door above, which means that C. A. Bulkley was located on Marshall Street. However, because Fox's exact location is unknown, C. A. Bulkley cannot be precisely located. A good possibility is the storehouse on the northeast corner of Marshall and Dallas that had been abandoned by Kohn & May in late 1855 and could have been occupied by Speake & Smoker from late 1855 through early 1857.

Robert Loughery visited Bulkley's grocery store in February 1857 and reports as follows:

YOU CAN TAKE MY HAT.—We were forcibly reminded of this expression a day or two ago. While in Jefferson we came across our enterprizing friend Mr. C. A. Bulkley, who invited us into his store, and treated us to one of the finest and most decidedly handsome HATS we have seen in many a day. A handsome hat is a handsome thing. We have felt decidedly amiable ever since we put it on, and cannot tell which we admire most, Mr. Bulkley or ourself. By the way, we were somewhat surprised to see him there. Although he has a small lot of clothing and hats on hand, he is not in that line. He has a large grocery store, having taken the house formerly occupied by Messrs. SPEAKE & SMOKER. He has a very fine stock on hand, and his prices are exceedingly low. Call on him, and you will be certain to purchase.

Advertisements dated June 13 that appear in the November 7, 1857, *Eastern Texas Gazette* indicate that Bulkley had expanded into dry goods and was at the same location. Bulkley's stock and location were acquired by H. Rhine & Brothers in May 1858. A January 13, 1858, conveyance of Lot 12 in Block 6 (formerly occupied by Joseph T. Prewitt & Company) from John Shaw to John Ligon and Chester Bulkley indicates that they were in business together under the name Ligon & Bulkley. The nature of this firm is unknown. Ligon transferred his portion of Lot 12 in Block 6 to Bulkley in August 1858 (indicating dissolution of the partnership), and Bulkley transferred Lot 12 in Block 6 to Richard Manwaring in April 1859. In any case, Bulkley was back in the dry goods business in December 1858 at a stand recently occupied by C. D. Morris, as advertised in the January 7, 1859, *Harrison Flag*. Bulkley purchased St. Catherine's Island in September 1858, sold it in May 1859, was back in Galveston by early 1859, and reappeared in Jefferson during the Civil War.

Charles Stanley was one of Jefferson's earliest merchants and had entered into the receiving and forwarding business in the landing area in 1853 and established a commission and forwarding business in January 1855 in a warehouse at the foot of Houston Street (east side) near the Jefferson bridge. Samuel Nimmo was in the receiving and forwarding business in 1852 and entered the dry goods and groceries business in 1853. The Stanley & Nimmo wholesale and retail furniture store was established in early 1856 in the warehouse formerly occupied by Stanley. The initial advertisement in the March 1, 1856, *Texas Republican* claimed that they had "just received from the manufactories in the Eastern cities, and will be constantly receiving throughout the season, the largest, most complete, and superb lot of Furniture ever brought into Eastern Texas." In stock were

> Bureaus, with and without marble tops; side-boards; sofas; tete-a-tetes; mirrors, from the largest and most splendidly gilded to the plainest; secretaries; desks; chairs of all kinds, from the finest rose-wood and mahogany to the cheapest and most durable; bed-steads, from the most elegant and finished patterns to the plainest; a superb lot of chairs, embracing several hundred of every variety. They have a choice selection of pianos, which for beauty of finish and richness of tone cannot be surpassed.

An advertisement in the November 29, 1856, *Texas Republican* indicates that Stanley & Nimmo had expanded into jewelry, with Loughery pointing out that "This enterprizing firm has also received a large and splendid lot of furniture, embracing every article in that line which may be desired. We received from them a few days ago a large gilded mirror, as beautiful and substantial an article as can be procured in New Orleans. Their stock of furniture cannot be excelled, and persons desiring to fit up rooms would do well to patronize them." In 1858, the warehouse was modified, and Stanley & Nimmo went into the meat-packing business, which lasted only two packing seasons and went heavily into debt. Stanley does not appear in the 1860 census. Nimmo is shown as a 28-year-old merchant born in Tennessee with a wife and two children and real and personal estate valued at $6,500.

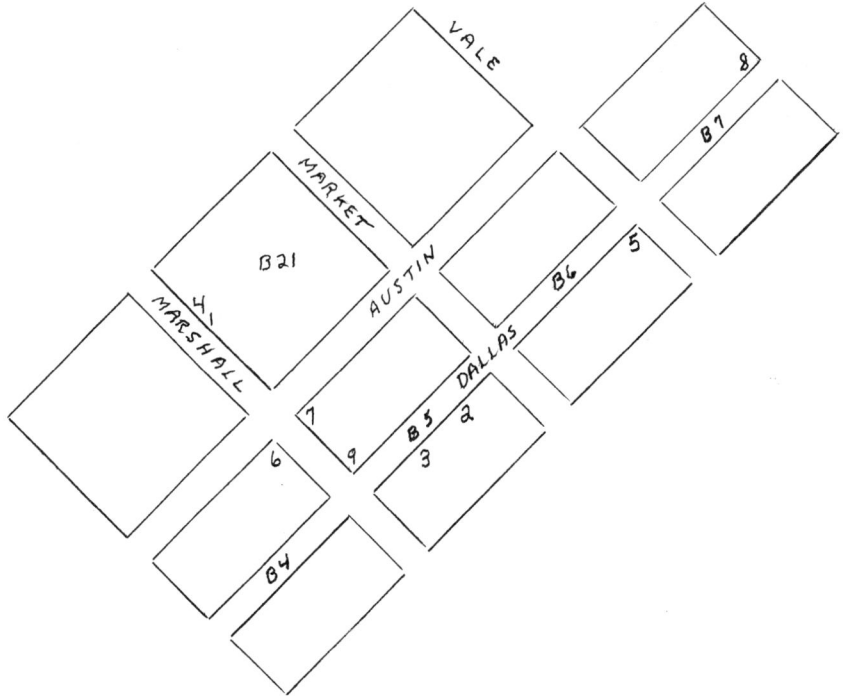

Fig. 22-2. Middle 1850s Merchants
KEY:
1. Sabine & Frazor (1856); Frazor & Company (1857)
2. William Torrans (1854)
3. William Torrans (1855)
4. T. & W. F. Smith (1854); Charles Peele (1855); R. W. Walker (1857)
5. Joseph T. Prewitt & Company (1854); Ligon & Bulkley (1858)
6. Walker & Sayre (1854); J. C. Preston & Company (1855)
7. J. L. & S. C. Smith (1854)
8. Spilker & Company (1857)
9. Speake & Smoker (1855); Chester Bulkley (1857)

28. Late Merchants

The Cass County tax rolls indicate ownership of town lots and value of merchandise in stock as of January 1 only for 1857. The value of merchandise is not given for 1858 and 1859. The Marion County tax rolls do not provide value of merchandise for 1860. Persons with town lots and merchandise in 1857 include E. M. Jenkins (1857); J. W. Turner (1857); and Saufley & Batte (1857). Persons without town lots but with merchandise and known to have been Jefferson merchants include Bryan & Clark (1857); O. C. Frazor (1857); Theophilus Nichols (1857); and Stanley & Nimmo (1857).

Merchants advertising in the November 7, 1857, *Eastern Texas Gazette* include Frazor & Company, dry goods; A. D. Taylor & Company, dry goods; Pinsky & Kallisher, dry goods; Dr. A. Prewitt, drugs; Saufley & Batte; H. Rhine & Brothers, dry goods and groceries; Reece Hughes, dry goods; and D. N. Alley, dry goods and groceries.

Merchants advertising in various newspapers from late 1857 through late 1860 include: Reece Hughes, dry goods and groceries (September 1857); H. Rhine & Brothers, dry goods and groceries (April 1858); W. P. Torrans, groceries (April 1858); John Speake, receiving, forwarding, and commission merchant (January 1859); R. Manwaring & Company, dry goods and groceries (February 1860); J. B. Ligon & Company, furniture and buggies (February 1860); Bob C. Hughes, dry goods and groceries (May 1860); T. D. Sedberry, dry goods and groceries (June 1860); W. K. Vining, hardware (July 1860); and Thomas Ferrell, at Speake's warehouse (November 1860).

Jefferson merchants listed in the 1860 census include A. B. Bayless, B. C. Hughes, John Smith, Samuel Smith, Jacob Sterne, B. H. Jacobs, Robert Green, William Smithson, Robert McWilliams, Theophilus Nichols, A. Bredig, Thomas Sedberry, John Pitkin, Joseph McDermott, James Brown, Elisha Price, A. B. Morris, Peter Morris, W. N. Klyce, Frederick Schluter, F. E. Taylor, George Taylor, Joel Hughes, S. Nussbaum, J. Nussbaum, Thomas Turner, D. C. Phillips, John Wallace, Jeptha Crawford, William Crawford, Lazarus Rosenzweig, Morris Rosenzweig, W. K. Vining, Samuel Nimmo, William Phillip, Moses Steinlein, Gus Hodge, John Murphy, Benjamin Terry, J. H. Faucett, William Torrans, John Speake, Richard Waterhouse, James Durr, Williamson Freeman, David Smith, John Reed, William Saufley, James Murphy, and William Nichols. Abraham Kohn and John Ligon are listed as merchants living in the vicinity of Jefferson.

Saufley & Batte, which was composed of William Saufley and William Batte, is listed in the 1857 tax rolls as owning $7,000 in merchandise and two town lots valued at $1,500. Saufley and Batte issued a notice in the March 14, 1857, *Eastern Texas Gazette* requesting that people owing Saufley & Batte and the old firm of Saufley & Nimmo pay up in cash, stressing that "We have been very liberal with our friends for the last five years, and have allowed ourselves pressed to save them; and we shall now expect in return for our indulgence to them, they will come forward and assist us." They advertised in the November 7, 1857, *Eastern Texas Gazette*, with the advertisement dated 1856, that they featured Smith's Tonic Syrup sold at wholesale and retail. This firm was probably in the dry goods and groceries business.

Saufley & Batte was obviously a successor to Saufley & Nimmo. William Saufley had been a partner in 1851 in the dry goods and groceries business of Saufley & Hudgins, continued in the same line of business by himself in May 1851, and joined with John Speake and Samuel Nimmo in a receiving, forwarding, and commission business in September 1852. The latter partnership apparently did not last very long, and Saufley and Nimmo entered into the dry goods and groceries business under the name Saufley & Nimmo in 1853, which was succeeded by Saufley & Batte at least by March 1856 when Nimmo went into the furniture business with Charles Stanley.

On February 5, 1853, Saufley and Nimmo purchased from Jeptha Crawford for $1,750 in cash and dry goods the lot on the northwest corner of Marshall and Austin known as Crawford's corner, which contained a storehouse and barber shop. This was obviously the inception of Saufley & Nimmo. Thomas Ferrell sold Lot 4 in Block 21 at the corner of Marshall and Lafayette to Saufley & Batte in October 1856. The transaction does not mention a storehouse, and the sales price was too low to account for one. Batte, who was a resident of Titus County, became dissatisfied with Saufley's management of the business and sued him in district court. A February 14, 1860, agreement between Saufley and Batte liquidated the firm's assets, including the lot on the corner of Marshall and Austin that contained their storehouse, confirming that Saufley & Batte was located at Crawford's corner.

Manwaring & Company, composed of Richard Manwaring and J. L. Thompson of Red River County, advertised in the February 18, 1860, *Texas Republican* as wholesale and retail dealers in dry goods and groceries located at the old stand of W. Stewart & Company. James Brown was in charge of the store. Emphasis was placed on filling orders for interior merchants, planters, and farmers. Highest market prices were offered for cotton, hides, pelts, wool, etc. Manwaring & Company was located on Lot 12 in Block 6. When Richard Manwaring purchased this lot from Chester Bulkley on April 12, 1859, the transaction indicates that Manwaring & Company was already in residence and that the storehouse had previously been let to William Stewart & Company. Manwaring does not appear in the 1860 census. James Brown is listed as a merchant.

Dr. Anselm Prewitt acquired the stock of J. C. Preston & Company and began operating the old drugstore near the southwest corner of Marshall and Austin in March 1857. In an advertisement dated March 21, 1857, that appeared in the November 7, 1857, *Eastern Texas Gazette*, Prewitt indicated that he had returned from New Orleans with a fresh supply of drugs, medicines, and stationery. The November 7, 1857, *Eastern Texas Gazette* indicates that Prewitt was then in the dry goods business in the lower portion of the McNab building (middle of Lot

12 in Block 22), with the upper part of the building occupied by the newspaper. Prewitt does not appear in the 1860 census. The drugstore was occupied by December 1859 by Taylor & Witherspoon.

Taylor & Witherspoon was composed of the 20-year-old druggist E. W. Taylor and the 30-year-old physician and surgeon Dr. Hamilton Witherspoon, both of whom appear in the 1860 census. Their occupancy of the property near the southwest corner of Marshall and Austin is mentioned in four deed records running from December 1859 to October 1860 that were filed by Charles Stanley and his brother Isaac. Charles Stanley owned the property, which fronted 30 feet on Marshall and ran back 50 feet, and was the lower portion of the original 50-foot lot. Stanley built a storehouse on the property in 1853, which was occupied during that year by Thomas Pugh, then by Walker & Sayre in 1854, J. C. Preston & Company in 1855, Anselm Prewitt in 1857, and Taylor & Witherspoon in 1859. Two of the 1860 transactions indicate that the storehouse was two stories, with the lower floor occupied by the drugstore and the upper floor by offices.

A December 13, 1858, conveyance from Robert Walker to Richard Waterhouse and William Lockhart concerning the 20-foot by 50-foot lot on the southwest corner of Marshall and Austin above Stanley's drugstore property indicates that it was occupied at that time by Riley Chase's grocery house. A July 10, 1860, conveyance from Isaac Stanley and Sam Moseley to Richard Waterhouse, Jr., and William Lockhart mentions that Stanley & Moseley was occupying a storehouse in the rear of a lot fronting 25 feet on Austin and running back 50 feet that was in back of the property occupied by Taylor & Witherspoon. The Stanley & Moseley storehouse was located on Austin on the west half of Lot 2 in Block 4.

John Wallace is shown as a merchant in the 1860 census. Wallace was a partner in Waterhouse, Wallace & Company, with the other principals being Richard Waterhouse of San Augustine and his son Richard, Jr., temporarily in Jefferson. On February 16, 1859, Richard, Jr., sold to Waterhouse, Wallace & Company the east half of Lot 4 in Block 5 fronting 25 feet on Dallas and running back to Austin, mentioning that the company was already in existence in Jefferson. Wallace sold out to Waterhouse and his son in September 1860, with the transaction indicating that a storehouse was located on this property. The nature of this firm is unknown. Richard, Jr., appears in the 1860 census as a 27-year-old merchant born in Tennessee with a wife and child and $18,000 in real and personal estate. When the Waterhouses (both then in San Augustine) mortgaged their property to M. D. Cooper & Company of New Orleans in February 1861, the transaction indicates that the storehouse was two stories and built of brick. Wallace appears in the census as a married 28-year-old merchant born in Virginia with assets of $51,000 ($39,000 in real estate and $12,000 in personal estate), making him one of the wealthiest persons in Jefferson.

Daniel Alley is listed as a farmer outside of Jefferson in the 1850 census and a farmer in Jefferson in the 1860 census. When Alley moved to Jefferson is unknown. D. N. Alley advertised in the November 7, 1857, *Eastern Texas Gazette* as a wholesale and retail dealer in staple and fancy dry goods and groceries, with hides and pelts taken in exchange (Fig. 23-1). The location is given as the old stand of Cocke & Whitaker at the southwest corner of Marshall and Dallas, which was the facility occupied by Thomas Pugh as a drugstore in 1850.

Bryan & Clark advertised in the March 14, 1857, *Eastern Texas Gazette* as receiving, forwarding, and commission merchants on Dallas but is shown in the 1857 tax rolls with $2,000 in merchandise. The reason that this firm appears in the tax rolls is that, as its advertisement indicates, it also sold groceries and dry goods. Liberal cash advances were made on cotton left for shipment.

William and Theophilus (Theo) Nichols appear in the 1860 census as merchants born in Georgia. With Theo aged 35 and William aged 33, these were obviously brothers or cousins (Bass Nichols also, aged 30). William appears in the 1850 census; Theo does not. William had been one of Jefferson's earliest merchants, starting a grocery with Duncan McNab in 1849 on part of Lots 11 and 12 in Block 22 fronting 30 feet on Marshall and running back 75 feet. After this business dissolved, Theo went into business at the same location. Theophilus Nichols is listed in the 1857 tax rolls as owning no town lots and $4,000 in merchandise. The nature of this firm is unknown.

On March 22, 1859, the heirs of Duncan McNab sold to Theo the property in Block 22 with a storehouse then occupied by Theo. The

D. N. ALLEY,

WHOLSALE AND RETAIL DEALER

IN

Staple and Fancy Dry Goods, Groceries &c.

CORNER OF MARSHALL AND DALLAS STREETS.

(Stand formerly occupied by Cocke & Whitaker.)

JEFFERSON, TEXAS.

RESPECTFULLY announces to his friends and the public generally, that he has just received, and is now opening, the largest and most complete assortment of Staple and Fancy

DRY GOODS!

Ever brought to this market. The following articles comprise a part of his stock,

FOR THE LADIES.

Black, Plaid, Watered, Fancy and Florence Silks; Satins; Bereges; French Robes; Silk Trimmings; Fringe; Thule; Tarleton; Bishop Lawn; Book, Swiss and Cross Bar muslins; Ribbons; French worked Collors; Undersleeves; Chimisetts; Laces; Edgings; Linnin Cambric Handkerchiefs, Hemstitched, do; Brown and Bleeched Hollands; Alpacras, Ladies Kid, Silk and Pick Nic Gloves; Veils misses Flats; Chinese Fans; Fancy furnishing articles; Work Bags; Thimbles. Also a splendid lot of

FASHIONABLE BONNETS;

And many other articles for the Ladies, too numerous to mention.

HATS AND CAPS.

Of all styles and kinds.

SADDELERY.

Ladies and mens Saddles; Bridles and Bridle fittings; martingales; Trunks; Saddle-bags; Carpet-bags; Satchels; Whips of all kinds; Collars, and a general assortment of Saddle Trimings.

DOMESTIC DRY GOODS.

Lowels, Brown and Bleached Shirting and Sheeting; Bleached and Brown Drills; Canton Flannel; Brown and Bleached Sea Island shirting; Striped Lowels, Chickasaw and Choctaw Stripes. Denims; Nankeen cotton, etc. Cassimers; Jeans; Tweeds, spring and summer styles. Flannels all colors; Coat linings, Cotton and Silk Velvets; Cloths, Trimmings, etc.

BOOTS AND SHOES

Of the latest style of Ladies Gaiter Boots, with and without heels, Lasting do; colored do; Foxed Morrocco; and Silk do; misses Boots and Gaiters; Ladies and misses fancy, plain and colored Walking Shoes; Gents Boots and Shoes, of all styles; Russets, Kip and Calf, pegged, Brogans; Calf, sewed, Boots; Water Proof Boots and Children Shoes.

SPRING AND SUMMER

CLOTHING;

Of every style, for men and Boys.

HARDWARE AND CUTLERY.

Iron; Steel, Nails, castings, Trace and Log Chains, Weeding Hoes; Collin's Axes; spades and Shovels; Grubbing Hoes and mattocks; Fire Irons; Sad Irons; shovel and Tongs; steelyards and Ballances; Door Locks; Pad Locks; Butts and Screws; Door and shutter Bolts; Japaned and Brass Candle-sticks, Stirup Irons and Bridle Bitts; Spring Ballances; Tacks; Brads; cupboard Locks; Safe, do; Buckles, steel Springs, etc. Pocket Knives; Pen Knives; a variety of Table cutlery; carving Knives and Forks; Steels; shoe Knives; Hunting Knives; mill-saw and Hand-saw Files; Rasps; chisels; Augers and Hatchets. Hand and cross cut saws; mill, do; Drawing Knives; Scissors and Shears; and Truning Knives. Also complete sets of carpenters Tools, Blacksmiths Tools, etc.

STAPLE AND FANCY GROCERIES.

Coffee; Sugar; molasses; Whiskey; Salt; Tobacco; Lard; Rice; mackerel, kits and half barrels; Vinegar; champagne; claret; Porter; Ale; Lemon Syrup; Port wine; stoughton's Bitters; Brandy Fruits; Rasins; Figs; Preserves; candy; Spice; Pepper; Ginger; Pickles etc. Also a superior article of Brandy, for Medicinal purposes.

CROCKERY AND GLASSWARE.

Consisting of every thing in that line.

Also a few

Sets of China.

NOTIONS.

Combs of every variety, Violins; Violin strings; Tooth and Nail Brushes; Hair do; Shaving and Cloth do; Port Monaie; Dressing cases; Accordeons; Jewsharps; Beads; Necklaces and Braceletts. And every thing else in that line that ever was heard of. All of which will be sold at the lowest market price for Cash, or to punctual dealers on the usual time.

Hides and Peltries taken in exchange.

Jefferson, march 20th, '57.

Fig. 23-1. D. N. Alley Advertisement. Source: November 7, 1857, *Eastern Texas Gazette*

transaction mentions a two-story storehouse on apparently adjacent property (same block and lots) fronting 45 feet on Marshall and running back 75 feet, which describes the property on which the McNab building was located. A March 31, 1859, conveyance of the adjacent property from John McNab to William Nichols indicates that the two-story building was then occupied by the confectioners Shoenburgh and Murzbacher (i.e., Frederick Merzbacher). When William Nichols sold this property to Elizabeth Hughes on February 22, 1860, the transaction mentions that the two-story storehouse was then occupied by William. Theo and William apparently operated storehouses on the adjacent McNab properties.

A. D. Taylor & Brother advertised in the November 7, 1857, *Eastern Texas Gazette* as a new store offering staple and fancy dry goods, with the advertisement dated June 13. A. D. Taylor does not appear in the 1860 census. F. E. and George Taylor are listed as merchants. On April 2, 1860, George Taylor formed a two-year partnership with John Reed, with each partner putting up $3,500, to form a general mercantile business that would begin on April 2, 1861.

Pinski & Kallisher advertised in the November 7, 1857, *Eastern Texas Gazette* as a new dry goods store offering fall and winter clothing direct from New York at New Orleans prices. On December 16, 1862, John Speake sold to Henry Bilger and Alexander McKimens part of Lots 1 and 2 in Block 4 fronting 47 ½ feet on Marshall and running back 100 feet and described as the Veal & Jennings storehouse and lately occupied by Isaac Pinski as a dry goods store. This was the apparent location of Pinski & Kallisher. Neither Pinski nor Kallisher appears in the 1860 census. Pinski went into business with Samuel Sterne in 1862, died in 1867, and is buried in the Oakwood Cemetery, with the gravestone reading "The First President of the Hebrew Benevolent Association of Jefferson." Sterne was probably in business by 1860 because he is listed in the census as a merchant with the merchants B. H. Jacobs, Robert Green, William Smithson, and Robert McWilliams living in his house.

H. Rhine & Brothers, which had been in the dry goods and groceries business in Clarksville, advertised in the November 7, 1857, *Eastern Texas Gazette* (with the advertisement dated May 23) as in the wholesale and retail dry goods, groceries, and jewelry business, having engaged the services of Moses Steinlein and making advances on cotton shipped to Ward, Sanders & Hunt in New Orleans. H. Rhine & Brothers advertised in the April 10, 1858, Clarksville *Standard* as "having purchased the entire large stock of C. A. Bulkley, have added it to their own previously large supply of staple Goods, and now offer to the citizens of Northern Texas, and of all the counties trading to Jefferson, far the largest stock of merchandise ever brought together in one establishment." Charles DeMorse visited the large storehouse and four warehouses containing an immense stock of groceries in conjunction with the placement of the advertisement and reports that H. Rhine & Brothers was located at Bulkley's old stand.

J. B. Ligon & Company, composed of John Ligon and Gus Hodge, advertised in the February 18, 1860, *Texas Republican* as dealers in furniture and buggies on Dallas Street, featuring 75 buggies of almost every quality; harnesses complete to match; mahogany, rosewood, walnut, and cherry furniture; carpeting of the latest styles; a large assortment of beautiful paintings in gilt frames; and single and double mattresses. Loughery pointed out that "They have a large and beautiful assortment of furniture. The number and superior character of their buggies surprised us, for we had no idea there was such an establishment in the place. They claim to sell below New Orleans rates." John Ligon appears in the 1860 census as a 35-year-old merchant born in South Carolina with $9,000 in real and personal estate and living near Jefferson with a wife and three children. Gus Hodge appears as a 35-year-old merchant born in Kentucky with $13,500 in real and personal estate and living in Jefferson with a wife and two children. In June 1862, John B. Ligon & Company sold to William Perry Lot 9 in Block 6 fronting 50 feet on Dallas and running back to Lake, which was the probable location of the store.

T. D. Sedberry advertised in the June 30, 1860 *Texas Republican* as a dealer in dry goods and groceries located at the southwest corner of Dallas and Marshall, which was the storehouse occupied by Thomas Pugh in 1850. Thomas Sedberry appears in the 1860 census as a married 28-year-old merchant born in Alabama with $13,000 in real and personal estate and living in the house of A. D. Tullis.

W. K. Vining advertised in the July 7, 1860, *Standard* as a dealer in hardware and crockery located on Dallas, featuring mechanics tools, house furnishing hardware, nails, horse shoes, chains, mill and gin bands, window glass, white lead, grass and cotton rope, tinware, and crockery and glassware by the crate, or carefully packed and shipped in quantities to suit. Vining appears in the census as a 26-year-old merchant born in Tennessee with $5,000 in real and personal estate and living in the house of Jeptha Crawford. Vining advertised iron for sale during the Civil War.

Reece Hughes advertised in the September 5, 1857, *Standard*, with the advertisement dated August 27, that he was in the wholesale and retail dry goods and groceries business, with $100,000 worth of goods purchased in the East expressly for the Texas trade. Hughes employed William Brooks, who had been a dry goods and groceries merchant. A similar advertisement, dated August 29, appears in the November 7, 1857, *Eastern Texas Gazette,* but with the added information that the firm was located in the house formerly occupied by J. M. & J. C. Murphy near the steamboat landing. This was the frame structure on Lot 4 in Block 7 that had been occupied by J. M. & J. C. Murphy before they erected the brick structure in the landing area.

In July 1857, Hughes acquired the City Hotel property on Marshall, which encompassed the lower 103 feet of Lots 7–9 in Block 21. The hotel was located on the upper 73 feet of this property. William Brooks became the operator of the hotel in April 1858. Hughes erected a two-story brick storehouse on the lower 30 feet of this property fronting Marshall, which he began advertising in the April 10, 1858, *Standard*. Reece's brother Robert was a partner in the business. Reece and Robert do not appear in the 1860 census. Reece sold the storehouse property for $15,000 to George Prewitt in June 1860. The storehouse was then operated as a drugstore by the druggist James Campbell under the name Campbell & Company through at least September 1862, when it was also occupied by Frederick Merzbacher as a grocery store.

W. R. Hines & Company, which was composed of William and Isaac Hines, went back to at least August 1857, when the company purchased the property on which it was located from Francis Baker. When the property was sold to Henry Bilger on March 4, 1858, the transaction mentions that the storehouse was located on the west half of Lot 11 in Block 6 fronting 25 feet on Dallas and adjoining Frederick Schluter's old storehouse. Sometime before March 1859, William Hines joined with Elias Durlin and Hiram Cutrer to establish Durlin & Company, which was on Lot 1 in Block 6 between Dallas and Austin. Durlin was dead by January 1860, when the property was transferred by Cutrer to Henry Hall of New Orleans for debts. William Hines appears in the 1860 census as a married 23-year-old clerk born in Tennessee with $15,600 in real and personal estate.

In June 1860, the firm of M. Rosenzweig & Company (composed of Morris and Lazarus Rosenzweig), which was already operating in Jefferson, agreed to rent for $900 a year from William Hines a brick storehouse between Dallas and Austin that was one of a block of brick structures that had been built by Hines. The Rosenzweigs appear in the 1860 census as merchants in their twenties born in Russia and living in the house of Jeptha Crawford.

James Durr appears in the 1860 census as a 45-year-old merchant born in Georgia with $1,850 in real and personal estate and a wife and eight children, including a son who was a clerk. Durr operated a store on the southeast corner of Vale and Dallas on the east half of Lot 1 in Block 6, which was already in existence when the property (storehouse, lot, stock, accounts, and 22-year-old slave Caroline) was mortgaged by Durr to Lewis & Oglesby in May 1860. Durr's assets were seized for debt and auctioned in May 1861. The assets included $9,005.42 in notes due Durr from credit transactions, $5,933.57 in stock on hand on February 1, $3,000 for storehouse and lot, $1,000 for slave, $14.50 cash in hand on February 1, and 52 bales of unsold cotton. The list of auctioned stock indicates that Durr was in the groceries and general plantation supplies business. The east half of Lot 1 in Block 6 was occupied by Joseph McDermott as a dry goods store sometime prior to December 1861. McDermott appears in the 1860 census as a 19-year-old merchant born in Louisiana with $6,000 in real and personal estate.

On June 8, 1860, Williamson Freeman as agent for John Hobdy paid the balance of an agreement with A. C. Allen that allowed Hobdy to extend upward the brick wall of Allen's one-story storehouse, with the wall dividing Lots 2 and 3 in Block 6. When Allen mortgaged his property to George Connelly & Company of New Orleans in April 1861, the transaction mentions a brick grocery house on the west half of Lot 2 in Block 6 fronting Dallas and then occupied by Allen & Pitcher (with C. L. Pitcher). Allen does not appear in the 1860 census. Hobdy apparently completed the two-story brick structure on the east side of Lot 3, but he appears in the census as a farmer living in Jefferson.

A. Nussbaum appears in the 1860 census as a 27-year-old merchant born in Austria with $10,000 in real and personal estate. J. Nussbaum is listed as a 24-year-old merchant born in Austria. The Nussbaums were members of a firm called Nussbaum & Brother, composed of Bernhard Nussbaum of New York and Lewis Nussbaum of Norfolk, doing business in New York, Norfolk, and Jefferson. Nussbaum & Brother was heavily in debt and mortgaged all of its properties in May 1860 to Benjamin Bernhard and Levi Steinlein of New York. Firms named Nussbaum & Lindsey and S. Nussbaum & Brother operated in Jefferson during the Civil War.

In March 1858, John Webster established a bond for title to Gillespie, Brother & Company for part of Lots 1 and 2 in Block 4 fronting 22 ½ feet on Marshall running back 100 feet and 25 feet on Austin running back 50 feet. The firm was composed of Vincent and Nelson Gillespie and Jessie Freeman. The property was placed in trust and sold by Sam Moseley (trustee) to Isaac Stanley in January 1860 when the storehouse was occupied by Fred White. Frederick White appears in the 1860 census as a 56-year-old painter born in New York with $600 in real and personal estate and a wife and child.

An October 26, 1859, transaction by Gustavus Leavitt as administrator of the deceased Israel Leavitt's estate indicates that May & Company was then occupying the Leavitt building on Lot 6 in Block 5, which was a few doors above their original location. Whether Abraham Kohn was still associated with this firm is unknown. However, he sold to D. C. Phillips in March 1860 his entire stock of groceries valued at $5,400, hides and pelts valued at $1,400, 11 bales of cotton (then in Williamson Freeman's store), and the 17-year-old slave Isah valued at $1,600. D. C. Phillips appears in the 1860 census as a 40-year-old merchant born in Kentucky and living in the house of the merchant Thomas Turner.

In July 1860, James Linn and Moses McCall in business under the name of Linn & Company mortgaged to E. B. Wheelock & Company of New Orleans their stock, consisting of drugs, medicines, paints, oils, and dye stuffs. This firm was dissolved by December. James Linn is listed in the 1860 census as a 38-year-old druggist born in Pennsylvania with $20,500 in real and personal estate.

B. C. Hughes is listed in the 1860 census as a 37-year-old merchant born in Arkansas. Bob C. Hughes advertised in the April 27, 1860, Marshall *Harrison Flag* as a wholesale and retail dealer in dry goods and groceries, with an accompanying editorial note indicating that he was located in Jefferson. A September 3, 1862, sheriff sale transaction in the deed records indicates that Lot 6 in Block 5 was known as the Bob Hughes lot; however, the lot delineation is incorrect, and there is nothing to indicate where Hughes' establishment was located.

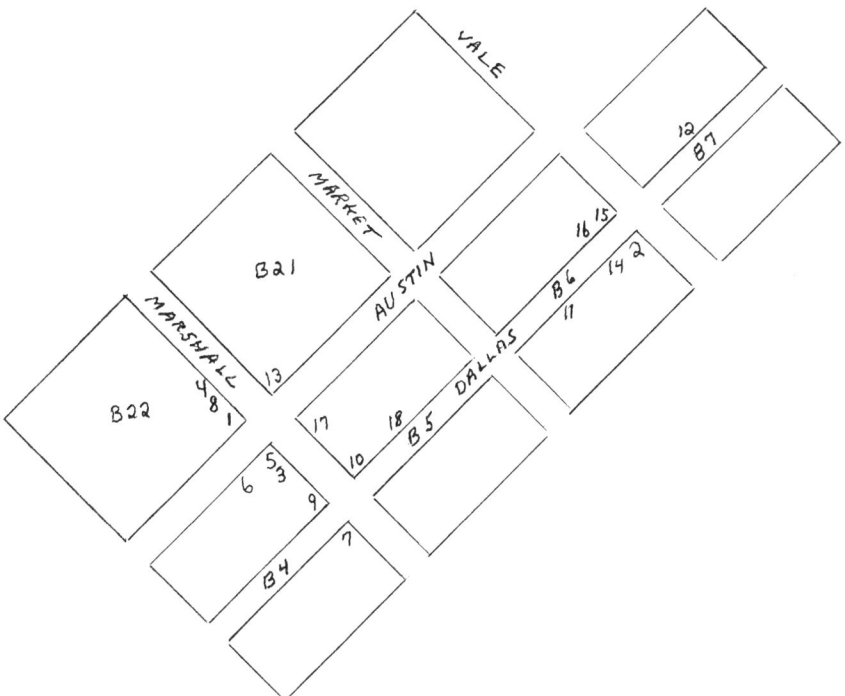

Fig. 23-2. Late Merchants
KEY:
1. Saufley & Nimmo (1853); Saufley & Batte (1856)
2. William Stewart & Company (1858); Manwaring & Company (1859)
3. Anselm Prewitt (1857); Taylor & Witherspoon (1859)
4. Anselm Prewitt (1857); Schoenburg & Merzbacher (1859); William Nichols (1860)
5. Riley Chase (1858)
6. Stanley & Moseley (1860)
7. Cocke & Whitaker (1856); D. N. Alley (1857); T. D. Sedberry (1860)
8. Theophilus Nichols (1857)
9. Pinski & Kallisher (1857); Isaac Pinski (1862)
10. H. Rhine & Brothers (1857)
11. J. B. Ligon & Company (1860)
12. Reece Hughes (1857)
13. Reece Hughes (1858); Campbell & Company (1860)
14. W. R. Hines & Company (1857)
15. Durlin & Company (1859); James Durr (1860); Joseph McDermott (1861)
16. A. C. Allen (1860); Allen & Pitcher (1861)
17. May & Company (1859)
18. Waterhouse, Wallace & Company (1859)

24. Miscellaneous Businesses

A perspective on the full array of business types and numbers is difficult to achieve in the absence of an antebellum business directory. Some business types did not advertise in the newspapers; and of those that did, many individual businesses within those types did not. Although most businesses were taxed, the county tax rolls provide insight only into the primary mercantile establishments. There are no extant tax rolls for the town.

The county and the town both imposed occupational taxes, but only for a limited number of occupations. Payment of these taxes resulted in a license to operate. Because people were brought before the courts for failure to obtain licenses, it is unlikely that an occupational tax list would be inclusive even for the types of businesses that were licensed.

A document titled "Old Officer's Fees Collected," which is in the Marion County courthouse, contains occupational taxes for 1860–1873. It is obvious that this is a county tax record because the issuance of some of the licenses is recorded in the minutes of the Marion County commissioners court. The list for 1860 includes 21 occupational licenses for six saloons, four restaurants, four peddlers, four auctioneers, one bowling alley, one ferry, and one circus.

Most, if not all, of these operations appear to have been in Jefferson, which would not be surprising given the absence of other large population centers in Marion County. The peddlers and the circus operator were not Jefferson residents, for obvious reasons. The only other persons who are not listed as Jefferson residents or nearby in the 1860 census were three of the four restaurant operators. However, because these persons are not listed anywhere in the county, it is probable that they operated in Jefferson.

Saloons

"Saloon" referred to any establishment that sold liquor in quantities less than a quart. The occupational license list indicates that there were at least six saloons in Jefferson in 1860. The operators were Richard Waterhouse & Company, George Prewitt, Richard Crump, James Henderson, T. W. Gardner, and John Neff. The 1860 census lists Waterhouse as a merchant, Prewitt as a farmer (Jefferson Post Office designation), Crump as a grocer, and Garner as a butcher. No occupational designations are given for Henderson and Neff. There were no occupational designations for saloon keeper in the census. The deed records indicate that Prewitt was actually operating a livery stable in Jefferson in 1860.

The occupational designations suggest that some saloons were not free-standing, but rather adjuncts to establishments that sold other goods and liquor on a wholesale and retail basis, which was certainly the case with Waterhouse & Company. The Marion County commissioners court minutes indicate that Gardner operated in a house adjoining the livery stable, that Neff operated the Horse Shoe Saloon, and that the Horse Shoe Saloon was operated in 1861 by the watchmaker E. L. Trickey.

There is no list of licenses prior to 1860. Taverns, which served alcoholic beverages, were operated in the earliest years by persons such as William Perry and William Russell. In 1856, the Cass County commissioners court issued licenses for sales of liquor in quantities less than a quart to Thomas Goyne, James Hosack, Thomas Owens, David Trice, and George Norris. The first two of these were Jefferson operators; one or more of the latter three may have operated in Linden, which as the county seat would certainly have had a saloon. The deed records indicate that Caleb Ragan operated a Bowling Saloon in the early 1850s that featured a bar, billiard table, and ten-pin alley and that Richard Crump operated a drinking and billiard saloon in the late 1850s and early 1860s that included a shooting gallery and ten-pin alley. This establishment was located immediately north of the City Hotel and was the reason Crump appears on the occupational tax list in 1860 and 1861.

The saloons in Jefferson probably began with taverns in the 1840s, which also provided food and overnight accommodations, and became more specialized in the early 1850s, but with the addition of billiard tables and, at least for one establishment, a bowling alley. On the other hand, at least some of them were adjuncts to other business operations. Crump's facility was a recreational center, featuring all of the above plus a shooting gallery. The sparse evidence with respect to location indicates that at least some of the saloons catered to the traveling public who used the hotels and livery stables.

Restaurants

The Eagle Restaurant, operated by Dick Cunliffe, advertised in the March 1, 1856, Marshall *Texas Republican* (Fig. 24-1), giving as its location Dallas Street, in the rear of Weaver's Coffeehouse (coffeehouses served liquor). The restaurant was recently opened, served meals at all hours of the day and night, featured oysters and game in season and boned turkey on all holiday occasions, and provided sleeping rooms. That it advertised in the Marshall newspaper indicates that it catered primarily to the traveling public. Loughery of the *Texas Republican* ate at this restaurant in September 1856, but it is not mentioned again. It

Fig. 24-1. Eagle Restaurant Advertisement. Source: March 1, 1856, *Texas Republican*

```
        EAGLE RESTAURANT.
    D I C K   C U N I L I F F E
    TAKES occasion to inform the
       public generally that he has
    opened a Restaurant in Jefferson, in
    the rear of Weavers's Coffee-house, on Dallas
    street, where he will be prepared to serve up
    meals at all hours, day or night.
       OYSTERS and GAME in proper sea-
    sons. Boned Turkey on all holiday occasions.
    ☞ Excellent sleeping rooms, well furnished,
    have recently been provided for this establish-
    ment.
       March 1st, 1856.                    n27 tf
```

does not appear in the two extant 1857 issues of the Jefferson *Eastern Texas Gazette*, and Cunliffe is not listed in the 1860 census.

It is obvious that there were many establishments in Jefferson for which there is no evidence; and the few mentions of non-mercantile businesses, such as Weaver's Coffeehouse, appear accidentally. There are no persons in the 1860 census with occupations that would suggest restaurant operation. Occupational licenses were provided in 1860 to S. Faber (restaurant, cook shop, and eating house), L. H. Ogletree (eating house), John Feidler (restaurant and bakery), and Nicholas Pusha (eating house and company). Only Pusha is listed in the 1860 census, but as a butcher born in France. The other three probably operated in Jefferson. In addition, there were a number of hotels that served fine meals and a number of taverns that would have provided some sort of food.

Barber Shops

There are no barbers listed for Precinct 1 in the 1850 census. Because this was a highly specialized occupation, it appears that there were no barbershops in Jefferson in 1850.

A February 5, 1853, conveyance from Jeptha Crawford to Samuel Nimmo and William Saufley mentions a barbershop on Crawford's corner, which fronted 30 feet on Marshall and ran back 70 feet on Austin. Because a storehouse occupied the immediate corner, the barbershop was probably on Austin on Lot 11 of Block 22. This was slightly northeast of the Jefferson Hotel on the corner of Dallas and Jackson and slightly east of the livery stable that serviced the hotel, which was located on the northeast corner of Austin and Jackson. This barbershop did not advertise in the May 14, 1853, *Jefferson Herald*.

Fritz Stutz advertised in the March 14, 1857, *Eastern Texas Gazette* as a fashionable hair cutter and barber located on Dallas Street one door below the Jefferson Hotel. This would have been the second structure east of Jackson on the north side of Dallas. The 30-year-old barber Frederick Stutz, born in Germany, is listed in the 1860 census with a wife and five children. Also listed in the household is the 21-year-old barber Henry Rodemic, also from Germany. It appears that Rodemic worked for Stutz and that the barbershop had two chairs.

Because Stutz and Rodemic are the only barbers listed in the census, it is apparent that there was only one barbershop in Jefferson in 1860 and probably only one barbershop from the early 1850s on. Both of the known barbershops were obviously located to secure the business of travelers in addition to that of the local population.

Watchmakers

W. J. Parker advertised as a watchmaker and jeweler in the May 14, 1853, *Jefferson Herald*, with the location given as over Pugh's drugstore. He also advertised in the March 14, 1857, *Eastern Texas Gazette* as a watchmaker and jeweler, with the location given as over Prewitt's drugstore. Parker is listed in the 1860 census as a 41-year-old watchmaker born in Georgia with $11,000 in real and personal estate. Also listed in the census is the 23-year-old watchmaker Moses Mills, born in Alabama, with $4,800 in real and personal estate, and the 23-year-old jeweler L. J. Morsler, born in Prussia, with $12,000 in real and personal estate, both of whom probably worked for Parker.

E. L. Trickey was a watchmaker and jeweler in Marshall who moved to Jefferson in November 1860. Because W. J. Parker was still operating in Jefferson in 1860, it is obvious that there were two watchmakers and jewelers in Jefferson on the eve of the Civil War. The ability to sustain two businesses of this type was a consequence of the flow of business travelers through Jefferson as much as the expanding numbers and wealth of the indigenous population. In addition, Trickey was not simply a craftsman, but also a jewelry merchant dealing in fine gold and silver watches, fine gold jewelry, silver tea and tablespoons, fine table cutlery, meerschaum pipes, cigar holders, and spectacles, as indicated in 1860 and 1861 advertisements in the *Texas Republican*. He also sold watchmaker tools and watch glasses to interior jewelers. His business was located one door below Taylor's drugstore.

Trickey was typical of the many businessmen who left regional towns to capitalize on the rapidly expanding commercial opportunities in Jefferson. He already had a successful business in Marshall and left for Jefferson "for the purpose and in the hope of finding more business," as he stated in a notice to his Marshall clients in the December 29, 1860, *Texas Republican*. He was able to establish himself immediately as a merchant in Jefferson because of the capital accumulated from his Marshall operation, and he continued to cultivate Marshall clients. And his craft skills served as a base for a larger commercial operation that was assisted by Jefferson's import capacities.

When Trickey left for Jefferson, his departure was noted by both of the Marshall newspapers. The *Texas Republican* stated that "His conduct while here made him many warm friends. We bespeak for him the good will and patronage of those who visit our neighboring city"; and the *Harrison Flag* stated that "We take pleasure in commending him to the patronage of the citizens of Jefferson and the surrounding country, as a good and faithful mechanic, and as an upright and reliable man." That these were not idle comments is indicated by the quality of Trickey's comments in his departure notice:

> I take this occasion of tendering my thanks to my friends and customers in Marshall; the former I thank for their personal kindness, the latter for their patronage.
>
> The Watches and Jewelry in my possession for repairs, were left in charge of M. Polock, who will deliver them to the owners on demand.
>
> All work done by me in Marshall which does not perform well, and all jewelry sold which does not hold good as represented, can be sent to me at Jefferson, where I will cheerfully fulfill all my contracts.

Photography

According to the *Handbook of Texas*, the first photographs in Texas were taken in Houston in December 1843. Photography was immensely popular, and photographic galleries proliferated throughout the state before the Civil War. There were two commercial photographers in Jefferson, both of whom operated in the late 1850s. The types of photographs mentioned were the ambrotype and the sphereotype. The ambrotype, which was patented in 1853, was a negative on glass with a backing of black paint that caused the silver image to be viewed as positive. The sphereotype, which was patented in 1856, was a positive on glass named for its spherical appearance after finishing and encasement. The brief mentions in the newspapers do not indicate anything about the operations of the galleries:

> While in Jefferson, we called in at Mr. MULLINS's Ambrotype and Sphereotype gallery, and were much pleased with the fine finish and truthful delineation of his pictures. But very few of our readers, we imagine, have seen the Sphereotype pictures. They resemble the Ambrotypes, with the exception that they seem to stand out from the plate, like a finely finished portrait upon ivory. We would advise our friends visiting Jefferson, to call upon Mr. Mullens. His pictures cannot be surpassed. (February 14, 1857, *Texas Republican*)
>
> We neglected to mention that Mr. A. C. Moestue, who, for seven or eight months has kept an Ambrotype Gallery over the drug store of Messrs. Saunders & Sears, has removed to Jefferson. We take pleasure in saying, that during his residence in Marshall, he secured the respect and confidence of the community. He is an accomplished artist. His pictures for faithfulness of design and fineness of finish, are equal to the best. Those desiring life-like portraits of themselves or friends should patronize him. (November 26, 1858, *Texas Republican*)

Moestue stayed in Jefferson only five months, probably because Jefferson could not support two photographic studios, and returned to Marshall. Mullins is not mentioned in the 1860 census.

Bookstores

Books and stationery were sold by many merchants in Jefferson. The May 14, 1853, *Jefferson Herald*, for example, contains a long descriptive advertisement of school books offered by the dry goods and groceries merchants Nichols & McNab, who featured William McGuffey's Eclectic Series of School Books, which covered reading and spelling and offered "chaste and instructive lessons in prose and poetry"; Pineo's English grammars; and Ray's arithmetic and algebra. Nichols &

McNab were obviously selling to a regional audience, including interior merchants. The first full-fledged bookstore in Jefferson was W. D. Stephenson & Company, composed of W. D. and J. C. Stephenson. The only time that this firm is mentioned in the newspapers is in the August 5, 1854, Clarksville *Standard* in connection with a promotional gift book received by DeMorse. It is listed in the 1855 tax rolls as having $2,118 in stock.

The largest bookstore before the Civil War was the Colt & Winans establishment, which was started in July 1860. The book line embraced law, medicine, science, history, biography, theology, fiction, and school books. Stationery and related items included blank books, ledgers, journals, cash books, day books, record books, Affleck's Plantation Books for Sugar and Cotton, memorandum and pass books, blank notes, drafts, receipts, transfer and copying books, letter and notarial presses, printing paper, inks, fluids, red carmine, letter paper, commercial and packet post, fools cap, legal cap, bill cap, note paper, card boards, blank cards, drawing papers, Bristol boards, blotting papers, bonnet boards, music paper, playing cards, envelopes, paper hangings, window shades, sheet music, and oil and linen shades. They also sold musical instruments such as piano fortes, guitars, drums, clarinets, melodions, flutes, fifes, violins, accordions, banjos, and tambourines. Orders were handled for magazines and newspapers. Terms were cash or approved credit.

The advertisement for the bookstore began to appear in the July 7, 1860, Clarksville *Standard* (Fig. 24-2), establishing a claim as "The Largest Book Establishment in Texas!" Given the stock list and the fact that the bookstore advertised in newspapers external to Jefferson, this was apparently a warranted claim. When the advertisement first appeared, the *Standard* noted its scope and regional orientation:

> We call attention to advertisement of new Book Establishment on a large scale opening in Jefferson. The advertisement is sufficient evidence of the grade of business intended to be carried on. Such an establishment selling at moderate prices might be of essential convenience to Northern Texas, and do well for its owners. The proprietors profess to understand their

business thoroughly, and to have facilities for carrying it on to the best advantage.

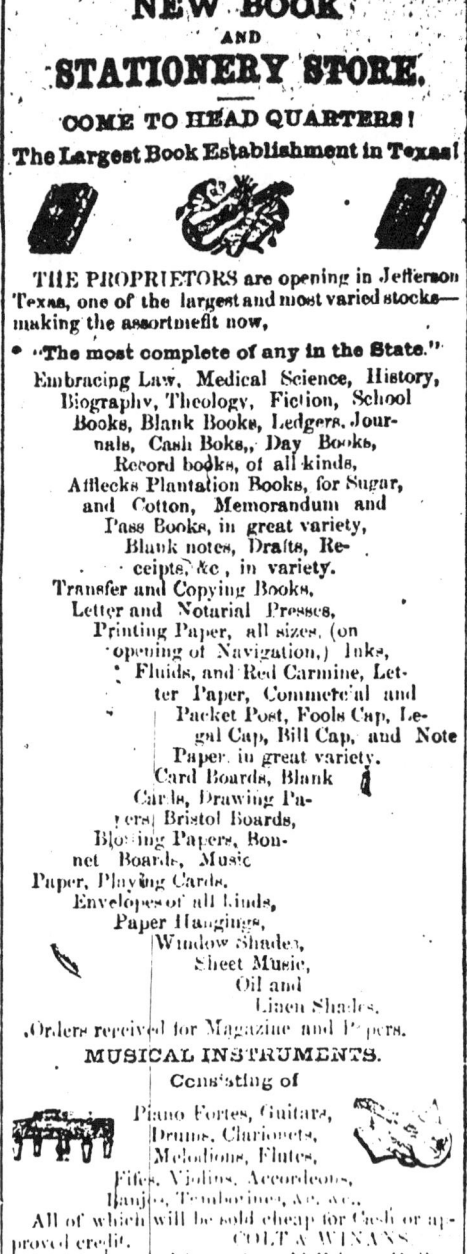

Fig. 24-2. Colt & Winans Bookstore Advertisement. Source: July 7, 1860, *Standard*

A few weeks later, the *Standard* noted that "the Book and Periodical establishment of Colt & Winans, at Jefferson, advertised in our columns, is now fully under way, and can supply customers with all the leading magazines and newspapers. Those who want to procure, Harper's magazine or Harper's weekly, The Atlantic, Graham's, the Eclectic, The Ledger, Mercury, Clipper, &c., can make their engagements through this house." The Colt & Winans Book and Stationery Store was located on Marshall Street under the Odd Fellows Hall, which was on Lot 12 in Block 22. Colt does not appear in the 1860 census. Joseph Winans is listed as a 24-year-old bookseller born in New York with $2,000 in real and personal estate.

Well Constructor

Richard Walker advertised in the November 7, 1857, *Eastern Texas Gazette* as a well and cistern digger, with curbing of wood, brick, or stone as desired. Walker is not listed in the 1860 census.

Machinist

William G. Dollar advertised as a millwright and machinist in the Jefferson, Marshall, and Clarksville newspapers from 1856 to 1859, with his first advertisement in May 1856 indicating that he had recently arrived in Jefferson from the Midwest and that he was constructing a flour mill for S. H. McFarland & Company near Jefferson. Dollar specialized in building and repairing saw, corn and flour mills; constructing mill dams; assembling wheat threshing machines, cotton gins, and cotton screws; and constructing railroad bridges, trestles, water tanks, and station houses. Dollar is not listed in the 1860 census.

Insurance Company

The March 10, 1860, Clarksville *Standard* indicates that the Texas Legislature had passed an Act to incorporate the Jefferson Insurance Company, which was an event of regional significance. The capital stock was $100,000 and the life of the corporation 20 years. Books of subscription were to be opened under the superintendence of Benjamin Terry, Harvey Black, John Speake, James Murphy, Williamson Freeman, and Charles Stanley. Insurance was to cover "steamboats and all other river crafts, and boats of every kind, and all goods, wares and merchandise, slaves, bullion, money and other property, against all maritime and river risks, and upon houses, stores and other buildings, goods, wares... against loss or damage by fire." This would have been an important addition to the business life of the city, but there is nothing to indicate that it came into existence before the war. After the war, the authority of the company was expanded to include life insurance.

25. Manufacturing

Context

Manufacturing refers to the making of things, usually from raw materials and through organized production processes and division of labor. The Old South was largely devoted to agriculture, with capital invested in land and slaves and towns largely devoted to agriculture-related business activities rather than to manufacturing. Newspapers constantly called for industrial expansion to strengthen the South as a region and to keep Southern money at home and also encouraged the purchase of the products of home manufacturers such as they existed (Fig. 25-1).

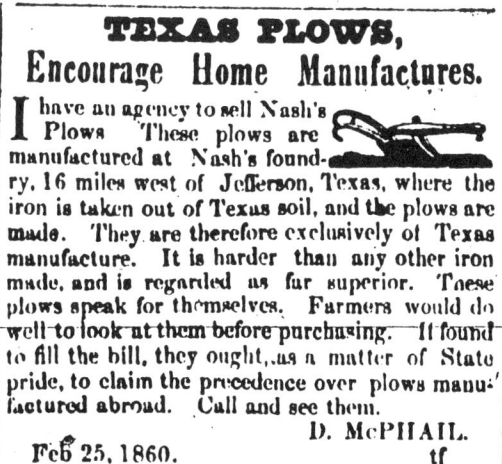

Fig. 25-1. Encourage Home Manufactures Advertisement. Source: February 25, 1860, *Texas Republican*

Comparisons between the North and the South are somewhat exaggerated because non-agricultural production on plantations was not included in the national industrial census. Blacksmith shops provide the clearest indication of the problem. They were included in the industrial census because they made such things as plows. Jefferson blacksmith shops are included in the industrial census; plantation blacksmith shops in the rest of the county are not because they were considered part of the agricultural enterprise. Nevertheless, the North did have more industry than the South.

The relative paucity of manufacturing in the South has been explained in terms of regional comparative advantages, the fact that there was money to be made in agriculture and particularly in the production of cotton, and the fact that Southerners were comfortable with agricultural activities and knew how to do them well. These reasons are true. To them should be added the scarcity of banks for capital and the fact that much of the capital of the South was tied up in slaves, which were secure and profitable investments.

Jefferson was primarily a commercial center. However, the town and its immediate vicinity were somewhat unusual because of the development of a base of small manufacturers in town, large meat packeries in and near town, and a large foundry 18 miles west of Jefferson that produced raw iron and manufactured items. These activities continued through and after the war. By 1870, Marion County was second among Texas counties only to Galveston County in the total value and value added of its manufactures.

A manufacturing enterprise comes into existence when a risk-taker assembles capital, raw materials, equipment, and skilled labor and is able to produce a product for a market at a competitive price or at some other competitive advantage such as quality or unique characteristics. The ability to produce things is an embodied skill rather than a theoretical knowledge, falling into the realm of *techne*, which refers to the making and doing of things. These skills are still important, but were much more important during the 1800s when the making and doing of things was not dependent on formal education.

The Jefferson area was populated by people who came from elsewhere, carrying skills they had previously acquired. It was a magnet for talent because it provided an opportunity situation. This is particularly evident in the case of merchants, most of whom had been merchants in other towns. It is not surprising that many of Jefferson's primary merchants were Jewish because mercantile activity was traditional among Jews. Because Jefferson dominated a large market area, it provided ideal conditions for those skills to flourish.

Manufacturers in the Jefferson area did not operate under advantageous conditions because all manufactured items needed in Jefferson and its market area were readily available from nationally competitive firms through importation. The two major industries were based on the availability of raw materials. Jefferson Nash's Texas Iron Works exploited iron deposits west of Jefferson and sold in a regional market on the basis of agricultural implements that were designed for local conditions. The meat packeries in and near Jefferson, which produced pickled beef in barrels that was sold in national markets, were based on the production of quality cattle in northeast Texas and the ability to transport products to national markets by water.

The earliest packers were Harvey Black, a sheep rancher from Kentucky who produced wool and probably knew something about the packing business, and Charles Stanley and Samuel Nimmo, who were furniture salesmen, demonstrated a high degree of enterprise, and went to the Midwest to learn the packing business. Black's 25 employees were skilled packers brought in from Louisville. Stanley & Nimmo brought in about 85 skilled packers from the Midwest. This was done because there were no local workers with the requisite technical skills and no capacity in a startup business to develop that talent through on-the-job training. Stanley & Nimmo even had to import barrel staves because the machinery for producing them was not available locally. The Stanley & Nimmo packery was a financial disaster, apparently because of their lack of experience.

There were meat packeries throughout Texas even though Texas was not a good place to pack meat because of the shortness of the cool packing season. These packeries were able to exist only because of the availability of quality cattle and particularly because it was impossible to transport these cattle to the traditional meatpacking centers in the Midwest that had a much longer packing season. When this transport became possible through the extension of railroads into the Kansas Territory, the great cattle drives started and the Texas meat packeries went out of business.

Most of the smaller manufacturers in Jefferson, such as wagon makers, that catered to local markets do not require explanation. However, there were three firms that dealt with regional markets, two of which sold wholesale as well as retail. The Stetson & Stewart planing mill, which produced sashes, blinds, doors, and furniture, apparently sold in Jefferson's market area as well as locally on a retail basis. Raw materials and production skills were readily available. There was a ready market for wood products in the wood-scarce western portion of Jefferson's market area, and such rough bulky products were not of sufficient value to justify import.

Haze Jolly manufactured tinware, almost certainly imported his raw materials, and sold retail in the local market and wholesale in the regional market. This apparently was a very small facility that operated primarily on the basis of job-work and did not last very long. Hugo Fox was a confectioner from Germany who sold retail locally and wholesale regionally. This was apparently a fairly large operation, as indicated by his employees and his advertisements. Fox's confectioners were born in Germany, and most of his clerks were from the United States. Fox was able to sell candy regionally because it was a speciality item known for its freshness and quality.

Most of the people who came to northeast Texas were agriculturalists seeking new opportunities. The primary group that came to Jefferson were merchants seeking new opportunities. Manufacturing started in the North, where the skills and collateral support facilities were concentrated. It was difficult to establish a firm in the South that could successfully enter into competition with a preexisting firm, particularly when the skills and collateral facilities were not available. That the packeries had to import labor is an indicator of half the problem. The other half is indicated by the shoe manufactories and other facilities that sprang up in the South with the necessities imposed by war, strong sectional demand, and the absence of competition from northern firms. The existence of manufacturing facilities in the Jefferson area suggests that southerners responded to opportunities afforded by raw materials and market demands when they were able to assemble the requisite skills and establish competitive operations.

Earliest Industries

Jefferson's earliest industry in the modern sense of the term was a steam saw and grist mill. This is not surprising given the fact that a growing town required sawn lumber for the erection of structures. The 1850 industry census indicates that saw mills for the cutting of lumber and gristmills for the grinding of grain were very common throughout Texas from the earliest years. These were usually independent; but cutting and grinding operations could be derived from the same power source, as was the case with the Jefferson facility. Power for mills was supplied by water, steam, which was quite common, and horses. The facilities using water power needed to be located on a stream. Those using steam or horse power could be located anywhere. The primary product of saw mills was pine lumber, but they also cut oak, gum, and cypress and probably cherry and walnut for cabinet makers and bois d'arc, ash, and hickory for wheelwrights. The grist mills ground mostly corn but also wheat, taking a portion of the product in payment.

A Steam Mill Company in Jefferson is first mentioned in a December 31, 1845, bond transfer from Berry Durham to the company owners William C. Baker, Job Baker, Isaac Stephens, and John O'Hara in connection with a May 30, 1845, bond for title from Durham to Arthur Hicks, including Lots 7–9 in Block 73 on the northeast corner of Marshall and Camp streets. The May 30 bond refers to Fractional Block 3 fronting on Marshall Street 125 feet from Lot 13 to the lake (i.e., Cypress Bayou); and on the back of this bond is a reference to the Steam Mill Company estate of Arthur Hicks. The lot and block designations are from the Jesse Cherry town plan and are equivalent to Lots 7–9 in Block 73 of the Hugh Hensey town plan.

The existence of the company in 1845 does not necessarily indicate the existence of a mill, and it is known that the first structures erected in Jefferson in early 1845 were log cabins. However, it is highly probable that Hicks operated a small saw and grist mill by mid-1845 and that this facility was taken over and improved by the Steam Mill Company in late 1845.

The first definite indication of the mill's existence is an October 1846 license from the Harrison County commissioners court to Isaac Stephens, William Baker, and John O'Hara to operate a ferry across Big Cypress at the steam mill; and in January 1847 the commissioners court proposed a road from Marshall to Jefferson beginning at the steam mill on Marshall Street. Job Baker appears to have paid taxes on four lots in Jefferson in 1846 as agent of the company. The 1847 tax rolls list O'Hara as agent of the company paying taxes on a steam mill valued at $3,040. In a June 26, 1848, deed record, the owners agreed to pay off the debts incurred in the erection of the mill proportionate to shares and to divide proceeds weekly. Of the $479.10 owed to Charles Dunn, Reuben Drake, Allen Urquhart, and Drummon of New Orleans, Stephens agreed to pay two-fifths, the Bakers agreed to pay two-fifths, and O'Hara agreed to pay one-fifth.

On June 26, 1848, Isaac Stephens and John O'Hara relinquished the "Hicks lots" to Job Baker. In a series of transactions on March 18, 1850, Job Baker and William C. Baker issued a quit claim deed on their two-fifths' interest in the steam mill owned in partnership with Isaac Stephens and John O'Hara to Gideon Baker, William W. Baker, and Benjamin Baker, including the lot on which the mill stood, three yoke of oxen, two wagons, and one set of extra gristmill irons; Gideon Baker and William W. Baker provided to Isaac Stephens a lien on their two-fifths' interest in the steam saw and grist mill, including a wagon carrylog, two yoke of oxen, and Lots 7–9 in Block 73 fronting on Marshall Street; and Stephens sold to Benjamin Baker his interest in the steam saw and grist mill, including one wagon and carrylog, five yoke of oxen, and Lots 7–9 in Block 73.

It can be determined from these transactions that the mill was located on the southwest quarter of Block 73 fronting Marshall Street. This was the "small saw and grist steam mill" mentioned by Edward Smith in his 1849 *Account of a Journey Through North-Eastern Texas*. It produced board lumber from the abundant forest resources of the region that was used primarily for building. The portion of the ground corn obtained by the mill in payment was probably sold to stores in Jefferson for sale to their customers.

The 1850 Cass County industry census lists two saw and grist mills, a water-powered mill, and a steam-powered mill operated by G. A. Mostacker. The Mostacker mill was apparently not the one owned by the Steam Mill Company but can serve as a representative operation for the period. This mill had a capital investment of $2,500, employed six men, paid average monthly wages of $72, and produced 300,000 feet of lumber valued at $4,500 and 1,000 bushels of meal valued at $1,000.

The Jefferson saw mill probably did not last for very long after 1849, because it does not appear in the 1850 census. Raw materials in the immediate vicinity had probably been exhausted by that time, and the land may have been too valuable to be used for industrial purposes as the town grew. Williamson Freeman was purchasing lumber from the McFarland mill southeast of Jefferson by 1850. According to Cass County district court records, Isaac Stephens sued Gideon, Benjamin, and William C. Baker for debts and secured a favorable judgment from the court in September 1851 that required the sale of their two-fifths' ownership, the mill, and the property. An April 19, 1859, conveyance from Francis Baker to Charles Stanley and Samuel Nimmo indicates that the property had become the location of Baker's warehouse.

Also listed in the 1850 Cass County industry census are one wagon maker (James Smith), one blacksmith and gunsmith (Alexander Holcomb, who lived well to the north of Jefferson), and five blacksmiths. One of the blacksmiths was Williamson Freeman, who lived on the outskirts of Jefferson in the area known as Paradise and is listed in the tax rolls as a resident of Cass County in 1848 and in the population census as a farmer in 1850. Freeman was proprietor of the blacksmith shop and not a blacksmith himself. Freeman's children owned a slave who was a blacksmith and wagon maker. The April 1850 probate court granted Freeman, as guardian of his children, the ability to establish a blacksmith shop 1 ¼ miles from Jefferson, which was done immediately. Proceeds from the blacksmith shop in 1850 were $750. The June 1851 probate court granted Freeman the ability to purchase town lots in Jefferson and to move the blacksmith shop to town where it could secure more business.

Blacksmiths are included in the industry census because they produced as well as repaired agricultural implements. The Freeman blacksmith shop produced plows. An April 23, 1856, conveyance from Horatio Walcott to Freeman indicates that Freeman's blacksmith shop was located on Lot 3 in Block 6 between Dallas and Austin streets.

Precinct 1 in the 1850 population census included Jefferson but also a much larger geographic area. Although occupations are listed, this does not necessarily mean that the person engaged in that occupation in a facility at that time. William C. Baker (Gideon's son), Benjamin Baker, and John Walker are listed as millers; Daniel McLaine and James Smith as wagon makers; and J. C. Hobbs as a carriage maker. Also listed are the blacksmiths May Pendleton, Thomas Cogdell, Joseph Macwacht, Joseph Jones, and E. Herring; the gunsmiths John Porter, John Peters, and J. C. Peters; the tanners James Davis and Milholand; the baker Charles Sharp; the tinner John Rather; and the cutlery maker Henry Hather. The blacksmith Pendleton and the tanners Davis and Milholand are known to be Jefferson residents, although there is nothing to indicate that they operated businesses. The gunsmith Porter arrived from England in 1849 and lived in Paradise. The baker Charles Sharp was the Charles Schaff who appears as a Jefferson confectioner in the 1860 census.

James Smith first appears in the 1847 Cass County tax rolls as an owner of one lot in Jefferson valued at $100 as well as shop tools, which were also taxed. It is apparent from the industry census, the population census, and the tax rolls that Smith was a wagon maker operating in Jefferson from 1847. He apparently acquired a steam engine in August 1848, which was transported aboard the *Maid of Osage*. Daniel McLaine, the other wagon maker listed in the population census, is known to have been a Jefferson resident because he is listed as a boarder in a hotel. McLaine, who was considerably younger, apparently worked for Smith, who owned the shop and the tools. These men produced hauling wagons that were made of oak and pine, with stock valued at $1,500 in 1850. They were probably joined by one or both of the wheelwrights listed in the 1850 population census. The location of this facility is uncertain because Smith's acquisition of the lot is not recorded in the deed records.

Other persons listed as owning town lots and shop tools from 1846 through 1850 include M. C. Martin, Chancy (i.e., Chauncey) Stetson,

Prentiss Stetson, Benjamin Miller, James Morris, and Isaac Tabor. Most of these men appear to have been blacksmiths. Mention is made, for example, of Chancy Stetson's blacksmith shop at the southwest corner of Lafayette and Canal streets in a November 20, 1848, deed record. The deed records suggest that there were others. Daniel Remington operated a blacksmith shop on Austin Street on the southwest half of Lot 9 in Block 22 in 1845 (sold to Amos Ury in January 1846, Joel Hughs in April, and John Sharp in August); there was a blacksmith shop on the half-block bounded by Lake, Dallas, Rusk, and Jackson (apparently Lot 6 in Block 3) in 1849 in which Simon Heald held an interest; Irwin and Jones occupied the old Remington shop in 1852; and John Ribold operated a blacksmith shop on the south end of Block A in the Alley Addition along Line Street at the intersection of Jackson and Lafayette in 1857 and 1858. Thomas Owens rented the Ribold shop and employed Ribold in 1857 according to a March 14, 1857, *Eastern Texas Gazette* advertisement. Ribold sold the lot and his blacksmith shop to Roberta Nichols for $750 in October 1858, with the transaction indicating that the lot fronted 30 feet on Line Street and ran back 65 feet to the Alley-Urquhart line.

The existence of a brick yard in Jefferson is first mentioned in a January 23, 1847, bond for title from Berry Durham to John Powell, which mentions a half lot near the southwest corner of the brick yard, fronting 25 feet on the east side of Clarksville Street (the old name for Rusk Street) and running back 150 feet to an alley. This lot was probably one of the unnumbered lots on Rusk Street in the area designated for a courthouse in Hugh Hensey's 1846 town plan. The brick yard was probably located on the southwest quadrant of Block 75 at the corner of Rusk and Camp streets. The only other information on the brick yard is an advertisement that appeared in the May 14, 1853, *Jefferson Herald* indicating that ownership had been transferred from W. P. Watson to Judge H. J. Bankston. Bricks were used at first for the erection of chimneys and from late 1854 on for the erection of buildings. Archibald Dunlap, who is known to have lived on the outskirts of Jefferson, is listed as a bricklayer in the 1850 population census.

There is nothing in the records from the early years to indicate that this was a production facility. Only two brick makers are listed for

Texas in the 1850 industry census, and both of these were in Harrison County, which contained abundant clay deposits. However, the deed records indicate that there was a brick kiln in Jefferson in 1860. In January 1861, Urquhart transferred to his daughter Margaret Block 120 in which her husband, Richard Figures, son of Bartholomew Figures, had established a brick yard in 1860. There was also a brick production facility in Paradise. In January 1851, the probate court granted Williamson Freeman as guardian of his minor children the right to purchase 1.5 acres near Jefferson "on which to make a brick yard and carry on the brick making business." In February 1861, William Perry sold to Williamson Freeman the 5 ½ acre Old Brick Yard Place in the southeast corner of the Archer headright, bounded on the north by the Daingerfield road, on the south by the Big Cypress Valley road, on the west by Freeman's plantation, and on the east by the Gillespie headright. In March 1862, Hinche Mabry sold his homestead in the Gillespie headright near Black Cypress Bayou to William Haygood for $8,000, with payment to be made in one million bricks. These transactions, along with the building of numerous brick structures in Jefferson during the 1850s, indicate that raw materials were readily available and that Jefferson had a production facility in 1846. The October 9, 1859, *Daily Picayune* quotes the *Jefferson Herald* to the effect that smoke from brick kilns could be seen in almost every direction on the outskirts of the town.

Jefferson's early industrial structure is what one would expect in an emerging Southern town in an agricultural area with a high flow-through of businessmen, immigrants, and ox-wagons. Most manufactured articles were imported from the Northeast, but there was a need for smaller industries to support local activities. Lumber and bricks were needed for construction. Wagon makers made and repaired wagons and buggies, with lumber supplied by local saw mills and ironwork supplied by local blacksmiths, who also provided agricultural services. Gunsmiths were needed during a period in which firearms were omnipresent.

These were not manufacturing facilities in the modern sense, engaging in the mass manufacturing of products for large markets. Blacksmiths, millers, and gunsmiths were actually in the services sector rather than in manufacturing. Product consumption was primarily at the local level, with very minor penetration of interior markets by commodities such as wagons. No Jefferson products appear to have been exported by steamboat to distant markets. One possible exception is indicated by the existence of tanners in Jefferson, and it is known that hides and skins were export commodities from the earliest years. Although there probably was a tannery on the outskirts of town, it would have produced leather for local saddle and harness making and repair rather than for export.

Contiguous Saw Mills

The disappearance of the saw mill in Jefferson during the early 1850s was the end of lumber production in the town. Land was becoming valuable, raw materials were not readily available, and it would have been difficult and costly to bring raw materials into the town by wagon. A planing mill was started in Jefferson in the late 1850s, but this facility produced finished items rather than raw lumber. The absence of a lumber mill in Jefferson was not a problem, because building materials were readily available from nearby mills to the east, west, and south.

There was a steam saw and grist mill in Harrison County one mile southeast of Jefferson on the road to Shreveport that was in existence at least by 1850 under the ownership of S. H. McFarland & Company. Various participants in ownership over the years included Samuel McFarland, Richard Crump, Lee Morris, and James Johnson, but the facility was generally known as the McFarland and Crump mill. The mill was sold to Thomas McAllenny in 1853. A May 14, 1853, *Jefferson Herald* advertisement notes operation of the mill by Thomas McAllenny and Joseph Mosby and indicates cash terms and that grinding would be attended to at nights and on Saturdays. This mill was sold to John O'Hara and Samuel Richardson in 1856 and by them to Harvey Black in 1859.

The same issue of the *Jefferson Herald* contains another advertisement for a steam saw mill on Black Cypress Bayou recently purchased by L. M. Rice from H. B. Heatherly, with the firm of Speake, Saufley, and Nimmo in Jefferson acting as agents for Rice. The advertisement is blemished, and stated prices, which probably relate to pine, are unreadable. However, a final note indicates that oak, gum, and other hardwoods were double the stated price of $15.

A February 10, 1857, trust deed from S. H. McFarland & Company to Anthony Owens indicates that there was a steam mill in the west half of the John Humphries headright immediately to the east of Jefferson. A road assignment in May 1855 Cass County commissioners court minutes indicates that the mill was located on the road between Jefferson and Smithland. The 1870 delineation of the city boundaries indicates that the mill was located on Big Cypress Bayou at the mouth of a small lake, which can be seen on the southern boundary of the Humphries headright in the General Land Office's 1943 map of Marion County (see Fig. 3-3). The company was composed of Samuel McFarland, Thomas Goyne, and John Dollahite. Early in 1858, Dollahite and Goyne sold their interests in the land and mill to McFarland, leaving him the sole owner.

A November 15, 1858, agreement between John Porter and George Young is concerned with the disposition of land and facilities in the Archer headright about 1 ½ miles west of Jefferson and immediately west of Williamson Freeman's property. The land was occupied by a recently erected steam saw and grist mill that had been run by Porter and Young as partners. Mentioned in connection with the mill are a two-horse wagon; a four-horse wagon; a sawed and unsawed stock of lumber; corn and meal; a circular saw mill made by Page & Company in Baltimore; a 12-horsepower portable engine, complete with boiler, made by Heard & Son in Waterhouse, New York; a 30-inch flouring mill, a 30-inch corn mill, an 18-inch corn and cob mill made by Strant in Cincinnati; and a 15-inch corn mill and one planing mill made by S. C. Hill of New York. A December 1860 court order in a suit by Porter forced Young to divest himself of his interest in the steam saw and grist mill. Porter secured this interest in January 1861 for $100.

A November 17, 1859, conveyance from the sheriff to John Watson mentions the William Hughes, Samuel Richardson, and John O'Hara Old Mill Tract about one mile west of Jefferson in the Thomas Gillespie headright. These men had been sued by Hiram Tomlin for debts owed, and the 110-acre tract was sold at auction through a court order by the

Manufacturing

sheriff to Watson. This saw and grist mill was probably in existence from December 18, 1851, when the articles of agreement were signed. The conditions of the partnership were arbitrated by Prentiss Stetson, William Nichols, and Hugo Fox in April 1861, with the findings indicating that this was a 107-acre tract in the Gillespie headright extending from the Daingerfield Road to Big Cypress Bayou.

Later Industries

Hugo Fox advertised candies, confectionaries, and fancy articles in the May 14, 1853, *Jefferson Herald*, with the advertisement dated January 30, 1852. Fox sold on a wholesale and retail basis, with particular attention paid to the needs of interior merchants. Fox was probably manufacturing candies at this time. He advertised staple and fancy groceries and home manufactured candy in the March 14, 1857, *Eastern Texas Gazette*, for cash or with pecans, hides, and pelts taken in exchange. He began advertising in the April 10, 1858, Clarksville *Standard* as a wholesale and retail family grocer and manufacturer of confectioneries, "manufacturing himself from the purest materials, Candies that will keep throughout the season and far superior to any imported." Fox also carried fruits, oysters, sardines, wines, sweetmeats, champagne, and fancy toys (Fig. 25-2).

Fox is shown in the 1853 tax rolls as owning $800 in merchandise, but no town lots. In 1854, he is listed as owning one lot valued

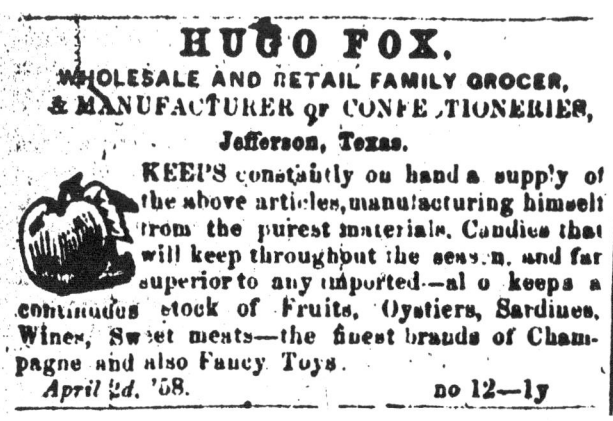

Fig. 25-2. Hugo Fox Advertisement. Source: February 5, 1859, *Standard*

at $1,000, but without merchandise. Merchandise and one town lot are shown in 1855 and 1856. In 1857, Fox had two town lots valued at $2,000 and $2,000 in merchandise. In an advertisement dated November 13, 1852, that appeared in the May 14, 1853, *Jefferson* Herald, Mayer Dopplemayer offered for sale two store houses and four offices on Marshall Street, including those then occupied by Moses Steinlein, Hugo Fox, and Charles Westmoreland. Fox's location in 1852 and 1853 was thus on Marshall Street. Fox's advertisement in the March 14, 1857, *Eastern Texas Gazette* indicates that he was located on Marshall one door above the stand of Speake & Smoker. Speake & Smoker's location is unknown. Fox may always have operated out of rental property. The only possibly relevant transaction I have been able to find is a March 6, 1858, purchase by Fox at a sheriff's sale parts of Lots 5 and 6 in Block 5 beginning 50 feet from Dallas, fronting 24 feet on Marshall, and running back 100 feet. However, this transaction took place after Fox's March 1857 advertisement.

Hugo Fuchs is listed in the 1860 census as a 38-year-old confectioner born in Germany, with $6,000 in real and personal estate, a wife, and two children. The name "Fox" is apparently an Anglicized version of the original German name, with both "Fox" and "Fuchs" appearing in the deed records. Also in the household were the baker William Zervas, born in Germany; the clerk Edward Klienbach, born in Germany; and the clerks Bob Briggs and John Vines, born in the United States. According to the September 1, 1876, *Jefferson Jimplecute*, Fox arrived in Jefferson between 1848 and 1851 and was still living there in 1876.

Also in the census were the confectioners Charles Schaff, born in Germany, and Frederick Merzbacher, born in Bavaria. Both of these probably had independent operations because they were a little older than Fox and had a fair degree of wealth. Merzbacher and Schoenburgh occupied the McNab two-story building on Marshall Street in 1859. An October 9, 1860, bond from Thomas and Caroline Goyne to Moses McCall indicates that Schaff was operating on Marshall Street on a 25-foot by 100-foot lot beginning 38 feet from Austin Street and occupying portions of Lots 5 and 6 in Block 5.

In a May 14, 1853, *Jefferson Herald* advertisement, William Matthews announced that he had purchased the interest of Lewis Carlton in a

Blacksmithing, Carriage & Wagon Making business, that he had some of the best workmen in the South, that he was prepared to "execute work in a neat and elegant manner, and on terms to suit Purchasers," and that he would soon have on hand a lot of wagons and carriages. This facility was probably on the northeast half of Lot 1 in Block 75 fronting 55 feet on Lake Street and running back 75 feet on Jackson, as indicated by a January 22, 1853, conveyance by Carlton to Matthews. Nothing is known about the prior existence of this facility. Carlton is listed in the 1850 census as a 24-year-old laborer born in Alabama.

An advertisement for Frank Clark's Tanyard appeared in the March 3, 1856, *Texas Republican*. The advertisement states that the tanyard was located near the Big Cypress bridge at the old mill of O'Hara, Richardson, and Hughes and that cash would be paid for sheep skins, calf skins, and well-cured dried beef hides. The next week Clark advertised for one or two tanners who would be given steady employment. The tanyard was located one mile west of Jefferson in the Gillespie headright.

The Branch Tan Yard, operated by Fisher & Mathews, advertised in the November 7, 1857, *Eastern Texas Gazette*. The advertisement states that the tanyard was located 3 ½ miles northwest of Jefferson near the Daingerfield road and was seeking 800–1,000 cow hides and pelts during the summer and fall from the areas to the north and northwest, for which 12 ½ cents would be paid per pound. This facility probably produced for the local market, because the repair and making of saddlery and other leather items had grown to substantial proportions by that time as an extension of the operations of livery stables.

The September 1, 1876, *Jefferson Jimplecute* indicates that John Kolster arrived in Jefferson between 1848 and 1851, but he is not included in the 1850 census. On April 4, 1851, Urquhart sold to Herman Kothe and John Kolster Lot 10 in Block 21. District court minutes for March 1852 indicate that Kothe and Kolster were partners in trade and manufacturing. Kothe sold his half interest in the lot and improvements in December 1852 to Arnold Heinemann, who sold it to Kolster in February 1853. District court minutes for March 1855 indicate that Kolster was occupying a house used as a tin shop. On July 21, 1856, John Kolster sold to Frederick Kolster the western half of this lot containing a frame house used as a tin shop. The same lot with the tin shop was sold to Samuel Locke of New Orleans on June 15, 1857. Kolster is listed in the 1860 census as a 37-year-old tinner with real estate valued at $2,000 and a personal estate valued at $5,000.

Haze Jolly advertised as a tinware manufacturer in the March 14, 1857, *Eastern Texas Gazette*. The advertisement indicates that Jolly sold cook, office, and parlor stoves and all kinds of tinware on a wholesale and retail basis. He also did job work with various metals, including sheet iron work to produce stoves, stove pipe, and stove pans. The advertisement says that Jolly's facility was located on Marshall Street. Jolly is listed in the 1860 census as a 36-year-old farmer born in Georgia with a wife and child.

A February 28, 1858, deed from John Cocke, administrator of the estate of William Cocke, to W. B. Mabry mentions a foundry and fixtures on Lots 7–9 of Block 46 of the Alley Addition that had been owned in a copartnership between William Cocke and Mabry. Cocke died in November 1856, and the Cocke & Mabry foundry is mentioned in his recently completed will and in the estate inventory filed in July 1857.

Prentiss Stetson & Charles Stewart's Sash, Blind, and Door Manufactory advertised in the April 10, 1858, Clarksville *Standard* as having machinery for the speedy manufacture of sash, blinds, doors, etc., for building and also plain furniture such as bedsteads, wardrobes, and safes (Fig. 25-3). Prices included 50 cents per square foot for blinds, one cent per inch for sash, $5 to $6 for doors with moulding, and $4.50 for doors without moulding. Charles DeMorse of the *Standard* saw this facility when he solicited the advertisement:

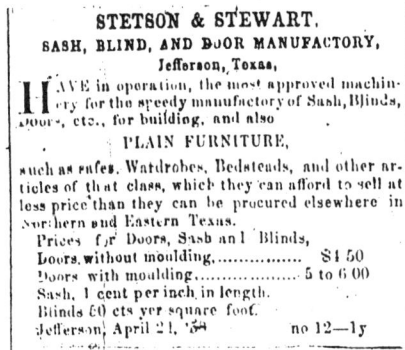

Fig. 25-3. Stetson & Stewart Advertisement. Source: April 10, 1858, *Standard*

> While at Jefferson, we called at the machine Sash and Blind manufactory, of Stetson & Stewart, whose card is to be found in our Jefferson column. Their various machines for ripping plank, planing, tongueing and grooving, mortising, etc., are very handsome as well as useful, and are all propelled by steam. It is the only establishment of the kind, we know of in north eastern Texas. Persons building, and needing Blinds, Sash, Doors, or plain furniture, would find it economical and convenient to purchase of them. Wagons hauling cotton down for shipment, could conveniently, bring return loads or parts of loads, made up of their manufacture.

De Morse's comments suggest that the Stetson & Stewart facility was the first in Jefferson to produce the woodwork that has been found in many northeast Texas towns. Prentiss Stetson is listed in the 1860 census as a 42-year-old carpenter born in Massachusetts with a wife and two children. Charles Stewart is listed as a 30-year-old county assessor and tax collector born in Virginia. A June 11, 1858, conveyance from Stetson to Stewart indicates that the facility was located on Lot 9 in Block 18, which had been sold to Stetson by J. H. Faucett and deeded by Urquhart to Stetson on February 24, 1857, and that Stetson and Stewart were no longer in business together. Stetson sold Lot 9 in Block 18 for $1,000 to E. S. Walker, wife of Robert Walker, on February 23, 1860, with the transaction indicating that Stetson was then operating a steam saw mill on the property.

Stetson apparently immediately went into business in a similar, but less sophisticated, operation with J. F. Warren. A March 1863 agreement between these men to arbitrate their differences indicates that for several years they had been operating a steam, grist, and planing mill, with a sideline in hogs, on Fractional Lots 6 and 7 in Block 70 at the corner of Broadway and Walnut. The arbitrators Daniel Alley, William Torrans, and James Durr determined that the property should be sold. The sale was advertised in the *Confederate News*, and the property was sold by the auctioneer James Hosack to Stetson and William Perry for

$8,000. Stetson and Perry sold the mill to Lewis Moody in May, and Moody sold the mill to Charles Stewart in June and August. The June transaction indicates that the Broadway extension through Block 70 was new.

Only seven facilities are listed in the 1860 Marion County census of industry: Jefferson Nash & Company's Texas Iron Works (castings, pig iron, plows); William Curry & Company's tanyard; Lewis Patillo's steam saw mill; Stewart and Lockett's iron foundry (castings, plows); George Kelly's bell factory (cow bells); Charles Stewart's bell factory (cow bells); and Samuel McFarland's steam saw mill. None of these facilities was located in Jefferson. This is in tension with the 1860 population census, which indicates a large number of machinists, civil engineers, confectioners, shoe and boot makers, bakers, butchers, tanners, saddlers, millers, coopers, carriage makers, and blacksmiths in Jefferson.

Although Jefferson's industries continued to produce products for local consumption, there was a decided shift in the late 1850s toward the interior market, as indicated by the wholesaling of tinware and candies and by the probable interior distribution of wagons, carriages, and finished wood products. This means that Jefferson manufacturers were able to compete in quality and price with national manufacturers, but only for the regional market, because there is no evidence that any of these products were exported by steamboat.

26. Packeries

Cotton was Jefferson's most important export commodity during the 1800s. Second to cotton in importance were cattle, beef and pork, and byproducts of slaughter such as hides and tallow. Of these, pickled beef in barrels was the most important. Pickled beef was somewhat like present-day corned beef and was cured in a brine solution. Such methods of preparation were absolutely essential for the shipment of meats before the introduction of artificial refrigeration. The cattle were driven to Jefferson from the plains to the north and northwest centering on the wiregrass prairies of the Sulphur Fork area. At Jefferson, they were slaughtered, and the meat was prepared by large packeries for shipment in barrels by steamboat. The packing operations required imports of salt and barrels or staves, and each exported barrel of beef contained 165 pounds of meat. Packing was conducted during the winter, which was the only time it was cool enough to limit spoilage.

The packeries were fairly large industrial operations, employing large crews of experienced butchers and packers to slaughter and process the cattle and a substantial number of coopers to construct the barrels in which the pickled beef was transported. Drivers brought the cattle to Jefferson, and steamboat crews carried off the finished product. Cattle from northeast Texas had traditionally been driven to Jefferson and Shreveport where they were placed on steamboats for transport to the New Orleans fresh meat market. The packeries increased the demand for cattle and provided an opportunity to achieve added value. Hides obtained from local slaughter in the north had always been an important export commodity through Jefferson; but the packeries increased the volume of hides exported and required tanyards for their preparation. Tallow was used in the production of soap.

There were two packeries in the vicinity of Jefferson before the Civil War, one new one during the war in addition to these two, and one after the war. The largest of these and the longest lasting was the post-war Wilson, Stoner & Company packery three miles downstream of Jefferson. The new Civil War packery, which was operated by James Dunn, was within the city, under contract to the Confederacy, and inconsequential in production. Of the two antebellum packeries, the first was started by Harvey Black in 1857 and was located across the bayou from Jefferson. The second was started by Charles Stanley and Samuel Nimmo in 1858 and was located at the foot of Rusk and Cypress streets. Because the source of supply was from the north, the antebellum packeries necessitated the movement of cattle through the city. Their exports were important factors in the level of steamboat activity at Jefferson in the years immediately before the war.

Black Packery

The brothers A. H. and H. H. Black advertised in the June 10, 1854, Clarksville *Standard* that they had Merino and Saxony sheep for sale to stock breeders and wool growers who were interested in improving the quality of their flocks. In a letter provided to the editor, Charles DeMorse, they explained that in 1852 they had driven from the northern states into Texas between 1,100 and 1,200 head of sheep. All but 250 were lost during the first season in acclimating, but the flock had increased to 500. The ranch was four miles west of Tarrant in Hopkins County, and the 1853 fleeces, averaging five pounds per sheep, had been sold in Jefferson for 40 cents a pound. Normal prices in eastern markets were 60–90 cents a pound, but the first fleeces were in poor condition because of the long drive from the north. DeMorse was provided samples of the 1854 fleeces to demonstrate their quality.

Beef packing was not a proven enterprise in the South, and there is nothing to suggest that Harvey Black was experienced in the business. Nevertheless, he started a small experimental operation in Shreveport in 1856 and a similar operation in Jefferson in late 1857. Black's initial advertisement for the Jefferson facility appeared in the September 5, 1857, Clarksville *Standard,* with Black's location given as Tarrant. The advertisement states that liberal prices would be paid in cash for all good, fat, heavy beef cattle delivered to Black in Jefferson in November, December, and the first part of January and that the facility had the capacity to handle 40–45 beeves per day (Fig. 26-1). A similar advertisement appears in the September 19, 1857, Marshall *Texas Republican,* but Black's location is given as Jefferson, and the facility is said to have the capacity to handle 45–50 beeves per day.

Articles accompanying the advertisements indicate that Black had become convinced in Shreveport of the efficacy of meat packing, but that he was still operating on an experimental basis. The newspapers celebrated the existence of a home market for Texas cattle, because stock raisers would always know what their cattle would bring at Jefferson. Transport to New Orleans by steamboat reduced the weight of cattle, and stock raisers could never be certain about the New Orleans cattle market. The editor of the Jefferson *Eastern Texas Gazette* visited

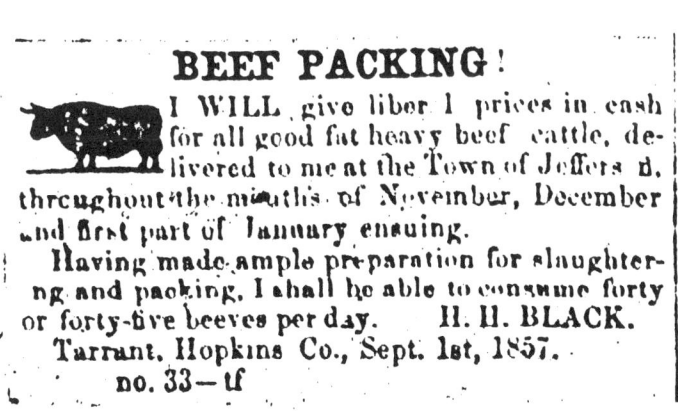

Fig. 26-1. Black Packery Advertisement. Source: September 5, 1857, *Standard*

the Black facility during its first season of operation and reports the following:

> We were down at Mr. Black's beef factory on yesterday. Beeves are slaughtered, skinned and cut up there in quick and scientific style. Mr. Black has made thorough preparations for his work before he commenced killing. We saw some 40 beeves already cleaned and ready to be cut up. It is a sight worth seeing.

The November 11, 1857, *Standard* states that Black employed 25 hands from Louisville, Kentucky, and that he expected to pack 3,000 beeves that winter, meeting his stated goals. The employees, as was the case with all of Jefferson's packeries, were not from Texas, because meatpacking required considerable expertise. The October 15, 1858, *Texas Republican* indicates that at least some of Black's product was sold overseas and "pronounced by competent judges equal to any grass fed beef in the United States." The *Jefferson Herald*, as quoted by the February 5, 1859, *Standard*, notes that Black had expanded his operations into pork packing at the end of the 1858 beef packing season:

> We are highly gratified to see the energy and industry manifested by Mr. Black, the proprietor of one of the Beef Packeries at this place; he has slaughtered this season three thousand beeves, and not content with being idle, has commenced on an extensive scale the packing of Pork. He has already killed about twelve hundred head, and still continues day by day adding to this number. We consider this one of the most important investments that has ever taken place in our progressive city. It not only adds much to the future interest of Jefferson, but it will hereafter be a market for all the hogs and cattle that can be raised in Northern Texas.

The last mention of Black's operation in the newspapers apparently occurs in connection with the 1859 packing season, which was the second season for the Stanley & Nimmo packery, and Black stopped advertising at the end of the year. On January 11, 1859, Black purchased the O'Hara & Richardson saw mill, which was located one mile southeast of Jefferson. On August 6, 1859, Ephraim Terry agreed to build brick walls for a warehouse on a lot to be chosen by Black. The March 1860 Marion County commissioners court minutes mention a Black and Crump tanyard. It appears that Black found his operation noncompetitive with the much larger Stanley & Nimmo packery and that he was entering into other lines of business.

In any case, he sold many lots in Jefferson, including the unfinished brick warehouse in Block 85, to the New Orleans firm of Fellows & Company of New Orleans, composed of Cornelius Fellows, David Logan, and Thompson Granfield, on June 30, 1860. He also sold the packery to the same firm on September 29, 1860. The deed record indicates that the facility was composed of a slaughterhouse and packery on land rented from Samuel Moseley on Big Cypress Bayou opposite Jefferson. The deed record also mentions that there were houses, sheds, shops, coopers' materials, beef, hides, tallow, and grease on the premises, as well as 3,500 cattle on the premises and at Shreveport and destined for Jefferson.

The November 17, 1860, *Harrison Flag*, citing the Jefferson *Herald and Gazette*, suggests that Black was still in operation at that time, but the reference is probably to the facility under its common name. Alternatively, Black may have been employed by the new owners. The facility is not listed in the 1860 Harrison County census of industry. It may have been acquired by the New Orleans firm of Hilliard, Summers & Company, which advertised in the December 21, 1861, Clarksville *Standard* that it had established a packery in Jefferson and was seeking fat cattle four years old and upward, with C. C. Alexander in Bonham acting as their purchasing agent. The Black facility was set on fire, apparently by an incendiary, on July 29, 1862.

Harvey Black is listed in the 1860 census as a 27-year-old stock raiser born in Kentucky. In June 1861, he joined the Marion Rifles as a 3rd Lieutenant. This was the first contingent of troops to leave Jefferson and became Company A of the 1st Texas Regiment, Hood's Brigade. Lt. Col. Black was killed on May 14, 1862, during a heavy skirmish at West Point.

Stanley & Nimmo Packery

Charles Stanley began advertising in January 1855 as a commission and forwarding merchant, and Stanley and Samuel Nimmo began advertising in March 1856 as furniture salesmen, with the showroom located in Stanley's warehouse on Cypress Bayou at the Houston Street Bridge. The warehouse was 15 feet above the water and had a door opening out onto the bayou. Before entering the meat packing business, Stanley visited model facilities in the North and Midwest, collecting information on technology, markets, and business practices and apparently also hiring employees. The warehouse was modified, an addition was constructed, barrels were made, thousands of sacks of salt were obtained, and the packery was opened in the winter of 1858.

The facilities and stockyards covered the whole of Block 93 and fractional Block O on the bayou east of Houston Street and south of Cypress Street (Fig. 26-2), with animal wastes apparently discharged directly into the bayou. In conjunction with the establishment of the packery, Stanley and Chester Bulkley cleared Cypress Bayou of obstructions from the warehouse of J. M. & J. C. Murphy in the landing area up to the packery; and a wharf was constructed at the foot of Marshall Street, which ended at the embayment formed by the upstream split of the bayou that created St. Catherine's Island. The editor of the *Jefferson Gazette*, who reported on these events, indicated that the bank of the bayou from Marshall Street to the packery was above high water and expected to see the entire area occupied by warehouses within the next two years. The reason that Bulkley participated in this project was that he purchased St. Catherine's Island from Allen Urquhart for $2,047 in September 1858 and expected to benefit from the provision of navigation above the landing area.

Robert Loughery of the Marshall *Texas Republican* visited the Stanley & Nimmo packery in October 1858 a few weeks before it went into production and found it "a model of convenience and economy" and that "Everything connected with it seems to contemplate the most rapid dispatch of business with the least cost of time." Loughery elaborated as follows:

> The building premises for packing, engine, and machinery, cover over three hundred feet square, while

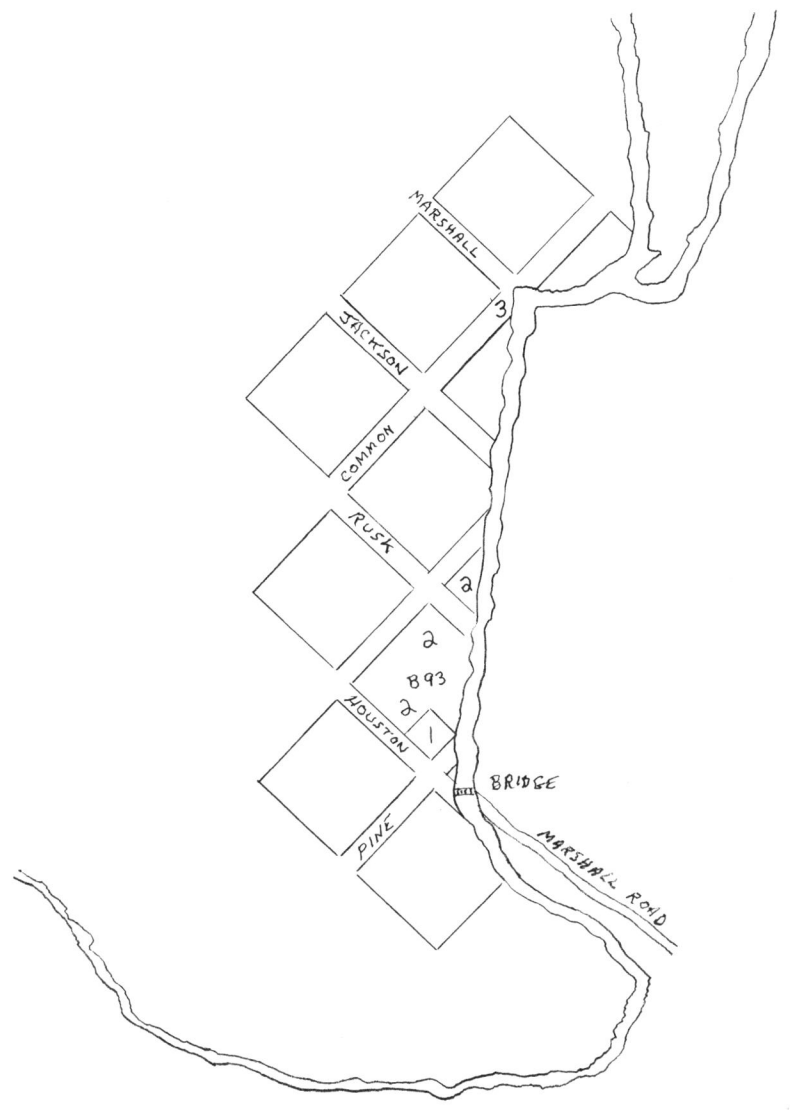

Fig. 26-2. Stanley & Nimmo Packery
KEY:
1. Charles Stanley's warehouse, 1855; Stanley & Nimmo furniture store, 1856
2. Packery property
3. Packery wharf

the area connected with the business of the establishment embraces several acres. Everything about the premises has an air of thrift and industry. We found the proprietors actively employed in putting their house in order. There are over one hundred thousand staves, which the coopers were working up into barrels. They have a superb steam engine and apparatus for tanking tallow, and in connection with this engine, they have water pipes to convey water to all parts of the building for packing or to use to advantage in case of fire. The tanks are of iron and constructed upon the latest and most improved plan. They have already on hand three or four thousand sacks of salt for commencing, so that they will be ready in a few weeks, or so soon as the weather will permit active operations.

Loughery was cognizant of the value to the region of a facility of this magnitude and optimistic about its business potentials because of the quality of its owners:

This is an enterprise which will prove of great advantage to this section of country, and particularly stock raisers. Messrs. Stanley & Nimmo are fully prepared and expect to slaughter over one hundred beef cattle a day. The business season for packing will embrace a period of from ninety to one hundred and twenty days, and will enable them, we presume, to dispose of from eight to ten thousand beeves. This establishment is situated immediately on the bayou, and they have nothing to do but to roll the beef when packed from the warehouse on board of a steamboat. That the business will prove a lucrative one, we do not entertain a doubt. As we before observed, the well known prudent character of the men, and the investigations which they made before they went into it, are a sufficient guaranty. We have known them for ten years, and if they are not successful, it will be the first failure they have ever yet made in business.

The first pickled beef was produced in January 1859. Loughery received a half-barrel sample, which he described as "remarkably firm, and richly flavored. Their packers understand the business thoroughly, and the beef which they put up is the finest in the country." This praise was not unwarranted. By March, Jefferson beef was in New York commanding high prices, as reported in the April 29, 1859, *Texas Republican*, quoting the *Galveston News*:

> TEXAS BEEF.—The New York papers of March 21st report sales of 500 tierces of Texas cured beef at $18.50 per tierce. A tierce we understand is equal to 1 ½ barrels, which makes the sale equal to $12.33 per barrel. The quality is quoted as good mess, and the price is that which is given for the best brands. We learn that this is probably the first Texas cured beef sold in New York, as Texas beef, though beef from this State has been sold before, with other brands. An experienced beef packer who has been in our city for some time past, informs us that this beef was put up in Jefferson, Cass county, and he entertains no doubt that Texas beef can be cured and shipped to markets abroad in the merchantable condition, so as to compare favorably with beef from any part of the world, and command the highest prices.

The *Galveston News* article indicates that the Stanley & Nimmo packery was the first Texas facility to sell on the New York market under its own brand name. The October 15, 1858, *Texas Republican* noted that the enterprise should be lucrative because "close proximity to the prairies will enable them to obtain the choicest beeves at comparatively little cost." Quality was attributed to packing techniques and conditions for cattle raising in northeast Texas: "The vast extent of the prairies, and the character of the grasses with which they are covered, keep the cattle which roam over them in excellent order all the year, without any cost to the owner, and always in a healthy condition." However, the editor of the *Jefferson Gazette* found it necessary in November 1859 to issue a warning to suppliers about the unacceptability of young cattle:

> THE CATTLE DROVERS.—We deem it a duty we owe to cattle drovers, to state that none but large and fat cattle will be received at the Packeries in this place. It is useless for them to drive two and three year olds here with the hope of finding a market. Our Packers will not injure their reputation abroad by putting up such cattle at any price. We hope this short notice will save some of our prairie friends the trouble of a useless and expensive journey.

The editor of the *Jefferson Gazette* was invited to Christmas dinner at the packery, which was held for some 80 or 90 employees, among whom he found "a pride of conscious merit." His description of the facility at the end of the packing season is contained in the January 14, 1860, *Texas Republican*:

> While on the subject, we may as well state that the slaughtering at this establishment is now pretty well over—four thousand head of cattle having been butchered for the season. And to show with what dispatch they transact business, we will state the fact that the morning of the 24th ult. found them with 177 cattle in the pen, and at 4 o'clock on the evening of the same day every beef was butchered, nicely cleaned, quartered and hanging in the cooling room. The reputation of this establishment with its extensive and convenient arrangements, has gone abroad. Men of experience, who have visited the best arranged packeries in the world, pronounce its whole construction unsurpassed by any thing of the kind in the country. Their cisterns are capacitated to hold, at the same time, two thousand head of six year old cattle, and every other arrangement is on a scale of equal magnitude. Their pumps are so arranged as to conduct water from the bayou to every department, enabling them to keep all things as clean and nice as their pride, comfort, or fancy may dictate. It is styled by competent judges a model pack-

ery, and we have no doubt, justly so. Their beef, we understand, has commanded the highest price in both the New York and Liverpool markets, and, it is well known, has secured an enviable reputation wherever it is known. This is their second season, and it is to be hoped that each succeeding one will bring to them enlarged profits and an extended reputation.

In spite of this promising beginning, the Stanley & Nimmo packery lasted only two packing seasons (1858–59 and 1859–60). The apparent cause of failure was a gross overextension of debt. By October 1860, Stanley and Nimmo owed $116,395.94 to various creditors, who brought suit. This was by far the largest recorded debt in the deed records. Part of the debt was shared by Charles' brother Isaac, a resident of Hartford, Connecticut, who appears to have been a partner in the firm shortly before it expired. The Stanley properties in Jefferson and vicinity, including the packery, were auctioned to satisfy the debt and were acquired by Elisha Price of New Orleans. The November 17, 1860, *Harrison Flag* reports that Price was renovating the packery and intended to begin slaughtering the next week.

By December 1860, Price was heavily in debt, with drafts drawn on the firm of Pilcher & Goodrich in New Orleans on the basis of the products of his packery. John Speake was selected as a trustee for the sale of these products on commission, including 268,000 pounds of unpacked pickled beef, 504 hides, 120 barrels of tallow, and 200 tierces and 100 barrels of pickled beef. A tierce was equivalent to 1 ½ barrels. Price advertised in the November 22, 1862, *Texas Republican* that he was packing pork for delivery to the government.

The packery is not listed in the 1860 industry census apparently because it was not in operation when the census was taken. Although Charles Stanley was a Jefferson resident from its beginning and was a prominent merchant, he is not listed in the 1850 or 1860 censuses. Samuel Nimmo was a 17-year-old clerk working for Jeptha Crawford in 1850 and is listed in the 1860 census as a 28-year-old merchant. He died on February 4, 1861, after a lengthy illness, leaving a wife and two children. Price is listed in the 1860 census as a 28-year-old merchant.

27. Structural Features

Construction Contracts

The early deed records and district court cases contain a few documents with information on antebellum construction.

In 1849, George Stark agreed to build for John Speake a two-story dwelling house for $1,000 and to provide all materials, except shingles and sills to be furnished by Speake, including locks, butts (?), hinges, screws, and nails. The house was to be 20 feet wide by 52 feet long and contain four rooms 20 feet in the clear with a 12-foot-wide passage in between. The first story was to have an 11-foot pitch and the second story was to have a nine-foot eight-inch pitch. Each room was to contain two windows in front and two in the rear, and the passage upstairs was to have two windows, one at each end. The windows were to contain 15 lights (panes), with the upstairs panes 12 by 14 inches and the downstairs panes 10 by 12 inches. There were to be two doors in the dining room and chamber, one door in each of the rooms upstairs, and two doors in the passageway, the first one having side and top panes. All doors were to be constructed in the latest style. The staircase was to be a neat ramp and knee with sides showing six inches and steps 10 inches. The floors were to be tongue and groove. The casing was to be palastered (?) downstairs and arctuies (?) upstairs. Blinds for said house to be venetian weatherboarding to show six inches. Cornice to be in proportion to the height and size of the house. Shingles to show six inches. Portices to be 14 feet long and eight feet, six inches wide showing a heavy seeking (?) and said cornice cased above house. Portices to have four columns and four palustrades opposite each column. Sash bourse (?) to show eight inches and a finish on top. Four mantel pieces made in a neat fashionable style. Sash front, weatherboarding, cornice, and portices to be made of seasoned lumber clear of knots and turpentine. Four closets or wardrobes upstairs adjoining the chimney. The house to be plastered and papered with neat and fashionable paper.

In 1850, Benjamin Kimble agreed to build for William Perry west of Jefferson two double-log dwelling houses with a 10-foot passage in between and with each room to be 16 feet square. Kimble also agreed to fence in a yard around the house with shade trees, to fence a garden 80 feet square, and to clear and fence 10 acres.

In 1851, George Loy and James Smith, the wagon maker, agreed to construct for Ithael Eason a 20-foot by 60-foot storehouse in Jefferson with a 10-foot pitch and a large house for themselves that would be connected with the Eason house in such a fashion as to constitute one building. Eason's part was to be built first with the following specifications: weatherboard; front to be dressed and the rest to be rough; roof; floor to be dressed and square-jointed; large double-pannel door in front; two show windows in front similar to those in Trawick's drugstore; batteu door and windows in the back.

In 1851, Augustus Lamprecht and George Cantrowinskey agreed to provide carpentry work valued at $320 for Bartholomew Figures in exchange for town lots. The work components and their valuation were as follows: six-pannel doors with frame and fashion ($6 each); five-pannel doors ($5 each); 10-foot by 12-foot windows (12 ½ cents per light); flooring dressed, tongued, and grooved and laid with broken joints ($2 per square); ceiling the same way ($2 per square); framing ($1.50 per square); shingling, including carrying them up to the roof ($1.50 per square); weatherboarding dressed ($1.50 per square); weatherboarding undressed ($1 per square); box and cornice fine and fashionable work (75 cents per foot); six-pannelled shutters ($5 per pair); table counters (50 cents per foot); pannelled counters (50 cents per foot); shelving (75 cents per foot).

In 1858, George Young agreed to build for John Porter and his wife west of Jefferson a dwelling house, a kitchen, a house constructed in two parts to serve as a blacksmith shop and workshop, a stable, and a corn crib. The dwelling house was to be 38 feet square, containing four rooms 14 feet square and two 10-foot passages intersecting at the center. Each room was to have a brick chimney and fireplace. The two front rooms were to have four windows each, and the two back rooms were to have three windows each. The kitchen was to be 14 feet square, in the rear of and 10 feet from the dwelling and connected to it by a 14-foot passage continuing the north-south passage running through the house. The kitchen was to have a brick chimney and four windows. The blacksmith shop was to be 14 feet by 16 feet, and the workshop was to be 16 feet by 20 feet. A well was to be constructed convenient to the dwelling.

In 1859, Ephraim Terry agreed to build for George Prewitt a brick wall for a stable for $200 with the following specifications: 64 feet by 80 feet from outside to outside; ten feet to the first joist extra wall 1 ½ feet high extending 18 feet both front and rear, including one side; wall to be 14 feet high and a brick and a half thick; parapet four feet high and the length of one brick in thickness the entire circumference; Prewitt to furnish water and plank for scaffolding. Also in that year, Terry agreed to build for Harvey Black brick walls for a warehouse on a lot to be chosen by Black with the following specifications: 100 feet by 185 feet; height not given; brick to be made by Terry; 21 brick to the cubic foot; Black to turn over lime, wood, and brick he has already collected for construction; to be built of good merchantable brick and materials.

In 1860, the carpenter and master workman M. H. Duncan agreed to build for Jesse Gillean and his wife a dwelling house in Marion County of the following description: "Two rooms eighteen feet square (measuring on the outside). One hall between said rooms twelve feet wide. Piazza twelve feet wide and forty-eight long, to be built on the east side in front of said rooms. The ceiling on the inside of said rooms to be put up undressed. The ceiling inside of the hall and on the east side of said rooms and overhead in piazza to be dressed and put up as said Gillean shall direct. The flooring throughout said building to be dressed and tongued and grooved or matched. Eight windows to be made in said rooms. Twelve lights, each fourteen inches by eighteen inches (each light). Said windows to be swung with weights and rollers (lower sash). Six square columns in front of piazza and banistering all the piazza. Base boards and case boards throughout the building to be made plain." The work was to be completed in three months at a cost of $375, with the materials to be furnished by Gillean.

In 1860, Robert Nesmith agreed to build at his own expense for Lewis Moody on Lot 7 in Fractional Block 23 at the corner of Jackson and Austin a 50-foot square two-story frame structure, one-half of which would be occupied by Moody and the other by Nesmith, which he would occupy rent-free for 10 years. Nesmith contracted the construction for $650 to the carpenter and master builder Abiel Morton, with Nesmith responsible for land clearing, foundation work, and materials expense. The contract called for finished weatherboarding on the two sides fronting the streets and rough weatherboarding on the other two sides; shingled roof in two sections; parapet wall tall enough to hide the roof on side fronting Jackson; floors of unfinished planks; partition running length of structure and encompassing both floors; three large double doors and three windows on Jackson side; three single doors and six windows on opposite side; two windows on Austin side and one on the opposite side; all windows and doors to have good batton (?) shutters.

In 1860, Ephraim Terry agreed to build for John Hobdy the brick walls for a building running 50 feet on Dallas Street and back 136 feet to Austin and connecting with A. C. Allen's one-story house. Terry was to put one story on the wall already built by Allen. Williamson Freeman as agent for Hobdy had secured this right from Allen in June, indicating that the wall to be extended was between Lots 2 and 3 in Block 6. The first floor was to be 12 feet high, and the second joint was to be 12 feet from the second floor. The first story was to be two bricks thick, and the second story was to be 1 ½ bricks thick, with a parapet run high enough to protect the roof. The foundation was to be dug at Hobdy's expense, and Hobdy was to supply brick to Terry at the kiln at $8 per thousand or at the worksite at $10.50 per thousand. Terry was to be paid $14 per thousand bricks, with 21 bricks to the square foot. Terry was to plaster the upper two rooms at 25 cents per square yard and the lower two rooms at 20 cents per square yard, apparently with a whitewash finish. This was the building that came to be known as Freeman's Hall.

In 1860, H. W. Hamil and Ephraim Terry agreed to build for Charles Graham a 30-foot by 138-foot two-story house, with payment of $14 per thousand brick at 21 bricks to the cubic foot, leaving openings for doors and windows. The foundation was to be 2 ½ bricks up to the joist, the first story two bricks, and the second story 1 ½ bricks, with the gables to be built up to show a parated (?) front.

Brick Structures

The vast majority of structures in Jefferson prior to the Civil War were of frame construction. However, brick began to be used in 1855 and dominated construction activities in the business district on the eve of the Civil War. The primary reason for the use of brick was fear of fire. This was particularly important for storehouses and warehouses in which the contents were often of greater value than the structure. Receiving and forwarding merchants with brick warehouses offered unique protection to their customers, which was emphasized in advertisements. Similar conditions prevailed for hotels. The documented brick structures in Jefferson prior to the war were

1. February 1855—J. M. & J. C. Murphy's warehouse on Lots 3 and 4 in Block 9. The February 17, 1855, *Texas Republican* says that this structure was two stories and 80 feet by 180 feet. The width is correct, indicating that the warehouse occupied two full lots. The length is apparently incorrect, because lots in this block were not 180 feet long. This structure appears to be shown on Brosius' 1872 *Bird's Eye View of Jefferson, Texas*.

2. January 1858—W. M. Freeman & Company's warehouse on Lots 5 and 6 in Block 10. This was a single-story structure running 100 feet by 140 feet, fully occupying two lots. This structure, expanded one lot to the east, appears to be shown on Brosius.

3. April 1858—Reece Hughes' storehouse on Marshall adjoining the City Hotel. The April 10, 1858, *Standard* says that this was a two-story structure. The storehouse occupied the lower parts of Lots 7–9 in Block 21, fronting 30 feet on Marshall and running back 108 feet on

Austin. The storehouse and lot were sold to George Prewitt for $15,000 in June 1860. This structure is not shown on Brosius.

4. April 1858—City Hotel on Marshall, owned by Reece Hughes and operated by William Brooks. The hotel property fronted 73 feet on Marshall and was immediately north of Hughes' brick storehouse. A brick addition to the original frame structure was completed in early 1858 in conjunction with the building of the storehouse. The March 16, 1861, *Texas Republican* notes that foundations were being laid for a three-story brick addition to the hotel that would contain 24 rooms. The latter addition does not appear to have been made. The City Hotel was destroyed by fire in January 1866, but a two-story brick structure is shown in the right place on Brosius.

5. October 1858—J. L. & S. C. Smith's storehouse. Robert Loughery of the *Texas Republican* saw this structure being built in early October and said that it would be completed in a few weeks. The Smiths were located from 1854–1857 in a frame storehouse on the southeast corner of Marshall and Austin. This property was acquired from Horatio Walcott in 1857 and is the probable location of the new brick structure. The attorney William Mason advertised in March 1861 that he was located on Dallas over the Smith store; however, the attorneys Patillo & Mason advertised in July of that year that they were located on Marshall over the Smith store. A two-story brick structure is shown on the southeast corner of Marshall and Austin in Brosius. In addition to the Smith storehouse, Loughery noted that the other brick buildings in town included the Murphys' warehouse, Freeman's warehouse, and Hughes' storehouse and that arrangements had been made for erecting five or six other large buildings.

6. In 1859, Ephraim Terry agreed to build for George Prewitt a 64-foot by 80-foot brick wall for a stable. This was a replacement for a newly completed frame structure at the corner of Jackson and Austin that had been destroyed by fire in December 1858 with a loss estimated at $5,000, including one horse, 1,800 bushels of corn, and a large amount of fodder. Prewitt's brick stable was located on Lots 7 and 8 in Block 22. Prewitt's stable continues to be shown on Graham's 1869 *Plan of the City of Jefferson, Texas*, but the brick structure is not shown on Brosius. Also in that year, Terry agreed to build for Harvey Black brick

walls for a warehouse that would be 100 feet by 185 feet. Black's brick warehouse was unfinished when he sold it in June 1860.

7. On February 27, 1860, William Perry sold to William Torrans for $1,500 Lot 6 in Block 9 with one-half of a brick wall built by Perry and David Culberson. Culberson was with the firm of B. J. Terry & Company, which purchased Lot 7 in Block 9 in October 1858. These adjoining brick structures were apparently built in late 1858 and may be shown on Brosius.

8. On June 8, 1860, Williamson Freeman as agent for John Hobdy paid A. C. Allen for one-half of the brick wall between Lots 2 and 3 in Block 6 with the right to extend the wall upward above Allen's one-story storehouse. Sometime prior to August 7, 1860, Hobdy entered into a contract with Ephraim Terry for the construction of a brick structure on Dallas and running back to Austin and adjoining Allen's structure. Allen's April 9, 1861, mortgage indicates that his brick grocery house was located on the west half of Lot 2 in Block 6. This structure appears to be shown on Brosius.

9. On June 16, 1860, Ephraim Terry agreed to build a two-story brick structure for Charles Graham.

10. On June 26, 1860, William Hines agreed to rent his brick storehouse to the merchants Morris and Lazarus Rosenzweig doing business under the name of M. Rosenzweig & Brother. The agreement mentions that this was one of a block of brick buildings recently built by Hines on Dallas and Austin.

11. On February 19, 1861, Richard Waterhouse and his son mortgaged to M. D. Cooper & Company the east half of Lot 4 in Block 5 fronting 25 feet on Dallas and containing a two-story brick storehouse that they had probably built in 1859. This structure does not appear in Brosius.

12. Loughery visited Jefferson in February 1860 and reports that "Quite a number of new store houses, mostly of brick, have gone up, and several others are about to be built." The editor of the *Harrison Flag* visited Jefferson in March and reports that "Several large brick buildings are going up." One of these structures was Freeman's Hall, which is shown on Graham's 1869 *Plan of the City of Jefferson, Texas* as occupying the west half of Lot 3 in Block 6 between Dallas and Austin and

Structural Features

running along the alley between Vale and Market. A two-story brick structure is shown in the appropriate place in Brosius. In connection with this structure, Williamson Freeman as agent for his son-in-law John Hobdy purchased one-half of a brick wall on June 8, 1860, and Hobdy reached a construction agreement with Ephraim Terry sometime prior to August 7.

Loughery mentioned the erection of a town hall in Jefferson in the July 7, 1860, *Texas Republican*, indicating that the grand opening had been scheduled for the Fourth with a ball. Loughery was quoting from the *Jefferson Gazette*, which said that the building was being fitted up by J. G. Richmond and that it would rank among the finest in the state. The first mention of the completed building was in the November 29, 1860, *Texas Republican*, which announced a supper, dinner, and fair that would be held in the hall on January 25, 1861, to raise money for building a Baptist Meeting House, with music provided by the Jefferson Brass Band. Loughery described the building in February 1861, indicating that it was a public building and served as the new Marion County courthouse:

> Our neighboring town of Jefferson has improved very much notwithstanding the short crops and hard times. We were agreeably surprised at the number and character of the new buildings. Among them, we noticed a house recently built by Mr. W. M. Freeman, which is forty by one hundred and twenty feet, and surmounted with a belfry or dome, in which the proprietor expects to place a town clock. The upper rooms are devoted to county and law offices. On the second floor there is a large room forty by seventy feet, which is used as a Court room, and in which the recent fairs were held. "Freeman's Hall," as it is called, is emphatically a great house, and we wish we had such a public building in Marshall. We noticed besides, one or two immense warehouses, which have been recently erected.

The brick for the erection of these buildings was produced by local yards. Much of the work would have been done by Ephraim Terry, a

49-year-old brick mason born in Massachusetts, and James Cotten, a 27-year-old brick mason born in Scotland, both of whom are listed in the 1860 census as Jefferson residents.

Fires

It is well known that Jefferson experienced a number of devastating fires in the business district during the Reconstruction period. The destructiveness of these fires was directly related to the density of structures, the prevalence of frame structures, and the lack of a fire department. It was common to attribute these fires to incendiaries, a charge that was never substantiated by any evidence. There were no conflagrations in Jefferson prior to the Civil War. Building density was not sufficient to support the spread of a fire. Residential fires would not have been reported in newspapers external to Jefferson. Because the burning of individual warehouses and storehouses would have been reported, it can be presumed that this did not happen.

As the war approached, many fires were reported throughout Texas. Most of these reports appear to have been based on rumor in the context of widespread assumptions about the activities of abolitionist emissaries engaged in direct action or inciting slaves to acts of violence. Fires provided the primary proof that abolitionists were at work, and assumptions that abolitionists were at work provided the primary reason for the rapid spread of rumors about fires. Within this context, real fires were reported that might at other times not have been reported, further enhancing rumor.

Truth in these matters is difficult to discern, beginning with the question of whether a fire actually occurred. Many towns were reported destroyed in which nothing happened. This is known to be the case when local newspapers repudiated the reports of other newspapers. For example, the *Mt. Pleasant Union* published in Titus County found it necessary to contradict a report in the *Jefferson Herald* that Mt. Vernon had been burned and reports in other papers that Daingerfield had been burned and that there had been hangings. The mindset operative in these reports is exemplified by the *Union*'s statement that Titus County had been blessed with quiet and order during the reign of terror.

Reports of fires must be dealt with on an individual basis. There were four reports of fires in Jefferson and vicinity from December 1858 through May 1859 and one in 1860. All of these actually happened because they were initially reported with details by the Jefferson newspapers. The one in 1860 concerned a residence and is of no interest other than the fact that it was used as further confirmation of incendiary activity. The other four were peculiar, particularly within the limited timeframe in which they occurred.

In May 1859, the Texas Iron Works owned by Nash, Doyle & Company 18 miles west of Jefferson burned to the ground without insurance, but was immediately rebuilt. The fire was thought to be the work of an incendiary. Also in May, the Female Academy in Jefferson was entirely consumed with $2,500 in damages. The newspapers reported that there were no clues as to how the fire originated.

These two fires occurred within the parameters of two fires involving stables. In December 1858, George Prewitt's new livery stable at the corner of Jackson and Austin sustained $5,000 in damages from a fire, with the loss of one horse and feed. At the same time, Nesmith & Booth's stable was found to be on fire but was saved by quick action. In early June 1859, the Nesmith & Booth stable was entirely consumed by flames, with $10,000 to $15,000 in damages and no insurance. Among the losses were 29 horses, five buggies, wagons, harnesses, and feed. The Shreveport *South-Western* reported that this fire was thought to be the work of an incendiary. The burning of the Nesmith & Booth stable was characterized as one of the most destructive fires that ever occurred within the city limits, which indicates that nonresidential single-structure fires had been rare and that there had never been a fire involving more than one structure.

Loughery of the *Texas Republican* concluded that these fires indicated an attempt to produce a general conflagration in Jefferson, with similar attempts in Tyler and Quitman and actual burnings of miscellaneous towns and farm houses in the northern portion of the state. This conclusion does not appear to be warranted. However, the initial fire in the Nesmith & Booth stable at the same time as the Prewitt stable fire and the subsequent burning of the Nesmith & Booth stable were certainly unusual occurrences, particularly within the context of two other major fires, one within and the other outside the city limits.

To complicate matters, there was a professed abolitionist by the name of Fory Arnold who was arrested in Jefferson in early January 1860, determined to have been tampering with slaves, and given 24 hours to leave town. What was happening, whether incendiaries were involved, and what their motives might have been cannot be determined without a more extensive study of fire reports and abolitionist activities on the eve of the Civil War.

28. The Professions

Law

Americans have always been litigious because of the heavy emphasis on rights, property, and individualism. Attorneys always appeared along with merchants and doctors at the inception of towns because disputes over land titles were characteristic of the expanding frontier. Jefferson's attorneys provided debt collection, probate (estate), and land title services and represented their clients in civil and criminal matters in the state district courts and the federal district and state supreme courts at Tyler. Non-advocacy services such as debt collection constituted the bulk of legal business. Most of the civil cases concerned debts and land disputes. Arguments in criminal cases were often like the present, with appeals based on assertions of procedural errors. Law degrees were not required, and prospective attorneys learned the trade by working in law offices. Men succeeded in the profession on the basis of natural ability and intelligence. Almost all were involved in political affairs; some went on to become judges and political office holders; many participated in other lines of business, with newspaper editorship as one of the preferred occupations.

The firm of T. J. & J. H. Rogers, attorneys and counsellors at law, began advertising in the May 26, 1847, Clarksville *Northern Standard* (Fig. 28-1). This firm was composed of the brothers Thomas, who was located in Jefferson, and James, who was located in Daingerfield. The firm advertised that it practiced in the 5th and 8th judicial districts and

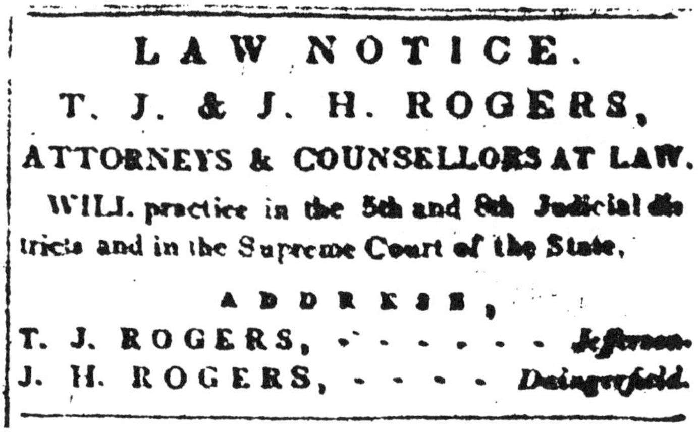

```
LAW NOTICE.
T. J. & J. H. ROGERS,
ATTORNEYS & COUNSELLORS AT LAW.
WILL practice in the 5th and 6th Judicial dis
tricts and in the Supreme Court of the State,
            ADDRESS,
T. J. ROGERS, - - - - - - Jefferson
J. H. ROGERS, - - - - - Daingerfield.
```

Fig. 28-1. First Attorney Advertisement. Source: May 26, 1847, *Northern Standard*

in the state supreme court. According to the *Handbook of Texas*, James settled at Daingerfield in 1843, was a brigadier general in the Texas militia, moved to Jefferson in 1851, was appointed special judge of the state supreme court in 1852, and married William Ochiltree's daughter Cozia in 1854. The November 7, 1857, *Eastern Texas Gazette* contains an advertisement for the sale of a farm previously occupied by Rogers two miles out of Jefferson on the Daingerfield Road. He is listed as a Jefferson attorney in the 1860 census.

There were at least four attorneys in Jefferson by 1848 who advertised in the *Spirit of the Age*. One name is indecipherable; another appears to be Martin Rogers, practicing in Cass, Bowie, Panola, Upshur, and Titus counties. The newly formed firm of Everett & Withers practiced in the U. S. district courts and in the state supreme court and was associated with R. W. Dixon in Titus County. John Everett was a Jefferson resident; Withers was apparently located elsewhere.

Edward Benners advertised in the October 12, 1850, *Texas Republican*. In May 1851, he joined with Samuel Moseley in Jefferson and M. J. Hall in Marshall to form the firm of Benners, Moseley & Hall, practicing in the several courts of the 6th judicial district and in the supreme and federal courts of the state at Tyler. Poindexter & Westmoreland advertised in September 1851 as practicing in the district courts and paying particular attention to collecting and probate business. Charles Westmoreland was a Jefferson resident; John Poindexter was a founding member of Christ Church in May 1851. Justice Ferris was a young lawyer who was editor of the *Jefferson Herald* in 1852.

Advertising in 1853 were Benners, Moseley & Hall, Poindexter & Westmoreland, Granville Lewis, H. L. Grinsted, and Summers & Clark. Granville Lewis was practicing in Jefferson by at least 1850 and left to go to Marshall in June 1853. Hiram Grinsted, with an office over the drugstore of Norris & Tackett, indicated that having permanently located at Jefferson, he "respectfully tenders his professional services to those having business in the 6th Judicial District, or in the Supreme or Federal Courts at Tyler. He hopes that a practice of several years in the courts of Texas well enable him to render entire satisfaction to those who may favor him with their patronage."

The firm of Summers & Clark was composed of John Summers in Clarksville and Frank Clark in Jefferson. They indicated "Particular attention paid to the Collection and Settlement of Claims from a distance. Letters requiring information in regard to Texas Lands, Titles, &c., when accompanied with a fee, will receive prompt attention." Summers moved to Jefferson in 1856, where he practiced independently under the name John A. Summers.

Bushrod Musgrove advertised in 1854 that his principal office was in Jefferson, that he would attend to the collection of all manner of debts west of Jefferson in north-eastern and western Texas, that he paid particular attention to the perfecting of land titles, and that he purchased and sold foreign accounts, with cash on hand sufficient to pay the purchase money on any old judgment.

The firm of Benners, Moseley & Hall dissolved by mutual consent in January 1857. Benners continued under the name E. G. Benners, practicing in Cass and neighboring counties and in the federal and supreme courts at Tyler. Moseley joined Seab (i.e., Seaborn) Wilkinson to form Moseley & Wilkinson, practicing in the 6th and 8th judicial districts and in the federal and supreme courts at Tyler. Hall continued to practice in Marshall and reestablished a partnership with Moseley in February 1858 under the name of Hall & Moseley.

Also in 1857, Michael Farley advertised that he had practiced law in Jefferson during the past few years and that he was located over Prewitt's store; Daniel McKay advertised that he practiced in the 6th judicial district; and Robert Ward advertised that he practiced in the 6th and 8th judicial districts and in the federal and supreme courts at Tyler. In 1858, Theodore Cameron, who had received his training in Clarksville, advertised that he practiced in the 6th and 8th judicial districts and in the federal and supreme courts at Tyler.

Seven persons were listed as lawyers in Precinct 1 in the 1850 Cass County census: R. J. Watson (aged 24 years); Justice Ferris (27); John Everett (45); James Maddox (23); John Eppinger (25); Martin Rogers (47); and Granville Lewis (45). Although Precinct 1 was considerably larger than Jefferson, it is apparent that most, if not all, of these persons practiced in Jefferson. Eppinger was killed in a hunting accident in November 1850, and a tribute of respect was prepared by John Everett, Edward Benners, Martin Rogers, B. F. Dennard, and Charles Westmoreland.

Twelve persons are listed as attorneys in Jefferson in the 1860 Marion County census: John Moseley (26); Seab Wilkinson (24); Theodore Cameron (24); Daniel McKay (36); Edward Benners (47); John Winslow (48); John Penman (40); Watts Cameron (26); Orville Yerger (36); Hinche Mabry (30); William Todd (50); George Todd (21); and James Rogers (45).

Medicine

Nothing was known about the causes of diseases before the Civil War, and they could not even be classified. As a consequence, medical practice attacked symptoms on the basis of the ancient theory that disease was the product of imbalances among bodily humors. Balance could be reachieved only by shocking the system. For mainstream physicians, medical procedures were largely limited to bloodletting, purgatives (laxatives), emitics (vomiting), and blistering (plastering to raise blisters that were punctured to release infectious agents). Purgatives and emitics involved large doses of dangerous chemicals such as calomel (mercury). Persons who used physicians and the physicians themselves assumed that medical practices were efficacious only if violent physiological changes were produced, which often resulted in death or debilitation.

The major reactions to mainstream practices were the Thomsonian movement, which relied heavily on botanics (folk medicine), and the homeopathic movement. Botanics were largely ineffective, but had the advantage of doing little harm. Homeopathy was a theory of how symptoms should be treated. Mainstream practices used drugs to produce reactions that were antithetical to the disease symptoms, which was called allopathy. Homeopathy asserted that "like cures like" and that drugs that caused particular symptoms to appear in healthy bodies should be applied to similar disease symptoms. It was equally invalid, but less harmful because it recommended small doses.

This was a period in which medical apprenticeship was giving way to medical schooling, through which an M.D. could be obtained. However, given the lack of knowledge, the schools had little to offer, education was brief and intermittent, and examinations were perfunctory. The only bright spots in medicine were the discovery of vaccination for smallpox, the use of cinchona bark (the source of quinine) in the treatment (but not the cure) of malaria, and surgery, which was largely devoted to bone setting and amputation without anesthesia that saved many lives. Many people did not use doctors and most did not use them often, but rather relied on botanics and patent medicines, which were wildly popular. Many patent medicines were alcohol- and opium-based.

Jefferson had a sizable number of doctors because it was an urban center with significant population and a large flow-through of businessmen, immigrants, ox-wagon drivers, and steamboatmen. Most of Jefferson's doctors were general practitioners operating alone or with a partner, but there was some specialization in dentistry. Many doctors operated drugstores, where they probably made most of their money. Two practiced the water cure, which involved such things as steam baths and wet sheets. Doctors competed with each other for clients and had difficulty in collecting bills.

Ithael Eason and Job Baker were apparently Jefferson's first doctors, because an 1876 article on Jefferson's history states that they settled in Jefferson prior to 1848 and that both were still in the town in

1876. Baker and Eason both advertised in the December 16, 1848, *Spirit of the Age* as having medical degrees and as offering medical services to the people of Jefferson and vicinity. Baker participated in the formation of the Steam Mill Company in 1845 and was apparently located in Francis Baker's establishment. Eason advertised that he was a physician, surgeon, and accoucheur (i.e., an obstetrician) and that he could always be found at his drugstore, which was adjacent to the printing office. He offered drugs and medicines, including patent and botanic, for cash or on time to select customers, indicating that the staple items were warranted as represented and that the patent medicines spoke for themselves.

Samuel Garey was the first person to appear with a "Dr." before his name in the extant texts, issuing an advertisement dated March 6, 1847, that he had acquired the drugs and medicines that had been previously stocked by Alexander & Chrisman. Although Garey did not advertise as a physician or surgeon in December 1848, he apparently had a medical degree because he is listed in the 1850 census as a 41-year-old physician. Garey advertised in October 1850 that he had practiced the allopathic system for the past 19 years, that he had recently discovered the superiority of hydropathy, that he was setting up special facilities for application of the water cure, and that he would continue allopathic services to patients who desired them (Fig. 28-2).

Dr. A. G. Brent advertised in March 1850 that he was a graduate of the University of Glasgow in Scotland, that he had been a practicing physician for 20 years, that he offered his services to the citizens of Cass County and vicinity, and that his office was located opposite the Soda Lake Hotel.

Listed as physicians in Precinct 1 in the 1850 Cass County census are: Thomas Pugh (aged 27 years); Samuel Garey (41); Nelson Trawick (40); George Echoles (48); James Durham (40); Robert Rogers (30); and Ithael Eason (33). Of these, only Echoles does not appear to have been a Jefferson resident. Trawick was from Marshall and was practicing in Shreveport by December 1853. The census designation does not necessarily mean that all of these men were practicing physicians. Rogers was the operator of the Star Hotel and did not advertise medical services. Pugh operated a drugstore and referred to himself in a May

Jefferson Water-Cure Establishment.

DR. SAMUEL GAREY would respectfully inform the citizens of Eastern Texas that he is now fitting up his buildings in this place for the reception of patients who are desirous of testing the practical application of the Water Cure.

Having practiced nineteen years under the Allopathic system, and for the last two years under the Water Cure, and having become fully convinced of the superiority of the latter over all other known practice, he flatters himself that he will be able to give general satisfaction to all those who are laboring under chronic, nervous, or acute diseases, of whatever type.

The wonderful cures effected by Hydropathy in the various countries of Europe, and in the Northern States, has established the fact that this practice is now no longer an experiment; and that nearly all the diseases incident to humanity can be treated more certainly, speedily, and effectually by this, than by any other known practice.

Many diseases pronounced incurable by medicines, or which have baffled the skill of the most eminent practitioners of other systems, have yielded, as if by magic, to the all-healing powers of the Water Cure.

Females laboring under complicated diseases peculiar to their sex, and who have failed to find relief from medicines, will find the Water Cure an invariably safe and efficacious remedy.

Those wishing information with a view to try the Water Cure at this establishment, or in reference to following a course of treatment at home, will meet with prompt attention by addressing (postage paid)

DR. SAMUEL GAREY,
Jefferson, Cass county, Texas.

N. B.—Dr. Garey will continue to practice in Jefferson and vicinity, as heretofore, under either system, as the patient may desire.

October 12, 1850.　　　　　　　　n18 y.

Fig. 28-2. Water Cure Advertisement. Source: October 12, 1850, *Texas Republican*

1853 advertisement as a druggist and apothecary. Also listed in the census is the 26-year-old druggist Isaac Eason, who was a Jefferson resident, and the 30-year-old dentist George Slaughter, who appears to have been a resident of Paradise in 1850 but was definitely a resident of Jefferson in 1851.

Dr. T. L. H. Cross advertised in March 1851 that he offered his services to the citizens of Jefferson and vicinity, that his office was nearly opposite the Jefferson Hotel, and that he could be found at the hotel at night. In printing the advertisement, Loughery noted that "Dr. C. is a well educated physician, and has had the best opportunity from his practice in the hospitals of New Orleans, of making himself familiar with the treatment of all diseases incident to a southern climate." In July 1851, Cross advertised as a physician, surgeon, and accoucheur and that his office was located in the Figures Building. By May 1853, Cross had relocated to Titus County near White Oak Bayou; and by May 1854, he was located permanently in Daingerfield. In connection with the latter move, Loughery noted that "Dr. C. is an excellent physician; a gentleman possessing a fine education, and one who has enjoyed superior advantages in acquiring a knowledge of his profession."

In January 1852, Dr. Samuel Norris moved the drugstore of Norris & Tackett from Marshall to Jefferson. There is nothing to indicate that Norris engaged in medical activities other than as a druggist. The drugstore was located on Marshall Street, and the stock was acquired by Elliott & Frith in early 1853. Drs. Frith and Robinson are mentioned as operating a drugstore at Eason's old location in October 1851.

Dr. E. P. M. Johnson, who apparently was a practicing physician in Jefferson for a number of years, moved to Marshall in August 1853, with the following comment in the *Jefferson Herald*:

> We regret very much the removal of Dr. E. P. M. Johnson from our town. He was one of our best and most esteemed citizens. His eminent success as a physician, has won for him in Jefferson, the most implicit confidence, of all who have tested his skill. He has left a very extensive practice here to settle in Marshall, where he hopes to have better health. We hope he may,

for there is no man better calculated to do good, either as a physician or a private citizen, than the Doctor. We recommend him to the citizens of Harrison county, and hope he may meet with that success he so justly deserves.

Four doctors advertised in the May 14, 1853, *Jefferson Herald*. Job and Francis Baker were in partnership in general medicine, with Job located in Paradise and Francis located in Jefferson. An M.D. does not appear after Francis' name. Dr. Glover advertised that he was a physician with an office on Lake Street. Drs. Johnson & Stephenson offered their professional services to the citizens of Jefferson and surrounding community, with an office in Dr. Pugh's drugstore. Dr. W. D. Stephenson died of pneumonia in January 1855. Dr. Thomas McAllenny advertised as a surgeon and physician in January 1854. McAllenny was also involved in a saw mill and contemplated establishing a hospital in Jefferson in March 1856. The May 12, 1855, *Texas Republican* reports that Drs. McKewen and McDonald, both of whom were dentists, moved from Marshall to Jefferson.

In the March 14, 1857, *Eastern Texas Gazette,* Dr. H. J. Witherspoon advertised as a physician and surgeon, located on Marshall Street opposite Frazor & Company and offering his services to the citizens of Jefferson and vicinity. Dr. R. W. Walker advertised in the same issue that he was still in Jefferson, that he was thankful for the patronage that had been afforded him in the past five years, and that he preferred day calls. Walker also advertised as a wholesale and retail dealer in staple and fancy drugs on Marshall Street one door above Frazor & Company. Walker also advertised in the October 15, 1858, *Texas Republican* as an Eclectic Physician offering the following services:

> THE CITIZENS OF JEFFERSON and surrounding country are respectfully informed that Dr. A. M. Walker has located in that place, where he will practice upon the HYDRO-ECLECTIC PRINCIPLE, using principally the Botanic or Vegetable medicines in the treatment of Acute Diseases, and Nature's Great Curative Agent, WATER, in Chronic Diseases; particularly

in Rheumatism, Nervous Affections, Spinal Diseases, Dyspepsia, Lung Diseases, Scrofula, Female Diseases, and indeed almost every form of disease. Water properly administered is an infallible remedy for Chronic Diarrhoea. Particular attention given to Ulcers on the Leg and Varicose Veins, WITHOUT CONFINEMENT. Also, to Cancerous Affections. He can be found at the City Hotel, Jefferson, at all times, when not professionally absent.

Following this statement are a number of testimonies, including cures for inflammation of the eyes, indigestion and dyspepsia, insanity, rheumatism, and cancer.

Dr. L. J. Graham advertised in the March 14, 1857, *Eastern Texas Gazette* as a practicing physician with his office at his drugstore on Marshall Street and as a wholesale and retail dealer in drugs, medicines, paints, oils, dye stuffs, books, stationery, etc. Some of the drugs offered were quinine, English calomel, blue mass, sulph morphine, rhubarb, aloes soc, gum camphor, sulphur, epsom salts, carb soda, soda powders, and Seidlitz powders. Also offered were all the popular patent medicines, including Jayne's Family Medicines, Bull's, Townsend's & Sand's Sarsparillas, Moffatt's Pills and Bitters, McLane's Pills and Vermifuge, Ayre's Cherry Pectoral, Wistar's Balsam, London & Co.'s Family Medicines, and Comstock & Company's Medicines. Dr. Anthony Owens is mentioned in September 1857 in connection with the death of his wife. Dr. Anselm Prewitt, Jr., advertised in the November 7, 1857, *Eastern Texas Gazette* as having returned from New Orleans with a fresh supply of drugs, medicines, books, and stationery.

Listed as doctors in Jefferson in the 1860 census are E. J. Northam (26); B. A. Bobo (25); Andrew Ewing (29); Ithael Eason (40); Hamilton Witherspoon (30); J. C. Cooper (28); C. Bullitt (38); and W. J. C. Rogers (42). Also listed is the dentist M. J. Odell (25) and the druggists James Campbell (53), E. W. Taylor (20), James Linn (38), B. R. Larn (23), and Joseph Preston (25).

29. Politics

Parties

The Democratic party was the dominant political party in Jefferson, as it was throughout Texas. The only other parties to exercise an influence on Texas politics were the Whig party, the American (or Know-Nothing) party, and the Constitutional Union (or Opposition) party. These were short-lived parties whose membership was constituted primarily by their predecessors. Personalities such as Sam Houston were also independent forces in Texas politics. Before 1848, elections in Texas were conducted without organized parties. Party structure did not become an important element in politics until 1855, when the Democratic convention was heavily attended because of an emerging threat by the Whigs.

The Whigs became established in Texas in 1848. Their national candidates, Zachary Taylor and Millard Fillmore, received strong support in northeast Texas and along the coast. Two of the most prominent Whigs were William Ochiltree, who was closely associated with Jefferson, and Benjamin Epperson, who moved to Jefferson after the Civil War. Ochiltree ran unsuccessfully for the U.S. Congress from the eastern district in 1851. As a national party, the Whigs became divided over issues connected with slavery. Ochiltree drew a substantial number of votes for governor of Texas in 1853, but the party was essentially dead in Texas by 1855.

The American party was the political manifestation of the anti-foreign, anti-Catholic secret society known as the Know-Nothing movement, which reached Texas in the mid-1850s. The party drew much of its membership from former Whigs and became strong in the western part of the eastern district, which elected the Clarksville attorney Lemuel Evans to the U.S. Congress in 1855, defeating the Democratic Jeffersonian Matt Ward. Evans and Benjamin Epperson attended the party's national convention in Philadelphia in 1856. The national party split over issues connected with slavery by 1857, with many former members supporting Houston's unsuccessful bid for governor during that year.

The Constitutional Union party, which included many former Whigs and Know-Nothings, emerged in Texas in 1859 and held its organizational meeting in Marshall. It successfully ran Houston for governor in 1859. In 1860, Evans and Epperson were delegates to the national convention in Baltimore and tried to get Houston nominated for the presidency, but the party nomination went to John Bell.

The Democratic party, which stood for the smallest possible federal government consistent with national security, was founded by Thomas Jefferson and was the dominant party nationally from 1800 until 1860, losing only to the Whig candidates William Harrison (over Martin Van Buren) in 1840 and Zachary Taylor (over Lewis Cass) in 1848. The party had northern and southern wings, which split over issues connected with slavery in 1860, with the northern wing supporting Stephen Douglas and the southern wing supporting John Breckinridge. The other two candidates in the 1860 election were the Republican Abraham Lincoln and the Constitutional Unionist John Bell. Breckinridge carried Texas by a heavy margin, and Lincoln was elected with less than half of the popular vote.

The Whigs and their successors should not be thought of as opposition parties to the Democrats. All parties in Texas were southern partisans, and Lincoln, who was not a radical, was not even on the ballot in 1860. Everyone venerated the Constitution and cherished the Union, and there was widespread agreement that the movement of the South toward secession was the unfortunate consequence of abolitionism. As a consequence, the issues that divided the parties in Texas were of far less importance than the sectional issues that were leading the national parties and the nation to an impasse; and, in spite of the dominance of the Democratic party, the other parties were able to have newspaper representation, to secure votes, and to occasionally win elections.

Context

Political activities related to state and national elections were important community activities during antebellum times and included meetings, speeches, debates, parades, singing, flag raisings, parades, balls, dances, and, in Texas, the mandatory barbecues and fish fries. Candidates were expected to confront each other in public at the community level, displaying their oratorical and analytical skills and wit, revealing their personal qualities, sharpening the issues, and fueling the competitive sentiments that are largely devoted to sports today. Speeches were often given outdoors, where it was cooler and a larger crowd could be accommodated, and were excessively long by today's standards, though filled with jokes and asides. Political festivals often lasted all day and well into the night.

Jefferson provided a setting for political activities because it was one of the largest and most important towns in Texas. When Jefferson was the county seat it was also the place at which the district court met. Attorneys, who were always politically active (Fig. 29-1), were drawn from throughout the region and provided opportunities for debate and for candidates to present their views. Newspapers were overtly political, the mercantile class had a sophisticated understanding of the issues, and citizens were more directly involved in politics than they are today.

It is not surprising that the first newspaper account of a trip to Jefferson, which was provided by Charles DeMorse of the *Northern Standard* in June 1847, was largely concerned with political reportage. DeMorse arrived on Monday the sixth, which was the first day of the district court, and found a much larger number of persons than he had expected. The place was "bubbling with political movement," with "a vast deal of political maneuvering going on." A resolution had been passed the previous week requesting the citizens of Red River, Titus, Bowie, and Harrison to meet with Cass and nominate a candidate

> **District Attorney.**
>
> ☞ SAMUEL F. MOSELEY, Esq., of Cass county, is a candidate for District Attorney, for the Sixth Judicial District, at the ensuing election.
>
> In due time, I will publish an address to the people of the District, setting forth *my opinions* of the *moral, personal,* and *legal qualifications,* that should characterize that officer; and the duties connected therewith.
>
> As soon as my health will permit, I will take pleasure in visiting the people, addressing them face to face, and making my views on this subject more fully known, as I deem that office to be second to none in the State, to sustain and vindicate the laws of the land, and in protecting the rights of her citizens. I wish—yea, I demand, at least for myself, that these things be fully discussed by the press and the people, and in so doing, that you " nothing extenuate nor aught set down in malice." Such is the ordeal I am of opinion all public officers *should pass through* before they are permitted to assume the powers thereby delegated, and enjoy the honors and profits arising therefrom. When the merits and qualifications of the candidates shall have undergone this test, then the people *need* have *no fears* that the office wlil not be filled by *one of merit.*
>
> SAMUEL F. MOSELEY.
> Jefferson, Texas, Oct. 21, 1851.   n27 tf

Fig. 29-1. Sam Moseley Statement. Source: January 10, 1852, *Star State Patriot*

for governor. Isaac Van Zandt was in town to put forth his claims for the governorship, and his supporters were there in large force. David Kaufman was also in town to provide an account of his activities as a state representative. Both made speeches.

On the next day, a public meeting was held at the courthouse to nominate a candidate for governor. Martin Rogers was elected chairman and Nat Burford secretary for this undertaking. John Chambers, J. W. Dabbs, and James Rogers of Titus County; Byrd Gray of Bowie; and John Elliott, Sam Moseley, and M. S. Mullens of Cass were appointed to consider the nominees and duly reported that Van Zandt was the best person for the job. Thomas Rogers, William Perry, and Charles Dunn were appointed to inform the nominee and convey his response. The meeting ended with a speech by Sam Moseley describing Van Zandt's character and abilities. At night, another meeting was held at the courthouse at which Berry Durham, who was about to announce his candidacy for state senator, spoke.

Democrats

The dominance of the Democratic party in Jefferson and the dimensions of politics as a community function are best illustrated through the planning and execution of a Democratic festival and barbecue at Jefferson in November 1856 in connection with the national election. A meeting was held at the beginning of the month to form a Buchanan and Breckinridge Club that would conduct a grand celebration toward the end of the month. James Rogers was elected president of the club; Daniel Alley, James Scott, Edward Benners, and Robert Ward were elected vice presidents; Henry Schluter, Ward Taylor, Jr., and Hiram Tomlin were elected secretaries; and John Cocke was elected treasurer. Committees were appointed for correspondence, platforms and resolutions, finances, arrangements, pole and flag raising, invitations, and arrangements for speakers.

Those participating in the meeting included most of the notables in and near Jefferson: Gus Foscue, John Sabine, William Mayberry, Robert Nesmith, Anthony Owens, Robert Cocke, Thomas Frazor, William Torrans, Gus Bowers, Richard Crump, Thomas Owens, Francis Clark, Charles Spilker, Thomas Goyne, James DeLahunty, M. C. Bradford, Nicholas Pusha, John Kolster, John Ribold, L. Sturm, Daniel McKay, W. Esteiker, W. Caberness, Frederick Kolster, N. F. Davis, Thomas Donohon, E. C. Cructher, Riley Chase, S. C. Neuman, James W. Alley (Daniel's son), W. Mason, Z. L. Durrum, B. Nussbaum, Abraham Kohn, William Clark, S. Rogers, W. Adkinson, W. B. Fonche, John Vines, William Johnson, James Elliott, L. T. Grey, J. T. Harrison, W. B. Frazior, O. C. Frazor, A. P. Mosby, John Harrison, C. F. Mosby, Marion Taylor, D. G. Frazor, J. M. Taylor, John Ward, E. S. Riley, W. C. Mason, J. Irwin, M. T. Slaughter, J. F. Morgan, Walter Swanson, Anselm Prewitt, Jr., W. Hongus, James

O'Neil, Thomas C. Alley (Daniel's son), J. J. Hatcher, George Bertrand, S. T. Harris, John Stewart, Samuel McFarland, S. J. Grey, Daniel Alley, Jr. (Daniel's son), William Cocke, Moses Steinlein, Benjamin Terry, Sam Moseley, J. B. McReynolds, Martin Rogers, Frederick Merzbacher, J. J. Mason, Jeptha Crawford, J. H. Boon, John O'Hara, Joseph Preston, Benjamin Foscue, J. C. Durham, John Terrell, John Aiken, Frank Mar, J. B. Frazor, J. W. Kemp, B. W. Patillo, D. C. Hughes, Samuel Nimmo, James Scott, W. D. F. Moore, C. Spilker, B. E. Adams, John Sentell, T. A. Clark, and C. T. Moseley.

Robert Loughery attended the celebration that followed ten days later as a representative from Harrison County and found it to be one of the most imposing and gratifying political demonstrations that he had witnessed:

> Between 10 and 11 o'clock, the Harrison delegation under the command of J. M. McREYNOLDS, as Marshal, arrived. They were welcomed by a troup on horse back, from Cass, over which Col. R. P. CRUMP, J. C. SCOTT, and H. TOMLIN, Esq., as Marshalls of the day, presided. They were formed into line, the horsemen in front, and the carriages in the rear, and headed by the Marshall brass band. With triumphal music the procession proceeded from the bridge into the town, where they were greeted with cheer after cheer from the animated and enthusiastic assemblage that thronged the streets. We do not know how many were present, but we may say this, that we have never before seen as many people in Jefferson on any public occasion.
>
> The splendid car in which the musicians were placed, was drawn by six beautiful iron greys, furnished and driven by R. W. Nesmith. A more beautiful team we have not seen in a long time. As they moved gracefully along, their feet seemed to keep time to the music of the band.
>
> The horses and carriages were disposed of, and the democrats *en masse* were formed into line on foot, and proceeded to the Democratic pole, which stands upon an

eminence overlooking the town. This pole is 151 feet in height, (48 feet higher than the K. N. pole,) and from its topmost height floats the gorgeous banner of the Union. There it stood floating triumphantly in the breeze, every star glittering in the glorious autumnal sun.

The procession having reached the ground, the delegations from Harrison and Cass were drawn up in lines facing each other, with ladies and gentlemen at each extremity, thus forming a complete square.

After a patriotic air from the band, GEN. JAMES H. ROGERS, as the organ of the democracy of Cass, welcomed the delegates from Harrison in an eloquent and soul-inspiring speech of some twenty minutes, at the conclusion of which the air resounded with enthusiastic cheers, when the band broke forth in a strain of patriotic music.

Col. C. M. ADAMS was then introduced to the audience, by Col. W. R. D. WARD, President of the Harrison Democratic Club, who responded, in behalf of the Democracy of Harrison in a felicitous and truly eloquent speech.

The procession then formed into marching order and proceeded to the place of speaking, which was a large warehouse open on one side that was filled to overflowing. Gen. Rogers announced that the Democrats welcomed discussion and invited Benjamin Epperson, or whoever the Know-Nothing or American party had chosen to represent its views, to come to the speaking stand, which Epperson did. M. D. Graham of Rusk County spoke for two hours and fifteen minutes in favor of the Democratic position. The meeting adjourned to another warehouse for barbecue, which was served on three tables two hundred feet long. After dinner, the party moved back to the place of speaking, where they heard from Epperson. After supper, Epperson spoke for an hour and was replied to by Pendleton Murrah of Marshall in a speech of the same length. Both parties concluded with speeches of thirty minutes each, and a ball was held that night.

Elections

In 1847, Cass County provided a majority for George Wood as governor, who was elected. In 1849, the vote for governor in the Jefferson precinct was 31 for John Mills, 26 for Wood, and 20 for Peter Bell, who was elected. In 1851, Cass County provided a majority for Bell as governor, a large majority for Matt Ward as lieutenant governor, and a large majority for Richardson Scurry over William Ochiltree for the U.S. House of Representatives. Bell and Scurry were elected along with Richard Crump as a state representative. In 1853, the Jefferson precinct provided a slight margin for the Democrat Elisha Pease (111) over the Whig William Ochiltree (107) as governor, but Ochiltree had a large majority over Pease in Cass County. Pease was elected. In 1855, the Jefferson precinct provided large majorities for Pease as governor, Hardin Runnels as lieutenant governor, the Democrat Matt Ward over the Know-Nothing Lemuel Evans for the U.S. House of Representatives, and the Democrat Marion Taylor over the Know-Nothing Hinche Mabry as state senator. The vote in Cass County was similar, with the exception of a near-tie between Ward and Evans. Pease, Runnels, Evans, and Taylor were elected. In 1857, Cass County provided large majorities for Runnels (555) over Sam Houston (355) as governor, the Democrat John Reagan over Evans for the U.S. House of Representatives, J. B. Henderson over Hinche Mabry as state representative, and Robert Ward over George Ury as floater (a person who represents an irregular constituency). A listing of representatives-elect shows J. B. Henderson as representative from Cass and Titus counties and Ward as representative from Cass County. In 1859, Cass County provided a smaller majority for Runnels (626) over Houston (528) as governor. The Jefferson precinct provided a slight margin for Runnels (210) over Houston (204) and modest majorities for Reagan (182) over Ochiltree (153) for the U.S. House of Representatives and Mabry (177) over Ward Taylor, Jr. (152) for state representative. Houston, Reagan, and Mabry were elected.

Matt Ward

Matthias Ward , who was always called Matt, was the only Jeffersonian prior to the Civil War to achieve a national political office. He was born in Georgia in 1805, came to Texas in 1836, was a merchant in Clarksville, and established the mercantile firm of Ury & Ward with Amos Ury in Jefferson in 1847, which lasted until 1852 when it moved to Clarksville. Ward was back in Jefferson in 1853, as indicated by a reference in an advertisement. He served in the seventh and eighth congresses of the Republic of Texas, was elected to the Texas Senate in 1849 (representing Cass, Bowie, and Titus), ran unsuccessfully for lieutenant governor in 1851, was a delegate to the national Democratic conventions in Baltimore in 1852 and Cincinnati in 1856, was president of the state Democratic convention in 1856, and ran unsuccessfully for the U.S. House of Representatives in 1855. The 1855 race with Lemuel Evans was close, with contested results, and the decision was made by the governor for Evans. U.S. senators were chosen by state legislatures rather than by popular vote at that time. Ward was appointed by Governor Runnels to replace the deceased James Pinckney Henderson as U.S. senator in September 1858, a position that he filled until December 1859. He sought his party's nomination for the Senate in 1859, but it was given to Louis Wigfall. Ward died in North Carolina 1861.

Ward's politics are best expressed in a circular covering national and state issues that he published in various newspapers for the election of 1855:

> I am what I have ever been, a Democrat, am in favor of a strict adherence to the Constitution claiming for every State in the Union, all the rights, privileges, and benefits guaranteed by that instrument.
>
> I was a member of the National Democratic Convention held at Baltimore in 1852, and voted for the platform then adopted as the constitution of the party. I was much pleased with its provisions and would not wish to change or remove a single plank from it.
>
> I am opposed to a System of Internal Improvement by the General Government where equal benefits cannot be extended to the whole people.
>
> I am opposed to a protective tariff, and in favor of raising no more revenue from the people by taxation or otherwise, than is actually necessary for the sup-

port of an economical Government, for the fact is too well established to be misunderstood, that an excess of money in a Treasury will create an anxiety in the mind of many for its disbursement, and oftener than otherwise it is appropriated to subserve party or sectional purposes.

I am in favor of the Nebraska-Kansas Bill as passed by Congress, which gives to the South additional strength and protection.

Ward was widely respected for his personal qualities, which limited his capacity for election. This is particularly evident in an 1852 *Jefferson Herald* endorsement of Ward for governor after his unsuccessful bid for lieutenant governor in 1851. The endorsement was made by the editor Justice Ferris and the proprietors Samuel Moseley and W. P. Watson, who were not in full agreement with Ward's politics:

We take pleasure in suggesting the name of Col. Matt Ward, a citizen of this place, as a suitable democratic candidate for Governor. The Colonel is an old Texan, was a member of Congress in the days of the Republic, and more recently a member of the Senate in our State Legislature. He has proved himself equal to every station he has filled; and wherever known he has left a favorable and enduring impress. He would make a Governor of which the State might be justly proud.

Col. Ward is no office-seeker. When he consented last year to become a candidate for Lieutenant Governor, it was only upon the urgent solicitations of his friends to allow them to use his name, and with the express understanding that his business would not justify him to canvass any portion of the State. Though remaining at home, he received a complimentary vote, and would undoubtedly have succeeded could he have mixed with the people. Should he become the democratic candidate for Governor, we believe he would accept the nomination and canvass the State thoroughly, to his and the party's triumphant success.

Robert Loughery of the Marshall *Texas Republican*, who had, as he said, "little disposition to flatter men, either in public or private life," described Ward on his return to Jefferson from the Democratic convention in Austin in 1856 as "An accomplished gentleman; sincere in his intercourse with the world, and distinguished for those sterling qualities of head and heart, which merit regard, he will always maintain the confidence and esteem of those who admire integrity and disingenuousness in public men."

When Ward was appointed senator, Loughery described him as follows: "He is a man of sound sense and exalted patriotism. A purer and more disinterested public man does not exist within the confines of the republic. He will make no long-winded speeches, or mingle to any great extent in the conflicts of debate. But we venture to say, that Texas has never had in the past, and is not likely to possess in the future, a representative at the Federal capital who will guard with greater faithfulness or fidelity her interests or her honor; or the South a firmer, more prudent, and devoted defender of her rights. The Senate of the United States, we feel assured, does not contain a more accomplished and amiable gentleman."

Finally, Loughery provided the following encomium at Ward's death: "The deceased was one of the purest public men the country has ever produced. He was a man of strict integrity, and of unbending devotion to principle; to which was united a warm, noble, genial disposition, that endeared him to all who came within the circle of his acquaintance. For upwards of twenty five years, his lot was cast in Texas, and thousands of hearts throughout the limits of the State will feel a pang of regret to hear of his death. We knew him intimately for upwards of thirteen years, and we are prepared to say, that we know of no man, public or private, whose death is more to be lamented."

The Robert Ward who was elected floater in 1857 was Matt's nephew and a Jefferson attorney. He began his political career in June 1855 at the age of 24 with a speech in Jefferson at Nichols & Hobdy's Auction Room and attended the state Democratic convention during that year. In 1857, Ward was a participant with the Jefferson attorney Michael Farley in the firm of Farley & Ward; and in 1858 and 1859, he was owner-editor of the *Jefferson Herald*.

Richard Crump

Richard Crump was born in 1816 in Virginia, came to Clarksville in March 1842, and participated in the abortive Santa Fe Expedition initiated by Sam Houston in connection with supposed Mexican violations of Republic of Texas territory. He participated in the war with Mexico in 1847 and was in Clarksville in January of that year to raise troops:

> SOLDIERS WANTED.—Mr. R. P. Crump, well known to many of our citizens, as a former resident of Clarksville, arrived in Town on Wednesday evening, from San Antonio. Mr. Crump is raising a company for service in Mexico. He has now about forty men enrolled. He wants only unmarried men, and is endeavoring to select a corps of the most effective and reliable sort.—Young gentlemen who wish a little glory mixed with hard fighting, have now an opportunity to put themselves in the way of it. We have no doubt that this will be a choice company. Mr. Crump's own reputation for cool and determined bravery, is of the best sort, and he is in every way a gentleman upon whose list any young man may place his name, with confidence that it is likely to gain credit, if there is any opportunity for it.

Crump began purchasing property in Jefferson in January 1845 and was definitely associated with the city in 1847, where he appears as agent for the *Northern Standard* and in the tax rolls as owner of one town lot. He appears in the 1848 tax rolls with $4,000 in merchandise and in the 1849 tax rolls with $1,800 in merchandise. The nature of this mercantile activity is unknown, but the small value of the stock suggests that he was in the liquor business. Whatever the nature of this business, it was not in Jefferson, but rather associated with his property near Black Cypress Bayou, as indicated by the 1850 tax rolls. The 1850 commissioners court minutes indicate that he lived near the

Black Cypress Road north of William Perry's field on a branch of Black Cypress Bayou. This location about two miles west of Jefferson is confirmed by the June 24, 1854, *Standard*, which contains an obituary for his brother William, who joined him at that place in 1847 after a distinguished public career.

Richard Crump became sheriff of Cass County in 1848 and is listed as such in the 1850 census. Crump was a Democrat. He was elected state representative in August 1851 and resigned, for reasons unknown, in December 1852. His replacement was Charles Westmoreland, a young Jefferson attorney who was vice president of the State and Southern Rights Association of Cass County formed to "aid in preserving the Constitution of the United States from violation, in protecting the rights of the people of the slave-holding States from oppression on the part of the General Government, with security and equality in the Union for the future." Westmoreland was editor of the *Jefferson Herald* until December 1851, leaving that position with the statement "I am done with politics."

Crump was a longtime member of the Missionary Baptist Church; part owner of the McFarland and Crump saw mill southeast of Jefferson in the early 1850s; part owner and captain of the *Grenada*, which he ran to Jefferson from March 1854 to May 1856; and local agent for the New Orleans liquor and tobacco dealers Thompson & Barnes in 1857. He operated a recreational saloon (bar, billiards, bowling alley, and shooting gallery) in Jefferson from 1859 to 1863; operated the Black & Crump tanyard with Harvey Black in 1860; was elected city alderman in 1860 but was not administered the oath of office (for reasons unknown); and conducted the 1860 Marion County census. The mortality component of the census records the death of his first wife Martha in June 1859 and the death of his infant son Richard in September 1859. Crump is listed in the 1860 census as a Jefferson grocer with $7,500 in real and personal estate, a wife, and three children. Grocer meant seller of liquor and in this case referred to his ownership of the recreational saloon, for which he acquired a license to sell liquor in quantities less than a quart in April 1860.

Crump became a Jefferson resident sometime between 1854 and 1860, with 1857 most likely, because he ceased operating the *Grenada* in 1856, was an agent for Thompson & Barnes in 1857, and is known to have been operating a store on Marshall by 1859. His bid to construct a public market house was accepted in 1861, but this project was not undertaken until after the war. He had a distinguished military career during the war, operated a furniture and grocery store on Dallas Street in 1866 that concentrated on bar stores, was incarcerated in the stockade during the infamous Reconstruction trials, became ill, was released, and was beginning an ice harvesting company when he died in October 1869. Crump is almost certainly buried in the Oakwood Cemetery in an unmarked grave near those of his wife and infant son.

Hinche Mabry

Hinche Mabry was born in Georgia in 1829 and does not appear in the 1850 Cass County census. He first appears in the newspaper record in August 1854 as custodian of election returns for the Jefferson box and is listed in the 1855 tax rolls as owner of three lots in Jefferson. He ran unsuccessfully for state senator in 1855 and state representative in 1857 before running successfully for state representative in 1859. He appears in the 1860 Jefferson census as an attorney with a wife and two children and real and personal estate valued at $17,000. He had a distinguished military career during the war, was elected district judge after the war, and built and operated the Haywood House in 1867. Although he moved from Jefferson in 1879, he is buried in the Oakwood Cemetery.

William Todd

William Todd was born in Virginia in 1808 and served in the Virginia legislature before moving to Texas. Todd began advertising in July 1843 in the *Northern Standard* as a Boston (Bowie County) attorney serving in the courts of the 7th judicial district and joined with Ebenezer Allen in December 1844 to form Allen & Todd, serving in the district courts and the Republic's supreme court. In March 1847, Todd associated with Burrell Smith in Clarksville, practicing in the 8th judicial district courts in Bowie, Titus, Hopkins, Grayson, Fannin, Lamar, and Red River and in the 5th district court in Cass. This advertisement continued to appear until September 1848, which may be taken as the approximate date for a move to Clarksville, where Todd's wife Eliza opened the Clarksville Female Institute in January 1849. Todd did not advertise as a Clarksville attorney and is known to have been involved in farming.

Todd was elected judge of the 8th judicial district in 1850, 1854, and 1858. His official duties brought him to many places in northeast Texas, including Marshall and Linden. Eliza died in late August or early September 1854. Todd moved to Jefferson in March 1857 and remarried in December of that year. The newspapers indicate that he was almost continuously ill (bleeding lungs, rheumatism, disease of the foot) from March 1858 on, which placed severe limitations on his ability to fulfill his duties. Todd is listed in the 1860 census as an attorney with a wife (Mary) and four children (all by his first marriage), including his 21-year-old son George, who was also an attorney. Todd served as the Marion County delegate to the secession convention in 1861. He retired from professional practice in 1862 because of ill health. William and Mary sold their house fronting Jefferson Avenue on Lots 8 and 9 in Block R of the Alley Addition to Bass Nichols in April 1864. Todd died in Jefferson in May 1864 at the age of 56 and is buried in the Oakwood Cemetery.

Loughery described Todd as "a good lawyer, and a man of talent and energy," "urbane and pleasant," and "as well calculated to adorn the festive board as to grace the bench" and reported that the lawyers who attended his court said that "while he is firm and able in the discharge of his duties, he is not unmindful of that courteous bearing which wins esteem." The January 11, 1852, *Texas Republican* contains an homage to Todd by 40 legal firms that stressed his "learning, patient attention, dignity, and good temper" and that the business of the court had been conducted "with the utmost regularity, decorum, and dispatch." Like most judges, Todd deprecated political issues in his contests for judgeships and based his claims solely on his merits and qualifications as a public officer.

DeMorse of the Clarksville *Standard* was to become critical of Todd when illness began to disrupt his official duties; but in March 1855 when Todd was at the height of his powers, DeMorse provided a commentary with quotes from the Marshall and Jefferson newspapers indicating Todd's popularity at home and abroad:

Judge Todd, of this District has been spending some days in Marshall and Jefferson.—From the papers below, we clip the following complimentary notices. It is pleasant to know that the choice of the people of this District, for their highest Judicial post, is so highly appreciated else where; and it would be superrogatory for us with our well known relations to the individual so endorsed, to add any testimonials of our appreciation. It will be sufficient for us to say, that throughout his District, the Judge, both in his official and personal capacity, is almost universally highly appreciated, and although elected by a large majority, after a warm canvass, is far more widely popular now than then.

"Hon. WM. S. TODD, of Red River Co., has been spending a week or two in Marshall. We were pleased to find him in the enjoyment of good health. As a polished gentleman—one of cultivated and refined intellect—and as a Jurist, he ranks among the first men of the State. His visits are ever welcome."—*Marshall Republican*.

"The Judge has been spending a few days in our city, but left on Sunday for his Court in Bowie.—We fully endorse the compliment paid Judge TODD, by the Republican. An intimate personal and professional acquaintance of long years' standing justifies us in the assertion that either as a lawyer and a private gentleman, William S. Todd has few equals and no superiors in the State."—*Jefferson Herald*.

William Ochiltree

William Ochiltree was born in North Carolina in 1811 and moved in 1839 to Nacogdoches, where he practiced law. During the days of the Republic, he was elected district judge and served as secretary of the treasury in 1844, adjutant general in 1845, and delegate to the Convention of 1845. After Texas entered the Union, he was elected state representative in 1855 while still a resident of Nacogdoches. By May 1849 he maintained a law office in Marshall with Louis Wigfall. His legal practice was geographically extensive, requiring attendance at various district courts and at the state supreme court in Tyler, which made him a frequent visitor at Jefferson, where he contemplated moving in September 1851. Two of his daughters were married at the family's residence in Nacogdoches in 1854. He moved permanently to Marshall at the death of his wife in August 1857, publishing an advertisement stating the move in the March 20, 1858, *Texas Republican*.

In December 1858, John Speake sold to John Ligon the south half of Block N of the Alley Addition (north side of Delta between Main and Bridge), referring to it as the Ochiltree place. Because Ochiltree never owned any property in Jefferson, this appears to have been a rental residence used by Ochiltree in his many trips to the area on legal business prior to his departure from Nacogdoches in late 1857.

Ochiltree advertised his house in Marshall for sale in November 1860 and is reported in the February 16, 1861, *Texas Republican* to have moved from Marshall. His family at that time was living a mile or two south of Jefferson in what was then a portion of Harrison County. This place was called Last Chance. Ochiltree was on his way to the secession convention in Austin and preparation for war. He was registered at the convention as a delegate from Harrison County, giving Jefferson as his place of residence, obviously because it was the nearest town. His son Tom became assistant editor of the *Star State Jeffersonian* in Jefferson in March 1861.

Ochiltree provided distinguished military and public service during the war and returned to Marshall in October 1865 to practice law, with an office opposite the Adkins House according to an advertisement in the *Texas Republican*. He was joined by a partner in December 1866, establishing the firm of Ochiltree & Shaw, with the advertisement in the *Harrison Flag* continuing until September 1867. Ochiltree died in December 1867 and is buried in the Oakwood Cemetery. His obituary appeared in the *Jefferson Times* and was republished in the January 4, 1868, *Texas Republican* with the comment that he died at his residence in Jefferson, suggesting that he had secured a home in Jefferson or that the family was still located at Last Chance:

> The name of the deceased is blended with the history of the State. For twenty-five years he has been a

prominent man in Texas—his early career commencing almost at the very dawn of the Republic. He was an able lawyer and a ready and powerful debater. The State, in his death, has lost one of its most gifted men. Society will mourn his death. Thousands throughout the State, who knew and esteemed him, will read the intelligence we have chronicled, with sadness. But his family, the charmed circle of which he was the sun and the center, mourn most deeply his demise. To them his loss is irreparable.

Charles DeMorse presented a portrait of Ochiltree in the June 25, 1859, *Standard* when Ochiltree was running (unsuccessfully) against John Reagan for the U.S. House. Although unflattering, it was not unjust because it described the course of politicians of Whig persuasion:

Hon. W. B. Ochiltree has announced himself as a candidate for Congress, in opposition to Judge Reagan. If our memory serves us right, this is the same Ochiltree who once before ran against a nominee of the Democratic Convention for the same office, and once sought the office of Governor in opposition to a Democratic aspirant. From the signs of the times it is apparent that he has less chance for succeeding than at any former time. His trumpeters having all expired, it remains for Ochiltree to blast for himself, and after the first Monday in August, the last blast of Ochiltree, the self-assumed trumpeter shall have been heard, and borne away upon the breeze, to return no more, and the recollection of the action only preserved as a memorial of an individual blowing himself out, without any real or artificial help. Once a violent Whig, next a Convention Democrat, and an independent Democrat, it only remains for an *apparent* popular breeze, to blow again in another direction before we have him in another character.

A more balanced perspective on his character and accomplishments is given by his colleagues in a tribute of respect in the August 21, 1868, *Texas Republican* that also mentions his residence in Jefferson:

> Judge Ochiltree, as a Statesman, was open, bold, and defiant in the expression of his views—never yielding principle for power or peace.
>
> As a Judge, he was firm, decided, and patient to hear the cause presented. However small the amount in controversy and however obscure the Attorneys of the parties, equal justice and an equal administration of the law were his rule of action.
>
> As an Attorney, his pleadings were accurate and presented the issues with clearness and perspicuity.
>
> As an advocate, he was original, clear, forcible, demonstrative, and eloquent.
>
> As a husband and parent, his kindness to his family was proverbial.

Houston at Jefferson

Senator Sam Houston ran as an independent for governor of Texas in 1857 against the Democratic candidate Hardin Runnels. For the campaign, Houston traveled throughout the then-settled portions of Texas in the buggy of his newly acquired friend Ed Sharp, giving 47 speeches over 67 days during late May through early August and camping out 58 nights. The weather was extremely hot, and the speeches were given to large crowds in the open. The speeches were basically the same everywhere, with modifications to suit the audience and the opportunities for joke and story telling. The speeches, as was common during this period, lasted from two to four hours. Houston was generally responded to by a Runnels supporter such as Louis Wigfall, who became a U. S. Senator in 1858.

Jefferson was on Houston's itinerary for Saturday, June 13, preceded by Marshall on the 12th and followed by Daingerfield on the 17th. Houston was well known throughout Texas but not a highly popular candidate, and Cass County, in which Jefferson was then located, was not Houston country. Houston was supported by Jefferson's *East-*

ern-Texas Gazette, but strongly opposed by the *Jefferson Herald*, which declared that "should Sam Houston be elected Governor of Texas, a shout of joy would go up from one end of the freesoil States to the other, and the day of his election be celebrated as the greatest victory ever achieved by the Black Republican party."

That Houston actually spoke at Jefferson on the appointed day is known from the June 20, 1857, Marshall *Texas Republican*: "General Houston spoke at Jefferson on Saturday. He was replied to by Col. Wigfall, in one of his happiest efforts. The Democracy of Cass are united and enthusiastic. Houston, we learn, lost ground there, as he has every where else he has gone." Houston probably camped out in the vicinity of Jefferson rather than staying at anyone's house. His speech was similar to that given in Marshall, a highly partisan account of which appears in the June 20, 1857, *Texas Republican*. Cass County voted 555 for Runnels and 355 for Houston with one box unreported, and Houston was soundly defeated in his bid for the governorship. Jeffersonians celebrated with a heavily attended Runnels Ball at the Alhambra Hall on September 24 that the governor-elect was unable to attend because his mother was ill.

Politicking

The techniques of politics have not changed very much. Two examples will suffice.

During the election of 1851, William Ochiltree was campaigning against Lemuel Evans. An anonymous article had appeared in a newspaper claiming that when Evans was participating in the framing of the Texas constitution, he attempted to deprive settlers of some of their rights to land. Ochiltree carried the article with him and read it from the stump during his encounters with Evans. The letter was doing a great deal of injury to Evans, who demanded of the newspaper editor the name of the person who had written the letter, only to be informed that it was Ochiltree.

When Runnels was running for governor in 1857, a rumor was circulated that he was a confirmed drunkard. A Jefferson preacher who knew Runnels was asked whether the rumor was true and replied that "he thought every body knew that." Testimonials to Runnels' sobriety were solicited from William Todd, Matt Ward, A. B. Bayless, Thomas Sedberry, John Cocke, Adam Haney, Joseph Preston, James Elliott, James W. Alley (Daniel's son), J. W. Aiken, Moses Steinlein, A. D. Taylor, Joseph Prewitt, L. J. Graham, and Hiram Tomlin and printed in the *Jefferson Herald*.

80. Fraternal Organizations

Voluntary organizations with social, political, cultural, religious, entertainment, and self-help purposes have always been a distinctive feature of American culture.

Independent Order of Odd Fellows

The Order of Oddfellows was a benevolent and self-help fraternal organization with lodges, initiatory rites, ceremonies, and grades of honor formed in England in the mid-1700s among persons interested in social unity during a period of sect and class formation. An offshoot, the Independent Order of Oddfellows, was formed in the early 1800s and introduced to the United States in 1819. The United States component severed the English association in 1842.

Ida Lodge No. 14 of the Independent Order of Odd Fellows advertised meetings every Monday night in the May 14, 1853, *Jefferson Herald*. The advertisement was signed by the secretary, Hiram Grinsted. In March 1853, Clinton Willard and George Tuttle mortgaged to a New Orleans firm various properties in Jefferson, including Lot 10 in Block 4 containing two storehouses, the upper stories of which were used as an Odd Fellows Hall and the printing offices of the *Jefferson Herald*. The organization was thus meeting in 1853 in the upper story of a storehouse on the lot between Dallas and Lake and running along the alley between Marshall and Jackson.

Fraternal Organizations

In January 1858, the New Orleans firm of Rawlins, Duncan & Company sold to the Ida Lodge No. 14 for $1,000 part of Lot 12 in Block 22 fronting 25 feet on Marshall and running back 50 feet along an alley, which had been purchased by them from Nelson Trawick. The price indicates the existence of a building, and this was the location of Frith & Robinson's drugstore in 1851. This was the permanent location for the Odd Fellows Hall. In July 1860, the Colt & Winans bookstore advertised a location on Marshall under the Odd Fellows Hall. The building was obviously two stories, the upper portion of which was occupied by the hall.

An Odd Fellows and Citizens ball was held at Jefferson in April 1853. Robert Loughery of the Marshall *Texas Republican* was unable to attend but reports that it was considered to be one of the gayest affairs of the season and that everything passed off in a manner calculated to inspire good feeling. Elizabeth Jackson of the Jefferson Hotel prepared the dinner and supper, which were represented as having been "unequalled by anything of the kind in Texas, either for variety, abundance, or the manner in which they were served."

Loughery was unable to attend another Odd Fellows celebration held in April 1856, but reports the departure of the Marshall contingent: "On Thursday morning quite a number of our citizens left for Jefferson to attend the Odd Fellows celebration. We noticed the elegant wagon containing the members of the Brass Band, and *some eight or ten others*, as it moved off drawn by six beautiful horses. We understand the days proceedings were to be embellished with a barbecue and an elegant ball."

These were obviously at least annual occasions. What this organization actually did is not reported in the newspapers. Ida Lodge No. 14, with John Smith as secretary, is mentioned in a February 1861 deed record.

Freemasons

Freemasonry is a secret society of ancient lineage, also with lodges, initiatory rites, ceremonies, and grades of honor. It entered the United States from England in the early 1700s with a strong non-sectarian religious emphasis and prohibition on political discussion.

Although the Jefferson Lodge, No. 38, of the Free and Accepted Masons begins to appear in the public records only in 1853, it probably went back to the origins of the town, because Masonry was prevalent throughout the region. December 1858 and June 1859 deed records mentioning the lodge do not enable a determination of location.

A Masonic celebration, ball, and barbecue was held at Jefferson on June 24, 1853. Loughery was again unable to attend, this time because all of the available transportation out of Marshall had been taken, but he provides an account of the proceedings in the July 2 *Texas Republican*:

> Those who attended the Masonic Ball and dinner, speak in terms of eulogy of the entire arrangements. The lady who presides over the Jefferson Hotel, comes in for a full share of compliments. The dinner is represented to us as having been an elegant affair, and to have been served up in the very best style. The supper at night was unequalled in Texas, and it is said could scarcely have been surpassed in New Orleans. The table presented a brilliant appearance, and was loaded not only with the delicacies of the season, but with everything that could be procured from New Orleans. They had a quantity of ice, and iced lemonades, ice-creams, bananas, oranges, &c. were on hand in abundance. And then to crown all, the music was of the richest kind. Messrs. Passier and Smith were in attendance. No one who has heard Mr. Passier touch the chords of his violin, but is willing to concede that he is one of the sweetest musicians he has ever heard....
>
> The Masonic fraternity at Jefferson is very numerous, and during the day they turned out in procession, which is described as having been very imposing....

A tribute of respect for the deceased Brother Levi Geer appears in the January 5, 1856, *Texas Republican* under the signatures of Clinton Willard, Perry Graham, and Francis Baker. The April 22, 1854, *Texas Republican* mentions that Masonic and Odd Fellows regalia, sashes, etc., were available at the dry goods and groceries establishment of P. M. Graham & Brother in Jefferson.

Independent Order of Good Samaritans

The only information in the newspapers on this organization is a tribute of respect for Caroline Hunt, deceased proprietess of the Jefferson Hotel, that appeared in the June 30, 1855, Clarksville *Standard* and Marshall *Texas Republican*. It is typical of the organizational eulogies of the day:

> *Lodge Room, Jefferson Lodge No. 34, Independent Order of Good Samaritans*
> *and Daughters of Samaria.*
>
> The Lodge met in obedience to a summon from the W. C. G. S., and was opened according to the usage of the Order, after which the object of the meeting having been explained, a motion was made and Sisters Walker, Vines, and Steele, were appointed a committee to draft resolutions suited to the occasion, which duty was immediately performed, and the following resolution reported, to wit:
>
> Whereas, This Lodge has learned with regret that our worthy Sister C. M. HUNT, departed this life on Wednesday morning, the 27th inst., and feeling most sensibly the severity of the loss our Lodge and the order generally has sustained in this afflictive dispensation of Providence, Be it therefore
>
> Resolved, That in the death of Sister HUNT, the Lodge has sustained an irreparable loss, and we deplore this sad event as having deprived us of one of our worthiest and most consistent members, who was ever ready to contribute to its good, and to carry into execution its benevolent designs.
>
> Resolved, That as a token of respect to the memory of Sister HUNT, the members of this Lodge wear the usual badge of mourning for fifteen days.
>
> Resolved, That the sincere condolence and sympa-

thy of this Lodge is hereby tendered to the afflicted family and relations of our deceased Sister,

Resolved, That these proceedings be published in the Jefferson Herald, and that the Texas Republican be requested to copy.

By order of the Lodge.

W. O. CONNELL, W. C.
H. KEYS, R. S.
Jefferson, June 27th, 1855.

Knights of the Golden Circle

The November 10, 1860, Marshall *Harrison Flag* reports that "General Buckley, whose position as President of the American Legion, or Knights of the Golden Circle, has rendered him a celebrity of the first magnitude, arrived in Marshall on Wednesday evening last by the western stage. He goes hence to Jefferson where he will address the people as to the objects of the mystic order over which he presides."

The Knights were a proslavery and later prosecession society formed in the North by southern sympathizers in the 1850s. The president of the first local branch, which was formed in 1854 in Cincinnati, was George Bickley. The military branch of the society was the American Legion, whose initial purpose was to establish a slave empire surrounding the Gulf of Mexico, referred to as the "Golden Circle." In 1860, the society shifted its attention to promoting secession in the Gulf and border states.

There is no evidence that a local chapter was formed in Jefferson.

31. Religion

When Edward Smith traveled throughout northeast Texas in 1849, he noted that "The presbyterians, methodists, baptists, episcopalians and other sects have extensive organizations in this part of Texas. No sect possesses any political advantages not enjoyed by another, but the presbyterians and the methodists appear to be now more influential than other bodies. The Sabbath is much respected, and the inhabitants conscientiously attend their places of worship, which are located within two or three miles of almost every residence. Some of these places are the houses of the settler, and others are chapels exclusively appropriated to religious and educational purposes."

The denominations and attendance are characteristic of Jefferson. House services and meetings at schoolhouses and other publicly accessible places preceded the erection of church buildings. The term "church" generally referred either to a church building or to a congregation that had achieved some sort of formal organization under the auspices of the larger religious body of which it was a part. Although there were some Catholics in Jefferson prior to the war, there was no Catholic church, which operates strictly in terms of sacerdotalism for the ministration of sacraments. Under circumstances in the United States where the Catholic church was not a national church, a priest could not be established in a community until there was a sufficient number of Catholics to support his activities, which are fulltime.

The Social Statistics section of the 1850 census indicates that there were 26 churches in Cass County, including 10 Methodist Episcopal with church property valued at $2,000, six Presbyterian with church property valued at $1,000, four Primitive Baptist with church property valued at $500, four Missionary Baptist with church property valued at $600, and two Christian Baptist. The 1860 census for Marion County lists the following churches: two Methodist accommodating 800 persons and with church property valued at $10,000, one Presbyterian accommodating 200 persons with church property valued at $550, one Baptist accommodating 230 persons with church property valued at $600, one Protestant Episcopal accommodating 430 persons with church property valued at $630, one Methodist accommodating 100 persons with church property valued at $200, one Protestant Episcopal accommodating 130 persons with church property valued at $300, one Cumberland Presbyterian accommodating 300 persons with church property valued at $800, and one Cumberland Presbyterian accommodating 550 persons with church property valued at $800.

William Saufley in an article on Marion County in the 1867 *Texas Almanac* says that there were three church buildings in Jefferson. These would be the Episcopal church built in 1867, the Methodist brick church built in 1860, and the Presbyterian chapel built in 1852.

Methodist

The Methodist Episcopal Church South was the first organized religious group in Jefferson because the Methodists had a well-developed system of traveling preachers who ministered to isolated settlers. The Methodist Episcopal Church was founded in 1784. The Methodist Episcopal Church South was formed in 1845 as a result of an 1844 split in the church over the issue of slavery. The Texas Conference of the Methodist Episcopal Church was formed in 1840, before the split. The East Texas Conference was formed in 1844, the year of the split.

Earline Burnett, in her 1954 Stephen F. Austin (Nacogdoches) MS thesis "A History of the First Methodist Church, Jefferson, Texas, 1844–1854," cites the "Minutes of the Annual Sessions of the East Texas Conference of the Methodist Episcopal Church, South" to the effect that the following preachers served Jefferson: James Baldridge, 1844–47;

Daniel Payne, 1847; Preston Hobbs, 1848; Robert Crawford, 1849; R. B. Wells, 1850; Samuel Lynch, 1851; Job Baker, 1855; L. R. Davis, 1855; and C. Hamill, 1856–58.

The December 6, 1849, *Texas Republican* indicates that the first 1850 quarterly meeting of the Methodist Episcopal Church South would be held on January 5 and 6 at Richland (about three miles east of Marshall) and that Robert Crawford would be the preacher at Jefferson assigned by the East Texas Conference. The December 13, 1851, *Texas Republican* indicates that Alexander Henkle had been appointed preacher for Marshall and Jefferson at an East Texas Conference recently held in Henderson.

The earliest preachers were obviously circuit preachers who served an organized congregation without a church building. Burnett indicates that a brick church was built in 1860 on the lot occupied by the present Methodist Church, but that it was preceded by another church building at the same site whose origin is unknown. The land was acquired by an April 4, 1848, deed of gift (for $100) from Allen Urquhart to Job Baker, Josiah Hill, Martin Rogers, and Frederick Schluter, trustees, Methodist Episcopal Church South, for Lot 10 in Block 47 fronting 50 feet on Henderson Street and running back 150 feet to the alley, for the purpose of erecting a house of worship.

Josiah Hill lived in Paradise and is listed as a Methodist Episcopal minister in the 1850 census. He purchased Fractional Lot 7 in Block 47 from Urquhart in May 1847 where he established, with William Crawford, the mercantile firm of Hill & Crawford. Job Baker was a physician and one of Jefferson's earliest residents, having participated in the establishment of the Steam Mill Company in December 1845. According to the January 17, 1852, *Star State Patriot*, the Rev. Dr. Job Baker of Jefferson gave the dedication sermon for the Methodist Church in Marshall. Martin Rogers was an attorney. The May 3, 1851, *Texas Republican* mentions that Martin Rogers of Jefferson was preaching at Quitman, and the June 20, 1857, *Texas Republican* mentions the Rev. Martin Rogers of Cass County.

In an editorial letter written in Jefferson on January 24, 1853, Robert Loughery of the Marshall *Texas Republican*, who was Methodist, reported that "On Sunday evening I visited the church, and had the pleasure of hearing Rev. Mr. Waskom preach a very interesting sermon, followed by an exhortation by Rev. J. M. Baker. The church was filled to overflowing." It is obvious that Loughery is speaking about a church building rather than a meeting place. However, the existence of a church building does not necessarily indicate that this was a Methodist church building; and it is likely that Loughery would have named it if it had been.

It is probable that the church visited by Loughery was an interdenominational chapel built by the Presbyterians in 1852 (for which there is firm evidence) and that the Methodists did not acquire a church building until 1860 that was constructed of brick. A September 1860 lot sale by Nathaniel Bradford to Frederick Schluter mentions the Methodist Episcopal Church adjoining Lot 11 in Block 47. A December 1860 sale of various properties by Bartholomew Figures to Frederick Schluter mentions the new brick Methodist Episcopal Church east of Lots 7–9 in Block 47.

The church also had a campground four miles west of Jefferson in the Reed headright, which was conveyed for $25 on January 1, 1852, by Thomas Watson to trustees William Aikin, Frederick Schluter, Martin Rogers, Josiah Hill, and Benjamin Kimball. The transaction mentions that the land had been surveyed by Allen Urquhart and that it could be used as a campground or place of worship. A September 26, 1853, transaction indicates that it was being used as a campground. This may have been the place near Jefferson reported by the October 14, 1854, *Texas Republican* in which "Thirty-five white persons, besides a number of blacks, professed religion." However, such camp meetings were fairly common, including a very large one near Daingerfield in September 1853 in which a large number of people were converted.

Baptist

Lucille Bullard in *The First Baptist Church, Jefferson, Texas, 1855–1985* states that the Missionary Baptist Church in Jefferson was formed in March 1855 and did not erect a church building until after the Civil War. However, in September 1850 by a deed of gift William Hughes conveyed to Williamson Freeman, Nelson Trawick, Clinton Willard, Jeptha Crawford, I. T. Owens, and Richard Crump, trustees of the

Religion

Missionary Baptist Church, one acre one mile from Jefferson on the Daingerfield Road in the Robert Hughes survey out of the Thomas Gillespie headright for the purpose of erecting a church. Although the church was apparently not built, it is obvious that some form of organizational structure preceded the March 1855 meeting.

Bullard indicates that the 1855 meeting was organized by the Marshall minister George Tucker and that the church covenant was signed by attendees Williamson Freeman, Drucilla Freeman, Lucy Freeman, Virginia Hobdy, Francis Harris, Martha Harris, Catherine Crawford, Eliza Jolly, Lotty Cotton, and Cyrus Cotton. This was largely a family affair, including Williamson Freeman, his wife Drucilla, his daughter Lucy, his daughter Virginia who was married to John Hobdy, and his sister Martha and her husband Francis Harris. Catherine Crawford was the wife of Jeptha Crawford.

They were joined in July 1855 by William Bateman and G. W. Spooner, in October 1856 by Benjamin Terry and his wife Mary, and in June 1857 by David Culberson, Sr., his wife Lucy, Alfred Badgett, and Ann Nichols, wife of Theophilus Nichols. Culberson began acting as pastor. Several slaves became members in June 1857, including the Badgett slaves Albert, Dinah, Stephen, and wife Silvey; the Culberson slaves Solomon and wife Charity, Jobe and wife Rodie, Giles, and Charles; Frederick Schluter's slave Richard; and the servants of Mrs. Wilkinson and Mr. Lanier. Americus Hay became pastor in 1860 when there were 26 members, including 11 slaves.

By the end of 1861, white membership had increased to 28 with the inclusion of Hay's wife, R. W. Bullard and his daughter Marietta, Henrietta Hathway, Turinda Rusk, and G. W. Allen, his wife Cynthia, and his daughter Nancy. Slave membership increased to 18 through the inclusion of William Mayberry's slave Jack, Benjamin Terry's slave Billy, W. M. Robinson's slave Jane, John Speake's slave Jane, Thomas Thornton's slave Nelly, A. D. Powell's slave Henry, and Douglas Walton's slave Patsy.

In September 1860, Allen Urquhart placed in trust (for $1) to Williamson Freeman and Benjamin Terry Fractional Block 69 in the Urquhart Addition for the use of the Missionary Baptist Church. In October, Daniel Alley as executor of Thomas Alley placed in trust (for $1) to Williamson Freeman and Benjamin Terry the block in the Alley Addition adjoining Fractional Block 69 with the requirement that a place of worship be erected by the Missionary Baptist Church within five years. The November 29, 1860, *Texas Republican* reported that a supper and dinner would be held at Freeman's Hall on January 25, 1861, to raise money for building a Baptist Meeting House. In June 1861, Freeman and Terry as trustees of the church purchased Lots 7–12 (5–10 in present delineations) in Block 69 for $2.50 in taxes owed by Urquhart. It was on this land on Polk Street that the church was built in 1869.

Presbyterian

Juanita Cawthon in a *History of the Presbyterian and Cumberland Presbyterian Churches, Jefferson, Texas* indicates that there were two Presbyterian groups in Jefferson prior to the Civil War: the Presbyterian Church, which was part of the Presbyterian Church USA (PCUSA), and the Cumberland Presbyterian Church, which was an offshoot of the PCUSA that began in the early 1800s in Kentucky and Tennessee with a massive outbreak of spontaneous preaching. The Cumberland Presbyterians do not appear to have had any major doctrinal differences with the PCUSA, and many of the Cumberland churches returned to the PCUSA in the early 1900s.

The Presbyterian Church in Jefferson was a member of the Eastern Texas Presbytery, which met in Marshall in January 1851. According to the Presbytery minutes, the church in Jefferson was formed in April 1851 by the Rev. M. W. Staples with six members and one elder. According to his personal records, Rev. Staples collected money to erect a chapel in 1852. Although a chapel was erected, I have been unable to find any deed record concerning a land conveyance.

The Presbytery met in Jefferson in November 1852 and secured colporteurs for the distribution of religious literature. Colporteurs were a feature of many denominations and active in places like Jefferson. According to the February 3, 1855, *Caddo Gazette* (also reported in the *Texas Republican*), a colporteur whose religious affiliation is not mentioned was tarred and feathered and run out of Jefferson for "taking unwarrantable liberties with some lady or ladies" and for having "obscene books among his bibles and other good books."

Religion

The earliest known minister was the Rev. Robert Byers, who served the church from April to December 1852. A historic sketch prepared by Mrs. Byers indicates that when she and her husband arrived in Jefferson in April 1852, there was no church organization, only six members, and several Cumberland Presbyterians. The members appear to have included William Nichols, his wife Eustatia, Thomas Pugh's wife Nancy, and someone by the name of Rountree (probably W. E. Roundtree). The church was weather-boarded and had six seats with backs, and services were held by all of the denominations in town. The Rev. and Mrs. Byers organized a Sabbath School uniting all of the denominations, achieving full attendance for a time.

The Rev. Marcus Wallace served the churches at Jefferson and Holly Branch (later Hickory Hill, now Avinger) from 1853 to 1855. James Harris of Jefferson was an elder in 1852, and his daughter Martha married the Rev. Wallace in May 1854. Harris moved to Hickory Hill, where he is listed in the 1860 census. Dr. Andrew Ewing, who is listed as a Jefferson resident and doctor in the 1860 census, was an elder in 1853. The church failed in 1855 because of lack of membership and was reorganized by the Rev. W. C. Dunlap of Marshall in 1860, when it consisted of eight members and one elder. A church building was constructed in the early 1870s, but the church was dissolved in the early 1900s because of a decline in membership.

The Cumberland Presbyterian Church apparently began in Jefferson through the activities of the Rev. S. R. Chadick of Daingerfield. The Rev. Chadwick is reported to have preached as early as 1850 in Jefferson and at a schoolhouse in Paradise, which would have been the Cass Academy. The church was probably formed about 1852 by the Rev. Chadick with six members. When the church was formed, the two elders were the lawyer Justice Ferris and a Mrs. Dr. Walker, obviously the wife of Dr. R. W. Walker, who became established in Jefferson in 1852.

In a July 1853 deed of gift, Daniel Alley conveyed to George Ury, E. B. Wilkins, and E. P. M. Johnson, church elders of the Cumberland Presbyterian Church, an 85-foot square on the northeast corner of the public square, for the promotion of the public good. No action was taken with respect to this property because Alley had conveyed the entire block to the county commissioners in April 1847. The return to Alley was not fully accomplished until February 1855, and there were still problems related to the block because the county commissioners had sold some lots, in some cases to persons who could not be remembered.

On July 12, 1859, Alley conveyed (for $1) to George Ury, E. B. Wilkins, and E. P. M. Johnson, elders of the Cumberland Presbyterian Church, an 80-foot square on the northeast corner of the public square, for the benefit of the church and the promotion of the public good. That a church was built on this property is known from a July 28, 1860, report in the *Texas Republican* that speeches were given in the Cumberland Presbyterian Church for the benefit of the Protestant Episcopal Church and in connection with a town proposal concerning the Memphis, El Paso & Pacific railroad.

The site became the location of a public market house after the Civil War and then the high school, which burned in 1915. The present church building is across the street slightly to the west. The land was acquired in June 1871, and the church is shown on Brosius's 1872 *Bird's Eye View of Jefferson, Texas*.

Episcopal

Dorothy Craver in *This Old Church: A History of Christ Church, Episcopal, Jefferson, Texas* indicates that a Protestant Episcopal congregation under the name of Christ Church Jefferson was formed on May 11, 1851. The articles of association were signed by Edward Benners, John Poindexter, James Brickell, Hiram Tomlin, Thomas Mebane, Joseph Moseley, Granville Lewis, Lucy Ann Jones, Samuel Friou, Mary Friou (his wife), Howard Burnside, Ardelia Burnside (his wife), Alfred Lander, and Ann Lander (his wife). Of the unfamiliar names, Joseph Moseley purchased lots in Jefferson in 1851 and 1852; L. A. Jones is listed as an unmarried 40-year-old female in the 1860 census. Benners was elected senior warden, Poindexter junior warden, and Burnside, Friou, Tomlin, and Moseley vestrymen.

The meeting was attended by the Rev. Henry Sansom, who had organized Trinity Episcopal in Marshall in January 1851, with the participation of Sam and Mary Friou, Howard Burnside, and Edward

Benners. Benners' wife Helen did not participate in either of these organizational meetings because she had remained with their young children in Alabama when he moved to Marshall in August 1852 to establish himself as an attorney. The Rev. Sansom became the rector of Trinity Episcopal in April 1851 and preached occasionally in Jefferson, but removed to Houston in September 1855. The group in Jefferson did not apply for admission into the Diocese of the Protestant Episcopal Church of the United States.

On June 8, 1860, friends of the Protestant Episcopal Church held a meeting in the Cumberland Presbyterian Church to organize the congregation on a firmer foundation; and, according to the July 18, 1860, *Texas Republican*, a fair was held for the benefit of the church (obviously to raise money for a church building), and speeches were given at the Cumberland Presbyterian Church. Articles of association were signed by Edward Benners, Helen Benners, Abbie Foscue, Adeline Pitkin, John Winslow, Amanda Winslow (his wife), Orville Yerger, Virginia Yerger (his wife), Jennie Duke, Emma Cox, Mary Virginia Todd, Harvey Black, W. J. C. Rogers, A. M. Walker, Alexander Storr, Martha Murphy, and Hamilton Witherspoon. The men of the church held their first meeting on June 11, with Benners as senior warden, Yerger as junior warden, Winslow as secretary, and Black, Judge William Todd (father of Mary Virginia by his first marriage), and Drs. Walker, Rogers, and Witherspoon as vestrymen.

Regular services were held on the second Sunday of the month by the Rev. Edwin Wagner of Marshall from February 1860 until December 1861. The first Episcopal marriage was held in April 1860, the first baptisms and confirmations in June, and the first infant baptism in September. Slaves baptized immediately before or during the war were Anne and Mary, slaves of H. A. Donaldson; Minerva, slave of Edward Benners (1863); Robert Waterhouse, slave of Richard Waterhouse (1864); and Rosa and Charles Johnson, children of Jack and Josephine Johnson, slaves of Edward Benners.

In March 1856, Allen Urquhart deeded in trust (for $1) to Edward Benners Lots 8–10 in Block 58 for any Protestant Episcopal Church that might be organized in Jefferson. Nothing appears to have been done with this property; and baptisms, confirmations, and services were held at the homes of members, at Freeman's Hall, and at the Cumberland Presbyterian Church, with Benners acting as lay reader. In October 1863, Daniel Alley as executor of Thomas Alley conveyed to the rector, warden, and vestry of Christ Church Jefferson for $1,000 Lots 1–3 in Block E of the Alley Addition and, for $10, Lots 4–6 in Block E of the Alley Addition. This was the property on Main Street on which the church building was completed in 1867.

Jewish

There were a number of Jewish merchants in Jefferson from the earliest years, beginning with Israel Leavitt by at least 1847. Congregation Har Sinai and the Mount Sinai Jewish Cemetery were not established until after the war. The formal congregation was preceded by the Hebrew Benevolent Association, with Isaac Pinski as first president (as indicated by his headstone). The association was apparently a late development, because Pinski does not appear in Jefferson until 1857. Fred Tarpley in his book on Jefferson indicates that the Jewish families tended to cluster along Houston Street in an area that came to be known as Jew Town. In July 1862, William and Matilda Brooks sold for $150 to Jacob Sterne, Isaac Pinski, Albert Kohn, A. Farber, Sam Sterne, Samuel Jacobs (of Marshall), and Henry Jacobs (of Sherman) 1.5 acres adjacent to the north boundary of the old graveyard, for the benefit of the Hebrew Benevolent Association. This land was adjacent to the Houston Street Jewish residential area and apparently was used as a graveyard, because the *Handbook of Texas* indicates that the benevolent associations were largely devoted to the establishment of cemeteries and that a Jewish cemetery was established in Jefferson in 1862.

32. Education

In January 1853, the editor of the *Jefferson Herald* cited the national census to the effect that there were 30,000 adults in Texas who could neither read or write. Robert Loughery of the Marshall *Texas Republican* felt constrained to respond as follows:

> The whole population of Texas does not, we believe, amount to thirty thousand.... we do not think that ignorance either of books or the ways of the world, can be considered a characteristic of our people. Look at the number of schools that are distributed throughout our young and growing State; look at the number of newspapers, and the extensive patronage they receive. In no place in the Union, of the same population as Marshall, is there a newspaper as large as the Republican; and yet there is another one published in the same place; one at Jefferson only sixteen miles distant; and another at Henderson, only forty-five miles from Marshall.

Loughery was correct in his observations, and there was a well-developed system of private academies throughout northeast Texas by the early 1850s, with the most notable in Jefferson, Clarksville, Marshall, and Daingerfield. However, there was no public education in the region prior to the Civil War. The Texas Legislature had established a land grant program as a basis for a public common school system, but there was little response to the opportunity other than to establish districts, acquire land, appoint trustees, and set up school funds. The Cass County commissioners court minutes for the 1840s and 1850s contain numerous references to such activities but never mention schoolhouses. A November 1, 1851, *Texas Republican* article attributes the lack of action to the fact that the legislature had prohibited sale or lease of the lands for 20 years, rendering them valueless.

In the absence of public education, people engaged in home schooling, including some education for slaves, and sent their children to private schools and academies that were sexually segregated. Most children in the 1850 and 1860 censuses are listed as students, although it is difficult to determine precisely what this means. The Social Statistics section of the 1850 census indicates that in Cass County there were six male academies with one teacher each and averaging 30 pupils, four female academies with one teacher each and averaging 40 pupils, and 15 common schools with one teacher each and averaging 33 pupils. None of the common schools received public funds. The Social Statistics section of the 1860 census indicates that in Marion County there were six common schools for males with one teacher each and averaging 30 pupils and seven common schools for females with one teacher each and averaging 25 pupils. None of the common schools received public funds.

The first mention of schools in the vicinity of Jefferson occurs in the commissioners court minutes, which refer to J. Williams' schoolhouse west of Jefferson in 1846 and Wilson's schoolhouse on the other side of Black Cypress Bayou in 1847. These were probably one-teacher operations. A larger operation is mentioned in a March 1848 deed record, which refers to the Gertrude Academy, north of Jefferson and in the vicinity of present-day Linden. This school did not advertise in the December 16, 1848, *Spirit of the Age*, which contains advertisements for academies in Kentucky and Virginia, and nothing is known about its operations.

On July 5, 1850, William Perry provided a gift of five acres in the Archer headright for the sake of establishing a school in the immediate vicinity of Jefferson. The gift was made to the Cass Academy Trustees Bartholomew Figures, Williamson Freeman, Thomas Watson, C.

Harrison, and Frederick Schluter, all of whom had property in Paradise. The deed of gift indicates that buildings for a male and female academy were already on the property. The Cass County Male and Female Academy was located near the Spring Branch about 1 ½ miles west of Jefferson on the south side of the Daingerfield Road and west of the Porter and Young steam saw and grist mill, which was west of Williamson Freeman's plantation. In the November 1849 term of the probate court, Freeman cited the existence of the school as the reason for his desire to purchase property near Jefferson.

John Steel is listed in Precinct 1 of the 1850 Cass County census as a 45-year-old teacher born in Virginia. A letter written from Jefferson to the editor in the July 13, 1850, *Texas Republican* describes the commencement examinations that were held by Mr. and Mrs. Steel and the attendant Fourth of July celebration:

> We had the pleasure of witnessing the interesting ceremonies of the public examination at the Academy of MR. STEEL, near this place, commencing on the 2d and continuing till the evening of the 4th instant.
>
> On the first two days, there was a very respectable audience in attendance, and the time was passed pleasantly and profitably, all in listening to the exercises and marking the evidences of improvement, particularly of the younger classes, the examination of which consumed the 2d, and the greater part of the 3d. We were not present on the 2d; but from what we saw on the 3d, and from what was told us, we feel safe in asserting that the examination was thorough, perfect, and entirely satisfactory. The little boys and girls throughout acquitted themselves in a manner that adds much to the already extensive and well earned reputation of Mr. S. and his accomplished lady. The satisfaction of the patrons of the school was general, and so was the proficiency exhibited by each and every pupil; yet we could mention some as being peculiarly interesting to the spectators, but we forbear from the fact that all acquitted themselves so well.

On the 4th, there was a very large audience in attendance, drawn together to aid in the celebration of the day, and to witness the *finale* of the school exercises. The ceremonies were commenced by speaking from the little boys, who distinguished themselves by the correctness of their gestures, and the perfect and distinct enunciation of every word—a part of education much overlooked and grievously slighted, we regret to say, in many of our high schools.

At half-past 9, Master Henry Hill, a lad and a pupil of the school, was introduced to the audience as the orator of the day, who delivered an original speech. We would not wish to be invidious, and must be allowed to be understood as expressing our *special* delight and pleasure at listening to him. Sentiments that would have reflected credit on an older head—an enunciation as clear and distinct as that of the most experienced speaker—an action in which every movement was expressive and graceful to the highest degree—impressed us, and the crowd generally, with the idea that, though much had been done for him by his accomplished teacher, *much more* had been given him by a higher source.

After this, the exercises were resumed and continued till 11, during which time, we would beg leave to notice a class of beautiful girls, or rather young ladies, who were examined in "Watt's on the Mind." In this, which is usually considered a dry and uninteresting study, there was much interest manifested by the class. The questions were selected from any and every part of the book, and there was not a single answer missed.

Mr. Wm. Henry Parsons then addressed the audience, in an elaborate speech of an hour and a half, on the subject of education. Mr. P. has already acquired a reputation as a public speaker. Of his style and manner it is useless to speak, from the fact that most of the citizens of Cass and Harrison have had the pleasure of hearing him. The sentiment was correct—perfect, we may say—and delivered in a creditable manner. In a word, he sustained himself with his usual ability.

After which, the audience adjourned to partake of a fine dinner, which had been prepared in a beautiful grove near the Academy. Every thing was served up in the most *recherche* style, and all partook with a zest that would have satisfied the Genius of Liberty that, notwithstanding how much soever we may be divided on matters of local interest, on an occasion like a public dinner, we are all purely *American*.

During the afternoon, the company was amused and entertained by a series of comical dialogues from the young men, in which all sustained themselves infinitely, we may say.

The company then dispersed, all leaving with regret, though happy in the belief that they had passed a pleasant day, and that they had something in the way of festivals to remember.

The July 12, 1851, *Texas Republican* reports that the academy was in a prosperous condition and that Howard Burnside and his wife Ardelia, lately of Marshall, were in charge of the Female Department. However, the academy soon fell into financial difficulties. In August 1852, the buildings and the five acres were sold for $20 to Archibald Dunlap by the Cass County sheriff in connection with a tax judgment against the academy. Dunlap sold the academy to Virgil Dubose for $200 in September 1852. In an advertisement dated August 1852, Dubose announced in the May 14, 1853, *Jefferson Herald* that he was opening a male and female academy at his residence 1 ½ miles west of Jefferson, that he taught all branches of a thorough English and classical education, and that the first session would begin in February 1853. This was obviously the old Cass Academy, which served as Dubose's residence. Dubose lectured in Jefferson before the Mutual Improvement Society in January 1853.

In October 1855, William Perry sold to Abraham Kohn a two-acre Female School House Lot in the Archer headright on the north side of the Spring Branch and Daingerfield Road that was surrounded on three sides by Horatio Walcott's property. This schoolhouse was on the old road to Daingerfield. The two-acre female academy or schoolhouse tract, but not the schoolhouse itself, continues to be mentioned in the deed records through 1861. This school appears to have been a replacement for the defunct Cass Academy, but nothing is known about its operation.

The first formal instructional program in Jefferson was Thomas Simms' penmanship school. Simms had been teaching in Marshall when he moved to Jefferson in February 1851. His lessons in Jefferson were probably similar to those provided in Marshall, which are advertised in the September 14, 1850, *Texas Republican*. Simms provided fifteen lessons in the art of penmanship for $5, with day and night classes offered. The January 4, 1851, *Texas Republican* reports that "Mr. S. has the praise of all who have taken lessons from him. We have seen several specimens of his skill, and should judge that the praise of his pupils is merited. The importance, and even the pleasure of being a good pensman, will naturally suggest itself to every one."

The August 22, 1857, *Texas Republican*, citing the *Jefferson Gazette*, reports that the theatrical troupe of Mr. Charles "played for the benefit of the Female Institute, a new school room, which is being erected in Jefferson." The Jefferson Female Academy advertised in the November 7, 1857, *Eastern Texas Gazette*, with the advertisement dated August 8 (Fig. 32-1). With Susan Foster as principal and C. W. Tarbox as assistant, the school offered two 20-week sessions at the following rates: Primary English branches, $12.50; Junior Class, $15.00; Senior Class, $20.00; and music, $25.00. Drawing and painting, embroidery, hair work, and French classes were offered at an additional $10 each. This was the first academic institution within the city limits and advertised that it would open on September 1. It was consumed by fire in May 1859, with $2,500 in losses.

On February 23, 1858, Daniel Alley sold for $100 Lots 1–3 of Block 34 in the Alley Addition as a site for a schoolhouse to the trustees John Murphy, Clinton Willard, Edward Benners, William Todd, Wil-

Education

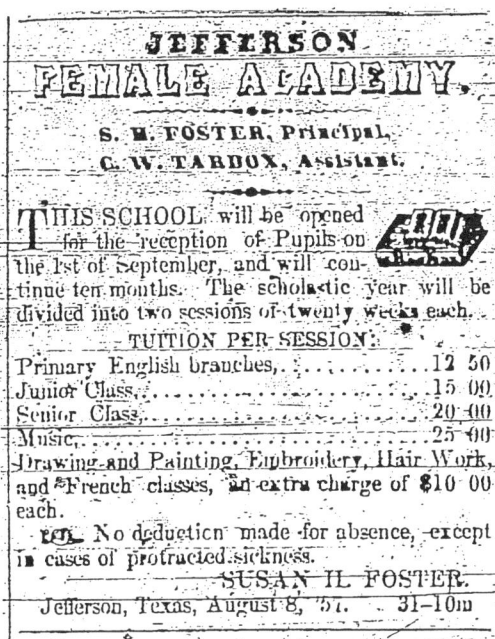

Fig. 32-1. First Academic Institution in Jefferson. Source: November 7, 1857, *Eastern Texas Gazette*

liam Perry, William Saufley, Robert Nesmith, Jesse Veal, James Rogers, Abraham Kohn, and Daniel Alley. It is unknown whether a schoolhouse was built on this property.

Listed in the 1860 population census for Jefferson are the teachers P. J. Carolin (30-year-old male), Henry Lidd (39-year-old male), and M. Marton (28-year-old female) and the music teacher Rachael Smither (18-year-old female). In addition to formal instruction, there were numerous public lectures on academic subjects, such as Prof. J. K. Henry's series on biology, which were given in Jefferson, Marshall, and Clarksville in September and October 1853.

88. Hotels

Hotels were common throughout early northeast Texas and usually one of the first structures to be erected in any town that contained mercantile establishments. People with business in town usually traveled by horseback or buggy over distances that required more than one day of travel. Business travelers needed a place to stay for the night and usually for more than one night. Ports such as Jefferson had the added need of accommodations for travelers leaving or entering the town by steamboat, particularly because steamboats were unscheduled carriers and seldom left when they said they would.

The horses of travelers needed to be fed and housed. This was done by stables that were integral to the hotel operation or else by independent stables nearby. The horses were cared for by hostlers, or ostlers as the word was spelled at that time. The long association between the hotel and the care of horses is indicated by the fact that the word "hotel" was derived from "hostler," which was the early term for innkeeper. All of Jefferson's hotels provided stables. The association of stables with hotels provided the circumstances in which stagecoach lines generally operated out of hotels.

Although hotels catered primarily to the traveling public, they also served as boarding houses. A boarding house was a paid residence, generally for an extended period, for persons who lived in the town in which it was located. It provided meals as well as lodging, as its name implies, because "board" is an old term that refers to the plank upon which meals were first served. Because the hotel boarders were permanent residents, they are listed in the 1850 and 1860 censuses. All of the boarders in Jefferson's hotels were unmarried males and almost all were professionals and craftsmen, a class that could afford lodging and a sex for which residence in a hotel was permissible. Most of Jefferson's private residences also contained boarders, but there do not appear to have been any boarding houses.

Although owners sometimes operated their hotels, they normally rented or leased them to professional hotel managers who referred to themselves as proprietors in the hotel advertisements. The traveling public that stayed at these hotels was probably dominated by interior merchants and planters and sometimes their families on their way to and from Jefferson by carriage and horseback and to and from New Orleans by steamboat. The hotels in Jefferson were near the business section and within a few blocks of each other, convenient to the steamboat landing, stagecoaches, and the road to Marshall.

Jefferson had one hotel in 1845, two in 1846, and three by 1850; and these three were in existence through 1860. There was also a hotel in Paradise from at least 1850. The first appears to have been a log hotel built by Ithael Eason and located on Line Street at the head of Marshall. It was probably called the Eason Hotel and later became the Star Hotel, then the Rising Sun Hotel, then the Planter's Hotel. The second was probably William Perry's Soda Lake Hotel, which was located on Dallas Street at the northeast corner of Dallas and Jackson. It later became the Jefferson Hotel. The third was probably the Figures Hotel, which was owned and operated by Bartholomew Figures and was located on Marshall at the northeast corner of Marshall and Austin. It later became the Planter's Hotel and then the City Hotel. Information on these hotels in the newspapers is somewhat confusing because two of them were owned at some time by Bartholomew Figures, and both of these operated at some time under the name Planter's Hotel.

Soda Lake Hotel/Jefferson Hotel

The Soda Lake Hotel was built, owned, and operated initially by William Perry and his wife Sardinia. The hotel fronted Dallas and was located on Lots 4–6 in Block 4 (at the northeast corner of Dallas and

Jackson) on land purchased by Perry from Berry Durham in December 1844. An advertisement for the hotel appears in the December 12, 1846, Clarksville *Northern Standard* (Fig. 33-1). The advertisement is dated November and mentions that the hotel had just been completed and "is now ready to accommodate the travelling community. Every means will be used to afford comfort to the tired traveller, and his table and larder will be furnished with the best that the country will warrant."

The advertisement points out that stables were connected with the hotel that were "large, airy and commodious" and that horses were "taken care of by an experienced person." Accommodations for horses were every bit as important as accommodations for travelers during this early period. The "experienced person" in charge of the stables was apparently Robert Nesmith, who was for many years the center of land-based travel in Jefferson, including a stagecoach line. The stables were located immediately across Austin Street on Lots 7, 8, and half of 9 in Block 22 (northeast corner of Austin and Jackson).

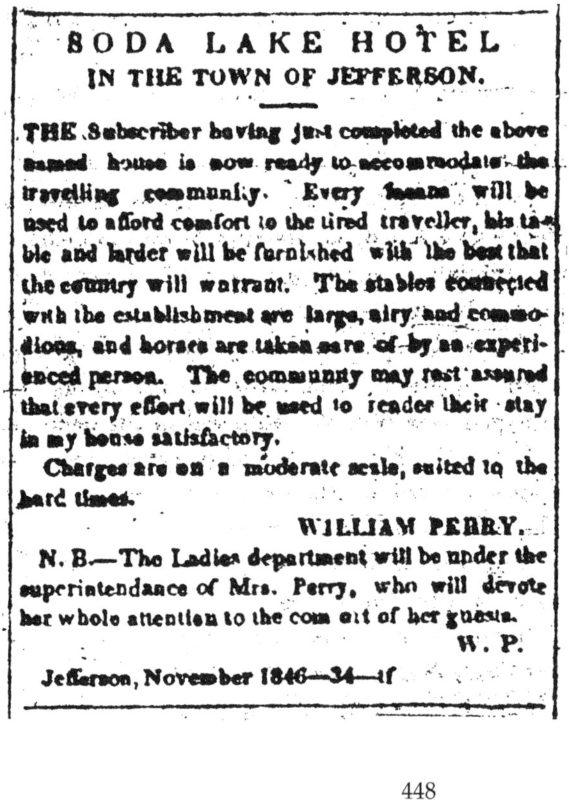

SODA LAKE HOTEL
IN THE TOWN OF JEFFERSON.

THE Subscriber having just completed the above named house is now ready to accommodate the travelling community. Every means will be used to afford comfort to the tired traveller, his table and larder will be furnished with the best that the country will warrant. The stables connected with the establishment are large, airy and commodious, and horses are taken care of by an experienced person. The community may rest assured that every effort will be used to render their stay in my house satisfactory.

Charges are on a moderate scale, suited to the hard times.

WILLIAM PERRY.

N. B.—The Ladies department will be under the superintendance of Mrs. Perry, who will devote her whole attention to the comfort of her guests.

W. P.

Jefferson, November 1846—34—tf

Fig. 33-1. Soda Lake Hotel Advertisement. Source: December 12, 1846, *Northern Standard*

A note mentions that "The Ladies department will be under the superintendance of Mrs. Perry, who will devote her whole attention to the comfort of her guests." The "ladies department" does not mean separate accommodations, but rather that Sardinia would devote special attention to female guests, which was an added feature that many hotels of the time could not provide. Charges for the hotel are mentioned as "on a moderate scale, suited to the hard times."

The name of the hotel was derived from an old name for Caddo Lake, which hydrologically reached up to the confluence of Big and Black Cypress bayous, only six miles below Jefferson. The advertisement appeared in the Clarksville newspaper because it was a regional newspaper with a circulation in all of the Texas counties north of Jefferson.

The advertisement indicates that the hotel was a large, sophisticated operation, and the fact that it was advertised in the Clarksville newspaper indicates that it appealed to an extensive traveling public. This impression is confirmed by Charles DeMorse, the editor of the *Northern Standard*, who stayed at the hotel in June 1847.

DeMorse had passed through Jefferson in July 1846 before the hotel was built and was not impressed. In June 1847, he was "agreeably surprised by the improved appearance of the place, since last summer, and the increased air of comfort which it has, from having a better supply of house room." DeMorse was particularly impressed by the formal gardens of the Soda Lake Hotel, which were occupied by exotic plants (apparently brought in by Sardinia from New Orleans):

> The Hotel of Mr. Perry is a large and commodious establishment, certainly well kept, and withal, having about it pleasant evidences of taste: rare shrubs and flowers, which greeted the eye, and refreshed the senses.—These things are rather rare in all the country East and North of Nacogdoches, and as the cultivation of them, is a recreation in which we take continual delight, it gave us pleasure to see them in so new a town as Jefferson, as it does to speak of them. Not that the grounds and walks were laid off in a manner to challenge criticism, but simply that they were decidedly

neat of arrangement, the plants many of them rare, and that they imparted delight from the general absence of such things in a region entirely new, and in which the trunks of the first pines felled, still lie in close contiguity to the town.

DeMorse was visiting Jefferson to attend the Cass County court. Cass County was created in April 1846. According to the Act that created the county, the court was directed to meet at William Perry's tavern house until a suitable structure could be erected. The first meeting of the court was indeed held in July 1846 at William Perry's tavern house. It appears that the Soda Lake Hotel was not under construction in July 1846 when DeMorse had previously passed through Jefferson, because this is the type of detail that he was fond of reporting.

What is surprising is the sophistication of this establishment only a year and a half after the first log cabin was completed in Jefferson. A large hotel in November 1846 indicates that the town was expanding rapidly. It is particularly fitting that the hotel was built by the Perrys. William was responsible for clearing out Cypress Bayou in late 1844, which enabled the town to come into existence. Sardinia reportedly gave birth to the first child born in Jefferson.

DeMorse visited Jefferson again in April 1848 and reports that the hotel had passed into the hands of Robert Nesmith and Robert Brownell and that it was "one of the most spacious in the Eastern part of the State." Nesmith and Brownell were probably renter-operators, because the hotel was not sold to them. Perry mortgaged the property to John Webster in September 1849 in connection with a $286 note owed to Webster and sold it to Stephen Ellis and Joseph Elliott for $3,100 in December 1849. An advertisement for the Soda Lake Hotel with Ellis and Elliott as proprietors appeared in the March 28, 1850, *Texas Republican*.

Elliott soon withdrew from participation and apparently left Jefferson or died, because he is not included in the 1850 census. As was typical of the period, the hotel not only served the traveling public, but was also the residence of its owner and boarders. The 1850 census lists Ellis as a 34-year-old innkeeper born in Virginia with real estate valued at $13,750, a considerable sum of money at that time; and the 1850 tax rolls indicate that he owned seven lots in Jefferson. Living with him at the hotel were his parents and sister.

In addition, there were 19 boarders: one painter (C. C. Robinson, 23); one blacksmith (May Pendleton, 21); one stable keeper (John McDaniel, 22); one warehouse keeper (Joseph Mosby, 40); two plasterers (F. Flynn, 30, and ___ Vandergrofft, 32); two lawyers (James Maddox, 23, and John Everett, 45); three carpenters (John Shook, 23, H. White, 40, and Henry Fusset, 40); three clerks (James Brickell, 40, Thomas Goyne, 25, and W. H. Childress, 40, with real estate valued at $3,920); and five merchants (George Tuttle, 25, Moses Ambros, 27, William Falk, 35, Perry Graham, 25, with real estate valued at $1,850, and Samuel Moseley, 27, with real estate valued at $20,000). The merchants and lawyers listed were among the most important and wealthiest men in Jefferson, indicating that the statements about the elegance of the hotel were justified.

The operation of the hotel under Ellis is described briefly in a letter that appeared in the June 20, 1850, Marshall *Texas Republican*: "By the way, I would not fail to speak of our neighbor, sir-named '*Stephe*,' the proprietor of the Soda Lake Hotel. The house is now conducted with more spirit, neatness, and order than ever before. With all the vegetables of a fine garden, and the best edibles the market affords, universal satisfaction is always given. The aforesaid 'Stephe,' alias Mr. Ellis, is also quite a pattern of the agreeable and lively gentleman. And he 'calls together the *ton* about town,' and the fair ones of Paradise or West Jefferson, when the pleasure loving can trip the fantastic toe to the enlivening music of the violin and 'win enough glory for one day.'" This letter and the July 13, 1850, *Texas Republican* indicate that numerous balls were held at the hotel, with catering provided by Ellis' mother and sisters, who also apparently provided the daily fare.

The advertisement for the Soda Lake Hotel disappeared in March 1851, and the hotel may have operated under someone other than Ellis for a short period. It reappeared in October 1851 under the name Jefferson Hotel, with the advertisement stating that Ellis had again taken charge and that he would be assisted by Captain Gooding, formerly of the Star Hotel in Clarksville. In March 1852, Henry Gooding advertised that he had taken charge for the ensuing year, that the hotel and furniture had been refurbished, and that Robert Nesmith provided stables connected with the hotel. Gooding is described in the November 1, 1851, *Northern Standard*:

> The old friends of *Captain* Gooding will find that he has re-hoisted his flag at the head of navigation on the Big Cypress, and is determined to treat them hospitably *if* they will let him. The Captain's rotundity of person, with a certain merry twinkle of the eye, and the unctuously complacent expression of the countenance, are the best possible indications that he appreciates good living himself, and will be likely to have it prepared for those who *will participate* with him.

Gooding was a renter-operator, and ownership remained in the hands of Ellis and Elliott. In July 1852, Ellis of Bowie County sold to Nelson Trawick for $5,750 Lots 4–6 in Block 4 containing the hotel and Lots 7, 8, and one-half of 9 in Block 22 containing the stables. In August, Elliott of Dallas County quit claimed to Ellis for $1,000 any interest he might have in these properties. Trawick sold the lots in Block 4 containing the hotel to Richard Patrick of New York for $5,000 in October 1852 and the lots in Block 22 containing the stables to Robert Nesmith for $700 in January 1853.

Gooding died in December 1852 at the age of 46, and J. W. Kemp and Elizabeth Jackson became renter-operators for a year in January 1853. Jackson had previously operated the Planter's Hotel in Marshall. Their advertisement mentions location in the center of town; large, pleasant, and commodious rooms; experienced cooks; attentive servants; the attached Nesmith's Livery Stable; and the following rates: board and lodging per day, $1.50; board and lodging per week, $7.00; board and lodging per month, $20; and board without lodging per month, $15. It should be noted that provision of food accounted for three-fourths of the cost. Boarders were required to settle accounts at the end of the week or month, and persons without baggage were required to pay in advance.

Robert Loughery of the *Texas Republican* took a stage run by Kemp from Marshall to Jefferson in January 1853 and stayed at the hotel:

> We arrived at Jefferson between two and three o'clock, and set down to an elegant dinner at the Jefferson Hotel, kept by Mrs. Jackson and Mr. J. W. Kemp. This house is very well managed, and is well patronized. We were surprised at the large amount of traveling custom which a hotel gets in this place. The house has been a perfect jam since we have been here.

The business relationship between Kemp and Jackson was dissolved in March according to the May 14, 1853, *Jefferson Herald*, and Jackson continued to operate the hotel by herself. Jackson catered (perhaps at the hotel) the Odd Fellows and Citizens Ball in April and the Masonic Ball in May. Jackson left the hotel before October and was mistakenly thought to have died of yellow fever during an epidemic in New Orleans, where she was residing. The *Jefferson Herald* apparently published an obituary, a not unusual mistake when communications were interrupted by quarantines.

John Speake, as agent, advertised the Jefferson Hotel for sale in the May 14, 1853, *Jefferson Herald*, with the advertisement dated November 1852 stating that the hotel "stands on the street leading from the Steamboat landing, and is convenient to the business part of town." Caroline Hunt purchased the Jefferson Hotel for $5,000 from Richard Patrick in November 1853, establishing a mortgage with Patrick on the same day. Hunt catered (perhaps at the hotel) the May Party and the Fourth of July Celebration and Lake Barbecue at the Alhambra in 1854. Her advertisement in February 1855 noted her long experience in the business and that she would be assisted by her son, L. L. Gwinn. Hunt died on June 27, 1855, and a tribute of respect from the Jefferson Lodge No. 34, Independent Order of Good Samaritans and Daughters of Samaria appeared in the July 14 *Texas Republican*. The probate records contain an inventory of the hotel's contents.

The hotel operated under M. B. Nash in March 1856. In connection with the placement of the advertisement, Loughery stated that "The Jefferson Hotel, under the direction of Mr. M. B. NASH, is a well conducted hotel, and a very desirable place to stop at. Every attention is paid to the comfort of guests, by the gentlemanly proprietor. The clerk of the establishment is an attentive, polite, business man. We wish this hotel success." Nash lasted only six weeks, and N. J. Moore began to operate the hotel in the middle of April 1856.

William Saufley as administrator of the Hunt estate conveyed the hotel property to Francis Harris in January 1858 for a $3,100 bid at public auction in October 1857. The Runnells Ball was held in October, and Loughery remarked that "At 11 o'clock supper was announced, and the gay throng repaired to the Jefferson Hotel, kept by Mr. F. T. HARRIS, where a table was set, which for artistic decoration, luxury, and profusion, we have seldom seen equalled. Everything that money could purchase, or art invent, to tempt the appetite, was furnished in abundance. The table was the theme of admiration and compliment." Moore either continued to be associated with this operation or resumed management after Harris' illness or death, because Loughery reported in April 1858 that the hotel under James Moore was filled to overflowing.

In October 1858, Robert Nesmith as executor of the estate of Francis Harris conveyed the hotel property to Lewis Boynton and Lewis Moody of Hunt County for $3,475. Moody advertised as proprietor of the Jefferson Hotel in January 1859:

> This COMMODIOUS HOTEL has lately been thoroughly repaired, and entirely refurnished, and is now open for the reception of travelers and boarders. The proprietor has spared neither pains nor expense in his preparations to render those who may patronize him comfortable. His table will always be supplied with the best the market affords, and served up by the most accomplished cooks. He has secured the best and most attentive servants, and flatters himself that by close attention to the wants of patrons, to render his house unsurpassed by any first class hotel in this section of country. Promising a good table, clean beds, and comfortable rooms, together with the best of attention, and moderate charges, he hopes to meet with public encouragement.

Boynton sold his half interest to Moody for $3,181 in March 1860, and Moody sold the entire property to Elizabeth Hughes, wife of Joel Hughes, for $5,819 in August. Hughes had also acquired half interest in the related stable (then of brick, with grocery house attached) from George Prewitt in January. Moody does not appear in the 1860 census, and William Brooks, who operated the City Hotel, is the only person listed as a hotel proprietor. The Jefferson Hotel was in existence after the Civil War.

Figures Hotel/Planter's Hotel/City Hotel

Bartholomew Figures appears in the 1849 tax roll as owning six lots in Jefferson valued at $1,200. He began operating the Figures Hotel at the corner of Marshall and Austin sometime before 1850. Figures is listed in the 1850 census as a 45-year-old innkeeper born in Tennessee with a property value of $6,000. When the census was taken, he was living in the hotel with his wife, six children, and eight boarders: one wagon maker (Samuel McLaine, 31); one laborer (Elisha Woodward, 27); two retired persons (James Wood, 65, and John Davis, 77); two tanners (James Davis, 28, and ___ Milholand, 30); and three carpenters (S. Simmon, 35, Augustus Lamprachts, 35, and Milton Mills, 30). These were all laborers, suggesting that the hotel was a very modest frame structure, because the log hotel was occupied by professionals. However, it was later to become one of Jefferson's finest hotels through brick additions.

Figures apparently continued to own this hotel until July 1857 and continued to operate it until early 1858. He became a tavern operator in Paradise on the south side of the Daingerfield Road in 1853. The tavern was referred to as the Figures Hotel, at least in 1856 according to an April 1859 conveyance from J. M. and J. C. Murphy to Lewis Northern. Because he owned two hotels in Jefferson, one of which he operated, and another in Paradise, he should be considered Jefferson's premier hotelier.

In July 1857, Figures sold to Reece Hughes for $6,000 Lots 7–9 in Block 21 (at the northeast corner of Marshall and Austin), with the exception of the northern 47 feet of each lot, which had been sold to August Lamprecht. Although the transaction does not mention the hotel, the price and location are certain indicators. The location is confirmed by the fact that the *Eastern Texas Gazette* moved its offices in early November 1857 to the McNab building across the street from the Figures Hotel, and it is known that the McNab building was located in the middle of Lot 12 in Block 22. The hotel was located on Marshall on the upper 73 feet of the 103 feet fronting Marshall, with a storehouse on the lower 30 feet at the corner of Marshall and Austin.

Hughes, who owned a large plantation northwest of Jefferson and was a wholesale and retail dealer in dry goods and groceries in Jefferson, advertised the Planter's Hotel for rent or lease in late October 1857, mentioning that it was presently occupied by Figures, that it was located in the business portion of town and convenient to the steamboat landing, that it was doing a large business, and that a new brick addition would be completed by January of the next year. Hughes was apparently responsible for changing the name from the Figures Hotel to the Planter's Hotel.

The Planter's Hotel was rented or leased by William Brooks from Hughes in early 1858. Brooks had been in the dry goods and groceries and in the receiving and forwarding businesses. When he took charge of the Planter's Hotel in 1858, he changed the name to City Hotel, as indicated by an April 10 advertisement in the Clarksville *Standard*. The advertisement mentions the new brick addition, new furniture, and convenience to the steamboat landing and stage office. Loughery visited Jefferson in April just before the name was changed and reports the hotel overflowing with travelers. J. W. Barrett, the editor of the Marshall *Harrison Flag*, visited Jefferson in September and reports that "We were kindly entertained by the gentlemanly proprietor of the City Hotel; and from experience we can recommend that as a No. 1 hotel; and the public seem to have found it out, from the patronage it receives." Loughery visited Jefferson in October and attended a party, apparently at the hotel, in connection with three marriages:

> Having comfortably quartered ourselves at the excellent hotel of our friend Mr. Brooks, we accepted an invitation kindly tendered by him to make one of the gay party. It has never been our fortune to witness an entertainment in which every one seemed to enjoy

themselves more, or to exhibit a greater freedom from undue restraint. The repast furnished by Mr. Brooks was excellent, and the music of the evening surpassed even our expectations. Every thing, in fact, passed off in good taste, and in a manner calculated to elicit emotions of pleasure.

A January 1859 advertisement says that the hotel was a brick structure located on the corner of Marshall and Austin, that a large number of rooms had been added and newly furnished, and that it contained the office for the stages. Brooks visited Barrett of the *Harrison Flag* in November, who reports that Brooks had been on a buying tour for his mercantile operation "and also something nice for those who may favor him with a call at the Jefferson City Hotel. There is no use in drumming for custom for the latter branch of his business. The knowledge of his bountifully supplied table precludes the idea of vacant chairs at the second ringing of the bell."

Brooks is listed in the 1860 census as a 42-year-old hotel proprietor with a wife and three children. Boarding in the hotel were three clerks (Robert Brooks, 26; Warren Ford, 21; Wayne Cotton, 24); one teacher (P. J. Carolin, 30); one sportsman (O. H. Whitman, 28); one fisherman (Anthony Owens, 40); and W. S. Deye, 45.

Foundations were laid for a three-story brick addition in March 1861. Reece Hughes offered the hotel for sale or rent in the November 27, 1861, Shreveport *South-Western*, with the advertisement mentioning that Brooks was still in charge. When Hughes sold the hotel to Jacob Sterne and Isaac Pinski in October 1863, the transaction indicates that Hughes' storehouse was on the first 30 feet from the corner of Marshall and Austin and that the hotel property occupied the next 73 feet on Marshall and ran back 150 feet to the alley. The City Hotel was destroyed in January 1866 in the first of many fires that were to devastate the town during the 1860s and 1870s.

Eason Hotel/Star Hotel/Rising Sun Hotel/Planter's Hotel

Dr. Ithael Eason, physician, surgeon, and druggist, was among Jefferson's earliest and longest residents, having established himself in Jefferson prior to 1848 and still living there in 1876. There are no newspaper records that would indicate when Eason began operating a hotel and what it was called, although it probably operated under the name of Eason House or Eason Hotel. What is known from the newspapers is that it began to be operated by Dr. Robert Rogers, formerly of Red River County, in December 1849 and advertised under the name Star Hotel in the Marshall and Clarksville newspapers in March 1850, featuring a stable with ostlers. The March 23 advertisement in the Clarksville *Northern Standard* states that this was the hotel "lately occupied by Dr. Eason."

Rogers is listed as a 30-year-old physician born in South Carolina in the 1850 census because this was his chief occupation. He lived in the hotel with his wife and four children. Also living in the hotel were one lawyer (Granville Lewis, 45); one druggist (Isaac Eason, 26, apparently Ithael's younger brother); and three clerks (Jacob Green, 22, Mortimer Ward, 40, and Richard Bailey, 25). Ithael Eason lived with his family in an adjacent structure. The Star Hotel had the least number of boarders in 1850 of the three hotels in Jefferson, but they were all members of the professional class.

Rogers was a renter-operator, and the hotel continued to be owned by Eason. In the March 1851 term of the district court, Daniel Alley received a judgment against Eason for nonpayment of debts that required Eason to sell the Star Hotel property on Fractional Block K in the Alley Addition fronting Jefferson Avenue on the south and Line Avenue on the west (immediately northeast of the courthouse square). Loughery reported only two hotels in Jefferson in September 1851, indicating that Eason's hotel was not in operation at that time.

I have not been able to find any deed records indicating who the hotel was sold to, but it must have been Bartholomew Figures, because he sold the hotel property in Fractional Block K to Frederick Schluter in December 1860, and the intervening hotel advertisements indicate that Figures was the owner. The interesting thing about the 1860 transaction is the mention that this was an old log hotel. This means that the Eason Hotel was probably built in 1845 and therefore was Jefferson's first hotel. There is no evidence for the construction of any log structures after that year, and there is evidence that a saw mill was in existence by at least December of that year.

Further evidence for the early existence of this hotel is a statement made by DeMorse in June 1847. DeMorse had passed through Jefferson in July 1846 and was not impressed. In June 1847, he was impressed, particularly because of the "increased air of comfort which it has, from having a better supply of house room," which was displayed in the Soda Lake Hotel. DeMorse apparently did not like the accommodations supplied by the log hotel in July 1846.

It is probable that Figures purchased the hotel from Eason in 1852 and named it Planter's Hotel. Dr. Samuel Garey rented the Planter's Hotel from Figures in January 1853 and began operating it under the name Rising Sun Hotel in February. Loughery mentions Garey as the operator of the Figures House in January, and the February advertisements for the Rising Sun Hotel state that it was the successor to the Planter's Hotel. The advertisements indicate that the hotel was located at the head of Marshall Street and offered stables and ostlers. The location indicates that this was the log hotel, because the south portion of Fractional Block K is at the head of Marshall Street, and this designation was used by Figures in the 1860 transaction.

Garey lived in a residence attached to the hotel. The following rates were listed: board and lodging per month, $15; board without lodging per month, $12.50; board and lodging per week, $5; board without lodging per week, $4.00; board and lodging per day, $1.00; board without lodging per day, $0.75; man and horse per night, $1.25; man and horse per day, $1.50; single meal, $0.40; horse per month, $12; horse per week, $4.00; and horse per day, $0.75. These were lower rates than those for the Jefferson Hotel.

Samuel Garey is listed in the 1850 census as a 41-year-old physician from Missouri with a wife and two children and property valued at $4,000. He acquired the Alexander & Chrisman drugstore in March 1847 and appears in the 1847 tax roll as having $1,300 in merchandise and owning seven lots in Jefferson valued at $700. He also served as Jefferson's postmaster in early 1853, but operated the postal services out of his storehouse rather than out of the hotel.

Garey left town in May 1853 owing people a lot of money and was assumed to be on his way out of state. His Jefferson properties were sold to satisfy his creditors. They did not include the hotel, which was still owned by Figures, who apparently operated it under the old name of Planter's Hotel.

The May 14, 1853, *Jefferson Herald* contains an undated advertisement for a Planter's Hotel under Joseph Taylor. Unfortunately, town and street locations are not given, and the newspaper contains advertisements for hotels in towns other than Jefferson. "Uncle Joe" Taylor was a well-known citizen of Marshall where he operated the Planter's Hotel. This was one of the most favored names for hotels in the South. He apparently took over the Planter's Hotel in Marshall when Elizabeth Jackson left to take over the Jefferson Hotel in January 1853. Immediately below the Planter's Hotel advertisement is an advertisement for Garey's Rising Sun Hotel stating that it was formerly known as the Planter's Hotel. Taylor's advertisement mentions that the eastern, northern, and western line of stages left from the hotel. This is descriptive of Marshall in 1853; but there does not appear to have been stage service to the north out of Jefferson in 1853.

J. Wright leased the Planter's House from Figures in July 1854, according to an advertisement that appeared in the *Texas Republican*. The advertisement stresses moderate terms and "the best of arrangements for providing for travelers' horses."

When Loughery visited Jefferson in April 1858, he states that "There are two excellent hotels in Jefferson, the Planters' Hotel kept by our old friend Wm. Brooks, and the Jefferson Hotel by James Moore, a very clever gentleman. The hotels are of a superior character, and were filled to overflowing." Loughery was visiting Jefferson at the time that Brooks was changing the name of the Planter's Hotel at the corner of Marshall and Austin to the City Hotel. Loughery's statement does not necessarily mean that the log hotel was not in operation in 1858. Although he wrote a great deal about the other two hotels over the years, he never mentions the log hotel or its operators, apparently because he did not consider it worthy of attention.

George Prewitt began advertising the Planter's Hotel in the January 28, 1859, *Harrison Flag*, stating that he had "just renovated and refurnished this well known house on Marshall Street, where he is prepared to entertain travelers and boarders in good style, at very reasonable prices." This advertisement appeared with advertisements for the City Hotel and the Jefferson Hotel through at least the end of 1860. As a consequence, this could not have been the Planter's Hotel on Marshall Street that came to be owned by Hughes and operated by Brooks under the name City Hotel. The Planter's Hotel operated by Prewitt is not mentioned in the newspapers other than in conjunction with the initial advertisement. Prewitt appears in the 1860 census, but as a farmer operating north of Jefferson.

Perry House

I have not been able to determine anything about the existence of a predecessor to the Excelsior House prior to the Civil War. In an advertisement dated January 29 that appeared in the April 30, 1867, *Semi-Weekly Jimplecute*, H. A. Cutrer announced that he had become the proprietor of the Perry House on Austin Street opposite Freeman's Hall, that the facility had been completely refurbished, and that it was then opening under the name Fulton House. It is obvious from this advertisement that the Perry House was a predecessor to the Excelsior House and that it had been in existence for some time. The Perry House is not mentioned in any documents prior to the Civil War. Lot 9 in Block 20 was purchased by Perry from Urquhart in February 1854, and Lots 4, 5, 6, 10, and 11 were purchased by Perry from Urquhart in September 1858. The sale prices indicate that the lots were not occupied by structures, and the significance of the purchases is lost against the background of Perry's many purchases.

Hotel in Paradise

Richard Ramsey is listed as an innkeeper in Precinct 1 in the 1850 census. Living with him were his wife and three children and three male boarders (B. Pendleton, J. M. Bentley, and T. A. Dicks). The surrounding inclusions in the census enumeration indicate that this hotel was located in Paradise. The number of boarders suggests that the hotel was very small. This was probably the tavern occupied by Bartholomew Figures in 1853 and operated under the name Figures Hotel in 1856, which was one-half mile west of town on the south side of the Daingerfield Road. The Figures Hotel in Paradise apparently continued in operation after 1856, because it is mentioned as a locator in a

January 20, 1864, sale by Lewis Northern of his one-acre homestead south of the Daingerfield Road and one-half mile west of the hotel.

It should be noted that the term "Jefferson" had no specificity in the deed records or in general usage and did not refer to the land within the city limits at that time. When speaking about land outside of the Urquhart and Alley portions of the town, the deed records generally refer to distance from the central business area. As a consequence, some deed records say that the Figures Hotel was in Jefferson. Actual locations of properties within Jefferson can be determined with precision from the deed records themselves because they reference lot and block numbers. Actual locations of properties outside of the lot and block designations can also be determined with precision on the basis of information in the deed records, but require an understanding of the on-the-ground locations of the reference points used in the deed records.

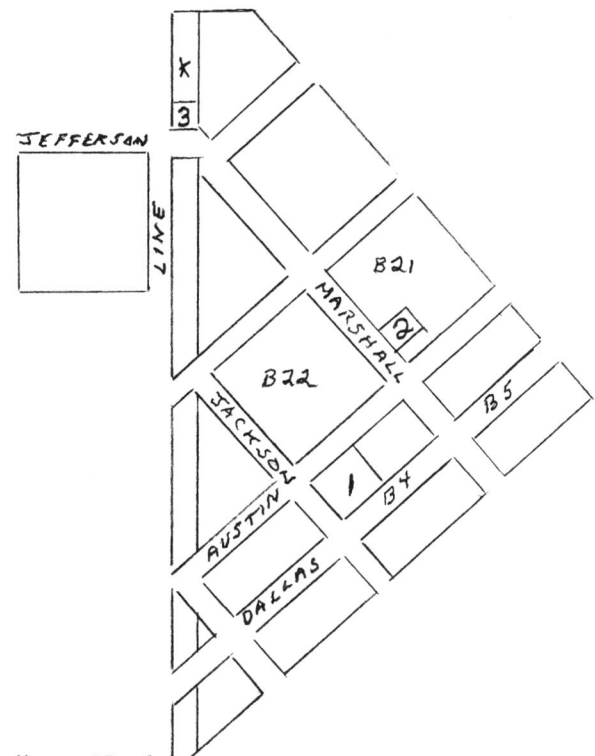

Fig. 33-2.
KEY:
1. Soda Lake Hotel/Jefferson Hotel
2. Figures Hotel/Planter's Hotel/City Hotel
3. Eason Hotel/Star Hotel/Rising Sun Hotel/Planter's Hotel

84. Stables

Horses were the primary means by which people traveled on land, either on horseback or else in carriages and buggies. Horses were sheltered, fed, and cared for in stables, which were attached to private residences and hotels or else were free-standing commercial operations that served the general public. Among the commercial operations, livery stables provided stabling, but also horses and transport vehicles for hire. It was a short step from renting to buying and selling horses, which gave rise to the sale and livery stable.

Many people passed through Jefferson on their way from and to New Orleans by steamboat or traveled to Jefferson on business. Stables were essential for the care of horses owned by the traveling public and for the rental of means of conveyance. Hotels that catered to the traveling public had to provide stabling services, which are usually given equal billing with personal accommodations in hotel advertisements. These services could be provided either by a stable run by the hotel or else by a nearby commercial operation.

The first commercial stables in Jefferson were two operated by William Russell by at least July 1845. Russell's lower (or downstream) stable was apparently on Dallas Street on Lot 1 in Block 8, because this lot was quit claimed by Russell to John Speake in 1852. The upper (or upstream) stable was larger and occupied the whole of Lot 7 in Block 74, fronting on Jackson Street at the northeast corner of Jackson and Camp. Russell sold the upper stable and adjacent Lot 8 to A. F. Alford and Thomas Hotchkiss for $1,200 in January 1847. Russell moved the lower stable to Lot 2 in Block 9 sometime before February 1853, when Hotchkiss sold his portion of the lot to John Speake and Clinton Willard. Russell is not mentioned in connection with stables after this point. It is probable that Russell rented horses and buggies, although his operation is not referred to as a livery stable.

The second mention of a stable in Jefferson occurs in a December 1846 advertisement for William Perry's Soda Lake Hotel, which was located on Dallas Street on Lots 4–6 of Block 4. The advertisement mentions "large, airy and commodious" stables connected with the hotel, with care of horses by an experienced person. This stable was immediately across Austin from the hotel and was on Lots 7 and 8 and part of Lot 9 in Block 22, fronting Jackson Street on the northeast corner of Austin and Jackson. It was probably a semi-independent operation, catering to a much larger public than the hotel guests.

Although Robert Nesmith is not mentioned specifically in connection with this stable until the 1850s, it is probable that he was the operator from the beginning. Nesmith and Robert Brownell operated the Soda Lake Hotel from at least April 1848 until it was sold by Perry in December 1849 to Stephen Ellis and Joseph Elliott, who changed the name to Jefferson Hotel. Nesmith is mentioned as the manager of the stable in a January 1852 advertisement for the Jefferson Hotel. He purchased the lots on which the stable was located from Nelson Trawick for $700 in January 1853, with clear title given in November of that year. Trawick is never mentioned in connection with stables, and it is obvious from the January 1852 advertisement that Nesmith was operating the stable before he became owner of the property.

In a February 1853 advertisement, Nesmith indicated that he had been in the stable business for a long time in both the North and South. He appears in the 1850 census as a 35-year-old farmer born in New Hampshire, with real estate valued at $1,000 and a wife and child. The occupational designation is correct, because Nesmith also operated a farm in Paradise, where he was living in 1850. A November 1853 conveyance from Allen Urquhart to Amos Ury concerning Lots 1–3 in Block 22 mentions that the house on the property had been occupied by Ury, but was at that time occupied by Nesmith. This property, which was not owned by Nesmith, was on the quadrant immediately to the northeast of the stable. During the late 1840s, the stable was probably only devoted to the care of horses. It became a sale and livery stable in January 1852, when the advertisement for the Jefferson Hotel mentions that Nesmith sold and exchanged horses and provided carriages, buggies, and riding horses for rent.

In February 1853, in conjunction with the land purchase, Nesmith began advertising independently from the Jefferson Hotel under the name Nesmith's Livery Stable (Fig. 34-1). The advertisement indicates that Nesmith had erected a new facility, that he was renting saddle horses and carriages, and that services were provided to the traveling public, including those stopping at the Jefferson Hotel. Rates for keeping horses were $12.50 per month, $4.50 per week, 75 cents per day, 50 cents per night, and 25 cents per single feed. The new facility was probably located across the street from the old one, on the corner lots in Block 23 at Austin and Jackson that had been acquired by Nesmith from Urquhart in December 1852. Nesmith probably continued to use the old property; however, it is certain that he was operating a stable on the corner of Block 23 in October 1856.

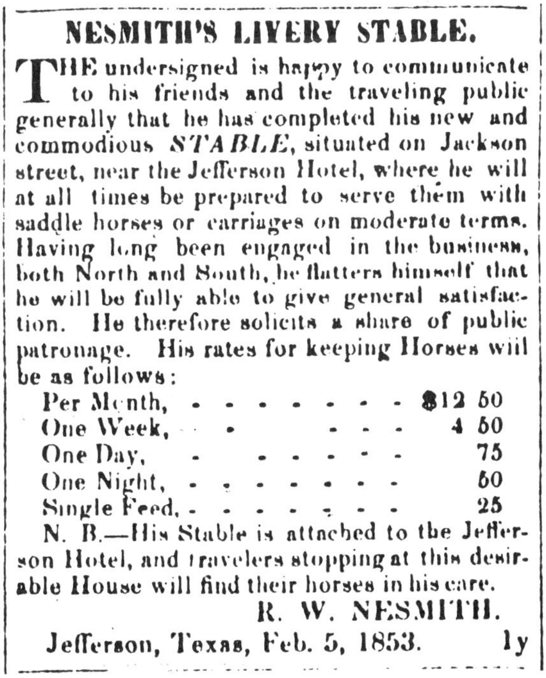

Fig. 34-1. Nesmith's Livery Stable Advertisement. Source: February 12, 1853, *Texas Republican*

NESMITH'S LIVERY STABLE.

THE undersigned is happy to communicate to his friends and the traveling public generally that he has completed his new and commodious *STABLE*, situated on Jackson street, near the Jefferson Hotel, where he will at all times be prepared to serve them with saddle horses or carriages on moderate terms. Having long been engaged in the business, both North and South, he flatters himself that he will be fully able to give general satisfaction. He therefore solicits a share of public patronage. His rates for keeping Horses will be as follows:

    Per Month, - - - - - - - $12 50
    One Week, - - - - - 4 50
    One Day, - - - - - - 75
    One Night, - - - - - - 50
    Single Feed, - - - - - - 25

N. B.—His Stable is attached to the Jefferson Hotel, and travelers stopping at this desirable House will find their horses in his care.

                      R. W. NESMITH.

Jefferson, Texas, Feb. 5, 1853.   1y

A stagecoach business was a logical extension of a stable. Robert Loughery took a stage from Marshall to Jefferson in January 1853. The regular driver was absent, and the stage driver was J. W. Kemp, co-proprietor of the Jefferson Hotel. This line did not advertise and was probably an adjunct to Nesmith's stable operation. By October 1857, Nesmith had secured a contract to carry the mails from Marshall to Jefferson, Daingerfield, and Mt. Pleasant and established the Forest Mail Stage Line. A December 1857 advertisement for this line states that "In connection with the stage Line, the Proprietor keeps an extensive Livery Stable, where travellers can procure hacks, carriages, buggies and saddle horses, at all times, on the most reasonable terms."

The stage line was extended to Clarksville in July 1858. Nesmith sold half of his interest in the Block 23 property to Anderson Booth, who had been operating a livery stable in Marshall, in September 1858. The Nesmith & Booth stable experienced a small fire in December 1858 and a large fire in June 1859 that consumed the entire operation. Among the losses were 29 horses, five buggies, wagons, harnesses, and feed. The losses were between $10,000 and $15,000 and there was no insurance. Nesmith sold the other half of his interest in the property to Lewis Moody for $2,000 in September 1859, and Booth sold his half interest to Moody in February 1860. By January 1860, the Forest Mail Stage Line was back in business with Nesmith and Shaw as proprietors, but stables are not mentioned in the advertisement.

On March 31, 1852, John Speake sold Lot 7 in Block 6 on the corner of Dallas and Market to Nelson Taylor, Richard Parmalee, and Daniel Coe for $200. This became the location of the Jefferson Livery Stable, which began advertising in the April 3, 1852, *Texas Republican* under the name of Nelson Taylor & Company. The advertisement states that the stable was recently built and "possesses more conveniences than any in Eastern Texas. Good ostlers will always be in attendance. The stable will be under the superintendance of one of the concern, whose experience enables him to please all who may favor them with a call." Rates for keeping horses given in the May 14, 1853, *Jefferson Herald* were $12.50 per month, $4.50 per week, 75 cents per day, 50 cents per night, and 25 cents for a single feed, the same as Nesmith's.

N. A. Birge & Company's Sale and Livery Stable began advertising in the July 12, 1856, *Texas Republican*. The owners were Noble Birge and Charles Hynson. The facility was located on Dallas Street on Lot 3 in Block 5, which was one block removed from the Jefferson Hotel. As indicated by the advertisement, Birge & Company rented saddle horses, buggies, hacks, and carriages; fed horses by the day or month; bought and sold horses on their own account and on commission; and broke horses on reasonable terms. In connection with the livery stable, they had a saddle and harness shop where any kind of work or repairing was done for cash.

Three advertisements by Birge & Company appear in the March 14, 1857, *Eastern Texas Gazette*. The advertisement for the sale and livery stable states that a new stable had been erected on Dallas Street and that "Persons from the country, with the intention of visiting New Orleans, or any point on the river, by leaving their animals at this stable, can have them carefully and attentively attended to." In addition to the saddle and harness shop, there was a black smith and wood shop. The black smith and wood shop appears in a companion advertisement, which indicates that the shop was located on the northwest corner of Jackson and Dallas and employed Tom Ward, "the best Blacksmith, in Eastern Texas," as well as a woodworkman.

A carriage repository in a red building adjoining the livery stable is featured in another advertisement. The repository sold buggies and other modes of conveyance, as well as harness, whips, and saddlery. The livery stable and blacksmith and woodshop advertisements continue into the November 7, 1857, *Eastern Texas Gazette* under the name of N. A. Birge & Company; but the N. A. Birge & Company Carriage Repository advertisement is replaced by an advertisement for Birge, Bradford & Co., "Dealers in Carriages, Buggies, And every thing pertaining to a Saddlery Business," with the location given as one door below Birge & Company's livery stable. This was the same carriage repository, but under new management and offering buggies, saddlery, trunks, valises, saddlebags, whips, collars, and harness.

In the April 10, 1858, Clarksville *Standard*, Birge & Company announced the recent completion of a two-story sale and livery stable. On March 25, 1859, one-half the interest in Lot 3 in Block 5 containing

N. A. Birge & Company's livery stable was sold for $1,000 by John McCamant and Esther Gooding to Nathaniel Bradford. An April 15, 1859, indenture from William Brooks to Nathaniel Bradford concerning Lot 3 in Block 5 mentions the livery stable formerly occupied by Birge and Hynson but then occupied by O. J. Bullock. A suit by a New Orleans firm against Noble Birge and Joseph Preston led to the sale in March 1860 of Lot 3 in Block 5 containing the livery stable. Birge appears as the county sheriff and Preston as a druggist in the 1860 census. Bullock, Bradford, and Hynson are not listed.

The October 15, 1858, *Texas Republican* notes that the existing stables were being enlarged and that a new one was about to be erected. In December 1858, George Prewitt's new livery stable at the corner of Jackson and Austin sustained $5,000 in damages from a fire, with the loss of one horse and feed. Prewitt continued in business, as is indicated by a June 1859 agreement with Ephraim Terry to build a brick wall for a stable. A June 9, 1860, deed of trust by Prewitt indicates that his stable was made of brick and that it was located on the property in Block 22 that had been previously occupied by Nesmith in connection with the Soda Lake Hotel and its successor, the Jefferson Hotel. In January 1860, Elizabeth Hughes purchased from Prewitt one-half interest in the livery stable business located in a brick building with grocery house attached on Lots 7, 8, and one-half of 9 in Block 22.

William Brooks operated a stable on Lot 8 in Block 26 according to a February 27, 1860, quit claim deed from Hugh Hensey to Bob Hughes. This stable was on Marshall Street about one block north of the City Hotel, which was operated by Brooks. Brooks apparently did not own the stable land. In October 1860, J. B. Ligon & Company agreed to build for William Hodge and James Moore a livery stable; to supply horses, mules, wagons, buggies, carts, etc.; and to rent or lease it to them fully furnished. An April 1861 deed record concerning William Perry and Hugh and Lucy Freeman mentions that Hodge's livery stable was on Lot 10 in Block 6.

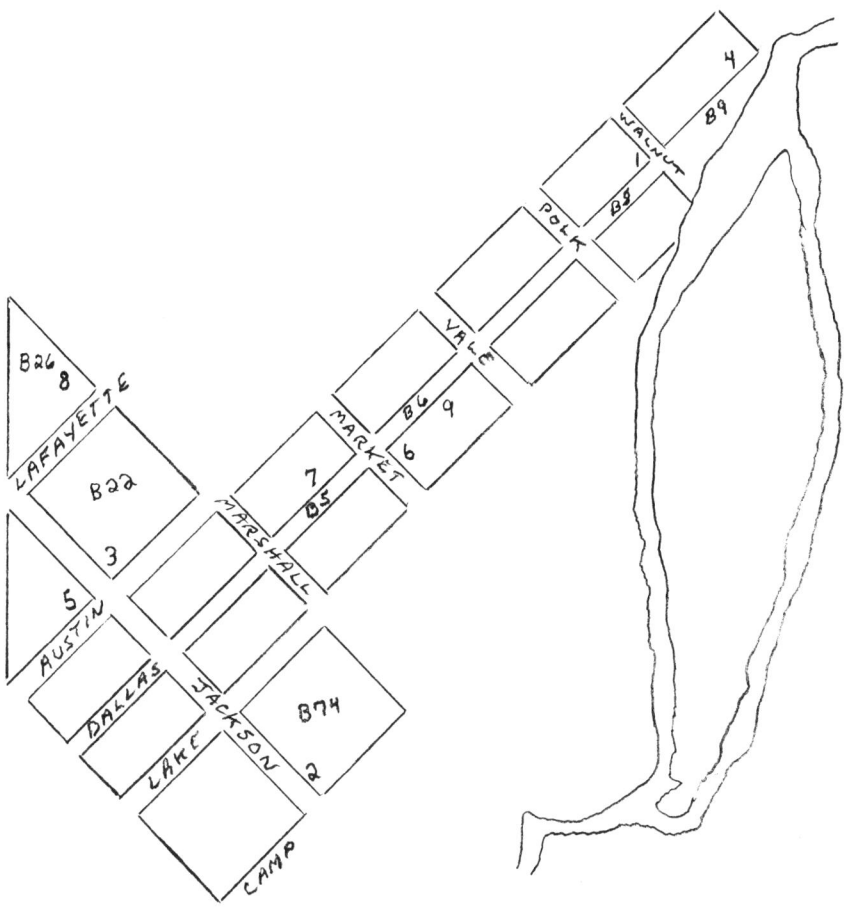

Fig. 34-2. Stables
KEY:
1. William Russell (lower), 1845
2. William Russell (upper), 1845
3. Robert Nesmith, 1846; George Prewitt, 1858
4. William Russell, 1853
5. Nesmith's Livery Stable, 1853; Nesmith & Booth, 1858
6. Jefferson Livery Stable, 1853
7. N. A. Birge & Company, 1856; O. J. Bullock, 1859
8. William Brooks, 1860
9. William Hodge, 1860

35. STAGECOACHES

The roads of northeast Texas were quagmires after heavy rains and rough and rutted during dry weather. Oxen that pulled the freight wagons were left on the roads when they died in transit. Stagecoaches were hot or cold, dusty, cramped, jolting, and often dangerous; but they provided a fairly rapid mode of overland transport and conveniences to the traveling public, particularly businessmen. They were also the primary means of interior transport for the mails. The establishment of stagecoach services between Shreveport and Jefferson was easily accomplished because of the existence of bridges over Little Cypress and Big Cypress bayous. Services between Jefferson and Clarksville were longer in coming because of the difficulty of erecting bridges over the Sulphur Fork.

The first mention of a stagecoach in connection with Jefferson occurs in the January 29, 1853, *Texas Republican*, which describes a trip from Marshall to Jefferson taken by the newspaper's editor, Robert Loughery:

> I left Marshall on Sunday morning, in the stage, for Jefferson. After proceeding about a mile and a half, with several disagreeable threatenings of being upset in the road, the body of the vehicle rolled completely to one side, and, on examination, we discovered that the stage was in a fair way to go to pieces, and could not possibly hold together much longer. Our stage driver,

who was an amateur, and not the regular one, (being no less a personage than friend Kemp of the Jefferson Hotel,) immediately drove the carriage to one side of the road, and started back to Marshall for another, leaving the passengers in the road to amuse themselves as they might think best. After waiting a considerable time, he once more made his appearance and we soon found ourselves under way. The road is none of the best; some parts of it, indeed, sadly need working. We sincerely hope that our Legislature will set themselves to work to reform our road laws; for certainly no country in the world is cursed with worse roads than Texas.

The account indicates that there was a regular stage line on the old road between Jefferson and Marshall by at least late 1852. The driver, who was not the regular one, was J. W. Kemp, co-operator of the Jefferson Hotel. It is possible that the stage line was operated by Robert Nesmith, who owned a livery stable that provided services to the hotel. However, there was a tri-weekly line between Marshall and Shreveport whose formation is mentioned in the September 28, 1850, *Texas Republican*. The May 14, 1853, *Texas Republican* indicates that this line was operated by Gibson and Swink and had been converted to a daily by the filling in of the intervening days by stage contractors from Georgia. Because the *Texas Republican* does not ever mention an extension of the Gibson and Swink tri-weekly to Jefferson, it is probable that the stage taken by Loughery was an independent tri-weekly operated by Nesmith.

The May 21, 1853, *Texas Republican* reports that "New life has been infused into the stage line in this section. We have now a daily stage line between Jefferson and Shreveport, by way of Marshall. The distance, 60 miles, is made in daylight. The enterprising gentlemen connected with these lines deserve encouragement." The entire line may have been run by Gibson and Swink and the stage contractors from Georgia. On the other hand, Nesmith may have run an independent tri-weekly, which is mentioned in November 1853, with the intervening days carried by the stage contractors from Georgia.

The April 2, 1856, Shreveport *South-Western* reports under the title "Daily Stages" that "Mr. Bradfield intends to run his four horse postcoaches hereafter daily between this place, Marshall and Jefferson. The trip will be made from Shreveport through to Jefferson in one day." This was the famous coachman William Bradfield. Bradfield's stage ran from Shreveport to Marshall directly west and from Shreveport to Jefferson on the road to the northwest out of Greenwood. Initially, the Bradfield stage to Jefferson may have been a tri-weekly, because the November 19, 1858, *Texas Republican* reports that Bradfield had just introduced a daily line between Shreveport and Jefferson and also between Henderson and Jefferson by way of Marshall.

By March 1856, the Post Master General had approved saddle horse mail service between Jefferson and Daingerfield, and consideration was being given to establishing saddle horse or coach mail service between Jefferson and Clarksville. Coach mail service between Clarksville and Mt. Pleasant was approved in June 1856. By September 1857, Robert Nesmith had received the contract to carry the mails between Marshall and Mt. Pleasant by way of Jefferson and Daingerfield and had established the Forest Mail Stage Line. Advertised prices in December were $2 to Jefferson, $5 to Daingerfield, and $7 to Mt. Pleasant (Fig. 35-1).

Nesmith's stages ran from Marshall to Jefferson daily and from Jefferson to Mt. Pleasant on Monday, Wednesday, and Friday, departing from Jefferson at 4 a.m. and returning at the same hour on Tuesday and Saturday. They connected with the Bradfield stages to Shreveport at Marshall and Jefferson, the Henderson and Tyler stages at Marshall, and the Clarksville stage at Mt. Pleasant. According to the advertisement, travelers from Shreveport could reach Mt. Pleasant "in one day, without the loss of sleep. Good teams, and careful drivers, always on the road. Persons traveling this line, will receive every kindness and attention necessary to insure their comfort."

The Forest Mail Stage Line was extended to Clarksville in July 1858, with the cost from Marshall to Clarksville at $12. The stages left Marshall at 4 a.m. on Tuesday, Thursday, and Saturday, arriving at Clarksville the next day. They left Clarksville at the same time on the same days, arriving in Jefferson in time to take the Shreveport stages.

FOREST MAIL STAGE LINE,

FROM MARSHALL TO JEFFERSON, DAINGERFIELD, AND MT. PLEASANT.

RATES OF FARE.

From Marshall to		Jefferson,	2
"	"	Daingerfield,	5
"	"	Mt. Pleasant,	7

THE above line will run in connection with the Shreveport stages and railroad, and Henderson and Tyler stages, and connect at Mt. Pleasant with the Clarksville and Western stages.

The stages run daily from Marshall to Jefferson, and depart from Jefferson for Mt. Pleasant, every Monday, Wednesday and Friday, at 4 o'clock, a. m., and return every Tuesday and Saturday at the same hour, always going through in one day, so as to connect with the stages at Mt. Pleasant.

By this arrangement, persons will be enabled to travel by Rail-road and stages, from Shreveport to Mt. Pleasant, in one day, without the loss of sleep. Good teams, and careful drivers, always on the road. Persons traveling this line, will receive every kindness and attention necessary to insure their comfort.

R. W. NESMITH,
Jefferson, Oct. 1, '57.   Proprietor,

☞ In connection with the stage Line, the Proprietor keeps an extensive Livery Stable, where travellers can procure hacks, carriages, buggies, and saddle horses, at all times, on the most reasonable terms.

☞ At Mt. Pleasant, Mr. M. Bowman, who is a host himself, keeps entertainment, for man and beast: travelers going West, will always find ready conveyances to any point to which they may wish to go.

no. 48—3ms

Fig. 35-1. Forest Mail Stage Line Advertisement. Source: December 19, 1857, *Standard*

The friendliness of the earlier advertisement was replaced by restrictions apparently born of experience in dealing with the general public during the intervening period:

No seat will be considered secured until paid for.

All bundles, packages and parcels, must be prepaid, or they will not be taken.

Fifty pounds of Baggage allowed to each passenger. One hundred and fifty pounds extra baggage will be charged the same as one passenger, and a lesser or greater quantity charged in the same proportion.

Nesmith's livery stable was destroyed by fire in June 1859. By January 1860, Nesmith was back in the stagecoach business with a man named Shaw under the old title Forest Mail Stage Line, which met the Bradfield stages to Shreveport at Jefferson. In July 1860, the name was changed to Forest Tri-Weekly Mail Stage Line. This line connected with the Bradfield stages at Jonesville by way of the Southern Pacific Railroad out of Marshall. Because of the scarcity of forage and attendant greater costs of operation, prices were increased to $2.50 from Marshall to Jefferson, $6.50 to Daingerfield, $8.50 to Mt. Pleasant, and $14.50 to Clarksville. Through tickets from Clarksville to Shreveport were $20.

Loughery described the line from Jefferson to Clarksville as "one of the best in the State" and the stages as "equal to any in the South." The October 13, 1860, Marshall *Texas Republican* reports that "The stage from Jefferson turned over on Thursday morning. There were four or five passengers, none of whom were severely injured." In late 1860, Nesmith mortgaged his home on Lots 7–9 in Block 46, two sets of harnesses worth $150, ten horses worth $1,000, a four-horse coach named Dick Runnelly, a Troy Coach, and a two-horse coach. These were coaches used by Nesmith in the mail route from Marshall to Jefferson. DeMorse of the Clarksville *Standard* described Nesmith as an "energetic gentleman." Nesmith appears in the 1860 census as a 45-year-old stage contractor born in North Carolina with $8,000 in real and personal estate and a wife and child.

36. Newspapers

Jefferson was the home of six newspapers prior to 1861, with continuous publication from May 1847, except for the period from late 1849 through late 1850. The first of these was the *Jefferson Democrat*, which was replaced by the *Spirit of the Age*, which was replaced by the *Independent Monitor*. After the period in which Jefferson had no newspaper, the *Jefferson Herald* started in September 1850. It was joined in January 1857 by the *Eastern Texas Gazette*, which changed its name to *Jefferson Gazette* in September 1858. The *Jefferson Herald* and *Jefferson Gazette* were consolidated into the *Herald and Gazette* in January 1860. These were all four-page weeklies that were distributed regionally.

Obviously, thousands of copies were issued; but there are only five extant copies, and two of these are incomplete. Fortunately, newspapers used each other as sources of information through an exchange system. When a newspaper was started, the first and subsequent issues were sent to regional newspapers, which announced the new arrival. Articles are summarized or taken verbatim, with attribution enabling insight on what was being published in Jefferson. In addition, editors knew each other and visited each other on their travels. These encounters are usually mentioned in the travel accounts. As a consequence, the sequence of the newspapers in Jefferson and something about what they contained can be known from external sources even if no antebellum Jefferson newspapers had survived.

Jefferson Democrat

Jefferson's first newspaper was the *Jefferson Democrat*, owned and edited by William Bishop. A prospectus for the newspaper first appeared in the May 5, 1847, Clarksville *Northern Standard* (Fig. 36-1), and the first issue appeared in May, only two years after Jefferson had come into existence. The paper changed hands in August, when Berry Durham became the owner and Robert Loughery the editor. It is last mentioned in the June 17, 1848, *Northern Standard*, and it was out of existence by August, when it was replaced by the *Spirit of the Age*. The demise of the newspaper was obviously related to Durham's death in November. There are no extant issues of the *Jefferson Democrat*, and there is little information on the newspaper in external newspapers such as the *Northern Standard*, which is not surprising given its brief life. However, there is sufficient evidence from the other newspapers of the period, from the prospectus, and from the comments in the *Northern Standard* to provide a characterization of the *Jefferson Democrat*.

With respect to the persons involved, Bishop was one of Jefferson's earliest residents and was instrumental in its development. Durham operated the ferry across Cypress Bayou before Jefferson became a town and was Jefferson's first resident. He became owner of the newspaper shortly after losing a bid for state political office. Bishop was Jefferson's first postmaster, appointed on May 22, 1846. He was replaced by Durham in January 1847 and he in turn replaced Durham in June. Loughery was associated with newspapers in New Orleans and Monroe, Louisiana, and came to Texas to edit the *Jefferson Democrat*. When it ceased to exist, he moved to Marshall, where he became the long-time owner and editor of the *Texas Republican*. He provided continuous coverage of Jefferson while in Marshall and returned to Jefferson in May 1867 to publish another newspaper.

Nothing can be determined from the quick change of ownership, because this was quite common for the period. Nor can anything be determined from its short life, because this was also quite common, with the cause usually being financial failure. The prospectus says that "The proprietors are aware of the disadvantages attending the establishment of a newspaper"; and they indicate that "The first number will be issued as soon as a sufficient number of subscribers can be

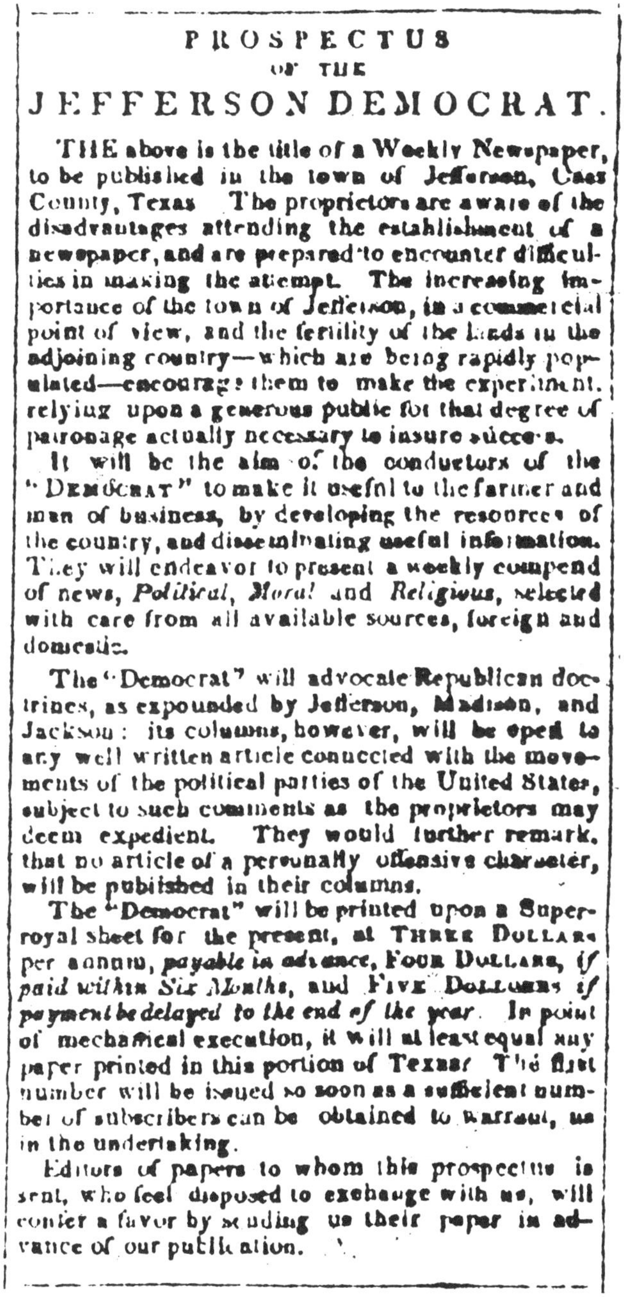

PROSPECTUS OF THE JEFFERSON DEMOCRAT.

THE above is the title of a Weekly Newspaper, to be published in the town of Jefferson, Cass County, Texas. The proprietors are aware of the disadvantages attending the establishment of a newspaper, and are prepared to encounter difficulties in making the attempt. The increasing importance of the town of Jefferson, in a commercial point of view, and the fertility of the lands in the adjoining country—which are being rapidly populated—encourage them to make the experiment, relying upon a generous public for that degree of patronage actually necessary to insure success.

It will be the aim of the conductors of the "DEMOCRAT" to make it useful to the farmer and man of business, by developing the resources of the country, and disseminating useful information. They will endeavor to present a weekly compend of news, Political, Moral and Religious, selected with care from all available sources, foreign and domestic.

The "Democrat" will advocate Republican doctrines, as expounded by Jefferson, Madison, and Jackson: its columns, however, will be open to any well written article connected with the movements of the political parties of the United States, subject to such comments as the proprietors may deem expedient. They would further remark, that no article of a personally offensive character, will be published in their columns.

The "Democrat" will be printed upon a Super-royal sheet for the present, at THREE DOLLARS per annum, *payable in advance*, FOUR DOLLARS, *if paid within Six Months*, and FIVE DOLLARS *if payment be delayed to the end of the year*. In point of mechanical execution, it will at least equal any paper printed in this portion of Texas. The first number will be issued so soon as a sufficient number of subscribers can be obtained to warrant us in the undertaking.

Editors of papers to whom this prospectus is sent, who feel disposed to exchange with us, will confer a favor by sending us their paper in advance of our publication.

Fig. 36-1. *Jefferson Democrat* Prospectus. Source: May 5, 1847, *Northern Standard*

obtained to warrant us in the undertaking." The number was obviously achieved, because the newspaper was established. Durham had sufficient capital to support a newspaper; and when it ceased, it was quickly replaced by another, indicating that there was sufficient community support.

The printing equipment for the *Jefferson Democrat* was quite sophisticated. The prospectus says that "In point of mechanical execution, it will at least equal any paper printed in this portion of Texas." DeMorse of the *Northern Standard* visited Bishop in June 1847 and "found him in possession of a fine stock of printing materials, new and costly. Indeed his establishment is of better quality than we had expected to see in so new a place." Loughery also reported retrospectively in January 1866 that it was "the wonder of the inhabitants of a large section of country."

The *Jefferson Democrat* was a weekly newspaper, which was the common publishing increment before the Civil War. It was a super royal sheet (19 by 27 inches) with a single fold to produce four pages. The first page would have been devoted to international and national news, with perhaps some serial story of romance or adventure, which was quite common, indicating that entertainment was integral to newspapers from the earliest times. The second page would have focused on state, regional, and local news and information and would have provided New Orleans market information. The last two pages would have been devoted primarily to advertisements, which were the main source of income, as they are today.

Information on local events would have been obtained by the editor through participation in the life of the community and would have been current. International, national, state, and regional news was a different matter. This was long before the telegraph. Editors had to rely on other newspapers for this information, which was presented as either direct (and usually extensive) quotes from other newspapers or else reportage on what they had to say. To obtain and use this information, all early newspapers were involved in an exchange system that functioned somewhat like the present-day press services. Participation in the exchange system was solicited before the first issue was published, because it was essential to the quality of the first issue. This is why the prospectus states that "Editors of papers to whom this prospectus is sent, who feel disposed to exchange with us, will confer a favor by sending us their paper in advance of our publication." Because the mails and transport modes were slow, the information obtained from these newspapers was always well out of date. This does not appear to have been a concern to anyone other than merchants and planters, who were forced to make economic decisions in the absence of knowledge about critical events that were occurring elsewhere.

As its title indicates, the *Jefferson Democrat* was a Jefferson newspaper. This does not mean simply that it was published in Jefferson, but, more importantly, that it was designed to promote the interests of Jefferson. As the *Northern Standard* expressed it on receiving the first issue, "We think the Democrat, a very respectable paper, so far as one may form an opinion from the first number, and decidedly calculated to advance the interests of the Town of Jefferson in which it is published." The promotion of Jefferson included making the community known to the larger world, notifying potential customers in the interior about the services offered by local merchants, and defending the community against any slights that might be published in other newspapers.

Although this was a Jefferson newspaper, it was not simply a community newspaper. All of the newspapers of the period were regional in readership and contained advertisements from regional towns and New Orleans, which was the source of regional imports and the destination of regional exports. Subscription lists from a small population center like Jefferson would have been small, and local advertisements would have been few if restricted to local customers. More importantly, a newspaper could not survive on the basis of local advertisements alone. To increase the advertising base, it was necessary to have a regional readership. Nevertheless, the existence of a population center like Jefferson was essential to the foundation and maintenance of a newspaper in the form of subscriptions, advertising accounts, and support services. The local and regional economics of newspaper viability were presented in the prospectus: "The increasing importance of the town of Jefferson, in a commercial point of view, and the fertility of the lands in the adjoining country—which are being rapidly populated—encourage them to make the experiment, relying upon a generous public for that degree of patronage actually necessary to insure success."

In addition to the pragmatics of the situation, there was a real concern with what we would call regional development; that is, a paper such as the *Jefferson Democrat* was not simply interested in promoting the interests of Jefferson, but also in promoting the interests of the surrounding country. As expressed by the prospectus, "It will be the aim of the conductors of the DEMOCRAT to make it useful to the farmer and man of business, by developing the resources of the country, and disseminating useful information." The term "country" was never used in this early period to refer to the United States, but rather to the region of interest and influence exercised by the town. As such, the "country" had no definite boundaries, changed over time, and referred to different geographic areas depending on who was using the term. The town, and its organ, the newspaper, thought of itself as the base for regional development, which in the case of Jefferson would have included the whole of northeast Texas. Because there were other population centers with their own newspapers in this area and at its fringes, there were equivalent and overlapping "countries" constituted by differing perspectives.

The selection and writing of articles would have been in the hands of Bishop and, later, Loughery. There were no reporters, and composition was always the responsibility of the editor (or editors) in these early newspapers. There would have been at least one type-setter. All of the newspapers of the period had agents in other towns. Their primary function was solicitation of subscriptions and perhaps some advertisements. However, new advertisements from other towns often appeared after an editor visited another town, indicating that advertisement solicitation was probably largely the responsibility of the editor.

With respect to content, the prospectus notes that the paper "will endeavor to present a weekly compendium of news, *Political, Moral* and *Religious*, selected with care from all available sources, foreign and domestic." From a modern perspective, notably absent is the dimension of sports. There were no team sports during this period, and the invention of baseball, which was the premier American sport, was many years away. Notably present from a modern perspective is the moral dimension. This was a period when character, correctness of thought, and right action were celebrated, and their opposites were condemned. The prospectus states that no articles of a personally offensive character would be published in the newspaper. Instructive stories and homilies were presented, and a moral perspective was integral to the interpretation of events. To give but one example, killings involving alcohol were fairly common. The facts of such killings were usually accompanied by editorials on the evils of drinking.

Another distinctive feature of the newspapers of the period was their political orientation. The *Jefferson Democrat* was a democratic newspaper. Because the parties have changed orientation, it is important to note that a Democrat of the past was more like a Republican of the present, emphasizing states rights, limited federal powers, and a strict interpretation of the Constitution. It also implied for the period adamant opposition to any concessions to the North concerning the institution of slavery and its political and social implications. The terminology of the period is particularly confusing because almost all democrats considered themselves republicans in the sense that they were strong supporters of the republican form of government as envisioned by the Founding Fathers, which included representative institutions and, as far as they were concerned, a limited franchise.

Almost all of the early newspapers expressed a political position, which usually was presented in their names, as was the case with the *Jefferson Democrat*. Given the importance of the political issues facing the nation both before and after the Civil War, it was difficult for a newspaper not to take a political position. Newspapers that attempted to be independent usually found themselves supporting a particular political position in addressing the issues of the day. This does not mean that they were party organs. A democratic newspaper would usually support the views of the Democratic party as a matter of principle, insofar as the party expressed the convictions of the newspaper's editor. But distance was maintained, and political positions were usually fine-tuned. In its prospectus, for example, the *Jefferson Democrat* emphasized that it would "advocate Republican doctrines, as expounded by Jefferson, Madison, and Jackson"; and DeMorse noted that Bishop considered himself a Democratic Republican of the Old School.

The idea of objective reportage was foreign to these newspapers and their readers. This is not to say that they were not interested in truth; and indeed, they were careful to retract any misstatements of fact. However, they would have repudiated the idea that facts can exist apart from an interpretive framework. It was necessary for a man to take a stand, to know where he stood, and to interpret the events of the day through a moral and political lens that was considered correct. Bias is an inappropriate charge for newspapers that expressed their principles in their names and statements of purpose and could only emerge under the assumption that newspapers had the capacity for objectivity.

Because newspapers were written by a single person (or by joint editors with similar views) who interpreted the events of the day in the light of specific political and moral principles, reading them is somewhat like reading a contemporary editorial page, but with one important exception: there was only one point of view. Modern newspapers present alternate viewpoints to increase readership, but also because of the entertainment value posed by conflict situations, which serve as the subtext for most straight reportage today. Conflicting interpretations of events are presented in early articles only when the editor is of a divided mind.

Alternative points of view were solicited in the prospectus for the *Jefferson Democrat*, but with the caveat that these commentaries would be "subject to such comments as the proprietors may deem expedient." However, it is unlikely that any such commentaries would have been submitted to the *Jefferson Democrat*. Submitted alternative points of view rarely appear in the pages of a particular newspaper and had their own organs of expression, at least within the context of the restricted range of opinion that was acceptable in the South before the Civil War. Alternative points of view were often introduced, but invariably for the sake of providing an occasion for refutation. Given the fine distinctions in political principle and its application, the *Jefferson Democrat* under Bishop felt obliged to respond to the *Northern Standard*'s interpretation of a political meeting in Jefferson, and the *Northern Standard* responded in kind.

For all of these reasons, the quality of an early newspaper was highly dependent on the quality of the editor. The old newspapers were generally of very high quality and a delight to read because the editors were thoughtful, learned, passionate, and good writers. This applies even to highly propagandistic newspapers like the *Jefferson Radical* published after the Civil War. Although this newspaper specialized in *ad hominem* attacks on its political opponents, it contains articles of profound insight on the issues facing the country during Reconstruction. From their largely self-taught and community based perspective, these editors were highly critical of the concept of professional journalism when it was introduced in the academic curriculum by Robert E. Lee after the Civil War.

DeMorse found the *Jefferson Democrat* at its inception to be "a respectable looking little sheet, nearly as large as the Soda Lake Herald, and is well filled with matter. The opening editorial is moderate and well expressed, and the selected matter is good.... We have a slight acquaintance with the editor of the Democrat, which induces us always to expect from him, a journal respectable in its character; reasonable, moderate and just in its editorials." However, he deprecated the change of hands, stating that the paper had "lost that nice appreciation of courtesy, which was a distinguishing characteristic of its former gentlemanly conductor." The occasion for this comment was an article apparently written by Loughery that lectured DeMorse on what it meant to be a good Democrat.

The readers of these newspapers were also of very high quality. They were expected to appreciate the details of political and moral commentary, to read the full text of important political speeches and writings, and to know when Shakespeare was being quoted and what he meant. The substantial and diverse subscriber lists for isolated minor towns like Monterey and industrial facilities like Nash's foundry indicate that general readership was much more sophisticated than might be expected. It can be assumed that the *Jefferson Democrat* was read by thoughtful readers throughout northeast Texas.

Spirit of the Age

The *Jefferson Democrat* was replaced by the *Spirit of the Age* in August 1848, undoubtedly using the existing press and equipment, and is last mentioned in March 1849. This was a weekly, published on Saturday evenings by W. C. Baker & Company. William Baker was apparently the editor, with participation in the company possibly by some of the investors in the Steam Mill Company. A poor-quality photographic copy of the December 16, 1848, issue can be seen at the *Jimplecute* office. This is number 19 of volume 1, as indicated by dates in the advertisements. The paper was small, with five columns and four pages 13 inches by 19 inches. Rates were $3 in advance, $4 in six months, and $5 in 12 months. The low rate on pre-payment reflects the greatest difficulty faced by editors—getting people to pay their bills. Professional cards (advertisements by doctors and lawyers) of eight lines or less were $10 per year. Candidate announcements were $10 for major offices and $5 for minor offices.

An advertisement by Ithael Eason within the newspaper indicates that he provided services as a physician and surgeon at his drugstore and that the printing office was adjacent to the drugstore (one door above or below). The drugstore was located at the north end of Lot 12 in Block 22, fronting 22 feet on Marshall Street and running back 50 feet.

The first page is devoted to national and international news, as was common practice. There is a long article on the proposed transcontinental Atlantic and Pacific Railroad. The rest of the first page is taken up by the "Farmer's Department," which is a long excerpt from the *Southern Cultivator*. Because the *Spirit of the Age* was sold regionally, it was not strictly a city newspaper and contained information of interest to interior planters. The right column is missing, but probably only completed the "Farmer's Department" article.

The second page is devoted to national and local news, again common practice. The national news is concerned with politics, elections, courts, newspapers, and western manufactures. Local news is concerned with the weather (pleasant, bayou continues to rise, navigation good), problems with the mails, navigation improvements, warehouse construction, and immigration to Cass and Harrison counties. There is also a short poem by Emily Judson to her father. Most old newspapers contained poems by locals, reflecting an interest in culture, and serialized fiction of love and adventure, reflecting an interest in entertainment.

The article on navigation improvements appears to be referring to a proposed bayou clearing effort from Black Cypress Bayou to Benton, but it may be referring to improvements to Black Cypress. Improvements to Cypress Bayou were a continuing concern to Jeffersonians, having been mentioned, for example, by the Clarksville *Northern Standard* in June 1847. The article on immigration appears to be providing a contrast between Cass and Harrison counties, but generally celebrating both. Mention is made of the iron resources of Cass, and the article appears to be saying that an iron works is under construction. This is compatible with a June 1847 *Northern Standard* article on a facility that was being developed 19 miles northwest of Jefferson by Jefferson Nash.

The article on warehouses indicates that two large, fine warehouses had been completed within the previous week, one 40 feet by 70 feet and the other 75 feet in depth. The article also mentions existing warehouses, which means that there were at least four in 1848. The article also says that interior merchants and planters would find it advantageous to ship their goods and cotton at Jefferson and that the present warehouses "will be amply sufficient to accommodate the merchants and planters who ship at this place."

The third and fourth pages are devoted entirely to advertisements and business matters, which was also common practice. National postal routes are announced, including the one from Fulton, Arkansas, to Moore's Ferry on Sulphur Fork and then to Jefferson by way of William's Bluff (later Monterey) and Clinton. There is a column on New Orleans market prices and advertisements for two New Orleans receiving and forwarding merchants. National newspaper and magazine advertisements include the *Scientific American*, the *Columbian Magazine*, the *Saturday Evening Post* (a newspaper), the *Daily Globe*, and *Godey's Lady's Book*. Planters and businessmen were well read, as is indicated by estate inventories. School advertisements include the Western Military Institute (Kentucky), the Collegiate Institute (Georgetown), and an academy in Lamar County. Planters and businessmen sent their sons to academies.

The dominant advertiser (in 10 sections, meant to catch the reader's eye) was C. Lewis & Company of Shreveport (flour, bacon, liquors, codfish, lime and cement). There is also an advertisement for a Shreveport receiving and forwarding merchant. James Todd of Smithland advertises new goods, including a good stock of boy's and youth's blankets and tweed coats. Todd mentions that full prices are allowed for cotton and that because of the poor cotton market during that year, credit would be extended on the next year's crop.

Official notices include an estray advertisement (a stray animal found by Ebenezer Frazier), which were very common in the newspapers. There are estate notices for Gray Blackburn (James Blackburn, administrator) and Ennis Ury (James Durrum, administrator). The official notices are issued by Clerk of Court Perry Graham. Sheriff Richard Crump issued a notice to Captain Sam Applegate of the steamer *Duck River* to appear in the district court at Jefferson under the petition of Williamson Freeman for $500 in damages to six boxes of merchandise shipped to E. T. Harris of Jefferson through the firm of Ury & Ward.

The Jefferson advertisements are by merchants, lawyers, and doctors, the dominant advertisers in all newspapers. Horatio Walcott, one of Jefferson's earliest and most important merchants, advertises dry goods and houseware, including bonnets and liquors, at apparently wholesale and retail prices. The dissolution of the firm of Stanley & Ward is announced, with Charles Stanley stating that persons in debt to the firm should make immediate payment, with J. H. Hill serving as agent in Stanley's absence.

Attorney advertisements include Martin Rogers and the newly formed firm of Everett & Withers. William McNeill advertises as a notary public. In addition, Nat Burford advertises that he lost a pocketbook on the road between Jefferson and Mt. Pleasant that, if found, should be returned through the office of Sam Moseley in Jefferson. J. M. Baker, M.D., offers his services to the people of Jefferson and vicinity, with his office at the house of W. C. Baker. Ithael Eason, who always appears under the initials I. G., has two advertisements, one as a physician and surgeon and the other as a pharmacist. The drugstore, where Eason practiced, was apparently adjacent to the printing office. Eason carried a large and well-selected stock of drugs and medicines, also patent and botanic concoctions, which were sold for cash or on credit to select customers. All staple articles were warranted as represented, but patent medicines would speak for themselves.

There are two steamboat advertisements. One is for a boat that ran between Alexandria and Hurricane Bluffs on Red River. The other is for the *Archer*, with Munroe as captain. The *Archer* advertisement is provisional (will operate when water levels permit). It appears to refer to a regular packet between New Orleans and Jefferson, but the text is damaged to such an extent that the meaning is unclear. There appears to be a Jefferson agent, but only the Shreveport firm of C. Lewis & Company is decipherable as an agent. This boat made documented trips to Jefferson in June and July 1848.

There is a prospectus for the *Jimplecute* (actually *Jim-ple-Cute*) that is long, damaged, and written in E. C. Beazley's bombastic style. A good copy is available in another newspaper. The prospectus is clear that Beazley intended to publish the *Jimplecute* in Marshall, where he lived. Two other prospectuses for a newspaper by this name appear in later years, and it did not begin to be published, in Jefferson, until 1865.

There is little information about the *Spirit of the Age* other than what appears in the extant issue. However, it was definitely Whig in politics, supporting the election of Zachary Taylor, a strong national government, and internal improvements. An extract published in the March 10, 1849, *Northern Standard* gives a sense of the editorial flavor of standard reportage in these early newspapers:

> THE LAST DAY OF DEMOCRACY.—This day closes the administration of the Democratic party. Thank kind Providence for the change.—The reckless experiments of the Democratic administration on the currency of the country ruined our temporal prospects. Thousands of energetic, enterprising, honest citizens shared the same fate. We looked forward with some impatience to the time when the Ruler of the Universe would restore the days of Washington, Jefferson, and Madison. Thank God the time has come. Democracy *run mad* has been signally defeated. The republican principles of Jefferson are again in the ascendant. On next Monday, General Taylor will be inaugurated President of the United States. Times, from that day,

will change for the better. Demagogues, intermeddling electioneering office holders, incompetent spooneyes, who have been leach-like sucking the heart's blood of the people, will all get their walking papers. Honest, competent, business men will take their places. The currency of the country will be improved, internal improvements will move like lightning—a railroad will be built to California—immigration will pour in like floods from Europe—education will be extended to all classes—missionaries "will run to and froe and knowledge shall increase"—agricultural and mechanical pursuits will prosper beyond a parallel in the history of nations.

Independent Monitor

The *Independent Monitor* replaced the *Spirit of the Age* in early June 1849, acquiring its equipment. The publishers were Dr. Job Baker and W. P. Watson, with Baker also serving as editor. The transition between the two papers was probably smooth, given the family and business relations between the Bakers. This weekly paper was "neutral in politics, and well filled" according to the June 16, 1849, *Northern Standard*. The May 22 term of the commissioners court ordered that the sale of lots in Linden be advertised in the *Independent Monitor*. Watson proposed in July to publish another newspaper in Dallas that would be called the *Texas Echo*, but this intent was apparently not realized. The *Independent Monitor* lasted only a few months. The October 18, 1849, *Texas Republican* provided a list of the 27 papers published in Texas, with a notation that the *Independent Monitor* had "died of congestive chill."

Jefferson Herald

Jefferson appears to have been without a newspaper from late 1849 to late 1850. In June 1850, a Jefferson resident wrote to Robert Loughery of the Marshall *Texas Republican* that his paper was "now in fact the principal means we have of obtaining the news." The first issue of the *Jefferson Herald* appeared in September 1850, with Samuel Moseley, B.

F. Dennard, and G. F. Wier as editors and publishers operating under the name Moseley, Dennard & Co. This weekly apparently used the high-quality equipment that was initially purchased for the *Jefferson Democrat*, because for neatness of appearance and typographical execution it was considered by the *Northern Standard* to be "not surpassed by any paper in the State."

The *Jefferson Herald* was Democratic in politics. The first issue caused some confusion because the editorials were lifted without attribution from the Whig Shreveport *Caddo Gazette* as an example of what the paper would look like. The next few issues were missed, and the paper did not begin to be published on a regular basis until late November, when DeMorse of the *Northern Standard* noted that "If it shall sustain the position and character of the present number, as we doubt not it will, it will deserve the liberal support of the people of Cass and the neighboring counties. At the outset it has taken a stand in behalf of correct principles—democratic ascendancy, the Union and the Constitution, the peaceful and legitimate enforcement of rights."

The *Jefferson Herald* quickly changed hands, with Robert Loughery of the *Texas Republican* indicating in March 1851 that ownership was then in the hands of Charles Westmoreland and W. P. Watson. Westmoreland was the editor, and Watson had been connected with the *Independent Monitor*. However, Watson must have assumed editorial responsibilities almost immediately because Westmoreland spent a good part of April and May visiting the lower Southern states. Articles supporting the right to secession appeared in June and July. Loughery reported in September that the *Jefferson Herald* was "going ahead finely," that Westmoreland was talented and popular, and that the proprietors were planning to enlarge the paper during the winter. DeMorse reported in December that Westmoreland had retired in November and that the paper had been suspended with a view to enlargement.

Loughery received the first issue of volume two of the *Jefferson Herald* at the beginning of 1852, greatly enlarged and with Justice Ferris, a "talented and courteous young lawyer," as editor and Watson and Moseley as proprietors. Loughery accused the paper of supporting Whig positions, but it replied that it was union democratic, with Watson and Moseley opposed to secession and disunion. The *Jefferson Herald* began supporting Sam Houston as a candidate for the presidency in March and was a strong advocate of internal improvements.

Watson expressed a desire in July 1852 to sell his interest in the paper. In December, W. A. Wortham purchased Watson's interest, joining Moseley as co-proprietor. Ferris retired as editor, continuing to practice law. Judge Hiram Grinsted, late of Brownsville and formerly a state legislator, became editor. Loughery stated that Grinsted "brought with him the reputation of being a gentleman of talent." Loughery indicated in January 1853 that Wortham was formerly of Marshall, that Grinsted "may be regarded as quite an accession to the Texas corps of editors," and that the paper was doing a prosperous business.

An extant issue of the May 14, 1853, *Jefferson Herald* is available in a paper copy. This was the 21st issue of volume three, and the paper was published on Saturday, with Grinsted as editor and Moseley and Wortham as proprietors. At 16 inches by 22 inches, this four-page weekly was equivalent in dimensions to a modern newspaper, but smaller in bulk and periodicity. The annual price was $2 in advance, $3 if paid at the end of six months, and $4 if paid at the end of 12 months. Advertisements were $1 per square (ten lines or less) for the first insertion and 50 cents for subsequent insertions. Small advertisements, called cards, were $10 per year. Candidate announcements were $10 for important offices and $5 for minor offices, both of which had to be paid in advance. Marriage and obituary notices greater than six lines were charged as advertisements. Printing work of all types was done on a cash basis.

The first page is devoted to international news, witticisms, moralistic stories, and the popular encouragement column by Fanny Fern. The second page contains the masthead column, with the first insertions devoted to political endorsements and local news. Most of the rest of the page is devoted to national and international news; but the right column contains advertisements, including official notices (court summons, trust sale). The third and fourth pages are devoted almost entirely to advertisements, which are largely grouped by category (e.g., law notices) or geographic area (e.g., New Orleans Advertisements). However, the left columns of the second page contain the newspapers terms and a long poem by Oliver Wendell Holmes. The advertisements for local businesses are not primarily for local customers, but rather for regional customers, particularly planters and interior merchants. There are numerous requests by merchants for customers to pay up on their debts, with some threats of legal action.

Loughery visited Jefferson again in June and reported that "We had the pleasure of calling on our friends of the Herald, by whom we were kindly received. The prospects of this excellent paper, we judge are flattering. Friend Wortham's countenance wears the same pleasant appearance as it did of yore, although we regret to find him in bad health. Judge Grinstead, the editor, is generally esteemed for his candor, talent, and moral worth, and the Herald cannot but acquire an enviable character under his management." Nevertheless, Grinsted withdrew from the editorial position in July, writing a valedictory suggesting interference with editorial prerogatives as his reason for leaving. It was necessary for Moseley to respond, stating that his letter to Grinsted was simply advisory and in keeping with his responsibilities as a proprietor.

In August, W. P. Watson reacquired an interest in the *Jefferson Herald*, and Frank Clark, a lawyer and former editor *pro tem* of the Clarksville *Standard*, became editor. DeMorse reported in September that "The Jefferson Herald is certainly improving under the new administration. It is full of editorial; much of it, of local interest; and will doubtless be very popular with the sovereigns in that region, if they have any proper appreciation of fancy, life and spirit." In the same month, Clark wrote an editorial claiming that the *Jefferson Herald* was "the commercial paper of Eastern Texas" and therefore a better place than Galveston for New Orleans merchants to place their advertisements.

A new press to print an enlarged sheet was ordered in January 1854 and delivered in March, with publication suspended for a few weeks so that volume four would appear in the new format. The *Jefferson Herald* entered its fourth year with the same editor, but with new owners. Moseley, Wortham & Company sold the paper in late February to W. P. Watson & Company, with Charles Norris and Benjamin Baker as the other proprietors. DeMorse reported in March that "It is now a sheet fully as large as the present size of the Standard, and greatly improved in its general appearance. With its usual spicy editorial, it will be a most readable sheet, and should prosper."

Clark became ill in April and went to Hot Springs, Arkansas, to regain his health, with Watson assuming the editorial chair. Clark returned to Jefferson in September, but with his health not much improved, resumed editorship, and purchased the paper in November. DeMorse characterized Clark as follows: "As a politician, he is a firm and tried Democrat—as a writer he is sprightly, and forcible, capable of 'doing good action' in time of need—as a social companion he is pleasing, with an inexhaustible fund of anecdote, and smart repartee—and as a young man of high literary acquirements he ranks high among those capable of estimating his worth. We anticipate for him a long career of usefulness in his present profession."

However, Clark's health continued to decline, and he apologized to his readers for his inability to vigorously pursue his editorial duties. When Loughery visited Jefferson in February 1855, he found Clark ill in bed and the paper reduced in size because of a temporary deficiency in paper supplies, which had been caused by the absence of navigation during that year. Clark married Annie Hawkins in April.

Two damaged pages of the May 29, 1855, *Jefferson Herald* under Clark's editorship are available on microfilm. This was number 28 of volume 1, new series. The paper was published on Tuesday and cost $3 in advance. The motto is "The Union—The World's Best Hope and Our Own." There are editorials opposing internal improvements and the Know Nothings, and mention is made of the fact that in the absence of navigation on Cypress Bayou, large quantities of cotton, hides, and pelts were being hauled to Shreveport for shipment to New Orleans.

Clark's health did not improve, and J. B. Hickey served as editor *pro tem*. Hickey purchased the paper in October, but it was under the proprietorship of Grinsted and Watson by February 1856, with Grinsted as editor. Frank Clark died of gastritia in Clarksville on August 20, 1856, at the age of 26, leaving a wife and young child. DeMorse's tribute indicates something of the quality of Jefferson's newspapermen:

> The deceased was formerly editor of the Jefferson
> Herald, and in his editorial position, known to many
> of the people of the State. He was born near the mouth

of Mill Creek, (now Bowie Co.) in this State, in April 1830, when this was an Indian border, undergoing all the dangers and inconveniences of a frontier. His Father, James Clark, the founder of this Town, was a man of active energy and influence, and had been a member of the Arkansas Legislature for several sessions. Frank Clark was liberally educated, had fine intellectual capacity, and had given promise of prominence; but disease had held its heavy hand upon him, for some years, and he has at last, with unexpected suddenness, fallen a victim, in early manhood. Impulsive, in a high degree, he had some faults, (as we all have,) but in his nature, there was *never* anything small, or ungenerous. He had a proud, high heart, which ever leaped to sustain Truth and manliness, and public and private virtue. As a slender boy of fifteen years, he enrolled himself in the service of the country, in the Mexican War, and was elected a Corporal by the Company raised in this Town, with which he went to service. Subsequent to this, he spent two years (graduating) at the Law school of Transylvania University, under the special tutelage of Judge Marshall, and as an inmate of his house. He commenced the practice of Law in this town, but a fondness for editorial life, contracted in an intimacy of years with the writer of this, and desultory occupation of his leisure hours, in this office, induced him to associate himself with Messrs. Moseley & Watson, in the Jefferson Herald, and subsequently, to purchase its entire proprietorship. He conducted that paper, we believe, about two years; and obtained much credit for sprightly writing, as its editor; and for his unqualified independence, regardless of personality or position. Tired of this, and enervated by disease, he sold the establishment to the present Proprietor, and for the past year had been unoccupied by business. Always a dutiful and affectionate son, his last wandering was, perhaps instinctively, towards the homestead; where under the gaze of the mother he had revered, his spirit made the mysterious transit from its mortal tenement into futurity, without a struggle, or an agitation of the countenance.

Grinsted ran into difficulties with a substantial number of the newspaper's subscribers by diverging from Democratic orthodoxy and sold his interest in the paper to Ward Taylor, Jr. Taylor had been associated with the *Jefferson Herald* 1854 when it was operated by W. P. Watson & Company and left in November when it was acquired by Clark to start a newspaper in Daingerfield called the *Lamplighter*, whose first issue appeared in July 1855. Taylor became the editor and proprietor of the *Jefferson Herald* in November 1856.

Taylor is last mentioned in connection with the *Jefferson Herald* in March 1857. J. T. Harrison, Jr., assumed the editorship sometime prior to August 1858 and may also have been the owner of the paper. Under any circumstances, the paper was staunchly Democratic, supporting Hiram Runnels for governor and Matt Ward for Congress. The paper passed into the hands of Robert and John Ward in August 1858, with Harrison citing failing health as the reason for his departure. The paper was owned and edited by the Wards, who continued to maintain a Democratic position. In August 1859, William Towers sold to Robert Ward the southwest half of Lot 11 in Block 22 fronting 25 feet on Austin Street and running back 150 feet in which the *Jefferson Herald* office was then located. The paper was sold to Harrison and Henry O'Neal, formerly of the *Linden Times*, in September 1859. In January 1860, the *Jefferson Herald* was sold to Shadrach Eggers, who united it with his *Jefferson Gazette* (formerly the *Eastern Texas Gazette*) to form the *Herald and Gazette*.

Eastern Texas Gazette / Jefferson Gazette

The *Eastern Texas Gazette* was started in January 1857, with W. J. Morgan and J. W. Nimmo as publishers and Nimmo and the attorney Daniel McKay as editors. Loughery reported that it was of respectable dimensions, well printed, edited with ability, and independent in politics. DeMorse reported that it was a neat looking sheet, about the size of the *Messenger*, quite readable, proposed to be a domestic journal without political bias, and sold at $2 per year in advance. The prospectus states that a new paper was needed in the region because "none of those heretofore established have met the entire wants of the community, but, instead of devoting a reasonable share of attention to domestic and local affairs, such as the advocacy of an energetic and speedy construction of Railroads, and other Internal Improvements, they have, as a general thing, launched out upon the boisterous and almost chartless sea of Politics, to the exclusion of almost every thing else of interest to the Planter, the Mechanic, the Artisan and the Domestic Circle."

The March 14, 1857, issue, with McKay and Nimmo as editors, is available on microfilm. This was the tenth issue of the first volume (Fig. 36-2). The location is given as Dallas Street, upstairs in Birge & Company's new building, which probably was on Lot 3 in Block 5. Advertisements were $1 per square of 10 lines or less and 50 cents for each subsequent insertion. Business cards of not more than 10 lines were $10 per year. Candidate announcements were $10 for state offices and $5 for county offices. Marriage and obituary notices were free. Job work was done at a slight advance on New Orleans prices and included bills of lading, bill heads, notes, receipts, business cards, and ball tickets. The newspaper advertised for "A negro Boy or Girl about 12 or 14 years of age, for the balance of the year, for whom good wages will be paid" (i.e., to the owner).

The cost was $2 a year in advance for most readers. However, special credit rates of $2.50 at the end of six months and $3 at the end of the year were given to subscribers in Titus and Cass counties and those portions of Harrison and Upshur counties from which businessmen traveled to Jefferson. The reason given for not extending credit to a larger region was the cost inefficiencies in collections. Agents for the newspaper, indicating its regional reach, were located in Linden, Gilmer, Tarrant, Bright Star, Black Jack Grove, Mt. Pleasant, Mt. Vernon, Marshall, Shreveport, Bonham, Paris, Clarksville, Red River County, Boston, New Orleans, and Brownstown, Arkansas. There was also a traveling agent.

EASTERN TEXAS GAZETTE.

THE subscribers propose to commence, at Jefferson, Texas, the publication of a newspaper, bearing the above title.

Should it be objected, that more Newspapers already exist in Texas than the requirements of the population demand, we would respectfully reply that in our opinion, few or none of those heretofore established have met the entire wants of the community, but, instead of devoting a reasonable share of attention to domestic and local affairs, such as the advocacy of an energetic and speedy construction of Railroads, and other Internal Improvements, they have, as a general thing, launched out upon the boisterous and almost chartless sea of Politics, to the exclusion of almost every thing else, of interest to the Planter, the Mechanic, the Artisan and the Domestic Circle.

Although the publishers of the Gazette do not arrogate to themselves the ability to supply this entire vacuum, they nevertheless, hope to be able to furnish such a paper as shall be a welcome weekly visitor to the various classes recited. It shall be their aim, as it will be their interest, to keep pace with the times, in supplying the latest and most reliable news; a regular and correct report of the state of the markets; recent improvements in agriculture and the mechanic arts, whilst the wants of the Family Circle shall receive a due share of attention.

In Politics the Gazette shall be for the present remain neutral. The nation has just emerged from a struggle such as shook the foundation of the Government to its centre. And it is hoped that we may be permitted to enjoy a season of quiet repose, in which the energies of our enterprising people may be devoted more undividedly to the peaceful pursuits of life, and the development of the exhaustless resources which nature has lavished upon our broad and noble State. Should a crisis arrive, however, in the future of our political affairs, in which the honor and the interest of the South should be involved, we trust that we would not be found laggards in the contest, or shielding ourselves behind the fortress of neutrality, but, nerving ourselves for the contest, our position should be boldly and fearlessly taken in defence of the rights and the honor of our own State and section.

With this brief and hasty outline of the course we intend to pursue, we earnestly and respectfully invoke the aid of our friends, and all those who may think us capable of redeeming the pledges herein made.

In order that the Eastern Texas Gazette may come within the means of those in the most limited circumstances, and with the view of giving it the broadest possible circulation, it will be afforded to *cash* subscribers at the very low price of Two Dollars a year, strictly in advance.

MORGAN & NIMMO, Proprietors.

The Eastern Texas Gazette

IS PUBLISHED EVERY SATURDAY BY

MORGAN & NIMMO,

DALLAS STREET, UP STAIRS, IN BIRGE & CO'S NEW BUILDING.

Terms—Two Dollars per annum, in Advance.

TERMS OF ADVERTISING.

Advertisements will be inserted at One Dollar per square of Ten Lines, or less, for the first insertion, and fifty cents for each continuance.

Business Cards, of not more than one square, will be inserted at Ten Dollars per annum.

All Advertisements, the publication of which is required by law, must be paid for in advance.

LEGAL NOTICES.—The twenty-second section of the law regulating fees of office, provides in all cases where citation, or other process, is required to be served by publication in a newspaper, the officer whose duty it may be to make such service, shall be furnished with the Printer's fee for such publication, before he shall be required to have such service made.

Announcing Candidates for State offices Ten Dollars; County offices Five Dollars.

Advertisements not marked with the time for which they are to be published, will be continued until forbid, and charged accordingly.

All personal and business communications promotive of individual interests, will be charged as Advertisement.

Marriage and Obituary notices inserted gratuitously.

AGENTS FOR THE GAZETTE.

S. H. Nance . . . . Linden, Cass, Co.
Messrs. A. V. Wright & Co. . . . Gilmer.
Eldridge & Bro. . . . . Tarrant.
Wiley Ferrill . . . . do
Bullion & Connally . . . . . Bright Star.
J. H. Dennard . . . . Black Jack Grove.
M. M. Bowman . . . . Mt. Pleasant.
M. H. Barnett . . . . do
A. H. Halbert . . . . Mt. Vernon.
Dr. J. C. Harris . . . . Marshall.
J. N. Howell & Co. . . . . . Shreveport.
R. S. Hunt . . . . Bonham.
Jacob Long . . . . Paris.
Dr. G. H. Wooten . . . . . . Clarksville.
John E. Trimble . . . . Red River.
R. M. Lindsay, Esq. . . . . . Boston.
H. K. Brown . . . . Brownstown, Ark.
C. S. Sabine . . . . New Orleans.
A. J. Bateman . . . . do
T. J. Clayton . . . . Our traveling Agent.

Fig. 36-2. Prospectus and Masthead column for *Eastern Texas Gazette*. Source: March 14, 1857, *Eastern Texas Gazette*

In addition to the proprietors column, the first page contains jokes and articles on a thrilling adventure in a gaming house, bashful men, why girls should learn to keep house, Indian depredations, and the camels brought by the U. S. government into Texas for transport experimentation. The second page contains the masthead column with small articles of local interest. There is a poem, a letter to the editor on southern rights and the impending conflict, and articles on credit and banking, Col. Matt Ward for Congress, the Dred Scott case, and the presidential inauguration. The third and fourth pages are devoted almost entirely to advertisements by Jefferson and New Orleans merchants, doctors, lawyers, and steamboats. In addition, there is a listing of the salaries of state officials, a listing of the arrival and departure of mails, and a commercial column showing the current market prices in New Orleans and Jefferson for various commodities and the names of persons for whom merchandise was being held by Jefferson's receiving and forwarding merchants.

As was usually the case, political neutrality did not last long, and the paper came out in support of Sam Houston as governor and Lemuel Evans for Congress in April. McKay informed Loughery that he had been connected with the *Gazette* on a temporary basis for the duration of the election. In spite of his political passions, Loughery recognized quality in his adversaries: "The Gazette under its present editors has been conducted with marked ability; and while we differ with our accomplished friend politically, we embrace the occasion to express our high appreciation of him personally and for his ability as a writer."

Michael Farley became part owner (with Morgan) and editor of the *Gazette* at least by August 1857. The November 7, 1857, issue, with Farley as editor, is available on microfilm. This was the 44th issue of the first volume. The newspaper offices had been moved to Marshall Street on the upper floor of the McNab building, opposite the Figures Hotel, and over the dry goods store of Dr. Anselm Prewitt. The McNab building was located in the middle of Lot 12 in Block 22. This issue was quite similar to the previous extant issue, with the exception of advertisements in the left two columns of the first page, which was common practice, and a list of unclaimed letters at the post office.

The July 18 *Texas Republican* identifies the political positions of Texas newspapers, most of which were Democratic. The *Gazette* is listed as formerly Know Nothing and now in support of the opposition ticket of Houston, Grimes, and Crosby. Although the paper supported Fillmore for the presidency, attempts in the north to reverse the Dred Scott decision by reconstituting the Supreme Court led it to adopt disunion as the appropriate course of action: "Disunion is the only hope of safety for the South. In the Union we are unsafe; out of it we can protect ourselves."

The *Eastern Texas Gazette* came under the editorial control of Shadrach Eggers in April 1858 according to Loughery: "We perceive from the last Jefferson Gazette that Michael Farley, Esq., has sold his interest in that journal to Mr. S. R. Eggers, a gentleman who recently resided in Marshall, and was connected with the Harrison Flag. Mr. Farley takes a pleasing farewell of his readers, in a well written valedictory. The best wishes of confreres of the press, we feel assured, will attend him in his retirement. Mr. Eggers has been, we learn, connected with several newspapers. He is an excellent practical printer, a good writer, a sensible and energetic man. We wish him abundant success in his new home." Eggers owned half interest in the newspaper.

The *Eastern Texas Gazette* changed its name to the *Jefferson Gazette* in September 1858, probably to avoid associations with the eastern seaboard as sectional conflict heightened. DeMorse had taken a similar step in dropping *"Northern"* from the *Northern Standard*. Loughery reported that the paper under its new name arrived "in a new and beautiful dress" and that it was produced with ability and industry. The Marshall *Harrison Flag* was equal in its praise: "The name of the Eastern Texas Gazette has been changed to that of the Jefferson Gazette. It appeared on the first inst., in an entire new and elegant dress. In point of appearance it now has not a superior anywhere. Of its merits we so often spoke while conducted in its former name we need not now repeat. If the success of its industrious, ingenious and gentlemanly proprietors is equal to their merits, their success will be equal to their most sanguine expectations."

The political position of the *Jefferson Gazette* is best expressed by a quote from it that appeared in the March 11, 1859, *Texas Republican*:

"In our two last issues we have made about fifty grave charges against modern Democracy—sufficient, we think, to forever damn any party."

Herald and Gazette

In January 1860, Shadrach Eggers of the *Jefferson Gazette* purchased the *Jefferson Herald* and united the two papers under the title *Herald and Gazette* :

> A DEMOCRATIC PAPER WINKED OUT.—S. R. Eggers, the proprietor of the Jefferson Gazette, has purchased the Jefferson Herald, and united the two papers under the name of the Herald and Gazette. The Herald was the Democratic paper. The subscription lists of the two have been united. Messrs. O'Neal and Harrison, late proprietors of the Herald, give as a reason for selling out, that "there is no money in two printing offices in Jefferson." In other words, the Democrats are unable to sustain a newspaper there. In that case, we hope our Democratic friends in Cass county will not think it immodest or presumptuous in us to say, "Gentlemen we stand ready to serve you." The (?) promises to be a year (?) in political interest. The events at the federal capital, the approaching State election, and the Presidential campaign, nearly at hand, require the circulation of newspapers that will advocate good, wholesome democratic doctrine. It is no time for neutrality, either for individuals or newspapers.

Loughery pointed out in February that the consolidated paper was doing an excellent business and that it better represented the commercial interests of Jefferson. The Social Statistics schedule of the 1860 census indicates that circulation was 1,080. Eggers is listed in the 1860 population census as a 35-year-old printer born in Alabama, with a wife and six children. Living with him was his staff of printers: W. A. Hamilton, 39, born in Louisiana; W. H. George, 19, born in Mississippi; R. Smithson, 18, born in England; and Allen Kirbie, 32, born in Maine.

Also listed in the census is the 21-year-old printer J. E. Duke, born in Alabama and living in the house of James Elliott.

Eggers became the first chief justice of the commissioners court when Marion County was created in early 1860. Loughery reported in August that Eggers was running for reelection and that he came in third (succeeded by James Durr). Eggers was in debt to Robert Ward and William Perry and sold the newspaper for $6,000 to Henry O'Neal in October 1860, including the printing press, job press, type cases, and stand. O'Neal sold the newspaper for $6,000 to A. M. Walker in February 1861, and it appeared under the editorship of Walker & Allen Kirby in March. The *Herald and Gazette* continued to be published in 1861 but disappeared at the end of the year because of paper, advertiser, and subscriber deficits as the nation entered deeply into war. The last record concerning this newspaper is a January 1862 purchase by John Carpenter of Titus County.

Locations

Jefferson's newspapers appear to have been located in buildings that were owned by other people and that were used for other purposes. The only exception is the *Jefferson Herald* in late 1859, when the newspaper purchased the building in which it had been operating.

The *Spirit of the Age* is known to have been located adjacent to Ithael Eason's drugstore, which was on Marshall Street on the northern end of Lot 12 in Block 22. Given the continuity between the *Spirit of the Age* and its predecessor (the *Jefferson Democrat*) and successor (the *Independent Monitor*), it is probable that Jefferson's first three newspapers were located in the same place. The *Jefferson Herald* was located in 1853 on Lot 10 in Block 4 according to a March 1853 mortgage of the property by Clinton Willard and George Tuttle and in 1859 on the southwest half of Lot 11 in Block 22 on Austin Street. The *Eastern Texas Gazette* was located in early 1857 in Birge & Company's building on Dallas Street on Lot 3 in Block 5 and in late 1857 in the McNab building. There is nothing to suggest that it changed its location when it changed its name to the *Jefferson Gazette* in 1857 or that the location changed when the *Jefferson Herald* and *Jefferson Gazette* were consolidated into the *Herald and Gazette* in 1860.

Newspapers

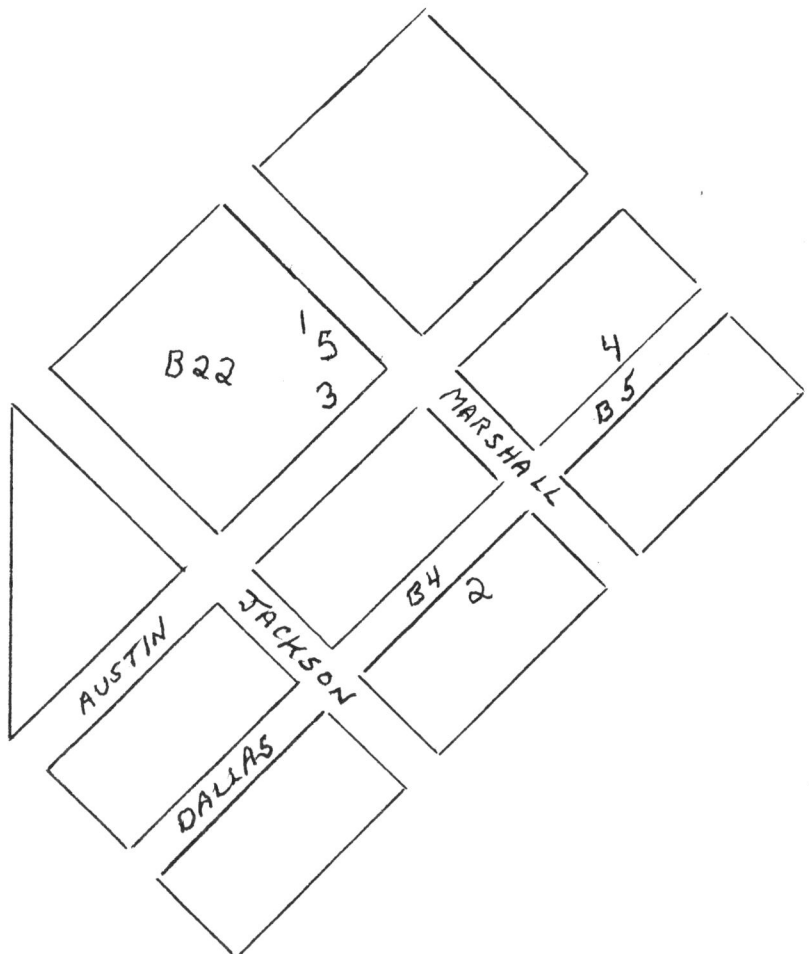

Fig. 36-3. Newspapers
KEY:
1. *Jefferson Democrat*, 1847; *Spirit of the Age*, 1848; *Independent Monitor*, 1849
2. *Jefferson Herald*, 1853
3. *Jefferson Herald*, 1859
4. *Eastern Texas Gazette*, January 1857
5. *Eastern Texas Gazette*, November 1857; *Jefferson Gazette*, 1858; *Herald and Gazette*, 1860

87. Postal Services

Postal System

Before the introduction of the telegraph, long-distance communication to and from places like Jefferson was restricted to the mails, which carried business and personal correspondence. Postal services were one of the primary means by which the extraordinary isolation of a dispersed population over a large continent was mollified. Postal services from the outset were a federal monopoly, but otherwise bore little resemblance to the postal services of today. There were no free-standing public buildings that served as post offices, there was no home or business delivery, postal workers were not federal employees, mail was transported to and from towns through a contracting system with private carriers, postal charges were paid by the receiver rather than the sender until 1855, and stamps were not mandated until January 1856.

As a public agency intended primarily to bind the nation through the diffusion of knowledge, the postal system almost automatically gave rise to subsidies. The primary subsidy was from the North to the South and West. The North had sufficient population masses and attendant correspondence needs to support a postal system. The South and West did not. Nevertheless, new towns like Jefferson demanded and received postal services even if there was insufficient business to cover costs. The first post office was established in Jefferson in May 1846, only one year after the town had come into existence and its population was minuscule.

The other modes of subsidy were in the dissemination of federal political materials and the promotion of newspapers. Newspapers were dependent on the mails, by which they received other newspapers from which they drew most of their information and by which they sent their products to their customers. Low postal rates were instrumental in the proliferation and survival of early newspapers. Weekly newspapers were granted free distribution in their county of publication in 1851. It is not surprising, then, that the bulk of early mail was constituted by political materials and newspapers rather than by personal and business correspondence.

As a nonprofit enterprise, the early national postal system was often in deficit. The bulk of the costs was borne by personal and business correspondence, for which charges were high. The cost of mail was determined by number of pages and distance sent, which is why most early letters were written in cramped styles fully on both sides of the page and are often difficult to read. Sectional imbalances gave rise to widespread illegal carriage of mail in the northeast in the 1840s. High costs also produced illegal carriage in the South, and the personal transmission of letters by steamboat captains and clerks appears to be one of the important means by which they ingratiated themselves to the public.

Postmasters

Postmasters were not federal employees. The federal Civil Service was not established until 1873, and postmasters were not covered until well into the next century. Postmasters were political appointees and part of the patronage system that governed most public appointments. They owed their jobs to their congressmen and lost their jobs when party power changed in Washington. This is one of the reasons why there was rapid changeover of postmasters in towns like Jefferson. Postmasters were paid a percentage of receipts. A salary system was introduced in July 1864, but this was based on the previous two years of income, with salaries adjusted every two years. For a modest town like Jefferson, this must have been a fairly low-paying position that was desirable because of the added income, business opportunity, and prestige that it provided.

Prestige came from the fact that the postmaster was usually the only person in town with a direct relation with the national government. As political appointees, postmasters were generally heavily involved in politics, serving as agents for their sponsors and as officers and members of various local organizations. The post office was a center of political activity at the local level, at least for members of the reigning party. Postmasters knew everyone in town and a lot about their affairs through the monitoring of correspondence. The following is a list of Jefferson's postmasters from 1846 through 1860 and their dates of appointment:

William Bishop	May 22, 1846
Berry Durham	January 26, 1847
William Bishop	June 15, 1847
Perry Graham	February 26, 1849
George Crump	May 2, 1849
Caleb Ragan	December 31, 1849
John Waskom	August 4, 1851
Stephen Ellis	March 31, 1852
Samuel Garey	December 30, 1852
Williamson Freeman	September 9, 1853
Jacob Fleming	April 25, 1854
William Moore	May 7, 1855
James Elliott	February 4, 1857

Elliott is listed as a postmaster in the 1860 census, and the position was not filled by someone else until after the Civil War.

Post Offices

Free letter-carrying service to homes and businesses was not introduced until 1863, and that only in the largest cities of the North. The introduction of this service would have been impossible without the Civil War, because Southern congressmen would have demanded similar services for Southern cities where the cost would have been prohibitive. It was not until 1887 that free delivery was established throughout the nation, but then only for towns with populations of

10,000 or greater. During the early days, there were no postal boxes on street corners, and it was necessary for people, including town and rural residents, to pick up and send their mail at the post office. Because people did not know when mail had been sent to them, early newspapers often contained columns listing unclaimed letters (Fig. 37-1).

Post offices were not buildings but literally offices established in existing businesses or even homes. Rural postmasters were generally storekeepers, newspaper editors, or politically oriented farmers. Storekeepers were particularly interested in becoming postmasters because the necessity for picking up and sending mail at the post office provided an additional flow-through of customers. William Bishop almost certainly operated the post office out of his residence on Lot 4 in Block 8 fronting Polk Street, and Berry Durham almost certainly operated the post office out of his residence on Lots 8 and 9 in Block 3 fronting Jackson Street, although he was reported to have been an avid fisherman who kept the mail in his hat. The post office operated by Samuel Garey was in the back of his drugstore on Lake Street on the southeast half of Lot 2 in Block 74, as indicated by an 1853 trust sale. Elliott provided notification in the November 7, 1857, *Eastern Texas Gazette* that the post office would thereafter be open on Sundays only from 8 a.m. to 10 a.m. and indicated that the post office provided boxes.

Carriage

An "Arrivals & Departures of the Mails" notice signed by James Elliott appears in the March 14, 1857, *Eastern Texas Gazette* (Fig. 37-2). In that year, Jefferson's overland mail to and from the south and east arrived on Tuesdays, Thursdays, and Saturdays and left on Wednesdays, Fridays, and Sundays. Mail to and from the north and west arrived on Tuesdays, Thursdays, and Saturdays and left on Mondays, Wednesdays, and Fridays. The Boston, Linden, Gilmer, Coffeeville, Port Caddo, Monterey, and Smithland mails left on Tuesdays and arrived on Saturdays.

The mails of the United States were originally carried by private enterprises operating under contract to the federal government. Jefferson's mail to and from New Orleans during the earliest years was apparently carried by horseback through Mansfield and Fort Jessup

(left) Fig. 37-1. Unclaimed Letters List. Source: November 7, 1857, *Eastern Texas Gazette*

LIST OF LETTERS,

REMAINING in the Post Office at Jefferson, at the end of the third quarter. Ending 30th Sept., 1857.

Alford, Moses	Henderson J B 2
Allen L B	Hamlett F M
Allen Mary Miss	Harris James
Alford Moses P	Johnson Wm
Buddy J J	Jones T A
Brown Dr	Johnson Henry
Britton J D	King Wm C
Berryman J W 2	Kinbrough
Bagett Wm	Kinbrough O L
Butt Elny	Kenedy Ana Eliza
Ball P Jane Miss	Kelly Geo A
Boynton L B	Leek Aylesberry
Bishop T W	Lewis W G
Batt E P	Lee John
Blyski J T	Leak A B
Brown Daniel	Lewis Wm
Batt James E P	Lee Lilla
Bayett John M	Lemons Adaline
Barton James	McAlaxander S B
Charles J S	Meredith W H
Clark Thos A & C	Morgan John F
Crow Isaac	Meadows Edward
Colemans Wm H	Morris J G
Campbell John	McCartney A G
Campbell Amanda	Martin Walker
Chapel Archey	Marshall Jesse S
Carson N 2	McElhath J A
Clark Mr	Montgomery J
Campbell Charlet W	McCoy M E
Conly Richard	Mebain Maria
Clapp Emory	Perkies E S
Cole M F Rev	Popkin D E
Carrington M F D	Pzle R W
Clark Robert A	Procto Rebecca Mrs
Clerk D C G Co	Riley P S 2
Dollar Wm G	Riley J
Davis Col N F	Ross Thomas 2
Daniels J W	Rossborough James
DeWitt Baney	Rogers Emily Mrs
East Wm	Rowell Anna A
Elliton Robert	Sheriff Cass Co.
Frensh Geo W	Sheppard Thaddias
Griffin C R	Stamps M W
Grimes Wm	Stegar Mary A
Gafford Samuel	Slugater F A
Gafford W L	Smith & Lawrence
Gill James	Smith F P
Gillmere James	Stephen Wm.
Griffin H E	Smith C M Mrs
Green Elizabeth Miss	Slaton Sanford
Gent Wm	Sullivan Wm
Hening A D	Stamps M W 2
Heard Mary A	Swain Josiah
Hynson W E Col	Sturm L
Hynson Geo W	Smiley R A
Hinas R E	Stephenson WD&JC
Tillman Wm	White John L
Teaches Sarah A	Williams J S
Trawick Dr	Wilson Thos A C
Trawick	Wimberly Wm P
Taylor Isack Dr	Wilson Henry
Try Thomas A	Willisons John L
Vickers John	Walker John C
Watts John 2	Watson W P
Womel Sarah	Windson Lenard

Person calling for the above letters will please say they are advertised.

J. S. ELLIOT, P. M.
Jefferson Sept. 2nd, 1857.

(below) Fig. 37-2. Arrivals and Departures of the Mails. Source: March 14, 1857, *Eastern Texas Gazette*

Arrivals & Departures of the Mails.

SOUTHERN & EASTERN MAIL
ARRIVES: Tuesdays, Thursdays, Saturdays.
DEPARTS: Wednesdays, Fridays, Sundays.

NORTHERN & WESTERN MAIL
ARRIVES: Tuesdays, Thursdays, and Saturdays.
DEPARTS: Mondays, Wednesdays, and Fridays.

LINDEN & BOSTON MAIL
Gilmer & Coffeeville, Port Caddo, Monterey and Smithland Mails,
LEAVES: on Tuesdays.
ARRIVES: on Saturdays.

J. S. ELLIOTT, P. M.

and then through Shreveport and/or Marshall. Regional overland mails to and from Jefferson were carried first by horseback and then by stagecoach. These were lucrative contracts and were particularly important in the development of stagecoach lines. Horseback carriage from Shreveport to Jefferson was provided from the beginning. A mail-carrying stagecoach line, probably operated through Robert Nesmith's livery stable in Jefferson, ran from Marshall to Jefferson by at least late 1852; and in 1857 Nesmith received a contract to carry the mail between Marshall and Mt. Pleasant. By March 1860, the *Fleta* provided services as a tri-weekly U. S. mail steamer from Shreveport to Jefferson, making contact with New Orleans boats at Shreveport.

Contracts for mail carriage were secured by bids. The routes and the specifics of carriage were advertised in local newspapers to allow citizens the opportunity to bid. Requests for proposals for mail carriage in northeast Texas appeared in the Clarksville newspaper. The requests contain a great deal of information on the towns of northeast Texas, including many that have disappeared, and show their emergence into prominence over time and the development of their relationships.

Of particular interest in the requests for proposals related to Jefferson are the old towns of Gertrude, Clinton, Williams' Bluff, and Gallatin. Gertrude was a predecessor to Linden and is mentioned in the requests for 1847 and 1849. Clinton was a steamboat port on the northern edge of Clinton Lake and is mentioned in the requests for 1849. Williams' Bluff, which is mentioned in the same year, was an old name for Monterey (also called Point Monterey) on Jim's Bayou. Gallatin, which is mentioned in the requests for 1854 and 1858, is shown in *The Official Military Atlas of the Civil War* on Cypress Bayou in the vicinity of Port Caddo. The proposals relevant to Jefferson were as follows:

1847–1850

Proposals for carrying the mails from July 1, 1847, to June 30, 1850, were advertised in the April 1, 1847, *Northern Standard*:

From Jefferson, by Port Caddo, to Shreveport, 45 miles and back, once a week. Leave Jefferson every Monday at 5 a.m.; arrive at Shreveport next day by noon; leave Shreveport every Tuesday at 1 p.m.; arrive at Jefferson next day by 6 p.m.

From Jefferson, by Cass County Courthouse, Daingerfield, Mount Pleasant (Titus County Courthouse), Tarrant (Hopkins County Courthouse), and Hunt County Courthouse, to Dallas, 120 miles and back, once in two weeks. Leave Jefferson every other Tuesday at 1 p.m.; arrive at Dallas next Friday by 6 p.m.; leave Dallas every other Tuesday at 1 p.m.; arrive at Jefferson next Friday by 6 p.m.

From Marshall, by Jefferson, Hughes Springs, Daingerfield, Weaver's, and Dunham's, to Boston, 90 miles and back, once a week.

1849–1850

Proposals for carrying mails from July 1, 1849, to June 30, 1850, were advertised in the March 17, 1849, *Northern Standard*:

From Fulton at 11 a.m. on Thursday, by Moore's Ferry on Sulphur Fork, Williams' Bluff, and Clinton in Cass County, to Jefferson by 3 p.m., 90 miles and back, between 6 a.m. Tuesday and 10 a.m. Thursday.

From Mooresville in Bowie County at 7 a.m. Thursday, by Old Hickory, Clear Springs, and Gertrude, to Jefferson, by noon Friday, 50 miles and back, between 1 p.m. Friday and 6 p.m. Saturday.

1851–1854

Proposals for carrying the mails from July 1, 1851, to June 30, 1854, were advertised in the March 8, 1851, *Northern Standard*:

From Jefferson at 7 a.m. once a week on Tuesday, by Alley's Mills and Coffeeville, to Gilmer by 11 a.m. next day, 45 miles and back, between 1 p.m. Wednesday and 5 p.m. next day.

1854–1858

Proposals for carrying the mails from July 1, 1854, to June 30, 1858 were advertised in the February 18, 1854, *Standard*:

From Jefferson, by Union Springs, Marshall, Concord, Powelton, and Greenwood, to Shreveport, 59 miles and back, three times a week. Leave Jefferson every Tuesday, Thursday, and Saturday at noon; arrive at Shreveport next days by 4 p.m.; leave Shreveport every Tuesday, Thursday, and Saturday at 11 a.m.; arrive at Jefferson next days by 4 p.m.

From Jefferson, by Hickory Hill, to Daingerfield, 31 miles and back, three times a week. Leave Jefferson every Tuesday, Thursday, and Saturday at noon; arrive at Daingerfield next days by noon; leave

Daingerfield every Wednesday, Friday, and Sunday at 1 p.m.; arrive at Jefferson next days by 11 a.m.

From Jefferson, by Smithland, to Point Monterey, 25 miles and back, once a week. Leave Jefferson every Friday at 3 p.m.; arrive at Point Monterey next day by 11 a.m.; leave Point Monterey every Saturday at noon; arrive at Jefferson next day by 11 a.m.

From Jefferson, by Gallatin, Port Caddo, Cook's Store, and Jonesville, to Powelton, 48 miles and back, once a week. Leave Jefferson every Saturday at 6 a.m.; arrive at Powelton next day by 11 a.m.; leave Powelton every Sunday at 1 p.m.; arrive at Jefferson next day by 5 p.m.

From Jefferson, by Coffeeville, to Gilmer, 48 miles and back, once a week. Leave Jefferson every Tuesday at 10 a.m.; arrive at Gilmer next day by 1 p.m.; leave Gilmer every Wednesday at 2 p.m.; arrive at Jefferson next day by 9 a.m.

From Boston, by Forest Home and Linden, to Jefferson, 39 miles and back, once a week. Leave Boston every Thursday at 7 a.m.; arrive at Jefferson next day by 1 p.m.; leave Jefferson every Tuesday at 1 p.m.; arrive at Boston next day at 6 p.m.

<u>1858–1862</u>

Proposals for carrying the mails from July 1, 1858, to June 30, 1862, were advertised in the February 20, 1858, *Standard*:

From Jefferson, by Floyd's Ferry on Red River, to Fulton, 90 miles and back, once a week. Leave Jefferson on Monday at 6 a.m.; arrive at Fulton next Wednesday by 10 a.m.; leave Fulton on Wednesday at noon; arrive at Jefferson next Friday by 5 p.m.

From Jefferson, by Alley's Mills and Coffeeville, to Gilmer, 45 miles and back, three times a week. Leave Jefferson on Monday, Wednesday, and Friday at 10 a.m.; arrive at Gilmer next days at 1 p.m.; leave Gilmer on Monday, Wednesday, and Friday at 10 a.m.; arrive at Jefferson next days by (?) p.m.

From Jefferson, by Smithland, to Point Monterey, 25 miles and back, once a week. Leave Jefferson on Friday at 3 p.m.; arrive at Point Monterey next day by 11 a.m.; leave Point Monterey on Saturday at noon; arrive at Jefferson next day by 11 a.m.

From Jefferson, by Gallatin, Port Caddo, Cook's Store, and Jonesville, to Powelton, 48 miles and back, three times a week. Leave Jefferson on Monday, Wednesday, and Friday at 6 a.m.; arrive at Powelton next days by 11 a.m.; leave Powelton on Tuesday, Thursday, and Saturday at 1 p.m.; arrive at Jefferson next days by 5 p.m.

From Boston, by Douglasville, Havana, Forest Home, and Linden, to Jefferson 80 miles and back, once a week. Leave Boston on Thursday at 6 a.m.; arrive at Jefferson next day at 6 p.m.; leave Jefferson on Friday at 6 a.m.; arrive at Boston next day by 6 p.m.

From Marshall, by Jefferson, Hickory Hill, Daingerfield, Snow Hill, Mt. Pleasant, and Gouldsboro, to Clarksville, 120 miles and back, three times a week.

Service

Newspaper reports make it clear that the elaborate schedules were often not kept. There are a number of complaints about mail service through the early 1850s. These complaints centered on the slowness or nondelivery of mails in some instances and the slowness in the development of the delivery system and particularly in the utilization of more efficient modes of transport. These problems are reasonable in the context of a newly emerging system in a fairly remote area with poor roads. Decisions on post offices, postal routes, and modes of carriage were in the hands of the federal Postal Service rather than in the hands of locals and generally needed congressional approval. The Postal Service operated through field agents who made recommendations for changes and monitored activities.

The first recorded complaint is in the December 16, 1848, *Spirit of the Age* and was made by the newspaper itself: "The Southern mail failed to bring any New Orleans papers yesterday. We wish we knew who is so frequently guilty or negligent in detaining our important papers from the City." In December 1849, Loughery of the *Texas Republican*, who was critical of mail service in northeast Texas, indicated that "One of our subscribers at Jefferson desires us to state that the mails leading to that place are in a wretched situation; that from all quarters there are nothing but failures and mismanagement." Loughery received a letter in March 1850 that placed part of the blame for the situation on Marshall:

> You have frequently spoken of the notorious failures of the mails "in these latter days." You may not be aware of the fact that the people of Jefferson suffer most from the malfeasance of the "Officers of the mail bag" between this place and Marshall. The truth of this has been satisfactorily ascertained. I have on several occasions, read the *Weekly Delta*, received by mail in Harrison county, and have then waited some three or four weeks, before I could receive the same numbers in my name—and this too, when the mail would be crossing the Bayous. The same applies to a great extent to other mail matters; and I assure you it is a matter of great complaint by our citizens. If the mail contractor, or postmasters in your county cannot do their duty, they should be ousted indignantly and others put in who can perform all the duties incumbent upon them.

Loughery protested that the problem in receiving New Orleans papers was not in Marshall, but rather in Mansfield and Fort Jessup; but he later indicated that Marshall papers were not being sent expeditiously because of the perverseness of the mail contractor, a Mr. C. Allen, who refused to carry them because they were put in a separate bag.

The greater concern was with route development, because something was better than nothing, and particularly with the establishment of stagecoach services. The Postal Service agent J. W. Scott was in Jefferson in July 1853 with a sprained ankle that interrupted his inspection tour of northeast Texas. Scott wrote to DeMorse in Clarksville that he desired to extend the present service by stagecoach from Shreveport through Marshall to Jefferson up to Clarksville by way of Daingerfield and Linden and that this could be done either by hack (light saddle horse) or stagecoach. He also indicated that his recommendation would be strongly influenced by the disposition of the people of the area to construct roads and bridges. In conjunction with this visit, the *Jefferson Herald* issued a bold proposal:

> Last week, in noticing the arrival of our mail agent, Maj. SCOTT, among other things, we remarked that

there were many routes that should be established, and the service increased on others and additional compensation allowed, which, we understand, led to the belief that he had the power to do all this himself. This is an error. He can recommend to Congress, if, in his judgment, they are proper, which would have a tendency to give more weight to them. We do hope that, before the adjournment of the next Congress, some relief will be afforded this section in the way of mail facilities. The mail stage route, for instance, from Shreveport to Jefferson should continue to Clarksville, where it would intersect with the Washington (Ark.) mail line, and a tri-weekly stage route from Jefferson to Dallas. These changes are needed worse than any other mail arrangements in Texas. We have often insisted upon them within the last 12 or 18 months but as yet they have received no attention from the proper authorities. This is a *shameful neglect*. The mail facilities on these routes are wholly inadequate. One great means of influencing their establishment we would suggest, is the improvement of the roads over which they must run; and this is an excellent time for it, as the crops are now laid by.

It is probable that coach mail service between Marshall and Jefferson was in place by late 1852. By March 1856, the Post Master General had approved saddle horse mail service between Jefferson and Daingerfield, and consideration was being given to establish saddle horse or coach mail service between Jefferson and Clarksville. Coach mail service between Clarksville and Mt. Pleasant was approved in June 1856. By September 1857, Robert Nesmith had received the contract to carry the mails between Marshall and Mt. Pleasant by way of Jefferson and Daingerfield and had established the Forest Mail Stage Line, running from Marshall to Jefferson daily and from Jefferson to Mt. Pleasant on Monday, Wednesday, and Friday. The Forest Mail Stage Line was extended to Clarksville in July 1858.

38. Telegraph

Communication in early Texas was slow and depended on transmission by word of mouth or by printed materials such as newspapers. Newspapers from outside the region were generally received in Jefferson by stagecoach and steamboat, sometimes weeks after they had been published. The telegraph offered the first technology for near-instantaneous transmission of information. In reviewing the advantages of the telegraph, the March 5, 1853, *Texas Republican* pointed out that one of its primary uses would be to obtain up-to-date information on the volatile cotton market. Merchants in interior towns like Marshall wanted to buy cotton but were deterred from doing so because they did not know the current market prices. Purchases under such circumstances were risky.

New York and New Orleans were connected by telegraph by way of Mobile in July 1848. In January 1853, the contractors T. C. H. Smith and George Ward proposed a line from New Orleans to Shreveport, Marshall, Houston, and Galveston. Stock subscriptions were being taken for the line between New Orleans and Shreveport in April 1853. By July, posts had been completed to Shreveport and the wire was at Shreveport ready to be strung. However, these activities were interrupted by a yellow fever epidemic in Shreveport, and the telegraph between Shreveport and New Orleans was not reported in operation by the *Texas Republican* until February 11, 1854.

In the meantime, construction of the line was progressing in Texas. By July 1853, work was being done west of Shreveport, and another crew was commencing at Galveston to work toward the northeast, with completion between Galveston and Shreveport expected in October. By August, subscriptions were being sought in the affected towns, posts had been erected six miles beyond Henderson, and wire for the Texas portion of the line was being sent to Shreveport. On September 12, a Texas and Red River Telegraph Company, with W. R. D. Ward of Marshall as president, met in Crockett. Stock had been sold, but a charter had not yet been obtained. Wire was strung between Crockett and Shreveport in September, providing linkage between Marshall and Shreveport.

The February 11, 1854, *Texas Republican* reports that there was already a telegraph office in Marshall and that the telegraph was expected to be in operation within the next few days. The line between Shreveport and Marshall had been completed by at least January 28, but was non-functional because of destruction by ox-wagon drivers, who used the poles for firewood. The February 18 *Texas Republican* reports that the telegraph office had become fully functional on Tuesday, February 14:

> The Magnetic telegraph is at length in operation between Marshall and New Orleans. We are no longer cut off from the balance of the world by low water and slow mails. But in the twinkling of an eye—in less time than it takes to talk about it—a dispatch can be sent and received from the most distant portions of the Union where this wonder-working machine is in operation.
>
> Who will now wait a week for intelligence from New Orleans, when by taking a Marshall paper they can get intelligence from that city of the day previous? We shall give weekly dispatches, and hope that for this additional expense we will be amply remunerated by an increase of our subscription list.
>
> On Tuesday the office commenced operations at this place, and throughout the day was thronged with visitors. In the course of two hours twenty dollars were re-

ceived, and since then the Telegraph has done a thriving business. We had no idea that the office would pay expense; but we are now satisfied that the stock in this line will pay a handsome dividend.

However, the same issue reports continuing destruction of the line between Shreveport and Mansfield, Louisiana. This is the first issue of the *Texas Republican* with a column of telegraphic dispatches, but the dispatches were obtained from the telegraph office at Alexandria, rather than directly from New Orleans. The line between Shreveport and Marshall was fully functional only in late February and during the month of March. The February 25 *Texas Republican* reports that "The Telegraph is working wondrously well, and our people begin to experience its advantages," with emphasis on the recentness of cotton market information from New York and New Orleans. However, by April 1, the *Texas Republican* was obtaining its dispatches from the *Shreveport Democrat*, and even this activity came to an end in early May. There is no evidence that Marshall had an operating telegraph after March 1854. The February 4, 1856, *South-Western* contains a sheriff sale advertisement for the property of the Texas and Red River Telegraph Line.

In early 1854, Jefferson attempted to join the developing system. The March 18, 1854, Clarksville *Standard* reports that a Marshall and Jefferson Telegraph Company had been formed with John Waskom as president and Frank Clark as secretary, that the stock necessary for the completion of the telegraph between Marshall and Jefferson had been taken in the latter place, and that work would begin immediately. The April 4 *Jefferson Herald*, as quoted by the April 8 *Texas Republican*, reports that "The Telegraph between Houston and Galveston is completed, and in successful operation. We confidently hope that it may not be long before we can say the same thing for Jefferson and Marshall, two of the most thriving and business towns in Eastern Texas. Gentlemen, it will never do to lag behind; it is not in keeping with our business and commercial character."

Loughery responded that "A place of the commercial importance of Jefferson should certainly not be without the telegraph." The *Jefferson Herald* included Marshall in its hope, and Loughery did not object to the statement because the telegraph at Marshall was no longer functional. There is no evidence for the operation of a telegraph at Jefferson prior to the Civil War, and as late as March 1860, the latest news from New Orleans was still being received by steamboat. It appears that the efforts of the Marshall and Jefferson Telegraph Company came to naught in the context of the inability of the overall system to provide continuing service to Marshall.

39. Railroads

The legend of Jay Gould has given rise to the impression that early Jeffersonians were not interested in railroads. This is not the case. Until the 1870s, Jefferson was one of the most important trade centers in Texas. Like everyone else, Jefferson's businessmen and public officials were railroad enthusiasts. The wealth and political influence of the town enabled it to secure one of the earliest railroad charters granted in Texas. The antebellum development of rails in Texas was restricted to the northeast and southern portions of the state, where ports like Galveston and Jefferson attempted to extend and consolidate their trade hinterlands and to tie into the transcontinental roads advancing from the east.

The Jefferson Railroad Company was chartered by the State of Texas on February 2, 1854, only nine years after Jefferson came into existence. The incorporators were John Speake, Daniel Alley, Hiram Tomlin, William Baker, William Brooks, James Murphy, William Aikin, Edwin Rogers, S. J. Pounds, William Batte, and Orin Conner. The line was to begin at Jefferson and connect with the east through the Mississippi & Pacific Railroad or the Vicksburg & El Paso Railroad (usually referred to as the Texas Western and later the Southern Pacific). By charter amendment in 1855, it was allowed to connect with the Vicksburg, Shreveport & Texas Railroad.

What the incorporators had in mind is obvious. The main purpose was to tie Jefferson by a north-south line into one of the projected east-west transcontinental lines, if none of these lines chose to proceed through Jefferson. This would provide Jefferson with relationships to the east and to the far west to the Pacific. The Mississippi & Pacific was projected to run north of Jefferson out of the Fulton, Arkansas, area to El Paso. The Texas Western was projected to run south of Jefferson in the general vicinity of Marshall. The Vicksburg, Shreveport & Texas was chartered in Louisiana to run west through Shreveport, where it would join the Texas Western at the state line. On the south, Jefferson had the opportunity to connect through a north-south line with the Texas Western or through a northwest-southeast line with the Vicksburg, Shreveport & Texas at the state line.

The Jefferson Railroad and the Mississippi & Pacific were never built. On the south, the Texas Western was begun under the name Southern Pacific. This was the road that began at Swanson's Landing on Caddo Lake and then ran south to Jonesville, thence west to Marshall in October 1858, before activities were interrupted by the Civil War.

The Texas Western (under the name Vicksburg & El Paso) received its charter in February 1852, but work was not begun until November 1855 under the name Southern Pacific. In early 1855, when the route that would be taken by the line was still uncertain, Jeffersonians were working politically and with the railroad company to have the line run through Jefferson. A meeting was held in Jefferson in April to determine the level of public interest in taking stock and supplying labor for grading a line beginning at Jefferson and extending to the state line or to the west. The local organizers of this effort were Frank Clark, John Waskom, John Murphy, John Speake, John Smedley, and Williamson Freeman.

The expectations of Jeffersonians were not unreasonable. Because of the immense difficulties in transporting railroad iron over land, railroads were built from existing lines or from ports, where the iron could be brought in by steamboats. The Southern Pacific was begun at Swanson's Landing because the Vicksburg, Shreveport & Texas had not even reached Shreveport, and the Southern Pacific would lose its charter if a portion of the line was not completed within a specified period. Benton on Cypress Bayou was surveyed in August 1854 for the line to Marshall that was eventually developed out of Swanson's Landing. Jefferson was in the running, but its proposal was rejected by the company because of the high cost and time that would be involved in bridging the Cypress bayous.

The Jefferson Railroad apparently allowed its charter to expire, in part because the Swanson's Landing to Jonesville and Jonesville to Marshall portions of the Southern Pacific were nothing but local roads as long as the Vicksburg, Shreveport & Texas was not complete, and that was a long way off. More importantly, new opportunities emerged through a local line, the Metropolitan Railroad, and another transcontinental line to the north, The Memphis, El Paso & Pacific (ME&P).

The Metropolitan Railroad was incorporated on February 1860 to run from Texarkana, through Jefferson and Marshall, and on to Austin. Although this was not specifically a Jefferson project, it provided Jefferson two opportunities. As a local road between Jefferson and Texarkana, the Metropolitan would capture all of the upper Red River trade, which went to Jefferson only when low water made the upper Red River inaccessible to steamboats. More importantly, the Metropolitan provided an opportunity to tie in with a transcontinental line. The ME&P was chartered in February 1853 and, by amendment in February 1856, was to begin near Texarkana, joining with such roads as the Cairo & Fulton advancing from the east and proceeding west over the northern tier of Texas counties to El Paso and thence to the Pacific.

A meeting in connection with the raising of additional stock for the Metropolitan was held in Linden in May 1860, with William Saufley, Daniel McKay, and Cols. Orville Yerger and Willerson (probably Seaborn Wilkinson) from Jefferson in attendance. Saufley read the charter, and Saufley, Yerger, and Willerson gave speeches emphasizing the importance of the road to the development of northeast Texas. Clarksville, the trade center on the upper Red River, was not happy about the prospects for this local line, because it would shift trade to the south and eliminate steamboat activity on the upper Red River.

The Metropolitan was not built under its own name, but became absorbed in the effort to construct the ME&P. The latter line was to start at Texarkana and run north of Clarksville to Paris, Texas. As was the case with the Southern Pacific, there was as yet no line from the east to Texarkana. As a consequence, it was necessary to begin at some port where rails could be brought in by water. Railroad iron could not be transported to Texarkana on the Red River because of a shallow place in the river above the mouth of the Sulphur Fork that could not be negotiated by heavily laden steamboats.

The company decided to import railroad iron at Moore's Landing on the Sulphur Fork, a tributary of the Red River running in a west-east direction below Clarksville and above Jefferson. A branch line was to run north from Moore's Landing to Texarkana, and the ME&P would then be constructed to the west. A locomotive, three construction cars, and chairs (ties) and spikes for six miles of the ME&P arrived at Moore's Landing in April 1860. The *Southerlin*, the steamboat that had brought up these materials, was to begin bringing rails, which had been purchased from the Mt. Savage Iron Works in Maryland. Then nature intervened.

In May 1860, the Great Raft on the Red River advanced beyond the mouth of Red Bayou, a distributary of the Red that was used to bypass the raft on the west. The Sulphur Fork was no longer accessible. Although plans were soon underway to develop another outlet farther north above the raft, the ME&P could not wait. It soon became obvious that the only way to stay on schedule was to begin a branch line at Jefferson, advancing north to Moore's Landing, thence to Texarkana.

In late May, the meeting was held in Linden to discuss the future of the Metropolitan. In June, Thomas Bates, the contractor for the ME&P rails, agreed to ship them to Jefferson and take the contract for building the Metropolitan's rails. In September, John Speake was appointed sub-treasurer of the ME&P under president Simpson Morgan, with John Murphy, William Perry, James Blackburn, and Robert Ward acting as sureties for the proper execution of his duties. The ME&P advertised in October for contractors to provide the grading, referring to the Metropolitan as the Jefferson Division of the ME&P. The entire contract for the project, with the exception of actually furnishing the rails, was taken by Capt. J. H. Pratt in November, as reported in a *Jefferson Gazette* excerpt in the *Texas Republican* of the 17th:

> OUR RAILROAD.—The work on the Road to connect this point with the Memphis and El Paso Railroad

is progressing rapidly. The grading is already commenced and the prospect of its speedy completion, is very flattering. In the course of next week about three hundred hands will be at work, and Capt. Pratt, who has taken the entire contract, with the exception of furnishing the iron, is daily letting out small contracts, endeavoring to give employment to the hands of every planter who has been so unfortunate as to make a small crop. No man doubts that this connection, the most important in the State, will be completed, and in running order, in less than fifteen months from to-day, giving Jefferson one hundred miles of road through the finest country in the world.

No point, in the State of Texas, can boast of a future so flattering as that of Jefferson, and taking every thing into consideration, no point in the entire South has increased in both business and population, within the past twelve months, as rapidly. Notwithstanding the sorry crops, in every portion of our city new buildings are springing up like magic, new business men are pouring in, and ere another 12 months has rolled around the oldest inhabitant will scarcely recognize the little Bayou City of today.

By March 1861, the Texas Legislature had formally recognized the absorption of the Metropolitan by the ME&P. Also by March, Capt. Pratt was at work on the grading, and Judge H. A. Bennett, the new president of the ME&P, was on his way to secure rails for the main road and the Jefferson branch. In April, Pratt attended a meeting of the ME&P in Paris and wrote to Samuel Moseley in Jefferson that the board had decided to concentrate all of its energies on the Jefferson branch and that all of the iron would be sent to Jefferson. In August, Urquhart granted an 80-foot right of way within Jefferson beginning at the southwest corner of Block 15 (corner of Lafayette and Washington) and running to the north through Blocks 33, 41, 62, and 112. At the same time, Pratt purchased from

Urquhart Block 103 for $1,800, apparently as a stationing area for the development of the railroad.

There is no firm record of any railroad iron having been sent to Jefferson. The Civil War began in April, and the rails for the ME&P that were in New Orleans and on the Red and Mississippi rivers, which were in possession of the then alien enemy Thomas Bates, were seized by the Confederate government in May. Bates had actually been a Jefferson resident in 1860, with the census listing him as a 43-year-old railroad contractor from New Jersey. Capt. George Kouns of the famous steamboat family was at the Confederate Congress in Montgomery and, with the assistance of Judge William Ochiltree from the Jefferson area, was able to get the seized rails transferred to the ME&P, as indicated in a letter to Bennett written from New Orleans on May 25.

Kouns said that he would transport the iron to Shreveport on the *Saracen* and then bring it to Moore's Landing when the fall rise provided better navigation conditions, suggesting that no iron was sent to Jefferson. However, low water prevailed through February of 1862, and there is no mention in the Clarksville papers of any iron having reached Moore's Landing, an event that surely would have been noted.

The only concrete evidence for a rail out of Jefferson is a Texas Railroad Commission record that six miles of track were completed by the ME&P in 1861 between Moore's Landing and Jefferson. The track was obviously laid north out of Jefferson rather than south out of Moore's Landing. Any construction out of Moore's Landing would have taken place to the north, because the whole point of starting at Jefferson was the inability to build north out of Moore's Landing. The completion of this small rail segment out of Jefferson is confirmed by the 1868 *Texas Almanac*.

The grading for the Jefferson Division of the ME&P was completed almost to Moore's Landing. This grading, and particularly the portion out of Jefferson that included the rails, cannot be seen at the present time because the Texas and Pacific was built along the same route after the Civil War. The fate of the rails is another matter.

In early 1862, the Confederacy was in desperate need to secure railroad iron to complete the casements of the ironclads *Louisiana* and *Mississippi* in New Orleans. According to the March 21 and April 1 issues of the *Semi-Weekly Shreveport News*, the *Era No. 5*, a Kouns boat, arrived from New Orleans, discontinued her regular trips, made a special trip to Jefferson, and departed for New Orleans from Shreveport on March 29 "with iron for the gunboats." The April 5 New Orleans *Daily Picayune* notes the arrival of the *Era No. 5* from Jefferson carrying 108 pieces of iron for W. H. McComb and 1,127 pieces for E. Rousseau.

Although some of this iron could have been secured at Shreveport, Jefferson is the apparent source, including the six miles of track and whatever was in storage for laying. However, it should be noted that the official state records do not indicate abandonment of the six miles of track until 1873. Because the 1868 *Texas Almanac* reports that all of the iron destined for the ME&P was seized by the Confederacy to build the gunboats, it is apparent that all iron in transit as well as the portion already at Jefferson would have been seized. Jefferson's first railroad was an accidental undertaking that extended only six miles into the wilderness and was apparently destroyed to defend the Confederacy.

40. Sports

A sport may be defined loosely as any skilled physical activity conducted for pleasure. Sports may be team or individual, competitive or noncompetitive, participatory or spectator, indoor or outdoor, with combinations of these elements. Sports as participatory and spectator phenomena have come to be so quintessentially American that their near absence in the South prior to the Civil War is one of its most striking cultural features. In particular, there were no competitive team sports such as baseball, football, or basketball. Baseball, the premier American sport, was popular in the Northeast well before the Civil War, but it does not begin to be mentioned in the newspapers of northeast Texas until the 1870s.

Athleticism in general and competitive athleticism in particular appear to have been of little interest to anyone. Few people knew how to swim, which is why drownings were frequent. People fought with their fists, but there are no reports of boxing in the papers of northeast Texas. People shot animals and undoubtedly engaged in target practice with some competition, but there are no reports of competitive marksmanship. People ran, but there are no reports of challenge races. That this lack of interest was real and not an artifact of reportage is indicated by the fact that challenge footraces between local champions (and often ringers) were reported when they began to occur in the 1870s.

The newspapers of the period mention only five sports that Jeffersonians participated in: hunting, fishing, bowling, billiards, and horse racing. The most popular were hunting and fishing. They were probably equivalent to card playing as leisure activities, but the latter activity was not a sport because it required skill but not physical exertion. All of these sports had very strong social dimensions that rendered them conducive to conviviality as opposed to competition.

Hunting and Fishing

Hunting and fishing were widely practiced individually and socially. There are no reports of fishing and hunting clubs, and it is doubtful they existed, because access to resources was readily available. Fishing excursions to Caddo Lake by steamboat came to be an important annual event out of Shreveport, but there is nothing of a similar nature mentioned in connection with Jefferson. Something of the nature of these resources is indicated by Edward Smith in his 1849 *Account of a Journey Through Northeastern Texas*:

> Game, of every variety, is in countless numbers over the country. Deer, in herds, occupy every wood, and at dawn of day and at night, may be seen browsing on the open prairie. Their number is much diminished, but even now the huntsman needs never to return without his game. Wild turkeys weighing 30 lbs. frequently crossed our path. Ducks and geese are said to be innumerable. Partridges exist everywhere, and were constantly running in front of our horses. The prairie hen is very abundant, and is about the size of a common fowl, but much more delicious. Woodcocks, snipes, and every other known variety of game are met with on all hands. Squirrels are very numerous, and are accounted a great luxury, and to my untutored taste the flesh is very rich. I shot six of these creatures in a very short time, and the large fox-tail squirrel, the grey and the black squirrel are equally prized. Game has long ceased to be profitable to the settler, since more useful occupations than hunting have presented themselves; and it is still too abundant to be valued as a luxury.

The 1860 census lists three Jefferson residents as sportsmen (O. H. Whitman, 28, born in New York; Frank Marr, 24, born in Kentucky; E. O. Kidd, 19, born in Missouri) and one as a fisherman (Anthony Owens, 40, born in North Carolina), but the latter was probably involved in a commercial operation. Hunting and fishing are mentioned only occasionally in the newspapers, and there are only two extant larger accounts, both of which are concerned with other matters. This is not surprising given the fact that hunting and fishing were common and therefore not worthy of reportage unless they involved unusual circumstances. The first of these accounts concerns the accidental killing of the young lawyer John Eppinger on a November 1850 hunting trip at night:

> MELANCHOLY ACCIDENT.—We learn from J. C. EVERETT, just from Jefferson, that in a fire hunt on Wednesday night, JOHN EPINGER, a citizen and promising lawyer of that place was accidentally killed by Dr. N. TRAWICK. It appears that TRAWICK had dismounted and followed some deer off, and EPINGER holding his mule moved from the place he left him, and on TRAWICK'S seeing the mule's eyes shot, killing the mule horse and EPINGER. There were two other gentlemen in company.

The second account is a condensed version of story by Hiram Grinsted, editor of the *Jefferson Herald*, about a May 1856 fishing trip. The account plays on the term storm party, which was a surprise party that was held at the home of and paid for by the person surprised:

> A STORM PARTY.—*Oh Meet Me by Moonlight Alone*—The editor of the Jefferson Herald gives an account of an interesting storm party, in which he was one of the principal actors, which we thus condense.
>
> 1. Started down Cypress Bayou on Friday morning, (unlucky day!) in an open skiff with a gentleman and two Africans; upon a crusade against trout, white perch, and all other fishes.
>
> 2. Discharged one African mile from town, on the ground of incompetency.

3. Sun broiling hot. Arrived at Smithland in two hours. Found gentlemen—and ladies fishing; up to snuff—couldn't fool him—had other objects in view, besides hook and line exercise on the piscatory tribe—in a word, thinks it was a courting expedition.

4. Staid half an hour, when storm broke forth. Party absconded. Editor, gentlemen and darkey took a boat. Left for Jefferson. Storm increased—winds raged—trees fell, waters lashed the shore—had seen many sights, including a few at sea—red lightnings glared—demons of the tempest bellowed in the blast—took advantage of the flashes of lightning, and got home "about nine o'clock at night, drenched with rain, covered with mud, and ravenous as wolves."

In next issue expect to hear what became of gentleman and the darkey. Supposition is, that they were *both lost!*

Bowling and Billiards

There was at least one bowling alley in Jefferson in the early 1850s. It was part of the Bowling Saloon owned by Caleb Ragan that featured, besides a ten-pin alley, a bar and billiard table. Bowling alleys and billiard tables were enticements for establishments whose primary purpose was the sale of liquor. This building, which was located on parts of Lots 5 and 6 in Block 5 fronting 50 feet on Marshall and 100 feet on Dallas, was sold by Ragan to May & Company for $6,500 in March 1854. This was the old building occupied by Charles Dunn as a storehouse and Ragan as a grocery store in 1847 and by Ragan as a grocery store through 1851, the last year in which he appears as a merchant. It is probable that Ragan converted the storehouse into a bowling saloon in 1852 and that it operated as such until March 1854 when it was reconverted by May & Company into a storehouse for their large wholesale and retail dry goods and groceries business.

Bowling was popularized by the Germans. There is nothing to indicate that there were any bowling leagues in Jefferson, and the Bowling Saloon appears to have had only one lane. Bowling and billiards were probably individual sports with some degree of competition and spectatorship. It can be presumed that there were billiards tables at other saloons and in some private residences. There may have been other bowling alleys; but this is the only one that advertised, and one may have been enough to accommodate the level of interest in the early 1850s.

Charles Merryman received a license in November 1860 to operate a ten-pin alley, and a similar license was received by James Moody in March 1863. In November 1863, Richard Crump transferred to John Mills for $6,500 a recently acquired drinking and billiard saloon, shooting gallery, and bowling alley located on the northern part of Lots 7-9 in Block 21. The saloon was 25 feet south of the alley, fronted Marshall 25 feet, ran back 125 feet to an alley, and was immediately north of the City Hotel. The property was originally purchased by August Lamprecht from Bartholomew Figures in April 1851. An October 1859 mortgage of the property for $2,050 from Crump to Mills of Harrison County indicates that Crump had been operating out of a store on the property. A January 1861 deed record concerning William Fisher and Caroline Figures indicates that Crump had erected a building on the property that he had a right to operate from December 1859 until December 1863. December 1859 was obviously the inception of Crump's saloon.

Horseracing

Fred Tarpley, on the basis of family reminiscences, says that Daniel Alley built Jefferson's racetrack. There appears to have been only one racetrack over time, in the northern part of the Alley Addition, as shown in the northeast corner of Brosius' 1872 *Bird's Eye View of Jefferson* (see Fig. 6-4). Alley advertised in the November 7, 1857, *Eastern Texas Gazette* as a wholesale and retail dealer in dry goods and groceries located at the corner of Marshall and Dallas at the old stand of Cocke and Whitaker and is listed in the 1860 census as a Jefferson resident.

The racetrack was in existence prior to the Civil War, as indicated by a December 8, 1860, Marshall *Harrison Flag* article quoting the Jefferson *Herald and Gazette*: "The late races over the Jefferson course have passed off smoothly to the entire satisfaction and edification of all present. A great many ladies graced the track with their smiles and beauty, which seemed to encourage the fleetfooted steed and bear him on like the winds of a stormy March." There were probably some facilities in conjunction with the racetrack prior to the Civil War, but this cannot be documented.

Horse racing was intrinsically competitive. There is no information about who participated in the Jefferson races. They probably involved local competitors as well as regional and nonregional competitors against each other and against local horses. Horse racing was popular throughout Texas, racetracks were numerous, and horses were bred for competition. As the article in the *Herald and Gazette* indicates, horse racing was also heavily oriented toward spectator participation, undoubtedly with gambling, given the propensity of people at that time to bet on almost anything. Early racetracks evolved out of individual challenges on straight courses, with the oval shape enabling spectators to see the entire race. Racing was the only true spectator sport in Jefferson prior to the Civil War.

41. CULTURE AND ENTERTAINMENT

Jefferson did not have much in the way of culture, and what little there was shaded off into entertainment. This should not be surprising for a new town on the edge of the frontier with a free adult population of 435 in 1860 in a young, pragmatic, and expanding country with little interest in culture. However, even by the standards of the time and place, Jefferson was found to be somewhat deficient by friendly observers like Charles DeMorse of Clarksville. Jeffersonians, according to DeMorse, did not have time for the "finer things of life" because they were too busy making money. This is a valid observation. Jefferson was not a town of small shopkeepers but of major merchants in expanding businesses, and merchants typically worked late into the night with their clerks. Hard work and restiveness looks to entertainment for the expenditure of leisure time, because culture requires effort.

Culture is both personal and public. On the personal side, travelers to East Texas were always struck by the high quality of libraries in even fairly modest plantation homes. These libraries usually contained bibles, religious tracts, political tracts, classical literature, poetry, histories, biographies, and books on agriculture and political theory. A few hints from estate accounts in Jefferson suggest similar literature, but with such things as medical and legal texts replacing books on agriculture for the professional class. Academies provided training in music, painting, and drawing. There are a few mentions of pianos in private residences. Newspapers contained poems by local and nationally recognized poets and stories of adventure and romance, usually with moral points. Magazines such as *Harper's* and *The Atlantic* were popular and widely read. A large bookstore was established in Jefferson in 1860 with a wide range of books and musical instruments.

On the public side, Jefferson did not have a theater, in spite of the fact that people like Urquhart and Alley were generous in their donations of land to schools and churches. Theatrical performances, which were fairly numerous, were apparently conducted in places like the Alhambra Hall.

Painting

The first mention of a cultural event in Jefferson is provided by Robert Loughery of the Marshall *Texas Republican* in October 1849. This was apparently a traveling exhibit of paintings, because the artist was not a Jefferson resident: "We neglected to notice at the proper time, from the crowd of political matter, our pleasant visit to Jefferson. While there, we had the pleasure of seeing Mr. Sala's exhibition of paintings. They are well worthy of an extended notice, which we would give if we had room. The audience was very large, and all who witnessed them, were pleased and edified." One artist by the name of J. G. Richmond (36-year-old male born in Connecticut) is listed in the 1860 census, but nothing is known about his activities other than that he was responsible for the decor in Freeman's Hall.

Music

There are no mentions of concerts or musical presentations of any type. One musician, the 22-year-old male L. Keizer born in Prussia, is listed in the 1860 census. Although the nature of his activities is unknown, he was apparently a professional musician. Rachael Smither, an 18-year-old music teacher, is also listed in the census. She was apparently teaching out of her home, because she was married and does not appear to have been associated with a school. The fiddle was, of course, always a component of dances and balls, and bands accompanied parades.

Theater

Thespians were very common amateur dramatic groups that were formed by young people who engaged in local presentations, usually for benefits. There was a Thespian corps in Jefferson before September 1851 when they appeared in a benefit that was being held by a Mrs. Strong. They engaged in skits and comic and dramatic dialogue. As with most other clubs of the 1800s, membership was restricted to males. Mutual improvement was the internal goal, and entertainment was the societal goal. The Thespian corps in Jefferson was presumably intermittent, because it reformed in 1853 and 1854.

The Strongs were apparently directors of a professional troupe that traveled from town to town presenting light comedy. Loughery attended one of their performances in Jefferson in September 1851: "On Wednesday evening, we had an interesting theatrical performance, under the direction of Mr. and Mrs. Strong. The audience was very large, many being unable to find seats. The excellent comedy of the 'Golden Farmer,' followed by the laughable farce of the 'Irish Tutor,' formed the night's entertainment. These pieces were really well played, and elicited merited applause. Every character was well sustained. We understand that Mr. and Mrs. Strong intend visiting Henderson soon."

J. S. Charles managed an eight-person theatrical company that operated out of Shreveport and Alexandria and later Marshall. It traveled throughout northeast Texas in 1857 giving multiple-night presentations of tragedy, comedy, and farce in places like Jefferson, Henderson, and Tyler. Among the plays mentioned were *The Lady of Lyons, Fazio, Ingomar the Barbarian, The Wife, Lucille, The Hunchback, Mr. and Mrs. White,* and *Cousin Carie,* the latter a farce written by one of the actresses, Virginia Smith, who was also a dancer. Loughery judged Charles' company as "by far the best company we have ever seen this side of New Orleans" and "decidedly the best theatrical corps we have ever seen in Texas," stating that "We have seen much worse, and seldom as fine acting, on the best New Orleans boards."

This troupe gave presentations in Jefferson in August 1857, including a benefit for the construction of the Female Institute. When it returned to Marshall, Loughery commented on the morality of the two theaters in Marshall:

Culture and Entertainment

No one can doubt, we think, that a theatre conducted on proper principles, is a source of improvement and of innocent recreation. The objections urged against them are, that modesty is not always consulted, and that sentiments are sometimes expressed which are reprehensible. These, where they occur, are easily corrected, if society would set its face against the abuse; for without the countenance and support of respectable people they would be compelled to close their doors. Our Marshall theatres have been remarkably free from these acts. Another thing to be deprecated is late hours. Our theatres are blamable in this. They should either commence earlier, or cut short their plays.

The troupe returned to Jefferson in May 1859 with an orchestra and Harry Macarthy, the Irish comedian, dancer, and vocalist, furnishing "Irish Dramas and Vaudevilles, light musical Farces, singing and dancing, together with fun in general." Loughery reports that the troupe played to crowded houses in Jefferson for a full week and then moved to Marshall:

CHARLES'S DRAMATIC COMPANY.—This popular company commenced a series of entertainments on Monday last, at Raines's Hall, in this city, much to the delight of our theatre going population. Mr. CHARLES has always been a favorite in this community, arising from the propriety of his management, his agreeable manners, and his ability as an actor. There are few men who possess such a versatile genius. His present troupe is a very efficient one, and contains a number of actors of superior merit, such as are seldom seen in the interior. Miss SUSAN DENIN, for instance, has attained the highest reputation in the first theatres of the Union. She possesses a sweet voice, a correct taste, and her acting is graceful and natural. Mrs. LYNNE exhibits the proper attention and study, and acquits herself creditably in the characters she personates. The other actors also display a knowledge of their profession. Mr. TRAVERS is a fine tragedian; Mr. DURIVAGE an excellent comedian; and Mr. BAYDON is superior in the character of an "old man." The scenery and decorations are creditable, and what has pleased us very much is the decorum manifested by the entire troupe. Everything calculated to shock a refined taste has been studiously excluded by them. This is correct, for no theatre that selects plays of questionable morality or permits the indulgence of vulgarity, deserves the flattering notice of the press or the patronage of the public.

In spite of this praise and apparent success, Charles' troupe did not receive sufficient support in Marshall to meet expenses and disappeared from the scene.

The travesty of Shakespeare described by Mark Twain in *Huckleberry Finn* was not a caricature, but rather the way in which Shakespeare was presented in rural communities by itinerant dramatists who charged an entrance fee. DeMorse of the Clarksville *Standard* saw a presentation of this type when he visited Jefferson in April 1858:

The population here has been regaled for the winter, by something termed a theatre. It has dwindled down, of late, to one stick of a fellow, who advertised a dramatic performance, in which all the parts of Macbeth to Wm. Tell were to be performed by himself—not read, but acted.—Drawn into presence by circumstances, and not by any personal inclination to witness the inevitble butchery, I went, last night, and beheld a personage with distinguished *legs*, and a visage like a Prairie Bull, which, whether he appeared as male or female, hero, woman, or sailor, *never changed*, but had the same unalterable expression of his prototype, through the most comical tragedy, and tragical comedy, that it has ever been my fate to suffer under the infliction of. A bad scenic representation of a modern parlor, served for battle field, castle hall, mountain crag, and shipboard: the spectator having to imagine all these localities, while looking at the curtained windows represented upon the canvas. Reciting the stage directions as he went along, the entrances and exits, accompanied by a felicitious running commentary upon the momentous events that the audience must *imagine* to ensue, he commenced with Lady Macbeth's

"Come to my woman's breasts
And take my milk for gall."
and further on,
"I have given suck and know,
How tender 'tis to love the babe that milks me."

dressed in a plaid kilt, with the steel corslet of a soldier, upon his breast. It would have required the utmost stretch of a most fertile imagination, to have given effect to this, and fancied the woman's breasts under that heavy corslet, and with the dull eyes of that bull's head, peering out above. Added to this a most majestic stage stride, of the tragic cast, which never varied, whoever was supposed to be represented, male or female, and you have a conception of the *"theatrical"* performance, which concluded by a sailor's Hornpipe, done with a distinct disregard of the time of the music to which it purported to be danced. Nearly all the Ladies rose and left while one of the most tragic scenes was in full blast; but the undaunted performer was in no degree disconcerted by so slight an unappreciation. Occasionally the boys called eh! eh! while some intense declamatory agony was startling the affrighted air; but the great actor never quailed—never! He is a hero, and will doubtless succeed—in humbugging other audiences. Theatrical performances in small villages, cannot well be worth seeing, except some of a broad farce character; and a small community should never humbug itself with the idea that any such amusement, in places of limited population, can by any possibility, be supported in a style to repay in interest, those who pay out their money to see it. Then, the butchery of such words as Shakespeare puts into the mouths of his characters, in their utterances by mere sticks of actors

"Who for the most part, are capable

of nothing but inexplicable dumb show, and noise" is an outrage upon common propriety, and "cannot but make the judicious grieve." Indeed the performance that I saw, is so happily described by Hamlet in his directions to the players, that it is most fit for repetition in this connection.

"O, there be players that I have seen play—and heard others praise, and that highly,—not to speak it profanely, that neither having the accent of christians, nor the gait of christian, Pagan, nor man, have so strutted, and bellowed, that I have thought some of Nature's journeymen had made men, and not made them well, they imitated humanity so abominably."

This, you perceive, describes in brief, all that I have said with less force and pertinence, and here, I wish you pleasant dreams, and leave you.

This presentation was apparently given by the Phoenix Theatrical Company. Loughery reported in May that the company was giving presentations in Jefferson, that the company would soon be in Marshall, and that the *Jefferson Herald* had spoken favorably of its efforts.

Readings

Miss Eloise Bridges traveled extensively giving dramatic readings and recitations with paid admission. She was a woman of great beauty and considerable talent who was well known throughout northeast Texas where her engagements were universally well received. She appeared in Jefferson at least once, in April 1859, prior to an appearance at Marshall. Shadrach Eggers of the Jefferson *Eastern Texas Gazette* noted that "a look at her beautiful face was ample recommendation for the admission fee."

The *Banjo*

The *Banjo* was a 115-foot by 25-foot sidewheel showboat with a stage and seating for 800 that traveled to Jefferson at least once and probably twice. Showboats were extremely popular because they could bring professional troupes to remote places and provided their own theater. The *Banjo* was built expressly for Ned Davis' Olio Minstrels at a cost of $18,000. She appeared at Shreveport in February 1856, advertising afternoon and evening performances at 50 cents with children and servants at half price, a 12-person ensemble, an illuminated levee for the evening performance, and a brass band (Fig. 41-1).

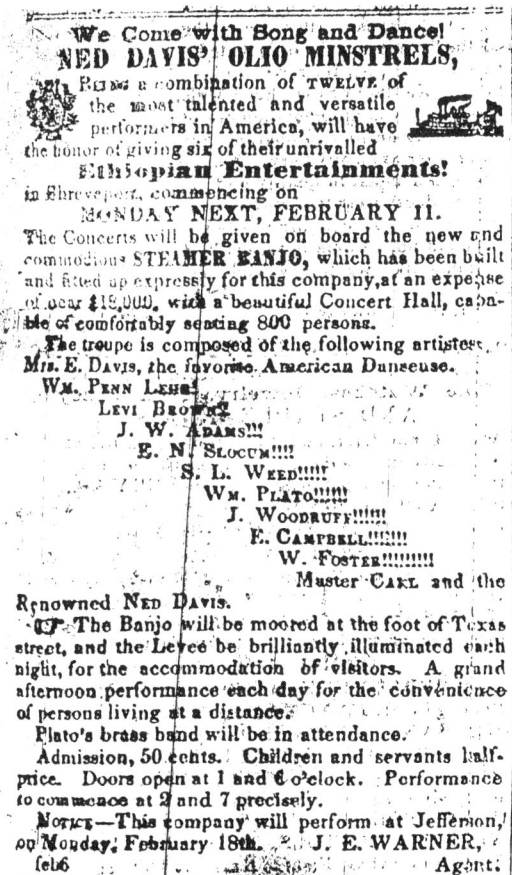

Fig. 41-1. Olio Minstrels Advertisement. Source: February 6, 1846, *South-Western*

The *Banjo* attempted to reach Jefferson but experienced difficulties in Twelvemile Bayou and had to return to Shreveport. She returned to Shreveport a year later, with the owners, Spalding & Rogers, indicating that they had concentrated all of their circuses, museums, minstrel bands, and steamboats in the south and west for the 1857 season and that these exhibits would be coming to the Shreveport area. The *Banjo* had been refitted in recherche style and featured a stage, music saloon, and cushioned seats, and Ned Davis' troupe had been increased by two. This time the *Banjo* was able to reach Jefferson after drawing crowded audiences at Albany, Mooring's Landing, Port Caddo, Benton, and Smithland. An excellent description of the nature of the presentation is given in the February 20, 1856, *South-Western* when the *Banjo* first arrived at Shreveport:

> THE BANJO.—Our citizens were delighted during the past week with the unique entertainments of Ned Davis' Ethiopian minstrels, and we know of no company that has visited us who have given such universal satisfaction.—Mr. Davis surpasses any delineator of the negro race we have witnessed, and appears equally inimitable as the darkey dandy of Chartres street, the uncouth, blundering plantation boy, or as the intelligent, saucy, well-fed house-servant; while his witticisms, contortions, and fancy touches on the tamborine would make the coldest cynic that ever breathed laugh until he grew fat. It is marvellous to listen to one of his "fast" harangues. His "gombo-French" version of Susannah will create a furor in the lower parishes. Mr. W. Penn Lehr is a master performer and has shown what sweet music the banjo can discourse; and Mr. Weed, as a bone-player and jig-dancer, has few equals.—Mrs. Davis' dancing gave great satisfaction. The manager on Saturday afternoon gave benefit to the methodist church, which yielded $112.70, and proved most acceptable to the congregation, as will be seen by the card from the stewards.

The *Banjo* arrived back in Shreveport in February 1859 and almost certainly proceeded on to Jefferson with a new troupe, as described in the *South-Western*:

> THE BANJO BACK AGAIN.—The steamer Banjo, having on board Donetti's celebrated company of acting monkeys, dogs and goats, will arrive to-morrow, and exhibitions will be given on Thursday, Friday and Saturday. Donetti's monkeys have displayed their training in all the principal cities of Europe and America to crowded audiences. They are well worth seeing. Wood's Minstrels will also give a grand display of negro minstrelsy, plantation melodies, burlesques, etc.

Circus

The circus, with its mix of excitement, beauty, skill, and danger, was the most important public entertainment medium during the antebellum period. It was something in which everyone in a community, including slaves, could and did participate, providing the only occasion other than national and Texas holidays for a community-wide celebration. Circuses were particularly liked because they provided wholesome family entertainment, a characteristic they emphasized in their advertisements. Robinson's Circus and Menagerie was in Marshall in March 1857 and almost certainly included Jefferson in its itinerary:

> THE CIRCUS RETURNING.—Robinson's Circus and Menagerie, which was exhibited here during the past week, will return again on its way through Texas and give another exhibition at this place on Monday next. A great many who had no opportunity of witnessing the performances of this troup, will doubtless avail themselves of this occasion. They will see many very interesting sights. There are several excellent actors in the company whose performances are worth seeing. The riding here was good; the vaulting seldom excelled. The Chinese juggler, and the man with the barrel and chairs, created great applause. We like to go to a circus just to see the crowd, witness the gyrations

of the clown, and to see other people laugh. The last is a decided luxury.

Orton & Older's Great Southern Circus exhibited at Marshall on October 28, 1859, and at Jefferson the next Thursday, with admission at 50 cents and half price for children and servants (Fig. 41-2). The circus, according to its advertisement, featured the largest acrobatic corps ever combined in one company; equestrians, herculeans, and dramatists culled from the stars of Europe and America; the fearless and graceful Madame Marietta with her trick horse, Jupiter; Professor Tubbe with his pet leopard, Washington; and the celebrated and well-trained ponies, Cherry and Fair Star. The circus was preceded by the morning entrance into town of Able's Military Band on a chariot drawn by 12 horses and followed by the Sable Harmonists' grand concert consisting of songs, dances, burlesques, and comicalities.

Fig. 41-2. Circus Advertisement. Source: October 21, 1859, *Harrison Flag*

42. Balls and Dances

Balls and dances were the primary form of social interaction between men and women in Jefferson. Balls and major dances in Jefferson involved surrounding communities such as Marshall. Music was provided by fiddlers, among whom the Jefferson dancing masters Sam and Hun Williams were the most prominent. They were always accompanied by food, with lavish outlays for the balls and major dances, which were catered by Jefferson's hotel operators. They were held in the Alhambra Hall, in hotels, in private residences, in schools, and occasionally in business warehouses.

Dancing was popular among all ages. All of the major parties involved dancing, although there were obviously occasions such as Christmas parties at private residences that did not. One of the most popular types was the storm party, which usually included dancing. Storm parties were surprise parties in which the house of the guest of honor was invaded and that person was expected to cover the cost. Almost anything could serve as a pretext for a storm party. Loughery reported in April 1858 that "These parties... are gotten up by the young folks every eight or ten days, and are exceedingly pleasant"; and DeMorse reported during the same month that preparations had to be made very quickly and that "these affairs are frequent, and got up here with great celerity."

Loughery identified sociability (friendliness and pleasant social relations) as one of Jefferson's primary virtues and balls as the primary manifestation of sociability: "Balls have occurred with frequency during the entire winter, and I know of no place where the entire population is on better terms of pleasantness each with the other, than this. It shows what good may be done, by a right start, and the residence of a few genial persons giving a right social turn to intercourse, at the inception of a new place." Although Loughery does not use the term, his descriptions of the balls he attended in Jefferson indicate conviviality (feasting, drinking, and good company) as another virtue. There are no reports of unpleasantness at any balls or dances. A few of the better descriptions will be used to characterize these occasions.

A ball held in the Soda Lake Hotel in connection with the Fourth of July celebration is described in the July 13, 1850, *Texas Republican*:

> But how shall we describe it? In what "set phrase of speech" shall we couch what is indescribable? We were there, and "saw it all," but of what shall we speak? We *could* talk forever of the beautiful ladies that thronged the dancing room; we could speak of a supper that would have tempted a Grahamite; we could speak of such music as the Mussulman hears, as in his opium dream he sees the Houris that gem the "gay parterre" of Paradise—all of this we could speak. But the occasion is too recent for us to make ourself coherent or intelligible; we forego it. The party assembled—danced till 10—had supper—danced till 2—had a lunch—danced "till day-light"—and then in the "morning" the young gents "went home with the *ladies*."

The October 3, 1857, *Texas Republican* reports on a ball that was held at the Alhambra Hall with a late supper at the Jefferson Hotel in connection with the election of Governor Runnels, who was unable to attend. A thousand tickets had been sent to women in Cass and nearby counties:

> We had the pleasure of attending the Runnels Ball at Jefferson, on the 24th ult., and seldom has it been our fortune in Texas to witness a more pleasant, and we may say with propriety, a more brilliant reunion. From

the amount of sickness prevailing in the country, it was feared that it would prove a failure. His Excellency, the Governor elect, was not present, owing to the illness of his mother, and his absence, and the cause which created it, was a matter calculated to throw a damper over the hilarity of the joyous occasion. Nevertheless, when the gay throng, were set in motion by the witching notes of the viol, care for the time was forgotten, and the scene was one of animation and beauty. The music was superb. The inimitable Sam Williams, and his brother, and a gentleman whose name we do not recollect, were the performers. The attendance, at the Ball, for the reason mentioned, was not large, but sufficiently so to render the occasion more agreeable than if there had been a large crowd. There were many lovely ladies in this attractive coterie, embracing, in addition to those of Cass, a few from Harrison and other adjoining counties. The large and elegant Alhambra Hall, brightly lighted, was used as the dancing saloon, and as many "sets," as could find room upon the floor, were organized. At 11 o'clock supper was announced, and the gay throng repaired to the Jefferson Hotel, kept by Mr. F. T. HARRIS, where a table was set, which for artistic decoration, luxury, and profusion, we have seldom seen equalled. Everything that money could purchase, or art invent, to tempt the appetite, was furnished in abundance. The table was the theme of admiration and compliment.

 After supper, dancing was resumed, and continued, how long deponent sayeth not, as he retired a short time afterwards, leaving the gay company in the full title of enjoyment. Suffice it, in a plain prose way, to say, that the Runnels Ball was one that will be remembered with delight by those who had the pleasure of attending it.

A storm party, including a fish fry, was held for Charles Stanley as reported in the April 10, 1858, *Standard*. Stanley was about to leave for the north to investigate meat packeries. The party was held at the Stanley & Nimmo furniture warehouse on Cypress Bayou at the foot of Houston Street. The warehouse, which was 15 feet above the bayou and had a large door opening to it, had been built for cotton storage and was soon to be converted into a meat packery. Stanley had to scramble to prepare for the party, which had been announced in the morning and began at 10 a.m. with a buffet of fish, ham, tongue, cakes, and champagne. The party lasted only until 4 p.m., at which time the participants left to prepare for a ball that night at the Alhambra Hall that continued till near morning:

> Sam Williams and Brother were there with violins, and the dancing was spirited and luxurious. The glowing sunlight could not penetrate the broad warehouse, which was darkened by the large space which it excluded from the direct rays of light, and also by the trees around. Then, the music, by the margin of the water, had of course, an increased melodiousness, as every one knows who has ever heard music softened by the contiguity of water. There were *fast* dances, and then conversational spells, the communicants being broken into parties, dispersed about the large building; then there was sometimes a song, with or without a banjo accompaniment. The party was entirely genial; every one's face had a pleasant glow; and I am sure that none who were present but will reckon the day with a white stone, as one of the few deliciously spent. Mr. Stanley, the proprietor of the warehouse, getting short notice, had gone to work with all the force at his disposal, and put out of the way as much as possible the stock of furniture, now much thinned out; and occasional sofas and chairs left in place beside the walls, were of course eminently useful. Late in the afternoon the party dispersed, to prepare for the Ball at night, under the immediate auspices of Old Sam.

Balls and Dances

A New Year's Eve party was held for the children of the town by Gen. James Rogers' wife (Cozia, eldest daughter of William Ochiltree), as reported in the January 7, 1859, *Harrison Flag*:

> You may talk of your balls for the grown ladies and the (?) beaux, but let me tell you, "there is none so rare as can compare" with such as was given to the juveniles of the city of Jefferson, on the night of the 1st of the new year, by that excellent lady, Mrs. General Rogers. There were about one hundred and twenty between the ages of six and eleven, the opposite sexes being about even. Now imagine you see young America making partners for a cotillion; then about four sets moving to music, discoursed from a Piano Forte, under the promptings of an accomplished lady; and, nothing is left for us to tell, except to inform you that at the proper time, (for youngsters of their ages,) they were introduced to an excellent supper, and soon thereafter admonished that sleep was the last restorer of nature, while we, old folks, talked about the rising generation, and sipped a little champagne, while felicitating ourselves upon the favorable indications of those to succeed us; and to whose hands the prosperity of our institutions is soon to be confided.

48. Crime

When Edward Smith traveled throughout the region, including Jefferson, in 1849, he reported that "The most perfect security to life and property reigns throughout N. E. Texas, far more perfect than can be found in the Eastern States, or in Europe, or indeed in any well-peopled country." By September 1858, Robert Loughery of the Marshall *Texas Republican* found that murder was common throughout Texas, giving as the primary reason the unwillingness of juries to uphold the law. Throughout the antebellum period, Jefferson was more like the condition described by Smith than the condition described by Loughery, in spite of the fact that it was a port town frequented by steamboat crews and ox-wagon drivers.

Criminal cases were handled through the district court, with the county court restricted to probate (inheritance) issues. There do not appear to be any surviving records of criminal cases below the district court level, which was regional in scope and dealt with the most serious crimes. Most of the efforts of the district court were devoted to civil matters, particularly land disputes and debt. Criminal cases included murder, assault with intent to kill, assault and battery, aggravated assault, burglary, theft, larceny, rape, adultery, incest, and malicious mischief. Few of these cases involved Jefferson residents.

By far the largest number of criminal cases brought before the district court involved gambling and neglect of road maintenance duties. This was a time in which maintenance of public roads was a citizen responsibility and gambling was illegal in Texas. From the number of cases brought before the court, it is obvious that gambling was immensely popular in Jefferson and throughout northeast Texas. Many of Jefferson's most prominent citizens, beginning with William Perry, were brought before the court on charges of card playing, operating a faro bank, betting on rondo, playing roulet and chuckaluck, and even, in the case of Nelson Trawick, betting on an election. Fines were generally modest and repeat offenses common.

Significant instances of criminal activity in Jefferson were covered by the external newspapers. There were only a few reported killings, and only two of these appear to have involved Jefferson residents.

David Douthit was a Jefferson merchant located on Marshall Street in Block 21 in August 1851 and on the same street in Block 74 by August 1852. In early January 1853, Douthit killed an orphan boy by the name of Baker who was working in one of the livery stables, as reported in the Marshall *Texas Republican*. Douthit was charged with manslaughter according to the newspaper, bond was set at $2,000 with Francis and William Baker as sureties, and the accused was to appear in the next term of the district court.

In the absence of a jail, the prisoner was housed with Francis Baker. The case of State of Texas versus David Douthit for murder was to be held in March 1854. The accused and his sureties did not appear in court on the appointed day, and the bond was forfeited, with the court stating that Douthit and the Bakers should appear on the first day of the next district court if they did not wish the judgment to be made final. There do not appear to be any later records concerning this case. Douthit apparently disappeared, because he is not mentioned again in any documents concerning Jefferson; but Francis Baker was paid by the commissioners court in May 1855 for having previously housed the prisoner. If the newspaper was correct that this was an instance of manslaughter, it is probable that Douthit fatally struck the boy during an altercation involving his services in the livery stable.

In late 1853, Dr. Alfred R. Lander, a Cass County physician, killed Eli Ussery on the streets of Jefferson. Ussery operated a plantation northwest of Jefferson. Although I have not seen anything to indicate that Lander practiced in Jefferson, he was a founding member of Christ

Church in Jefferson. The circumstances of the killing are not reported in the newspapers.

The trial was held in the March 1854 term of the district court. Lander pleaded not guilty and was found guilty of second degree murder and sentenced to five years in the State Penitentiary. The case was taken on appeal to the Texas Supreme Court on the grounds that there was an error in the charge of the judge to the jury. In May, the Supreme Court, sitting in Tyler, affirmed the lower court's decision.

After conviction, Lander was placed on bail at $8,000, with William Hill, James Henderson, Charles Jackson, James Scott, and Morrys Hagger as securities. In the absence of a jail, he was housed with John Ligon. Lander and his sureties did not appear as ordered in the September term of the court. He had escaped in August, and the sheriff offered a $500 reward for his capture. In October, Loughery of the *Texas Republican* reported rumors that the prisoner had never been in irons, that he had been allowed to practice medicine, and that he had even attended a ball a few nights before his escape. Loughery inquired of the *Jefferson Herald* whether these rumors were true. There was no response, and Lander is not mentioned thereafter.

Hiram Grinsted of the *Jefferson Herald* and Henry Parsons of the *Tyler Telegraph* got into an editor's quarrel that resulted in a duel, with Richard Crump acting as second for Grinsted. A number of notices appeared in the newspapers in which Parsons and Crump attacked each other. In one of these, Crump asserted that Parsons was a coward because he did not respond to an insult to his wife that was meant to provoke a response from him. Parsons replied that the man who insulted his wife had permitted the seduction of his own sister without defending her honor. The allusion was understood by everyone to refer to John Morgan of the firm of Morgan & Tomlin, who had provided the initial insult.

In January 1854, Parsons was in Jefferson to attend the funeral of his brother-in-law, Frank Dennard. Rather than leaving after the funeral, Parsons went downtown, visited Owens & McLeroy's store on the corner of Austin and Marshall, and proceeded towards Morgan & Tomlin's. On reaching the corner, he started to cross the street in the direction of Saufley & Nimmo's. The unobserved Morgan was advancing upon him. They both started across the street at the same time. About midway, Morgan called to Parsons; and when Parsons turned around, Morgan shot him with a double-barrel shotgun, breaking one of his legs and inflicting a flesh wound in the other.

The January 28, 1854, *Texas Republican* reports that "Morgan surrendered himself promptly to the sheriff, and will have no difficulty in giving bond, as he has numerous friends, in town and throughout the county, who hold him in high esteem." Morgan was brought before the district court in April on a charge of assault and battery with attempt to kill and placed on bail at $8,000, with James Scott, John Farley, and Gus Hodge as sureties. In September, he pleaded not guilty, was found guilty of assault and battery by the jury, and was fined one cent. The court, with judicial propriety, instructed that Morgan be placed in the hands of the sheriff until the fine was paid.

The jury's verdict was not a matter of friendship. Parsons' attacks on Grinsted and others had been scurrilous from the beginning, going downtown was a deliberate provocation and perhaps a threat, and it is unclear that Morgan attempted to kill Parsons. The one cent fine indicated that the jury thought that Parsons got what he deserved in an affair of honor.

In early July 1858, William Perry's *Bloomer* was in port, and the body of an Irish deckhand was found in the bayou horribly mangled through beating with a pine knot or other heavy instrument. The mate A. L. Johnson and the second mate Real Wilcox were arrested. While examinations of the accused were underway, the court adjourned, and the prisoners were brought on board the *Bloomer* for lunch. Wilcox took the opportunity to escape, jumping into a yawl, proceeding to the opposite shore, and then running downstream to McFarland's sawmill above Black Cypress Bayou, where he crossed over Big Cypress Bayou and ran up Black Cypress Bayou and spent part of the night in a tree.

Pursuit was immediately undertaken with dogs. Wilcox was only a short distance ahead of his pursuers, and a number of shots were fired. Descending the tree while it was still dark, Wilcox headed for Shreveport, but was seen by some slaves, who gave the alarm, and was captured about five miles from Jefferson at Jack Morgan's plantation.

The court dismissed Johnson, but Judge Todd ordered him immediately rearrested with a bail of $2,000, which was soon paid. Wilcox was unable to meet a bail of $7,500 and was placed in confinement. The *Jefferson Gazette* stated that "Our town was, from the discovery of the dead body, up to the close of the trials, the scene of intense excitement. The public indignation was roused to the utmost tension. As for ourself, we believe that Johnson is innocent of the murder, and that his trial will result in full acquital." The outcome of the trial is not mentioned in the newspapers, and I have been unable to find any account in the district court records.

The Stanley & Nimmo packery brought its employees in from the Midwest because meat packing required skilled labor. During late December 1859, an altercation occurred between members of this workforce in a rough area of town in which one man was killed and two were arrested. The only information on this incident is a highly corrupt text in the January 6, 1860, Marshall *Harrison Flag* quoting the *Jefferson Herald*:

> On Christmas day, the "five points" of this city was the (?) of a bloody affray. The persons implicated in the matter were men in the employ of Messrs. Stanly & Nimmo, in their packery, but who meting at the "points" (?), several words passed between them, when with (?) urging the other, blows, (?) and a (?) was the result. Two men are now in custody charged with the murder, but at the present writing Judge Ury has not given facts in investigation of the case.

There was one other possible murder mentioned in the newspapers about which nothing is known other than the report in the June 23, 1860, *Texas Republican* taken from the *Jefferson Herald*:

> BODY FOUND.—The dead body of a man was found in the timber on the north side of town on Saturday morning last. The corpse was in an advanced state of decomposition and had been partially devoured by hogs. Two wounds were found upon the body, either one of which was sufficient to have produced death. Of

the circumstances attending the death of the deceased nothing is known.

Only three instances of theft were considered important enough to be mentioned in the newspapers, and only one of these could have been perpetrated by a Jefferson resident.

The first is from the October 27, 1855, *Texas Republican*: "At Jefferson, we learn from the Herald, that M. Steinlein & Co., on the night of the 11th lost a negro, who left, taking with him a valuable horse and a revolving pistol, the property of Dr. I. G. Eason. Another horse belonging to Mr. F. M. Martin was stolen, and a negro belonging to Mr. Turner and one belonging to Mr. J. H. Boone, left about the same time." These and other disappearances of slaves and horses were attributed by the newspaper to bands of thieves scattered over Texas and Louisiana.

The second is from the April 4, 1857, *Texas Republican*: "A young man by the name of McShaun *alias* Whitfield recently hired a buggy and a pair of horses from Messrs. N. A. Birge & Co., of Jefferson, under the pretence of going a few miles in the country for his sister. Instead of having any such business, he proceeded to Shreveport and sold the horses and buggy to Mr. Hitchcock."

The third is from the August 13, 1859, *Texas Republican*: "BOLD ROBBERY.—The dwelling of Mr. Gus. Hodge, in Jefferson, was entered a few nights ago, and the keys of his iron safe abstracted from his pantaloons pocket, while he was asleep. The next morning he found the keys, and the papers which had been placed in the safe, some distance from the store. The thief, after stealing the money in the safe, amounting to about $2,000, had locked the store and safe, and doubtless after examining the papers, had placed the keys and papers in a place where they could be readily found. This was certainly a daring piece of villainy."

Lastly, counterfeit money, obviously not produced by Jefferson residents, was circulated in Jefferson, as reported in the September 23, 1854, *Texas Republican*, quoting the *Jefferson Herald*: "Counterfeit half dollars of the new coinage are in circulation here. They look well, have a very clear ring when struck, but are very light. They are well executed, and calculated to deceive."

These records confirm the observations by persons external to Jefferson that it was a fairly peaceful town. The low incidence of serious crime, most of which was conducted by nonresidents, should not be surprising. The population never reached 1,000 before the Civil War, and more than a quarter of the population were slaves. The community was close knit, civil ordinances were enforced, merchants worked late into the night on their books, almost all males were employed, and slaves were kept under strict supervision.

Premeditated murder was rare in northeast Texas, and murder in connection with theft was unknown. Violence, such as it occurred in Jefferson, generally appeared through random encounters on the city streets between parties to long-standing quarrels involving honor and reputation, such as the one reported in the September 1, 1860, *Texas Republican*: "We are informed that a difficulty occurred in Jefferson a day or two ago between Mr. Thos. Boykin and a lawyer by the name of Cameron. Cameron shot twice at Boykin, when Boykin threw a brick bat at Cameron, which struck him in the head. At the last accounts Cameron's life was despaired of."

Acts of violence that were an outrage to the moral sense of the community mobilized citizens and people in the general area to apprehend the criminal. Justice appears to have been served in the major cases that came before the court. Acts of violence that were in keeping with the moral sense of the community resulted in formal convictions with light penalties. The major thing that was lacking in the administration of justice was a jail.

There was no jail in Jefferson when it was the seat of Cass County from 1846 to 1852, and there was no jail in Linden, the new county seat, until 1856. During that decade, prisoners were housed in Jefferson in hotels, stores, and probably stables. The only prisoners mentioned in the commissioners court minutes are those that were involved in capital cases. Although they were guarded, security was lax, particularly in the case of prominent citizens, and escapes were frequent. This was a particular concern of Robert Loughery of the Marshall *Texas Republican*, as expressed, for example in the September 2, 1854, issue:

> Dr. A. L. Lander, who was convicted of the murder
> of Eli Ussery, at the last term of the District Court of

Cass county, and who was sentenced to five years imprisonment in the Penitentiary, effected his escape on the night of the 16th ult. The Sheriff offers a reward of $500 for his arrest. We have been in Texas five years, and although a goodly number have been killed in this portion of it, no one, as yet, has been punished. Jordan, in Wood county, was sentenced to be hung, but made his escape before the day of execution. Shell, convicted two years ago in Cass county of murder, and sentenced to the Penitentiary for ten years, made his escape. And the same may be said of others; persons notoriously guilty of crimes of this character have been suffered to escape, when they might have been arrested. How can we expect law and order to triumph, when such things are permitted? Have we any reason to be astonished at the number of murders, when the chances of punishment are as remote as they are in Texas?

We believe the late Sheriff of Cass, Mr. George Ury, to be a conscientious, clever gentleman, and to have made a good officer. We expect that he used his best exertions (there being no jail in Cass) to retain Lander. But what we deem particularly objectionable is, not this particular case alone, but that all escape. Out of the number of murders and deeds of violence, not one is punished.

A jail was proposed for the new county seat in Linden in December 1852, with work to be contracted to the lowest bidder. Bid specifications were advertised in August 1854 in the *Jefferson Herald*, and design plans were posted in Linden and at Saufley & Nimmo's store in Jefferson. The jail was not completed until July 1856, with formal adoption by the commissioners on August 1. Prisoners were still being housed in Jefferson as late as May 1855 by persons such as Thomas Goyne and Francis Baker. The construction of the jail actually fell under two major contracts, one for the structure and the other for an iron cage. The latter was the most important, because structures had already proven to be unsatisfactory as places of retention.

The structure was completed by David Carpenter at a cost of $1,572.70, with the assistance of John Ribold at a cost of $132.30, both of whom were from Jefferson. The cage was constructed by J. H. Updegraff at a cost of $560, with the following specifications:

> Seven feet long, four feet and a half wide, and seven feet high. To be made of bar iron two inches wide and a half inch thick, to be crossed and riveted at each crossing, and to be made so as to be a space of four inches between bars. The cage is to be made after the plan of the one in Marshall, Texas; door, shutter, hinges, and such after the same plan and to be furnished after like plan.

There was no county jail in Jefferson when it became the seat of Marion County in February 1860, and prisoners were housed in private facilities. A decision to build a jail was made in August 1860, with specifications advertised in the *Herald and Gazette* and proposals to be submitted in November. Although there are no records pertaining to subsequent actions, the jail apparently was built, because the sheriff Noble Birge was authorized in February and August 1861 to repair the jailhouse floor. In addition, the town apparently had its own jail, because James Hosack was paid $1 for putting a lock in the jail in March 1860, which was many months before the decision to build a county jail was made.

44. Vice

Vice implies moral fault: it is behavior that is both a manifestation of moral degradation and conducive to moral degradation. Attitudes toward vice were ambivalent. There was a widespread attitude that people should mind their own business; but they were acutely conscious of the personal, family, and social ramifications of vice and expressed strong opinions on these matters. Coercion was disdained, but people were not reluctant to legislate morality. Widespread support for public policies was coupled with indifference to enforcement, apparently under the recognition that popular vices could not be extirpated by laws. The primary reliance was on moral suasion, particularly in the form of large social movements such as temperance.

There is evidence for the existence of a particular section of Jefferson in which vice was prominent. When smallpox struck the town in early 1859, the *Harrison Flag* reported that "it only existed in a portion of the town inhabited by persons of impure habits, a sort of hell's half acre." In late 1859, the "five points" was the scene of a bloody affray that involved employees of the Stanley & Nimmo meatpacking plant, in which at least one person was killed. The "five points" was probably the hell's half acre. From the smallpox reports, the area was separated from the business section of town. This area may have been near the intersections of Broadway, Line, and Walnut, which provide a geographic setting for five points; however, it is more probable that the name was derived from the notorious Five Points in New York and does not refer to geography.

Gambling

People loved to gamble and apparently were willing to bet on just about anything. Gambling was against state law. Many Jeffersonians were brought into court on charges of gambling (mostly card playing and operating faro banks), paid modest fines, and went back to their practices. The number of persons brought to court, which was quite large, represented an infinitesimally small portion of the infractions. State-sponsored gambling would have been considered by Texans to be an inversion of the moral order.

When Loughery visited Jefferson in January 1853, he pointed out that "Gambling is carried on here pretty extensively, as it is all over Texas, notwithstanding the stringency of our laws." The favored game at the time was Rondo, which was played openly, because the State Supreme Court had declared (in violation of the clear intent of the law according to Loughery) that forms of gambling not specifically mentioned in the state law were legal. Rondo was played with a billiard table, two open pockets, and small balls that were rolled from one to the other pocket. If an even number of balls remained outside the pockets, the house won. If the house lost, it took a percentage of the winnings.

Loughery pointed out that legislation against gambling was ineffectual as long as it was countenanced by public opinion, but that the law at least kept gambling out of public places. He was not concerned about the professional gamblers, who were honest about what they were and who didn't need to cheat because of their superior skills, but rather by the "gentlemen" gamblers, who tended to cheat and corrupted themselves and the youth:

> He is the man that decoys and ruins youth—if not by persuasion, at least by example. A young man of 18 or 19 cannot think a practice very bad when he finds himself sustained by and in the company of the most respectable men in the place. We should, therefore, make laws punishing more severely the respectable gentlemen who give their influence, and spend their time

in gaming, instead of the professional gamester who takes no pains to conceal his vocation, and who will most certainly get the money of those with him, unless they understand the whole machinery of cards. I do not mean to assert that those who gamble are dishonest in the full sense of the word. When men gamble, there is a tacit understanding that the smartest man gets the money; and many of those who would, under such circumstances use all their ingenuity to carry their point, would not in their business affairs be guilty of any thing disreputable. I know many who have been very succesful in play, who are considered high minded liberal men. Yet the practice is pernicious and demoralizing and ought to be exterminated. It makes a man selfish and covetous, and has a greater tendency to harden his heart than any other vice. At least, such is my opinion.

Drinking

The consumption of alcoholic beverages was widespread and persistent, affecting all social classes, sexes, ages, and occupational settings. Americans preferred distilled spirits, in contradistinction to Europeans who favored wine and beer. Consumption was continuous, but usually moderate, or else no one would have been able to function; falling-down drunkenness was for afterhours. The favored drink was whiskey, which could be obtained at most stores and in the numerous saloons. Chester Bulkley's grocery advertisement was typical, offering superior old brandy from $2.50 to $8 per gallon, imitation and American brandy from 75 cents to $1 per gallon, Holland gin, common whiskey, Dexter & Rye whiskey, Cocke whiskey, bourbon whiskey, old Rye whiskey, cider, ale, porter, port, Madeira, sherry, Malaga, claret, champagne, white wine, Jamaica rum, schnapps, brandy, cherries, black berry brandy, cordials, and Stoughton, Gouley and Boke's bitters. When the drygoods and groceries merchant Ephraim Beckett died in 1853, his store inventory included more than 3,000 gallons of whiskey. Loughery pointed out that many forms of alcohol were adulterated with other substances. Alcohol was also available through the popular patent medicines, which were consumed by teetotalers among others.

In 1854, the Texas Legislature allowed counties by majority vote to prohibit sale of liquor in quantities less than a quart, which was aimed at the saloons. Jeffersonians voted overwhelmingly (225 to 33) for the prohibition, but the law was declared unconstitutional at the state level and never went into effect. The town had the capacity to regulate the sale of liquor independently. Loughery reported in May 1855 that the corporate authorities had put an end to the liquor traffic by passing an ordinance that closed the saloons; but he retracted the statement in June when informed by the *Jefferson Herald* that this was not the case. There were at least six saloons in Jefferson in 1860.

Apart from whatever pleasure people derived from consumption of alcohol in moderate quantities, Loughery was probably correct when he pointed out in the April 7, 1855, *Texas Republican* that there was widespread agreement on the overall deleterious effects of drinking: "There are no two sides to this question. From its very nature, there can be but one. The sale of intoxicating drinks benefits no one. On the contrary it is productive of incalculable mischief. The dram seller and the dram drinker are both willing to confess this." The extent of alcoholism is unknown. However, it must have been quite large because it precipitated the formation of the Sons of Temperance in Texas in 1848. Like all temperance movements, this was a misnomer, because it called for pledges of abstinence (rather than moderation) from all alcoholic beverages. There must have been a chapter in Jefferson, because they were quite common throughout Texas. In February 1855, James Young, a Louisville temperance lecturer, spoke at Jefferson.

Drugs

Opium, its alkaloid morphine, and its tincture laudanum were readily available in patent medicines and over the counter without prescription in drugstores, and opium was used extensively by doctors for the relief of pain. The level of use by the public cannot be ascertained. Overdoses of laudanum appear to have been the preferred course of suicide by women. Addiction appears to have been an occupational hazard for doctors. Morphine occasionally appears in the property listings for probated estates. Addiction is not mentioned in the newspapers because it was not recognized as a social problem until after the Civil War. Consumption before the war was oral; hypodermic injection of morphine, which produced a more powerful effect, became popular during the war.

Prostitution

The large number of unattached young males in Jefferson and the fact that it was an ox-wagon and steamboat destination provided conditions for prostitution, and the existence of "persons of impure habits" suggests that they might have been present. However, the 1854 ordinances do not address prostitution, there is no firm evidence for any prostitutes in town, and the 1860 census does not contain any persons who might qualify. Loughery and DeMorse, who visited Jefferson often and provided moral commentaries on what they saw, do not mention any houses of prostitution.

The newspapers of the day were not reluctant to report on such matters. The February 7, 1857, *Texas Republican* contains a reprint of an article from the Shreveport *Caddo Gazette* concerning a shooting at a bawdy house involving steamboatmen and Texas wagoners. This was a place in which someone had been recently killed. The *Caddo Gazette* comments: "We advise persons who desire to be shot to go to that same house; it surely is the best place in town for such accommodations."

In spite of the lack of firm evidence, it can be assumed that there were houses of prostitution within the corporate boundaries because the aldermen passed an ordinance in August 1858 stipulating a fine of $50 for any person or persons "guilty of keeping a disorderly house or a house of ill fame for the purpose of prostitution." Prostitution was considered a nuisance, particularly when conducive to other forms of disorder. The mayor had the power to tell prostitutes to leave the town within five days, with the problem then turned over to the town marshal.

The mayor also had the power to allow prostitutes to remain "upon their entering into such bond with good security as may be required by the Mayor conditional upon their good behavior." I have not seen a bond of this nature, perhaps because the Transcribed Deed Records deal almost entirely with property transactions. This was an obvious concession to practicality and a reasonable alternative to attempts at exclusion, which were usually not successful in other towns. The aldermen were not concerned with prostitution per se, but rather with the collateral disorderly activities normally generated by houses of prostitution. This is confirmed by the 1870 *Digest of the Laws of the City of Jefferson, Texas*, which provided for the expulsion of "houses of ill fame within the city of Jefferson that shall be conducted in an indecent manner, or conducted so as to become a nuisance."

It is important to note that the ordinance dealt only with in-town prostitution. There were no restrictions on such activities external to the corporate limits; and the geographic range probably extended as far as Four Mile Branch, where the ox-wagons stopped. The need for an in-town ordinance suggests that the demand for prostitutes was great by 1858.

Tobacco

Tobacco was widely used in antebellum times in the form of chewing tobacco, pipes, snuff, and cigars, with chewing tobacco being the most common and women using all forms but favoring the first three. Tobacco stains from spitting were omnipresent. Spitting in church was common and condemned. The smoking of cigars in closed spaces such as stagecoaches was objected to from time to time; but the ritual of men retiring to a smoking room after dinner was primarily a matter of male bonding rather than the result of objections from women. Cigars were much favored by businessmen. Loughery, when he received a box of cigars from John Sabine, expressed the particular pleasure afforded by cigars when he spoke of "the delicious fragrance spreading beatitude over our countenance." When the drygoods and groceries merchant Ephraim Beckett died in 1853, his store inventory included nearly 2,000 pounds of tobacco and 700 cigars.

Many people during the 1800s considered the use of tobacco to be a vice. An excellent, lengthy diatribe by a woman from Honey Grove is contained in the February 26, 1859, *Standard*. The section concentrating on chewing tobacco will be quoted because it is no longer as common:

It is not alone the unfortunate inebriate entangled in the meshes of intemperance, from the use of Alcoholic drinks, thereby rendering himself a drone in the hive of society, a pest to himself, and a curse to his family, and friends that claims our attention. There is a much larger class, who are slaves to a vice, not much inferior in magnitude, and one too, that exerts a most baneful influence, on man's intellectual powers; often sowing the seeds of disease in their systems, and hurrying many to a premature grave. I allude to the use of *Tobacco*.—Go where you may, to the private parlor, the public walks, the stores, or shops, and even to the sanctuary of the Most High, and your olfactories are offended by a Regalia, or perchance a pipe; 'tis true, they do not enter the house of God, with the lighted cigar, or pipe, but hang about the doors, and windows, from which the fragrance readily finds its way within, rendering its sacred precincts almost unbearable, to many within its walls. Its place when laid aside even for that brief period, is usually supplied with a quid, creating around them a pool of ambier, which makes it almost impossible for those in their vicinity, to worship God by kneeling, even in time of prayer. And is it possible, think you Mr. Editor, for a lady to walk your streets, or enter any of your business houses, without danger of her dress coming in contact with a similar pool? And then ye devotees of the quid, look at your own personal appearance, mouths that at each corner, display unmistakeable evidence of the contents within; your stained teeth, that no dentifrice can whiten; your soiled garments, and your utter inability, even to pass the common salutations of the day, with a lady acquaintance, whom you might chance to meet, without first, ejecting from the mouth, a stream of the noxious fluid.

45. HEALTH AND WELFARE

Health

When A. W. Moore visited Jefferson in January 1846, he observed that it had "the appearance of being as sickly a place as exists under the sun." Josiah Gregg made a similar statement in August 1841: "all the country bordering the lake and either branch of the cypress must always be very unhealthy, owing to the stagnancy of the waters, and the marshiness of their borders." Moore and Gregg were apparently basing their observations on contemporary theories of miasmatic causes of disease in which swamps were often considered the culprit. The primary killers in the south were yellow fever, cholera, and smallpox. All diseases that affected groups of people were thought to be contagious.

Jefferson was, in fact, a very healthy place. There appear to have been a few cases of cholera in January 1850, but there were no reported deaths. There is only one instance of an outbreak of disease prior to the Civil War that could be considered an epidemic and that caused deaths. We can be certain that this was the only occurrence because all towns were quick to identify problems in other towns and to establish quarantines. Towns were diligent in informing others of disease outbreaks, although sometimes the initial reportage understated the conditions, perhaps out of hope. On the other hand, rumors of disease that were false were immediately quashed by town officials because they quickly led to suspension of business activity.

Health and Welfare

The only instance in Jefferson was a minor smallpox epidemic in late February 1859 that affected 10 persons and killed three. The outbreak occurred in a hotel and was thought to have reached the town through a business traveler. The *Jefferson Herald* immediately issued a warning:

> SMALL POX.—We are sorry to announce to the public that this troublesome disease is now raging in our city. Up to the present time there has been but eight or nine cases reported. The disease is in a mild form and yields readily to medical treatment. The city authorities have passed laws, which if carried in effect will no doubt put a stop to its further spreading. We are truly sorry that this sad calamity has befallen our prosperous city; but it is the fate of all places, of any commercial importance. We will from week to week, give our readers the true condition of the disease, and hope soon to announce that all is healthy again.

Robert Nesmith reported that Jefferson immediately began to be depopulated, which was the normal course of action for residents during an epidemic. A handbill was prepared and sent to Marshall, which established a quarantine. Men were placed on every road likely to be traveled by persons from the infected region. A young man from Marshall by the name of Stone who had been in Jefferson became ill on the way home and collapsed about a mile and a half from town. Citizens of Marshall went to his assistance, built a shanty for him, and provided for his needs. Within a few days, however, favorable news was reached from Jefferson, and the quarantine was lifted.

The favorable news was that the epidemic had been contained and that there was little danger to visitors. The *Jefferson Herald* reported that cotton receipts were light because the prevalence of the disease had been exaggerated and that it was, in fact, small and "confined to a locality which will prevent its further spreading." In early March, Mayor Saufley issued a proclamation that persons visiting Jefferson need not fear contraction of the disease. The proclamation was followed by a circular issued in late March under the signature of 85 citizens and businessmen that only 10 persons had been affected, three had died, and only two were still in danger (a negro woman and a boy, who eventually became well) and that they had been "safely secured from any intercourse whatever with any portion of the community."

Shadrach Eggers, the editor of the *Jefferson Gazette*, visited Marshall in early April and reported to the editor of the Marshall *Harrison Flag* that business had improved rapidly after the smallpox panic had ended. The editor of the *Harrison Flag* visited Jefferson shortly thereafter and provides the last newspaper mention of the epidemic:

> SMALL-POX IN JEFFERSON.—We paid a flying visit to Jefferson, in the early part of the present week. There is some small-pox there, though it does not prevail to any great extent. We were informed that it only existed in a portion of the town inhabited by persons of impure habits, a sort of hell's half acre. How many cases there are, we are unable to state; but this we may be permitted to say, the people out side of the "half acre" seem to have no fears whatever. Business is not as lively there as it would be in the absence of the disease, or rumors of its prevalence.

The absence of major epidemics in Jefferson should not be taken to mean that people were healthy. Americans prior to the Civil War were not healthy, and illness was common. Diets were poor, waste disposal was primitive, water supplies were often polluted, food and its preparation were often unsanitary, mosquitoes and flies were omnipresent, poor housing subjected people to the elements, and bathing and exercise were unpopular. The primary endemic diseases in the South were malaria, dysentery, chronic diarrhea, pneumonia, and influenza. Jeffersonians probably had better diets than the general population, there was an insufficient mass of persons to generate slum conditions, and the sanitation ordinances established by the town were probably important limitations on disease if they were enforced.

There are no records of medical conditions in the town. However, there are numerous mentions in the newspapers of persons who were interrupted in their activities by illness, sometimes over long periods of time, with multiple ailments, and terminating in death. It appears that illness was a normal part of life and death always close at hand.

Poison Spring

Reports on poison springs were quite common and usually bogus. There was a spring on the road to Daingerfield that obviously was dangerous, because it was reported contemporaneously in the *Jefferson Herald*, as reprinted in the June 12, 1852, *Texas Republican*:

> THE POISON SPRING.—On the road leading from Jefferson to Dangerfield there is a spring known by the old setlers as "the poison spring." The letter P is plainly marked upon several trees to designate the spot and warn the traveling community. Several years ago a family of emigrants camped by it, and drank largely of its waters. The following day all were taken suddenly sick and a part died. Sometime afterwards during a dry season, the greater part of a large drove of cattle drank of its waters and died in a few hours afterwards. The water runs slowly from a sink or gulch; and its color indicates that it is tinctured with a mineral, which at particular stages of the water and during a dry season operates as a poison. During the wet season, and when the water runs freely, it is said to be harmless.

Public Assistance and Charity

Work was readily available to everyone in Jefferson, and almost everyone worked. The population was not large, the community was close knit, and there were no slums. Conditions for the development of a dependent class did not exist. Edward Smith noted in 1849 that many small farmers in northeast Texas were poor, but attributed these conditions to lack of enterprise resulting from a preference for leisure. This was a condition throughout the South, where game was abundant, the land produced corn with little effort, and hogs foraged freely in the woods and were slaughtered when needed. Poor immigrants passing through Jefferson appear to have been the major group in need.

Texas counties had public assistance programs for the destitute. The commissioners courts provided assistance in the form of food and shelter to persons in dire need who were classified as paupers. Only three instances of such assistance are mentioned in the Cass County commissioners court minutes. In August 1851, Bartholomew Figures was paid $12 for the board of Erastus Montague, a pauper, in his hotel. In August 1856, Thomas Wilkins and James Wornell, paupers, were allowed $50 and $75, respectively, for support for one year.

Jefferson did not provide any public assistance. Charity was provided by fraternal and beneficent organizations, churches, and individuals. Women are often noted in their obituaries for their charitable activities. A particularly notable instance of assistance involved Richard Crump of Jefferson, who was at the time captain of the *Grenada*, as reported in the June 16, 1855, *Texas Republican*:

> Two orphan children, a boy about 9 and a girl 11 years old, passed through this place, a few weeks ago, in charge of Capt. R. P. Crump, who sent them to M. D. Ector, Esq., of Henderson, by whom they were kindly received. They were the children of a poor woman who was making her way to her parents in Rusk county, but was taken with cholera on the boat, coming up Red River, and died. Alas! had she succeeded in getting to Rusk county, she would have found herself pennyless and in a land of strangers. Her name was Mrs. Emeline Graham, the daughter of Martin Johnson of Rusk county. She was without means. Mr. Crump and the passengers of the boat raised $60 for the children, and forwarded them to Henderson.

46. Mortality

Deaths

There are no public records of deaths in Jefferson prior to the war. The tombstone inscriptions for Oakwood Cemetery recorded in the *Cemetery Records of Marion County, Texas,* are obviously not inclusive because they are few in number, many graves are unmarked, and some of the inscriptions are illegible. The recorded deaths ordered by date of death are:

Rev. Benjamin Foscue, March 25, 1798–January 4, 1850

Hattie Hail, July 18, 1850

Talbot R. Amoss, December 10, 1819–July 11, 1852

Nancy Ann Waskom, November 13, 1819–July 14, 1852

Samuel Walter Oliver, son of W. A. and C. R. Oliver, January 23, 1843–September 23, 1852

James W. Smith, June 10, 1789–December 26, 1852

Lucy Eason, wife of I. G. Eason, November 16, 1821–January 2, 1853

Mary Hamblin, died March 12, 1853, aged 50 years

John J. Murphy, died June 1853, aged one year

Berryman H. Murphey, November 2, 1851–May 16, 1854

Robert S. Elliott, son of Mary R. and J. S. Elliott, 1853–1854

Ann Eliza Henrie Bateman, daughter of A. J. and L. D. Bateman, October 19, 1852–January 27, 1855

Charley Bigham, July 2, 1855–July 30, 1855, aged four weeks

Little Battie Saufley, daughter of W. P. and Eliza Saufley, March 25, 1854–August 1, 1855, aged 16 months

Lucy T. Murphy, March 20, 1854–August 29, 1855

S. S. Harris, died November 12, 1855, aged about 44 years

Elizabeth Geer, November 15, 1795–January 1, 1856

Edward Clyde Nichols, infant son of Ann D. and Theo Nichols, February 27, 1855–January 11, 1856

James Alley, December 8, 1783–February 29, 1856

Willie Geer, infant son of H. M. and M. B. Geer, July 9, 1855–September 27, 1856

Lucy L. Schaf, wife of Charles Schaf, May 26, 1827–April 14, 1857

Ellen A. Freeman, April 25, 1846–April 17, 1857

Sophia Marion Browning Speake, wife of John Speake, September 19, 1827–April 20, 1857

James Browning Speake, son of J. and S. M. Speake, died July 8, 1857, aged 11 months

Sarah N. Owens, April 1, 1812–September 4, 1857

Jeanie Torrans, daughter of W. P. and C. D. Torrans, March 24, 1852–September 5, 1857

Lucy H. Smith, November 26, 1789–November 3, 1857

Adams, infant son of Lucy Jane and James M. Adams, February 17, 1858–February 24, 1858

Martha P. C. Freeman, June 1, 1840–August 3, 1858

Eppie Geer, daughter of H. N. and M. B. Geer, July 16, 1852–August 27, 1858

Thomas H. Owens, February 27, 1824–September 12, 1858

Ella Schluter, daughter of F. A. and A. T. Schluter, died January 22, 1859, aged 11 years

Ethelbert C. Crutcher, April 20, 1825–January 30, 1859

Ann A. Schluter, infant daughter of F. A. and A. T. Schluter, died February 23, 1859, aged one month

Martha A. Crump, January 1, 1828–June 23, 1859

Eliza G. Saufley, wife of W. P. Saufley, died August 4, 1859, aged 23 years, and infant Eliza Spire

Willie Torrans, daughter of W. P. and C. D. Torrans, November 3, 1856–August 16, 1859

C. I. Willard, died 1859

W. M. Freeman, August 3, 1807–January 14, 1860

Emma Kitchen, died February 19, 1860, aged eight years

Catherine Alley, wife of James Alley, May 2, 1789–February 26, 1860

Thomas O. Alley, son of Daniel N. and Lucy A. Alley, January 6, 1836–April 10, 1860

Hervey, infant son of J. P. and F. P. Hervey, May 12, 1860–May 15, 1860

Mary Nichols, daughter of W. H. and Eustatia Nichols, died June 30, 1860

Thomas Nichols, died September 28, 1860, and Willis Nichols, died October 1, 1860, twin brothers, sons of W. H. and Eustatia Nichols

W. Goodloe Williams, June 29, 1846–October 9, 1860

Christiana Kolster, February 1, 1858–October 28, 1860

Mary Tullis, infant daughter of A. D. and M. J. Tullis, died November 3, 1860, aged four months

Mary Schluter, infant daughter of F. A. and A. T. Schluter, July 1, 1860–November 20, 1860

John Henry Wright, 1858–1860

The newspapers record the deaths of Eliza Todd, 40, wife of William Todd, September 1854; Dr. W. D. Stephenson, of pneumonia, January 1855; Caroline Hunt, July 1855; Levi Geer, December 1855; Frank Clark, 26, of gastritia, August 1856; Sarah Owens, wife of Anthony Owens, August 1857; Kate Nimmo, infant daughter of Samuel and Rebecca Nimmo, October 1857; Lucy Smith, mother-in-law of William Perry; J. B. Hickey, January 1859; Mittie C., 16, daughter of William and Anne Gillean, July 1859; Eliza Saufley, 23, wife of William Saufley, and newborn daughter Eliza, August 1859; Sallie Clark, four, daughter of Anna and Frank Clark, October 1860; and Samuel Nimmo, February 1861 (Fig. 46-1).

The 1860 mortality census contains a list of 34 persons, including 11 unnamed slaves, who died in Jefferson during the year ending June 1, 1860. Of the 34, 19 were males, 18 were under age eight, and only

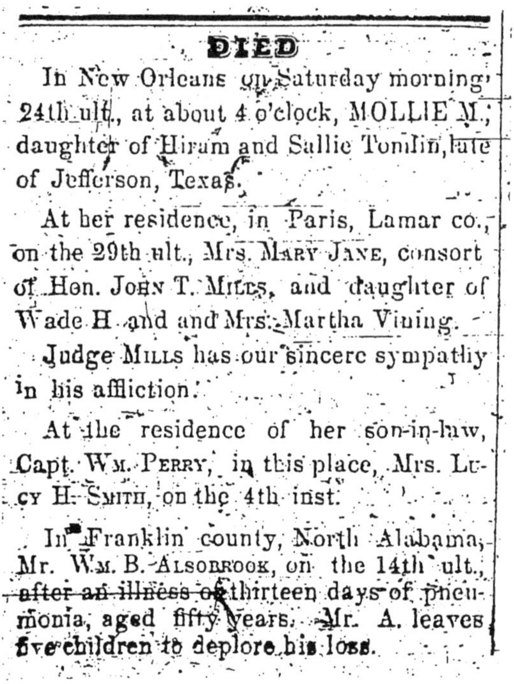

> **DIED**
>
> In New Orleans on Saturday morning 24th ult., at about 4 o'clock, MOLLIE M., daughter of Hiram and Sallie Tomlin, late of Jefferson, Texas.
>
> At her residence, in Paris, Lamar co., on the 29th ult., Mrs. MARY JANE, consort of Hon. JOHN T. MILLS, and daughter of Wade H. and and Mrs. Martha Vining.
>
> Judge MILLS has our sincere sympathy in his affliction.
>
> At the residence of her son-in-law, Capt. WM. PERRY, in this place, Mrs. LUCY H. SMITH, on the 4th inst.
>
> In Franklin county, North Alabama, Mr. WM. B. ALSOBROOK, on the 14th ult., after an illness of thirteen days of pneumonia, aged fifty years. Mr. A. leaves five children to deplore his loss.

Fig. 46-1. Death Notice. Source: November 7, 1857, *Eastern Texas Gazette*

seven were over age 17, the oldest of whom was 73. The causes of death were scarlet fever (7), measles (4), unknown (4), pneumonia (3), fever (3), flux (2), cough (2), congestion (2), and one each for spasms, brain fever, dropsy, apoplexy, childbirth, consumption, and fall from house. There was no particular pattern in the month of death. There were no significant differences between slaves and free whites with respect to cause or age of death. The 1850 census indicates that there was a minor cholera epidemic in an area of Cass County outside of Jefferson that killed both slaves and free whites.

Anyone who has visited old graveyards knows that mortality among infants and children was high and that women often died in childbirth. Reductions in early deaths is the primary cause of increased life expectancies, which are often mistakenly thought to mean increased life spans. The only thing not encountered in the Jefferson record is whole families wiped out by epidemics.

Suicides

People killed themselves in the past pretty much for the same reasons they do today: disappointments in love and business, or depression often exacerbated by alcohol or drugs. There are only three cases of suicide reported in the newspapers, and only two involved Jefferson residents, neither of whom were prominent. This low reportage is probably partly the result of the near absence of Jefferson newspapers. On the other hand, external newspapers were interested in such matters, probably much more than they are today because the population was small and there was greater community sentiment.

If any prominent citizen had killed himself, it would have been reported in newspapers external to Jefferson. Businesses failed constantly, but businessmen apparently considered this part of the natural order and simply started again. Religious faith was a strong impediment to suicide in cases of physical suffering, and the elderly were not isolated. As has always been the case, the burden of suicide fell on family and friends. The cases reported in the newspapers are as follows:

> On the morning of the 30th ultimo, about 8 o'clock, a tailor in this place, by the name of J. G. Snyder, committed suicide, by placing the muzzle of a gun in his mouth, and firing it off. The ball passed clear through his head, killing him instantly. The cause, so far as we have been able to ascertain, was a mental derangement, induced by drinking. He leaves a wife and child, nearly destitute, to mourn his untimely death. (*Jefferson Herald*, as quoted by the August 10, 1851, *Texas Republican*)

> On Tuesday evening the 17th inst., Mr. THOMAS HARPER, a resident of Jefferson, committed suicide at that place. The mind of the deceased was operated upon by a morbid melancholy, indulged in for a long time, and which resulted, at last in the rash act which terminated his existence. On the evening in question he was laboring more than usual, under this monoma-

nia. He invited some of his friends to supper with him, none of them dreaming the purpose he had in view. At the termination of the repast, he arose from his chair, drew a revolver, and shot himself through the body. He lived about thirty hours. Mr. Harper was a young man in the prime of life; warm hearted but impetuous, with many noble traits of character. His parents reside in Caddo parish La. Upon them the blow falls heavily. (January 28, 1854, *Texas Republican*)

On Thursday, September 30th, a gentleman came to Jefferson, put up at the City Hotel, and registered his name as J. A. Sylvester, of Louisiana. He deported himself in a very gentlemanly manner, and was quite communicative to the book-keeper of the hotel, Mr. W. H. Duke, reading to him several letters that contained evidence of his respectability. On Friday evening he went into the store at Waterhouse, Wallace & Co., and purchased a pocket knife with a single blade, some two and a half inches long. He ate his supper, exhibited no unusual manifestations—after which he was seen sitting in the door of a grocery store, opposite the hotel. About 8 o'clock, he came over and went up stairs to his room, without calling for a candle. In a short time after, one of the servants came down to the book keeper and said there was some one making a dreadful noise in No. 2. He was requested to go back and wake the gentleman up, as he probably had the nightmare. The boy went up, but soon returned, stating that the gentleman was under the bed—whereupon Mr. Nesmith, stage contractor, took a candle, went up to the room, and found the sad horrible spectacle of a man lying on the floor in a pool of blood. His throat was cut from ear to ear, and one of his arms gashed in a most horrible manner. The bed was completely saturated with blood, and the knife he had that evening purchased was found on it. He left the following note, the last line of which was written with a pencil:

"JEFFERSON, TEXAS, OCT. 1, '58.—I am out of business, and my health is in a awful state, and I don't think I care to live after losing my character, and I have no doubt that he will try to ruin me, and they no telling that J. C.

I will swear that I never did any thing."

The jury of inquest rendered a verdict in accordance with the facts above stated. He had a double cased silver watch and twenty-three dollars in cash, and was decently interred. (*Jefferson Gazette*, as quoted by the October 13, 1858, *South-Western*)

Passing On

In the August 11, 1906, *Jimplecute*, the long-time Jefferson auctioneer James Hosack used an October 9, 1852, *Jefferson Herald* to list the prominent men of the day: Frederick Schluter, Perry Graham, John Sabine, Ward Taylor, Jr., Jesse Veal, Thomas Goyne, James Hosack, Samuel Moseley, James Murphy, William Nichols, Edward Benners, Ithael Eason, L. A. Ellis, Job Baker, William Towers, William C. Baker, Hugo Fox, Francis Baker, William Saufley, James Rogers, Moses Steinlein, Hiram Grinstead, W. P. Watson, Anthony Owens, William Brooks, Bartholomew Figures, Thomas Pugh, John Morgan, Hiram Tomlin, William Cocke, John Cocke, Ephraim Beckett, W. J. Parker, J. R. Watson, James Elliott, John Murphy, Clinton Willard, Robert Nesmith, Richard Crump, Samuel McFarland, Joseph Mosby, Labon Bayless, Williamson Freeman, John Hobdy, Daniel McKay (attorney), Daniel McKay (painter), Samuel Nimmo, John Speake, George Tuttle, W. E. Roundtree, Charles Stanley, John Waskom, Nelson Taylor, T. H. Taylor, John Pitkin, Horatio Walcott, Justice Ferris, Virgil Dubose, Granville Lewis, Nat Burford, Thomas White, Haze Jolly, Samuel Norris and his partner Tackett, August May, Abraham Kohn, John McNab, L. M. Carlton, H. F. Peters, E. P. M. Johnson, T. L. H. Cross, and Charles Westmoreland. Hosack characterized them as "a grand set of men" who "contributed with means, effort and good work to the foundation and building up of Jefferson, Texas, then the largest place, commercially speaking, of its size in the United States."

In the March 4, 1905, *Jimplecute,* Hosack compared the 1852 list to the persons mentioned in the July 19, 1873, *Daily Tribune.* The persons still in Jefferson in 1873 were: Frederick Schluter, Perry Graham, John Sabine, Ward Taylor, Jr., Jesse Veal, Thomas Goyne, James Hosack, Samuel Moseley, James Murphy, William Nichols, Edward Benners, Ithael Eason, L. A. Ellis, Job Baker, William Towers, William C. Baker, Hugo Fox, Francis Baker, William Saufley, James Rogers, and Moses Steinlein. Those dead by July 1873 were: Hiram Grinstead, W. P. Watson, Anthony Owens, William Brooks, Bartholomew Figures, Thomas Pugh, John Morgan, Hiram Tomlin, William Cocke, John Cocke, Ephraim Beckett, W. J. Parker, J. R. Watson, James Elliott, John Murphy, Clinton Willard, Robert Nesmith, Richard Crump, Samuel McFarland, Joseph Mosby, Labon Bayless, Williamson Freeman, John Hobdy, Daniel McKay (attorney), Daniel McKay (painter), Samuel Nimmo, and John Speake. Those living elsewhere by July 1873 were: George Tuttle, W. E. Roundtree, Charles Stanley, John Waskom, Nelson Taylor, T. H. Taylor, John Pitkin, Justice Ferris, Virgil Dubose, Granville Lewis, Nat Burford, Thomas White, and Haze Jolly. Not known to be living or dead were: Samuel Norris and his partner Tackett, August May, Abraham Kohn, John McNab, L. M. Carlton, H. F. Peter, E. P. M. Johnson, T. L. H. Cross, and Charles Westmoreland. Hosack characterized them as "good men and friends of one brotherhood who stood as friends of the once great city at the head of navigation for northeast Texas."

In March 1905, Hosack was living in Cleburne, Texas, and Hugo Fox was still alive. By August 1906, Fox had died, and Hosack was the only survivor from the prominent Jefferson men of October 1852.

APPENDIX: SOURCES

APPROACH

The present study is an outgrowth of *A History of Navigation on Cypress Bayou and the Lakes*. The navigation history covered all of the ports and landings west of Shreveport and all navigation activities from 1800 to the present. Jefferson, as the major port on the route, served as a unifying element for the narrative. However, a large amount of information on Jefferson that had been obtained from regional newspapers could not be incorporated in the text. In addition, as the navigation history was being prepared for production, W. W. Withenbury's Red River reminiscences were obtained from the *Cincinnati Commercial*, which provided clues with respect to the first steamboats on Caddo Lake and a firm date for the arrival of the first steamboat at Jefferson. In the interim, a considerable amount of time has been spent collecting materials for a history of navigation on the Upper Red River and as a base for the publication of Withenbury's reminiscences, which deal primarily with trips to the Upper Red River. These efforts have provided a greater understanding of Jefferson's role in regional trade.

The present study was originally intended as a narrative history that would cover the period of Jefferson's commercial primacy, from 1845 to 1874. The intention was abandoned with the discovery of the extraordinary resources available for local histories in the federal censuses; city records; and county tax rolls, deed records, probate records, district court minutes, and commissioners court minutes. The volume of materials and the detailed analysis needed to make them useful required that the present text end with the advent of the Civil War and that a topical rather than a narrative approach be used for the presentation of the materials. A topical approach lacks the drama of narrative, but provides a different sort of intensity as one encounters many of the same people in different roles in different chapters.

The present study is based primarily on public records and regional and Jefferson newspapers that were purchased on microfilm from state and commercial sources and reviewed on a reader at home. The only absolutely essential source that was not available on microfilm is the city records, which are housed in the City Hall. The author of the present study is not a Jefferson resident or an academician and works fulltime in applied research on matters unrelated to history. Microfilm is ideally suited to night and weekend work and historical investigations at a geographic distance. Because these are public records, there are similar records for towns other than Jefferson; and, with the availability of microfilm, an opportunity for similar investigations by persons similarly situated.

The navigation history was heavily dependent on federal manuscripts housed at Louisiana State University, the present study on public records available on microfilm, and documentation for Withenbury's reminiscences on Internet sources. The future of historic research will obviously be heavily dependent on the Internet, signaled in Texas by the conversion of the *Handbook of Texas* to an electronic format. The conversion of paper, microfilm, and map sources (including many of those used in the present study) to an electronic format is proceeding at a rapid pace. Eventually, most important sources will be instantaneously available everywhere and, with the power of search engines, the ability to readily identify items of interest will be given to anyone interested in the information. The Internet was not used in the present study, with the exception of the *Handbook of Texas Online* and the acquisition of important information on Berry Durham.

The present study is based almost entirely on primary sources, which are mentioned in the text rather than in footnotes. All of the newspaper articles on Jefferson from Jefferson and regional newspapers for the period 1842–1875 have been typed into an electronic format and are on file with the Historic Jefferson Foundation, along with paper copies of all advertisements. Only one chapter (Religion) relies heavily on secondary sources. Secondary sources were used primarily to confirm or clarify impressions (such as the near absence of participatory sports in the antebellum South) gathered from the reading of thousands of regional newspapers. The major sources and how they were used are discussed in the following sections. The discussion of secondary sources is not intended as a review of the literature on each topic, but rather limited to works that were found helpful by the author or might be of interest to the reader.

JEFFERSON AND MARION COUNTY HISTORIOGRAPHY

The first history of Jefferson appeared in 1936 in booklet form under the authorship of Mrs. Arch McKay and Mrs. H. A. Spellings and under the title *A History of Jefferson, Marion County, Texas, 1836–1936*. It was followed in 1953 by Willie Dean's *Jefferson, Texas: Queen of the Cypress*; in 1965 by Ben Cooner's North Texas State University thesis "The Rise and Decline of Jefferson, Texas," which was the first to demonstrate that Jefferson declined because its trade was captured by the railroads; in 1966 by Rebecca Cameron and Ruth Lester's *Jefferson on the Bayou*; and in 1967 by Judy Watson's 1967 Texas Christian University thesis "Jefferson: Rise and Decline of the Cypress Port." All of these have been superseded by Fred Tarpley's 1983 *Jefferson: Riverport to the Southwest*, which has been summarized in booklet form. Additional comments on Jefferson can be found in the *Handbook of Texas Online* and in Keith Guthrie's *Texas Forgotten Ports*.

None of these works are period specific. Tarpley provides the best coverage of the antebellum period using some of the documentation provided by the present study. However, the historiography of antebellum Jefferson has not reached a stage at which much can be said in terms of theses and counter theses. Tarpley correctly treats as an undocumented tradition the idea that Jefferson was first occupied by Smithland residents escaping faulty land titles. The author of the present study was not able to advance beyond what Tarpley has to say on the naming of Jefferson.

Particularly valuable to the present study were works by local historians on some of Jefferson's major churches. These include: Earline Burnett's 1954 Stephen F. Austin thesis "A History of the First Methodist Church, Jefferson, Texas, 1844–1854"; Lucille Bullard's 1986 *The First Baptist Church, Jefferson, Texas, 1855–1985*; Juanita Cawthon's 1993 *History of the Presbyterian and Cumberland Presbyterian Churches, Jefferson, Texas*; and Dorothy Craver's 1980 *This Old Church: A History of Christ Church, Episcopal, Jefferson, Texas*.

There are no comprehensive histories of Marion County. T. C. Richardson's *East Texas: Its History and Its Makers* contains a chapter on Marion County. The *Inventory of the County Archives of Texas: Marion County* (prepared by the Texas Historical Records Survey in 1940) contains a brief historical sketch of the county, as well as a valuable digest of state laws pertaining to the county and Jefferson derived from Gammel's *The Laws of Texas*. Lucille Bullard's 1965 *Marion County, Texas, 1860–1870* deals primarily with the Civil War period. The *Cemetery Records of Marion County, Texas*, published by the Martha McGraw chapter of the DAR in 1961, contains a comprehensive list of tombstone inscriptions in Jefferson's Oakwood Cemetery. The accompanying map showing the sections of the cemetery is based on an 1872 cloth original in the City Hall vault.

PUBLIC RECORDS

An investigation into the public records connected with Jefferson is complicated by the fact that Marion County was preceded by Cass County, which was preceded by Bowie County, which was preceded by Red River County. As a practical matter, however, Jefferson came into existence in 1845, Cass County was formed out of Bowie County in 1846, and Marion County was formed in 1860. Consequently, most of the materials for an antebellum history of Jefferson are contained in the Cass County records. This is particularly fortunate because the early Bowie County records were destroyed by fire.

The most important of the county records from the perspective of the present study were the deed records, which cover property transactions. Deed records relevant to Marion County from prior counties (including Bowie) were transcribed in the early 1870s and are part of a special set in the Marion County deed records. In addition, there is important information in the Harrison County public records concerning cross-boundary features such as roads, bridges, and ferries, and part of Marion County was once part of Harrison County.

This investigation could not have been conducted were it not for the fact that most of the primary county materials were available at that time on microfilm from the Texas State Library and Archives Commission. As a non-resident, review of materials at various courthouses would have been a practical impossibility. Although some of these materials (e.g., the deed records) are indexed, the type of information presented in the present study could only be acquired by a complete review of each set of records.

The present study used federal, county, and local records, which were equally important.

Federal

Almost all of the federal documents used in this investigation were obtained on microfilm from Heritage Quest Genealogical Services in Bountiful, Utah. These include the 1850 Cass County population census, the 1860 Marion County population census, the 1850 social statistics census for Cass County, the 1860 social statistics census for Marion County, the 1850 agricultural census for Cass County, the 1860 agricultural census for Marion County, the 1850 slave schedule for Cass County, the 1860 slave schedule for Marion County, the 1850 products of industry census for Cass County, the 1860 products of industry census for Marion County, and the 1860 mortality census for Marion County. Because these are decennial censuses, they provide information for only two years, but are invaluable because of the nature of their contents and the ability to identify trends.

The censuses of free white inhabitants were conducted for the June 1 population and are organized on the basis of households and families, with more than one family sometimes appearing in a household. Heads of families appear first, followed by wives and then children, so that the composition of each household is apparent, including unrelated inhabitants. Names are provided for each person in each household, along with age, sex, color (white only), occupation of persons over 15, value of real estate, value of personal estate (not in 1850 census), place of birth (state, territory, or country), married within the year, attended school within the year, illiteracy, and impairment. Jefferson is enumerated as a separate entity only in the 1860 Marion County census.

During the initial phase of the investigation, renditions of the 1850 and 1860 censuses with indexes prepared by the local historian Lucille Bullard (deceased) were found to be useful. However, it became necessary to refer back to the original census tapes and prepare a special rendition of the assumed composition of Jefferson in 1850 and the actual population of Jefferson in 1860. These renditions, which are on file with the Historic Jefferson Foundation, are not full transcriptions, but rather limited to name, age, sex, occupation, value of real estate (plus personal estate in 1860), and place of birth for heads of households, employed adult male children, and nonfamily members, along with the names of wives and number of minor children. This information was used in many different chapters, but primarily in chapters 7 (Censuses) and 8 (Women).

The social statistics census contains information on total value of real and personal property, annual taxes by type, average crop yields, schools (type, number, number of teachers, number of pupils, and income sources), libraries, newspapers (name, character, publication, and circulation), churches (type, number, facility capacity, and value of church property), pauperism, crime, and prevailing wages for various labor types. This information was used primarily in chapters 31 (Religion), 32 (Education), and 36 (Newspapers).

The agricultural census contains information on owner or agent/manager of farm, improved and unimproved acres, value of farm and implements/machinery, number of livestock (by type) as of June 1, value of livestock, produce quantities (by type, including ginned cotton in 400 lb. bales) for the year ending June 1, and value of animals slaughtered. This information was used to characterize the operations of large landholders who were closely associated with Jefferson.

The slave schedules list number of slaves (sequential numbering) by owner and indicate age, sex, and color for each slave, but without providing any slave names. There are also columns for fugitive, freed, and impaired slaves, but these columns are blank in the 1850 Cass

County and the 1860 Marion County slave schedules (obviously disregarded). The 1860 schedule includes an additional column for number of slave cabins and a separate enumeration for Jefferson. Because these were population censuses paralleling the order of the white population censuses, the listings apparently reflect location rather than actual ownership. This information was used primarily in Chapter 9 (Slaves).

The products of industry census lists industries with products valued at $500 or greater and includes information on type, capital investment, raw materials, motive power, employment, wages, and quantity, kind, and value of annual products. This information was used in Chapter 25 (Industry).

The mortality census covers cause of death for whites and slaves for the year ending June 1 and includes the name and age of the deceased. The 1850 mortality census for Cass County was not useful because Jefferson is not identified as a separate entity. The 1860 Marion County mortality census contributed to chapters 45 (Health and Welfare) and 46 (Mortality).

County

All of the records in the Marion County Courthouse are cataloged and described in the *Inventory of the County Archives of Texas: Marion County,* which was prepared by the Texas Historical Records Survey in 1940. This is a useful positioning document for anyone interested in using the courthouse records. It was used in the present study to identify materials that should be obtained from the Texas State Library and Archives Commission. Although no inventory was completed for Cass County, the record types of county courthouses across the state are fairly uniform, with the exception of those that have been lost by fire or other causes.

The deed records are primarily concerned with transfer of lands by sale, but also include such things as mortgages, judgments, and deeds of trust. The Marion County deed records begin with a ten-volume set referred to as the "Transcribed Deed Records." The first seven volumes contain deeds relevant to Marion County from the predecessor counties of Cass, Bowie, Paschal, and Red River. The last three volumes were transcribed in the 1880s and cover the areas acquired from Harrison County in 1863 and 1874. They are followed by the deeds related to Marion County proper, beginning March 3, 1860. Because the many transactions related to Jefferson are embedded in a multitude of transactions concerning land outside the city, the deed records had to be read in their entirety. There may be additional records relevant to Jefferson in the Cass County Courthouse in Linden and the Red River County Courthouse in Clarksville, although only one has been brought to the author's attention (a bond related to fulfillment of duties). The Port Jefferson Abstract and Title Company has a set of volumes that lists sequentially the deeds related to each town lot, which provides an overview of the transactions. Information from the deed records was used primarily in the chapters in which facility locations were identified: chapters 19 (Warehouse District); 20 (Earliest Merchants); 21 (Early 1850s Merchants); 22 (Middle 1850s Merchants); 23 (Late Merchants); 26 (Packeries); 33 (Hotels); 34 (Stables); and 36 (Newspapers).

The commissioners court was the governing body of the county and was headed by the county judge. Commissioners courts were responsible for the establishment of courthouses and jails, setting tax rates, issuing bonds, administering county welfare services, and constructing or licensing roads, bridges, and ferries. The commissioners court minutes for Cass County extend back to 1846 and were obtained on microfilm. Microfilm is not available for the Marion County and Harrison County commissioners court minutes, which were read in their respective courthouses. Information from the commissioners court minutes was used in many chapters, but particularly chapters 10 (Roads and Bridges) and 11 (County Seat).

Tax rolls were developed on an annual basis by tax assessor-collectors, with a copy deposited in Austin because they included state tax assessments. Tax rolls are available on microfilm for Bowie County from 1846, Cass County from 1846, and Marion County from 1860. Although Bowie County came into existence in 1840, the tax rolls do not begin until 1846. However, Bowie County and Paschal County are included in the Red River County tax rolls beginning in 1841. All but the earliest of the tax rolls are arranged alphabetically (but not alphabetically under each letter). Information is provided for each person on real property (land and town lots), personal property (negroes, horses, cattle, money at interest, value of merchandise on hand as of January 1, and miscellaneous property), total value, poll tax, state tax, and county tax. A separate section is devoted to real property owned in other counties. The tax rolls provide an annual census of persons important enough to pay taxes, identify number and value of town lots owned, and enable merchants and their relative size (by value of merchandise) to be identified. Information from the tax rolls was used in many chapters, but particularly those concerned with the development of businesses: chapters 20 (Earliest Merchants); 21 (Early 1850s Merchants); 22 (Middle 1850s Merchants); and 23 (Late Merchants).

The district courts were trial courts that dealt with civil and criminal matters (felonies, misdemeanors, divorces, property disputes, election contests, and civil actions). The minutes of the district court for Cass County extend back to 1847 and were obtained on microfilm, along with the minutes for the Marion County court. The court cases cover a wide range of topics and occasionally include evidence from earlier periods. Consequently, they provided key pieces of information for many chapters, but were particularly important in Chapter 39 (Crime).

The county court dealt primarily with probate matters (the disposition of estates of persons who have died). Although the county courts also had criminal and civil jurisdiction, there do not appear to be any documents of this type in the court minutes, which were obtained on microfilm for Cass County (back to 1846) and Marion County. The *Inventory of the County Archives of Texas: Marion County* classifies these minutes as county court records. The minutes available on microfilm are called probate court minutes, and the court is referred to as the probate court in the records. The county (probate) court minutes did not prove to be particularly valuable. The Cass and Marion County courthouses contain full probate case files, only a few of which were used.

The survey records contain the documents related to the original land surveys conducted by the county surveyor, including property descriptions as well as inset maps showing the configurations of the surveys. The Marion County survey records contain copies of the predecessor counties of Bowie, Cass, Paschal, and Red River. The survey records are not available on microfilm and were read in the courthouse. This information was used primarily in Chapter 3 (Foundations).

City

The city records are housed in the City Hall vault and are available for review at the City Hall. These are original records, and no copies have been made. The extent of the original records is unknown because the earliest records were destroyed by fire after the Civil War. Volume 1 of the city records covers the period November 4, 1857, to January 2, 1871; and Volume 2 covers the period January 3, 1871 to July 11, 1873. These two volumes were read and formed the basis of Chapter 12 (Civic Affairs), as well as providing important information for other chapters.

NEWSPAPERS

Newspapers are an important primary source for local history. Indeed, with a continuous newspaper record, the major events in a town's development are readily discerned. Jefferson had many newspapers during its period of commercial primacy through 1874, but most have disappeared, and the situation is particularly bad before the Civil War. Fortunately, there were important towns in the general region (Clarksville and Marshall in Texas, Shreveport in Louisiana, and Washington in Arkansas) that had their own newspapers and were interested in Jefferson. This interest was manifest in articles about Jefferson based on visits and by the reprinting of articles from Jefferson newspapers. Many Jefferson merchants advertised in these newspapers, whose extant issues are much more voluminous than those of Jefferson.

Most of the extant Jefferson newspapers are available on microfilm from the Center for American History at the University of Texas. The Clarksville and Marshall newspapers are available on microfilm from public sources and also from commercial sources such as Southwest Micropublishing. The Washington newspapers are available on microfilm from the Arkansas History Commission. The Louisiana newspapers can be reviewed at the Special Collections department of the Louisiana State University library system. None of these newspapers is indexed. However, all of the articles on Jefferson from Jefferson and regional newspapers for the period 1842–1875 have been typed into an electronic format and are on file with the Historic Jefferson Foundation, along with paper copies of all advertisements.

There are only five extant copies of antebellum Jefferson newspapers. The December 16, 1848, issue of the *Spirit of the Age* was obtained as a paper copy from the *Jimplecute* office in Jefferson. The May 14, 1853, issue of the *Jefferson Herald* was obtained as a paper copy from the local historian Catherine Wise (deceased). The May 29, 1855, issue of the *Jefferson Herald* and the March 14 and April 7, 1857, issues of the *Eastern Texas Gazette* were obtained on microfilm from the Center for American History. In addition, the September 1, 1876, issue of the *Daily Jimplecute*, available on microfilm from the Center for American History, contains an article on the City of Jefferson that includes important information on the antebellum period. The Jefferson newspapers were read through the early 1900s.

Of the regional newspapers, those from Marshall and Clarksville are the most important, particularly from an antebellum perspective. The Marshall *Texas Republican* covers the period 1849–1869, and the Marshall *Harrison Flag* covers the period 1858–1868. The Clarksville *Northern Standard* and its continuation the *Standard* cover the period 1842–1873. The *Washington Telegraph* covers the period 1841–1865. Miscellaneous Shreveport newspapers extend back to the 1830s; however, the most important Shreveport antebellum newspaper is the *South-Western*, which covers the period 1854–1871. The *South-Western* was followed by the *Shreveport Times*. The regional newspapers were read through the 1870s. They provided the bulk of commentary on Jefferson and numerous advertisements, as well as a general understanding of the life of the times.

MAPS

The Texas General Land Office in Austin contains all of the records related to the transfer of public lands in Texas to private ownership. These records include the original land grants, surveys and resurveys, and county maps showing the distribution of land grants over time. The county maps include Marion and all predecessor counties extending back to the early years; and the more recent maps, which extend into the 1900s, include information of historic importance. The holdings include Texas and some city maps, many of which are part of the Texas State Library and Archives Commission collection. The maps can be reviewed online, but not at a sufficient degree of resolution for details to be observed. The maps are for sale at modest cost directly from the General Land Office.

The Texas State Library and Archives Commission in Austin has a collection of historic state, county, and city maps; however, only a few of these can be reviewed online. The David Rumsey Collection, which is available online, contains many thousands of historic maps, including more than 100 for the state of Texas alone. The reproductions are of high quality, the details of each map are readily observable through enhancement tools, and there is no cost for their use.

The present study includes hand-drawn maps, maps from collections, and maps obtained from the deed records. There are no extant antebellum city maps of the Alley portion, nor any antebellum maps showing the Urquhart and Alley portions together, which is why it was necessary to incorporate a postbellum map to indicate the full dimensions of the city.

Two maps were obtained from the deed records: Hensey's 1846 town plan (Figs. 6-1 and 6-2) and the 1867 map showing the embayment at the foot of Houston Street (Fig. 4-3). The latter was given to the author because it pertained to a period in the deed records that had not been covered. There may be additional maps in the postbellum deed records that provide insight into antebellum conditions. The Hensey map is important as a town plan, but even more important as a property allocation map, providing key evidence with respect to the relative importance of Durham and Urquhart in the founding of the city.

Urquhart's 1841 (Fig. 3-1) and 1849 (Fig. 3-2) survey maps were obtained as part of the Urquhart files from the Texas General Land Office. A similar set of materials is available for Alley, including a survey map that was not used because it does not contain any details of interest. The representations of headrights (Fig. 3-3), Trammel's Trace (Fig. 3-4), and the Old Daingerfield Road (Fig. 4-1) are different parts of a 1943 map of Marion County obtained from the General Land Office and illustrate the incorporation of historic materials in more recent maps.

Eppinger's 1850 map of the Urquhart portion of Jefferson (Fig. 6-3) was also obtained from the General Land Office. This is the only extant antebellum Jefferson map other than Hensey. Portions of this map were also used to illustrate various historic features, such as the bridge (Fig. 10-2) and the early cemetery (Fig. 12-3). This map is also available through the Texas State Library and Archives Commission.

A plan of the city of Jefferson and a map of the city of Jefferson were prepared by S. Graham in May and July 1869, respectively. The May map was used to show the location of the present cemetery (Fig. 12-4), and the July map was used to show the location of the Old Daingerfield Road (Fig. 4-2) and the full dimensions of the city during the antebellum period (Fig. 12-1). Copies of these maps were provided to the author many years ago by the local historian Catherine Wise. The originals are in the Jefferson Historical Museum and do not appear to be available elsewhere. Mrs. Wise also provided the author a copy of the 1844 Morse and Breese map of Texas (Fig. 4-12).

Figs. 4-4 showing the roads south from Jefferson and 4-5 showing the roads to Greenwood and Shreveport were obtained from the Louisiana State Archives and are part of a large collection of captured Civil War maps for Louisiana organized on a parish-by-parish basis. These maps are distinguished by a high degree of detail.

Fig. 2-1 used to illustrate Jefferson's market area was obtained from the Texas State Library and Archives Commission and is titled *Part of North Eastern Texas Shewing the Route of the Inspectors*. Smith was an Englishman commissioned to determine the suitability of northeast Texas for a colony. The map shows the route taken by Smith and accompanies his *Account of a Journey Through North-Eastern Texas Undertaken in 1849*.

Brosius' 1872 *Bird's Eye View of Jefferson* (Fig. 6-4) was obtained as a black and white photograph from the Library of Congress. An original colored map is on display in the Jefferson Historical Museum. Although the map represents Jefferson in its primacy, it provides important clues to antebellum conditions and facilities.

Almost all of the hand-drawn maps showing the locations of various facilities are based on Epperson's 1850 map of Jefferson, which provides a clear delineation of the lots and blocks (see Fig. 6-3). In a few cases, a contemporary lots and blocks map prepared by the East Texas Council of Governments was used when it was necessary to include portions of the Alley Addition. This contemporary map can be seen at City Hall and purchased from the city.

Helmuth Holtz's 1867 map of the state of Texas is based primarily on Charles Pressler's 1857 map of the state of Texas. The Holtz map contains a high degree of detail for northeast Texas and was used partly to prepare the map of the road system (Fig 10-1). It can be obtained from the Historic Print and Map Company as part of the CD "Antique Maps of Texas." However, it should be used with caution because it contains information from disparate periods.

Fig. 1-1 showing northeast Texas in 1826 was obtained from a law office in Jefferson. The map is titled *Map of Part of the Country between Sabine & Red Rivers with Some of the Surveys of Lands in Texas*. The map is not dated. A typed description titles it "Map of the Caddo Lake Area" and suggests about 1826. According to the description, the original was found in the Raguet family papers and was given by Charles Raguet to the historian Hobart Key.

SECONDARY SOURCES

The chapter "Empire State of the South, 1846–1861" in Randolph Campbell's *Gone to Texas: A History of the Lone Star State* covers the economy, social structure, health and medical care, slaves, social institutions and life, and politics during the antebellum period. See also the article by Campbell on antebellum Texas in the *Handbook of Texas Online*. The chapter "Pioneer Institutions" in Rupert Richardson's *Texas: The Lone Star State* (seventh edition) covers the people; occupations; slavery and the plantation system; life on the farms; the towns; transportation; health; amusements; crime, vice, and reform; education; newspapers, literature, and art; and religion. For conditions in a nearby county, see the chapter on "Community Institutions and Social Life" in Randolph Campbell's *A Southern Community in Crisis: Harrison County, Texas, 1850–1880*. For comparative features in the emergence and development of Galveston, Houston, Austin, and San Antonio, see Kenneth Wheeler, *To Wear a City's Crown: The Beginnings of Urban Growth in Texas, 1836–1865*. For the continuity of various social features such as entertainment, see William Hogan, *The Texas Republic: A Social and Economic History*.

Secondary sources that were helpful in each chapter or that may be of interest to the reader are as follows:

1. Background—For fuller information on the development of the area, see my *A History of Navigation on Cypress Bayou and the Lakes*. Articles on Haden Edwards and Frost Thorn can be found in the *Handbook of Texas Online*. Josiah Gregg's comments are in Maurice Fulton, ed., *Diary and Letters of Josiah Gregg*.

2. What Jefferson Was—This chapter summarizes the main points about Jefferson and is based entirely on subsequent chapters.

3. Foundations—On the headright system in Texas, see the article on land grants in the *Handbook of Texas Online*. On Trammel's Trace, see Jack Jackson, "Nicholas Trammell's Difficulties in Mexican Texas," *East Texas Historical Journal* 38, no. 2. On transportation as a critical factor in town locations, see the article on urbanization in the *Handbook of Texas Online*.

4. Townsite—Articles on ferries and on Paschal County can be found in the *Handbook of Texas Online*. Information on Durham family genealogy can be found at various sites on the Internet. "Rip" Ford's comments are in Stephen Oates, ed., *Rip Ford's Texas*.

5. Emergence—Buck Barry's comments are in James Greer, ed., *Buck Barry: Texas Ranger and Frontiersman*.

6. Development—Edward Smith's comments are in his *Account of a Journey Through North-Eastern Texas*. A. W. Moore's comments are in "A Reconnaissance in Texas in 1846," *Southwestern Historical Quarterly* 30, no. 4. John McLean's comments are in his *Reminiscences of Rev. Jno. H. McLean, A.M., D.D.* Melinda Rankin's comments are in her *Texas in 1850*. Albert Leonard's comments are in his "Memoirs," a manuscript located in the archives department at Northwestern State University in Natchitoches, Louisiana. William Logan's letter is reproduced in the *Inventory of the County Archives of Texas: Marion County*.

7. Censuses—A profile of regional immigrants based on the census

can be found in Barnes Lathrop, *Migration Into East Texas, 1835–1860*. See also Ralph Wooster, "Foreigners in the Principal Towns of Ante-Bellum Texas," *Southwestern Historical Quarterly* 66, no. 2. On Rebecca Hagerty, see Judith McArthur, "Myth, Reality, and Anomaly: The Complex World of Rebecca Hagerty," *East Texas Historical Journal* 24 (Fall 1986).

8. Women—See Fane Downs, "'Tryels and Trubbles': Women in Early Nineteenth Century Texas," *Southwestern Historical Quarterly* 90, no. 1. See also Mark Carroll, *Homesteads Ungovernable: Families, Sex, Race, and Law in Frontier Texas, 1823–1960*.

9. Slaves—Although the literature on slavery is vast, almost all of the city studies are concerned with the slave trade and therefore deal with matters that are not directly related to a city like Jefferson. Randolph Campbell provides a comprehensive analysis in *An Empire for Slavery: The Peculiar Institution in Texas, 1821–1865*. Frederick Bancroft's *Slave Trading in the Old South* provides a detailed analysis of the types of information found in newspapers. James McGettigan in "Boone County Slaves: Sales, Estate Divisions and Families, 1820–1865" (*Missouri Historical Review* 72, nos. 2 and 3) offers one of the few county level analyses. See also the chapter on "Urban Blacks" in John Moore, *The Emergence of the Cotton Kingdom in the Old Southwest: Mississippi, 1770–1860*. To achieve clarity with respect to slavery in Jefferson, it was necessary to conduct a systematic analysis of the evidence in the Shreveport newspapers concerning slavery in Shreveport.

10. Roads and Bridges—On the condition of early roads, see Charles Potts, "Transportation in Texas," in Eugene Barker, ed., *History of Texas*.

11. County Seat—See the articles on county organization, county courthouses, and the county commissioners court in the *Handbook of Texas Online*.

12. Municipal Affairs—See the articles on city government and mayor-council form of city government in the *Handbook of Texas Online*.

13. Wharves—The remnants of these wharves have been found, as recorded in Geo-Marine's 2003 report for the Fort Worth District Corps of Engineers, *Archeological Assessment of Big Cypress Bayou Fish and Wildlife Habitat Restoration Area, Jefferson, Texas*.

14. The best book on steamboats is Louis Hunter's *Steamboats on the Western Rivers*. For additional information on the boats, see my *A History of Navigation on Cypress Bayou and the Lakes*.

15. Navigation Controversies—The extended context of these controversies is presented in my *A History of Navigation on Cypress Bayou and the Lakes*.

16. Market Area—Josiah Gregg's comments are in Maurice Fulton, ed., *Diary and Letters of Josiah Gregg*. Jefferson's market area is described in the state context in S. G. Reed, *A History of the Texas Railroads* and in Charles Potts, "Transportation in Texas," in Eugene Barker, ed., *History of Texas*. The best description of the internal features of the market area is Edward Smith's 1849 *Account of a Journey Through North-Eastern Texas*, which includes coverage of slavery, markets, water, minerals, labor, security, laws, taxes, health, disease, and the people.

17. Primary Business Types—On commission merchants in the Houston/Galveston area, see Abigail Holbrook, "Cotton Marketing in Antebellum Texas," *Southwestern Historical Quarterly* 73, no. 4. On commission merchants in the antebellum urban centers of Mississippi, see John Moore, *The Emergence of the Cotton Kingdom in the Old Southwest: Mississippi, 1770–1860*. Marilyn Lavin in her 1977 Columbia University dissertation "William Bostwick, Connecticut Yankee in Antebellum Georgia" provides a detailed analysis of the activities of an Augusta commission merchant and wholesaler/retailer. On how merchants were evaluated for credit, see Lewis Atherton, "The Problem of Credit Rating in the Ante-Bellum South," *Journal of Southern History* 12, no. 4. Kenneth Greenburg in *Honor and Slavery* indicates that loans and endorsement of notes were components of gift exchange in an honor culture. On the importance of slaves as collateral, see Richard Kilbourne, *Debt, Investment, Slaves: Credit Relations in East Feliciana Parish, Louisiana, 1825–1885*.

18. Commodity Markets—There are no studies that would enable a ready interpretation of the available evidence with respect to the cotton market in Jefferson. The best coverage of market factors in the United States continues to be Matthew Hammond's 1897 *The Cotton Industry*, particularly Chapter 10, "The Evolution of the Cotton Market." The international context is covered in Part IV ("Financing and

Marketing the Cotton Crop") in Stuart Bruchy's *Cotton and the Growth of the American Economy, 1790–1860*. Lynn Willoughby's *Fair to Middlin': The Antebellum Cotton Trade of the Apalachicola/Chatahouchee River Valley* offers insight into participants and mechanisms in a regional setting. Harold Woodman's *King Cotton and His Retainers: Financing and Marketing the Cotton Crop of the South, 1800–1925* concentrates on the cotton factorage system. On commission merchants as buyers of cotton, see Ralph Haskins, "Planter and Cotton Factor in the Old South: Some Areas of Friction," *Agricultural History* 29, no. 1. To achieve some degree of clarity with respect to the cotton market in Jefferson, it was necessary to conduct a systematic analysis of the evidence in the Shreveport newspapers concerning the cotton market in Shreveport, most of which, unfortunately, is related to the postbellum situation.

19. Warehouse District—Perspectives on the types of merchants found in Jefferson's warehouse district can be found in Abigail Holbrook, "Cotton Marketing in Antebellum Texas," *Southwestern Historical Quarterly* 73, no. 4; Lynn Willoughby, *Fair to Middlin': The Antebellum Cotton Trade of the Apalachicola/Chatahouchee River Valley*; and Harriet Amos, *Cotton City: Urban Development in Antebellum Mobile*.

20. Earliest Merchants—Interest in the Southern economy has centered on cotton production, the plantation system, and slavery. Lewis Atherton's 1949 *The Southern Country Store, 1800–1860* was the first to emphasize the importance of merchants. However, only in recent years have merchants begun to receive the attention they deserve. See, in particular, Jonathan Wells' 2004 *The Origins of the Southern Middle Class, 1800–1861* and Frank Byrne's 2006 *Becoming Bourgeois: Merchant Culture in the South, 1820–1865*. However, neither of these works provides a clear picture of how mercantile establishments functioned as businesses (for example, terms of credit with northeastern suppliers). A detailed analysis of the activities of an Augusta merchant is provided by Marilyn Lavin in her 1977 Columbia University dissertation "William Bostwick, Connecticut Yankee in Antebellum Georgia." For particular features of Texas mercantile activity, see Suzanne Summers' "The Geographic and Social Origins of Antebellum Merchants in Houston and Galveston, Texas, 1836–1860" (*Essays in Economic and Business History* 15, p. 95) and "Public Policy and Economic Growth in Antebellum

Texas: The Role of Houston-Galveston Merchants" (*Essays in Economic and Business History* 16, p. 127).

21. Early 1850s Merchants—See the references for Chapter 20. On John Pitkin, see Albert Pitkin, *Pitkin Family of America: A Genealogy of the Descendants of William Pitkin.*

22. Middle 1850s Merchants—See the references for Chapter 20.

23. Late Merchants—See the references for Chapter 20.

24. Miscellaneous Businesses—See the articles on prohibition and on photography in the *Handbook of Texas Online*.

25. Manufacturing—An overview of manufacturing in Texas is provided by the article on manufacturing industries in the *Handbook of Texas Online*. Vera Dugas in "Texas Industry, 1860–1880" (*Southwestern Historical Quarterly* 59, no. 2) provides a degree of commentary on the situation before the war. Jefferson Nash's foundry is covered in Robert Jones, "The First Iron Furnace in Texas" (*Southwestern Historical Quarterly* 63, no. 2).

26. Packeries—For an overview of the meat packing industry, see Rudolph Clemen, *The American Livestock and Meat Industry*. For the source of the cattle that were processed in Jefferson's packeries, see the chapter "The Northwest Texas Prairies" in Terry Jordan's *Trails to Texas: Southern Roots of Western Cattle Ranching*.

27. Structural Features—See Gordon Echols, *Early Texas Architecture* and Dorothy Bracken, *Early Texas Homes* (both of which include photographs of Jefferson residences). The significance of the fires has now been addressed by Donald Reynolds in *Texas Terror: The Slave Insurrection Panic of 1860 and the Secession of the Lower South*.

28. The Professions—On the legal profession, see Lawrence Friedman, *A History of American Law*. See also the article on James Harrison Rogers in the *Handbook of Texas Online*. On medicine, see Pat Nixon, *The Medical History of Early Texas, 1528–1853* and Steven Stowe, *Doctoring the South: Southern Physicians and Everyday Medicine in the Mid-Nineteenth Century*. See also the articles on health and medicine, medical education, and medical quackery in the *Handbook of Texas Online*.

29. Politics—See the articles in the *Handbook of Texas Online* on the Democratic Party, the American Party, the Whig Party, Matthias Ward, Hinche Parham Mabry, William Smith Todd, and William Beck Ochiltree.

30. Fraternal Organizations—See the articles on Freemasonry and on the Knights of the Golden Circle in the *Handbook of Texas Online*.

31. Religion—This chapter relied primarily on the work of local historians: Earline Burnett's 1954 Stephen F. Austin thesis "A History of the First Methodist Church, Jefferson, Texas, 1844–1854"; Lucille Bullard's 1986 *The First Baptist Church, Jefferson, Texas, 1855–1985*; Juanita Cawthon's 1993 *History of the Presbyterian and Cumberland Presbyterian Churches, Jefferson, Texas*; and Dorothy Craver's 1980 *This Old Church: A History of Christ Church, Episcopal, Jefferson, Texas*. See also J. A. R. Moseley's 1946 *The Presbyterian Church in Jefferson*. In an unpublished 1996 paper on the "Mount Sinai Cemetery, Jefferson, Texas," the Shreveport historian Eric Brock covers the establishment of the cemetery in 1866 by the Hebrew Benevolent Association, which was a forerunner to Congregation Har Sinai. For an overview of the various denominations, see the article on religion in the *Handbook of Texas Online*.

32. Education—See Frederick Eby, *The Development of Education in Texas* and Cecil Evans, *The Story of Texas Schools*. See also the article on education in the *Handbook of Texas Online*.

33. Hotels—For conditions nationally and in the South, see the chapter on "Boarding and Lodging" in Edgar Martin's *The Standard of Living in 1860—American Consumption Levels on the Eve of the Civil War*.

34. Stables—Although stables have been described in connection with barns, their function in early transportation has not been addressed.

35. Stagecoaches—Stagecoaches and routes are described in Charles Potts, "Transportation in Texas," in Eugene Barker, ed., *History of Texas* and in S. G. Reed, *A History of the Texas Railroads*. See also the article on stagecoach lines in the *Handbook of Texas Online*. The route between Marshall and Jefferson is described in Max Lale, "Stagecoach Roads to Marshall," *East Texas Historical Journal* 17, no. 2.

36. Newspapers—See Marilyn Sibley, *Lone Star State Gazettes: Texas Newspapers Before the Civil War* and Joe Frantz, *History of the Texas Press and the Texas Press Association*. The *Northern Standard* and its editor are covered by Ernest Wallace, *Charles DeMorse: Pioneer Editor and Statesman*. See also the article on newspapers in the *Handbook of Texas Online*.

37. Postal Services—See the article on stagecoach lines in the *Handbook of Texas Online* and LeRoy Hafen, *The Overland Mail, 1849–1869*.

38. Telegraph—The national context for the development of the telegraph is covered in Robert Thompson, *Wiring a Continent*. The regional context is covered in Charles Dillon, "The Arrival of the Telegraph in Texas," *Southwestern Historical Quarterly* 64, no. 2. See also the article on telegraph service in the *Handbook of Texas Online*.

39. Railroads—On the general development of the rails in Texas, see Charles Zlatcovich, *Texas Railroads: A Record of Construction and Abandonment* and S. G. Reed, *A History of the Texas Railroads*. See also the article on railroads in the *Handbook of Texas Online*. Regional development is covered in A. B. Armstrong, "Origins of the Texas and Pacific Railway" (*Southwestern Historical Quarterly* 56, no. 4) and in Emilia Means, "East Texas and the Transcontinental Railroad" (*East Texas Historical Journal* 25, no. 2).

40. Sports—See Elliott Gorn and Warren Goldstein, *A Brief History of American Sports*. See also the article on sports in the *Handbook of Texas Online*.

41. Culture and Entertainment—For conditions nationally and in the South, see the chapter on "Leisure and Recreation" in Edgar Martin's *The Standard of Living in 1860 — American Consumption Levels on the Eve of the Civil War*. For conditions in Texas, see the articles on music and on theater in the *Handbook of Texas Online*. A photograph of the *Banjo* can be found in my *A History of Navigation on Cypress Bayou and the Lakes*.

42. Balls and Dances—See the article on folk dance in the *Handbook of Texas Online*.

43. Crime—See Edward Ayers, *Vengeance and Justice: Crime and Punishment in the Nineteenth Century American South* and Dickson Bruce, *Violence and Culture in the Antebellum South*.

44. Vice—See the articles on prostitution and on drinking and beverages in nineteenth-century Texas in the *Handbook of Texas Online*.

45. Health and Welfare—The comments by A. W. Moore are in his "A Reconnaissance in Texas in 1846," *Southwestern Historical Quarterly* 30, no. 3. See the article on epidemic diseases in the *Handbook of Texas Online*.

46. Mortality—See Gerald Grob, *Disease and Death in America*. See also the articles on women and health and on epidemic diseases in the *Handbook of Texas Online*.

SOURCES NOT USED

There were three sources that were not used that could provide additional information on Jefferson's antebellum history.

R. G. Dun & Co. was a predecessor to Dun & Bradstreet and in the business of evaluating companies. The R. G. Dun collection is housed at Harvard's Baker Library, with limited access. The collection includes credit report ledgers for Marion County and its predecessor Cass County back to 1847. They would provide insight into the nature of Jefferson's businesses, financial status, and the character of owners.

Jefferson is mentioned in 18 of the collection descriptions in Chester Kielman's *The University of Texas Archives: A Guide to the Historical Manuscripts Collections in the University of Texas Archives*. Most of these materials are concerned with the Civil War and the postbellum period and with persons who were not Jefferson residents. Of particular interest are the Culberson, Epperson, Frazor, and Ochiltree family papers.

The trade relation between Jefferson and Dallas has long been assumed but never investigated. There does not appear to be anything of particular interest related to Jefferson in the Dallas Public Library. Dallas newspapers extending back to 1855 are available on microfilm.

INDEX

Page numbers in *italics* refer to illustrations.

A

Account of a Journey Through North-Eastern Texas Undertaken in 1849 (Smith), 19, 293, 358, 525. *See also* Smith, Edward
Adams-Onis Treaty, 9
A. D. Taylor & Brother, 335
Alban, George, 83, 84
alcohol: types sold, 557–58; evils condemned, 481, 558
Alexander, Alexander, 276
Alexander, Capt. E, 207
Alexander & Chrisman, 276, 277; advertisement, *277*; location, *296*, *297*
Alhambra Hall, 531, 541, 542, 543
Alley, Daniel, 28, 33, 34, 35, 36, 55, 109, 154, 156, 333, 408, 435, 458
Alley, James, 33, 35, 53
Alley, Thomas, 34
Alley Addition, 53, 55, 96, 97, 104, 109, 110, 154; role as residential section overemphasized, 114
Alligator (steamboat), 199
American Party, 404
Ames, Harriet, 13, 15
Arberry, Robert, 67, 153, 154
Archer (steamboat), 487
Atherton, Lewis, 223
attorneys, 393–96
Austin Street, 58, 105, 257, 287, 293, 321, 345, 385, 448, 464

B

Bails, Hiram ("Bails the Bee Hunter"), 15
Baker, Francis, 97, 292, 301, 302, 398, 401
Baker, Job, 292. 358, 397–98, 431, 488
Baker, William, 55, 111, 112, 271, 284, 292, 301, 302, 358, 574; editor of *Spirit of the Age,* 484
Banjo (showboat), 537–39
banks, 237
Baptist churches, 432–34

barber shops, 345–46
Barry, Buck, 81, 83, 86, 91
baseball, 524
Bayless, Labon, 271, 312
Beazley, E. C., 487
Beckett, Ephraim, 301; inventory at death of, 557, 560
Beckett & Company, 301
beef packing, 24, 221, 242, 355, 371–81; locations, *377*. *See also individual meat packing companies*
Belle Gates (steamboat), 199, 208
Benners, Edward, 135, 394–95
Benners, Moseley & Hall, 394–95
Benton, TX, 5, 13, 16, 78, 141, 203, 214, 518
Big Cypress Bayou. *See* Cypress Bayou
Big Cypress Valley Road, 42, 55, 142, 150, 161; on map, 54
billiards, 343, 344, 527–28
Birge, Noble, 161, 173, 467, 468, 554
Bird's Eye View of Jefferson, Texas (Brosius), 106, 107, 108, 149, 386–87, 436, 587
Bishop, William, 61, 69–71, 76, 87, 105, 504, 505; opertates ferry, 45, 66, 145; as postmaster, 64, 258, 504, 505; residence location, *275*; editor of *Jefferson Democrat*, 476–83
B. J. Terry & Company, 224, 267, 324; location, *275*
Black, Harvey, 199, 355, 372–75, 384
Black and Crump tanyard, 375
Black Cypress Bayou, 33, 93, 147, 161, 196, 363, 414, 449
Black Packery, 372–75; advertisement, *373*

blacksmiths, 354, 359–60, 361, 384
Bloomer (steamboat), 199, 549; advertisement for, *200*
Bois d'Arc (steamboat), 16, 75, 85
bois d'arc (tree and seeds), 59, 218, 241, 255, 357
bookstores, 348–51
Bowie County, 6, 7–8, 14, 35, 38, 70, 140, 151, 278
bowling, 343, 344, 527–28
Boynton, Lewis, 454–55
Branch Tan Yard, 367
brick, 26, 177, 267, 268, 272, 338, 339; first brick structure, 263–65; warehouse advertisement, *264*; location of warehouses, *275*; manufacturing, 361–62; structures, 386–90
Brickell, James, 172–73
bridges, 145–50; location, *146*; toll rates, 45, 53, 145, 147, 148
Bridges, Eloise, 536–37
Brooks, Brother & Mabry, 270, 306, 317; location, *275*
Brooks, John, 270
Brooks, Joseph, 306
Brooks, William, 133, 136, 270, 337, 387, 455, 456–57, 468; captain of *Belle Gates*, 199, 208; location, *469*
Brown, William, 71, 72, 259, 289
Bryan, John, 271
Bryan & Clark, 224, 271–72, 333; advertisement, *235*
Bulkley, Chester, 325
Bullard, Lucille, 159
Butt, George, 279, 280
Byers, Robert, 435

C

C. A. Bulkley, 224, 325–26
Caddo Indians, 5, 10, 12–13; village, 10
Caddo Lake, 1, 13, 15, 29–30, 77, 182, 203, 518, 525; Texas borderlines through, 1, 9; navigation on, 15, 84, 195–96, 203, 575
Cairo & Fulton Railroad, 4, 519
Camp Street, 58, 60
Campti settlement, 10, 11
Cass County, 151–59
Cass County Male and Female Academy, 107, 124, 441–43
Catholic church, 429
cattle, 24, 212, 218, 220, 242, 355, 371–75, 380; ferry and bridge rates for, 45, 53, 145, 147, 148. *See also* hides, tallow, meat packing
cemetery, 179, 181, 567; location, *179, 180*; Jewish, 438
Census, of 1850, 100, 102, 116–17; merchants listed in, 279; lawyers listed in, 396; doctors listed in, 398
Census, of 1860, 100, 102, 117–22, 134; merchants listed in, 330, 343, 346; lawyers listed in, 396; doctors listed in, 402
census of industry, 1860, 370
Charles, J. S., theater troop, 532–33
Charter, By-Laws and Ordinances of the City of Jefferson, 168
Cherry, Jesse, town plan, 6, 38, 56–58, 59, 60, 62, 66, 71, 93, 99–100, 105, 109, 257, 357
Chrisman, John, 276
circus, 539–40
City Hotel, 337, 387, 455–57, 461; location, *462*
city records, 172–73, 578–79
C. J. Willard & Company, 281; location, *296, 297*
Clapp, George, 272
Clark, Frank, 126, 367, 395, 491; obituary by DeMorse, 492–94
Clarksville (street and town), 14, 29, 58, 76, 78, 99, 102, 182, 205, 210–11, 361, 470, 472, 519; town compared with Jefferson, 228. *See also* Northern Standard.
Clarksville Female Institute, 417
Clinton, TX, 84, 280, 507
Clinton Lake, 280–81
Colt & Winans, 349–51; advertisement, *350*
commission merchants, 24, 130, 131, 207, 245, 246, 251, 254. *See also* receiving, forwarding, and commission merchants
commodity markets, 23, 241–56
Constitutional Union Party, 404
construction contracts, 382–86
cotton, 1–3, 15, 25, 74, 75, 82, 85, 129, 160, 195, 199, 212, 213, 220, 236, 261, 272; dollar value of, 8, 75, 79, 219, 252; transportation of, 15, 20–22, 24, 74, 75, 76, 143–44, 195, 199, 218–19, 236–37; compared with population, 219, 222; factors of, 24, 232–33, 245; market of, 218–19, 242–55, 514, 515; receipts in Jefferson, 272–74
counterfeit money, 551

Crawford, Jeptha, 78, 283, 285; location, *296, 297*
credit system, 238–39
Cross, T. L. H., 400
Cross Lake, plan to drain, 208–10
Crump, Richard, 154, 181, 207, 279, 288–89, 344, 414–16, 528, 548; conducts census, 117–18; captain of *Grenada*, 199, 208, 415, 566
Cunliffe, Dick, 344–45
Cypress Bayou, 1, 20, 30, 53, 147, 167, 196, 470; removal of obstructions from, 6, 7, 77–82, 187–88, 200–1, 203, 484–85; navigation on, 194–204. *See also* bridges; ferries; steamboats
Cypress Bayou and the Lakes navigation route, 2–4, 13, 195–96, 201, 203, 205–6

D

Daily Jimplecute, 43, 55, 64, 83, 84, 88, 105, 164, 172, 296, 585
Daingerfield, 29, 46, 63; meeting at to organize Jefferson, 76–78
Daingerfield Road, 30, 35, 108, 140, 565; location, *47, 48*
Dallas Street, 26, 58, 69, 88, 99, 103, 105, 107, 109, 114, 177, 293, 296; as part of warehouse district, 257–77. *See also individual merchants*
Darby, William, 9
deaths, listed, 567–70; causes of, listed, 570; of prominent men, listed, 573–74
debts, 237–40, 295

Democratic Party, 403, 404, 407–9, 481, 487; list of members, 407–8
DeMorse, Charles, quoted on Jefferson, 52, 74, 78, 81, 101–2, 104, 126, 152, 201, 228, 315, 368, 405, 417–18, 449, 459, 478, 530; on Ochiltree, 420; on *Jefferson Democrat*, 483; on *Jefferson Herald*, 489, 491; on Frank Clark, 492–94; on performance of Shakespeare play, 534–36
Digest of the Laws of the City of Jefferson, Texas, 560
disorderly conduct, 167, 168–69
D. N. Alley, 333; advertisement, *334*
dollars, conversion into current values, 8
Dopplemayer, Mayer, 303
Douthit, David, 301, 547; location, *296, 297, 316*
Drake, Reuben, 285, 295; location, *296, 297*
D. R. Carroll (steamboat), 198
Durham, Berryman Hicks (Berry), 6, 36, 37, 63–68, 71, 72, 76, 79, 87, 95, 96, 407; operates ferry, 6, 30, 35, 44–45; first inhabitant of Jefferson, 43, 44, 55, 66; sells interest in ferry, 46; relationship with Allen Urquhart, 6, 37, 58–63; locations, *65*; buys *Jefferson Democrat*, 68, 476, 478; postmaster, 64, 504, 505
Durham, Eliza, 67, 132
Durham, James, 67, 277, 398
Durlin, Elias, 338
Durlin & Company, 338; location, *341*

600

Durr, James, 161, 338; location, *341*

E

Eagle Restaurant, 344–45
Eason, Ithael, 120, 132, 294, 383, 397–98, 457–58; location, *296, 297*
Eason Hotel, 457–61; location, *462*
Eastern Texas Gazette, 494–99
Echo (steamboat), 15, 196, 303
Edwards, Haden, 10, 589
Edwards, Larkin, 16
Eggers, Shadrach, 161, 494, 498, 499–500
election results, 410
Elliott, Joseph, 450, 452, 464
Elliott & Frith, 307, 400
Ellis, Stephen, 155, 164, 450–51; first mayor, 172; operates Jefferson Hotel, 451; as postmaster, 504
English, William, 16
Episcopal churches, 436–38
Epperson, Benjamin, 404, 409
Eppinger, John, 102, 396; death of, 526
Eppinger's *Map of Jefferson*, 98–99, 146, 165, *179*

F

factors, cotton, 24, 232–33, 245
Falk, William, 291–92
Farley, Michael, 396, 497
Female Academy, 391, 443, 444
ferries, 43–56, 66, 74, 76, 95, 140, 143, 145, 173, 182, 183, 192; toll rates, 45, 52, 147, 148; locations, *53*; described by DeMorse, 52. *See also under,* Durham, Berryman Hicks; Bishop, William
Figures, Bartholomew, 383, 447, 455–57, 459, 460, 461
Figures, Richard, 362
Figures Hotel, 107–8, 447, 455–57, 461–62; location, *462*
Financier (steamboat), 198
fire department, 178, 390
fires, 390–92; laws to prevent, 170, 178, 184; of Nesmith & Booth stable, 391, 466; of City Hotel, 457
fishing, 525–27
"five points," 137, 550, 555
flatboats, 2, 15, 74, 194
Fleta (steamboat), 199, 507
Ford, John Salmon "Rip," 74
Forest Mail Stage Line, 466, 472, 512; advertisement, *473*
Fox, Hugo, 299, 325, 356, 365; advertisement, *365*; death of, 574
Frazor, O. C., 312, 318
Frazor, Thomas D., 312–13, 318
Frazor & Company, 312, 318; location, *316, 328*
Fredonian Rebellion, 10
Freeman, Williamson, 118, 131, 172, 189–91, 246, 252, 362, 569; business location, *275*; as blacksmith, 359–60
Freemasons, 425–27
Friou, Samuel, 110, 306
Friou Street, 110, 150
Frith, John, 305, 307, 400
Frith & Robinson, 294, 307, 425; location, *296, 297, 316*
Fuchs, Hugo. *See* Fox, Hugo

G

gambling, 529, 546, 556–57
Garey, Samuel, 226, 287, 292–93, 398; advertisement, *227, 399*; location, *296, 297*; runs hotel, 459–60; as postmaster, 504, 505
Gazelle, 86, 91, 196
Gillian, James, 312
Gooding, Henry, 452
Graham, Charles, 116
Graham, L. J., 324, 402
Graham, Perry, 283–84, 486; location, *296, 297*; term as postmaster, 504
Graham, Robert, 96
graveyard. *See* cemetery
Great Raft (on Red River), 5, 7, 10–13, 90, 195–96, 205, 208, 209, 210–11, 520
Gregg, Josiah, 17, 38, 212, 562, 591
Grenada, 199, 208, 415, 566
Grinsted, Hiram, 202, 395, 490, 491, 494, 526, 548

H

Hagerty, Rebecca, 16, 121, 122, 590
Hagerty, Spire, 16, 122
Hamilton, William, 29, 34, 44
Harmon, J. T., 29
Harris, F. (Francis) T., 454, 543
Harrison County, 14; 44, 52, 53, 140, 143, 167, 214, 362, 363; cotton production of, 16, 219, 249, 250
Harrison Flag, 39, 149, 204, 231, 250, 252, 269, 272, 326, 340, 347, 375, 381, 388, 419, 428, 456, 457, 460, 498, 528, 545, 550, 555, 564, 585
Hebrew Benevolent Association, 335, 438
Henderson Street, 58, 60, 99
Hensey, Hugh, town plan of, 61, 62, 66, 93–95, *97,* 98, 99, 100, 153, 179, 361
Herald and Gazette, 175, 375, 475, 494, 499–500, 529, 554
hides, cattle, 3, 23, 24, 218, 241, 255–56, 371–72
High Street (now Henderson), 99
Highway 59, 42, 48, 51
Hill, David, 61, 96
Hill, Josiah, 286–87, 431
Hines, Isaac, 337
Hines, William, 337, 338
Historic Jefferson Foundation, 4, 5, 577, 580, 585
History of Navigation on Cypress Bayou and the Lakes (Bagur), 4, 575
Hobdy, John, 188, 338, 389, 433
Hodge, Gus, 336, 551
Hodge, William, 173, 317; location, *469*
homeopathy, 397
Homer (steamboat), 199; advertisement, *200*
horseracing, 528–29
Hosack, James, 131–32, 574
Houston Street, 47, 48, 60, 64, 69, 99, 107, 140, 141, 187, 438; embayment, *49*
Howell, John, 67
H. Rhine & Brothers, 224, 235, 335–36; advertisement, *229*; location, *341*
Hughes, Bob C., 340

Hughes, Isaac, 77
Hughes, Reece, 74, 75, 91, 224, 228, 337, 386, 387; location, *341*; runs Planter's Hotel, 455–57
Hughes, William, 34, 37
Humphries, John, 32, 363
Humphries, William, 37
Humphries tract, 44
Hunt, Caroline, 124, 427, 453; advertisement, *125*
Hunter Transfer, 216–17
hunting, 525–27

I

I. G. Eason & Son drugstore, 294, 307
incendiaries, rumors of, 390
Independent Monitor, 488
Independent Order of Good Samaritans, 427–28
Independent Order of Odd Fellows, 424–25
insurance company, 351–52
iron works, 355, 391

J

Jackson, Elizabeth, 124, 425, 452, 453
jail, 552–54
J. (John) B. Ligon & Company, 336; location, *341*
J. C. Preston & Company, 321; advertisement, *322*; location, *328*
Jefferson, TX, significant dates, 5–7; as port, 18, 21, 77, 194; map of market area, *19*, 217; founding date of, 6, 35, 64, 66, 76; first mention in survey, 38–39; naming of, 39–40; first appearance on map, 72–73; first buildings constructed, 80–81, 87; first steamboat arrives, 82–86; second steamboat arrives, 86–88; first merchant, 88–92; first warehouse built, 105, 259–61; residential development, 109–115; as seat of Cass County, 151–59; as seat of Marion County, 161–62; incorporation of, 163–67; original boundaries, 165–67; "five points," 137, 550, 555; steamboats to, listed, 573–74. *See also* population, of Jefferson; streets; wards; Census, of 1850; Census, of 1860; ordinances; town plans; taxes
Jefferson Daily Democrat, 82, 83, 86
Jefferson Democrat, 68, 70, 153, 475, 476–83
Jefferson Female Academy, 124, 391, 444; advertisement, *445*
Jefferson Gazette, 102, 175, 187–88, 215, 250, 268, 302, 376, 379–80, 389, 444, 475, 494–99, 520, 550, 564, 573. *See also* Herald and Gazette
Jefferson Herald, 126, 148, 157, 158, 175, 239, 422, 488–94, 500, 585; on map, *501*. *See also* Herald and Gazette
Jefferson Hotel, 451–55, 464; location, *462*
Jefferson Insurance Company, 351–52
Jefferson Jimplecute, 37, 63, 299, 366, 367, 487, 585. *See also*

Daily Jimplecute; Weekly Jimplecute; Semi-Weekly Jimplecute
Jefferson Livery Stable, 466
Jefferson Railroad Company, 517
Jefferson Town Company, 6, 34, 35, 36–38, 45, 59
Jenkins, E. M., 323
Jesse Cherry Town Plan. *See* Cherry, Jesse, town plan
Jewish congregations, 438
Jimplecute. See Jefferson Jimplecute
Jim's Bayou, 12, 84, 284, 507
J. L. & S. C. Smith, 286, 321–22; location, *328*
J. M. & J. C. Murphy, 187, 237, 243, 251, 262, 265, 274, 386; advertisements, *262, 264*; location, *275*
J. Mosby & Company, 271; location, *275*
John H. Bills (steamboat), 16
Johnson, James and Asa, 46, 69, 145, 147
Johnson's Bridge, 99, 145–46; location, *146*
Jolly, Haze, 356, 368
Jones, Edward, 199
Jones, Erastus, 217–18
Jones, M. J., 300
Jordan, Levi, 30, 33, 34, 38, 53, 55
Joseph T. Prewitt & Company, 320; location, *328*
Julia (steamboat), 198
J. W. Pitkin & Company, 224, 310, 312; advertisement, *311*; location, *316*

K

keelboats, 2, 11, 194
Kemp, J. W., 323, 452–53
Kitchen, John, 16
Knights of the Golden Circle, 428
Kohn, Abraham, 111, 114, 271, 339; contents of house listed, 115
Kolster, John, 367
Kothe, Herman, 367

L

Lafayette Street, 58, 361
Lake O' the Pines, 142
Lake Street, 57, 58, 60, 88, 100, 110, 294, 367, 505
Lama, 75, 82–86, 91, 280
Lander, Alfred R., 547–48
Larkin Edwards, 196
laudanum, 558–59
lawyers, 393–96
Leavitt, Israel, 153, 155, 288, 339, 438; location, *296, 297*
Lewis, Granville, 395
libraries, in private homes, 530
Ligon, John, 112, 118, 336
Linden, TX, as Cass County seat, 7, 94, 149, 151–59, 343, 552, 553; roads to, 142, 161
Lilly, Joseph, 35, 53
Linden Times, 494
Linn, James, 340
Little Cypress Bayou, 42, 48, 51, 141, 147, 470
L. J. Graham & Company, 324
Lone Star (steamboat), 199
Loughery, Robert, 68, 158, 408, 413; quoted on Jefferson, 108, 125, 144, 147, 155, 167, 174–

75, 188, 209, 242, 263, 325–26, 376–77, 387, 425, 431–32, 439, 453, 454, 470–71, , 476, 489, 531, 552–53; quoted on gambling, 556–57
Louisiana, Arkansas and Texas Navigation company, 210–11
Louisiana Purchase, 9, 11
Lowenstein, Casper, 42

M

Mabry, Hinche, 135, 170, 177, 306, 410, 416
Mabry's Bridge, 150
machinist, 351
mail delivery routes, 507–10
Manchester (steamboat), 15
Manker Lot, 69; on map, 70
Manwaring, Richard, 331
Manwaring & Company, 248, 331; location, *341*
Map of Jefferson (Eppinger). *See* Eppinger's *Map of Jefferson.*
Marion County, 1, 4, 7, 8, 31, 117, 132, 159–62, 220, 329, 342, 354, 364, 430, 440, 500, 578–79, 581–84; map of, *47*; debate over name, 159–60
Marion County, Texas, 1860–1870, 159
market house, 181
Market Street, 58, 100, 107, 296
Marshall Street (Jefferson), 26, 55, 56, 58, 71, 92, 99, 105, 106, 107, 114, 126, 155, 168, 177, 188, 261, 376, 386; merchants located on, 282–341, 345, 351, 357, 358, 366, 368, 386, 387, 400, 401, 447, 455–57, 484; location, *57, 296, 341*

Marshall, TX, 14, 26, 39, 48, 51, 64, 72, 99, 102, 129, 130, 143, 152, 168, 206, 346–47, 394, 510–11; stage line between Jefferson and, 470–72, 474, 507; telegraph to, 514–16. *See also* Harrison Flag; Texas Republican
Marton, M., 121, 123, 125
Masons. *See* Freemasons
Matthews, Mansell, 77, 78
May, August, 291
May & Company, 226, 235, 236, 247, 255, 291; advertisement, *226*; location, *296, 297, 341*
May & Kohn, 114
Mayberry, William, 150, 183, 188, 190
Mayberry Bridge, 150
McAllenny, Thomas, 401
McCown, James, 75, 305
McDermott, Joseoph, 338; location, *341*
McLaughlin, Levi, 42, 55
McLean, John, 278
McNab, Duncan, 290, 333
McNeill, William, 261, 486; location, *275*
meat packing, 24, 221, 242, 355, 371–81; locations, *377. See also individual meat packing companies*
medicine, 396–402
Memphis, El Paso & Pacific Railroad (ME&P), 182, 519–23
Merzbacher, Frederick, 335, 366
Methodist churches, 430–32
Metropolitan Railroad, 519, 520, 521
mills, steam, 357–64
Mississippi & Pacific Railroad, 518

Monterey, 84, 196
Moody, Lewis, 44–55
Moore, A. W., 101, 562
Morgan, John, 314–15, 548–49
Morgan, W. J., 494, 497
Morgan & Tomlin, 314; location, *316*
Morris, C. D., 325
Mosby & Kohn, 271; advertisement, *232*; location, *275*
Mosby, Joseph, 271
Mosby, Schluter & Company, 271, 323; location, *275*
Moseley, Samuel, 112, 272, 294, 395, 407, 488–89, 491; statement, *406*
Moseley's Bridge, 167
Mostacker steam mill, 359
M. Rosenzweig & Company / Brother, 338, 388
M. Steinlein & Company, 248–50, 302, 303–4, 315, 551; advertisement, *249*; location, *296, 297, 316*
Murphy, James, 111, 113, 132, 262; one of richest people, 120
Murphy, John, 111, 112, 132, 262
Musgrove, Bushrod, 395
music, 531

N

N. A. Birge & Company's Sale and Livery Stable, 467–68; location, *469*

Nash, M. B., 453–54
Natchitoches, LA, 10
Nave, Jesse, 61, 62, 66, 74, 96; warehouse, 260, 261, 262

Nelson Taylor & Company, 466
Nesmith, Robert, 135–36, 238, 385, 448, 464–65, 466, 472, 474; advertisement, *465*; location, *469*
Nesmith & Booth stable: fire at, 391, 466; location, *469*
New Madrid earthquake, 13
New Orleans, 100, 210, 513; as shipping and business center, 1, 4, 12, 16, 18, 21–24, 75, 84, 85, 198, 206–7, 214, 231–32, 236, 241, 243, 245, 254–55, 291, 371, 373, 485
Nichols, Theophilus, 333
Nichols, William, 290, 333; location, *341*
Nichols & McNab, 290, 295, 348, location, *296, 297*
Nimmo, J. W., 494
Nimmo, Samuel, 174, 327; death of, 569. *See also* Stanley & Nimmo
Norris, Samuel, 307, 308, 400
Norris & Tackett, 307, 308
Northern Standard (Clarksville newspaper), 52, 64, 71, 74, 76, 78, 80, 81, 101–2, 104, 126, 152, 201, 228, 315, 368, 405, 417–18, 420, 449, 459, 479, 482, 487, 498, 491, 530, 534
N. Trawick & Company, 305; location, *316*
Nussbaum, A., 339
Nussbaum, J., 339

O

Ochiltree, William, 149, 403, 410, 418–21, 422
O'Hara, John, 55

Index

opium, 558–59
ordinances, of Jefferson, 168–71, 174, 184
Orton, Harry, 256
Overton, Reddick, 37, 167
Owens, Anthony, 290
Owens & McElroy, 290; location, *296, 297*
ox-wagon drivers, 25, 84, 101, 126, 244, 397, 514, 546, 560
ox-wagons, 18, 20, 21, 22, 42, 46, 108, 195, 231; slowness of, 2, 77, 143

P

packeries, meat, 371–81. *See also* meat packing; individual company names
Page, Harriet. *See* Ames, Harriet
paintings, 531
Paradise, 104, 107–8, 126, 165, 461–62
Parker, Burrell, 39, 44
Parker, W. J., 346
Parsons, Henry, 314, 442–43, 548
Peele, Charles, 199, 319; location, *328*
Perry, Sardinia, 124, 447, 449, 450
Perry, William, 34, 37, 84, 91, 104, 116, 122, 174, 289, 383, 447, 464, 547; tavern as meeting place, 151–53, 450; clearing bayou, 60, 79, 182, 201, 202, 203; building wharf, 188–89; captain of *Bloomer*, 199, 549; property transactions, 81, 82, 87, 88, 190, 259, 267, 282, 283, 362, 444; location, *296, 297*
Perry Claim, 190, 191, 192
Perry House (hotel), 461

photography, 347–48
pickled beef, 3, 25, 218, 221, 355, 371, 379
Pinski, Isaac, 335, 438
Pinski & Kallisher, 335; location, *341*
Pitkin, John, 116, 228, 309–12. *See also* J. W. Pitkin & Company
Plan of the City of Jefferson, Texas, 47, 48, 165; illustrated, *166*
Planter's Hotel, 447, 455–57, 459, 460, 461; location, *462*
P. M. Graham & Brother, 284; advertisement, *284*; location, *296, 297*
Poindexter, John, 395
Poindexter & Westmoreland, 395
poison spring, 565
Polk Street Bridge, 41, 47, 103
population, of Jefferson, 3, 7, 25, 100–3, 116–22, 129; decline in, 4. *See also* women; slaves; Census, of 1850; Census, of 1860
population, of market area, 219–20, 222
Port Caddo, 5–6, 15, 16, 46, 74, 84, 85, 198, 214; on map, *14*
postal delivery routes, 507–10
postmasters, 503–4
post office, first, 6, 502, 504–5
Potter, Robert, 13, 67
Potter's Point, 13, 15; on map, *14*
Presbyterian churches, 434–36
Prewitt, Anselm, 331
Prewitt, George, 460–61
"Price Current" columns in newspapers, 224–25, 241, 242, 254–55; illustrated, *225, 251, 253*
prominent men listed, 573–74

prostitution, 559–60
Pugh, Thomas, 293, 310; location, *296, 297*
public assistance, 565–66
public education, 439–40

R

Ragan, Caleb, 109, 287–88, 343, 527; location, *296, 297*; as postmaster, 504
Ragan, Gilbert, 109, 287
railroads, 7, 182, 184, 309, 356, 517–23, 595; effect on market, 4. *See also names of individual lines*
Ramsey, Richard, 461
Ray's Bluff (Benton), 5, 14, 16
receiving and forwarding merchants, 3, 21–24, 213, 223, 230–37, 243, 245, 246, 254, 261, 262, 263, 265, 269, 270, 274, 386. *See also individual merchant names*
receiving, forwarding, and commission merchants, 3, 21, 223, 230–37, 246, 274; as quintessential Jefferson business, 23. *See also individual merchant names*
Red River, 1, 11, 13, 21, 83, 195, 196, 203, 209, 214, 519. *See also* Great Raft
Red River Association, 205–8
Red River County, 5, 6, 7, 14, 29, 37; part of Second Senatorial District, 67; cotton production in, 222
Reece Hughes wholesalers. *See* Hughes, Reece
Relief (steamboat), 15, 84, 85

Republic of Texas, 5, 9, 13, 14, 28, 78, 86
restaurants, 344–45; licensing taxes on, 176
Rising Sun Hotel, 457–61; location, *462*
roads, county, 140–45
Robert T. Lytle (steamboat), 16
Robbins, John, 37
Rogers, Edwin, 60, 61, 78
Rogers, Martin, 154, 431
Rogers, Robert, 398, 458
Rogers, Thomas, 266–67, 268, 324, 393; advertisement, *234, 394*; business location, *275*
Rogers, W. J. C., 178
Rondo (game), 556
Rosenzweig, Lazarus, 338
Rosenzweig, Morris, 338
Ross, Joseph, 15
Rusk Street, 57, 61, 99, 112, 361, 372
Russell, William, 69, 82, 105, 152, 258, 463–64; stable location, *275, 469*
R. W. Powell (steamboat), 198
R. W. Walker, wholesalers, 224; location, *328*

S

Sabine, John, 312–13, 315
Sabine & Frazor, 312, 318; location, *316, 328*
saloons, 176, 289, 343–44, 558
Saufley, Eliza, obituary of, 127–28
Saufley, William, 168, 300, 330–31; as mayor, 173, 300
Saufley & Batte, 330–31; location, *341*
Saufley & Hudgins, 138, 298, 300

Index

sawmills. *See* mills, steam
Schaff, Charles, 360, 366
Schluter, Frederick, 107, 134, 294, 299–300; business location, *296, 297*; one of richest people, 120
Schluter, Henry, 271, 322–23
Schoenburg & Merzbacher, location, *341*
Sedberry, Thomas, 336
Semi-Weekly Jimplecute, 461
Seymour, Daniel, 269
Shakespeare, William, performances, 534–36
Sharp, Charles. *See* Schaff, Charles
Shelby County, 14
Shreve, Capt. Henry, 12, 13, 194, 210
Shreveport, LA, 1, 12, 13, 14–15, 46, 74, 198, 224, 472, 513, 514, 515; condition of landing, 187; and plan to drain Cross Lake, 205, 209; competitive with Jefferson, 213, 242; as cotton market, 243–44, 255. *See also* Great Raft
Slaughter, George, 110, 117, 400
slaves, 20, 129–39, 178, 238, 354, 433; price of, 8, 129–30, 339; as proportion of population, 27, 100, 102, 117, 552; enumerations by owners, 132–133; self-hiring, 136–38
smallpox, 7, 178, 397, 555, 562, 563–64
Smith, Edward, 19, 81, 101, 102, 260–61, 278, 293, 358, 429, 525, 546, 565
Smith, Eliza, 110, 304
Smith, George, 110, 304

Smith, James, 116, 360, 382
Smith, John, 174, 286, 321–22
Smith, Samuel, 286, 321–22
Smith, Sidney, 199
Smith, Stephen, 29, 33, 35, 38, 42, 53, 55
Smither, Rachael, 121, 123, 531
Smithland, 6, 14, 16, 17, 21, 38, 72, 77–78, 83, 85–86, 212
Smoker, John, 325
Soda Lake (extinct), 1, 13, 90, 195–96, 203, 208–9
Soda Lake Hotel, 124, 152, 153, 277, 289, 447–55, 464, 542; on timeline, 6; advertisement, *448*; location, *462*
Soda Street, 58, 100, 103, 105, 187, 257
Southern Country Store, The (Atherton), 223
Spanish influence, 9, 10
Speake, John, 68, 83, 84, 106, 120, 173, 269, 280, 281–82, 381, 382, 520; advertisement, *231*; business location, *274–75, 296, 297*
Speake & Smoker, 325, 326; location, *328*
Speake & Willard, 278, 281; location, *296, 297*
Speake, Saufley, & Nimmo, 215, 269, 282, 298, 306; location, *274–75*
Spilker & Company, 248, 324; location, *275, 328*
Spirit of the Age, 68, 201, 283, 292, 475, 476, 483–88, 500, 585
Spring Street. *See* Marshall Street.
St. Catherine's Island, 95, 99, 103, 376
stables, 446, 448, 463–469; taxes

on, 176; location, *274, 275*; fires at, 391. *See also* Nesmith, Robert; stagecoach line
stagecoach line, 466, 470–74
Stanley, Charles, 187, 269, 326–27, 332, 355, 376, 381, 544; location, *377*
Stanley & Nimmo Packery, 187, 188, 224, 327, 355, 376–81; location, *377*
Stanley & Seymour, 269; location, *275*
Stanley & Ward, 277, 283, 486; location, *296, 297*
Staples, M. W., 434
Star Hotel, 457–61; location, *462*
State and Southern Rights Association, 415
Steam Mill Company, 292, 357–59
steamboat monopoly, 205–8
steamboat turning basin, 77, 103, 185
steamboats, 15, 16, 18, 21–22, 25, 74, 75, 77, 86–88, 169, 170, 171, 281; importance to Jefferson, 1–3, 21, 212–13, 224; role in trade replaced by rail, 4, 519–20; firsts, 5, 6, 9, 15, 16, 46, 82–86; wharves for, 184–86; role in navigation, 194–204; list of known boats, 196–98; sizes of, 198. *See also individual boat names;* Withenbury, Capt. W. W. ; steamboat monopoly
Steel, John, 441
Steinlein, Moses, 302, 304
Stephens, Isaac, 55, 357, 358, 359
Stetson, Prentiss, 71, 112, 368, 369, 370

Stetson & Stewart Sash, Blind, and Door Manufactory, 356, 368–69; advertisement, *368*
storm party, 526–27, 541, 544
street names, 99–100
streets, conditions of, 25, 26, 32–33, 101, 126, 163–64, 176–77; names of, 99. *See also individual street names*
suicide, 571–73
Summers & Clark, 395
Sunday prohibitions, 170, 171
surveyors' records, 34–36
Swanson, Peter, 13
Swanson, Thomas, 173
Swanson's Landing, 5, 13, 15, 16, 17, 184, 206, 214, 518–19

T

tallow, 372
tanyards, 367, 375
Tarpley, Fred, 41, 159, 438, 528, 577
taxes, in early Jefferson, 163, 169, 175–76, 342
Taylor, E. W., 332
Taylor, Marion, 161, 211, 410
Taylor & Witherspoon, 332; location, *341*
T. D. Sedberry, 336; location, *341*
telegraph, 245, 513–16
Terry, Benjamin, 174, 266, 267, 324
Terry & Rogers, 266–67, 324; advertisement, *234*; location, *275*
Texas & Pacific Railroad, 4
Texas and Red River Telegraph Line, 514, 515
Texas General Land Office, 28, 44, 47, 585

Texas Iron Works, 355, 391
Texas Republican (Marshall), 68, 145–46, 148, 149, 168, 213, 215, 218, 221, 271, 347, 476, 515, 585; first issue, 201. *See also* Loughery, Robert
Texas Western Railroad, 518
theater, 532–36
theft, 551
thespians, 532–36
Thorn, Frost, 10, 589
Tillus, Mary, 121, 123
T. J. & J. H. Rogers, 393–94; advertisement, *394*
tobacco, 560–61
Todd, James, 85, 116, 308–9, 485–86
Todd, William, 416–18
Todd & Brander, 85
Tomlin, Hiram, 288, 314
Torrans, William, 319; location, *328*
town hall, construction, 389
town plans: Hensey's, 61, 62, 66, 93, 95, 98, 99, 100, 153, 179, 361; illustrated, *94, 97*; Cherry's, 6, 38, 56–58, 59, 60, 62, 66, 71, 93, 99–100, 105, 109, 257, 357
Trammel, Nicholas, 10, 41
Trammel's Trace, 10, 35, 41–42, 55
Trawick, Nelson, 304–5, 526, 547
Trickey, E. L., 346–47
Tryon, N. G., 256; advertisement, *256*
Turner, J. W., 323
Turner & Jenkins, 323
Tuttle, George, 282
Twelvemile Bayou, 1, 195, 538; removal of raft to, 5, 12, 13

U

Urquhart, Allen, 6, 34, 35, 36, 37, 43, 44, 58, 66, 77, 90, 93, 95, 147, 164, 165, 182; land acquisitions of, 28–33, 63, 71, 190; illustrations of surveys, 30, 31; mention of Jefferson in survey, 38–39, 43–44, 76; operates ferry, 45, 46, 55, 56, 76, 145, 147; relationship with Berry Durham, 58–63; as Jefferson's "founder," 63, 66; operates tollbridge, 147–49, 183; builds wharf, 188–92. *See also* Jefferson Town Company; Durham, Berryman Hicks; Urquhart Addition
Urquhart Addition, 56, 114, 167
Urquhart's Bridge, 147–48
Ury, Amos, 82, 84, 88, 90–91, 105, 109; locations, *89, 274–75, 296, 297*
Ury, Ennis, 60, 61, 67, 109, 260
Ury & Ward, 92, 106, 279, 304, 305, 411; locations, *89, 296, 297*
U.S.-Republic of Texas boundary, 9

V

Vandergrift, S. W., 86
Veal & Jennings, 248, 282, 303, 313; location, *296, 297, 316*

W

wagon makers, 360
Walcott, Horatio N. (business and person), 247, 261–62,

285–86; advertisement, *247*; location on map, *275*
Walcott & McNeill, 261, 286
Walker, Dr. R. W., 320, 401
Walker & Sayre, 320; location, *328*
Wallace, John, 332–33; one of richest people, 120
Wallace, Marcus, 435
Ward, Clark, 216
Ward, Leonard, 37
Ward, Matthias (Matt), 203, 410–14
Ward, Robert, 413–14
wards, voting, 114, 172, 174
warehouses, 231, 386, 485; first constructed, 105, 259–61; warehouse district, 257–75; location, *275*
Waskom, John, 168, 246, 269, 306, 515; location, *274–75*; as postmaster, 504
watchmakers, 346–47
water cure, 398; advertisement, *399*
Watson, W. P., 361, 412, 488, 489, 490, 491
W. Brooks & Brother, 270, 306. *See also* Brooks, Brother & Mabry
W.(illiam) C. Baker & Company, 271, 292, 301–2, 317, 484; location, *296, 297, 316*
W. D. Stephenson & Company, 349
Weaver, Tinsly, 37, 45
Weekly Jimplecute, 131
well constructor, 351

Westmoreland, Charles, 395, 415, 489
Wharf Street, 58, 99, 100
wharves, 104, 126, 183, 184–93, 590; dates of, 7; tax for, 169, 175–76, 184–85; public, 186–87; packery, 187–88; private, 188–92; locations, *186, 191, 377*
Whig Party, 403, 404
wholesale merchants, 21, 22–23, 26, 223–30, 233, 234, 236, 270; 274, 276, 295. *See also individual merchant names*
Whetstone, Peter, 14
Wilcox, Real, 549–50
Willard, Clinton, 135, 280, 313
Willard & Tuttle, 282, 303, 313; location, *296, 297*
Withenbury, Capt. Wellington W., 15–16, 74, 75, 82, 83–84, 85, 86, 101, 207, 575
Withee, John, 37, 45, 71, 72, 77, 78, 79, 81, 87, 289
Witherspoon, Hamilton, 332, 401
W. K. Vining, 337
W. M. Freeman & Co., 224, 265–66, 268, 274, 386; advertisement, *266*; location, *275*
women, 119, 123–28; occupations of, 27, 121; not included in ferry rates, 45; suicides of, 558
W. R. Hines & Company, 337; location, *341*

F
314
.J3
B34
2012